THE

DOCUMENTARY HISTORY

OF THE

ARRANGED UNDER DIRECTION OF THE

HON. CHRISTOPHER MORGAN,
Secretary of State.

BY E. B. O'CALLAGHAN, M. D.

VOLUME I.

ALBANY:
WEED, PARSONS & CO., PUBLIC PRINTERS.
1850.

*** The Map facing the Title page of this Volume is taken from one of North America, engraved by Lucini, an Italian artist, originally on four sheets, three of which belong to the Warden Collection of the State Library.

It will be perceived from its Title that it is a Map of New Belgium (now New-York,) and part of New England, the former of which Provinces was claimed at the time, to extend from Cape Cod to the Capes of Delaware. The absence of any date renders it difficult, however, to ascertain precisely the year it was engraved and this point can be determined only by other evidence.

Boston, which was settled in 1630, is found laid down, but there is no mention of Maryland, the Province of Virginia forming the southern Boundary of New Belgium.

As Maryland was first granted in 1632, it is evident the date of this Map must be some year between that and the settlement of Boston. Most probably, it was engraved in 1631.

In point of time, it may be considered the third oldest Map of the Province extant, having, as far as yet known, been preceded by only two Dutch Maps, one of 1616 and one of 1618, transcripts of which are in the office of the Secretary of State, and of one of which this Italian Map is evidently an improved copy.

CONTENTS.

INDEX TO ILLUSTRATIONS.

I.

PAPERS

RELATING TO

The Iroquois and other Indian Tribes.

1666—1675.

THE NINE IROQUOIS TRIBES. 1666.

[Paris Doc. 1.]

The Iroquois Nation consists of nine tribes, which form two divisions; one of four tribes, and the other of five.

They call the first division Guey-niotiteshesgué, which means the four tribes; and the second division they call it Ouiche-niotiteshesgué, which means the five tribes.

The first is that of the Tortoise, which calls itself *Atiniathin*. It is the first, because they pretend, when the Master of Life made the Earth, that he placed it on a tortoise; and when there are earth-quakes, it is the tortoise that stirs.

The second tribe is that of the Wolf, and calls itself *Enanthayonni*, or *Cahenhisenhonon*, and brother of the Tortoise tribe. When there is question of war they deliberate together; and if the affair is of great moment, they communicate it to the other tribes to deliberate together thereupon, so of all the other tribes. They assemble in the hut of a war-chief when the question is of war, and in the hut of a council-chief when it is for ordinary matters of state.

The third tribe is that of the Bear, which they call *Atinionguin*.

The fourth tribe is that of the Beaver, and brother to that of the Bear. These four tribes compose the first division, which they call *Guey-niotiteshesgué*.

SECOND DIVISION.

The fifth tribe is that of the Deer, which they call *Canendeshé*.

The sixth is that of the Potatoe, which they call *Schoneschioronon*.

The seventh is that of the Great Plover, which they call *Otinanchahé*.

The eighth is that of the Little Plover, which they call *Asco*, or *Nicohes*.

The ninth is that of the Kiliou [Eagle], which they call *Chanon-chahonronon*. They call these five tribes *Ouiche-niotiteshesgué*.

These nine tribes formerly occupied nine villages, which were finally collected together in order to sustain war more easily.

The ninth tribe derives its origin from a cabin that was in the interior (*dans les terres*), and composed of several fires or establishments. In the middle of the cabin was a partition which divided the cabin in two.

Weary of knowing no one, and consequently unable to marry, they all married among themselves; which is the reason that their name signifies two cabins united together.

Each tribe has in the gable end of its cabin, the animal of the tribe painted; some in black, others in red.

When they assemble together for consultation, the first Division ranges itself on one side of the fire in a cabin; and the other Division places itself on the other side.

When the matter on which they have met has been discussed on one side and the other, they accompany the decision with much ceremony.

The Division which decides the matter gives two opinions, so that the best may be adopted, and offers all possible opposition in proposing its opinions, in order to show that it has well considered what it says.

They adopt, usually, the first opinion, unless there be some strong motive to the contrary.

When they go to war, and wish to inform those of the party who may pass their path, they make a representation of the animal of their tribe, with a hatchet in his dexter paw; sometimes a sabre or a club; and if there be a number of tribes together of the same party, each draws the animal of his tribe, and their number, all on a tree from which they remove the bark. The animal of the tribe which heads the expedition is always the foremost.

They generally have a rendezvous when they propose to strike a blow, where in case of pursuit, they leave a part of their clothes and ammunition. When they fight, they are very Molochs, and have merely the waistcloth on, with a pair of mocasins on the feet.

When the expedition is numerous they often leave a party a hundred or a hundred and fifty leagues (*lieues*, qy. paces?) from the village which they are about to attack. When they have finished, if they have casse-tetes or clubs, they plant them against the corpse inclining a little towards the village of the slain.

On their return, if they have prisoners or scalps, they paint the animal of the tribe to which they belong, rampant, (*debout*) with a staff on the shoulder along which are strung the scalps they may have, and in the same number. After the animal are the prisoners they have made, with a *chichicois*, (or gourd filled with beans which rattle), in the right hand. If they be women, they represent them with a *Cadenette* or queue and a waistcloth.

If there be several tribes in the war party, each paints the animal of his tribe with the scalps and prisoners it has made, as before, but always after that which is head of the party.

When they have scalps they give them to one or two men who suspend them behind them to their girdle.

These men who carry these scalps follow the others at a distance, that is to say, at a quarter of a league, because they pretend that when they retreat and have scalps, if these precede the others they cannot march any further because they are seized with terror at the sight of the dripping blood. But this is only the first day, sometimes the second and third when they are pursued.

When they come again together, they proceed to notify the others and then each one takes his station or awaits the enemy. When night falls they make a hole in the earth where they kindle a fire with bark to cook their meat, if they have any, and that during three or four days.

They tie the prisoners to stakes set in the ground, into which they fix their leg or rather foot, and this stake is closed by another tied together at a man's height. They place a man at each side who sleeps near them and who is careful to visit the prisoners from time to time during the night.

When they have lost any men on the field of battle they paint the men with the legs in the air, and without heads and in the same number as they have lost; and to denote the tribe to which they belonged, they paint the animal of the tribe of the deceased on its back, the paws in the air, and if it be the chief of the party that is dead, the animal is without the head.

If there be only wounded, they paint a broken gun which however is connected with the stock, or even an arrow, and to denote where they have been wounded, they paint the animal of the tribe to which the wounded belong with an arrow piercing the part in which the wound is located; and if it be a gunshot they make the mark of the ball on the body of a different color.

Engraved & Printed by Gavit & Duthie, Albany.

(The Tribe of the Tortoise)
Famille de la Tortue

(The Tribe of the Wolf)
La Famille du Loup

(The Tribe of the Bear)
La Famille de l'Ours

(The Tribe of the Beaver)
La Famille du Castor

K

G

If they have sick, and are obliged to carry them, they paint litters (*boyards*) of the same number as the sick, because they carry only one on each litter.

When they are thirty or forty leagues[1] from their village they send notice of their approach, and of what has happened them. Then every one prepares to receive the prisoners, when there are any, and to torment each as they deem proper.

Those who are condemned to be burnt are conveyed to the cabin which has been given them. All the warriors assemble in a war cabin and afterwards send for them to make them sing, dance, and to torment them until they are carried to the stake.

During this time two or three young men are preparing the stake, placing the fuel near and keep their guns loaded.

When every thing is ready, he is brought and tied to the stake and finally burnt. When he is burnt up to the stomach they detach him, break all his fingers, raise the scalp which was left hanging behind by a small tongue of skin to the head. They put him to death in these agonies, after which each takes his morsel and proceeds to make merry.

Explanation of the First Designs.

A. This is a person returning from war who has taken a prisoner, killed a man and a woman whose scalps hang from the end of a stick that he carries.

B. The prisoner.

C. *Chichicois* (or a gourd), which he holds in the hand.

D. These are cords attached to his neck, arms and girdle.

E. This is the scalp of a man, what is joined on one side is the scalp lock.

F. This is the scalp of a woman; they paint it with the hair thin.

G. Council of war between the tribe of the Bear and that of the Beaver; they are brothers.

H. A Bear.

I. A Beaver.

L. Is a belt which he holds in his paws to avenge the death of some one and he is conferring about it with his brother, the Beaver.

K. Council for affairs of state.

M. The Bear.

N. The Council fire.

O. The Tortoise; so of the other tribes, each ranges at its own side.

P. Canoe going to war.

Q. Paddles. They know hereby how many men there are in the canoe, because they place as many paddles as there are men. Over these is painted the animal of the tribe to which they belong.

R. The Canoe.

S. This is a man returning from hunting who has slept two nights on the hunting ground and killed three does; for when they are bucks, they add their antlers.

What is on his back, is his bundle.

T. Deer's head. This is the way they paint them.

V. This is the manner they mark the time they have been hunting. Each mark or rather each bar is a day.

Y. Fashion of painting the dead; the two first are men and the third is a woman who is distinguished only by the waistcloth that she has.

As regards the dead, they inter them with all they have. When it is a man they paint red calumets, calumets of peace on the tomb; some times they plant a stake on which they paint how

1 Three or four miles.—Colden.

often he has been in battle; how many prisoners he has taken; the post ordinarily is only four or five feet high and much embellished.

a. These are punctures on his body.

b. This is the way they mark when they have been to war, and when there is a bar extending from one mark to the other, it signifies that after having been in battle, he did not come back to his village and that he returned with other parties whom he met or formed.

c. This arrow, which is broken, denotes that they were wounded in this expedition.

d. Thus they denote that the belts which they gave to raise a war party and to avenge the death of some one, belong to them or some of the same tribe.

e. He has gone back to fight without having entered his village.

f. A man whom he killed on the field of battle who had a bow and arrows.

g. These are two men whom he took prisoners, one of whom had a hatchet, and the other a gun in his hand.

g. g. This is a woman who is designated only by a species of waistcloth.

h. This is the way they distinguish her from the men.

Such is the mode in which they draw their portraits.

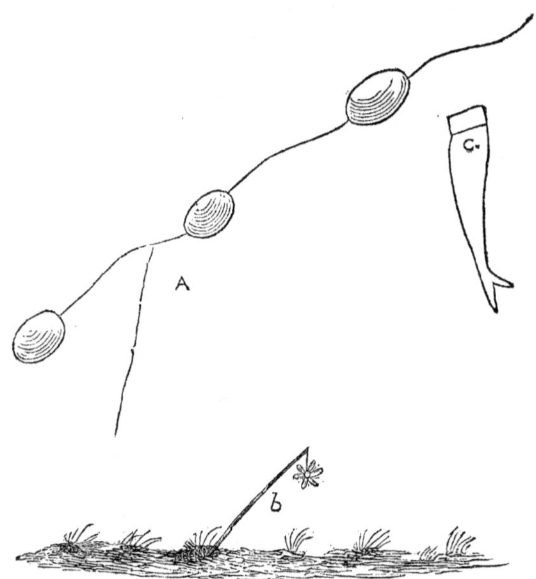

A. This is the manner they paint the tribe of the Potatoe and not as it is on the other plate.

b. Is a stick set in the ground to the extremity of which two or three pieces of wood are attached, to note the direction in which they went when they are hunting; and on the nearest tree they paint the animal of the tribe to which they belong, with the numbers of guns they have; that is to say if they are three men, they paint three guns, if they are more and there are some who have a bow and no gun, they put down a bow.

When they return from hunting and are near the village they do the same thing and add the number of beasts they have killed—that is to say, they paint the Deer, and the Stag from the head to the neck; if some are male they add antlers; they paint the other animals entire; if they are some days at the chase they mark the number as you see on the other plate.

c. Club which they use to break the skull when they are at war.

Stake to tie the prisoners. They place his leg between these two posts in the hollow of the larger—that is the two posts catch the leg above the ankle, and they afterwards join one to the other and tie them at a man's height—sometimes higher, so that it is impossible to withdraw the foot without untying the cords.

OBSERVATIONS OF WENTWORTH GREENHALGH,

IN A JOURNEY FROM ALBANY TO Y^e INDIANS, WESTWARD; BEGUN MAY 20th 1667, AND ENDED JULY Y^e 14, FOLLOWING.

[Lond. Doc. III.]

The Maquaes have four townes, vict. Cahaniaga, Canagora, Canajorha, Tionondogue, besides one small village about 110 miles from Albany.

Cahaniaga is double stockadoed round; has four forts, [ports?] about four foot wide a piece, conteyns about 24 houses, and is situate upon the edge of an hill, about a bow shott from the river side.

Canagora is only singly stockadoed; has four ports like the former, conteyns about 16 houses; itt is situated upon a ffatt, a stone's throw from ye waters side.

Canajorha is also singly stockadoed; and the like man^r of ports and quantity of houses as Canagora; the like situacôn; only about two miles distant from the water.

Tionondogue is double stockadoed around, has four ports, four foot wide a piece, contains a^bt 30 houses; is scituated on a hill a bow shott from ye River.

The small village is without ffence, and conteyns abôut ten houses; lyes close by the river side, on the north side, as do all the former.

The Maquaes pass in all for about 300 fighting men.

Their corn grows close by the River side.

Of the Situacôn of the Oneydas and Onondagoes and their Strength.

The Onyades have but one town, which lys about 130 miles westward of the Maques. Itt is situate about twenty miles from a small river which comes out of the hills to the southward, and runs into lake Teshiroque, and about 30 miles distant from the Maquaes river, which lyes to the northward; the town is newly settled, double stockadoed, but little cleared ground, so thatt they are forced to send to the Onondages to buy corne; The towne consists of about 100 houses. They are said to have about 200 fighting men, Their Corne grows round about the towne.

The Onondagoes have butt one towne, butt itt is very large; consisting of about 140 houses, nott fenced; is situate upon a hill thatt is very large, the banke on each side extending itself att least two miles, all cleared land, whereon the corne is planted. They have likewise a small village about two miles beyond that, consisting of about 24 houses. They ly to the southward of ye west, about 36 miles from the Onyades. They plant abundance of Corne, which they sell to the Onyades. The Onondagos are said to be about 350 fighting men. They ly about 15 miles from Tshiroqui.

Of the Caiougos and Senecques, their Situacôn and Strength, &c.

The Caiougos have three townes about a mile distant from each other; they are not stockadoed. They do in all consist of about 100 houses; they ly about 60 miles to the southward of ye Onondagos; they intend the next spring to build all their houses together and stockade them; they have abundance of Corne; they ly within two or three miles of the lake Tichero. They pass for about 300 fighting men.

The Senecques have four townes, vict. Canagora, Tiotohatton, Canoenda and Keint-he. Canagora and Tiotohatton lye within 30 miles of ye Lake ffrontenacque, and ye other two ly about four or five miles apiece to ye Southward of those. They have abundance of Corne. None of their towns are stockadoed.

Canagorah lyes on the top of a great hill, and in that, as well as in the bignesse, much like Onondago, contayning 150 houses, northwestward of Caiougo, 72 miles. Here ye Indians were very desirous to see us ride our horses, wch wee did: they made great feasts and dancing, and invited us y^t^ when all ye maides were together, both wee and our Indyans might choose such as lyked us to ly with.

Tiotohattan lyes on the brincke or edge of a hill; has not much cleared ground; is near the river Tiotehatton, wch signifies bending. It lyes to Westward of Canagorah about 30 miles, containing about 120 houses, being ye largest of all the houses wee saw, ye ordinary being 50@60 foot long with 12@13 fires in one house. They have good store of corne, growing about a mile to the Northward of the towne.

Being at this place the 17 of June, there came 50 prisoners from the Southwestward. They were of two nations, some whereof have few guns; the other none at all. One nation is about 10 days journey from any Christians and trade only with one greatt house, nott far from the sea, and the other trade only, as they say, with a black people. This day of them was burnt two women, and a man and a child killed with a stone. Att night we heard a great noyse as if ye houses had all fallen, butt itt was onely ye Inhabitants driving away ye ghosts of ye murthered.

The 18th going to Canagorah, wee overtook ye prisoners; when the soudiers saw us they stopped each his prisoner, and made him sing, and cutt off their fingers, and slasht their bodies wth a knife, and when they had sung each man confessed how many men in his time hee had killed. Thatt day att Canagorah, there were most cruelly burnt four men, four women and one boy. The cruelty lasted aboutt seven hours. When they were almost dead letting them loose to the mercy of ye boys, and taking the hearts of such as were dead to feast on.

Canoenada lyes about four miles to ye Southward of Canagorah; conteynes about 30 houses, well furnished with Corne.

Keint-he lyes about four or five miles to y^e^ Southward of Tietehatton; contayns about 24 houses well furnished with corne.

The Senecques are counted to bee in all about 1000 fighting men.

The French call the

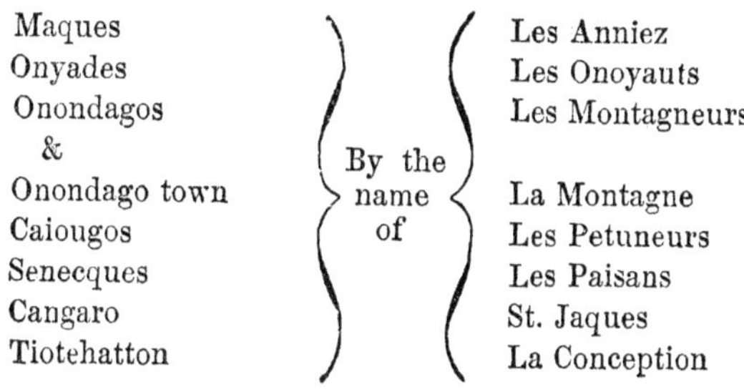

Maques	By the name of	Les Anniez
Onyades		Les Onoyauts
Onondagos & Onondago town		Les Montagneurs / La Montagne
Caiougos		Les Petuneurs
Senecques		Les Paisans
Cangaro		St. Jaques
Tiotehatton		La Conception

Note. The above paper will be found also in Chalmers' Political Annals, in which however, Greenhalgh's name is misspelt. That paper differs likewise in other respects from the MS. now followed.

ENUMERATION OF THE INDIAN TRIBES

CONNECTED WITH THE GOVERNMENT OF CANADA; THE WARRIORS AND ARMORIAL BEARINGS OF EACH NATION. 1736.

[Paris, Doc. VIII.]

The Eskimaux,
The Micmacs,
The Amaleates or rather the Maneus. } These Nations are below Quebec, and beyond my knowledge.

At Quebec.

The Hurons. - 1 Village 60 *a* 70 men bearing arms, - - - - - - - 60

At the River St. John, near the English.

The Abenabis. - - 1 Village called Panaȣamsket towards the mouth of said river. Warriors. 200

The ȣbenakis at the head of said River.

1 Village called Narentchȣan. Warriors. - - - - - - - - - 150

Becancour. The Abenakis. 1 Village. Warriors. - - - - - - - - 60

The ȣbenakis. At St. Francis. 1 Village. War. - - - - - - - - - 180

including those of Michikoui and those who migrate.

The armorial bearings (Totums) of this Nation, which is divided into two sections, are the Pigeon (*toutre*) and the Bear.

There are besides some tribes who carry the Partridge, the Beaver and the Otter.

650

650

At Three Rivers. See Montreal.

The Algonquins. - fifteen men. - - - - - - - - - - - - - - 15

The Têtes de Boule or tribes of the Interior.

These are wandering Savages who have no knowledge either of the order or form of villages, and those who evince the least intellect (*esprit*); they inhabit the mountains and the lakes, from Three Rivers, in the interior, to Lake Superior. Their armorial bearings (Totums) are unknown, if they have any.

Boston and Orange.

The Loups (Mohegans) who understand the ȣabenakis and whom the ȣbenakis understand are dispersed from Boston to Virginia, which is equal to from Lake Champlain to the head of Lake Erie—300 leagues. This nation may be six hundred men, under British rule. No person could give me any information of their customs. This only by way of remark.

Montreal.

Algonquins. They are twenty men settled with the Iroquois of the Two Mountains; this is all that remains of a nation the most warlike, most polished and the most attached to the French. They have for armorial bearings an Evergreen Oak (*chêne vert.*) - 20

At the Lake of the Two Mountains.

The Nepissingues. A part of this Tribe is incorporated with the Iroquois. The remainder has its village at the lake of the same name. There are here fifty men bearing arms. 50

The armorial bearings of this Nation are the Heron for the *Achagué*, or Heron tribe; the Beaver for the Amekoves; the Birch for the Bark tribe (*la famille de l'Ecorce*); Blood for the Miskouaha or the Bloody people.

Remark, Sir, if you please, that besides the bearings of the principal stocks to which I exclusively confine myself, leisure not permitting me to obtain thorough details, each tribe distinguishes itself by peculiar devices. The Iroquois who are masters of this village, amount to no more than sixty-three—I mean warriors. - - - - - - - - - 60

At Sault St. Louis.

The Iroquois, who compose exclusively the village are nearly three hundred and three bearing arms. - - - - - - - - - - - - - - - - - 300

These two villages proceeding from the Iroquois of Lake Ontario, or Frontenac, have the same armorial devices. Three principal tribes carry the Wolf, the Bear and the Tortoise.

Note.—*Argent*, to the Wolf *gules*, &c.

They usually ornament them merely with charcoal.

The Great river of the Outawas.

At Lake Nepissingue there is one small village of thirty men, who bear a Squirrel, *Atchitam8*. 30

River and Lake Themiscaming.

The Tabittibis are one hundred warriors. - - - - - - - - - - - - - 100

They have for device an Eagle.

At the mouth of the Themiscaming there are twenty warriors. - - - - - 20

At the head of the Lake twenty domiciled. - - - - - - - - - 20

1265

1265

These savages are what are called *Tetês de Boule*, who amount to over six hundred in the Northern country. - - - - - - - - - - - - - - - 600

I shall speak of them hereafter without reference to their numbers.

At Missilimakinak.

The Outawas of this village amount to one hundred and eighty warriors; the two principal branches are Kiskakous (1) and Sinago (2); the Bear (1) and Black Squirrel (2). 180

River Missisagué.

The Missisagués on the river number thirty men, and twenty men on the Island called Manitouatim of Lake Huron. - - - - - - - - - - - - - - 50

And have for device, a Crane.

Lake Superior—At the Mouth.

At Sault St. Mary are the Sauteurs, to the number of thirty; they are in two divisions, and have for devices, the Crane and the Vine, (*la Barbue.*) - - - - - 30

North of this Lake is Michipicoton.

The Papinakois and those of the interior; the first are twenty warriors, and have for device, a Hare. - - - - - - - - - - - - - - - 20

River Ounepigon.

The Oskemanettigons are domiciled there to the number of forty warriors. - - - 40

They have for device, the bird called the Fisher.

The Monsonies, who are migratory, estimate themselves two hundred men, and have for device, the Moose. - - - - - - - - - - - - - - - 200

The Abettibis and the *Tètes de Boule* come there also. Some have informed me that the first have for arms the Partridge with the Eagle. I have already stated that they are in all one hundred warriors.

The Nameßilinis have one hundred and fifty fit to bear arms. They have for device, a Sturgeon. - - - - - - - - - - - - - - - 150

The tribes of the Savannas, one hnndred and forty warriors strong, have for armorial device, a Hare. - - - - - - - - - - - - - - - 140

Gamanettigoya.

The Ouaceé are in number sixty men, and have for device a Vine, (*une Barbue.*) - - 60

Tecamomiouen, or Rainy Lake—(Lac de la Pluie.)

These savages are the same as those who come to Nepigon. They are about this lake to the number of one hundred men. - - - - - - - - - - - 100

Lake of the Woods—(Lac des Bois.)

The Cristinaux are scattered hereabout, to the number of two hundred warriors. They have for device the Bustard, (*l'Outarde.*) - - - - - - - - - 200

Lake Ounepigon.

The Cristinaux are around this lake to the number of sixty men. - - - - - - 60

Assenipoels. See *Scioux.*

3095

3095

South of Lake Superior.

Kiouanan. In this quarter there are domiciled forty Sauters, who have for device the Crane and the Stag. - - - - - - - - - - - - - - - - 40

The Sauters of Point Chagouamigon are one hundred and fifty warriors, - - - - 150

The Scioux are at the head of this lake in the woods and along the lakes. Though scattered they are computed at three hundred men. - - - - - - - - 300

The Scioux of the Prairies are, in the opinion of voyageurs, over two thousand men, - - 2000
Their armorial devices are the Buffalo, the Black Dog, and the Otter.

The Assenipoels, or Pouans according to others, can vie with the Scioux, from whom they formerly sprung. They number one hundred and fifty to the south of Lake 150
Ounepigon, and have for device, a Big Stone or a Rock.

The Puans have withdrawn, since 1728, to the Scioux, to the number of eighty; they have for armorial bearings, the Stag, the Polecat (*Pichoux*), the Tiger, - - - - 80

The head of Lake Superior.

The Ayoȣois are settled at the south of the River de Missouris, at the other side of the Mississippi. They are no more than eighty. They have for device a Fox. 80

Lake Michigan with its dependancies.

The Folles Avoines, north of this lake, number one hundred and sixty warriors. The most considerable tribes have for device, the Large tailed Bear, the Stag, a Kiliou—that is 160
a species of Eagle (the most beautiful bird in this country,) perched on a cross.

In explanation of a cross forming the armorial bearings of the savages, it is stated that formerly a Chief of the Folles Avoines finding himself dangerously sick, consented, after trying the ordinary remedies, to see a Missionary, who, cross in hand, prayed to God for his recovery, and obtained it from his mercy. In gratitude for this benefit, the Chief desired that to his arms should be added a Cross on which the Kiliou has ever since been always perched.

Pouteȣatanis. In 1728 there was a village of this name retired on an island to the number of 20
The Bay. At the head of this Lake is the sojourn, or rather the country of the Sakis.
This nation could put under arms one hundred and fifty men. Others do not count but one 150
hundred and twenty. They have for device, a Crab, a Wolf, and a She-Bear.

Fox River.

Fox river discharges into this Lake. This nation now migratory, consists, when not separated, still of one hundred men bearing arms, - - - - - - - - - - 100
They have for device, a Fox.

The Kickapous, formerly their allies, may be eighty men. They bear for device the Pheasant and the Otter, - - - - - - - - - - - - - - - - 80

The Maskoutin has for armorial device the Wolf and the Stag. This nation is estimated at sixty men, - - - - - - - - - - - - - - - - 60

River St. Joseph, south of Lake Michigan.

The Potteȣatamies, who call themselves the Governor's eldest sons, compose the village of St. Joseph, to the number of one hundred warriors, - - - - - - - - 100

The principal families have for device the Golden Carp, the Frog, the Crab, the Tortoise.

6565

6565

There are in the village about ten Miamis who bear in their arms, a Crane, - - 10

Eight Illinois Kaskakias are also included whose device is a feather of an arrow, notched; (+) or two arrows supported one against the other in *saltier* (like a St. Andrew's cross.)

These are the nations best known to us as well along the great river of the Outawas as north and south of Lakes Superior and Michigan. I propose now proceeding again from Montreal by way of the Lakes to Missilimakinak.

From Montreal on the Lake route, I spoke of Sault St. Louis, on the first sheet.

Toniata.

Some Iroquois, to the number of eight or ten men have retired to this quarter. Their device is without doubt, like that of the village from which issue the Deer, the Plover, &c., as hereafter, - - - - - - - - - - - - - - 10

Lake Ontario, or South of Frontenac.

There are no more Iroquois settled.

The Mississagués are dispersed along this lake, some at Kenté, others at the River Toronto, and finally at the head of the Lake, to the number of one hundred and fifty in all, and at Matchedach, - . - - - - - - - - - - - - 150

The principal tribe is that of the Crane.

North of Lake Ontario.

The Iroquois are in the interior and in five villages, about fifteen leagues from the Lake, on a pretty straight line, altho' one days journey distant from each other. This nation, though much diminished, is still powerful.

South of Lake Frontenac.

The Onondagoes number two hundred warriors. The device of the village is a Cabin on the top of a mountain, - - - - - - - - - - - - - 200

The Mohawks, towards New-England, not far from Orange (Albany) are eighty men, and have for device of the village a *Battefeu* [a Steel] and a flint, - - - - - 80

The Oneidas, their neighbors, number one hundred men or a hundred warriors, - - 100

This village has for device a Stone in a fork of a tree, or in a tree notched with some blows of an axe.

The Cayugas form a village of one hundred and twenty warriors. Their device generally is a very large Calumet, - - - - - - - - - - - - - - 120

The Senecas form two villages in which are three hundred and fifty men. Their device is a big mountain, - - - - - - - - - - - - - - 350

Besides the arms of each village, each tribe has its own, and every man has his particular mark to designate him. Thus the Oneida designates his village by a Stone [in] a fork—next he designates his tribe by the bird or animal, and finally he denotes himself by his punctures. See the designs which I had the honor to send you in 1732 by Father Francois, the Recollet.

The five villages which belong to the same tribe, have for their arms in common, the Plover, to which I belong;[1] the Bear, the Tortoise, the Eel, the Deer, the Beaver, the Potatoe, the Falcon, the Lark, and the Partridge.

7585

1 M. De Joncaire, the supposed author of this Report, is here thought to be alluded to. He was adopted at an early period by the Senecas, among whom he had much influence.

7585

I doubt not but the other nations are as well distinguished, but our voyaguers, having little curiosity in these matters, have not been able to give me any information.

The Tuscarorens have a village of two hundred and fifty men near the Onondagoes, who brought them along. I know not their hieroglyphics, - - - - - - 250

The Iroquois have some cabins at the Portage, (Niagara, Lake Ontario.)

Lake Erie and Dependancies on the South Side.

The Chaouanons towards Carolina, are two hundred men, - - - - - - - 200

The Flatheads, Cherakis, Chicachas, Totiris, are included under the name of Flatheads by the Iroquois, who estimate them at over six thousand men, in more than thirty villages, - - - - - - - - - - - - - - - - - 6000

They have told me they had for device a vessel, (*un Vaisseau.*)

The Ontationoué, that is those who speak the language of men; so called by the Iroquois because they understand each other—may be fifty men. I am ignorant of them. 50

The Miamis have for device the Hind and the Crane. These are the two principal tribes. There is likewise that of the Bear. They are two hundred men, bearing arms. - 200

The Ouyattanons, Peanguichias, Petikokias, are the same Nation, though in different villages. They can place under arms three hundred and fifty men. - - - - - - 350

The devices of these savages are the Serpent, the Deer, and the Small Acorn.

The Illinois, Metchigamias at Fort Chartres, number two hundred and fifty men. - - 250

The Kaskakias, six leagues below, have a village of one hundred warriors. - - - 100

The Peorias, at the Rock, are fifty men. - - - - - - - - - - - - - - 50

The Kaokias, or Tamarois, can furnish two hundred men, - - - - - - - 200

All those savages comprehended under the name of Illinois have, for device, the Crane, the Bear, the White Hind, the Fork, the Tortoise.

River of the Missouris.

The Missouris.

The Okams or Kamsé, the Sotos, and the Panis.

This only as a note, not knowing any thing of these Nations except the name.

Lake Erie—The Detroit.

The Hurons at present are two hundred men, bearing arms. - - - - - - - 200

They mark the Tortoise, the Bear and the Plover.

The Pouteouatamis have a village there of one hundred and eighty men.* They bear for device the Golden Carp, the Frog, the Crab, the Tortoise. (See *South of Lake Michigan: River St. Joseph.*) - - - - - - - - - - - - - 180

The Outawas there have two villages, composed one of the tribe of Sinagos; the other of Kiskakous, and may count two hundred warriors. - - - - - - - - 200

They have the same devices as those of Missilimakinac; that is to say, the Bear and Black Squirrel.

15815

Note in Orig. Instead of 180, only 100 men must be counted.

15815

Lake St. Clair, which leads to Lake Huron.

At the end of the Little Lake St. Clair, there is a small village of Mississagués, which numbers sixty men. - - - - - - - - - - - - - - - - - 60

They have the same devices as the Mississagués of Manitouatin and of Lake Ontario; that is to say, a Crane.

Lake Huron.

I have spoken before of the Missisagués who are to the North of this Lake.

I do not know, on the South side, but the Outawas, who have at Saguinan a village of eighty men, and for device the Bear and Squirrel. - - - - - - - - 80

15955

Less, - - - - - - - - - - - - 80

15875

Remark.

All the Northern Nations have this in common; that a man who goes to war denotes himself as much by the device of his wife's tribe as by that of his own, and never marries a woman who carries a similar device to his.

If time permitted, you would, Sir, have been better satisfied with my researches.

I would have written to the Interpreters of the Posts, who would have furnished me with more certain information than that I could obtain from the *Voyageurs* whom I questioned. I am engaged at the history of the Scioux, which you have asked from Monsieur de Linerot.

Missilimakinak.

PRESENT STATE OF THE NORTHERN INDIANS

IN THE DEPAR[t] OF SIR WILLIAM JOHNSON BART., COMPREHENDED UNDER THE SIX NATIONS AND OTTAWA CONFEDERACIES, ETC, CONTAINING THE NAMES, NUMBERS AND SCITUATION OF EACH NATION, WITH REMARKS. NOV. 18, 1763.

[Lond. Doc. XXXVI.]

SIX NATION CONFEDERACY COMPREHENDING THAT OF CANADA, OHIO, &c.

Names.	*Number of men.*	*Scituation.*	*Remarks.*
Mohocks,	160	Two villages on the Mohock river, with a few emigrants at Schohare about 16 miles from Fort Hunter.	Of the Six Nations the Mohawks or Mohocks, Onondages and Senecas are considered as the chief and elder branches. The Oneidas, Cayugas and Tuscaroras are younger; the last mentioned Nation having many years ago retired from the South, and were admitted into the confederacy with the then Five Nations, the Oneidas giving them land and they now enjoy all priviledges with the rest.
Oneidas,	250	Two villages, one 25 miles from Fort Stanwix, the other twelve miles west of Oneida Lake, with emigrants in several places towards the Susquehanna river.	
Tuscaroras,	140	One village 6 miles from the first Oneidas, and several others about the Susquehanna.	
Onondagas,	150	One large village 6 miles from the lake of their name (which is the place of Congress for the confederates) with a smaller at some distance.	
Cayugas,	200	One large village near the Lake of their name with several others from thence to the Susquehanna.	
Senecas,	1050	Have several villages, beginning about 50 m. from Cayuga, and from thence to Chenussio, the largest about 70 m. from Niagara, with others thence to the Ohio.	Of the Senecas two villages are still in our interest, vizt. Kanadasero and Kanaderagey, the rest have joined the Western Nations.
Oswegachys,	80	Emigrants from the Six Nations chiefly Onondages settled at La Galette on the river St. Lawrence.	These are at peace with the English.
Nanticokes, Conoys, Tutecoes, Saponeys, ettc.	200	A people removed from the Southward, and settled on and about the Susquehanna on lands allotted by the Six Nations.	These people are immediately under the direction of the Six Nations, and at peace with the English.
		INDIANS OF CANADA IN ALLIANCE WITH THE SIX NATIONS.	
Caghnawagas,	300	Emigrants from the Mohocks, settled at Soult St. Louis near Montreal, with emigrants at Aghquissasne, below la Galette which is the seat of a Mission.	All these Nations are in alliance with the Six Nations, and warmly attached to the British Interest, as are all the other Indians in Canada. Caghnawaga is the seat of a Mission, as is the village of Lac du deux Montagnes.
Canassadagas, Arundacks, Algonkins,	150	These three Nations now reside together, at the Lac du deux Montagnes at the mouth of the Ottawa river near Montreal.	
Abenaquis,	100	Their village having been burned at St. Francis below Montreal during the war, they have since lived scattered except a few.	These Indians are originally from New-England: if they were all collected they would amount to more than is represented. They have likewise a Missionary who is a Jesuit.
Skaghquanoghronos,	40	Reside at Trois Rivieres, they are originally Algonkins.	
Hurons,	40	Reside at Loretto near Quebec, a very civilized people.	(There are several other Nations to the Northward, who avoid any connection with the white people; and as they have no fixed residence, their numbers, though considerable, cannot be ascertained.)

SIX NATION CONFEDERACY—CONTINUED.

Names.	Number of men.	Scituation.	Remarks.
		INDIANS OF OHIO.	
Shawnese,	300	Removed to the River Sciota and other Branches.	These people are greatly influenced by the Senecas, and reside on lands allotted them by the permission of the Six Nations. They are now at war with the English.
Delawares,	600	In several villages on and about the Susquehanna, Muskingum, ettc. and thence to Lake Erie.	
Wiandots, ettc.	200	Some villages in the neighborhood of Sandusky Fort near Lake Erie.	
Total,	3960	There are also in the Six Nation Confederacy, many Indians whose numbers cannot be computed as they have no fixed residence.	

OTTOWAY CONFEDERACY COMPREHENDING THE TWIGHTWEES, ETTC.

Names.	Number of men.	Scituation.	Remarks.
Wyandots or Hurons,	250	Reside opposite Detroit, their village is the seat of a Jesuit Mission, their language bears affinity with that of the Six Nations.	This Nation has a great influence over the rest, and has been greatly instigated by the neighbouring French to commit acts of hostility.
Powtewatamis, in the neighbourhood of Detroit.	150	Resided about a mile below the Fort, but abandoned their village on the commencement of hostilities.	
In the neighbourhood of St. Joseph.	200	A little below the Fort.	
Ottawas, residing in the neighbourhood of Detroit.	300	Resided about Detroit, but with the former, form a flying camp.	With these and the above Indians are joined several others, who form a flying camp under *Pondiac*, an Ottawa Chief.
In the neighbourhood of Michilimackinac.	250	Resided in different villages, but are now probably with the former. Michilimakinac is the seat of a Mission.	The Ottawas in the neighbourhood of Michilimakinac are well attached to us for the most part.
In the neighbourhood of Fort St. Joseph.	150	Resided at a small distance after the reduction of the Fort probably joined the rest.	
Chippeweighs or Mississagais: in the neighbourhood of Detroit.	320	Resided above the Detroit, now probably in arms with the rest.	These are the most numerous of all the Ottawa Confederacy and have many villages about Lakes Superior, Huron, Erie, ettc. whose numbers cannot at present be ascertained with exactness.
In the neighbourhood of Michilinac.	400	Had several different villages in that country, and the environs of the Lake Huron.	
Meynomenys	110	All these nations reside on the west side of La Baye at Lake Michigan and in the neighborhood of the fort there.	These nations are at present in alliance with the Ottawa Confederacy, but appear inclined to our interest, nor did they take the Fort at La Baye, the officer abandoning it on the news of the rupture, as he could make no defence.
Folsavoins	110		
Puans	360		
Sakis	300		
Foxes	320		
		MIAMIS OR TWIGHTWEES.	
Twightwees,	230	Near the Fort on the Miamis river.	The Twightwees were originally a very powerful people, who having been subdued by the Six Nations were permitted to enjoy their possessions. There are many tribes and villages of them, but these are all who are perfectly known.
Kickapous	180	These nations reside in the neighbourhood of the Fort at Wawaighta, and about the Walache river.	
Mascoutens	90		
Piankashaws	100		
Wawiaghtonos	200		
Ottawas, Chippeweighs, ettc.	4000	Residing through all the extent of country from the Lakes to the Great Ottawa river, and about Lake Superior, ettc.	This is the most exact computation that can be made of these numerous people, who are scattered throughout the Northern Parts and who having few places of fixed residence, subsisting entirely by hunting, cannot be ascertained as those of their confederacy, residing near the outposts.

OTTAWA CONFEDERACY—CONTINUED.

Names.	*Number of men.*	*Scituation.*	*Remarks.*
Illinois number uncertain.		Reside about the Illinois River and hence to the Mississippi.	We have hitherto had nothing to do with these people, who are numerous and variously computed. The Six Nations claim their country, but their right of conquest thereto does not appear so clear as to the rest, as represented in the letter herewith.
Sioux number uncertain.		Reside in the country westward of [*One line cut off here* Mississippi, they are much addicted to wandering and live mostly in camps.	The Sioux who are the most numerous of the Northern Indians, are little known to us, they *in binding the original.*] not appear well affected to the Western Indians, and promise to send Deputies to me in the spring.
Total, ...	8020		

November 18th, 1763. WILLIAM JOHNSON.

II.

PAPERS

RELATING TO

The First Settlement at Onondaga,

AND

THE DISCOVERY OF THE SALT SPRINGS AT SALINA.

Anno 1654—8.

VOYAGE OF FATHER SIMON LE MOINE

TO THE COUNTRY OF THE IROQUOIS ONONDAGOES, IN JULY, AUGUST AND SEPTEMBER, 1654.

[Relation de la N. France ès années, 1653 and 1654.]

On the second day of the month of July, the festival of the Visitation of the Most Holy Virgin always friendly to our undertakings, Father Le Moine departed from Quebec on a voyage to the Iroquois Onondagoes. He passed Three Rivers, and from thence by Montreal, where a young man of good courage, and an old *habitant*, joined him, with much piety. I shall follow the Father's Journal for greater facility.

On the 17th day of July, St. Alexis' day, we left home with this great and holy traveller, and departed for a land unknown to us. On the 18th, following always the course of the River St. Lawrence, we met nothing but breakers and impetuous rapids, all strewed with rocks and shoals.

The 19th. This river grows wider and forms a lake, agreeable to the view, from eight to ten leagues in length. At night, an army of troublesome musquitoes forboded the rain which poured down on us the whole of the night. To be in such circumstances without any shelter except the trees, which Nature has produced ever since the creation of the world, is a pastime more innocent and agreeable than could be anticipated.

20th. Nothing but islands, in appearance the most beautiful, which intersect here and there this very quiet river. The land on the north bank appears to us excellent; there is a range of high mountains towards the east, which we called St. Margaret's.

21st. Continuation of the islands. In the evening we break our bark canoe; it rains all night. The naked rocks serve us for bed, mattrass and all. Whoever hath God with him reposes quietly every where.

22d. The precipices of water which for a while are no longer navigable oblige us to carry on our shoulders both our baggage and the canoe which carried us. At the other side of the rapid, I perceived a herd of wild cows which were passing at their ease in great state. Five or six hundred are seen sometimes in these regions in one drove.

23d and 24th of the month. Our pilot being hurt, we must remain a prey to the musquitoes, and have patience, often more difficult in regard to the inconveniences which have no intermission neither night nor day, than to behold death before one's eyes.

25th. The river is so very rapid that we are obliged to throw ourselves in the stream to drag our canoe after us, amid the rocks, as a cavalier, dismounting, leads his horse by the bridle. At night we arrive at the entrance of Lake St. Ignatius, in which eels abound in a prodigious quantity.

26th. A high wind with rain forces us to debark, after having made four leagues. A hut is soon built. The neighboring trees are stript of their bark; this is thrown on poles set in the ground on either side, bringing them together in the form of an arbor; and then our house is built. Ambition finds no entrance into this palace. It failed not to be as agreeable to us as if the roof was all covered with gold.

27th. We coasted along the shores of the lake; they are rocks on one side and the other, of an immense height, now frightful, now pleasing to the sight. It is wonderful how large trees can find root among so many rocks.

28th. Thunder, lightning and a deluge of rain oblige us to shelter ourselves under our canoe, which being inverted, serves us for a house.

29th and 30th July. A rain storm continues, which arrests us at the entrance of a great lake, called Ontario. We call it the Lake of the Iroquois, because they have their villages on the south side there. The Hurons are on the other shore, farther on in the interior. This lake is twenty leagues wide; its length about forty.

31st. St. Ignatius' day. The rain and storm force us to seek for lost roads. We cross long islands, carrying our baggage, provisions and canoe on our shoulders. The road seems long to a poor weary man.

On the first day of the month of August, some Iroquois fishermen having perceived us from a distance, get together to receive us. One of them runs towards us, advancing a half a league to communicate the earliest news and the state of the country. It is a Huron prisoner, and a good Christian, whom I formerly instructed during a winter that I passed among the savages. This poor lad could not believe that it was he whom he never hoped to see again. We disembarked at a little village of fishermen. They crowd as to who shall carry our baggage. But alas! they are apparently only Huron squaws, and for the most part Christian women, formerly rich and at their ease, whom captivity has reduced to servitude. They requested me to pray to God, and I had the consolation to confess there at my leisure Hostagehtak, our antient host of the Petun Nation. His sentiments and devotion drew tears from my eyes; he is the fruit of the labors of Father Charles Garnier, that holy missionary whose death has been so precious before God.

The second day of August. We walked about twelve to fifteen leagues in the woods. We camp where the day closes.

The 3d. At noon we find ourselves on the bank of a river, one hundred or one hundred and twenty paces wide, beyond which there was a hamlet of fishermen. An Iroquois whom I at one time had treated kindly at Montreal, put me across in his canoe, and through respect carried me on his shoulders, being unwilling to suffer me to wet my feet. Every one received me with joy, and these poor people enriched me from their poverty. I was conducted to another village a league distant, where there was a young man of consideration who made a feast for me because I bore his father's name, Ondessonk. The Chiefs came to harangue us, the one after the other. I baptized little skeletons who awaited, perhaps, only this drop of the precious blood of Jesus Christ.

4th. They ask me why we are dressed in black? and I take occasion to speak to them of our mysteries with great attention They bring me a little moribund whom I call Dominick. The time is passed when they used to hide the little innocents from us. They took me for a great Medicine-man, having no other remedy for the sick but a pinch of sugar. We pursued our route—in the middle of which we found our dinner waiting for us. The nephew of the first Chief of the country, who is to lodge me in his cabin, is deputed by his uncle to escort us, bringing us every delicacy that the season could afford, especially new corn bread, and ears (of corn) which we had roasted at the fire. We slept again that day by the beautiful light of the stars.

5th. We had to make four leagues before arriving at the principal Onondaga village. There is nothing but comers and goers on the road who come to salute me. One treats me as brother; another as uncle—never did I have such a number of relations. A quarter of a league from the village I began a harangue, which gained me much credit. I named all the Chiefs; the families and persons of note in a drawling voice and with the tone of a chief. I told them that Peace walked along with me; that I drove War afar off among the distant nations, and that Joy accompanied me. Two Chief made their speech to me on my arrival, but with a gladness and cheerfulness of countenance which I never had seen among savages. Men, women and children, all were respectful and friendly.

At night I called the principal men together to make them two presents. The first to wipe their faces, so that they may regard me with a kindly eye, and that I may never see a trace of sorrow on their foreheads. The second to clear out the little gall which they still might have in their hearts. After several other discourses they retired to consult together, and finally they responded to my presents by two other presents richer than mine.

6th. I was called to divers quarters to administer my medicine to weakly and hectic little things. I baptized some of them. I confessed some of our old Huron Christians, and found God every where, and that he pleased to work himself in hearts where faith reigns. He builds himself a temple there, where he is adored in spirit and truth. Be He blessed for ever.

At night our host draws me aside and tells me very affectionately that he always loved us, that finally his heart was satisfied, seeing all the tribes of his nation demanded nothing but peace: that the Seneca had recently come to exhort them to manage this matter well for peace, and that with that view he had made splendid presents: that the Cayuga had brought three belts for that purpose, and that the Oneida was glad to be rid of such a bad affair through his means, and that he desired nothing but peace: that the Mohawk would, no doubt, follow the others, and thus I might take courage, since I bore with me the happiness of the whole land.

7th. A good Christian named Terese, a Huron captive, wishing to pour out her soul to me away from noise and in silence, invited me to visit her in a field cabin where she lived. My God! What sweet consolation to witness so much faith in savage hearts, in captivity, and without other assistance than that of heaven. God raises up Apostles every where. This good Christian woman had with her a young captive of the neutral nation (*de la Nation Neutre*), whom she loved as her own daughter. She had so well instructed her in the mysteries of the faith, and in sentiments of piety, in the prayers they made in this holy solitude, that I was much surprised. Eh! sister, I asked, why did you not baptise her, since she has the faith like you, and she is Christian in her morals, and she wishes to die a Christian? Alas, brother, this happy captive replied, I did not think it was allowed me to baptise, except in danger of death. Baptise her now, yourself, since you consider her worthy, and give her my name. This was the first adult baptism at Onondaga; we are indebted for it to the piety of a Huron.

* * * * * * * * * * *

GENERAL COUNCIL OF PEACE WITH THE FOUR IROQUOIS NATIONS,

AND THE SUBSEQUENT RETURN OF FATHER SIMON LE MOINE FROM HIS VOYAGE.

[From the Same.]

On the 10th day of August, the deputies of the three neighbouring Nations having arrived, after the usual summons of the Chiefs that all should assemble in Ondessonk's cabin, I opened the proceedings (says the Father, continuing his Journal) by public prayer, which I said on my knees and in a loud voice, all in the Huron tongue. I invoked the Great Master of heaven and of earth to inspire us with what should be for his glory and our good; I cursed all the demons of hell who are spirits of division; I prayed the tutelar angels of the whole country to touch the hearts of those who heard me, when my words should strike their ear.

I greatly astonished them when they heard me naming all by nations, by tribes, by families and each particular individual of any note, and all by aid of my manuscript, which was a matter as wonderful as it was new. I told them I was the bearer of nineteen words to them.

The first: That it was Onnonthio, M. de Lauzon, Governor of New France, who spoke by my mouth, and then the Hurons and the Algonquins as well as the French, for all these three nations had Onnonthio for their Great Chief. A large belt of wampum, one hundred little tubes or pipes of red glass, the diamonds of the country, and a caribou's hide being passed: these three presents made but one word.

My second word was, to cut the bonds of the eight Seneca prisoners, taken by our allies and brought to Montreal as already stated.

The third was, to break the bonds of the Mohegans also, captured about the same time.

The fourth; to thank those of Onontago for having brought our prisoner back.

The fifth present was, to thank the Senecas for having saved him from the scaffold.

The sixth for the Cayuga Iroquois, for having also contributed.

The seventh, for the Oneidas for having broken the bonds which kept him a prisoner.

The 8th, 9th, 10th and 11th presents to be given to the four Iroquois Nations, a hatchet to each, for the new war they were waging against the Cat Nation.

The twelfth present was to heal the head of the Seneca who had lost some of his people.

The thirteenth, to strengthen his palisades; to wit, that he may be in a state of defence against the enemy.

The fourteenth, to ornament his face: for it is the custom of warriors here never to go to battle unless with the face painted, some black, some red, others with various other colors, each having herein as if particular liveries to which they cling even unto death.

The fifteenth to concentrate all their thoughts. I made three presents for this occasion; one wampum belt, little glass beads and an elk hide.

The sixteenth—I opened Annonchiasse's door to all the Nations; that is, they would be welcome among us.

The seventeenth. I exhorted them to become acquainted with the truths of our faith, and made three presents for this object.

The eighteenth. I asked them not to prepare henceforward any ambushes for the Algonquin and Huron Nations, who would come to visit us in our French settlement. I made three presents for this purpose.

Finally, by the nineteenth present I wiped away the tears of all the young warriors for the death of their great Chief Annencraos, a short time prisoner with the Cat Nation.

At each present they heaved a powerful ejaculation from the bottom of the chest in testimony of their joy. I was full two hours making my whole speech, talking like a chief, and walking about like an actor on a stage, as is their custom.

After that they grouped together apart in nations and tribes, calling to them a Mohawk who by good luck was there. They consulted together for the space of two hours longer. Finally they called me among them and seated me in an honorable place.

The Chief who is the tongue of the country, repeats faithfully as orator the substance of all my words. Then all set to singing in token of their gratification; I was told to pray God on my side, which I did very willingly. After these songs he spoke to me in the name of his Nation. 1. He thanked Onnontio for his good disposition towards them, and brought forward for this purpose two large belts of wampum.

2. He thanked us in the name of the Mohawk Iroquois for having given their lives to five of their allies of the Mohegan nation. Two other belts for that.

3. He thanked us in the name of the Seneca Iroquois for having drawn five of their tribe out of the fire. Two more belts. Ejaculations from the whole assembly follow each present.

Another Captain of the Oneida Nation rises: Onnontio, said he—speaking of M. de Lauzon our Governor—Onnontio thou art the pillar of the Earth; thy spirit is a spirit of peace and thy words soften the hearts of the most rebellious spirits. After other compliments expressed in a tone animated by love and respect, he produced four large belts to thank Onnontio for having encouraged them to fight bravely against their new enemies of the Cat Nation, and for having exhorted them never again to war against the French. Thy voice, said he, Onnontio is wonderful, to produce in my breast at one time two effects entirely dissimilar; thou animatest me to war, and softenest my heart by the thoughts of peace; thou art great both in peace and war, mild to those whom thou lovest, and terrible to thine enemies. We wish thee to love us, and we will love the French for thy sake.

In concluding these thanks, the Onontaga Chief took up the word. Listen Ondessonk, said he to me; five entire nations speak to thee through my mouth. My breast contains the sentiments of the Iroquois Nations, and my tongue responds faithfully to my breast. Thou wilt tell Onnontio four things, the sum of all our councils.

1. We are willing to acknowledge Him of whom thou hast spoken, who is the master of our lives, who is unknown to us.

2. Our council tree is this day planted at Onnontaga—meaning that that would be, henceforth, the place of their meetings and of their negotiations for peace.

3. We conjure you to select on the banks of our great lake an advantageous site for a French settlement. Fix yourself in the heart of the country, since you ought to possess our hearts. There we shall go for instruction, and from that point you will be able to spread yourself abroad in every direction. Be unto us careful as fathers and we shall be unto you submissive as children.

4. We are engaged in new wars; Onnontio encourages us. We shall entertain no other thought towards him than those of peace.

They reserved their richest presents for these last four words; but I can assure you their countenances told more than their tongues, and expressed joy mingled with so much mildness that my heart was full. What appeared to me most endearing in all this was that all our Huron Christians and the captive women, lighted this fire which melts the hearts of the Iroquois. They told them so much good of us, and spoke so often of the great value of the Faith, that they prize it without being acquainted with it; and they love us in the hope that we shall be for them what we have been for the Indians. To return to the Father's Journal:

The 11th day of August. There is nothing but feasts and rejoicings every where. A misfortune occurred, however, at night. A cabin catching fire, no one knew how, an impetuous wind drove the flames to the others, and in less than two hours more than twenty were reduced to ashes, and the remainder of the village was in danger of being burnt. God preserved all hearts however in the joy of the preceding day, and their dispositions as calm towards me as if this misfortune had never happened.

The 12th. Our Christian captives wishing to confess before my departure gave me employment, or rather repose which I wished for. I baptized a little girl of four years who was dying. I recovered from the hands of these barbarians, the New Testament of the late Father Jean de Brebouf, whom they put to a cruel death five years ago, and a small book of devotion which was used by the late Father Charles Garnier whom they also killed four years ago.

* * * * * * * * * * * * * * * *

The 13th. Came the leave taking. Observing the custom of friends on similar occasions, having convoked the Council, I made them two presents to console them. And with this view I first planted in the name of Achiendassé (which is the appellation of the General Superior of all our Society's Missions in these countries) the first post on which to begin a cabin. This is like laying the first stone in France of a house one intends to build. My second present was to throw down the first bark that is to cover the cabin. This evidence of affection satisfied them, and three of their chiefs thanked me publicly in speeches which one could not be persuaded issued from the lips of men called savages.

* * * * * * * * * * * * * * * *

Nevertheless they seek me every where to give me my parting feast, all the men and women of consideration being invited in my name into our cabin, according to the custom of the country, in order to do honor to my departure. We part in good company. After the public cry of the Chief, every one vies to carry our little baggage.

About half a league from there we found a group of old men, all Chiefs of the Council, who waited to bid me Adieu hoping for my return for which they ardently testified their wishes.

16th. We arrive at the entrance of a small lake in a large half dried basin; we taste the water of a spring that they durst not drink, saying that there is a Demon in it which renders it fœtid; having tasted it I found it was a fountain of Salt water; and in fact we made salt from it as natural as that from the sea; of which we carried a sample to Quebec. This lake abounds in fish—in salmon trout and other fish.

17th. We enter their river, and at a quarter of a league meet at the left the Seneca river, which increases this; it leads, they say, to Cayuga (Onioen) and to Seneca in two sunsets. At three leagues of a fine road from there, we leave the river Oneida (Oneiout) which appears to us very deep. Finally a good league lower down we meet a rapid which gives the name to a village of fishermen. I found there some of our Christians and some Huron Christian women whom I had not yet seen.

* * * * * * * * * * * * * * * *

19th. We proceed on our journey on the same river which is of a fine width and deep throughout, except some shoals where we must get into the water and draw the canoe lest the rocks break it.

20. We arrive at the Great Lake, Ontario, called the Lake of the Iroquois.

21. This lake is in a fury in consequence of the violence of the winds after a storm of rain.

22. Coasting quietly the shores of this Great Lake, my sailors kill with a shot from a gun, a large stag: my companion and I content ourselves looking at them broiling their stakes, it being Saturday, a day of abstinence for us.

23. We arrive at the place which is fixed on for our house and a French settlement. Beautiful prairies, good fishing; a resort of all Nations. There I found new Christians who confessed themselves and furnished me with devotion in their sentiments of piety.

24 and 25. Being windbound, one of our canoes foundered on the 26, our sailors having embarked before the tempest had abated, and we thought we should have perished—finally we cast ourselves on an island where we dried ourselves at our leisure.

27. In the evening a little lull afforded us time to regain the main land.

28 and 29. The chase stops our sailors who are in the best possible humor; for flesh is the paradise of the man of flesh.

30 and last of August. The rain and wind seriously inconvenience poor travellers, who having worked all day are badly provided for at night.

1st day of Sept. I never saw so many deer, but we had no inclination to hunt. My companion killed three as if against his will. What a pity! for we left all the venison there, reserving the hides and some of the most delicate morsels.

2d of the month. Travelling through vast prairies, we saw in divers quarters immense herds of wild bulls and cows; their horns resemble in some respect the antlers of the stag.

3d and 4th. Our game does not leave us; it seems that venison and game follow us every where. Droves of twenty cows plunge into the water as if to meet us. Some are killed, for sake of amusement, by blows of an axe.

5. In one day we travel over the road which took us two long days ascending the rapids and breakers.

6. Our Sault St. Louis frightens my folks. They land me four leagues above the settlement of Montreal, and God gave me sufficient strength to arrive before noon, and to celebrate mass, of which I was deprived during my whole voyage.

7. I proceed and descend to Three Rivers where my sailors desire to go. We arrived at Quebec on the eleventh day of the month of September of this year, 1654.

JOURNAL OF WHAT OCCURRED BETWEEN THE FRENCH AND SAVAGES.

[Relation, &c. 1657 and 1658.]

The word *Onnota*, which signifies, in the Iroquois tongue, a Mountain, has given the name to the village called Onnontaé, or as others call it, Onnontagué, because it is on a mountain; and the people who inhabit it consequently style themselves Onnontae-ronnons, or Onnontagué-ronnons.

These people have for a long time and earnestly demanded that some priests of our Society
1655. be sent to their country. Finally, Father Joseph Chaumont and Father Claude Dablon were
granted to them, in the year 1655. They embarked on the 19th Sept., and arrived at Onnontagué the 5th November of the same year 1655.

These two good fathers finding themselves listened to with approval and kindness, Father
1656. Dablon left Onnontagué on the second day of March of the following year 1656, to look for
help at Quebec, where he arrived in the beginning of April, and departed thence on the 17th May, in company with three Fathers and two brothers of the Society, and a good number of Frenchmen, who all proceeded towards this new country, where they arrived on the 11th day of July of the same year, 1656.

In the year 1657, the harvest appearing plentiful in all the villages of the upper Iroquois,
1657. the common people listening to the words of the gospel with simplicity and the Chiefs with
a well disguised dissimulation, Father Paul Ragueneau, Father François Du Peron, some Frenchmen and several Hurons, departed from Montreal the 26th July, to aid their brethren and compatriots.

On the 3d day of the month of August of the same year 1657, the perfidy of the Iroquois began to develop itself by the massacre which they made of the poor Hurons whom they brought into their country, after thousands of protestations of kindness and thousands of oaths, in their style, that they should treat them as brothers. And had not a number of Iroquois remained among the French, near Quebec, to endeavor to bring with them the rest of the Hurons, who distrusting these traitors, would not embark with the others, the Fathers and the Frenchmen who ascended with them would have then been destroyed; and all those who remained on the banks of Lake Ganantaa, near to Onnontagué, would shortly after have shared the same fate. But the fear that the French would wreak vengeance on their countrymen, staid their design, of which our fathers had had secret intelligence immediately on their arrival in the country. Even a captain who was acquainted with the secret of the chiefs, having taken some liking to the preachings of the Gospel, and finding himself very sick, demanded Baptism ; having received it with sufficient instruction, he discovered the evil designs of his countrymen to those who attended him, and went a short time afterwards to Heaven.

* * * * * * * * *

The 9th of the month of September. Our fathers at Onnontagué sent two canoes to Quebec with intelligence of the massacre of the poor Huron Christians, treacherously put to death by these barbarians, as we remarked above, 3 August of the year 1657.

* * * * * * * * *

The 7th of the month of November. Two Mohawks departed from Quebec, and took a third at Three Rivers. . . . . . A number of letters from divers quarters were given to them for Father Le Moine, part of which were to be sent to our Fathers and our French of Onnontagué thro' the medium of the Mohawks, who often go to that country.

* * * * * * * * *

It is true that the Mohawks faithfully delivered the letters to Ondessonk, because they feared evil for their people detained by the French. But for the letters addressed to our French at Onnontagué, the Mohawk who was the bearer thereof, threw them in the river, or gave them, probably to the chiefs of the country. But these good fellows, who wished to rid themselves of the preachers of the gospel and of those who assisted them, threw them into the fire.

The Onnontagué sent by Monsieur de Maisonneuve did still worse: for he told the chiefs of the nation, that the French were leagued principally with the Algonquins to make war on them, and that they had killed his comrade. It was an Algonquin killed him on his way to war as we have remarked on the 3d November. Nothing more was necessary to excite these furious men, who had already concluded on the death of some and the captivity of others. They were desirous, however, to act in concert with the Mohawks, who could, no more than the others, reconcile themselves to the detention of their people, believing it very unjust.

Our poor French were, meanwhile, much astonished at receiving no certain news either from Quebec, Three Rivers, or Montreal. These barbarians had entirely cut off all communication, so that Monsr. de Dailleboust's orders were not delivered to Monsr. Du Puis, who commanded the soldiers, nor a letter to any of the French whomsoever.

OF THE RETURN OF OUR FATHERS AND OF OUR FRENCHMEN FROM THE COUNTRY OF THE ONNONTAGUES.

[From the Same.]

Though it be true that the Iroquois are subtle, adroit and great cheats, I nevertheless cannot persuade myself that they possess so much intelligence, so much tact, and that they are such great politicians as to have had recourse to the ruses and intrigues imputed to them to destroy the French, the Hurons, the Algonquins, and their allies.

They urged for many years with incredible persistence; with evidences of especial affection and even with threats of rupture and war, if their friendship were despised and their demand rejected; they insisted, I say, and solicited that a goodly number of French should accompany them into their country, the one to instruct, the others to protect them against their enemies, as a token of peace and alliance with them.

The Mohawks desired to thwart this scheme; they fought the one against the other even unto polluting the earth with blood and murder. Some believed that all that was mere feint, the better to mask their game; but it would seem to me not a very pleasant game when the stakes are life and blood. I strongly doubt that Iroquoy policy should extend so far as that, and that Barbarians who repose but little confidence in each other, should so long conceal their intrigues. I believe rather that the Onnontagué Iroquois demanded some Frenchmen in sincerity, but with views very different. The Chiefs finding themselves engaged in heavy wars against a number of nations whom they had provoked, asked for Hurons as reinforcements to their warriors; they wished for the French to obtain firearms from them, and to repair those which might be broken. Further, as the Mohawks treated them sometimes very ill when passing through their villages to trade with the Dutch, they were anxious to rise out of this dependence in opening a trade with the French. This is not all, the fate of arms being fickle, they demanded that our Frenchmen should erect a vast fort in their country to serve as a retreat for them, or at least for their wives and children in case their enemies pressed too close on them. Here are the views of the Iroquois politicians. The common people did not penetrate so far ahead; curiosity to see strangers come from such a distance, the hope of deriving some little profit, created a desire to see them; but the Christian Hurons and captives among the people, and those who approved their lives and conversations which they sometimes held regarding our belief, breathed nothing in the world so much as the coming of Preachers of the Gospel who had brought them forth unto Jesus Christ.

But so soon as the Captains and Chiefs became masters of their enemies, having crushed all the Nations who had attacked them; so soon as they believed that nothing could resist their arms, the recollection of the wrongs they pretended to have formerly experienced from the Hurons; the glory of triumphing over Europeans as well as Americans, caused them to take the resolution to revenge themselves on the one and destroy the other; so that at the very moment they saw the dreaded Cat Nation subjugated by their arms and by the power of the Senecas, their allies, they would have massacred all the French at Onnontagué, were it not that they pretended to make use of them as a decoy to attract some Hurons and to massacre them as they had already done. And if the influence of some of their tribe, then resident at Quebec, had not staid them, the path to Onnontagué had become the tomb to Frenchmen as well as to Hurons, as will be seen hereafter. From that time forth our people, having discovered their conspiracy, and perceived that their death was concluded on, bethought them on their retreat, which shall be described in the following letter.

FATHER PAUL RAGUENEAU

TO THE REV. FATHER JACQUES RENAULT, PROVINCIAL OF THE SOCIETY OF JESUS IN THE PROVINCE OF FRANCE.

Pax Christi.

My R. Father,

The present is to inform Y. R. of our return from the Iroquois mission, loaded with some spoils rescued from Hell. We bear in our hands more than five hundred children and a number of adults, the most part of whom died after Baptism. We have reëstablished Faith and piety in the hearts of a poor captive church, the first foundation of which we had laid in the Huron Country. We have proclaimed the gospel unto all the Iroquois Nations so that they are henceforth without excuse, and God will be fully justified against them at the great day of judgment.

The Devil enraged at seeing us reap so fine a harvest and enjoy so amply the fruits of our enterprise, made use of the inconstancy of the Iroquois to drive us from the centre of his estates; for these Barbarians, without other motive than to follow their volatile humor, renewed the war against the French, the first blows of which were discharged on our worthy Christian Hurons, who went up with us to Onnontagué at the close of the last summer, and who were cruelly massacred in our arms and in our bosom by the most signal treason imaginable. They then made prisoners of their poor wives and even burned some of them with their children of three and four years, at a slow fire.

This bloody execution was followed by the murder of three Frenchmen at Montreal by the Oneidas, who scalped them and carried these as if in triumph into their villages in token of declared war. This act of hostility having obliged M. Dailleboust, then commanding in this country, to cause a dozen of Iroquois, in part Onnontagués and mostly Mohawks, to be arrested and put in irons at Montreal, Three Rivers and Quebec, where they happened to be at the time, both Iroquois Nations became irritated at this detention of their people, pretending that it was unjust; and to cruelly avenge themselves convoked a secret Council where they formed the scheme of an implacable war against the French. Yet, they judged it fitting to dissimulate for some time until through the return of Father Simon Le Moine, then with the Mohawks, they should have obtained the delivery of their folks who were in irons. In that Council they even looked on our persons as precious hostages, either for the exchange of some of their tribe who were in prison, or obtainment of whatever pleased them when within view of our French settlements they should make us feel the effects of their cruelty; doubting not that these horrible spectacles and the lamentations of forty and fifty innocent French would touch with compassion and distress the Governor and inhabitants of what place so ever.

We were only privately acquainted with these disastrous designs of the Iroquois, but we openly saw their spirits prepared for war; and in the month of February divers bands took the field for that purpose, 200 Mohawks on the one side, 40 Oneidas on the other; some Onnontagué warriors had already gone forward whilst the main body of the army was assembling.

We could not expect, speaking humanly, to extricate from these dangers, by which we were surrounded on all sides, some fifty Frenchmen who had entrusted to us their lives and for whom we should feel ourselves responsible before God and men. What distressed us the most was, not so much the flames into which a part of our Frenchmen would be cast, as the unfortunate captivity to which the most of them were destined by the Iroquois, in which the salvation of their souls was more to be dreaded than the loss of their bodies. This is what the greater number most especially apprehended, who already seeing themselves prisoners, coveted rather the stroke of the hatchet or even the flames, than this captivity. They were determined in order to avoid this last misfortune, even to risk all and to fly each, his way in the woods, to perish there of hunger and wretchedness or to attempt to reach some of the French settlements.

In these circumstances so precipitous, our Fathers and I and a gentleman named Monsieur du Puys, who commanded all our Frenchmen and a garrison of soldiers, nine of whom had already of themselves resolved to abandon us, concluded that it would be better to withdraw in a body, either to encourage one another to die or to sell life more dearly. For that reason it became necessary to depart without breathing a syllable about it; for the least suspicion that the Iroquois would have had of our retreat, would hurry down on us the disaster we would avoid. But how hope to be able to depart without being discovered, being in the heart of the country, and always beset by a number of these Barbarians who left not our house so as to watch our countenances in this conjuncture? It is true they never imagined that we should have had the courage to undertake this exploit, knowing well that we had neither canoes, nor sailors, and that we were unacquainted with the paths topped by precipices where a dozen Iroquois could easily defeat us: Besides, the season was insupportable on account of the cold of the frozen water through which, under all circumstances, the canoes were to be dragged, throwing ourselves into the river and remaining there entire hours, sometimes up to the neck, and we never had undertaken such expeditions without having savages for guides.

Notwithstanding these obstacles which appeared insurmountable to them as well as to us, God, who holds in His hands all the moments of our lives, so happily inspired us with all that was necessary to be done, that having departed on the 20th day of March from our house of *Ste. Marie*, near Onnontagué, at eleven o'clock at night, His divine providence guiding us, as if by a continued miracle, in the midst of all imaginable dangers, we arrived at Quebec on the 23[d] of the month of April, having passed Montreal and Three Rivers before any canoe could be launched, the river not having been open for navigation until the very day that we made our appearance.

From the same to the same.

Your Rev. will be glad to learn the particulars of our departure from *Ste. Marie* of the Iroquois. * * * * * The resolution being taken to quit that country where God took through us, the small number of his disciples, the difficulties appeared insurmountable in their execution for which every thing failed us.

To supply the want of canoes, we had built, in secret, two Batteaux of a novel and excellent structure to pass the rapids; these Batteaux drew but very little water and carried considerable freight, fourteen or fifteen men each, amounting to fifteen to sixteen hundred weight. We had moreover four Algonquin and four Iroquois canoes, which were to compose our little fleet of fifty-three Frenchmen.

But the difficulty was to embark unperceived by the Iroquois who constantly beset us. The batteaux, canoes and all the equipage could not be conveyed without great noise, and yet without secrecy there was nothing to be expected save a general massacre of all of us the moment it would be discovered that we entertained the least thought of withdrawing.

On that account we invited all the savages in our neighborhood to a solemn feast at which we employed all our industry, and spared neither the noise of drums nor instruments of music to deceive them by harmless device. He who presided at this ceremony played his part with so much address and success, that all were desirous to contribute to the publick joy: Every one vied in uttering the most piercing cries, now of war, anon of rejoicing. The savages, through complaisance, sung and danced after the French fashion and the French in the Indian style. To encourage them the more in this fine play, presents were distributed among those who acted best their parts and who made the greatest noise to drown that caused by about forty of our people outside who were engaged in removing all our equipage. The embarcation being completed, the feast was concluded at a fixed time; the guests retired, and sleep having soon overwhelmed them, we withdrew from our house by a back door and embarked with very little noise, without bidding adieu to the Savages, who were acting cunning parts and were thinking to amuse us to the hour of our massacre with fair appearances and evidences of good will.

Our little Lake on which we silently sailed in the darkness of the night, froze according as we advanced and caused us to fear being stopt by the ice after having evaded the fires of the Iroquois. God, however, delivered us, and after having advanced all night and all the following day through frightful precipices and waterfalls, we arrived finally in the evening at the great Lake Ontario, twenty leagues from the place of our departure. This first day was the most dangerous, for had the Iroquois discovered our departure they would have intercepted us, and had they been ten or twelve it would have been easy for them to have thrown us into disorder, the river being very narrow, and terminating after travelling ten leagues in a frightful precipice where we were obliged to land and carry our baggage and canoes during four hours, through unknown roads covered with a thick forest which could have served the enemy for a Fort, whence at each step he could have struck and fired on us without being perceived. God's protection visibly accompanied us during the remainder of the road, in which we walked through perils which made us shudder after we escaped them, having at night no other bed except the snow after having passed entire days in the water and amid the ice.

Ten days after our departure we found Lake Ontario on which we floated, still frozen at its mouth. We were obliged to break the ice, axe in hand, to make an opening, to enter two days afterwards a rapid where our little fleet had well nigh foundered. For having entered a Great *Sault* without knowing it, we found ourselves in the midst of breakers which, meeting a quantity of big rocks, threw up mountains of water and cast us on as many precipices as we gave strokes of paddles. Our batteaux which drew scarcely half a foot, were soon filled with water and all our people in such confusion, that their cries mingled with the roar of the torrent presented to us the spectacle of a dreadful wreck. It became imperative, however, to extricate oureslves, the violence of the current dragging us despite ourselves into the large rapids and through passes in which we had never been. Terror redoubled at the sight of one of our canoes being engulfed in a breaker which barred the entire rapid and which, notwithstanding, was the course that all the others must keep. Three Frenchmen were drowned there, a fourth fortunately escaped, having held on to the canoe and being saved at the foot of the *Sault* when at the point of letting go his hold, his strength being exhausted. * * * The 3d of April we landed at Montreal, in the beginning of the night.

* * * * * * * * * * *

You noticed above....how our Fathers and our Frenchmen withdrew from their habitation built on the banks of Lake Ganantaa, near Onnontagué. That happened at night, and without noise and with so much address, that the Iroquois, who cabined at the doors of our house, never perceived the removal of the canoes and batteaux and baggage which were launched, nor the embarcation of fifty-three persons. Sleep in which they were deeply enveloped, after considerable singing and dancing, deprived them of all consciousness; but at length night having given place to day, darkness to light, sleep to awaking, these Barbarians left their cabins, and roving round our well locked house, were astonished at the profound silence of the Frenchmen. They saw no one going out to work; they heard no voice. They thought at first that they were all at prayer, or in council, but the day advancing and these prayers not getting to an end, they knocked at the door. The dogs, which our Frenchmen designedly left behind, answered by barking. The cock's crow which they heard in the morning and the noise of the dogs, made them think that the masters of these animals were not far off; they recovered the patience which they had lost. But at length the sun began to decline and no person answering neither to the voice of men nor to the cries of animals, they scaled the house to see the condition of our people in this terrible silence. Astonishment now gave place to fright and trouble. They open the door; the chiefs enter every where; ascend the garret; descend to the cellar; not a Frenchman makes his appearance dead or alive. They regard one another—terror seizes them; they imagine they have to do with Devils. They saw no batteau, and even if they saw it they could not imagine that our Frenchmen would be so rash as to precipitate themselves into rapids and breakers, among rocks and horrible dangers in which themselves though very expert in passing through *Saults* and Cascades, often lose their lives. They persuade themselves either that they walked on the waves, or fled through the air; or as seemed most probable, that they concealed themselves in the woods. They seek for them; nothing appears. They are quasi convinced that they rendered themselves invisible; and as they suddenly departed, so will they pounce as suddenly on their village.

III.

PAPERS

RELATING TO

De Courcelles' and De Tracy's Expeditions

AGAINST

THE MOHAWK INDIANS.

Anno 1665—6.

OF THE FIRST FORTS ERECTED ON THE IROQUOIS RIVER.

[Relation de ce qui s'est passé en la Nouvelle France ès années 1664 and 1665.]

At the same time that the Outaouaks embarked to return to their country, the wind becoming more favorable, the soldiers who had been obliged to stop at Three Rivers likewise embarked; and after having navigated Lake St. Peter arrived at the mouth of the River Richelieu, which leads to the Iroquois of the Mohawk.

The plan entertained at this first campaign was to erect on the route some forts, which were considered absolutely necessary as well to secure the passage and liberty of trade as to serve for stores for the troops and retreats for sick and wounded soldiers. For this purpose three advantageous posts were selected. The first at the mouth of the Iroquois River; the second seventeen leagues higher up, at the foot of a current of water called the *Sault de Richelieu*: the third about three leagues above this current.

The first fort, named Richelieu, was built by Mons. de Chamblay, who commanded five companies which Monsieur de Tracy sent there. The second fort, named St. Louis, because it was commenced the week of the celebration of the festival of that great saint, protector of our Kings and of France, was built by M. de Sorel, who commanded five other companies of the Regiment of the Carignan Salières. . . . The [third] fort was fortunately finished in the month of October on St. Theresa's day, whence it derived its name. From this third fort of St. Therese we can easily reach Lake Champlain without meeting any rapids to stop the batteaux.

This Lake, after a length of sixty leagues, finally terminates in the country of the Mohawk Iroquois. It is still intended to build there, early next spring, a fourth fort, which will command those countries, and from which continual attacks can be made on the enemy, if they do not listen to reason.

We shall give at the end of the next chapter, the plan of these three forts, with the map of the Iroquois country[1] which has not been as yet seen, after having given some particulars of those people, who thwart us so long a time, because they have never been efficiently attacked.

OF THE IROQUOIS COUNTRY AND THE ROUTES LEADING THITHER.

It must be premised that the Iroquois are composed of five Nations, of which the nearest to the Dutch is that of the Mohawk consisting of two or three villages containing about three to four hundred men capable of bearing arms. These have always been at war with us, though they sometimes pretended to sue for peace.

1 For the Map above referred to, see the Vol. of Relations in the State Library.

Proceeding towards the West, at a distance of forty-five leagues, is found the second Nation, called Oneida, which has no more, at most, than one hundred and forty warriors, and has never wished to listen to any negotiations for peace; on the contrary it has always embarrassed affairs when they appeared about to be arranged.

Fifteen leagues towards sunset is Onnontagué, which has full three hundred men. We have been formerly received there as friends and treated as enemies, which obliged us to abandon that post, where we remained two years, as if in the centre of all the Iroquois Nations, whence we proclaimed the gospel to all those poor people, assisted by a garrison of Frenchmen sent by Monsieur de Lauzon, then Governor of New France, to take possession of those countries in his Majesty's name.

At twenty or thirty leagues from there still towards the West is the village of Cayuga, of three hundred warriors, where in the year 1657, we had a mission which formed a little church filled with piety in the midst of these Barbarians.

Towards the termination of the Great Lake, called Ontario, is located the most numerous of the Five Iroquois Nations, named the Senecas, which contains full twelve hundred men in two or three villages of which it is composed.

These last two nations have never openly made war on us, and have always remained neuter.

All that extent of country is partly south, partly west of the French settlements, at a distance of from one hundred to one hundred and fifty leagues. It is for the most part fertile, covered with fine timber; among the rest entire forests of chestnut and hickory (*noyer,*) intersected by numerous lakes and rivers abounding in fish. The air is temperate; the seasons regular as in France, capable of bearing all the fruits of Touraine and Provence. The snows are not deep nor of long duration. The three winters which we passed there among the Onnontagués, were mild compared with the winters at Quebec where the ground is covered five months with snow, three, four and five feet deep. As we inhabit the Northern part of New France and the Iroquois the South, it is not surprising that their lands are more agreeable and more capable of cultivation and of bearing better fruit.

There are two principal rivers leading to the Iroquois: one to those which are near New Netherland and this is the Richelieu river of which we shall speak hereafter; the second conducts to the other Nations more distant from us, always ascending our great river St. Lawrence which divides, above Montreal, as if into two branches, whereof one goes to the antient country of the Hurons, the other to that of the Iroquois.

This is one of the most important rivers that can be seen, whether we regard its beauty or its convenience; for we meet there almost throughout, a vast number of beautiful Islands, some large, others small, but all covered with fine timber and full of deer, bears, wild cows which supply abundance of provisions necessary for the travellers who find it every where, and some times entire herds of fallow deer. The banks of the main land are ordinarily shaded by huge oaks and other lofty timber covering a good soil.

Before arriving at the Great Lake Ontario, two others are traversed, one of which adjoins the Island of Montreal, the other is amidway. It is ten leagues long by six wide. It is terminated by a great many little islands very pleasing to the sight, and we have named it Lake St. Francis.

But what renders this river inconvenient is the water falls and rapids which extend for the space of forty leagues, to wit from Montreal to the entrance of Lake Ontario, there being only the two lakes just mentioned of easy navigation. To surmount these torrents, we must often debark from the canoe and walk in the river whose waters are sufficiently low in these quarters, chiefly towards the banks. We take the canoe in hand dragging it after us. Ordinarily two men suffice, one forward at the bow, the other behind at the stern; and as the canoe is very light, being made merely of the bark of trees, and as it is not loaded, it glides more smoothly over the water, not meeting great resistance. Some times the canoe is to be landed and carried some distance, one man in front, the other in the rear; the first carrying one end of the canoe on the right shoulder, the second carrying the other end on the left. It becomes necessary to do this either on meeting cascades and entire rivers which fall sometimes perpendicularly from a prodigious height or when the current is too rapid; or when the water thereabout being too deep, we cannot walk, dragging the canoe along by the hand; or when the country is to be crossed from one river to the other.

But when the mouth of the Great Lake is reached, the navigation is easy, when the waters are tranquil, becoming insensibly wider at first; then about two-thirds, next one half and finally out of sight (of land); especially after one has passed an infinity of little islands which are at the entrance of the Lake, in such great number and in such a variety that the most experienced Iroquois Pilots sometimes lose themselves there, and experience considerable difficulty in distinguishing the course to be steered, in the confusion and as it were in the labyrinth formed by the islands, which otherwise have nothing agreeable beyond their multitude. For these are only huge rocks rising out the water, covered merely by moss, or a few spruce or other stunted wood whose roots spring from the clefts of the rocks which can supply no other aliment or moisture to these barren trees than what the rains furnish them.

After leaving this melancholy abode, the Lake is discovered appearing like unto a sea without islands or bounds, where barks and ships can sail in all safety; so that the communication would be easy between all the French colonies that could be established on the borders of this Great Lake which is more than a hundred leagues long by thirty to forty wide.

It is from this point that all the Iroquois Nations can be reached, by various directions, except the Mohawks, the route to whom is by the River Richelieu, of which we can safely say two words since they regard it, that our troops have already constructed the three forts of which we have spoken. It is called the Richelieu River because of the fort of the same name which was erected there at its mouth at the commencement of the wars; and which has been rebuilt anew to secure the entrance of that river. It likewise bears the name of the River of the Iroquois, because it is the route which leads thither, and it is by it these Barbarians used most ordinarily come to attack us. The bed of this river is one hundred to one hundred and fifty paces wide almost throughout, though at its mouth it is somewhat narrower: its borders are decorated with beautiful pines through which we can walk with ease; as in fact fifty of our men have done a foot by land nearly twenty leagues of the way from the mouth of the river to the *Sault*, which is so called, though it is not properly a waterfall but only an impetuous rapid full of rocks, that arrest its course and render the navigation almost impossible for three quarters of a league. In time however its passage may be facilitated. The remainder of the river has from the beginning a very fine bottom; as many as eight islands are to be met with before arriving at the basin, which is at the foot of the *Sault*. This basin is like a little lake, a league and a half in circumference and six to eight feet deep, where fish abounds almost at all seasons.

To the right of this basin in going up, is seen Fort Saint Louis, built quite recently here, which is very convenient for the design entertained against the Iroquois, since its position renders it almost impregnable and causes it to command the whole river.

After passing the rapids of the *Sault* which extend three leagues, the third fort is visible that terminates all these rapids: for the river afterwards is very beautiful and quite navigable to the Lake called Champlain, at the extremities of which we enter on the lands of the Mohawk Iroquois.

OF THE WAR AND THE TREATIES OF PEACE OF THE FRENCH WITH THE IROQUOIS.

[Relation, &c., ès années, 1665, 1666.]

The great varieties of Nations which are in these countries, the changeable and perfidious disposition of the Iroquois and the barbarism of all these tribes not permitting us to hope for any stable peace with them except inasmuch as it can be maintained by the terror of the king's arms, it is not to be wondered at that peace succeeds war so easily, and that wars terminate so quickly in peace.

The ambassadors of five different nations were seen in one year at Quebec, who came there to solicit peace; yet these did not prevent us punishing by a good war those who answered badly by their conduct the promises of their deputies.

The first of these Ambassadors who came from the Upper Iroquois, were presented to M. de Tracy in the month of December of the year 1665, and the most influential among them was a famous Captain, called Garacontié, who always signalized his zeal for the French, and employed the credit which he has among all these tribes, in extricating our prisoners from their hands, as he has liberated very recently Sieur Le Moine, an inhabitant of Montreal, who had been captured three months ago by these Barbarians.

M. de Tracy having notified him by the usual presents that he would give him a friendly audience, he pronounced a harangue full of good sense and an eloquence evincing no trace of the barbarous. It contained nothing but courtesies and offers of friendship and service on the part of all his tribe; wishes for a new Jesuit Mission, and expressions of condolence on the death of the late Father Le Moine, the intelligence of which he had just received.

* * * * * * * * * * *

However as no advantage can be expected from these Nations except in so far as we appear able to injure them, preparations were made for a military expedition against those with whom no peace could be concluded. Monsieur de Courcelles, who commanded, used every possible diligence so that he was ready to start on the 9th January of the year 1666, accompanied by M. du Gas, whom he took for his Lieutenant; by M. de Salamper, Gentleman Volunteer; by Father Pierre Raffeix, Jesuit; by 300 men of the Regiment of Carignan Salières and 200 Volunteers, *habitans* of the French Colonies. This march could not but be tedious, every one having snow shoes on his feet, to the use of which none were accustomed, and all, not excepting the officers not even M. de Courcelles himself, being loaded, each with from 25 to 30 pounds of biscuit, clothing and other necessary supplies.

A more difficult or longer march than that of this little army, can scarcely be met with in any history, and it required a French courage and the perseverance of M. de Courcelles, to undertake it. In addition to the embarrassment caused by the snow shoes, which is a species of great inconvenience and that of the burthen which each one was obliged to carry, it was necessary to walk three hundred leagues on the snow; cross lakes and rivers continually on the ice in danger of making as many falls as steps; sleep only on the snow in the midst of the forest and endure a cold surpassing by many degrees in severity that of the most rigorous European winters.

Our troops, however, having gone the first day to Sillery to recommend the success of their enterprize to St. Michael the Archangel the patron of that place; many had, as early as the third day, the nose, the ears, the knees and the fingers or other parts entirely frozen and the remainder of the body covered with cicatrixes, and some others wholly overcome and benumbed by the cold would have perished in the snow, had they not been carried, though with considerable difficulty, to the place where they were to pass the night.

Sieurs De la Fouille, Maximin and Lobiac, Captains in the Carignan regiment, having joined this little army on the 24th January, each with 20 soldiers of their companies and some *habitans* of the place were treated by the cold, on the day following, worse than any had previously been, and many soldiers were obliged to be brought back, of whom some had the legs cut by the ice and others the hands or the arms or other parts of the body altogether frozen. These losses were repaired by Sieurs de Chambly, Petit and Rogemont, Captains of the same regiment, and by the Sieurs Mignardi, Lieutenant of the Colonel's company which was withdrawn from Forts St. Louis and St. Therese, where the troops rendezvoused on the 30th of the same month. So that the army being still 500 men strong finally arrived on the 14th of February, with the same difficulties and the same dangers, as before, in the enemy's country, at 20 leagues distance from their villages. The journey yet to be travelled, was very long in consequence of the prodigious depth of the snow and the delay of the Algonquin guides, in whose absence unknown routes were to be tried and continual mistakes experienced.

Finally information was received from prisoners who were taken in some detached cabins, and from the Commandant of a hamlet inhabited by the Dutch of New Netherland, that the greater part of the Mohawks and Oneidas having gone to a distance to make war against other tribes called the Wampum Makers, (*les faiseurs de porcelaine*) had left in their villages only the children and the helpless old men; and it was considered useless to push further forward an expedition which had all the effect intended by the terror it spread among all the tribes, who were haughty and perfidious only because they considered themselves inaccessible to our troops. Before returning however we killed several savages who from time to time made their appearance along the skirts of the forest for the purpose of skirmishing with our people. Sieur Aiguemorte and some of our soldiers were also killed pursuing them.

The effects of the terror produced by his Majesty's arms on the hearts of these savages were apparent at Quebec in the month of May following, by the arrival of ambassadors from the Senecas, (*Sonnontouaeronnons*) who demanded the King's protection for their nation and the continuation of peace, which they pretended they never violated by any hostile act. M. de Tracy had already refused 34 presents that they had tendered him, but perceiving that it affected them sensibly and that they considered it the greatest insult that could be offered, he finally accepted their wampum belts, repeating to them that it was neither their presents nor their goods that the King desired, but their true happiness and salvation; that they would derive all sorts of advantages from their confidence in his goodness which should be extended to the other Nations also, that they might experience its most favorable effects, if they took the same care in imploring it by sending their ambassadors forthwith.

These were soon succeeded by those of other tribes; among the rest by those from the Oneida and even by those from the Mohawk, so that the deputies from the Five Iroquois Nations were almost at the same time at Quebec, as if to confirm by one common accord a durable peace with France.

In order the better to accomplish this it was deemed proper to send some Frenchmen with the Oneida Ambassadors, who were also responsible for the conduct of the Mohawks, and even gave hostages for them. The Dutch of New Netherland had likewise written in their hehalf and went security for the faithful observance by all those Barbarians of the articles of peace entered into with them. These French delegates had orders to inform themselves of every thing carefully on the spot, and to learn if it were safe to confide again on the Savages, so that His Majesty's arms should not be retarded by an illusive hope of peace.

But scarcely were the Ambassadors two or three days journey from Quebec, when news came of the surprisal by the Mohawks of some Frenchmen belonging to Fort St. Anne who had gone to the chase, and of the murder of Sieur de Traversy, Captain in the Carignan Regiment and Sieur de

Chusy, and that some volunteers had been taken prisoners. The French delegates were at once recalled, and the Oneida savages who remained as hostages whose heads could have been at once split by axes according to the laws of war in this country, were imprisoned. But without having recourse to these barbarous laws, means were adopted to derive greater advantage from this treachery; and M. de Sorel, Captain in the Carignan Regiment, immediately collected a party of three hundred men, whom he led by forced marches into the enemy's country, resolved to put all every where, to the sword. But when only 20 leagues distant from their villages he encountered new Ambassadors bringing back the Frenchmen taken near Fort St. Anne, and who were coming to offer every satisfaction for the murder of those who were slain and new guarantees for peace, so that this Captain having returned with his troops, there was no more talk but of peace, which they pretended to conclude by a general council of all the Tribes who had at the time delegates at Quebec.

These treaties had not, however, all the success which was expected from them, and M. de Tracy concluded that, to ensure their success, it was necessary to render the Mohawks by force of arms more tractable, for they always opposed new obstacles to the publick tranquility. He wished, despite his advanced age, to lead in person against these Barbarians, an army composed of 600 soldiers drafted from all the companies, of six hundred *habitans* of the country and one hundred Huron and Algonquin savages. Through the exertions of M. Talon, all the preparations for this war were completed by the 14th Septr, the day fixed on for departure, being that of the exaltation and triumph of the cross, for whose glory this expedition was determined on. The general rendezvous was fixed for the 28th of Sept, at Fort St. Anne recently constructed by Sieur La Mothe, Captain in the Carignan Regiment, on an Island in Lake Champlain. Some of the troops not being able to come up in sufficient time, M. de Tracy would not proceed before the 3d of October, with the main body of the army. But M. de Courcelles impelled by his characteristic impatience for the fight, started some days ahead with 400 men, and Sieurs De Chambly and Berthier, commandants of the Forts St. Louis and Assumption were left to follow M. de Tracy, four days afterwards, with the rear guard. As it was necessary to march one hundred and twenty leagues into the interior to find the enemy's villages, and as several large lakes and many considerable rivers were to be crossed before arriving there, it was necessary to be provided with conveniences for land and water. Vessels requisite for this expedition had been prepared. Three hundred were ready; consisting partly of very light batteaux, and partly of bark canoes, each of which carried at most five or six persons. On crossing a river or lake, each was obliged to take charge of his own canoe and to carry the batteaux by main strength. This caused less labor than two small pieces of artillery which were conveyed even to the farthest Iroquois villages, to force more easily all the fortifications.

Notwithstanding the care taken to accomplish this march with little noise, we could not prevent some Iroquois, despatched from 30 to 40 leagues to discover our troops, seeing from the mountain tops this little naval expedition, and running to warn the first village of it; so that the alarm spreading afterwards from village to village, our troops found them abandoned, and these barbarians were only seen on the mountains at a distance uttering great cries and firing some random shots at our soldiers.

Our army halting only for refreshment at all these villages, which were found void of men but full of grain and provisions, expected to meet with a vigorous resistance at the last which we prepared to attack in regular form, because the barbarians evinced by the great firing they made there, and the fortifications they had erected, every disposition for a desperate defence. But our people were again disappointed in their hope; for scarcely had the enemy seen the vanguard approach, when they immediately fled to the woods where night prevented our troops pursuing them. A triple palisade, surrounding their stronghold, twenty feet in height and flanked by four bastions, their prodigious quantities of provisions and the abundant supply of water they had provided in bark tanks to extinguish fire when necessary, afforded sufficient evidence that their first resolution had been quite different from that which the terror of our arms had caused them so suddenly to adopt. A few persons whom their advanced age had prevented withdrawing from the village two days previously with all the women and children, and the remains of two or three savages of another tribe whom they had half roasted at a slow fire with their accustomed fury, were all that were found. After having planted the Cross and celebrated Mass and sung the *Te Deum* on the spot, all that remained was to fire the palisades and cabins and to destroy all the stores of Indian corn, beans and other produce of the country found there. The other villages were again visited where as well as throughout the whole country, the same devastation was committed; so that those who are acquainted with the mode of living of these barbarians doubt not but famine will cause as many to perish as would have been destroyed by the arms of our soldiery had they dared to await them, and that those who survive will be reduced by terror to peaceful conditions and to a demeanor more difficult to be obtained from them by mere sanguinary victories.

The return route of our troops was more disagreeable than that taken in going, because the rivers being swollen some seven or eight feet by the rains, were found much more difficult to cross, and a storm which arose on Lake Champlain wrecked two canoes with eight persons, amongst whom was to be particularly regretted Sieur de Lugues, Lieutenant of a company, who made frequent displays of his valour in France as well as in Canada.

The courage of our troops was ever wonderfully excited in the hardships of this expedition and in the face of danger, by the examples of M. de Tracy, M. de Courcelles and M. de Salliere, Quarter Master (*Mestre de Camp*) of the regiment and of Chevalier de Chaumont who desired always on approaching the villages to be of the forlorn hope; and their generosity was animated by the zeal and pious sentiments with which Messrs. Du Bois and Cosson, secular Priests, and Fathers Albanel and Rafaix, Jesuits, endeavored to inspire them.

Our excellent Prelate who had his hands ever raised to Heaven and had called every one to prayers, during the absence of our troops, caused thanks to be given to God and the *Te Deum* sung on their return. Every body here has conceived renewed hopes in consequence of the King's goodness towards the country and of the manner in which the West India Company, to whom his Majesty has confided it, is affected towards it. So that we doubt not but we shall very soon see most populous towns in the place of these extensive forests, and Jesus Christ worshipped in all these vast countries.

END.

A RELATION OF THE GOVERNOR[R] OF CANADA

HIS MARCH WITH 600 VOLUNTEIRS INTO Y[e] TERRYTORYES OF HIS ROYAL HIGHNESSE THE DUKE OF YORKE IN AMERICA.

[Lond. Doc. II.]

Upon the 29th of Xber last, Monsier Coarsell the Governour of Canada, in Nova ffrancia begun his march with near 600 men, to seeke out their inveterate ennemyes called the Mohauke Indians in their owne country and forts, there to take reuenge upon them for the seuerall murthers and spoyles which the Barbarians had for many yeares exercised in Cannada upon the French, and the Indians of those parts even to the ruine of most, but to the insufferable discouragement of all those Inhabbitants, who being taken alive were usually tortured and eaten, or burnt by the Mauhaukes; If not taken, yet liv[d] in perpetuall alarums to see their dwelling houses burnt, their Cattell and Corne destroyed. All which powerfull arguments furnish't y[e] french with heate enough to march over the ffrozen lake of Canada, lying in the 6th degree of northerne latitude, and taking their tyme that the snow upon the ground was hard frozen (though in most places 4 foote deep) made use of Indian snow shoes w[ch] hath the very form of a Rackett tyed to each foote, whereby y[e] body and feet are kept from sinking into the snow, and because it was not possible for horses to pass, or subsist in the snow, or for the soldiers to carry their necessary provisions on their backes, and had lesse expectation to meete wth any reliefe in the vaste wilderness, the Governo[r] caused slight sledges to be made in good number, laying provisions upon them, drew them over the snow with mastive doggs, all these difficultyes put together impeded his march, and by the mistake of his guides hapned to fall short of the castles of the Mauhaukes, and to take up his quarters or rather incamp upon the 9th of February within 2 myles of a small village called Schonectade, lying wth in the woods beyond fort Albany in y[e] terrytoryes of his Royall highness, and 3 dayss march from the first castle of the Mohaukes.

The French suposed they were then come to their designed place, and the rather because y[t] evening they did rancounter wth a party of the Mohaukes who made appearance of retreating from the French, whereupon a party of 60 of their best Fuzileers after them, but that small party drew the French into an ambuscade of near 200 Mohaukes planted behind trees, (who taking their advantage as it fell into their hands,) at one volley slew eleuen French men whereof one was a Lieutent[t]. wounded divers others, the french party made an hono[r]able retreit to their body, w[ch] was marching after them close at hand, w[ch] gave the Mohaukes tyme and opportunity to march off w[th] the loss of only 3 slaine upon the plaice and 6 wounded, the report whereof was soon brought to Schonecktade by those Indians, with the heads of 4 of the ffrench to the Commissary of the Village who immediately despatched the newes to Fort Albany, from whence the next day 3 of the principle inhabitants were sent to Monsier Coursell the Governo[r] of Canada to inquire of his intention to bring such a body of armed men into the dominions of his Ma[tie] of Great Brittaine, w[th]out accquainting the Governo[r] of these parts w[th] his designes. The Governo[r] reply[d] that he come to seeke out and destroy his ennemyes the Mohaukes without intention of visiting their plantations, or else to molest any of his Ma[ties] subjects, and that [he] had not heard of the reducing those parts to his Ma[ties] obedience, but desired that hee and his soldiers might bee supplied with provisions for their money, and that his wounded men might be sucoured, and taken care for in Albany; To all which the Emissaryes freely consented and made a small but acceptable present of wine and provisions to him, further offering the best accommodations ye poore village afforded, wch was civilly refus'd, in regard there was not accommodacôn for his soldyers, with whom he had marcht and campt under the blew canopye of the heavens full six weeks, but hee prudently foresaw a greater inconvenience if hee had brought his weary and half starv'd people within the smell of a chimney corner, whom hee now cold keepe from stragling or running away, not knowing whither to runn for feare of y[e] Indians; The next day Monsieur Corsell sent his men to the village where they were carefully drest and sent to Albany, being seaven in number, the Dutch bores carryed to the camp such provisions as they had, and were too well paid for it; Especially peaz and bread, of w[ch] a good quantity was brought; y[e] Mohaukes were all gone to their Castles, with resolution to fight it out against the french, who being refresht and supplied wth the aforesaid provisions made a shew of marching towards the Mohaukes Castles, but with faces about and great sylence and dilligence return'd towards Cannada.

Upon the 12th of February, whether a Panick feare, some mutiny, or y[e] probability of the thawing of the lake, caus'd this sudden (w[ch] the Indians call a dishonorable retreit) I cannot learne, but surely so bould and hardy an attempt (circumstances considered) hath not hapned in any age. All w[ch] vanisht like false fyer, and hath given new courage to their old enemyes y[e] Mauhaukes who by their spyes hearing of y[e] retreat of y[e] French pursued them back to the Lake, but the French making more speed to them from Canada, the Mohaukes did noe considerable prejudice to them, onely took 3 one of w[ch] at his own request they slew, not being able to march, the other they kept prisoners, they found 5 others dead in the way with hunger and cold, but according to their manner brought the crownes of their heads away. those who observed the words and countenance of Monsieur Coursell, saw him disturbed in minde that the king was Master of these parts of the Country, where hee expected to have found the Dutch interest uppermost, saying that the king of England did graspe at all America, but hee did not beleive to see the Dutch the masters ere long; he enquired what garrison or what fort was at Albany, 'twas told him a Captain and 60 English soldyers with 9 peece of ordinance in a small fort of foure Bastions, and that the Cap[t] thereof Cap[t] Baker had sent for 20 men from another garrison of the Kings at the Sopes, who probably might be arrived at Albany the same hower, thus finding his men tyr'd, the Mohaukes resolute, and something doubtfull, without tryall of the good will of the English Garrison, because y[e] reports were strong that the French King and States of Holland were united against His Ma[tie] of England, Monsieur Coursell found it reasonable to returne home nothing effected, the 2 prisoners taken by the Mohaukes in the retreate tell them y[t] this summer another attempt will be made upon their country with a greater force and supplyes of men, the truth or success of which I shall not now discourse upon, having given y[e] trew relation of what past from y[e] 29th December to the 12th of February.

[From Paris Doc. I.]

On the seventh of the month of July of the year 1666, the Iroquois of the Oneida Nation, having learned from the Mohawks, their neighbors and allies and by the Dutch of Fort Orange that the troops of Louis the fourteenth by the grace of God Most Christian King of France and Navarre, had in the month of February of the said year carried his Majesty's arms, over the snow and ice near unto Fort Orange in New Netherland, under the command of Messire Daniel de Courcelle, Lieutenant General of his armies, pursuant to orders which they received from Messire Alexandre de Prouville knight, Lord de Tracy, member of his Majesty's councils and Lieut. Genl. of his armies, both in the Islands and mainland of South and North America, as well by sea as by land, to fight and destroy the Mohawks, which probably they would have accomplished, had not the mistake of their guides caused them to take one road for the other, came down to Quebec to solicit peace as well in their own name as in that of the Mohawks by ten of their Ambassadors, by name Soenres,

Tsoenserouanne, Gannoukouenioton, Asaregouenioton, Asaregouaune, Tsendiagou, Achinnhara, Togoukouaras, Oskaraquets, Akouehen, And after having communicated by the mouth of their Orator and Chief Soenres, the object of their Embassy by ten talks expressed by as many presents, and having handed to us the letters from the officers of New Netherland, have unanimously requested, acknowledging the force of his Majesty's arms and their weakness and the condition of the forts advanced towards them, and moreover aware that the three upper Iroquois Nations have always experienced great benefit from the protection which they formerly received from the said Lord the King, that his Majesty would be pleased to extend to them the same favour by granting them the same protection and receiving them among the number of his true subjects, demanding that the Treaties formerly made as well by the said Nations as by theirs, have the same force and validity for that of the Mohawks, who have required of us to solicit this with great importunity, as they should have themselves done by means of their Ambassadors had they not been apprehensive of bad treatment at our hands, ratifying on their part all the said treaties in all their points and articles, which have been read to them in the Iroquois tongue by Joseph Marie Chaumont, priest, member of the Society of Jesus; adding, moreover, to all the said articles what the protest effecting in good faith what they offered by their said presents, especially to restore all the Frenchmen, Algonquins and Hurons whom they hold prisoners among them of what condition and quality they may be, and as long as any are detained there, even on the part of the Mohawks, to send families from among them to serve, like those of other nations as the most strict hostages for their persons and dispositions to the orders of those who shall in this Country have authority from the said Lord the King whom they acknowledge from this time as their Sovereign; demanding reciprocally among all other things the restoration to them in good faith, of all those of their Nation who are prisoners at Quebec, Montreal and Three Rivers, that French families and some Black gowns, that is Jesuits be sent to them, to preach the gospel to them and to make known to them the God of the French whom they promise to love and adore; also that trade and commerce be open to them with New France, by the Lake *du Saint Sacrement*, (L. George) with the assurance on their part that they will provide in their country, a sure retreat as well to the said families as to the trading merchants, not only by preparing cabins to lodge them in, but also by assisting to erect forts to shelter them from their common enemies the Andastaeronnons and others. And that the present Treaty, made on their part in ratification of the preceding, may be stable and known unto all, they have signed it with the separate and distinctive marks of their Tribes, after which what they solicited from the said Lord the King was granted to them in his name by Messire Alexandre de Prouville, Knight, Lord de Tracy member of the King's Councils, &c. (as above) in the presence and assisted by M. Daniel de Remey Siegneur de Courcelles, King's Councillor, &c., &c., and of M. Jean Talon also Councillor, &c. who have signed with the said Lord de Tracy; and as Witnesses, François le Mercier, Priest, Member and Superior of the Society of Jesus at Quebec and Joseph Marie Chaumont likewise Priest and Member of the said Society, Interpreters of the Iroquois and Huron languages. Done at Quebec the 12 July, 1666.

ACTE OF POSSESSION

BY SIEUR DU BOIS IN THE NAME OF THE KING (OF FRANCE) OF THE FORTS TAKEN FROM THE IROQUOIS.

In the year 1666, the 17th day of Octob., the King's troops commanded by Messire Alexander de Prouville Knight, Lord de Tracy Lieut. General of His Maties Naval armies both in the Islands and Continent of South and North America as well by sea as by land, aided by Messire Daniel de Remy Knight, Seigneur de Courcelles, Governor and Lieut. General for the King in New France, being drawn up in battle array before the Fort of Andaraque, Jean Baptiste du Bois Esqrs Sieur de Cocreaumont and de St. Morice, Commandant of the Artillery of the army, presented himself at the head of the army by order of Mons. Lord de Tracy and deputed by M. Jean Talon, King's Councillor in his State and Privy Councils, Intendant General of Justice, Police and Finance in New France, for the review and direction of the Supplies of the Troops, who declared and said that at the request of Monsr Talon he took possession of said Fort and of all the lands in the neighborhood as far and in as great a quantity as they may extend, and of the other four forts which have been conquered from the Iroquois in the name of the King, and in token thereof hath planted a cross before the doors of said forts and near this hath erected a post and to these hath affixed the King's arms, of which and of all the above the said Sieur du Bois has required acte of the undersigned Royal Notary commanded in the said army for His Majesty's service. Done at the aforesaid Fort of Andaraque the day and year above written, in presence of Messire Alexander de Chaumont, Knight Seigneur of said place, Aid de Camp of his Majesty's armies, and of Hector d'Andigny, Knight of Grande Fontaine, Captain of a Company of Infantry in the Carignan Regiment, of the Nobleman Antoine de Contrecour Capn of a Company of Infantry in said Regiment, of Francois Massé Sieur de Wally Jean du Gal Esqrs Sieur du Fresne Major of Canada, Jean Louis Chevalier du Glas Lieut of a Company of said Regimt, Rene Louis Chartier Esqr, Sieur de Lobinire Lieutenant of a Militia Company from Quebec, Dominique le Feure Esqr Sieur de Quesquelin Lieutenant in said Regiment, Witnesses undersigned with the said Seigneur du Bois and the Notary. Signed, Chaumont, le Chevalier de Grand Fontain, de Contrecour, du Gal, Wally, Chevlier du Glas, du Güesclin, Rene Louis Chartier, Lobiniere, du Bois and du Guet Royal Notary.

GOV. NICOLLS TO CHEV. TRACY, AT QUEBEC.

[London Doc. II.]

Monsieur,

I was in some measure surprized in february last with the newes of so considerable a force of forreiners under the commând of Monsieur de Courcelle so farre advanct in these His Maties Dominions without my Knowledge and Consent, or the least notice given of yr intentions to any of His Maties Colonies then in amity with the French Nation: although yr proceedings heerin were not conformable to the practise in Europe, yet all my officers both Military and Civill soon resolu'd to succor and relieve your Campe with such meane provisions as the Country affords [and] from a small village could bee expected and as they have in all former times been very affectionate with Christian Charity to ransome or by any other meanes to convey divers French prisoners out of the hands of their barbarous Enemies so also their Intentions towards you is manifest in their letter of the 20th March last wherein their purpose was to give you a speedy notice that the Maquaes were at last wrought upon to treat of peace if you on your parts were so disposed, but it seems (by a sad accident intervening,) you are pleas'd to lay a greater burden upon them than they deserve after their sincere affections to your yeace. To both yr Letters directed to the Captain and Commissaries at Albany themselves will return answer but hearing that you had Emploied Le Sr Couture with yr Letters I tooke a suddaine Resolution to have discourse with him to wch purpose I came hither but find that he is return'd without the Knowledge of the Capt. or Commissarie. I could have wisht that hee had staid for mee, or that I could wait his coming for I now want the opportunity of enlarging myself to him and by him to yrselfe with how much Integrity I shall constantly attend the European Interest amidst the heathen in America as becomes a good Christian, provided that the bounds and limits of these His Majesties of Englands dominions be not invaded or the Peace and Safety of his subjects interrupted, In all other points I shall be found to entertaine yr Correspondence with Mutuall Civility and respect the rather because the reputation of yr honour hath spread itself in all these parts of the world, as well as it is known in Europe, whereof I can beare some Testimony, when I had the honour to attend my master his R. H. the Duke of York and Albany a few years in the french army, and now that I serve the same Master in his interest in this part of the World, I should count my selfe very fortunate in an opportunity at least to acknowledge some part of yr great civilities to my Master and all his Servants in their low estate and condition of Exile, The Memory whereof obligeth me (a reasonable time and good occasion concurring) to give you certaine proofe with how much truth I am, Sir,

Yor Most affte. Servant

RICHARD NICOLLS.

20th Aug: St; Vet;
In fort Albany 1666.

A Monsieur, Monsieur Le Chevalier et Seigneur de Tracy Lt. Generall Du Roy tres Chrestien dans toute L'Amerique.

A Quebec.

M. TALON TO M. COLBERT, 13 Nov. 1666.

[Paris Doc. I.]

Monsieur de Tracy and Monsieur de Courcelles are returned from their Expedition, the Iroquois having concluded to retreat and abandon their settlements. The said M. de Tracy could do nothing else than burn their forts and lay waste everything. These two gentlemen will inform you of whatever occurred throughout their march which occupied fifty-three days. What I learn from public opinion is that in what has been performed nothing has been left undone, and that the King's orders had been executed and his expectations entirely realized had those savages stood their ground. It would, in truth, have been desirable that a part had been defeated and some others taken prisoners.

The advanced age of M. de Tracy must greatly enhance the merit of the service he has rendered the King, by assuming in a broken down frame such as his, a fatigue of which no correct idea can be formed. I am assured that throughout the whole march of three hundred leagues, including the return, he suffered himself to be carried only during two days, and then he was forced to do so by the gout. M. de Courcelles, though stronger than he, could not help being carried in like manner, having been attacked by a contraction of the nerves. Both in truth have endured all the fatigue that human nature is capable of.

M. de Tracy incurred some expenses on his march for the conveyance of the cannon and other extraordinary services rendered the troops, which I wished to reimburse, but his modesty would not suffer it.

M. TRACY TO GOV. NICOLLS.

[London Doc. I.]

Sir

In answer to yor letter of 31. August, [N. S.] I shall tell you that Monsr de Courcelle Governo^r General of this Countrey, signifying to mee that hee had a desire to make some inroad upon the Maquas, to put a stopp to their barbarous Insolencies; I gave my consent to further the design, that hee might take with him so many officers and souldiers as he thought fit, either of his Maties Companyes, or those of ye Countrey. Whereupon hee advanced within fifteen or twenty leagues of the villages of ye Anniés. But fortunately for them his guides conducting him a wrong way, hee did not meete with them, till he came neare the village which you name in yor Letter, neither had he known there was any of them there, until he had surprized all the Indyans that were in two small Hutts at some distance from that place. This truth is sufficiently convincing, to justify Monsr de Courcelle, that hee had no intention to infringe the Peace, that was then between us, for that hee thought himself in the Maquas land. The Moderacôn which he used in the said hutts (although the persons under his command were driven to the uttermost extremity, for want of Provisions) hath sufficiently manifested the consideracôns wee have always had for our allyes (for until then we had no intelligence, that New Holland was under any other Dominion than that of the States of the United Belgick Provinces) and understanding that hee was upon the Lands belonging to the Dutch, hee tooke great care to hinder his companyes from falling into the village, by which means alone the Maquaes that were there saved themselves.

Hee also had so much care and authority as to hinder the souldiers from Killing the Poultry, and taking away Provisions that were in the said hutts, to satisfy their hunger. Thus farr, I ought to vindicate the truth upon this subject.

The ffrench nation is too much inclined to acknowledge curtesies, not to confess that the Dutch have had very much charity for the ffrench, who have been Prisoners with the Maquaes, and that they have redeemed divers, who had been burnt wi^thout their succour; They ought also to be assured of our gratitude towards them, and to any others who shall exercise such Christian Deedes, as they have done.

I am also persuaded that they had a sincere intention for the conclusion of a firme peace between us and the Maques. They ought in like manner to believe, that wee have always expressly forbid ye Algonquins to make warr upon or kill them.

Since the Dutch Gent. did send you ye Lrês which I writt unto them, you have known the candour of my thoughts, and the confidance which I had in their ffriendship, by that of the 14th July 1666 as also by the Request I made to the Reverend Father Bechefer (who is a person of great meritt) accompanied with three considerable persons, to transport himself upon the place, to conclude a peace, thereby to ease them of the trouble of côming to Quebec.

Its true the displeasure I received by the death of some Gent'men, who went a fowling upon confidence, of that article wch is in the same letter those Gent'men sent mee, the second time, dated the 26th March 1666, the which I had published in our Garrison [we have acquainted the Maquaes, that they are to forbear all acts of Hostility, during the time that the Messenger shall be absent which they have promised to observe] did give mee a just griefe, and a great deale of discontent, It being evident that those Gent'men had not put themselves upon that hazard, without the assurance: wch would have served amongst Europeans as well as the most authentick Passeport that could be had, the which also wee had caus'd the Algonquins to observe.

Such an unexpected misfortune obliged mee to chang the designe I had of adventuring the person of the reverend Father Bechefer, and the rest that accompanied him, & I resolv'd to send only the Sieur Cousture (who had been a Prisoner among the Maques) with a letter to the Dutch Gent. of the 22d July 1666. The said Cousture having no other employ than what was in his Instruction which hath or might have been seene, since I gave him leave to shew it.

I had never the thought of accusing those Dutch Gent'men either directly or indirectly, nor any other person, of holding intelligence with the Maques in so foule an action as was committed by them; But writt onely to oblige them, and those other Gent'men who serve under yor command at Albany, (for we were then in peace,) to councell the Maques, as Neighbours, to deliver up into our power, the actors of that murder, wch was a satisfaction that with reason I might promise myselfe on that occasion.

My L're of the 22d July to those Gent'men at Albany, might have informed you what the Sr Cousture was; ffor it had not beene prudent after the death of those Gent'men, to hazard a person of quality. And I am very sorry that you tooke the paines to leave the place of yr usual residence to make a voyage to Albany, to have discourse with an ordinary Messenger who had nothing of Trust committed to him.

The intention you signify to have of Embracing Allwayes the Interest of Europe, against the barbarous Indyans of America, is very commendable and befitting a person of your Quality and a good Christian: That Passion which you likewise expresse, for the interest of his Maty of Great Brittaine, is to be esteemed, and there is no man of reason, who doth not approve yr judgmt therein, & that hath not the like for his Prince.

I returne you thanks in particular for those obliging termes you are pleas'd to use on my behalfe, as also for the assurances you give mee of a desire to hold a mutuall Correspondence of civility and respect with mee to ye end before proposed: If I was particularly knowne to you I might feare you would alter your opinion of mee, for that Reputacôn doth very often give us advantages which wee do not deserve.

I had the honor to serve the King in Germany, in the most considerable commands of his Army, at the time when my son (that was hee and not mee) was knowne unto you, in those which served in fflanders, where he commanded His Maties Cavalry of Strangers: Hee had a very particular respect for the person, and for the great meritt of his Royal Highness, the Duke of York, who seemed to bee well pleased with his respectful carriage towards him: You have no reasons to expect lesse services from mee, that you might have received from my son, upon all occasions where those of the King will permit mee to render them.

It cannot bee but you must have heard from divers of your Nation that have been in the Islands of America, how I have done them courtesyes with passion, and with as much civility as may bee; I have cause enough to complaine that the same hath not been practised towards me; ffor that a vessell which went out of Boston, took in the Gulfe of St. Laurence, towards the latter end of June, or the beginning of July 1665, (near upon five months before the declaracôn of the warre) a barque of between 25 and 30 tunnes, wch belonged to mee, being laden with a good quantity of strong Waters, and other refreshments which come from France: But as I know no other interest than that of the service of his Maty who bestows many benefits upon mee, I shall easily forgett that losse, 'till the conclusion of Peace, you may also believe that I am wth a great deale of esteeme,

Sr Your thrice affectionate

and humble Servt.

TRACY.

Quebec
Apr. 30, 1667.

IV.

REPORTS

ON

The Province of New York.

About 1669; 1678.

GOV. NICOLLS' ANSWERS TO THE SEVERAL QUERIES

RELATING TO THE PLANTERS IN THE TERRITORIES OF HIS R. HS THE DUKE OF YORKE IN AMERICA.

[Lond. Doc. II.]

1st. The Governour and Councell with the High Sheriffe and the Justices of the Peace in the Court of the Generall assizes haue the Supreame Power of making, altering, and abolishing any Laws in this Government. The Country Sessions are held by Justices upon the Bench, Particular Town Courts by a constable and Eight Overseers. The City Court of N. Yorke by a Mayor and Aldermen. All causes tried by Juries.

2nd. The Land is naturally apt to produce Corne & Cattle so that the severall proportions or dividents of Land are alwaies allowed with respect to the numbers of the Planters, what they are able to manage, and in wt time to accomplish their undertaking, the feed of Cattell is free in commonage to all Townships, The Lots of Meadow or Corne Ground are peculiar to each Planter.

3rd. The Tenure of lands is derived from his R. H.s who gives and grants lands to Planters as their freehold forever, they paying the customary rates and duties with others towards the defraying of publique charges. The highes Rent or acknowledgment to his R. H.s will bee one penny *pr* acre for Lands purchased by his R. H.s, the least two shillings sixe pence for each hundred acres, whereof the Planters themselves are purchasers from the Indyans.

4. The Governour gives liberty to Planters to find out and buy lands from the Indyans where it pleaseth best the Planters, but the seating of Towns together is necessary in these parts of America, especially upon the Maine Land.

5. Liberty of Conscience is graunted and assured with the same Provisoe exprest in the Querie.

6. Liberty of ffishing and fowling is free to all by the Patent.

7. All Causes are tried by Juries, no Lawes contrary to the Lawes of England. Souldyers onely are tryable by a Court Marshall, and none others except in cases of suddaine invasion, mutiny or rebellion as his Maties Lieutenants in any of his Countries of England may or ought to exercise.

8th. As to this point there is no taxe, toledge, Imposte or Custome payable upon the Planters upon Corne or Cattle: the Country at present hath little other product, the Rate for publicke charges was agreed unto in a generall Assembly, and is now managed by the Governour his Councell and the Justices in the Court of Assizes to that onely behoofe.

9th. The obtaining all thes priviledges is long since recomēnded to his R. H.s as the next necessary encouragement to these his Territories, whereof a good answer is expected.

10th. Every man who desires to trade for ffurs at his request hath liberty so to doe.

ANSWERS OF GOV. ANDROS TO ENQUIRIES ABOUT NEW YORK; 1678.

[Lond. Doc. III.]

Answers to the Inquiries of Plantacôns for New Yorke.

1. The Governo^{r} is to have a Councill not exceeding tenn, wth whose advice to act for the safety & good of the country, and in every towne, village or parish a Petty Court, & Courts of Sessions in the Severall precincts being three, on Long Island, & Townes of New Yorke, Albany & Esopus, and some smale or poore Islands & out places; and the Generall court of assizes composed of the Governo^{r} & Councill & all the Justices & magistrates att New York once a yeare, the Petty courts Judge of five pounds, & then may appeale to Sessions, they to twenty pounds & then may appeale to assizes to ye King, al sd courts as by Law.

2. The court of Admiralty hath been by speciall comission or by the Court of Mayor and Aldermen at New Yorke.

The chiefe Legislative power there is in the Governo^{r} with advice of the Councell the executive power Judgm^{ts} given by ye courts is in the sheriffs and other civil officers.

4. The law booke in force was made by the Governo^{r} and Assembly, att Hempstead in 1665, and since confirmed by his Royal Highnesse.

5. The Militia is about 2000 of wch about 140 horse in three troopes the foote formed into companyes, most under 100 men each all indifferently armed with fire-armes of all sizes, ordered and excersized according to Law, and are good fire men, one standing company of Souldiers with gunners and other officers for the fforts of New York & Albany always victualled in October & November for a yeare.

6. Forteresses are James fforte seated upon a point of New Yorke towne between Hudson's River & ye Sound, its a square with stone walls, foure bastions almost regular, and in it 46 gunnes mounted and stores for service accordingly. Albany is a smale long stockadoed forte with foure bastions in it, 12 gunns, sufficient ag^{t} Indians, and lately a wooden redout & out worke at Pemaquid wth 7 gunns, s'd Garrisons victualled for a yeare, wth suff^{t} stores.

7. There are no privateers about o^{r} Coasts.

8. Our Neighbours westward are Maryland populous and strong but doe not live in townes, their produce tobacco, Northwest the Maques &^{c}. Indians ye most warr like in all the Northern Parts of Amereca, their trade beavers and furrs. Northward the ffrench of Canada trade as wee with our Indians; Eastward Connecticut in a good condition and populous, their produce provisions of wheate, beefe & porke, some pease, o^{r} south bounds the Sea.

9. Wee keepe good Correspondence with all o^{r} neighbours as to Civill, legall or judiciall proceedings, but differ with Connecticut for o^{r} bounds and mutuall assistance wch they nor Massachusetts will not admitt.

10. Our boundaries are South, the Sea, West Delaware; North to ye Lakes or ffrench; East Connecticut river, but most usurped and yett possêd by s'd Connecticut some Islands Eastward & a tract beyond Kennebeck River called Pemaquid, &c. New Yorke is in 40^{d} 35^{m}; Albany ab^{t} 43^{d}; the Colony is in severall long narrow stripes of wch a greate parte of the settlem^{t} made by adventurers before any Regulacôn by wch Incroachm^{ts} without pattents wch townes have lately taken but by reason of continuall warrs noe Survey made & [qu. of the] wildernesse, noe certaine computacôn can be made of the planted and implanted, these last 2 yeares about 20,000 acres taken up and pattented for particuler persons besides Delaware, most of the land taken up except upon Long Island is improued & unlesse the bounds of the Duke's pattent be asserted noe great quantityes att hand undisposed.

11. Our principall places of Trade are New Yorke and South'ton except Albany for the Indyans, our buildings most wood, some lately stone & brick, good country houses & strong of their severall kindes.

12. Wee haue about 24 townes, villages or parishes in Six Precincts, Divisions, Rydeings, or Courts of Sessions.

13. Wee haue severall Rivers, Harbours and Roades, Hudson's River the chiefest & is ab^{t}. 4 fathom water att coming in butt six, tenn or more within & very good soundings & anchorage either in Hudson's River or in the Sound, the usuall roade before the town and moulde.

14. Our produce is land provisions of all sorts as of wheate exported yearly about 60000 bushells, pease, beefe, pork, & some Refuse fish, Tobacco, beavers, peltry or furrs from the Indians, Deale & oake timber, plankes, pipestaues, lumber, horses, & pitch & tarr lately begunn to be made, Commôdityes imported are all sorts of English manufacture for Christians & blanketts, Duffells &^{c}. for Indians about 50000^{lb} yearly, Pemaquid afords merchantable ffish & masts.

15. Wee haue noe Experience or skill of Salt Peter to be had in Quantityes.

16. Our Merch^{ts} are not many but with inhabitants & planters about 2000, able to beare armes, old inhabitants of the place or of England, Except in & neere New Yorke of Dutch Extraction & some few of all nations, but few Serv^{ts}, much wanted & but very few slaves.

17. Noe persons whateuer are to come from any place but according to act off Parl^{t} wch the magistrates and officers of the severall townes or places are to take care of, accordingly the plantacôn in these late yeares increased, but noe Generall acc^{t} hath been taken soe is not knowne how much nor what persons. Some few slaues are sometimes brought from Barbadoes, most for Provisions and sould att a^{bt} 30^{lb} or 35^{lb} Country pay.

18. Ministers have been soe scarce & Religions many that noe acc^{t} cann be giuen of Children's births or christenings.

19. Scarcity of Ministers and Law admitting marriages by Justices, noe acc^{t} cann be giuen of the number marryed.

20. Noe acc^{t} cann be giuen of burialls, formes of burialls not being generally obserued & few ministers till very lately.

21. A merch^{t} worth 1000^{lb} or 500^{lb} is accompted a good substantiall merchant and a planter worthe halfe that in moveables accompted [rich ?] with all the Estates may be valued at about £150,000.

22. There may lately haue traded to ye Collony in a yeare from tenn to fifteen shipps or vessells of about togeather 100 tunns each, English new England and our owne built of wch 5 small shipps and a Ketch now belonging to New Yorke foure of them built there.

23. Obstruccôns to Improuem^{t} of planters, trade, Navigacôn and mutuall assistance are ye distinction of Collonies for our owne produce, as if different nations and people, though next neighbours upon the same tract of land, and His Maties subjects, we obserueing acts of trade & navigacôn &c.

24. Aduantages, Incouragem^{t} & Improuem^{t} of Planters trade & Navigacôn would be more if next neighbours of o^{r} own Nation the King's subjects on the same tract of land might without distinction, supply each other with our owne produce, punctually obserueing all acts of parliam^{t} for Exportacôn & would dispose all persons the better for mutuall assistance.

25. Rates or dutyes upon Goods exported are 2^{s} for each hhd of Tobacco & 1^{s} 3^{d} on a beaver skin & other peltry proportionably, Provisions and all else paye nothing, Goods imported payes 2 per cent except Liquors particulerly rated something more, & Indian trade goeing up the river payes 3 per cent, there are some few quitt-rents, as also Excise or license moneys for retaileing stronge drinke & a way house or publique Scale: all applyed to ye Garrison and publique charge, to which it hath not hitherto sufficed by a greate deale.

26. There are Religions of all sorts, one church of England, Several Presbiterians & Independents, Quakers & Anabaptists of Severall sects, some Jews but presbiterians & Independ[ts] most numerous & Substantiall.

27. The Duke maintaines a chapline w[ch] is all the certaine allowance or Church of England, but peoples free gifts to y[e] Ministry, and all places obliged to build Churches & provide for a minister, in w[ch] most very wanting, but presbiterians & Independ[ts] desierous to have and maintaine them if to be had, There are ab[t] 20 Churches or Meeting places of w[ch] aboue halfe vacant their allowance like to be from 40[lb] to 70[lb] a yeare and a house and garden. Noe Beggars but all poore cared ffor. If good Ministers could be had to goe thither might doe well & gaine much upon those people.

Endorsed

"Answers of inquiries of New-York
Rec[d] from S[r] Edm. Andros on the 16th
of Ap. 1678."

Note.—Chalmers gives in his annals what purport to be copies of these Reports, but they will be found to be rather abstracts when compared with the official MSS. which are now published in full, it is believed for the first time.

V.

PAPERS

RELATING TO

M. de la Barre's Expedition to Hungry Bay,

JEFFERSON COUNTY.

1684.

EXTRACT OF THE INSTRUCTIONS GIVEN BY THE KING TO M. DE LA BARRE.

[Paris Doc. Vol. II.]

Versailles, 10th May, 1682.

He is equally informed that the Savages nearest adjoining to the French Settlements are the Algonquins and the Iroquois, that the latter had repeatedly troubled the peace and tranquility of the Colonies of New France until His Majesty having waged a severe war against them, they were finally constrained to submit and to live in peace and quietness without making any incursions on the lands inhabited by the French. But as these restless and warlike tribes cannot be kept down except by terror, and as His Majesty has even been informed by the last despatches, that the Onnontagués and Senecas—Iroquois tribes—have killed a Recollet and committed many other violences and that it is to be feared that they will push their audacity even further; It is very important that the said Sieur de la Barre put himself in a condition to proceed as early as possible, with 5 or 600 of the militia most favorably situated for this expedition along the shores of Lake Frontenac at the mouth of Lake Conty, to exhibit himself to those Iroquois Settlements in a condition to restrain them within their duty and even to attack them should they do any thing against the French, wherein he must observe that he is not to break with them without a very pressing necessity and an entire certitude to promptly and advantageously finish a war that he will have undertaken against them.

He must not only apply himself to prevent the violences of the Iroquois against the French. He must also endeavor to keep the Savages at peace among themselves, and prevent the Iroquois by all means making war on the Illinois and other tribes, neighbors to them, being very certain that if these Nations whose furs, the principal trade of Canada, are destroyed, should see themselves secure against the violence of the Iroquois by the protection they would receive from the French, they might be so much the more excited to wear their merchandizes and will thereby increase trade.

At the meeting held the tenth October, 1682, composed of M. the Governor, M. the Intendant, M. the Bishop of Quebec, M. Dollier Superior of the Seminary of St. Sulpice at Montreal, the Rev. Fathers Beschefer Superior, D'Ablon and Fremin, Jesuits, M. the Major of the City, Mess[rs]. de Varenne Governor of the Three Rivers, de Brussy, Dalibout, Duguet, Lemoine, Ladurantais, Bizard, Chailly, Vieuxpont, Duluth, de Sorel, Derepentigny, Berthier, and Boucher.

It is proposed by M. the Governor, that from the records which M. the Count de Frontenac was pleased to deposit in his hands of what had passed at Montreal on the 12 Sept. last, between him and the Deputy of the Onontagué Iroquois, it is easy to infer that these people are inclined to follow the object of their enterprize, which is to destroy all the Nations in alliance with us, the one after the other, whilst they keep us in uncertainty and with folded arms; so that, after having deprived us of the entire fur trade which they wish alone to carry on with the English and Dutch established at Manate and Orange, they may attack us isolated, and ruin the Colony in obliging it to contract itself and abandon all the separate settlements, and thus arrest the cultivation of the soil which cannot bear grain nor be cultivated as meadow except in quarters where it is of good quality.

As he is not informed in the short time since his arrival from France, of the state of these tribes and of the Colony, he requests them to acquaint him with all they know of these things in order that he may inform his Majesty thereof, and represent to him the necessities of this Colony, for the purpose as well of averting this war as for terminating and finishing it advantageously should it be necessary to wage it; Whereupon the Meeting after being informed by the Rev[d] Jesuit fathers of what had passed during five years among the Iroquois Nations, whence they had recently arrived, and by M. Dollier of what occurred for some years at Montreal, remained unanimously and all of one accord, that the English have omitted nothing for four years to induce the Iroquois, either by the great number of presents which they made them or by the cheapness with which they gave them provisions and especially guns, powder and lead, to declare war against us, and which the Iroquois have been two or three times ready to undertake; But having reflected that, should they attack us before they had ruined in fact the allied nations, their neighbours, these would rally and, uniting together, would fall on them and destroy their villages whilst occupied against us, they judged it wiser to defer and amuse us whilst they were attacking those Nations, and having commenced, with that view, to attack the Illinois last year, they had so great an advantage over them that besides three or four hundred killed, they took nine hundred of them prisoners, so that marching this year with a corps of twelve hundred men, well armed and good warriors, there was no doubt but they would exterminate them altogether, and attack, on their return, the Miamis and the Kiskakous and by their defeat render themselves masters of Missilimackina and the lakes Hérié and Huron, and Bay des Puans and thereby deprive us of all the trade drawn from that country by destroying, at the same time, all the Christian Missions established among those nations; and therefore it became necessary to make a last effort to prevent them ruining those Nations as they had formerly the Algonquins, the Andastez, the Loups (Mohegans), the Abenaquis and others, the remains of whom we have at the settlements of Sillery, Laurette, Lake Champlain and others scattered among us. That to accomplish that object, the state of the Colony was to be considered, and the means to be most usefully adopted against the enemy; that as to the Colony we could bring together a thousand good men, bearing arms and accustomed to manage canoes like the Iroquois, but when drawn from their settlements, it must be considered that the cultivation of the soil would be arrested during the whole period of their absence, and that it is necessary, before making them march, to have supplies of provisions necessary in places distant from the settlements, so as to support them in the enemy's country a time sufficiently long to effectually destroy that nation, and to act no more by them as had been done seventeen years ago, making them partially afraid without weakening them. That we have advantages now which we had not then; the French accustomed to the woods, acquainted with all the roads through them, and the road to Fort Frontenac open to fall in forty hours on the Senecas, the strongest of the five Iroquois Nations, since they alone can furnish fifteen hundred warriors, well armed; that there must be provisions at Fort Frontenac, three or four vessels to load them and embark five hundred men on Lake Ontario, whilst five hundred others would go in Canoes and post themselves on the Seneca shore; but this expedition cannot succeed unless by His Majesty's aid with a small body of two or three hundred soldiers to serve as a garrison for Forts Frontenac and La Galette, to escort provisions and keep the head of the country guarded and furnished whilst the interior would be deprived of its good soldiers; a hundred or a hundred and fifty hired men, to be distributed among the settlements to help those who will remain at home to cultivate the ground, in order that famine may not get into the land; and funds necessary to collect supplies and build two or three barks, without which and that of Sieur de Lesalle, it is impossible to undertake any thing of utility: That it is a war which is not to be commenced to be left imperfect, because knowing each other better than seventeen years ago, if it were to be undertaken without finishing it the conservation of the Colony is not to be expected, the Iroquois not being apt to return. That the failure of all aid from France had begun to create contempt for us among the said Iroquois, who believed that we were abandoned by the great Onontio, our Master, and if they saw us assisted by him, they would, probably, change their minds and let our allies be in peace and consent not to hunt on their grounds, or bring all their peltries to the French, which they trade at present with the English at Orange; and thus by a small aid from his Majesty we could prevent war and subject these fierce and hot spirits, which would be the greatest advantage that could be procured for the Country. That notwithstanding, it was important to arm the militia and in this year of abundant harvest to oblige them to furnish guns which they could all advantageously use when occasion required.

Done in the house of the Rev[d] Jesuit Fathers at Quebec, the day and year above stated.

Compared with the original remaining in my hands.

LE FE BURE DE LABARRE.

FATHER LAMBERVILLE TO M. DE LA BARRE.

[Paris Doc. II.]

February 10, 1684.

* * * * The Governor of New York is to come, they say, next summer to the Mohawk and speak there to the Iroquois. We'll see what he'll say. He has sent a shabby ship's flag to the Mohawk to be planted there. This is the coat of arms of England. This flag is still in the public chest of the Mohawks. I know not when it will see day.

M. DE LA BARRE TO GOV. DONGAN.

Montreal 15th June 1684.

Sir—The unexpected attack which the Iroquois, Senecas and Cayugas have made on one of my forts whither I had sent a gentleman of my household to withdraw Sieur de la Salle therefrom, whom I sent at their request to France, and the wholesale plunder of seven French canoes laden with merchandize for the Trade, and the detention during ten days of 14 Frenchmen who were conducting them up, and that in a time when I was in a quiet and peaceable negotiation with them, oblige me to attack them as people from whose promises we have nothing to expect but murder and treason; but I did not wish to do so without advising you of it, and telling you at the same time, that the Mohawks and Oneidas, neighbours of Albany, having done me no wrong, I intend to remain at peace with them and not attack them.

The letters which I have rec[d] from France inform me as does that which you were pleased to honor me with, that our two Kings desire that we should live in Union and Fraternity together.

I shall contribute with the greatest joy, and with a punctuality with which you will be satisfied. I think that on the present occasion you can well grant me the request I make to forbid those at Albany selling any Arms, Powder or Lead to the Iroquois who attacked us and to the other tribes who may trade with them.

This proceeding alone may intimidate them, and when they see the Christians united on this subject they will shew them more respect than they have done hitherto.

If you have any cause of complaint against their conduct, you can advance it now, & I shall consider your interests as those of my master, as soon as I shall hear from you I will answer regarding what you may require from my ministry in a manner entirely satisfactory to you, esteeming nothing in the world more highly than the opportunity to testify to you how truly I am

Sir

Your very humble servt

(Signed) LE FEBURE DE LA BARRE.

GOV. DONGAN TO M. DE LA BARRE.

[N. Y. Council Min. V.]

New York June ye 24th 1684.

Sr—Yrs dated the 15th I received the 23d of S. V. of this Instant; & am very sorry that I did not know sooner of the misunderstanding between you and the Indians that so I might (as really I would) haue vsed all just measures to prevent it

those Indians are under this Governmt as doth appeare by his Rll Highss his patent from his Maty the King of England and their submitting themselves to this Governmt as is manifest by or Records, his Rll Highnesses territories reaching as far as the River of Canada and yet notwithstanding the people of yr Govermt Come upon the great lake as allso on this side of both lakes, a thing which will scarcely be beleeved in England

I desire you to hinder them from so doing; and I will strictly forbidde the people of this Province to go on your side of the lakes this I haue hinted that there may be no occasion, as there shall not undoubtedly of mine, to break that desirable and faire Correspondence between the two Kings our Masters. I am so heartily bent to promote the Quiet and tranquillity of this Country & yours that I intend forthwith to go myselfe to Albany on purpose; and there send for the Indians, & require of them to do what is iust in order to a satisfaction to yr pretences; if they will not I shall not uniustly protect them, but do for yr Governmt all that can be reasonably expected from me; & in the mean time to continue & preserue a good Amity between us I think it convenient & desire that no Acts of hostility be cômitted, such differences are of so weighty a concerne that they are most proper to be decided at home and not by us.

I do assure you Sr that no body liueing hath a greater desire that there should be a strict friendshipp betwixt the subjects of this Govermt & yours than I haue and no body more willing upon all Occasions ivstly to approue myselffe Sr

Yr humble Servt

THO. DONGAN.

THE SAME TO THE SAME.

[Lond. Doc. V.]

Fort Albany, July 1684.

Sir—I came to this town with an intention to sent for the Senequaes but was prevented by some of their Sachims being come hither expressly to meet me.

They tell me that your Intentions are to make warr against them and they believe that you have already entered their countrey which repport I can scarcely give creditt to, after my last letter written to you.

You cannot be ignorant that those Indians are under this Goverm^{t} and I do assure you they have againe voluntarily given up both themselves and their lands to it, and in their application which they make to me, do offer, that if they have done anything amisse they will readily give all reasonable satisfaction.

S^{r} I should be very sorry to hear that you invade the Duke's Territories, after so just and honest an offer, and my promisse, that the Indians shall punctually perform whatever can be in justice required for all these injuries which you complaine they have committed.

I do not doubt but that if you please, this affair may be quietly reconciled between you and the Indians, if not, as I wrote in my former, wee have Masters in Europe to whom we should properly referr.

To prevent as much as I can all the inconveniencyes that may happen. I have sent the bearer with this letter and have ordered the Coates of Armes of His Royal Highnesse the Duke of York to be put up in the Indyan Castles which may diswade you from acting anything that may create a misunderstanding between us

Sir
I am with all respect
Most humble & affectionate
Servant

(Signed) THO DONGAN

M. DE LA BARRE TO GOV. DONGAN.

[Paris Doc. II.; Lond. Doc. V.]

Camp at Lachine, 24 July 1684.

Sir—I was much astonished by the receipt of your two letters of the fifth of July, New Stile, seeing one in French written by you, which I knew came from you as from friend to friend, and that written in English which I knew came from your Council and not from people disposed to maintain the union of our two Kings.

I sent Sieur Bourbon to you to advise you of the vengeance which I was about to wreak for the insult inflicted on the Christian name by the Senecas and Cayugas, and you answer me about pretensions to the possessions of lands of which neither you nor I are judges, but our own two Kings who have sent us, and of which there is no question at present, having no thought of conquering countries but of making the Christian name and the French people to be respected, in which I will spill the last drop of my blood.

I have great esteem for your person, and considerable desire to preserve the honor of his Brittannick Majesty's good graces as well as those of my Lord the Duke of York, and I even believe that they will greatly appreciate my chastisement of those who insult you and capture you every day as they have done this winter in Merilande. But if I was so unfortunate as that you desired to protect robbers, assassins and traitors, I could not distinguish their protector from themselves. I pray you, then, to attach faith to the credit which I give Sieur de Salavye to explain everything to you; and, if the Senecas and Cayugas wish your services as their intecessor to take security from them, not in the Indian but in the European fashion, without which and the honor of hearing from you, I shall attack them towards the 20th of the month of August, New Stile.

Sir

Your very humble Servant,

LE FEBURE DE LA BARRE.

[Par. Doc. II.; Lond. Doc. V.]

INSTRUCTIONS

WHICH SIEUR DE LA BARRE KING'S COUNCILLOR IN HIS COUNCILS, GOVERNOR & HIS LIEUTENANT GENERAL IN ALL THE COUNTRIES OF NEW FRANCE AND ACADIA, GIVES TO SIEUR DE SALVAYE HIS AMBASSADOR TO COLONEL DONGAN, GOVERNOR OF NEW YORK, TO EXPLAIN TO HIM THE UNFAITHFULNESS AND VIOLENCES COMMITTED BY THE SENECAS AND CAYUGAS AGAINST THE FRENCH.

He is, in the first place, to make known to him the quarter where the pillage of the seven canoes was perpetrated, and that it is more than 400 leagues distant from here and an equal distance, at least, Southwest from Albany, in the 39th or 40th degree.

That the place has been occupied over 25 years by the French who there established Catholic Missions of the Jesuit Fathers, and traded there (*on fait la traitte*) since that time, without the English having ever known, or spoken of, that country.

That the question is not about the country of the Iroquois, nor the Eastern shores of Lake Erie.

That the Iroquois having lived, previous to the arrival of M. de la Barre, with little consideration for the French, he was desirous to speak with them, to see if they were friends or foes, and for that purpose they were all assembled at Montreal last August where every thing was arranged on a friendly basis; even the Senecas and Cayugas had demanded the said Sieur de la Barre to withdraw Sieur de la Salle from the government of Fort St. Louis, in Illinois; which he caused to be done and he had the said Sieur de la Salle sent to France in the month of last November.

That notwithstanding this, and all the protestations they had made, a band of 200 warriors, Senecas and Cayugas having met in the month of March of this year, seven canoes manned by 14 Frenchmen, with fifteen or sixteen thousand pounds of Merchandize, who were going to trade with the Scious, towards the Southwest, pillaged them and took them prisoners, without any resistance from the said Frenchmen, who considered them as friends, and after having detained them nine days, with thousands of taunts and insults, released them without having given them either arms or canoes for provisions and to cross the rivers. After which the said Iroquois went and attacked Fort St. Louis, where Sieur Chevalier de Blangy was in the place of said Sieur de la Salle who had been withdrawn at their request. Having made three assaults and been vigorously repulsed, they withdrew from before the said Fort the 29th of said month of March.

That Sieur de la Barre having seen these acts of hostility committed in time of established peace and which Teganeout their Ambassador was coming to him to confirm, he might have adopted two courses, one to detain the said ambassador, and the other to wage war against them, not being able to eudure a treachery of that description against the Christian name and French Nation.

That, things being in this condition, he could not believe that Colonel Dongan would interfere therein in any way, if it were not to unite with him in destroying these traitors and Infidels.

That the Mohawks and Oneidas, neighbours of Albany, have no part in all this war, and that he has envoys at Onontagué to see if they will take a part.

That his troops being assembled and on the march, he cannot postpone attacking the Senecas unless by losing the campaign.

That in despatches dated the 5th of August last, the King his master was pleased to communicate to him the information which he had received from the King of England, of the appointment of Colonel Dongan as Governor of New York, with express orders to maintain good understanding and correspondence with said Sieur de la Barre, who, on that account, could have no idea that he had any intention to protect a treachery and injustice similar to that committed by villains on Frenchmen.

Done at the Camp of Lachine the 24th July, 1684.

Signed, LE FEBURE DE LA BARRE.
And lower down by M. REGNAUT.

GOV. DONGAN TO M. DE LA BARRE.

[Lond. Doc. V.]

1. It is not intended that I will justify the wrong the Indians have done to the French so farr to the southwest as 400 leagues from Mont Royall or in any other place whatsoever, though in all probability if we were to dispute these countreys so farr to the south west are more likely to be ours than the French, haveing English Colonies much nearer them.

2. The pretences you make to that countrey by your 25 years possession, and sending Jesuits amongst them are very slender, and it may bee, you may have the same to other countries as for Jesuits living amongst them, how charitable soever it may bee, it gives no right or title, and it is a great wonder that the English who so well know America should neither hear nor see in a long time the treaty you speak of.

3. But if the matter in debate bee not concerning the land on the side of the lake of Canida, it is desired to know what it is concerning since the Indians offer to give satisfaction for what injuries can be prooved to be cômitted by them as they say they have formerly done in such cases, and if they do not I never promised them any countenance from this government.

I wonder that Monsr de la Barr should send for any Indians who ouned themselves under this Government to know whether they were friends or ennemies, since this Government at that time and at this present hath enjoyed for aught I know a full and perfect peace with the Government of Canida; as for the case of La Salle I am not concerned in it but wonder you should send him to France upon the bare complaint of the Indians.

As for the injuries, affronts, insolencyes and robberyes committed by the Indians upon the French, I have earnestly pressed them to make a submission and satisfaction, and that out of a true consideration of the misseryes that may happen by having a warr with such Savages.

I could heartily wish that the Sieur de la Barre had sooner given me notice of the act of hostility before he had detained Taganeout there Ambassadour, or made warr against them, that I might have used all just methods to prevent a warr that may be destructive to either party—

That the Governor of Canida does very well in believing what truly he ought that I will not interest myselfe in any manner to countenance such villanyes and if I did not think there was a middle way to compose that difference myselfe, I would be willing to joyne against them.

I am glad you assured me that the neighbouring Indians to Albany have no share in that warr, but I am sorry the troops are in soe great forwardness, that if my former advice had bin taken, there had been no absolute necessity to attaque the Indians or loose the campaigne.

That it is very true, I ought to have a good correspondence with the Sieur de la Barr, and it is not nor ever shall be my fault if I have not, and I againe must tell you that I have no thought or inclination to protect any villany whatsoever.

EXTRACT OF A LETTER ADDRESSED BY LOUIS XIV. TO MONSIEUR DE LA BARRE, THE 21st JULY, 1684.

[Paris Doc. II.]

Monsieur De la barre

I have seen by your letters of the 5th June last, the resolution you have taken to attack the Iroquois, and the reasons which moved you to it, and though it is a grave misfortune for the Colony of New France which will interrupt the trade of my subjects and divert them from the cultivation of the land and expose them to frequent insults on the part of the Iroquois Savages, who can frequently surprise them in distant settlements, without your being even in a state to succor them; I do not hesitate to approve your adoption of that resolution since, by the insult they offered the fifteen Frenchmen whom they pillaged, and the attack on Fort St. Louis, you have had reason to believe that they seriously intended declaring war, and as I wish to place you in a position to sustain it, and bring it to a speedy termination, I have given orders for equipping the Ship L'Emerillon, on board which I have caused to be embarked three hundred soldiers quartered in the ports of Brest and Rochefort with the number of Officers and Marines contained in the lists which you will find annexed, and this reinforcement with that sent to you by the last vessels from Rochelle, and which you have learned from my preceding letters, will furnish you means to fight advantageously, and to destroy utterly those people, or at least to place them in a state, after having punished them for their insolence, to receive peace on the conditions which you will impose on them.

You must observe as regards this war that even though you prosecute it with advantage, if you do not find means to wage it promptly, it will not the less cause the ruin of the colony, the people of which cannot subsist in the continual disquietude of being attacked by the Savages, and in the impossibility in which they find themselves of applying themselves to trade and the cultivation of their farms. Therefore whatever advantage you may derive for the glory of my arms and the entire destruction of the Savages by the continuation of this war, you ought to prefer peace which restoring quietness to my subjects will place you in a condition to increase the Colony by the means pointed out to you in my preceding letters.

I write to my ambassador in England to procure orders from the Duke of York to prevent him who commands at Baston assisting the Savages with troops, arms or ammunition, and I have reason to believe that orders will be despatched as soon as representations on my part will have been made.

I am very glad to tell you that from every thing I learn of what has occurred in Canada, the fault which you committed in not punctually executing my orders relative to the number of twenty-five licenses to be granted to my subjects, and the great number you have sent on all sides, in order to favor persons belonging to yourself, appears to me to have been the principal cause of what has happened on the part of the Iroquois. I hope you will repair this fault by giving a prompt and glorious termination to this war.

* * * * * * * * * * *

It appears to me also that one of the principal causes of the war arises from one Du Lhut having caused two Iroquois to be killed who had assassinated two Frenchmen in Lake Superior, and you sufficiently see how much this man's voyage, which cannot produce any advantage to the Colony, and which was permitted only in the interest of some private persons, has contributed to disturb the repose of the Colony.

As it concerns the good of my service to diminish as much as possible the number of the Iroquois, and as these Savages who are stout and robust, will, moreover, serve with advantage in my galleys, I wish you to do every thing in your power to make a great number of them prisoners of war, and that you have them shipped by every opportunity which will offer for their removal to France.

* * * * * * * * * * *

I desire likewise that you leave Fort Frontenac in the possession of Sieur de la Salle or those who are there for him, and that you do nothing in opposition to the interest of that man whom I take under my special protection.

MEMOIR OF M. DE LA BARRE

AS TO WHAT HAD OCCURRED AND HAD BEEN DONE REGARDING THE WAR AGAINST THE SENECAS.

[Paris Doc. II.]

Having been obliged to leave early in June, in conformity to the resolution adopted by the Intendant, the Bishop, the heads of the country and myself, to wage war against the Senecas for having, in cold blood, pillaged seven hundred canoes belonging to Frenchmen ; arrested and detained the latter to the number of fourteen, as prisoners for nine days, and finally attacked Fort St. Louis of the Illinois, where the Chevalier de Bangy gallantly defended himself, and having resolved, at the same time, to seize Teganeout, one of their chiefs and his twelve companions who had come to ratify the peace made last year, who left their country before they heard of this attack, which circumstance would oblige me not to treat them ill, but merely to secure their persons, we considered three things necessary : First, to endeavor to divide the Iroquois among themselves, and for this purpose, to send persons expressly to communicate my sentiments to the Revd Jesuit Fathers who are Missionaries there and to request them to act ; the second, to send to the Outaouacs to engage our French to come to my assistance by the South, by Lake Erie and to bring as many as they could of the Savages, our allies ; and thirdly, to advise Colonel Dongan, Governor of New-York of what we were obliged to do, whilst at the same time I would throw a considerable reinforcement of men into Fort Frontenac to secure it. Being arrived at Montreal the tenth of the said month, we sent for Mr. Dollier, Superior of the Seminary of said town and of the Mission to the Indians of the Mountain, and the Reverend Pere Briare, Superior of the Mission of the Sault Saint Louis, who having concurred with us, furnished seven Christian Iroquois, friendly to the French and pretty shrewd, two of whom we sent with some belts of Wampum to the Mohawks, and two to the Oneidas, to say to them that we were resolved to observe the peace made with them—that we were very willing to live there as with friends, and that we requested them not to interfere in the war which we were about to wage against the Senecas, who had cruelly insulted us in the person of the frenchmen whom they had plundered and seized, and fort St. Louis which they had attacked, since, and in violation of the peace made last year at Montreal; we sent the three others to Onontagué to explain the same things, and finally I despatched Sieurs Guillet and Hebert to the Outaouacs to advise Sieurs Ladurantaye and Dulhut of my design and of the need I had of their assistance, and sent my orders to the Rev. Father Enjalran, Superior of said Missions, to operate there and send orders to different quarters according to his usual zeal and capacity, whilst I despatched Sieur Bourbon to Orange or Manette to notify Colonel Dongan of the insult the French had received from the Senecas, which obliged me to march against them, of which I gave him notice, assuring him that if he wished to revenge the twenty-six Englishmen of Merilande, whom they had killed last winter, I would promise him that I would unite my forces to his, that he may obtain satisfaction for it, or avenge them.

I next despatched Sieur Dutast, first captain of the King's troops, on the twentieth of the same month with five or six picked soldiers and six mechanics, carpenters and masons, with provisions and ammunition of war to throw themselves into Fort Frontenac and put it, in all haste, beyond insult; after which, having caused all to embark at la Chine, I proceeded from Montreal, on St. John's day, to return to Quebec were I had requested the Intendant to make out the detachments of Militia which should follow me to the war, without inconvenience to the Country; I arrived there on the twenty-sixth, having used great diligence on the route, and found the people ordered and some canoes purchased; but as they were not sufficient for the embarcation of all, we caused fifteen flat (bottomed) pine batteaux, suitable for the conveyance, each, of fourteen or fifteen men, to be constructed in a hurry.

I divided all my small force into three divisions, I placed myself at the head of the first which I commanded to lead the van. I left the management of the second to Mr. D'Orvilliers, antient Captain of Infantry; the third being composed of troops from the Island of Montreal and the environs, was commanded by Sieur Dugue, antient Captain of Carignan. Sieur D'Orvilliers had been, since the fore part of spring, reconnoitering Lake Ontario and the Seneca Country, to see where the descent should be made and in what direction we should march to their two principal villages, of which he had made a faithful and exact plan. I selected as Major of the Brigade which I commanded, Sieur de Villebon-Beccancour, formerly Captain of the King's Dragoons, so that acting in my place, as I was obliged to have an eye to all, I could confide in him; he succeeded with all possible diligence and experience.

I left Quebec the ninth of July, at the head of Three hundred militiamen, accompanied by the said Sieur de Villebon, and arrived at Montreal the 16th, where I was joined by Sieur D'Orvilliers on the twenty-first, who brought me, in addition to two hundred and fifty militia, batteaux to embark the King's troops. Thus after having issued every possible order for the conveyance of provisions, in which I had much difficulty in consequence of the scarcity of canoes and of experienced persons to conduct them in the portages of the Rapids, I detached Sieur de Villebon to take the lead with my brigade, and the two companies of King's troops, and ordered them to pass the first and second portages, where I should join them, so that on the thirtieth I passed their encampment beyond the said second portage, and we marched next day, both brigades together, Sieur D'Orvilliers bringing up the rear with the third one day behind us, so that being, on the 1st of August in Lake St. Francis with about two hundred canoes and our fifteen batteaux, I was joined there by the Rev. Father Lamberville, Junior, coming on behalf of his Brother from Onontagué, and by the Rev. Father Millet, from the Oneidas.

By the annexed letters from Onontagué, you will learn that these people having been joined by the Oneidas and Cayugas, had obliged the Senecas to make them Mediators as to the reparation suitable to be made to me for the insult which had unfortunately been committed against the French in the month of March ; and prayed me to send Mr. le Moine to them, with whom they could terminate this affair. This obliged me immediately to dispatch a canoe to Fort Frontenac in all haste, to send me from there the new bark which I had built in the winter, in order to freight her with the provisions I brought, and to send the canoes in which they were loaded to fetch others from la Chine.

We arrived on the second, at the Portage of the Long Sault, which I found very difficult, notwithstanding the care I taken to send fifty men ahead thither, to cut the trees on the bank of the river and prevented those passing who were to drag the canoes and batteaux ; because the stream being voluminous and the bank precipitous the people were in the water the moment they abandoned the shore, and were not strong enough to draw said batteaux ; this necessitated my sojourn at that place, where having been joined by the Christian Iroquois of the Sault and of Montreal, they undertook, for a few presents of Brandy and Tobacco, to pass the said batteaux and the largest canoes, which they fortunately accomplished in two days without any accident.

On the morning of the fifth I found the new bark arrived at La Galette where I had all the provisions discharged from the canoes before eight o'clock in the morning, and these despatched at the same time on their return to la Chine to reload there. The strong winds from the South West, which constantly prevailed all this time, and which obstinately continued during the remainder of the month, were the cause of the great diligence that the bark had made, and likewise delayed our march so much, that I could not arrive, at the fort, with my canoes alone until the ninth. I was joined there by Father de Lamberville whom I despatched next day to his brother at Onnontague whom I instructed to assure those of that Nation that I had so much respect for their request and for those of the other two, that I should prefer their mediation to war, provided they made me a reasonable satisfaction.

Three things obliged me to adopt this resolution : the first, because it appeared by letters I had received from Colonel Dongan, in answer to the message by the man named Bourbon, that he was very far from the good understanding of which His Majesty had assured me ; but much disposed to interfere as our enemy in this matter. The second, because I had few provisions, and I did not see that any effort was made to forward flour to me, with any diligence, from Montreal ; and the third, because the wind prevailed so strong from the South east, that my bark did not return from La Galette, and I could not despatch another to Lake Ontario, to notify the army of the South, which was to arrive forthwith at Niagara, of my arrival at Fort Frontenac with that of the North.

I afterwards reviewed all our troops, as annexed, and Sieur le Moine having overtaken me on the same day with the remainder of the Christian Iroquois who had not previously arrived, I despatched him on the sixteenth to Onnontague and placed in his hands, Tegancourt, the ambassador from the Senecas, whom I had arrested at Quebec. Seeing the wind always contrary I sent on the preceding day, eight of the largest canoes that I had to the bark at La Galette to bring me ten thousand weight of flour, bread beginning to fail which caused me a good deal of uneasiness and created considerable murmurs among the troops and the militia. Finally on the 21st my canoes arrived with what I sent them for. I set to work immediately with all possible diligence to have bread and biscuit baked, and sent off forthwith, the King's troops, D'Orvilliers' and Dugué's two brigades, and two hundred Christian savages to encamp at La Famine [Hungry bay], a post favorable for fishing and hunting and four leagues from Onontagué, so as to be nearer the enemy and to be able to refresh our troops by fishing and the chase, whilst we were short of provisions, intending to join them, myself, with about three hundred Frenchmen whom I had remaining.

On the 25th the canoes which I had detached from La Galette to Montreal, arrived, but in far less number than I had looked for, and brought me but eight or nine thousand weight of flour, instead of twenty thousand which I expected, having left them ready for loading when I departed. I caused bread and biscuit to be immediately made of it for the support of our troops who were at the place called La Famine.

On the 27th at four o'clock in the afternoon, a canoe of M. Lemoine's men arrived from Onnontagué with Tegancourt who reported to me, that the Onnontagués had received orders from Col. Dongan which he sent by the person named Arnaud, forbidding them to enter into any treaty with me without his express permission, considering them the Duke of York's subjects, and that he had caused the Arms of the said Duke to be planted three days before, in their village; that the Council had been convened at the said place of Onontague and Sieur Lemoine invited to repair thither, in which the matter having been debated, these savages got into a furious rage, with some danger to the English delegate, saying they were free, and that God, who had created the Earth, had granted them theirs without subjecting them to any person, and they requested the elder Father Lamberville to write to Colonel Dongan the annexed letter, and the said Sieur Lemoine having well sustained the French interests; they unanimously resolved to start in two days, to conclude with me at La Famine. On the receipt of this news I immediately called out my canoes in order to depart and was accompanied by a dozen of others, having caused six of the largest to be loaded with bread and biscuit for the army.

After having been beaten by bad weather and high wind, we arrived in two days at La Famine. I found there tertian and double tertian fever which broke out among our people so that more than one hundred and fifty men were attacked by it; I had also left some of them at the fort, which caused me to despatch, on arriving, a Christian savage to Onontague to M. Lemoine, to request him to cause the instant departure of those who were to come to meet me, which he did with so much diligence, though he and his children were sick, that he arrived as early as the third of September with fourteen Deputies; nine from Onontague, three from Oneida and two Cayugas, who paid me their respects and whom I entertained the best manner I was able, postponing until the morrow morning the talk about business, at which matters were fully discussed and peace concluded after six hours deliberation, three in the morning and as many after dinner, Father Brias speaking for us and Hotrehonati and Garagonkier for the Iroquois; Tegancout, a Seneca present, the other Senecas not daring to come in order not to displease Col. Dongan, who sent to promise them a reinforcement of four hundred horse and four hundred foot, if we attacked them. The treaty was concluded in the evening on the conditions annexed, and I promised to decamp the next day and withdraw my troops from their vicinity; which I was, indeed, obliged to do by the number of sick which had augmented to such a degree that it was with difficulty I found enough of persons in health to remove the sick to the canoes, besides the scarcity of provisions having no more than the trifle of bread which I brought them.

I allowed the Onontagues to light the Council fire at this post without extinguishing that at Montreal, in order to be entitled to take possession of it by their consent when the King should desire it and thereby exclude the English and Col. Dongan from their pretensions.

On leaving the Fort I had ordered one of the barks to go to Niagara to notify the army of the South to return by Lake Erie towards Missilimakinack. She had a favorable passage; found it arrived only six hours previously to the number of seven hundred men, viz: one hundred and fifty French and the remainder Indians.

I departed on the sixth, having had all the sick of my troops embarked before day (so as not to be seen by the Indians) to the number of one hundred and fifty canoes and twelve flat batteaux and arrived in the evening of the same day at Fort Frontenac, where I found one hundred and ten men of the number I had left there, already departed, all sick, for Montreal, and having given the necessary orders as to the number of soldiers to be left there for the security of that post, until the arrival from France of Sieur de la Forest, Major thereof, I started, about nine or ten o'clock in the morning, on my return. Shortly after my departure, the bark arrived from Niagara with some French officers of the army who brought me news from it at night, and assured me that the Chiefs of all the savages had accompanied them to the Fort, desirous to see me, and that they would visit me at Montreal, where I should await them. The Rev. Father de Lamberville Sen[r] came, likewise, with these Gentlemen on account of some difficulties which he was very glad to arrange for Onontague whither he had returned. We worked some hours together; I then sent him back to the fort with some of the arrived French; the others being desirous to leave and come down again into the country.

After having waited some time for Mess[rs] du Tast and de Cahonet to whom I gave one of my canoes and two of my attendants well acquainted with the navigation, to pilot their batteaux and troops in safety through the rapids, I resumed my journey down the river. I likewise took on board one of my canoes the Sieur Le Moine whose fever had seriously augmented, and who had served the King in this affair with so much zeal and affection, aided by the intimate knowledge he had of the Iroquois language, that it may be said the entire Colony owe him a debt of eternal gratitude.

Finally, in my return of three days I accomplished what cost us thirteen in ascending, and found in the stores at Montreal and la Chine, forty-five thousand weight of flour, which, had we received it, would have enabled us to have made a longer sojourn in the upper country.

Done at Quebec the 1st day of October 1684.

LE FEBURE DE LA BARE.

PRESENTS MADE BY THE ONNONTAGUES TO ONONTIO, AT LA FAMINE, THE 5th 7ber 1684.*

[From the same.]

The Onnontagués, whose mediation between the French and the Senecas the General accepted, having repaired to a place called La Famine about 25 leagues from their country, Sieur Hateouati, who is the Orator of that Nation, spoke by fifteen presents, not only on behalf of the Senecas, but also for the other Iroquois Nations.

1st *Word of the Iroquois.* After having taken God to witness the sincerity of his heart, and having assured Onontio of the truth of his words, he spoke in this wise:

I give you a Beverage devoid of bitterness, to purify whatever inconvenience you may have experienced during the voyage, and to dispel whatever bad air you may have breathed between Montreal and this place.

Answer of Onontio to the words of Hoteouaté:—As I have placed in your hands the mediation with the Senecas, I wish, truly to do what you ask me. I, therefore, lay down my Hatchet and refer to you to obtain a reasonable satisfaction.

2[d] *Word.* I remove the hatchet with which you threaten to strike the Senecas. Remember he is your child, and that you are his father.

3[d] *Word.* Mr. Lemoine, your ordinary envoy, having come last year, and speaking to us in your name, cut a deep ditch into which he told us you and we should cast all the unkind things that

* Endorsed by the Minister, "These letters must be kept secret."

might occur; I have not forgotten this word, and in obedience to it, I request you to throw into that ditch the Seneca robbery, and that it may disturb neither our country nor yours.

Answer. That ditch is well cut, but as your young men have no sense, and as they may make this a pretext for committing acts of hostility anew, after having cast the Seneca robbery into that ditch, as you desire; arrest, then, your young men, as I shall restrain mine. I cover it up forever.

4th *Word.* I set up again the tree of peace, which we planted at Montreal, in the conference we had the honor to have with you last summer.

Answer. It is not I who think of throwing it down: it is your nephews who have seriously shaken it. I strengthen it.

5th *Word.* I exhort you, Father, to sustain it strongly, in order that nothing may shake it.

6th *Word.* I again tie up (*je rattache*) the Sun which was altogether obscured: I dispel all the clouds and mists that concealed it from our view.

7th *Word.* The robbery committed by the Senecas on your nephews, is not a sufficient motive to make war against them. Where has blood been shed? I promise you that satisfaction shall be afforded you for the loss the French have experienced by the pillage of their merchandize.

Answer of Onontio. It is good that you promise me satisfaction: deceive me not. The first thing that I expect of you is, that you restore me the two prisoners of Etionnontaté who are with the Seneca, and a third who remains at Cayuga.

8th *Word.* Onontio, my father, I feel uneasy and cannot pluck up courage, whatever kindnesses you have the goodness to show me. What disquiets me, is to behold Soldiers, hear drums, etc. I pray you return to Quebec, so that your children may sleep in peace.

Answer. I depart to-morrow and quit this country, to show you what deference I pay to your demands.

9th *Word.* The fires of peace and the halls of our Councils were at Frontenac or at Montreal. The former is a poor country where the Grasshoppers prevent me sleeping, and the second is far away for our old men. I kindle the fires of peace on this spot, which is the most agreeable that we can select, where there is good fishing, hunting, &c.

Answer. I accept the selection you have made of this place for our conferences, without, however, extinguishing the fire which I keep burning at Montreal.

10th *Word.* Our warriors have, as well as our other chiefs, accepted the peace. I bear their words by this belt.

Answer. You need not doubt the obedience of my soldiers; endeavour to make yourselves obeyed by your own. To prove to you that I maintain uphold the tree of peace, I sent to Niagara to cause the army to return which was coming from that direction.

11th *Word.* You told us, last summer, to strike the enemy no more. We heard your voice. We shall not go to war again in that quarter.

Answer. Remember that the Maskoutenek is brother to the Oumeami. Therefore strike neither the one nor the other.

12th *Word.* He has killed some, this spring, in divers rencounters, but as you bound my arms I allowed myself to be beaten, without defending myself.

Answer. That's good; you need not pursue the Oumeami who struck you; I shall send him word not to commit any more acts of hostility.

13th *Word.* Regarding the Illinois, I am at war with him; we shall, both of us, die fighting.

Answer. Take heed, in firing at the Illinois, not to strike the French whom you meet on your path and in the neighbourhood of Fort St. Louis.

14th *Word.* Restore to us the Missionaries whom you have withdrawn from our villages.

Answer. They shall not be taken from you who are our mediators; and when the Senecas shall have commenced to give me satisfaction, they shall be restored to them as well as to the other nations.

15th *and last Word.* Prevent the Christians of the *Sault* and of the Mountain coming any more among us, to seduce our people to Montreal; let them cease to dismember our country as they do every year.

Answer. It is not my children of the *Sault* nor of the mountain who dismember your country; it is yourselves who dismember it by your drunkenness and superstitions. Besides, there is full liberty to come and reside among us; no person is retained by force.

The General added two presents to the above.

By the first he said: You see the consideration which I have for the request you have made me. I ask you in return, if the Seneca, Cayuga or any other commit a similar insult against me, that you first give him some sense, and if he will not hear you, that you abandon him as one disaffected.

By the last belt, he exhorted them to listen not to evil sayings, and told them to conduct Tegannehout back to Seneca and to inform those of the above conclusions.

M. DE MULLES TO THE MINISTER.

[From the same.]

My Lord—I thought you would be impatient to learn the success and result of the war the General had undertaken against the Iroquois which rendered it necessary for him to call a part of the people of this country together and make all necessary preparation, at his Majesty's expense, for this expedition. The troops have been as far as a place called La Famine, thirty leagues beyond Fort Frontenac. The army consisted of nine hundred French and three hundred Savages, and from the Niagara side there was another army of six hundred men, one third of whom were French and the remainder Ottawas and Hurons, amounting in all to eighteen hundred men.

What Indians there were evinced the best disposition to fight the Iroquois to the death. Sieur de la Durantaye who brought the last six hundred men from Missilimakinak, has informed us that he learned from a Miami Chief that more than a thousand Illinois were coming to our aid on learning that we were about to fight the Iroquois, to such a degree are they their irreconcilable enemies. Certainly, never was there remarked a better disposition to fight and conquer them and purge the country of that nation which will be eternally our enemy. All the French breathed nothing but war, and though they saw themselves obliged to abandon their families, they consoled themselves with the hope of liberating them by one victory from a nation so odious as the Iroquois, at whose hands they constantly dreaded ambushes and destruction. But the General did not think proper to push matters any farther, and without any necessity sent Sieur Le Moyne to the said Iroquois to treat of peace at a time when every one was in good health, and when all necessary provision was made of food, &c. to dare every enterprize; and finally after various comings and goings on one side and the other, the General concluded peace such as you will see by the articles which I take the liberty to send you as written by the hand of his Secretary.

This peace, my Lord, has astonished all the officers who had the command in that army and all those who composed it, who have testified so deep a displeasure and so sovereign a contempt for the General's person that they could not prevent themselves evincing it to him. I assure you, my Lord, that had I strayed ever so little from my duty and not exhibited exteriorly, since his return, the respect I owe his character, the whole world would have risen against him and would have been guilty of some excess.

The said General excuses himself because of the sick and even says that the troops lacked food; to which I feel obliged to answer, being certain that he seeks every pretext and has recourse to every expedient to exculpate himself and perhaps to put the blame on me.

'Tis certain that there was a great number of sick among the Militia which he took with him to Fort Frontenac, who were in perfect good health on arriving there, but having encamped them for a fortnight in prairies between the woods and a pond, it is not surprising that some fell sick.— Again he made them camp at La Famine in places that were never inhabited, entirely surrounded by swamps, which contributed still considerably to the sickness in his army; and had he remained there longer he would not have saved a man. This has caused every one to say that he did not care, that he had not the least desire to make war; that he made no use of his long sojourns except employing them in his negociations. Had he seriously wished to make war on the said Iroquois he would not have remained ten to twelve days at Montreal, fourteen or fiften at Fort Frontenac and as many at La Famine, but would have remained merely a day or two, and would have used the greatest despatch to fight the Iroquois, and not uselessly consumed all his provisions; he would have, indubitably surprised the said Iroquois who did not expect this war, especially as the greater number of their young men had been at war in the beginning of the spring.

He says he lacked provisions; though that were true, he would be the cause and could not but accuse himself of imprudence, having supplied him, generally, with whatever he required of me, of which the whole country is a witness, and with a little precaution or rather good faith he would have had every thing in abundance. He had determined not to leave until the 15th of August; he departed on the 15th of July. That did not prevent me furnishing all that he required of me, such as batteaux, canoes, arms, ammunition, and all the provisions he desired. This is so true that there yet remained at the end of the island of Montreal, at a place called La Chine thirty-five thousand weight of flour and five of biscuit which he found on his return, and which he had requested me to retain for him at Montreal. Had he not halted, and had he been disposed to push into the Iroquois Country, the first convoy of provisions which accompanied him had sufficed, the greater number of the militia, unwilling to wait for the King's supplies having laid in their own private stock, the greater part of which they brought back with them, which all the Captains in command will certify. This convoy consisted of eighteen canoes full of biscuit, pork, brandy and apparently other things which I do not precisely know having been loaded at Montreal whilst I was at Quebec where I issued orders for the provisions that the General had demanded of me and for attending to the harvest of those who had gone to the war.

If it had been the General's design to make war, he should not have caused the cargoes of the eighteen canoes I have mentioned to be put into barks thirty leagues from Montreal above the Rapids, instead of letting the voyage be continued by the canoemen who were paid to go to Fort Frontenac and who had already accomplished the roughest half of the road, and who, without a doubt, would have arrived in three days at the Fort, which was represented to him by all the officers who stated to him that the barks required wind which being contrary would keep them more than three weeks from arriving. This turned out to be true. Notwithstanding all these reasons he absolutely insisted that all the said provisions should be put in the barks. Some have assured me that the canoes of said convoy were partly laden with merchandize, and not being very desirous to let the circumstance be known, he had caused the said barks to precede the canoes to put the goods secretly into them and keep the knowledge of it from every body. By these means he made use of these canoes to convey these merchandises to the Fort at the King's expense, which he has always practised for two years, ever pretending certain necessity to transport munitions of war, and to make use, by this means, of the conveyances for which the King is made to pay, under pretext to keep the Fort in good order. It is impossible to conceive the quantity of Brandy that he has caused to be conveyed thither during eighteen months, of which I have had most positive information, and of which I had the honor to advise you in my last. Others supposed that he had the said provisions put on board those barks in order to obtain time and by this address, to negotiate a peace with the Iroquois, as he had sent Sieur Le Moyne to them who is a very brave man and who despaired of all these negotiations, stating openly that they ought to be whipt. All the delays at Montreal, the Fort, and at La Famine caused the useless consumption of a portion of the supplies which, however, did not fail; other convoys having been received from time to time, but these were always wasted without any thing having been done.

After the said General had determined in his own mind on this war, he sent the man named Bourbon, an inhabitant of this country to Colonel Dongan to advise him that he was obliged to wage war against the Iroquois, requesting him not to afford them any aid; which he confided to me eight days after the departure of the said Bourbon. This obliged me to tell him that I was astonished that he should have thus proceeded; that the Iroquois having insulted us and intending to fight with and destroy them, I should not have deemed it proper to inform neighbours who have an interest in our destruction; and that he afforded thereby an opportunity to Col. Dongan, who is an Englishman, and consequently our born enemy, to give underhand information of our designs to the Iroquois, and convey secretly to them all that may be necessary for their defence against us. I asked him if he did not perceive that the English would never desire our advantage, and that they would contribute all in their power to destroy us, though at peace as regards France; that they would always be jealous of the Fur trade prosecuted by us in this Country, which would make them protect the Iroquois always against us.

This Bourbon negotiation gave Colonel Dongan occasion to use some rhodomontade as the General has informed me; and this assuredly it was that obliged him, having this information, to send an Englishman, who is in the habit of trading among the said Indians, to plant the Duke of York's arms among the Onontagués, which is an Iroquois village, wishing by that act to take the first possession of the Country. We have not heard talk of any other movement on the English side, and it is even certain that they will never cause us any dread from that quarter and that they could not prevent us to achieve that conquest this year, had the General been willing to fight.

You can hardly believe, my Lord, that the General has, alone, undertaken the war without having consulted any person, neither officers of the army nor gentlemen, nor the people of the country who are the most interested, nor any individual whosoever he might be, except Sieur de la Chesnayne, with whom he acts in concert for the entire destruction and ruin of the country. He has again made peace in this manner without any communication with any of the officers or others of those who were near his person. What seems a wonder in the country is that one individual, subject of his Majesty like others, should, of his own will, make war and peace without having consulted or demanded the opinion of any person. His Majesty never acted thus. He has his Council of War, and when he is about to wage it, he demands advice of those of his council, in communicating to them the reasons which he may have to do so, and even causes the publication of manifests throughout the kingdom, wishing to communicate to his people the justice of his undertakings. But the General has treated of peace, like a sovereign, with the said Iroquois, having employed none of those who were nigh him and who were acquainted with the Iroquois tongue, except as Interpreters. He dare not consult the officers, being certain that they would all have concluded on war; and but little was necessary to make them select a chief from among themselves to attack the enemy.

The said General proceeds at the head of a small force to make war against the Iroquois, and far from doing that, he grants them all they ask. His principal design was to attack the Senecas, but instead of showing him any civility, they did not even condescend to come and meet him, and gave an insolent answer to those who proposed it to them. If people had any thing to say to them, let them take the trouble and come and meet them. There came altogether on this embassy only a certain sycophant who seeks merely a good dinner, and a real buffoon called among the French *Le Grande Gueule* [Big Throat,] accompanied by eight or ten miserable fellows who fooled the General in a most shameful manner, which you will perceive by the articles of peace I have the honour to send you, and which I doubt not he also will send you. They will assuredly excite your pity. You will see he abandons the Illinois among whom M. de la Salle is about to establish himself and who are the cause of this war, inasmuch as the Iroquois attacked them even in Fort St. Louis which the said Sieur de la Salle had erected among them, and of which the General took possession, having ousted and driven away those whom the said Sieur de la Salle had left in command there, and whither he sent Sieur de Bangy, his lieutenant of the guards, who is still there.

When he concluded this peace he already had His Majesty's letter eight days in his possession, but so far from conforming to its intentions, he consents to the slaughter of the Illinois who are our allies, and where His Majesty designed to plant a new Colony or some powerful establishment under M. de la Salle's direction. I consider it also my duty to inform your Lordship that the General quit La Famine the moment the peace was concluded without taking the least care of the troops, abandoning them altogether to their own guidance, forbidding them on pain of death to leave the place until a long time after him, fearing to be surprised by the Iroquois, and having (so to say) lost his wits, caring little what became of the army. Certain it is that he went up to the Fort without taking information about any thing and returned in the same manner.

The worst of this affair is the loss of the trade which I find inevitable, because the Outawas and other Savages who came to our aid will hereafter entertain no respect for us, and will regard us as a people without courage and without resolution. I doubt not, my lord, but the General sends you a letter which he received from Father Lamberville, Jesuit, who is a missionary in an Iroquois village at Onontagué, whence those ambassadors came with whom peace was negotiated. The Father, who had learned the General's intentions from Sieur Le Moyne, has been wise and sufficiently discreet, anticipating his design, to write to him in accordance with his views, and to ingeniously solicit that which must flatter and highly please him. But one thing is certain that all the Jesuits at Quebec, and particularly Father Bechefer have openly stated in Quebec for six weeks that the country was destroyed if peace were concluded ; which is so true, that having communicated to him the two letters I wrote to the General, he highly approved of them and advised me to send them to the fort. I shall take leave to send you copies of them, requesting you very respectfully, to be persuaded that I speak to you without passion, and that I state nothing to you but what is most true and reliable, and because I feel obliged to let you know the truth as regards all things, without which you will never have the least confidence in me.

I should wish, my Lord, to avoid explaining myself in this manner, fearing you might infer that we were, the General and I, greatly disunited, which is quite contrary to the manner in which we live together, since it is certain that we never had, personally, the least difference, wishing in that to conform myself to your wishes and His Majesty's orders, aware that it is the most assured means that I can take to be agreeable to you, which is the sole ambition I have in the world, and to prove to you that no person can be with more profound respect and greater devotedness than I, my Lord,

Your very humble and ob: serv[t].

This, my Lord, is only incidentally. I defer informing you of what has occurred in this country during this year, until the departure of the vessels.

Quebec, the 10th, 8[ber], 1684.

DEMEULLES.

FATHER LAMBERVILLE, MISSIONARY AT ONONDAGA, TO M. DE LA BARRE.

[Onondaga,] July 10, 1684.

Sir,—A general Assembly of all the Iroquois will be held here at which it is intended to unite against you, and to inform the Senecas that you wished to persuade the four Iroquois Nations not to aid them in case of war. I am surprised that M. Le Moyne or some other persons have not told you that all the villages were confederated, and that one could not be attacked without becoming embroiled with the others.

Did affairs permit, I should have much wished to tell you my thoughts on many things. My brother will inform you of all when he will have the honor to see you. The On [non] tagués who have been spoken to, would like much to settle matters ; this is the reason my brother goes to you, whilst I still keep them disposed to give you satisfaction, in order to avoid if possible an infinitude of evils which will overtake Canada, and as I know not whether you desire war without listening to proposals for peace, I wish to understand whether it is not fitter that I withdraw, if possible, rather than give occasion to the Iroquois to say that I deceived them, by propositions for peace. The Onontagués and other nations say, that it grieves them to take up arms against you who are their neighbour, and who form almost one country with them.

They acknowledge that the Senecas are proud and insolent on account of their great number of warriors, but if you are desirous to maintain peace by some satisfaction which they will induce the Senecas to make you, it will be very acceptable, so as not to be obliged to come to extremities which will be very disastrous. If war occurs, Sir, all those who have houses apart from fortified places must at once abandon their dwellings, for the grain and the houses will be burned, and many will otherwise be brought away prisoners to be cruelly tormented and insulted. I always think that peace ought to be most precious to you, and that all the advantages that can be held out ought to cause you to shrink from war. A delay in order to arrange everything more at leisure and after having received assistance from France, would extricate you from much embarrassment which will follow from all sides. Pardon me if I give free expression to my thoughts ; you will not at least disapprove of the zeal with wch I am with much respect and submission

Your very humble and
Very Obedient Servant
(Signed) DeLambervile.

FROM THE SAME TO THE SAME.

11 July 1684.

Sir,—A troop of Senecas on their way to buy their supplies and munitions of powder, lead and arms are two days [distance] from here. They are expected in order to talk fully of affairs and to endeavour for the preservation of peace to induce them to give to you satisfaction. I believe if you are really desirous to come to an arrangement in which an effort will be made to satisfy you, and wherein will be prescribed the boundaries of war and trade, you would have leisure to provide with less trouble and embarrassment for the security of Canada, either by erecting forts at La Famine or towards the Senecas under the pretext of establishing a blacksmith, or at La Galette according as you think proper.

I do not believe that you will derive any advantage this year from war, if you wage it; for not only will almost the whole of the Iroquois prosecute the war in Canada, but you will not find the Senecas in their villages, in which they give out they will not shut themselves up, but conceal themselves in the grass and prepare ambuscades every where for you. Regarding your declaration to the Iroquois that you had no ill will except against the Senecas, they convoked a general Diet here, where they will conclude to league themselves against you, if you will not accept the propositions of peace for which the Onontagué wishes to obtain the consent of the Seneca who has already placed in security the old grain, and made a retreat in the woods for the children, women and old men, of which you will be ignorant.

The Warriors are to prowl every where, killing without if possible being killed. If their Indian corn be cut, it will cost much blood and men—You must also resolve to lose the harvest of the French grain to which the Iroquois will set fire. As for the French settlements, the Iroquois suppose that they are all abandoned and that the people have retired within the forts; otherwise, they would be a prey to the enemy. It is the opinion that if you begin the war, it will be of long duration, and that to feed those in Canada you will have to bring provisions from France. The Iroquois believes that he will destroy the Colony in case of war, for he will never fight by rule against us and will not shut himself up in any fort in which he might be stormed. Thus they are under the impression that no person daring to come into unknown forests to pursue them, they can neither be destroyed nor captured, having a vast hunting ground in their rear, towards Merilande and Virginia, as well as places adjoining their villages, wholly unknown to the French. If winter were not so cold in this country, that would be the time to wage war, for one can then see all around, and the trail cannot be concealed; but every thing must be carried—provisions, arms, powder and lead. You can not believe, Sir, with what joy the Senecas learned that you would, possibly, determine on war; and from the report the savages make them of the preparations apparent at Kataroskouy, they say, that the French have a great desire to be stript, roasted and eaten; and that they will see if their flesh, which they say is salt on account of the salt they make use of be as good as that of their other enemies whom they devour.

The envoy of the Governor of New York who is here promises the Iroquois goods at a considerable reduction; 7 *a* 8 lbs. of powder for a Beaver; as much lead as a man can carry for a Beaver, and so with the rest.

Every thing considered, Sir, if you will be content with a satisfaction which we will endeavor to obtain for you from the Senecas, you will prevent great evils which must fall on Canada in case of war; you will divert from it famine and many misfortunes, especially will you avoid much confusion and great suffering to the French who will fall into the hands of the Iroquois, who, as you are aware, exercise the most cruel and shameful cruelties towards their captives. Independent of there being no profit in fighting with this sort of banditti whom you, assuredly, will not catch and who will catch many of your people who will be surprised in every quarter.

The man called Hannatakta and some others of influence told me they pitied you. These are their words—they besought you not to force them to wage war against you; that the five Nations would be obliged to unite against you; that the French and the Iroquois being so near the one to the other, the war would be too disastrous to you, because, say they, our mode of fighting, of harrassing, of living, of surprising and flying to the woods will be the ruin of the French who are accustomed to fight against towns capable of defence or against armies who appear in the plains; if there be misunderstanding it ought to be settled. All the Iroquois are persuaded that before going to war you will try the ways of mildness and tell the Senecas to appease your anger for what they have plundered; that if you begin by a desire to wage war and will not act as a father towards your children, they have already declared beforehand that they will all unite against you.

FROM THE SAME TO THE SAME.

J ly 13. 1684.

My Lord—I have the honor to write to you by Father Millet who passes here in retiring from among the Iroquois who cannot be persuaded that you have determined on waging war against them, not having demanded any satisfaction of them for the merchandize of the Frenchmen whom the Senecas plundered. To turn away the scourge of war and the miseries which must follow it, especially among the French who will find themselves attacked by all the Iroquois if any hostile act is committed against the Senecas, I have strongly urged the Onnontagues to give you satisfaction according to the instructions which the Christian Iroquois, your deputies here, had. To-morrow a great number of Senecas are expected with several Cayugas and the Ambassadors from the two Lower Nations to talk about business.

The Senecas consequent on the declaration you made to them that you would proceed to their country, have concealed their old grain, prepared a distant retreat in the wooden fort for the security of their old men, women and children, and conveyed whatever they have of value out of their villages. The Warriors in great number have heard this news with much joy; they are determined to fight, not in their forts for they have none, and will not shut themselves up any where, but under cover, behind trees, and in the grass where they will try to do you considerable injury, if you want war. The Onnontagues—men of business—wish to arrange matters, especially having lost nothing of theirs, except only some goods. Must the father and children, they ask, cut each others throats for clothes? The children must satisfy the father to whom they owe honor and respect.

Further, I, last year, guarantied by two Wampum belts—one to the Senecas and the other here—that if the Iroquois army met the French who were towards Illinois, and any acts of hostility should follow on one side or the other, they would mutually arrange the difficulty without it leading to any consequences, and this is what we are endeavoring to persuade the Senecas to do. Father Millet, to whom I communicated all, and who has just passed, will tell you every thing and how apropos it would be that M. le Moine should come here to fetch those Chiefs and Warriors who will most willingly meet you under the safe conduct which you will give them through M. le Moine (who can come here in all surety and without any fear) to be conducted to your rendezvous near Seneca, or to the Fort, in order to settle matters in a friendly manner.

The Iroquois say they will not commit any act of hostility against you, unless you commence either by attacking the Senecas or by refusing all satisfaction, for they remark, it is painful to come to blows with their Father. They all say that their mode of warfare will be disastrous to you, but that the respect they entertain towards you, and which we insinuate among them, withholds them until they are forced, they add, to wage a sorrowful war, despite themselves, against you. They wish, first of all, they say, to avoid the reproach of not having kept their word which they gave. I told M. le Moine of the above.

My brother expects to leave with your deputies to carry to you the result of the Iroquois Diet, where the Onnontagué who assumes to be a moderator, pretends to force the Senecas to disavow what two of their captains caused their warriors to do, and to quieten again your mind; that is, they say, by some satisfaction which may afford you an honorable pretext to pay a friendly visit to Kaniatarontagouat [now, Irondequoit Bay] and not to appear there as an enemy.

I forgot to inform you that the Iroquois say they have accepted the satisfaction they received for the death of their captain, Hannhenhax, killed by the Kiskakous, and that it would seem very strange to them that you should refuse the satisfaction they wish to induce the Senecas to give you for the pillaged merchandize which, in their estimation is next to nothing compared with that important [council] fire in your children's cabin. I pray God that He conduct matters for His glory and the country's good and that He preserve you long, which is the wish, my Lord, of

Your very humble & very obt Servt,

J. DE LAMBERVILLE.

FROM THE SAME TO THE SAME.

18 July, 1684.

Sir—The Council convoked at Onnontagué was, at length, held on the 16th and 17th of July. You will see by the memoir I enclose in this letter what you said to the Onnontagués and what they reply by three Belts. Since you spoke, or I have made you speak to the Senecas assembled here in a body, Chiefs and Warriors, and their answer, we have spoken to them by three Belts and they have answered you by nine.

These are twelve Belts which your ambassadors take to you. I know not if you will accept the trifling pains we have taken to cause satisfaction to be given you, and to extricate you from the fatigues, the embarrassments and consequences of a disastrous war, and procure at the same time freedom of trade; for the Senecas informed me at night, by express, that they would give you more satisfaction than you expected, because they wished through respect for you, not to wage war any more against the Oumiamis, if you so wish it, and even any other nation if you insist on it. In fine, they do not wage war save but to secure a good peace. They return without striking a blow, without shedding blood, etc. The Seneca Iroquois offer you more than you would have believed.

The Onnontagués considered their honor engaged to this meeting, and have put all sorts of machinery in motion to induce the Senecas to condescend to place their affairs in their hands. On the first day of the Council every thing was almost despaired of, and the plenipotentiaries all excited came to see me, saying they gained nothing on the Senecas, and that up to that time they most willingly accepted war; that they rejected the presents which you and they had made them. They sent me back a collection of belts, that the chiefs and warriors acted with great zeal in combating the obstinacy of the Senecas so that having gained the Oneidas and Cayugas over to their side, they came to high words. Deputies, notwithstanding, succeeded one another to sound me on the state of affairs and to learn the true cause of the withdrawal of our Missionaries. Finally I told them that the real cause was, that the displeasure which they perceived you felt, and which they also entertained at being disparaged by the Senecas, had caused them to withdraw to you, until they should have satisfied you. At length the Onnontagués persuaded them to confide in them and to place their affairs in their hands—that if you did not accept their mediation, they should unite according to their policy, with all the other Iroquois against you. La Grande Gueule and his triumvirate have assuredly signalized themselves in this rencounter. My brother, who will inform you of every thing, will relate matters more in detail. We, however, await your orders which you will please convey to us by M. le Moine whom the Onnontagués request you to send instantly to them at Choueguen [Oswego] in all security and without the least fear.

FROM THE SAME TO THE SAME.

Onontague, this 17th August, 1684.

My Lord—Your people have brought my brother back here with the greatest possible diligence, having been wind bound three days, at one island. In order not to cause you any delay, which could only produce a useless consumption of provisions by your army, they arrived here with Sieur le Duc at midnight and having passed the rest of the night in conferring together, we had the Chiefs and Warriors assembled at day light after having obtained information from *La Grande Gueule* and Garakontie.

We declared our intentions in the presence of several Senecas who departed the same day to return to their country where they will communicate our approach. They carry one of your belts to reassure those who are alarmed by your armament. The Onnontagués have despatched some of theirs to notify the Oneida, the Mohawk and the Cayuga to repair to Ochouegen [Oswego] to salute you and to reply to your proposals. They wish so much to see M. le Moine here whom you promised them would come, that it appears that nothing could be done should he not arrive. Also, as you advised them not to be troubled at the sight of your barks and Gendarmes, they give you notice, likewise, not to be surprised when you will see faces painted red and black at Ochouegen

I gave a Cayuga letters for you some eight or ten days ago. I do not know if he will have delivered them. I believe that I advised you that Colonel Dongan had the Duke of York's placards of protection (*des sauveguardes*) affixed to the three upper Iroquois villages, and that he styled himself Lord of the Iroquois. A drunken man here tore these proclamations down and nothing remains but the post to which the Duke of York's arms were attached.

I gave La Grande Gueule your belt under hand, and remarked to him the things which you wished him to effect. He calls himself your best friend and you have done well to have attached to you this *hoc*, who has the strongest head and loudest voice among the Iroquois.

The over coats (*capots*) and shirts which you have been so good as to send to be used on occasions are a most efficaciaus means to gain over, or to preserve public opinion. An honorable peace will be more advantageous to Canada than a war very uncertain as to its success. I am of opinion, whatever the Mess[rs] the Merchants may say, that you do them a good turn by inducing the Iroquois to give you satisfaction, and that the war would be very prejudicial to them.

I am with all sort of respect and submission, My Lord,

Your very humble and very obedient servant,

J. DE LAMBERVILLE, Jesuit.

FROM THE SAME TO THE SAME.

Onontague, this 28th August 1684.

My Lord—M. Le Moine's arrival has much pleased our burgomasters who have exhibited towards him many attentions, and have promised to terminate matters with you in the manner you desire. The Onontagués have called the Deputies of each Nation together as I have advised you. The Cayugas came here the first, with two young Tionnoutatés to restore them to you. We expect the Senecas, and as we were hoping that the Oneidas would arrive to-day, one Arnaud[1] whom Father Bruyas is well acquaintainted with, came here on horseback from Mr. Dongan to tell the Iroquois that he did not wish them to talk with you without his permission, being com-

1 Arnold Cornelis'n Viele, a citizen of Albany, who acted as Interpreter between the Whites and Indians. For his service in this capacity he had already obtained from the latter, 26th Septr. 1683, a tract of land called Wachkeerhoha, on the north bank of the Mohawk above Schenectady, the grant of which is in Alb. Deed Book C, 199.—TR.

plete master of their land and conduct towards you; that they belonged to the King of England and the Duke of York, and that their Council fires were lighted at Albany and that he absolutely forbad them talking with you.

Two words which we whispered in the ears of your pensioner, La Grande Guele, caused us to see at once how unreasonable, in his opinion, was so strange a proceeding as that of Mr. Dongan, after having himself exhorted the Iroquois to give us satisfaction in order to avoid a disastrous war which would have very bad [consequences.] When M. le Moine and I shall have the honour to see you, we shall give you the particulars of these things, and how La Grande Gueule came to high words against this Messenger, exhorting all the warriors and chiefs not to listen to the proposals of a man who seemed to be drunk, so opposed to all reason was what he uttered.

We being two or three day's journey from here, the said Messenger produced three belts of Wampum. The first and second are from the Mohawks and Oneidas, who have promised Mr. Dongan that they should not go to meet us; the third was for the Onnontagués to exhort them to give their wampum belt also, as assurance of the same thing. They answered by La Grande Gueule, that they esteemed themselves too highly honored by your having granted to them the embassy of M. Le Moine and by your having placed the affairs of the peace in their hands, to commit so cowardly an action and so grave a fault as that which he seemed willing they should perpetrate. After many disputes, the Onnontagués councilled among themselves, and concluded to enquire of M. le Moine if he would not wait the permission which Mr. Dongan wished the Iroquois to have from him to talk with you, and if he would not tarry ten days more, and you remain at the Lake, to learn Mr. Dongan's final will. This is a piece of Iroquois cunning not to embroil themselves with Mr. Dongan, and to follow entirely what M. le Moine should say, whom they well knew would not wait so long, matters having advanced to the point at which they are, and knowing moreover that delay was directly contrary to your instructions. The Iroquois requested M. le Moine himself to communicate their opinion to the Cavalier, which he certainly did in an excellent manner, and which you will be glad to learn when he will give an account of his negotiation.

He has thought proper to send you one of his canoes at once to inform you hereof, and to assure you that as soon as the Onontagué deputies shall have arrived here, he will endeavor to despatch them hence at the earliest moment to conduct them to you. If not he will leave with the Senecas who are here. Tegannehout acted his part very well and harrangued strongly against Mr. Dongan's messenger and in favor of Onontio. Good cheer, and the way you regaled him was a strengthening medicine which sustained his voice when it might perhaps have failed in another who had not experienced proofs of your friendship such as you did him the honor to give him. He will return with M. le Moine.

The cavalier says that before returning to his Master, he wishes to speak to the Senecas who are expected here. I caress somewhat Tegannehout in order that he may win those of his Nation over to his opinion and not to suffer them to yield to the solicitations of Sieur Arnaud to whom the Onnontagués have given two wretched belts to say to Mr. Dongan that they could not do other than what he himself had urged them to do; to wit, to settle matters peaceably with you, and to soothe his spirit if he were dissatisfied with them for not going to Albany whence they had returned very recently. A letter is sent you which he has given to M. le Moine.

Whatever Sieur Arnaud may say, we have not neglected to send for the Oneida deputies whom we expect to-morrow. Monsieur le Moine will use the greatest possible diligence to return to you, inasmuch as this delay is not very agreeable to him.

I am always, my Lord,

Your very humble and very obedient servant,

J. DE LAMBERVILLE.

FROM THE SAME TO THE SAME.

Onontague, 27 Sept. 1684.

My Lord,—I return here after having been delayed ten days in the Lake by very strong head winds. A day before the Iroquois deputies met here, the Senecas sent Belts to the Iroquois villages to declare to them that should you disembark in their country, they would attack you. Six or seven Mohegans (*Loups*) were preparing to go to the assistance of the Iroquois, as the Outaoutes were aiding the French. The Seneca scouts have been as far as Kaionhouagué, where you had concluded the peace, to be certain of the place at which your army had encamped. The Onnontagués believed for several days that they had killed me. Tegannehout's arrival in this country will have calmed the minds in communicating your peace to them. No news have as yet been received from the Seneca. Some say they will shortly come hither to confer on important matters. If any one come from the Fort there I shall inform you of whatever I will have learned.

Sieur Arnaud, Mr. Dongan's deputy, has not re-appeared here since my departure from Onnontaé, though he had assured me that he should return in ten days. 'Tis said that his delay is caused by not having found his master at Orange (Albany), and that he has gone to Manath to inform him of the proceedings of the Onnontagué and of your arrival at Gainhouagué, [Hungry Bay.]

I had the honour of writing to you from the Fort whence I sent you a wampum belt from the Tionnontatés. I gave Sieur Hannataksa the belt of Wampum and the red Calumet in your name, to whom I said that you would be ever obliged to him if he would turn his arms to the left of Fort St. Louis, where the Illinois are mingled with the Oumiamis, so as to give no cause of complaint.

Uncertain as I was regarding matters on the side of the Senecas, and fearful that the Senecas would create confusion on arriving here, I made some presents in your name to some captains who could best curb their insolence, so as to prevent the brewing of the storm.

Your man of business, I mean La Grande Gueule, is not concerned at any thing; he is a venal being whom you do well to keep in pay. I assured him that you would send him the jerkin you promised. The Cayugas who are gone to war to the borders of Merinlande and Virginia have sent home some of their warriors to say that the English had killed three of their men, and that they having taken five Englishmen alive, had cut their throats after subjecting them to some bad treatment, and that they were still in the English country.

After having spoken to you of others, I must acquit myself of a part of my duty, by thanking you very humbly for all the kindnesses you have been pleased to shower on me. I should have wished you, in addition to the good health in which it pleased God to preserve you in the midst of an army weakened by diseases, greater satisfaction for the trouble you have taken for the public good. Individuals assuredly know that if you had not accepted peace, which is very favorable since no one has been killed on either side, the Colony would have been exposed to the mercy of the Iroquois who would pounce, in different directions, on defenceless settlements, the people of which they would carry off in order to pitilessly burn them. I pray God, who knows the sincerity of your intentions, to be your reward and to heap His blessings on you to the extent of the wishes of him who is entirely, my Lord

Your very humble and very obedient servant,

J. DE LAMBERVILLE.

I told Colin that you would remember him and his comrade.

The Tionnontatés have sent to thank the Onnontagués for having, by their obliging disposition, gained you over to treat for peace, and thus preserve the lives of many, and that they were attached to Onnonthio. Sieur la Grande [Gueule] has pronounced your panegyric here, and professes to keep the promise he made you, to cause the articles of peace to be observed. Some furs are to be collected this fall. He is treating on this subject with Hannagoge and Ganakontié. There is no news yet from the Senecas.

FROM THE SAME TO THE SAME.

Onnontague, this 9th Octob. 1684.

My Lord,—The message you sent here by three canoemen from Montreal shows you to be in reality a man of your word. Sieur Grande Gueule has been informed by express, who is gone to find him at his fishery eight leagues from here, that you have written. I shall cause him when he returns particularly to recollect his promise to you to have satisfaction given you. I have spoken in his absence both privately and publicly, to influential persons and obtained promises from the chiefs and warriors that they would send two strings of wampum to the Senecas in three days to put them in mind of the word which the leader of those who pillaged the French canoes had himself brought here, from those of his own nation, that they had accepted all you had concluded at La Famine. I told them what you had concluded and had ordered me to acquaint them with. The report about the thousand Illinois is a mere rumor without any foundation, and M. du Lut told me at Katarakoui, that he did not believe the truth of this news; besides there cannot be any apprehension that they could have dared to undertake any thing, having met neither Frenchmen nor Outaouas. All that they could make a demonstration against have more fuzileers than they.

A party of 40 warriors will leave here in six days to attack the Illinois whom they may find among the Chaouennons. I have presented the Captain a shirt in your name, to exhort the Senecas through whom he will pass, to keep their word with you. He has assured me that he will not lead his troop towards the quarter you forbad him. I notified him as well as the others that you had despatched a canoe to inform the Oumiamies and the Maskenses that you had included them in the peace, and that they could remain secure at the place where they had been before they were at war with the Iroquois. The Senecas shall be equally notified of this in a few days. You may rest assured, my Lord, that I shall spare no pains to have that satisfaction given you which you expect from the Iroquois The frenchmen who came here told me that whilst you were at La Famine a false alarm reached Montreal that the Iroquois were coming; that there was nothing but horror, flight and weeping at Montreal. What would so many poor people have done in their settlements if merely six hundred Iroquois had made an irruption into the country in the condition in which it is. You form a better opinion than one hundred manufacturers of rhodomontades who were not acquainted with the Iroquois, and who reflect not that the country, such as it is, is not in a condition to defend itself. Had I the honor to converse with you longer than your little leisure allowed me, I should have convinced you that you could not have advanced to Paniaforontogouat [Irondequoit bay] without having been utterly defeated in the state your army was in—which was rather an hospital than a camp. To attack people within their entrenchments and fight banditti in the bush will require one thousand men more than you have. Then you can accomplish nothing without having a number of disciplined savages. I gave you already my thoughts, and believe I told you the truth, and that you deserved the title of "Liberator of the Country" by making peace at a conjuncture when you would have beheld the ruin of the country without preventing it. The Senecas had double pallisades stronger than the pickets of the fort and the first could not have been forced without great loss. Their plan was to keep only 300 men inside, and with 1200 others perpetually harass you. All the

Iroquois were to collect together and fire only at the legs of your people to master them, and burn them at their leisure; and after having cut them off by a hundred ambuscades among the foliage and grass, pursue you in your retreat even to Montreal to spread desolation throughout its vicinity also; and they had prepared for that purpose a quantity of canoes of eighteen men each which they kept concealed. But let us all speak of this war to thank God that He has preserved our Governor in the midst of so much sickness, and that He had compassion on Canada from which He turned away the scourge of war which would have laid it entirely desolate.

The English of Merinlande who had killed three Iroquois, and of whom the English Iroquois had killed five, are about to have difficulties with that belligerent nation which has already killed more than twenty-nine of their men, and has been threatened with war should it continue to insult them. We shall see what the English of that quarter will do.

Garakontie returned to day from Orange, where he told by a belt of Wampum how you had given peace to the public; also how Colonel Dongan had urged the Iroquois to secure it by the satisfaction which he advised them to give you. M. Dongan left Orange when those who brought the Duke of York's Safeguards came to this place; it is supposed that Arnaud's visit here to prevent the Iroquois going to see you and to get them to hold a Council at Orange, was an intrigue of the Orange merchants who feared that their trade would be diminished by a conference held with you with arms in your hands; for M. Dongan had probably departed from Orange when Arnaud left to come here. What the Iroquois know is, after having heard M. Dongan who exhorted them to an arrangement with you, it was in no wise probable that on the eve of a negotiation, he should have forbidden them to visit you without his permission.

A man named La Croix, in Indian Tegaiatannhara, who answered Garakontie on behalf of the Dutch, said that had you not made peace, knowing that the Safeguards of England were on the Iroquois, 800 Englishmen and 1200 Mohegans, (*Loups*) who are between Merinland and New York, entirely distinct from the Cannongageh-ronnons whom you have with you, were all ready to march at the first word to aid the Iroquois. This man La Croix passes with the Iroquois for a great liar; he, possibly may have advanced this of his own accord, as well as many other things he has stated, which M. Dongan perhaps would not approve, were he acquainted with them.

I thank you most humbly for having furnished an opportunity for the transportation to us of a part of our necessaries. It is a continuance of your kindness towards us and towards me in particular, who am sincerely and with much respect, My Lord,

Your very humble & very obedient Servant,

DE LAMBERVILLE.

I shall give La Grande Gueule your jerkin as soon as he returns here. I had the honor to write to you by Colin ten days since.

FROM THE MINISTER TO M. BARILLON, FRENCH AMBASSADOR AT LONDON.

[Paris Doc. III.]

Versailles, 10 March, 1685.

Sir—The King has learned that the Governor of New York, instead of maintaining good correspondence with Sieur de la Barre, Governor of Canada, in conformity with the orders of the late King of England, has done what he could to prevent the Iroquois treating with him ; that he offered them troops to serve against the French, and that he caused standards (flags) to be planted in their villages, though these nations had been always subject to France since their country was discovered by the French, without the English objecting thereto.

His majesty desires you to present his complaints to the King of England and to demand of him precise orders to oblige this governor to confine himself within the limits of his government, and to observe different conduct towards Sieur Denonville, who is selected by His Majesty to succeed the said Sieur de la Barre.

VI.

Gov. Dongan's Report

ON

THE PROVINCE OF NEW-YORK.

1687.

GOV. DONGAN'S REPORT

TO THE COMMITTEE OF TRADE ON THE PROVINCE OF NEW-YORK, DATED 22D FEBRUARY, 1687.

[Lond. Doc. V.]

My Lords—I have received the heads of inquiry your Lo'ps sent to mee and indeed I have been as industrious as possibly I could to make myself capable of giving you satisfaction. And wherein I am short of answering your Lo'ps expectation I question not but youl pardon it when you consider that to give a distinct answer to several of your queries must require a longer time than I have yet had since their arrival here. However to such of them as I am at present capable to make an answer, I herein give yor Lo'ps I hope the satisfaction required which are as follow

In answer to the first of your Lo'ps Querys.

Courts of Justice. The Courts of Justice are most established by Act of Assembly and they are

1. The Court of Chancery consisting of the Governor and Council in the Supreme court of this province to which appeals may be brought from any other court

2. The Assembly finding the inconvenience of bringing of ye peace, Sheriffs, Constables @ other prsons concerned from the remote parts of this government to New York did instead of the Court of Assizes which was yearly held for the whole Government of this province erect a Court of Oyer and Terminer to be held once every year within each County for the determining of such matters as should arise within them respectively, the members of which Court were appointed to bee one of the two judges of this province assisted by three justices of the peace of that county wherein such court is held. Which Court of Oyer & Terminer has likewise power to hear appeals from any inferior court

3. There is likewise in New York @ Albany a Court of Mayor @ Aldermen held once in every fortnight from whence there can be noe appeal unless the cause of action bee above the value of Twenty Pounds, who have likewise priviledges to make such by-laws for ye regulation of their own affairs as they think fitt, soe as the same be approved of by ye Govr @ Council.

Their Mayor, Recorders, town-clerks @ Sheriffs are appointed by the Governor.

4. There is likewise in every County twice in every year (except in New York where it is four times @ in Albany where its thrice) Courts of Sessions held by the Justices of the Peace for the resp'ive countys as in Engld.

5. In every Town wtn ye Government there are 3 Commissioners appointed to hear and determine all matters of difference not exceeding the value of five pounds which shall happen within the respective towns.

6. Besides these, my Lords, I finding that many great inconveniences daily hapned in the managemt of his Mats particular concerns within this province relating to his Lands, Rents, Rights, Profits @ Revenues by reason of the great distance betwixt the Cursory settled Courts @ of the long delay which thereon consequently ensued besides the great hazard of venturing the matter on

country Jurors who over @ above that they are generally ignorant enough @ and for the most part linked together by affinity are too much swayed by their particular humors @ interests, I thought fit in Feb. last by @ with ye advice @ consent of ye Council to settle and establish a Court which we call the court of Judicature [Exchequer] to bee held before ye Govr @ Council for the time being or before such @ soe many as the Govr should for the purpose authorise, cômisionat @ appoint on the first Monday in every month at New York, which Court hath full power and authority to hear, try @ determine suits matters @ variances arising betwixt his Ma^ty^ @ ye Inhabitants of the said Province concerning the said lands, rents, rights, profits @ revenues

In answer to the Second.

Laws in Force.

The Laws in force are ye Laws called his Royal Highnesses Laws and the acts of the General Assembly the most of which I presume y^r^ Lop^s^ have seen @ the rest I now send over by m^r^ Sprag to whom I refer your Lop^s^ in this point.

In answer to the Third.

In this Governm^nt^ there are about four thousand foot @ three hundred horse besides one company of Dragoons of which I shall be able to give a more particular account when the Mustermaster shall make his return.

In answer to the Fourth

At New York there is a fortification of four bastions built formerly against the Indians of dry stone @ earth with sods as a breast-work well @ pleasantly situated for the defence of the Harbor on a point made by Hudsons River on the one side and by the sound on the other, It has Thirty-nine Gunns, two Mortar pieces, thirty Barils of Powder five hundred ball some Bomb-shells @ Granados small arms for three hundred men, one Flanker, the face of the North Bastion, and three points of Bastions @ a Courlin has been done @ are rebuilt by mee with lime @ mortar @ all the rest of the Fort pinnd @ rough-cast with lime since my coming here.

And the most of the Guns I found dismounted @ some of them yet continue to bee soe which I hope to have mounted soe soon as the mills can sawe

I am forced to renew all the Batterys with three-inch Plank @ have spoke for new planks for that purpose

And the breast-work upon the wall is so moultered away that its likewise needful to make a reparation thereof. The Officers quarters had formerly a flat roof which I finding to be chargeable to maintain @ that it could not be kept high, [qu. dry ?] have caused a new roof to bee upon it, as alsoe finding water to run through the arch of the Gate I have been forc't to put a Roof over it, I am forc't every day by reason of the roteness of the Timber @ Boards to bee making reparations in the Soldiers quarters or my own.

The ground that the Fort stands upon @ that belongs to it contains in quantity about two acres o^r^ thereabouts about which I have instead of Palisadoes put a fence of Palls which is more lasting.

Thò this Fortification be inconsiderable, yet I could wish the King had severall of them in these parts, the people growing every day more numerous @ they generaly of a turbulent disposition.

In this Country there is a woman yet alive from whose Loynes there are upwards of three hundred @ sixty persons now living.

The men that are here have generally lusty strong bodies.

At Albany there is a Fort made of pine trees fifteen foot high @ foot over with Batterys and conveniences made for men to walk about, where are nine guns, small arms for forty men four Barils of powder with great and small Shott in proportion, The Timber & Boards being rotten were renewed this year, In my opinion it were better that fort were built up of Stone & Lime which will not be double the charge of this years repair which will yet not last above 6 or 7 years before it will require the like again whereas on the contrary were it built of Lime & Stone it may bee far more easily maintained, And truly its very necessary to have a Fort there, it being a frontier place both to the Indians @ ffrench.

Pemaquid Fort and Connecticut.

At Pemaquid there is another Fort built after the same manner as I am informed a particular description whereof I am not capable of giving having never been been there however its a great charge to this Governmnt without being any thing of advantage to it, having officers there with twenty men always in pay, And which makes it yet more chargeable, I am forced to send from time to time provisions @ stores thither, altho' its near four hundred miles from this place If His Maty were pleased that I might draw of the men and arms from that place with the guns being of light carriage @ that I might have leave to put them further into the country I would place them where I will give your Lohp an acct hereafter

And then if his Maty were further pleased to annex that place to Boston, being very convenient for them in regard to its vicinity affording great store of Fishery @ Islands fit for that purpose lying all along to the eastward of them—And in lieu of that to add to this Government Connecticut @ Rhode Island, Connecticut being so conveniently situate in its adjacing to us and soe inconvenient for the people of Boston by reason of its being upwards of two hundred miles distance from thence, Besides Connecticut as it now is takes away from us almost all the land of value that lies adjoyneing to Hudsons River @ the best part of the river itself, Besides as wee found by experience if that place bee not annexed to that Government it will bee impossible to make any thing considerable of his Matys customs @ revenues in Long Island they carry away witht entring all our oyles which is the greatest part of what wee have to make returns of from this place : And from Albany and that way up the river—our Beaver & Peltry.

This Government too has an undoubted right to it by charter which his late Maty of Blessed Memory granted to our present King, and indeed if the form of the Government bee altered these people will rather choose to come under this than that Governmt of Boston as yr Lo'ps will p'ceive by their present Govrs lres directed to me

East and West Jersey.

And as for East Jersey it being situate on the other side of Hudsons river @ between us @ where the river disembogues itself into the sea paying noe custom @ having likewise the advantage of having better land @ most of the settlers there out of this Govermt. We are like to bee deserted by a great many of our merchants whoe intend to settle there if not annexed to this Government—

Last year two or three ships came in there with goods @ I am sure that that Country cannot, noe not with the help of West Jersey consume one thousand £b in goods in two years soe that the rest of their goods must have been run into this Government without paying his Matys customs and indeed theres no possibility of preventing it.

And as for Beaver & Peltry its impossible to hinder its being carried thither, the Indians value not the length of their journey soe as they can come to a good market, which these people can better afford than wee they paying noe custom or excise inwards or outwards.

An other inconveniency by the Governments remaining as it does is that privateers and others can come within Sandy Hook and take what Provisions & goods they please from that side. Alsoe very often ships bound to this place break bulk there & run their goods into that Colony with intent afterwards to import the same privately & at more leisure into this Province notwithstanding their oath, they salving themselves with this evasion that that place is not in this Governt, To day an Interloper landed five tun & one half of teeth there, to prevent all which inconveniences & for the securing of this place from enemys, I desire to have an order to make up a small Fort with twelve guns upon Sandy-Hook the channell there being soe near the shore that noe vessel can goe in nor out but she must come soe neare the Point that from on board one might toss a biscuit cake on shore.

If the Proprietors would rightly consider it they would find it to their own interest that that place should bee annexed to this Government for they are at a greater charge for maintaining the present Govermt than the whole profits of the Province (which is by quit-rents) will amount unto; for they are at the whole charge the Country allowing nothing towards its support soe that had they not the charge of the Governmt, they might put that money into their own pockets.

And indeed to make Amboy a port will be no less inconvenient for the reasons afore mentioned neighboring colonys being not come to that P'fection but that one fort may sufficiently serve us all We in this Government look upon that bay that runs into the Sea at Sandy Hook to be Hudsons River therefore there being a clause in my instructions directing mee that I cause all vessels that come into Hudson's River to enter at New York I desire to know whether his Maty intends thereby those vessels that come within Sandy-Hook, the people of East-Jersey pretending a right to the river soe far as their province extends which is eighteen miles up the river to the northward of this place

Dutys to paid at Sandy Hook.

West Jersey remaining as it does will be no less inconvenient to this Govermt for the same reasons as East Jersey, they both making but one neck of land & that so near situate to us that its more for their convenience to have commerce here than any where else, & under these circumstances that if there were a warr either with Christians or Indians they would not bee able to defend themselves without the assistance of this Govermt.

To bee short, there is an absolute necessity those provinces and that of Connecticut be annexed

The three lower Countys of Pennsylvania have been a dependency on this place & a great many of the inhabitants persons that removed thither from this Govermt and I doe not believe it was his Matys intention to annex it to Pennsylvania, nor to have it subject to the same laws it being the King's own land, the doing whereof by mr Pen there has been of great detriment to this place in hindring the Tobacco to come hither as formerly, for then there came two shipps for one that comes now; Beaver & Peltry taking up but small Stowage in shipps

And indeed it were in my opinion very necessary for the advantage of this place & increase of his Matys revenues that it were soe ordered that the Tobacco of these countrys may bee imported hither without paying there the duty of one penny pr pound and then wee should not bee at such streights for returns, their trade would much increase, and this place become a magazine for the Neighboring provinces, & care taken that the Tobacco bee duly returned to England whereas now a great part of it goes another way & soe its very necessary that the Collector of this place should be Collector of that River for the enumerated commoditys, And wee will have such regard to the advantage of this port that we'll suffer noe fraud to bee committed there nor noe Tobacco to be exported but what goes either directly for England or this place.

Besides wee find the country to bee very inconvenient in this that whereas formerly the damnified Tobacco which came from thence not fit for England wee made up in rolls and sent ye same up the River to the Indians who in Exchange gave in Beaver & Peltry, for want whereof his Matys revenue here is much impaired inasmuch as the Indians are therefore forct either to Plant the tobacco themselves or to goe where they can be furnished with it & there carry their beavor & peltry (they being of that temper that they had rather want clothes than Tobacco) by which Meanes his Matys revenue sustains a double loss, one in the ten per cent such tobacco pays custom up the river & the other in the custom of such Beaver & peltry as the same would produce

Further if Pennsylvania bee continued as by charter running five degrees to the westward it will take in the most of the five nations that lye to the westward of Albany & the whole Beaver & Peltry trade of that place the consequence whereof will be the depopulation of this Govermt for the people must follow the trade. Those Indians and the people of this Govermt have been in continued peace & amity one with another these fifty years And those Indians about forty years agoe did annex their lands to this Governm^t @ have ever since constantly renewed the same with every Governor that has been here both in the time of the Dutch @ the English @ in particular to myself who have given them largely in consideration of their lands. And I am certainly informed that they have declared they will go & live on ye other side of the lake than be under any other Goverm^t on this than ours, Endeavors have been used (tho to noe purpose) to p'suade some of our Traders who speak the language to goe and live upon the Susquehanna river tho I cannot yet find out by whom this has been made.

The five Indian nations are the most warlike people in America, & are a bulwark between us & the French & all other Indians they goe as far as the South Sea the North West passage & Florida to warr. New England in their last warr with the Indians had been ruined had not Sir Edmund Andros sent some of those nations to their assistance, and indeed they are soe considerable that all the Indians in these parts of America are tributary to them. I suffer no Christians to converse with them any where but at Albany & that not without my license.

Since I came here the people of Boston have sent them presents in acknowledgement of their favor and friendship. & I was forc't to goe with my Lord Effingham to bury his hatchet and theirs which is their way of making a peace.

Indian proposal and present.

I have sent herewith what the nations that conquered the Susquehannas desired of the King in my Lord Effingham's presence and I believe it to be of dangerous consequence if denyed.

This Governm^t has always been and still is at a great charge to keep them peaceable & annexed to this government which is of that moment that upon any occasion I can have three or four thousand of their men at a call.

Pensylvania & for the Beaver Trade.

I cannot believe that ever it was the King's intention to grant away soe considerable a part of this government which has been so long appropriated to it and even the people think it as a part of themselves & would be much troubled at a separation from soe good & ancient neighbours that at first of their own free wills become soe and have ever since continued with such constancy to desire and maintain a mutual friendship and correspondence. If therefore his Ma^ty were pleased to have a line run from 41^d and 40^m in Delaware River to the Falls upon the Susquehanna and to let Mr. Pen keep all below that it would be sufficient for him the bounds below it being conjectured to contain more than all England, besides the louer Countys which is near upon 100 miles from the Cape up the river; and in bredth more than 30 miles as is generally believed.

To preserve the Beaver and Peltry trade for this & Albany and to be an encouragement to our Beaver hunters I desire I may have order to erect a Campayne Fort upon Delaware River in 41^d 40 m; another upon the Susquehanna where his Ma^ty shall think fit Mr. Penn's bounds shall terminate. And another at Oneigra near the great lake in the way where our people goe a Beaver hunting or trading or any where else where I shall think convenient it being very necessary for the support of trade, maintaining a correspondence with the further Indians, & in securing our right in the country the French making a pretence as far as the Bay of Mexico, for which they have no other argument than that they have had possession this twenty years by their fathers living so long among the Indians they have fathers still among the five nations aforementioned viz. the Maquaes, Sinicaes, Cayouges, Oneides, and Onondagues and have converted many of them to the Christian Faith and doe their utmost to draw them to Canada, to which place there are already 6 or 700 retired and more like to doe, to the great prejudice of this Goverm^t if not prevented. I have done my endeavours & have gone so far in it that I have prevailed with the Indians to consent to come back from Canada on condition that I procure for them a piece of land called Serachtagua lying upon Hudson's River about 40 miles above Albany & there furnish them with priests.

Indians from Canada.

Thereupon and upon a petition of the people of Albany to mee setting forth the reasonableness and conveniency of granting to the Indians there requests I have procured the land for them, altho it has been formerly patented to people at Albany & have promised the Indians that they shall have priests and that I will build them a church & have assured the people of Albany that I would address his Ma^ty as to your Lo^ps that care may be taken to send over by the first five or six it being a matter of great consequence.

These Indians have about 10 or 12 castles (as they term them) and those at a great distance from one another, soe that there is an absolute necessity of having soe many priests, that there bee three always travelling from castle to castle, & the rest to live with those that are Christians. By that means the French Priests will be obliged to retire to Canada, whereby the French will be divested of their pretence to ye Country & then wee shall enjoy that trade without any fear of being diverted.

I find a very small matter will serve the French for a pretence of right. About 30 years ago 6 or 700 of them taking advantage of the Indians being abroad soe farr as Cape Florida at warr came down & burnt a castle of the Maquaes wherein there were none but old men women & children which the rest of the Indians hearing pursued the French to a place called Sconectady about 20 miles above Albany where they had every man been cut off had not one Corlarr (a Dutchman so beloved of the Indians that in memory of him they call all Governors by that name) interposed.

However from that time they have fancied to themselves that they have a right to the country so farr as that place.

The great difference between us is about the Beaver trade and in truth they have the advantage of us in it & that by noe other means than by their industry in making discoveries in the country before us.

Before my coming hither noe man of our Governm^t ever went beyond the Sinicaes country. Last year some of our people went a trading among the farr Indians called the Ottowais inhabiting about three months journey to the West & W. N. W. of Albany from whence they brought a good many Beavers. They found their people more inclined to trade with them than the French the French not being able to protect them from the arms of our Indians, with whom they have had a continued warr, soe that our Indians brought away this very last year, a great many prisoners.

Last week I sent for some of our Indians to New York where when they came I obtained a promise from them that some of themselves would goe along with such of our people as goe from Albany & Esopus to there far nations & carry with them the captives they haue prisoners in order to the restoring them to their liberty & bury their haichetts with those of their enemys by which means a path may be opened for those farr Indians to come with safety to trade at Albany, and our people goe thither without any let or disturbance.

I hear the French have built a Wooden Fort or two in the Way thither & that there are two officers with men in them to obstruct our passage, I am sending a Scotch Gent called McGreger (that served formerly in France) along with our people, he has orders not to disturb or meddle with the French and I hope they will not meddle with him. Ever since my coming hither it has been no small trouble to keep the Sinicaes from making warr upon the French, Monsieur De la Barr was very hot upon it & brought a great many men to a place called Cadaraque lying on the lake with intent to fall on the Indians, who hearing of it came to me for leave to enter Canade with fire & sword, which I refused to permit but immediately wro^t to La Barr & let him know that those indians were his Mat^ys of Great Britain's subjects & that he must not molest them & that if the Indians had done the Governm^t of Canada any injury, upon his making the same appear, I would cause that hee should have satisfaction as also I sent the arms of his Royal Highness now his Majesty to bee put up in each castle as far as Oneigra which was accordingly done, & thereupon De la Barr retired without doing anything after having been at vast expense and all to no purpose.

The new Governor Monsr de Nonville has written mee that he desires to have a very good correspondence with this Governm^t & I hope hee will be as good as his word, notwithstanding he put a great deal of provisions into & keeps four or five hundred men at Cadaraque.

Last spring he sent one De la Croa with fifty soldiers & one hundred young men of Canada to the North West passage where as I am certainly informed from Canada they have taken three forts. About two years since there came a thousand men from France to Canada with the new Govr & three hundred came the year after. But the most part of them as I hear are since dead the country proving too cold for them. We need not feare them soe long as the Indians continue to bee our friends & the less if we can prevail with the Indians that are Christians to come from them to us, they being generally the youngest & lustiest men.

The number of French in Canada. Last year there was a list brought into the new Govr of 17000 French Inhabitants in Canada, men women & children of which 3000 fit to bear arms.

It will be very necessary for us to encourage our young men to goe a Beaver hunting as the French doe.

I send a Map by Mr. Spragg whereby your Lopps may see the several Governmts &c how they lye where the Beaver hunting is & where it will be necessary to erect our Country Forts for the securing of beaver trade & keeping the Indians in community with us.

Alsoe it points out where theres a great river discovered by one Lassel a Frenchman from Canada who thereupon went into France & as its reported brought two or three vessels with people to settle there which (if true) will prove not only very inconvenient to us but to the Spanish alsoe (the river running all along from our lakes by the back of Virginia & Carolina into the Bay Mexico) & its believed Nova Mexico can not be far from the mountain adjoining to it that place being in 36d North Latitude if your Lops thought it fit I could send a sloop or two from this place to discover that river.

In Answer to the Fifth

The strength of our neighbors This query is for the most part answered in the precedent what is not answered followeth here

Connecticut according to the nearest conjecture I can make may have about 3000 men able to bear arms

In it there are but few Indians having been generally destroyed or removed into this government in the time of the last warrs

They have but a small trade, what they have is to the West-Indies Boston and this place.

They have not above a Ketch or two and about 6 or 7 sloops belonging to the place.

The country is very good accommodated with several good harbors & two considerable rivers New London is & very good harbor for shipping where they ride secure from all winds As for their timber its the same as ours here.

To the Sixth

The Correspondence wee hold with our neighbors is very amicable & good wee on all occasions doing to each other all the offices of Friendship & Service wee cann; which has soe much endeared them to us that they desire nothing more than to be a part of this Govermt those of Connecticut choosing far rather to come under this Govermt than that of Boston for the reason afore mentioned and the Jerseys wishing the like as having once been a part of us. And seeing that in this separation they are not soe easy nor safe, as they might expect to bee, were they re-united to us

To the Seventh

What arms, &c It is answered in the answer to the Fourth

To the Eighth

What are the boundaries longitude & latitude &c For the longitude latitude and contents of this Govermt I refer yor Lops to the afore mentioned Map wherein you will see in what narrow bounds we are cooped up

The land of this Government is generally barren rocky land except the land wee have right to on the Susquehanna river & up into the country amongst our Indians where there are great quantities very good

What was good & did lye convenient and near the sea for ye most part is taken from us by Connecticut East and West Jersey

What is left is pretty well settled, as your Lops will perceive by the list of patents Mr. Sprag has with him

When I come to the Government, I found very little quit-rent reserved to his Maty however I have got the people with their own consent to the payment of a certainty as yor Lops may perceive by the afore mentioned list of patents. Such as pay noe quit-rents I bring into the aforementioned court for his Matys rents & revenues where in a short time they are easily induced to doe it, & I hope his Maty will have considerable revenue by it

To the Ninth

What are the principal towns &c

The principal towns within the Govermt are New York Albany & Kingston at Esopus All the rest are country villages the buildings in New-York & Albany are generally of stone & brick. In the country the houses are mostly new built, having two or three rooms on a floor The Dutch are great improvers of land New York and Albany live wholly upon trade with the Indians England and the West Indies. The returns for England are generally Beaver Peltry Oile & Tobacco when we can have it. To the West Indies we send Flower, Bread Pease pork & sometimes horses; the return from thence for the most part is rumm which pays the King a considerable excise & some molasses which serves the people to make drink & pays noe custom

Ships & vessels

There are about nine or ten three mast vessels of about 80 or 100 tons burthen two or three ketches & Barks of about 40 Tun: and about twenty sloops of about twenty or five & twenty Tun belonging to the Govermt All of which trade for England Holland & the West Indies except six or seven sloops that use the river trade to Albany & that way

How many parishes Precincts &c

The Tenth is answered in the answers to the four & twentieth

To the Eleventh

What rivers harbors or roads &c

A thousand ships may ride here safe from winds & weather, I send herewith to your Lodp a Map from the coming in of Sandy Hook to the northermost end of this Island wherein the Soundings are markt by which youil perceive the coming in & conveniency of this harbor Quit along the north side of Long Island are very good harbors & roads but on the south side none at all

To the Twelfth

What commodity &c

What account I can at present give of this is for the most part contained in my answer to the fourth of your Lops Queries

To the Thirteenth

What timber mast & other materials

Both our neighbors and we have conveniency sufficient either for transporting timber or building And for tryal if your Lodp think fit, I will send over boards of what dimensions you please the three inch planks I have for the Batteries cost me fifteen shillings the hundred foot

To the Fourteenth

Whether Salt Petre &c

I can give yr Lo noe account at present but by the next I may. I will make a diligent enquiry about it & when I have got any thing worthy of your Lops knowledge I will acquaint you with it

To the Fifteenth

What number of inhabitants.

Concerning the number of the Inhabitants merchants English and foreigners, Servants Slaves & how many able to bear arms it is not possible to give an exact account but in order to my being certainly informed I have issued forth several warrants to the Sheriffs within this government requiring them to make an inquiry thereof & to return the same to mee on which returns I shall not fail to give your Lord^{ps} the account required.

To the Sixteenth.

What number of English Scotch Irish or Forreigners have come to inhabit &c

I believe for these 7 years last past, there has not come over into this province twenty English Scotch or Irish familys. But on the contrary on Long Island the people encrease soe fast that they complain for want of land & many remove from thence into the neighboring province. But of French there have been since my coming here several familys come both from St. Christophers & England & a great many more are expected as alsoe from Holland are come several Dutch familys which is another great argument of the necessity of adding to this Goverm^{t} the Neighboring English Colonys, that a more equal ballance may be kept between his Mat^{ys} naturall born subjects and foreigners which latter are the most prevailing part of this Government

I send herewith a petition of the new come naturalized French

17 & 18 What number of Marriages Christenings and what number of people dyed &c

For answer to the Seventeenth & Eighteeenth.

I must refer your Lo^{ps} to my next by which time I doubt not but to be able to give ye desired account having to that end issued forth the like warrant to the Sheriff as aforesaid

To the Nineteenth.

What number of ships trade &c

As concerning ye vessels belonging to this place it is already answered in the answer of y^{r} Lo^{ps} ninth Querie & for others they are but few which are either from England New England or the West Indies

To the Twentieth.

What obstructions &c

What obstructions do you find to the improvement of trade &c.

Ans. a great obstruction to our trade is the hindring the importing Tobacco from the three lower Countrys in Delaware as I have already given your Lo^{ps} an account in answer to the fifth of your queries

It is likewise a great hindrance to our trade here & an inconveniency to the ships that come out of England and the fishery that his Mat^{y} keeps not an officer at Newfoundland for formerly there went every year Sloops with provisions thither & gave the provisions in exchange for their fish who again sold them to the Shipps for Bills of Exchange to England which made good returns from this place procuring back from England English goods which paid his Mat^{y} custom there

For the regulation of our trade we have made several rules among ourselves, the chief of which is that noe goods of the product of Europe or West Indies bee imported into this province unless it were directly from England or such part of the West Indies where such commoditys were produced, without paying as a custom to his Mat^{y} 10 per cent

To the one and Twentieth.

What advantage or improvements may be gained to your trade

This querie is sufficiently answered in the foregoing answers

To the two and Twentieth concerning the Revenue

What rates and dutyes &c

I shall give your Lo^{ps} an exact answer to this querie as its possible for me, and wherein I am deficient I shall acquaint your Lo^{ps} with the true causes of it

The Revenue except that of the Quit-Rents has been settled upon his Mat^{y} then his Royal Highness & his heirs by act of Assembly payable in manner folloving vizt

For every Gallon of Rum Brandy & distilled liquors to bee imported into the province & its dependencys fou pence currant money of the province

For every pipe of Madera, Fyal St George Canary Malaga Sherry & all sweet wines the summ of forty shillings current money aforesaid

Upon all other merchandizes imported into the province & dependencys the summ of forty shillings current money aforesaid for every hundred pounds valued at the prime cost except those hereafter specified viz[t]

Salt, Brick, Pan-tyles, Coals, Fish, Sugar Molasses, Cottonwool Ginger, Logwood, brasalette, ffustyk west-India hydes, Tobacco bullion & Plate

Upon all merchandize commonly called Indian Goods as Duffels, Strouds, Blanketts, plains, halfthicks, Woolen Stokins, White Ozenbriggs, kettles, hatchetts, hoes, Red Lead, vermillion, Cotton, Red Kersey, Knives, Indian Haberdashery & other Indian goods the sum of ten pounds current money aforesaid for every hundred pounds value prime cost carried up Hudsons river in any vessel sloops boats or canoes or any other way

Upon every baril of powder twelve shillings

Upon every lb. weight of lead six shillings

For every Gun or Gun Baril with a lock six shillings

For every Gall'. of Rum, Brandy or distilld Liquors that shall bee carried up Hudsons river aforesaid four pence current money aforesaid

And likewise by the said act is settled upon his Maty, his heirs & successors an excise upon all liquors (beer and cyder excepted) retailed under five gallons the sûm of twelve pence current money, aforesaid within ye city & county of New York per gallon as alsoe the excise of twelve pence current money aforesaid upon each gallon of liquor carried up Hudsons river. And also an excise of twelve pence on liquors retailed throughout the whole province & Depencies (beer and cyder only excepted)

As alsoe the custom & duty upon every beaver skin commonly called a whole Beaver, nine pence

And that all other furs & peltry bee valued accordingly that is for two half beavers nine pence for four lapps nine pence three drillings one shilling sixpence ten ratoons ninepence four foxes ninepence, four fishers nine pence, five catts ninepence, four & twenty mees-catts nine pence, ten mallers nine pence, twenty-four pounds of Moose & Deer Skin ninepence. And all other Peltry to be valued equivalent to the whole beaver exported out of this Province (bull & cowhides excepted)

And alsoe that all Indian traders throughout the whole province & dependencies doe pay for the value of each hundred pounds prime cost they traffick with the Indians for, ten pounds money aforesaid.

And for all Beer & Sider retailed throughout the Province & dependencies six shillings per baril, and for each baril of beer or sider that is sold to the Indians six shillings as if retailed

As for the Quit Rents at my arrival they were very inconsiderable most made by S[r] Edmund Andros, the greatest part whereof in Delaware River the most part of the patents granted by my predecessors were without any reservation of any Quit-Rents or acknowledgement to his Ma[ty] or very inconsiderable such as several of S[r] Edmond Andros's grants to great townships reserving the Quit-rent of our Land only & were but confirmations of former grants & Indian purchases, These people have renewed their patents under a greater Quit-Rent as will appear by the list sent herewith most of these patents granted by mee were confirmations alsoe

Quit Rents.

The methods that I took for the obliging them to this was finding several tracts of land in their townships not purchased of the Indians and soe at his Maty[s] disposal. They were willing rather to submit to a greater Quit Rent than have that unpurchased land disposed of to others than themselves

The persons that have had the collection receipt & management of his Maty's revenue for these three years past & upwards are Mr Lucas Santen by commission from his Ma[ty] then his Royal Highness, Collector & Receiver. John Smith one that he brought out of England was his deputy bookkeeper & surveyor for about three years & one John Harlow a servant of his, waiter & searcher

Santon

I gave order to Mr Santon that for the good management of this small revenue to y[e] best advantage hee should not make any journey into the country on pretence of the King's business whereby to put him to charge, but that when any thing occurred hee should acquaint me with it that I might order the sheriffs or Justices of the Peace of the Place to take care of it. And alsoe went up to Albany myself on purpose to settle his Maty[s] business there where I made one Robert Livingstone Collector & Receiver, with order to acc[t] w[th] & pay into Mr Santer w[t] money he sho[d] receive for which he was to have 1[s] per Pound of all such moneys as should pass through his hands, & alsoe made him Clerk of the Town that both places together might afford him a competent maintenance.

At Esopus one Thomas Garton was by Mr. Santon made collector & receiver who as I find by Mr Santons account had not accounted with him for these three years past. Upon wch I was forct to send an order of Council for his coming hither with his accts who when hee came gave in a scrole of paper containing a confused acct of about £200. pretending that his accts together with a great deal of corn & Peltry by him collected & received for his Matys customs excise & Quit-Rents were burnt in his house so that all the council & I could get from him for three years & on half past was a bond of £200.

Since that I have set the Excise of that country alone to Mr. Pawling sheriff for £110.

As for the county of Richmond I have noe acct thereof, as your Lo[ps] will see by the audit.

And for the county of West Chester one Collins is Collector & Receiver there, whoe (as your Lop[s] may likewise see by the audit) has not given any account—only this Mr Santen tells me that in Sept[r] last hee took two bonds for money payable in March next which I look upon to be nothing, & all the Revenue of that County lost the man having hardly bread to put in his mouth.

The first year there was £52. offered for the Excise of Long Island, but I thought it unreasonable it being the best peopled place in this Goverm[t] & wherein theres great consumption of Rumm & therefore I gave commission to Mr Nicolls & Mr Vaughton to gather it with whom I made this agreement that out of it they should have forty pounds, & that they should account with Mr Santon for the remainder.

Since that for these two years past one Henry Fillkin has been Collector & for his pains has a salary of £30 per ann. What returns he makes I referr to the audit most part of the people of that Island especially towards the East End are of the same stamp with those of New-England, refractory & very loath to have any commerce with this place to the great detrm[t] of his Matys revenue & ruin of our merchants. To prevent which the aforementioned act of Assembly imposing 10 pr cent upon all such goods as should be imported from any colony where such goods were not produced passed, which was intended chiefly to hinder their carrying their oyle to Boston & bringing goods from thence into this Goverm[t].

They thought it a hardship to be obliged as formerly to come to this citty to enter & clear & on their application were allowed to have a port where I made Mr Arnold Collector & Receiver, with order to be accomptable to Mr Santen—What returns he has given I likewise referr to the audit

I allowed him for 3 years & half past but £52 with which hee was well satisfied having had some Pquisits by Entrys & clearing there. Notwithstanding the desire of theirs was readily granted they refused to take our merchants money or goods & carried away their Oyle private to Boston & brought back goods from thence as formerly. Therefore with the advice of the Council I made an order that all people before they goe there shall enter & clear here and also I have bought a Bark that cruseth there with a master, two seamen a sergeant & six soldiers from the Garrison for which the soldiers are allowed no more than their pay except a little provision more than their former allowance, the master & two seamen I have listed in the Company alsoe & allow them something more than soldiers pay.

As for the Dukes county & county of Cornwall I refer to ye audit. What acct Mr Santen gives & Judge Palmer whom I sent thither last spring & has made his returns to Mr Santen among which theres an account of the seizure of wines and oyl made in the county of Cornwall

The first year I left every thing to the care of Mr Santon & what officers he thought fit to put in, but afterwards finding things ill managed I spake to Mr Santon several times, advising him as a friend to look better to the trust reposed in him.

What returns he has made mee for my kindness I will pass by & say noe more of them than I am obliged to doe for my own vindication having nothing of ill will against him

After the expiration of the year I desired him to bring in his accounts that they might bee audited which he promised me from time to time but in such manner as was not fit for him for always when I spoke to him of moneys & accompt he flew into a passion

Upon which I ordered him that since hee had no better government of himself he should refrain from coming into my company & after I frequently sent to him by the Sec^{y} for his accompts who likewise met with the same dilatory answers. Upon which I had him brought before the council 3 or 4 times where he was often ordered to bring in his accts but all to noe purpose for upwards of a year together as y^{r} Lop^{s} may see by the time of the audit & by the several orders of council herewith sent

At last when his accts came I shewed them to the council who were mightily surprised that for eighteen & upwards the Revenue should amount but to £3000 & odd pounds upon which I had them audited and thereby it was found that a great many frauds had been done to the King as your Lop^{s} may see by the said audit & the charge brought in & proved against Mr. Santon

Then I desired him to put John Smith from the office of surveyor and out of the custom house having the charity for mr Santon to believe that that man has cheated him as well as the King (I having had while in England this ill character of him from Sr Benjn Bathurst that for his misbehavior he had been turned out of a good employment) But he never wo^{d} comply with it notwithstanding several orders of councill to that affect until I put in one Thomas Coker to bee surveyor, upon which Smith being concerned at losing his surveyors place, grew very insolent and put Mr Santon upon worse measures as is believed, for which & other misdemeanors as y^{r} Lop^{s} may pceave by the Minutes of Council sent over by Mr Sprag he was turned wholly out of the Custom House

In Hatlow (Servt to Mr Santon) that was waiter and searcher he sent into England as I am informed to the commissioners of thee custom house for a commission to be collector for the enumerated comoditys here, & would force so much for his going & coming as y^{r} Lop^{s} may see charged in his acct brought in to the audit & likewise has brought in a note of his for four and twenty pounds odd money for going to the east end of Long Island in which he did not spend fourteen days time

The Auditor finding noe cheque upon the collector his book keeper being Surveyor called upon this Hatlow for his warrants who answered that hee had none or that if ever hee had any hee had left them in England.

Upon which I put in one Larkin in his stead who upon an order in Council set up in the Custom House commanding noe goods to goe off without a warrant refusing to lett some goods be exported on the verbal order of Mr Santon only was by him turned out of that place as your Lop^{s} will see by the aforementioned charge & the proofs thereto

After the audit of his first accts the others were demanded and with the same difficulty as the former obtained as y^{r} Lop^{s} may perceive by the said minutes of Council particularly the order for payment every Saturday which was occasioned thus The Council considering how dilatory Mr Santon was & with what difficulty he would be brought to account being satisfied that Mr Santon was then behindhand in his paym^{ts} & that in process of time he might bee yet more soe for the preventing of further embezlement of his Ma^{tys} revenue they ordered him that every Saturday he should acct with and pay into mee what he had received the preceding week which was a method taken in the time of Sr Edmond Andros with Capt Dyer the then Collector upon the like occasion tho' this had not the like effect thro Mr Santens disobedience, for as hee did with all other orders hee did with this hee took noe notice of it

As alsoe there were several orders of Council requiring him to have all his acts from the 25th of March to the 6th of October ready for Mr. Sprag to carry over audited with him who had agreed for his passage in a ship & kept her here on that purpose these two months past. But with all this he made noe compliance pretending that by a letter from my Lord Treasurer hee was satisfied his accomps were not to be audited here that hee was only obliged to leave a duplicate with me upon which the Council upon sight of the letter agreed that it was reasonable for him to send his accomps home but that nevertheless it was my duty to have them audited according to former instruction & soe to continue to doe until I should have orders to the contrary from Mr. Blathwayt to whom my Lord Treasurer in his letter refers it being otherwise impossible for me to answer this query.

Seeing soe many abuses done to his Maty & finding fair means to be wholly ineffectual to the making Mr. Santen discharge his duty & hee continuing still refractory & disobedient to the several orders of Council to him directed, the charge which yr Lops have herewith was drawn up against him to which hee answered in such manner as your Lops will see on perusal of the copy thereof herewith sent. Upon hearing of which charge and answer & ye proofs thereto herewith likewise sent, thee council made their report to mee under their hands, in manner as your Lops sees by the copy thereof which you have likewise herewith wherein altho' they positively say that he has been an unfaithful servt to his Maty in the management of his Revenue, yet I sent for him & advised him to give in security for the ballance of the acct that by the audit he was found behind hand. And for his better carriage for the future which if hee did I promised to pass by all former faults & make noe complaint against him. I not only told him this myself but from time to time sent messages to him to this effect sometimes by such of the council as were his particular friends sometimes by the ministers & often by the Secretary but all to noe purpose hee still continued obstinate

And what returns he made mee to these several instances of my kindness I shall not now trouble your Lops with

Nevertheless I forbare doing anything further against him till the expiration of the second audit proposing that then when I could know the whole amount of his debt I would at once doe my best to secure the Kings concerns from sustaining any loss by him

At last hee brought in a book without being signed and said he could not lieve them neither, they being to bee sent over to Mr. Blathwayt. Whereupon we were forct to give him 3 weeks longer to get them copied & then with great adoe he signed them & brought in with them an acct called a general acct, an acct so extravagant that your Lops have hardly seen the like

Then I pressing the auditors to make an end they desired that they might have his papers to compare with those books & accomps he had delivered in, which by order of council hee was required to deliver to them. But he refusing as appears by the testimony of 3 of the auditors herewith sent, It was ordered that his said papers should be seized and he suspended from the sd office of collector & receiver till his Matys pleasure should be known thereon & he taken into the Sheriff's custody and there remain till hee should give in such security as in the said orders is expressed as relation to the said orders had, may more at large appear

Upon search of the Pap's relating to his Matys revenue I found a charge drawn up against myself with letters to his Maty Lord T'sear Lord Chancellor & several other gentlemen stuft with complaints against me and other p'sons which are wholly false

Indeed its true the poor gentleman since his coming here has been troubled with 3 or 4 hypocondriack fitts, he was in one of them when his Matys nomination of the Council came over upon which they all thought it not convenient to have him sworn at least at that time as your Lopps will see by the minutes of council

And my lords to be short I must say this of him hes a man wholly unfit for business especially this wherein hee has noe more skill than a child, Soe that for the executing of it he must have his whole dependence upon another. I am sure I had not taken more care of the Revenue than hee did since I found his failure it had been more embezled than it is for though he received the money I was obliged to continual watching to guard against his carelessness and neglects

And truly what he takes very ill what there is neither president nor establishment for

In his commission hee has allowed him £200 pr annum the same allowance that Dyer had in the time of Sr Edmond Andros of which £100 was for the Surveyor Comptroller & Waiter therefore I finding no new establishment allow him no more than Dyer had for him & his officers Salary it being the sentiment of the Council that I could not alter the former practice with which they were well acquainted But he gives himself a far larger allowance he will have it that his salary is sterling; and to make it so of this country money he charges three & thirty Pr cent advance & one hundred pound more for his two under officers, Besides this Mr Smith being his Deputy-Surveyor & Book-keeper, hee would have allowance to him of £50 pr ann as his deputy £40 Pr ann as his accomptant £30 Pr ann for his transcribing his books £20 Pr annum Pr his diet besides his salary for Surveyor, For John Harlow hee would have allowed £30 Pr ann as waiter, £48 Pr ann as being employed in the Kings service where or how noe man Knows £20 pr ann for his Diet and £162 and two voyages made into England with despatches for his Maty all this & a great deal more such for his officers in the country, & the like your Lops will see in his last general acct a copy whereof is herewith sent,

Notwithstanding hee charges the King soe largely for his officers salaries, to some of them hee has paid nothing at all insomuch as they are making very great clamor for their money, and not getting it from him expect it from the King

Of his own head hee bought a little rotten tool of a sloop on pretence for his Matys service, which as your Lops may see by their audit, has stood the King in near £700 & now cannot be sold for thirty soe must either be laid up or burnt

In his instructions & by several orders from me & the council he was expressly forbid to trust out his Matys revenue notwithstanding I was forc't to take notes from him to the value of £800. besides a great many more which hee pretends still to be standing out as your Lops will perceive by the audit

Hee has likewise been negligent in taking the bonds required by the laws of the Government from the masters of ships one ill consequence whereof has been the New York Pink has carried off several Elephants teeth without entry, & the bond being inquired for there was none taken, How he has behaved himself touching an interloper that came in hither I have already given Sr Benj. Bathurst an account, and as for the debts for him pretended to too the auditors upon enquiry the most of them are found to bee received by him. and I believe of the rest, the twentieth part will never be had, they are soe ill

And besides notwithstanding his confused way of accounting & being without a cheque upon him as aforesaid, he is found by his own accounts brought into the audit to be £1758 15 shillings threepence and $\frac{5}{8}$ths of a penny in debt to the King as your Lops may see by the said audit which (as is to be feared) is all gone besides his salary and pquisits, on which he might have lived very handsomely.

Hee (as hee hath all along done) does to all persons he converseth with speak scurrilously & abusively of me & ye Council which considering his circumstances we let pass without taking any notice of

Hee is likewise very troublesome to the present management of his Matys customs

I desire that as soon as may bee I may know what his Matys pleasure is should bee done with him, what acct I have here given yr Lopps of him is as moderate as may bee farr short of what I might have represented & yet have spoken nothing but the truth. What I have done has not been out of malice, for I beare none to him rather pitty, but purely with an intent to doe his Maty service & to secure his interest, as I doubt not will appear to yr Lopps and if I bee to be blamed for any thing in the Series of this affair its for too much forbearance

Thus my Lords I have given you as good an account of the Revenue received, & by whom as I can, as also how the same in a great part of it has been mismanaged and by what meanes I shall therefore now proceed to give your Lopps an estimate of what charge the maintenance of this Govermt has been hitherto to mee & what will be requisite for its further support.

Its a very hard thing upon mee that coming over hither in troublesome times, finding noe revenue established & yet having three garrisons to look after & the forts in the condition before mentioned, & finding such contest between the Governmt of Canada & this about the Beaver Trade the Inland Country & the Indians, to purchase, as I was obliged by my instructions, sixty odd miles, upon the Hudsons River 17 or 18 miles into the land in one place from the Indians. In another place up the River 16 miles. And on the south side of Long-Island twelve miles, to give a great deal to the Indians for Susquehanna River to bee at great expences on the Assembly at their first sitting when they gave the revenue & on the Lord Howard of Effingham when here with his train Governor Pen, commissioners from Boston & other colonies, the Govr of Connecticut East and West Jersey, the running the line between this & East Jersey, and the like between Connecticut and this, tho' that last not yet finished besides the establishment as will appear by my books when audited & sent over, which shall be by the very first conveniency, & had been long ere now, had I got Mr. Santens sooner done

In the meantime yr Lops may be capable of making an estimate of the constant charge of the Govermt by the calculation thereof herewith sent in which you see that there is set down yearly for the Council Judges & Attorney General which tho' not at present allowed in my opinion with submission to your Lops there is a necessity there should. The Councilors being persons obliged to a constant attendance from their own business & the judges such as devote themselves wholly to that service & whose present salary is soe small to support them & their familys in that station as is set forth in their petition which I have herewith sent to his Maty for his consideration, neither can the Attorney-general's small perquisites bee able to maintain him in going thro his Matys concerns, which may take up his whole time, without the addition of such salary as his Maty shall think fitt to allow.

Your Lops taking all this into yr consideration, cannot but think his Maty must be in debt, which however would not have been very much had Mr. Santen done his duty.

What revenue there is is with the ease and satisfaction of the people & paid without grumbling, though as much as modesty can bee put upon them.

Soe that if Connecticut be not added to the Govermt it can be hardly able to support itself. But if it bee added, thee revenue will bee sufficient to keep the King wholly out of debt.

Mr. Santen taxes me with covetousness in not allowing sufficiently to the officers employed. Niggardly I have not been, but the revenue being soe small & having soe great a charge, I endeavored to bee as good a husband for the King as I could I'm sure better than I ever was for myself. And truly I have been put soe to it to make things doe that what small pquisits I got I have disburst, & not only soe, but have been forc't to engage my credit soe far as t'would goe & that not sparing to pawn my plate for money to carry on the King's affairs & now I have sent some of it home by Mr. Spragg to reimburse Sr Ben Bathurst what hee has paid for mee, & to provide clothes for the soldiers & some things for my own use.

Now My Lords before I proceed to answer the rest of your queries I will take occasion here to give your Lops satisfaction as to those articles Mr. Santer has been pleased to draw up against mee, a copie whereof I herewith send for yr Lopps perusal the scope of which being to charge with mismanagement of his Matys affairs, I thought noe place more proper for my making appear the falsity of his accusation than here, wherein I have been soe long treating of the mismanagement of the revenue in which this man himself had soe large a share, which answers follow distinctly with relation to such proofs as are herewith sent necessary for my vindication.

Answer to Capt. Santer's charges against me.

As to the FIRST *Article—concerning a copartnership in a trade to France, &c.*

For my justification & making appear the falsehood of this article is the testimony of Mr. John Sprag & Mr. Gabriel Minvielle taken before Mr. Swinton clerk of the Council hereunto annexed.

To the SECOND *concerning a partnership in trade to Newfoundland.*

This is noe less true than the other as appears by Major Brokhelles testimony, &c. & truly had I any such design I had not communicated with the King's collector especially to a man of his disposition & subject to soe many follies and infirmitys that he was never capable of concealing his own secrets from the very rabble of the town, and always made the debates of the Council (while he was a member of it) the subject matter of his Tavern discourse.

To the THIRD *concerning my going sharer with the Privateers.*

Wherein he does mee the honor to join mee in partnership with privateers. I dont believe that Frederick Flipson ever went sharer with any body in a ship & am sure Beekman never had a vessel nor a share in a vessel in his life. Had I had 2 or 3 men's shares of what was got upon the wreck I think it had been noe breach of Law or my instructions it being customary in such cases for the Govrs of plantations to have it. But Mr. Santen too was mistaken in this they did not clear for the wreck & least they should make incursion upon the Spaniards I took security from them that they should not, in short for my justification on this point I refer myself to the testimonies of Frederic Flipson & Beakman & the obligation aforesaid herewith sent.

To the FOURTH *Copartnership with Mr Antill for Jamaica.*

Hee does me wrong I never was concerned with Mr Antill in copartnership One Vaughan half brother to Mr Sprag that had been a volunteer 2 or 3 years on board Captn Temple, & happening to bee in London when I came away offered his service to come along with mee, whom finding a pretty ingenious young man & out of employment I promised to help him with a little money when hee stood in need of it for to put him into some way. Whereupon not long after this Antill purposed if he could get money from his brother or any other to purchase the half of a little ship then to bee sold hee would purchase the other & that Vaughton should goe master of her upon which hee came to me into the country where I then was & acquainted me with ye proposal and desired my assistance to enable him to comply with it. I demanded what security he could give mee, hee proposed to make over his share in the vessel for it. Upon which in kindness to him I let him have the money & took the vessel in security for it & by him sent as a venture ten Barils of Oyle of a drift Whale that came to my share, & thirteen half Barils of Flower, to purchase Sugar Molasses Sweetmeats Oranges and other necessaries for use in my family. And this (as Mr. Santen knows as well as I & most of the town) was all the concerns I ever had with Antil

To the FIFTH *concerning the Dogger.*

This Mr Beekman having a Sloop went from this place to Nevis & Sr William Stapleton hearing of a dutch privateer gave him a commisson to goe after him, which hee did & took a great ugly vessel ye dutch have for fishing with one deck & went back with her to Nevis. Whereupon Sr Wm in reward of his good service gave him the Kings & his own share in her soe hee brought her hither where shee being a Dutch built & and the man having a mind to sell her, had her condemned at a Court of Admiralty. Upon which I forgave him the Kings share which by appraizement amounted to as doth appear by Mr Beekman's testimony

To the SIXTH *concerning Heathcot's Sloop.*

Mr. Santon does me wrong in this for upon the word of a Christian, I know not at this minute who were the appraizers they having been appointed by the Court where the sloop & goods were condemned, & they too upon their oaths. Neither had I any advantage by that vessel as Mr Santon knows tho' he had by making George Heathcot pay him ninety pounds & charges which was more then the third part the condemnation came to soe that I hope this is not the voyage he charges the King with soe much for, tho' it is the only remarkable one hee ever made & yet but ten miles distant from this place

To the SEVENTH *concerning my Lord Neill Campbells goods*

My Lord Neill Campbell its true desired my bill of store for the 10 Pr cent which I did grant, but Mr. Santen does mee wrong to say that I ordered they should bee entered without examination to the best of my remembrance there was noe such thing: but here hee forgets what hee has done himself what goods he has admitted to entry without examination contrary to Act of Assembly & my order as appears by his own books to the great diminution of his Matys revenue in this Province: neither does he remember what bills of store he has granted notwithstanding several orders to the contrary

To the EIGHTH *concerning one Riddell*

Mr Santen does mee wrong in this, One Mr Riddell a poor Gentleman that brought into this city without entry (as a great many others have done without Mr Santen or his officers taking notice thereof) a small parcel of linen afterwards appraised to be of the value of 3 or 5 pounds, And after that this Riddell & one of the officers of the Custom House drinking drunk together, fell a quarrelling, on which the Officer went out & meeting with Vaughton about one or two in the morning, compelled him to goe along with him to seize uncostumed goods at Riddell's lodging, where when they came they broke open the door upon this Riddell who being still drunk endeavoured to keep them out & and in the struggling stabbed Mr Vaughton. Whereupon he was secured in prison where hee lay a long time till Vaughton recovered. Afterwards the poor man being in a starving condition on the application of Mr Vaughton & himself & Mr Sprag & several others hee was set at liberty, and on a petition of his to the Council his goods were ordered to bee released, he paying all charges which being more than the value of the goods Mr. Sprag in charity to Riddell paid the Surgeons their demands which was ten pounds without taking any thing from him

To the NINTH *concerning Capt. Santen's warrants to the Sheriffs &c*

Mr Santen knows himself that from time to time by order of Council, all the Sheriffs have been obliged to account with him for all rents, Quit rents & arrearages of rent &c yet this would not doe to make himself seem great, he would needs issue forth his own warrants, which poor man was done in one of his fitts & indeed they met with such reception as they deserved, the sheriffs took noe other notice of them than to send them to mee Whereupon I being somewhat surprised at his manner of procedure called him before the Council where (being asked how he came to issue forth such warrants) his answer was that to his knouledge the Lord Treasurer did soe in England, But here I would ask Capt Santen why he hath not given a better account of Such Quit rents &c as have passed through his hands

To the TENTH *concerning my covetousness as he is pleased to term it*

Here (if Mr. Santon speaks true in saying I have been covetous) it was in the management of this small revenue to the best advantage, & had Mr Santen been as just as I have been careful the King had not been in debt, as I had more in my pocket than now I have

It may be true when I called for the King's money & accompts from Mr Santen & I met with unbecoming returns I might use some passionat expressions

And as for my pinching Officers if hee means himself it was because he took it very ill that I would not allow him 7 or 800 pounds extravagant expenses, As for Fran. Barber I never spoke a word to him of salary in my life & leave it to the audit what acct hee gives of the Revenue of that County for three years & on half

To the ELEVENTH *concerning the excise of Long Island &c*

What Mr. Santen says concerning the offer of £52 for the excise p^r a year may bee true I thought it very unreasonable that the excise of three Countys should be farmed for soe little, therefore I fixed upon Mr Vaughton & Mr. Nicolls looking upon them to bee honest men & agreed with them for £20 P P^s & what they could make over & above they should deliver to Mr Santen That Dan. Whitehead offered me three pounds for my license it is false, or that I had £10, from Nicolls & Vaughton is likewise false as doth appear by Mr Nicolls testimony & would by that of Mr Vaughton were hee here. Neither had I even any money for licenses since I came into this Government except from Albany & this place £24, but on the contrary gave it all to the collectors of the respective countys for their encouragement

To the TWELFE *concerning Mr Pretty &c*

Mr. Pretty is Sheriff of that County & having a great deal of other concerns upon his hands for the King & countreys service, that being a frontier County to Canada, soe that hee could not possibly attend the Surveyors place I put in William Shaw who had that place before in the time of Sr Edmond Andros & as Mayor Brockhelles informs us behaved himself faithfully therein. And as to his allegation in his memorandums that Shaw was put in for satisfaction for two or three years pay due to him, it is wholly untrue as does appear by the testimony of Mayor Baxter, Mr Coker, & by the receipt under Shaws own hand

To the THIRTEENTH *concerning the deprivations of officers* &c

This John Smith is a man that if he were as honest as hee is able the king had had more justice done him & Mr. Santen more money in his pocket. What account Sr Ben Bathurst gave mee of him I have already acquainted y^r Lo^pps with, & for what reason hee was turned out of the Custom House is herein before given to your Lo^ps.

To the FOURTEENTH *concerning the Pasture of Albany &c*

As for this of the Pasture, he is mistaken, it was never yet in the King's hands, but hee that was the commander took some profits of it, which was a great grievance to the people it having been patented by governor Nicolls to several people & by them built upon whose buildings have been since carried away by the overflowing of the river, It does not contain above fifteen or sixteen acres. I doubt not but I shall make it appear that I have done nothing in this to his Mat^ys^ prejudice I conceive I have done the King very good service in Albany. The town of Albany lyes within the Ranslaers Colony, and to say truth the Ranslaers had the right to it for it was they settled the place, & upon a petition of one of them to our present King about Albany the petitioner was referred to his Mat^ys^ council at law who upon a perusal of the Ranslaers papers made their return that it was their opinion that it did belong to them Upon which there was an order sent over to Sr Edmund Andros that the Ranslaers should be put in possession of Albany, & that every house should pay some two beavers, some more some less according to their dimensions p^r^ annum, for thirty years, & afterwards the Ranslaers to put what rent upon them they could agree for—What reason Sr Edmond Andros has given for not putting these orders in execution I know not.

The Ranslaers came & brought me the same orders which I thought not convenient to execute judging it not for his Maty^s^ interest that the second town of the Goverment & which brings his Mat^y^ soe great a Revenue should be in the hands of any particular men. The town of itself is upon a barren sandy spot of land, & the inhabitants live wholly upon trade with the Indians. By the meanes of Mr James Graham Judge Palmer & Mr Cortlandt that have great influence on that people I got the Ranslaers to release their pretence to the town & sixteen miles into the country for commons to the King with liberty to cut firewood within the Colony for one & twenty years. After I had obtained this release of the Ranslaers I passed the patent for Albany wherein was included the afore mentioned pasture, to which the people apprehended they had so good a right that they expressed themselves discontented at my reserving a small spot of it for a garden for the use of the Garrison

That the people of Albany has given me £700. is untrue I am but promised £300, which is not near my P^r^quisits, viz, ten shillings for every house & the like for every hundred acres patented by me, established by a committee appointed by the Assembly for the establishing of all fees, where Capt Santen may remember himself was chairman, Alsoe what they have given to those other Gentlemen I know nothing of it & upon my word in Genl I have not got the fourth part of my Pquisits, chusing rather to want them than take from the poor people that cannot spare it

To the FIFTEENTH *concerning a farm at East Jersey belonging to his Mat^y^ &c*

Mr Santen might have given a better account of this if his malice had suffered him The Farm at East Jersey paid £10, p^r^ annum to his Mat^y^ & at a Rack-rent, the proprietors of East Jersey putting us to more trouble than the value of it, they constantly disturbing the Tenants on pretence that his Mat^y^ had granted that to them, so that I conclude it would be more inconvenient to keep it than to part with it. Therefore Judge Palmer having an interest in East-Jersey & an influence with the Governor there, on his giving mee his obligation to pay as a fine the summ of £60. to the King in case hee should not think fit to forgive it & the rent of twenty shillings p^r^ ann. & to defend the title, I gave him a lease of the Reversion of it

To the SIXTEENTH *concerning Rockaway Neck &c*

Mr Santen poor man neither understands his own nor others concerns, hee was one of the Council himself when Capt Palmer petitioned for licence to purchase this land, lying without the meers & bounds of Hempstead & when the same was granted, & before hee had had his patent granted, the people of Hempstead were summoned to appear to show cause, if they had any why it should not bee granted, Thereupon one person came to mee & told mee that it was his land & that it was within the meers & bounds of Hempstead on which I ordered him to put a Caveat in to the Secry^s^ office against the passing of Judge Palmers patent, and then the Surveyor went to survey the lands accompanied by some of the Inhabitants of Hempstead, to show him their bounds who returning this lands to bee without their meers & bounds the patent was passed in which Captn Palmer is expressly bounded where hee adjoins to Hempsted by their line, And, wherein hee says the Hempsted people were frighted to let their Suits fall, its quite otherwise, for this Pearsall, upon the granting of this Patent got into possession of this land, inasmuch as Judge Palmer was forcet to commence suits against him Where after it had sometime depended, Pearsall finding that to insist on his pretence would not avail him, suffered judgement to goe against him, and as for his being frightened into it by Captn Palmers being Judge, there's noe such thing for on purpose he withdrew himself & left the management of that Court to his Collegue Judge Nicolls and as for the lands being the only pasture of the town its wholly false for its noe pasture at all, being all woodland, and that town having a plain of upwards of 40,000 acres of good pasture without a stick upon it & as for its value I believe Judge Palmer would think himself obliged to Capt Santen or any others that would give him £200. for it.

To the SEVENTEENTH *concerning Mr Grahams insinuation*

Mr Santen is in the right that Mr. Graham is Attorney-general and supervisor of all Patents & soe made upon Mr Rudyard's going from this place to Barbadoes & is a person understanding in the law, it being his whole business Wherefore I thought it not fit to pass any patents without his perusal least I might doe prejudice to the King. It is likewise true that I have called in former patents & still continue to doe so, that I might see by what Tenure they hold their lands, which I find generally to be by none, they paying noe acknowledgment to the King Whereupon being convinced of that defect by the resolution of ye Judges the people for their own ease & quiet & that of their posterity which otherwise might have fallen under the lash of succeeding Governors, without the least murmuring have renewed their patents with a reservation of a certain Quit-Rent to the King to the noe small advancement of his Revenue, & this done with general satisfaction & of which none will in the least complain but on the contrary express themselves thankful for it

Mr. Santen sure when hee wrote this article against mee did not consider the obligation that was upon us both to advance the Kings interest in our several stations, far less how inconsistent it was with his office to bee the only pson aggrieved at the advancement of his Matys revenue, when the people themselves that are concerned are not only satisfied but pleased with it.

Again hee forgets that hee was a member of the Council when they gave it for their opinion that those former patents were insufficient & were then dayly consenting to the passing of new ones. As for sums of money exacted I own I have received £200 from Ranslaer, but its nothing to what my perquisits would have amounted to according to the aforementioned regulation he having a vast tract of land

From Hempted I recd one hundred pound by forty & that in Cattle which is far less than my pquisits they hauing upwards of 100,000 acres, I own alsoe I have received £300 from the citty of New York, & have granted them nothing more than what they had from my predecessors, & is now before his Maty for a confirmation.

The land that Mr Santen complains of to bee such a grievance, is the Dock which the town at their own proper charge have taken from the sea, & dayly are at vast expense to maintain, & what use they make of it is not my business to inquire, but as to their selling to the value of £1500 for my use its wholly false, And as for those other sums of 50, 30 & 20 pounds, its not soe. I was never covetous to take from the poor people what they could not well spare, the Secratary is my witness, but if I had it never amounted to my pquisits, according to the regulation aforesaid

Besides the charge herein before answered were found several memorandums of what Mr Santen intended to complain against me. Among which there being some things not mentioned in the said charge, the same as I presume not being perfected, I presume further to trouble your Lops with what I have to say therein in my vindication

Answer to Capt Santens Mem'dums

I am sorry Mr. Santen has not a better memory. The Kings share of Cobbys Ship came by ap-
Cobbys Ship prizement to £19 7^{s} 6^{d} which was by Judge Palmer paid into Captn Santens own hands as appears by the testimony of Capt Palmer

Meritts house As to Mr Merrits house it does not pay soe much rent as Capt Santen pretends & is too quite out of repaire, ready to drop down

And as to the Farm hee might have remembered that I showed him a letter from S^{r} B Bathurst
The Farm. wherein was intimated that his Royal Highness now his Mat^{y} was pleased I should have both the farm & the house during the time of my government of this place.

For Coker's house I am glad Captn Santen has found so considerable a rent, for my part I never
Coker's House received a peny for it, therefore I shall now charge £72, more, being four years rent to Capt Santens account for which he has not yet given the King credit. There was a cooper liv'd in the next house to it and paid 12 or 15 pound p^{r} ann for which I find no credit given to the King in Capt Santens books, since the cooper left the poorest p'son in town would not live in it it being ready to drop down & Cokers is not in a better condition, soe bad they are that its a wonder to every body that they stand yet, in soe much that when Dr. Junes brought me my Lord Middletons order to let him have them & I showed them to him hee would not live in them.

Two or three years agoe Sr John Worden sent me an order to give a long lease of them to any that would take it, I have not met with any such person & I am sure if rebuilt by the King, it would not give him the interest of his money & Merrits house is in the same condition, as appears by the return of the Survey made by some of the Council and Carpenters sent to view it.

As for the business between Mr. Santen & Mr. Antill its a thing so scandalous that I will not trouble
Antill's business your Lo^{ps} with an account of it, only this I'll say that Mr Antill sent severall to him and I spake to him myself to let him know that Mr. Antill would be satisfied with an acknowledgment that he had done him wrong in speaking those scandalous words & that it was the effects of drink. But Mr. Santens pride was such that hee would not doe it, but continued to justify what he had said. Whereupon Mr. Antill took out the execution against him (he not being then of the Council) but before the serving sent him ye like message as before with the same effect whereupon the execution was served.

Larkins Case. As for Larkins case I refer to the orders of Council herewith sent.

As for the King's concerns going in a right channel I am sure they never can where he has powers. As for desiring a list of his Mat^{ys} Quit-Rents & my denying it to him, its wholly untrue for he has a book with an acct of all the Quit-Rents that then were to bee found mentioned in the records of Patents kept in the Secretarys office, which I caused Coker to draw out on purpose for him.

Smith kept the key of the Granary & what corn I received for my own use or the use of the Garrison was taken out by Coker & it was shown to Mr. Smith where I gave credit to the King for it in my books. Afterwards finding that Santen gave no credit to the King for what corn came into the Granary I took the key from Smith & gave it to James Larkens with order to him to give receipts for what should be brought in & to give an account of it to Smith that he might enter it upon the books.

Hee does Judge Palmer & Mr. Graham wrong for they are psons look't upon by the Council as fittest for those employments they are in, viz. Palmer Judge & Graham attorney for the
Capt. Palmer & Mr. Ja Graham. King, And if Mr. Santen would speak truth he must needs say they both have been very serviceable for the King in the advancement of his Revenue, & that they still continue with their utmost endeavors soe to bee And though their way of living is by the law, yet their management has been such by arbitration & such other mild courses that where there was ten

actions formerly there is not one now. And the Council had soe good an opinion of Captn Palmer that hee was thought the fittest to be the Judge of ye court for the King's affairs.

As for sloops &c going from this to Newfoundland, if it was against the act of navigation hee did ill to admit so many to clear & enter to & from thence without soe much as taking notice of it, till he and Major Brockhelles falling out, he took occasion to sieze his sloop, which the Council & I looking upon to be only malicious discharged taking security from him till his Matys further pleasure were known. Mr. Mayne coming here & showing mee his instruction, noe vessel has gone from hence thither since,

And had I not relyed soe much upon Capt Santen none had gone, & for his sake I'll not trust to another soe much again

Mr Santen was in the right I was angry to find a cart-load of goods going off the bridge after shutting up the Custom House without entry & demanding of the man how long they had been there, he answered from seven in the morning, without any officers taking notice of them, Upon my speaking to Mr. Santen he fell excusing his officers & gave me ill words. What thereupon happened I refer to My Lord Neal & Mr Mayne's testimonies that were then witnesses of it

As for Woolsford's case I have already referred your Lops to the account given thereof to Sr Benjamin Bathurst.

The negro-story I refer to the record herewith sent I never did anything since I came into the government without the advice & consent of the Council

The ship Charts was cleared upon trial Mr Santen had nothing to allege against her

The sloop Lancaster is the same with that of Gov. Heathcot before mentioned

The Boat of D'Morex was condemned for going to the Mill with Corn without the Governmt & seized by Capt Santen

The Sloop Fortune was condemned & my own share as well as the Kings forgiven, the poor man having done what he did innocently

The Sloop Lewis came from Pettiquaves, & brought here some of our people who had been taken by the Spaniards, in going to Jamaica with provisions & had fled to Pettiquaves & the sloop coming hither the master sent up word from Sandy Hook that hee would willingly come & live here which I willingly granted him liberty to doe, & in consideration of his service in bringing home our people I forgave the Kings & my own part in the sloop after shee was condemned with the proviso that if his Maty did not approve of it hee should pay that share according to apprizement for which Bond was accordingly taken, as will appear to yr Lops by the attested copie herewith sent In short all that I'll say, hee's fitter for a retired life, than to be the Kings Collector

To the three & twentieth

What estimate you can make touching the estates &c

The answer thereof is referred to the next

In answer to the tenth & four & Twentieth querie

What persuasions in Religion &c

Every Town ought to have a Minister New York has first a Chaplain belonging to the Fort of the Church of England; Secondly, a Dutch Calvinist, thirdly a French Calvinist, fourthly a Dutch Lutheran—Here bee not many of the Church of England; few Roman Catholicks; abundance of Quakers preachers men & Women especially; Singing Quakers, Ranting Quakers, Sabbatarians; Antisabbatarians; Some Anabaptists some Independents; some Jews; in short of all sorts of opinions there are some, and the most part of none at all

The Church

The Great Church which serves both the English & the Dutch is within the Fort which is found to bee very inconvenient therefore I desire that there may bee an order for their building an other ground already being layd out for that purpose & they wanting not money in store wherewithall to build it

The most prevailing opinion is that of the Dutch Calvinists

To the five and twentieth

It is the endeavor of all Psons here to bring up their children and servants in that opinion which themselves, profess, but this I observe that they take no care of the conversion of their Slaves.

What course &c

Every Town and County are obliged to maintain their own poor, which makes them bee soe careful that noe Vagabonds, Beggers, nor Idle Persons are suffered to live here

But as for the Kings natural-born subjects that live on long-Island & other parts of the Government I find it a hard task to make them pay their Ministers.

THO. DONGAN.

MY LORDS

Since my writing of this, on Perusal of some Papers in the Secretary's office, I found some Memorandums of Sir Edmond Andros whereby I understand that in the year 167$\frac{5}{6}$ hee sent home Captn Salisbury for England to let his Royal Highness now his Ma^{ty} know how impossible it was, for this Government to subsist without the addition of Connecticut. And hee himself went with some soldiers to surprise them, intending when he had done it to keep possession by a Fort he designed to make at a place called Seabrook but was prevented by the opposition of two companys of men then lodged there ready to goe out agst the Indians with whom they were in Warr

Much less it can subsist now without it, being at more expense than in the time of Sir Edmond & having lost Delaware & soe consequently the Peltry Trade which is not much inferior to that of the Beaver, besides much Quit-rents & the Excise which would have been a very considerable Revenue And too, what helps, he had these from East & West Jersey.

Weighing this with the reasons aforementioned, I hope his Ma^{ty} will be graciously pleased to add that Colony to this which is the Centre of all *His Dominions* in America. And the people thereof have been more inclined to his Ma^{tys} service and have expressed upon all occasions more Loyalty than any other of these parts

Likewise I am to give y^{r} Lo^{ps} an account that since I received my Instructions, I caused a Vessel which came to Amboy to come hither & enter - It being the opinion of the Council, that it was both agreeable to my Instructions and former practise especially in the time of Sir Edm^{d} Andros

I am now informed that the people of Pensilvania have had last year from the Indians, upward of 200 packs of Beaver down to the Skonshill & will have more this, as I have reason to believe which if not prevented, his Ma^{ty} must not expect this Governm^{t} can maintain itself, besides that it will wholly depopulate both this Town & Albany

Pensilvania

One Rogers the Weighmaster being found indebted to the King in £190–17-$\frac{1}{2}$ I demanded the money from him to which hee returned for answer; that he was Mr. Santen's servant & would live & die by him & would not pay it without his order. On which an Extent was made out against him & hee taken thereupon and put into Prison; Where after many endeavors of Mr. Saten to the contrary as will appear by the Minutes of Council hee at last paid £140 of it which I was willing to take rather than lose the whole

I am afraid we shall not have soe good an account of the rest of the debts

Being informed that Mr. Smith has never accounted with Mr Santen & having the opinion of Captn Palmer & Mr Graham that he is accountable to the King at least for soe much of the money as he has received to his own use on pretence of Salary without any authority for the same. I have caused him to be arrested in an action of account at his Ma^{tys} suit, upon which hee lies a prisoner to answer it at the Court appointed for the management of his Mat^{ys} Revenue

Mr Santen since his commitm[t] hath been soe unruly & abusive to mee and the Council that in our own defence, Wee are force't to send him home, threatening us with Chains at least for what wee have done

Councilors The names of y[e] Councilors

Major Anthony Brockhells
Frederick Flipson
Stephen V Courtlandt
John Spragg
Gervis Baxter

The Council thought fit not to give Mr. Santen his oath as appears by the Minutes of Council

John Young had his oath given him but hee lives 150 miles from this, & has no estate of his own and very old, that it is a thing impossible for him to serve

There being a clause in my Instructions wherein I am limited not to act without five, therefore Mr John Spragg & Major Jervis Baxter going for England, and there not being a sufficient number to make a quorum, I have by Vertue of a clause in my letters Patents, impowering me in case of absence out of the Government death or Suspension to add of the principal Freeholders) given the oath to Judge Palmer and Nicolas Bayard the present Mayor to serve in the Council until his Ma[tys] pleasure be known

And whereas there is a clause in my instructions to send over the names of six persons more fitt to supply the vacancy of the Council six of the fittest I find in this Government are as followeth

Mathias Nichols Judge
James Graham
William Smith
Gabriel Minvielle
Francis Rumbouls
Major Nicolas Demyre

VII.

PAPERS

RELATING TO

M. de Denonville's Expedition

TO

THE GENESEE COUNTRY AND NIAGARA.

1687.

EXTRACT FROM THE KING'S INSTRUCTIONS TO THE MARQUIS DE DENONVILLE, March 10, 1685.

[Paris Doc. III.]

His principal object ought to be to establish the repose of the Colony by a firm and solid peace. But to render this peace durable he must lower the pride of the Iroquois, support the Illinois and the other allies whom Sr de la Barre has abandoned, and by a firm and vigorous policy to let the said Iroquois know that they will have every thing to fear if they do not submit to the conditions which he intends to impose on them.

He will, then, first declare to them that he shall protect with all his power the allies of the French; inform the Illinois, the Outaouacs, Miamis and others of the same thing, and should he deem it proper to back this declaration by troops and an expedition against the Senecas, His Majesty leaves it to him to adopt, in his regard, such resolutions as he shall deem most suitable, being well persuaded that he will follow the best course, and that his experience in war will place him in a position to bring that to a speedy conclusion if he be obliged to undertake it.

He ought to be informed that the Commandant of New York has pretended to aid the Iroquois and to extend the English domination even to the bank of the River St. Lawrence and over the whole extent of Country inhabited by those Savages. And though His Majesty doubts not but the King of England to whom he has made representations by his Ambassador, will give orders to his Commandant to put a stop to these unjust pretensions, he, notwithstanding, considers it necessary to explain to him that he ought to do every thing to maintain good understanding between the French and English: Yet should the latter, contrary to every appearance, rouse the Savages and afford them succor, he must act towards them as towards enemies, when he finds them in the Indian Country, without, however, attempting any thing in the countries under the King of England's obedience.

FATHER LAMBERVILLE TO GOV. DONGAN.

[Lond. Doc. V.]

From Onnontague, 10 Sept. 1685.

My Lord—I had the honour not long since to write to you—it was last month; since the despatch of my last letter, the Senecas who were desirous to make trouble and to persuade the Mohawks and other villages to unite with them against Monsr de la Barre, have changed their minds; since they were assured that the peace concluded last year, as you desired, should not be broken by M. de la Barre, as they were maliciously told, and as a hundred false reports which are never ceased being related would persuade them. To complete successfully what you have so well begun, it only remains to exhort the Senecas to add a few more peltries to the ten beavers and thirty otters which they left in deposit with the Onnontagués to satisfy Mr de la Barre, as you recommended them to do last year. Let your zeal for the public peace, and especially for the Christians of this America induce you, if you please, to put the finishing hand to this good work and to recommend the Senecas and other villages not to attach credit to the new floating rumors, since it is true that the Govr of Canada desires with all his heart that all things should be quiet and to second your just intentions. The Onnontagués and those who are of their opinions, have operated powerfully on the minds of the said Senecas to induce them to resume thoughts of peace, as well as Mr. Arnout, bearer of this letter, who was present at what was done and said; and who can inform you, and from whom you will be glad to receive this report.

Since peace, through your care, will apparently last, we shall continue to carry the Christian faith through this Country, and to solicit the Indians, whom you honor with your friendship, to embrace it as you yourself embrace it, for this is the sole object that has caused us to come here, that the blood of Jesus Christ, shed for all men, may be useful to them, and that His glory may be great throughout the earth.

If you will please to honour me with a line from your hand, you can have your letter given to one named Garakontié who is deputed from the Onnontagués to repair to the Diet which you have convoked at Albany. Do him the charity to exhort him to be a good Christian, as he was whose name he bears, and who was his brother. Recommend him I beseech you not to get drunk any more, as he promised when he was baptized, and to perform the duties of a Christian. One word from you will have a wonderful effect on his mind, and he will publish throughout that it is not true that the English forbid them to be Christians since you who command them will have exhorted them to persevere therein.

I pray God, who has given us the grace to be united in the same Catholic faith, to unite us also in Heaven; and that he may heap his graces on you here on earth, is the wish of him who is perfectly and with all manner of respect, My Lord,

Your very humble and
very obedient servant,
Jean de Lamberville,
of the order of Jesuits, (called in Indian, *Téiorhensere.*)

Oblige me, I request you, to have the enclosed sent to its address.

Please, My Lord, pardon me the liberty which I take to present my humble respects to the Governor of Virginia, who is called among the Indians, Big Sword or Cutlass, who I learn is with you at Albany, to whom, some time ago, I caused to be restored an Englishman named Rolelman, whom these Indians here had plundered and captured and whom I took into my hut to save him from the fury of some refractory people and from those who would make him their slave. It is the east service I would desire to render him.

MEMOIR CONCERNING THE PRESENT STATE OF CANADA

AND THE MEASURES THAT MAY BE ADOPTED FOR THE SECURITY OF THE COUNTRY. 12 NOVEMBER 1685.

(*Extract.*)

[Paris Doc. III.]

The most to be feared is the Iroquois who are the most powerful in consequence of the facility with which they obtain arms from the English in the number of slaves they make daily among their neighbors by carrying away at an early age their children, whom they adopt; this is the only means of their increase, for thro' their debaucheries of Brandy which lead them into frightful disorders, the few children their women raise could not of themselves assuredly sustain them, if they did not make prisoners.

The great trade in arms and ammunition at a low rate, among the English has given them hitherto that advantage which they have over other nations who in order to be disarmed have been destroyed by the former who are all of them insolent. Even the English in Virginia have suffered and still suffer from them every day; but the interest of the trader at Orange and Manatte supersedes the public interest, for if they would not sell them powder, that nation could be more easily conquered than any other. It consists of five principal villages, each of which have other smaller ones depen-dant on them; the first is called Annié (Mohawk) which can furnish two hundred men fit for service and are ten leagues from Orange (Albany); the second is Oneyoust (Oneida) which can furnish one hundred and fifty men at from 15 to 20 leagues from Annié; the third is Onnontagué which could bring out three hundred men, ('tis one hundred leagues from Montreal); the fourth is Goyoguoain (Cayuga) which could put two hundred men a-foot, at twelve leagues from Lake Ontario, and the Sonoutouans (Senecas) the fifth, who comprize, as is reported, twelve hundred men bearing arms, at five leagues South of the Lake.

The Senecas being the strongest, are the most insolent. The idea must not be entertained that this Nation can ever be reduced except by being in a position to pounce on them; which cannot be done without approaching them, occupying some posts where provisions can be placed for the troops who will be sent after them. To accomplish this sufficiently apropos without being perceived by the enemy, in consequence of the navigation of the river, which is full of Rapids and Cascades, impassable except by portages, independent of the distance—herein consists all the care and difficulty.

The post of Catarokuy appears to me the most advantageous, by placing it in a better state of defence than it is. It is at the entrance of Lake Ontario from the extremity of which the Senecas are distant only five or six leagues, in a beautiful country towards the South.

The position of this fort is sufficiently favorable to secure the barks against the storms and the attacks of the Indians at a trifling expense which will require to be made on it. The passage to be made through this lake is forty or fifty leagues before disembarking near the Senecas. The three barks at Catarokuy will be particularly useful in this enterprize by putting them in repair, for they have been much neglected.

* * * * * * * * * * *

It appears to me extremely important that the King render himself absolute master of this Lake, which is more than three hundred leagues in circumference. I am persuaded that the English would like particularly to have a post there, which would be immensely prejudicial to the Colony and the King's power on this Continent; his Majesty could easily make himself master of it, without any opposition, by the permanent establishment of a post, with vessels on this lake, and by another fort and vessels on lake Erie which is only two leagues distant, by the Niagara River, from this lake Ontario; but as this post cannot be established until after the Iroquois are conquered, I shall, before entering into a detail of the means of conquering that Nation, again say, regarding the importance of occupying these posts, that the English have so great a facility to establish themselves there that it is the power of the Iroquois alone which has prevented them having posts there, since Lake Ontario can be easily reached on horseback from Manette and Orange, there being a distance of only one hundred leagues through a fine country.

The importance of the post to be occupied on lake Erie is easily perceived, since we can easily go in vessels from that lake to Missilimakina which would be a great facility for the trade of the country, to keep the Outaouacs in check and in obedience to the King; besides, we shall have the means of reaching through this lake the Illinois, and surmount by this communication with ships many of the difficulties experienced in the Rivers in consequence of the number of portages. Being masters of these two lakes and cruising there with our vessels, the English would lose the Beaver trade in that quarter, of which they have abundance.

A durable peace with the Iroquois Indians would be more advantageous to the Colony than prosecuting a war; but this Nation has assumed such excessively insolent and haughty airs towards all the other tribes against whom they wage war and at whose expense they daily increase; and joined to that, the odds they have had from a disadvantageous peace concluded last year with us, has placed them in a position that, we may be assured, they will break with us on the first opportunity. It is yet more certain that if they be not checked, they will reassume their former insolent air the moment there will be no more troops in this country, however they may promise us at present, and will no doubt insult us, and subject us to all possible outrage.

It is necessary, then, to examine the most certain means of destroying and conquering their five villages, which according to the above estimate, may bring into the field about two thousand men bearing arms, and in a condition to go to war.

I consider that what troops we have, and what militia we can collect together, if we had them all with some of our Savages, would suffice to attack them; but as it is not sufficient to make them let go their foot, and it becomes necessary to deprive them of all means of disturbing us in our settlements, we must not go after them to chastise them by halves but to annihilate them if possible. This cannot be done without the aid of a number of Savages sufficiently great to pursue them in security to the distant forests towards Maryland and Andastes whither they will retreat if they find that we are more powerful than they; and as it is of extreme importance not to declare war against them until we are in a condition to vanquish them, it will be absolutely necessary to adopt measures with the Illinois, their enemies, and with the Savages our allies, to engage them to unite with us in attacking them and pursuing them into the woods whither they never fail to retire, daring not to stand against us. For as it would be very unfortunate not to vanquish them if we attack them, nothing ought to be neglected that can be done, to endeavor to destroy them and put it beyond their power to injure the Colony. If we succeed, I calculate the English will lose their trade in that quarter.

I find all our allies so discontented with us, and so dissatisfied on account of the idle march which we caused them to make last year, that according to what I learn, I do not believe that any of them can be relied on.

Before engaging in a war, then, I considered it prudent to permit the continuance of the negotiations of a certain Onontague savage, accredited by them and the other Iroquois, who is said to wish for nothing but peace. Notwithstanding I bethought me of managing the Illinois by promising them every protection, and as Chevalier de Tonty, who is in command at the fort on behalf of M. de Lasalle, has considerable influence among the Illinois, I have deemed it a duty to advise him of my arrival and of the necessity which exists that he should speak, as soon as possible, for the King's interest.

I likewise sent to M. de Ladurantaye who is at lake Superior under orders from M. de Labarre, and to Sieur Duluth who is also at a great distance in another direction, and all so far beyond reach that neither the one nor the other can have news from me this year, so that not being able to see them all, at soonest before next July, I considered it best not to think of undertaking any thing during the whole of next year, especially as a great number of our best men of the Colony are among the Outaouacs, and cannot return before the ensuing summer.

Moreover, learning that six tribes of our friends and allies are at war with each other, and as it is absolutely necessary to reconcile them before thinking of deriving any advantage from them, I sent presents and instructions to M. Ladurantaye to collect our French and put himself at their head, in order to support his reasoning and to have more authority to reconcile them in concert with Father Anjeblan Jesuit Missionary at Missilimakina.

We shall, however, lose no time in putting ourselves in a position to resent the insults that the Iroquois may offer the Colony, which would suffer very much if we were mastered, and we will not let pass any negotiations that offer so as to lull the Senecas who are the most insolent, and with whom there is no permanent peace to be expected, much less that they will observe it with our allies whose total destruction they contemplate.

Chevalier de Tonty commandant of M. de Lasalle's fort among the Illinois, coming next week, we shall agree together as to what is best to be done to secure the conquest of this Nation, which I understand can be done if he can march with a sufficiently large body of Illinois behind lake Erie and come to Niagara, as Sieur de la Forest who commanded at Fort Catarokvy told me could be done, who also assured me that powder and at least four or five hundred guns would be required to arm these people. This is but a loan, which the said Sieur de Laforest is certain will be rëimbursed in cash, by the said Sieur de Tonty.

The said Sieur de La Forest having demanded my permission to go and join said Sieur de Tonty on M. de Laselle's business, I deemed it proper to select a capable person to guarantee the safety of the Post of Catarokvy. I chose Sieur D'Orvilliers a very prudent and intelligent man and who has much experience, whose conduct during M de Labarre's administration is praised and approved by all persons of property in the country.

I gave him his company as a garrison, with some workmen as well to refit the vessels as to repair the barracks, and to put the fort in the best possible condition to pass the winter.

And as there is a great resort of Iroquois at that place, and as there is quite a number established there, I requested the Jesuit Fathers to station Father Milet there to act as Interpreter and to correspond with Father de Lamberville who is a Missionary among the Onontagues who evince a desire for peace.

In regard to Sieur Duluth I sent him orders to repair here so that I may learn from himself the number of savages on whom I may depend: he is accredited among them and rendered great services to M de Labarre by a considerable number of savages whom he brought to him to Niagara, who alone would have attacked the Senecas were it not for an express order from M de Labarre to the contrary.

On arriving here I found neither batteaux nor canoes for our troops, and as they are absolutely useless if not adapted to pass from one point to another; knowing by experience that the expense of canoes is too great and that they require too much attention and repair, I thought I could not do better than to order plank to be prepared for one hundred flat batteaux, which will carry twice more than canoes and will be much cheaper both in cost and repair, because a batteau that will carry two thousand pounds will not cost more than a canoe which will carry only one.

The means for preparing to wage war against the Iroquois, if the King approve of it, so that that Nation may not have any suspicion, remain to be considered.

It is very much to be desired that first of all, sufficient flour and other provisions might be put into Catarokvy next year, so as to have nothing to do the following year but to march against the enemy; but as I do not think it possible to convey the whole quantity of provisions necessary thither without the savages naturally suspicious taking umbrage, measures must be adopted to accomplish all in the same year with great diligence, which cannot be effected without trouble and expense, for in truth, the difficulties in surmounting rapids and cascades, twenty-five to thirty leagues in extent, are immense.

This, however, is not all; for it is well to consider that the arrangements are not easy to be made so as to secure punctuality, since from the Illinois country there are four hundred leagues to be travelled to arrive at Niagara, the place of rendezvous; and from the Outaouacs and Savages of lake Superior, three hundred leagues, and from Quebec nearly two hundred to the said place of Niagara. All this must make me think of putting myself in a condition to be, myself, sufficiently strong to fight them without any other aid than that of this country.

The conveyance of supplies and the expense are my sole difficulties. The neighborhood of Catarokvy indifferently fertile in grain, produces good peas; M. de Laforest assures me that he has nearly three hundred minots. I caused him to give orders to have them all sown, and M. d'Orvilliers not to allow any to be consumed, but will make the soldiers work and oblige them to plant some. That will be a trifling supply of four or five hundred minots for next year.

* * * * * * * * * * *

It will require considerable expense to render the river navigable; the Map I have caused to be made of it will afford some imperfect idea by remarking the pitch in several places there.

* * * * * * * * * * *

The surest remedy against the English of New York would be to purchase that place from the King of England who in the present state of his affairs, will, without doubt, require money of the King. By that means we should be masters of the Iroquois without waging war.

M. DE DENONVILLE TO THE MINISTER, 8 May 1686.

[Paris Doc. III.]

I learn that the news which I had the honour to send you of the appearance on Lakes Ontario and Erie of English Canoes accompanied by French Deserters on their way to the Outaouacs is true. There are ten of them loaded with merchandize. Thereupon, my Lord, I sent orders to Missilimakina, to Catarokouy and other places where we had Frenchmen, to run and seize them, and I am resolved to send another officer with twelve reliable men to join Sieur D'Orvilliers at Catarosky, who is to go with Sieur de Lasalle's bark to Niagara to treat there with the Iroquois Indians on their return from hunting. He will take some men with him. This officer, with the aid of this bark and some canoes which shall be furnished him, will post himself with twenty good men at the River, communicating from Lake Erié with that of Ontario, near Niagara by which place the English who ascend Lake Erié must of necessity pass on their return home with their peltries. I regard, my Lord, as of primary importance the prohibition of this trade to the English, who without doubt, would entirely ruin ours both by the cheaper bargains they could give the Indians and by attracting to them the Frenchmen of our Colony who are accustomed to go into the woods.

* * * * * * * * * * *

I am persuaded that the Iroquois are very anxious for peace now that they see troops, but I do not at all believe that they will submit not to make war any more against the other Nations our allies, therefore there is no doubt but we must prepare to humble them.

What I should consider most effectual to accomplish this, would be the establishment of a right good post at Niagara.

The manner in which the English have managed with the Iroquois hitherto, when desirous to establish themselves in their neighbourhood, has been to make them presents for the purchase of the soil and the property of the land they wish to occupy. What I see most certain is, whether we act so by them or have peace or war with them, they will submit with considerable impatience to see a fort built at Niagara which would secure to us the communication between the two lakes; would render us masters of the road the Senecas take in going to hunt for furs, none of which they have on their own grounds; it is likewise their rendezvous when hunting for their supplies of meat with which as well as with all sorts of fish, this country abounds.

This post would be of great advantage to the other nations who are at war with these, and who durst not approach them, having too long a road to travel when retreating. It would keep them in check and in obedience, especially by building a Fort sufficiently large to contain a force of 4 or 500 men to make war on them; this cannot be done without expense because it must be enclosed by a simple, ordinary picket fence to place it beyond all insult, not being in a position to be relieved by us.

To guarantee its construction, it must not be doubted for a moment, though at peace with them, but a guard would be necessary there for the security of the workmen. The freight of provisions as well for the garrison as the troops to be stationed there is very high, since a thousand pounds w[t] which is a load for a canoe, costs 110 liv. from Ville Marie on the Island of Montreal to Catarakouy. Independent of mere provisions, how many other necessaries and munitions are required!

This post, my Lord, would absolutely close the entire road to the Outaouacs against the English, and would enable us to prevent the Iroquois carrying their peltries to the latter; for with the redoubt at Catarokouy which would serve us as an Entrepot to shelter our barks from the storms in winter, we having posts at both sides of the Lake could render ourselves Masters of the hunting of that Nation who can support itself merely by that means and would draw but little from the English if it had no more peltries to give them: What is very certain, they would carry them much fewer than heretofore.

I propose to send Sieur D'Orvilliers to Niagara this year with Sieur de Villeneuve, the draughtsman whom you gave me, to draw the plan, and after I shall have seen the Iroquois at Villemarie on the Island of Montreal and we shall know what we have to expect from them, I'll see if I shall not be able to take a trip thither myself, in order to furnish you with a more certain report thereon; for to rely on Sieur de Villeneuve alone, he is a very good, very accurate, very faithful draughtsman, but in other respects he has not a very well ordered mind; it is too confined to be able to furnish out of his own head any ideas for the establishment of a post and its management.

I am assured that the land in the neighbourhood is very fine and fertile, easy of cultivation; it is situate about the 44th degree. Everything I learn confirms me in the opinion which I entertain, that this post would, in three years at furtherest, support itself. It is to be feared that fortifying it would draw war on us, if you wish to avoid it; but at the same time I believe that were the Senecas to see us well planted there, they would be more pliant.

Should this plan be agreeable to you, my Lord, please send masons and plenty of instruments to break up the ground and convey stone.

* * * * * * * * * * * *

You will be surprised, my Lord, to learn that Sieur de Chailly, of whom I had the honour to write you this fall, not being able to have his *congé* from me to retire to France with all his property which he sent off last year before my arrival, has fled and deserted the Country, to pass over to Orange (Albany) and thence without doubt by way of England to France.

* * * * * * * * * * *

What is disagreeable in it is, that he will have informed Governor Dongan of every thing he knows of our expedition to the *Baie du Nord* (Hudson's Bay) and has learned of the interests of the country and our designs. I beg of you, my Lord, to permit of the confiscation of whatever property may be found belonging to him for the benefit of the two hospitals of the Colony.

FROM GOV. DONGAN TO M. DE DENONVILLE.

[London Doc. V.; Par. Doc. III.]

Albany, May 22, 1686.

Sir—I have sent for the five Nations of Indians y[t] belongs to this Governm[t]. to meet me at this place, to give them in charge that they should not goe to your side of the Great Lakes nor disturbe your Indians and Traders, butt since my coming here I am informed that our Indians are apprehensive of warr by your putting stores into Cataract [Cataraqui] and ordering some forces to meet there. I know you are a man of judgment and that you will not attack the King of England's subjects. Being informed that those Indians with whom our Indians are engaged in war with, are to the West and Southwest of the Grate Lakes (if so) in reason you can have no pretence to them. It is my intention that our Indians shall not warr with the farr Indians. Whether they doe or not it docs not seem reasonable that you should ingage yourself in the quarrell of Indians we pretend to, against our own Indians. Whether these Territories belong to our or the French King is not to be decided here, but by our Masters at home; and your business & mine is to take Mapps of the Country so well as we can and to send them home for the limits to be adjusted there.

I am likewise informed that you are intended to build a ffort at a place called Ohniagero on this side of the Lake within my Masters territoryes without question (I cannot believe it,) that a person that has your reputation in the world would follow the steps of Mons[r] Labarre and be ill advised by some interested persons in your Governm[t] to make disturbance between our Masters subjects in these parts of the world for a little pillitree; when all these differences may be ended by an amicable correspondence between us, If there be any thing amiss I doe assure you it shall not be my fault, though we have suffered much, and doe dayly by your People's trading within the King of England's territoryes. I have had two letters from the two Fathers that lives amongst our Indians, and I find them somewhat disturbed with an apprehension of war, which is groundlesse, being resolved that it shall not begin here, and I hope your prudent conduct will prevent it there, and referr all differences home as I shall doe. I heare one of the Fathers is gone to you, and the other that staid I have sent for him here lest the Indians should insult over him, tho' its a thousand pittys that those that have made such progress in the service of God should be disturbed, and that by the fault of those that laid the foundation of Christianity amongst those barbarous people.

Setting apart the station I am in I am as much Mons[r] Desnonville's humble Servant as any friend he has, and will omit noe opportunity of manifesting the same

S[r]

Your humble Serv[t]

THO[s] DONGAN.

This Rumor of y^{r} coming to Cataracto has prevented my sending a gentleman to Quebec to congratulate your arryval in ye Governm^{t} soe am constrained to make use of ye Father for ye safe conveyance of this to your hands.

M. DE DENONVILLE TO GOV. DONGAN.

[Paris Doc. III.]

Ville marie, June 20, 1686.

I received, Sir, the letter which you did me the honour to write me on the 22d May last, You will sufficiently learn, in the end how devoid of all foundation are the advices which you have had of my pretended designs and that all that has been told you by the deserters from the Colony ought to be much suspected by you.

You are, Sir, too well acquainted with the service and the manner that things must be conducted, to take any umbrage at the supplies which I send to Cataracouy for the subsistence of the soldiers which I have there.

You know the savages sufficiently to be well assured that it would be very imprudent on my part to leave that place without having enough of supplies and munitions there for one year's time. You are not ignorant that it is impossible to get up there at all seasons; if I were to have them conveyed for a large force, I should have used other means.

The natural treachery of a people without faith and without religion, require us to be so far distrustful of them that you ought not to blame me for using precaution against their restlessness and caprice.

I had the honor to inform you by my letter of the 6th June last that the orders I have from my Master manifest merely the zeal which his Majesty entertains for the progress of Religion and for the support and maintenance of the Missionaries. I expect from your piety that you will not be opposed to that, knowing well how much you love religion. Do you think, Sir, that they will reap much fruit whilst the savages are allowed no peace in the villages in which our Missionaries are established?

When I came here, I thought Peace was assured between the Iroquois and us and our Savage allies. You see, Sir, what has been the conduct of the Iroquois in this rencounter. Can you say, Sir, that I am wrong in distrusting them?

They are alarmed at the war which they fancy I shall wage against them; their conscience only could have impressed them with this idea, since I have not done the least thing to make them believe that I want any thing else from them than to see peace well established throughout all the country. What have I done to cause them the least uneasiness? And what do they want?

In respect to the pretensions which you say you have to the lands of this country, certainly you are not well informed of all the entries into possession (*prises de possessions*) which have been made in the name of the King my Master, and of the establishments which we have of long standing on the lands and on the lakes; and as I have no doubt but our Masters will easily agree among themselves, seeing the union and good understanding that obtain between them, I willingly consent with you that their Majesties regulate the limits among themselves wishing nothing more than to live with you in good understanding; but to that end, Sir, it would be very apropos that a gentleman so worthy as you should not grant protection to all the rogues, vagabonds, and thieves who desert and seek refuge with you, and who, to acquire some merit with you believe they cannot do better than to tell you many impertinencies of us, which will have no end so long as you will listen to them.

The letter which the Rev. Father de Lamberville has been so kind as to be the bearer of from me on the 6th June last ought to suffice, Sir, to put you perfectly in possession of my intentions. It would be unnecessary that I should make any other reply to your last of the 22d of May, were it not that I was very glad hereby to prove to you again that I shall always feel a great pleasure in seizing every opportunity to show that I am

Sir,

Your very humble &
very obedient Servant.

COL. DONGAN TO M. DE DENONVILLE.

[Lond. Doc. V.; Par. Doc. III.]

New-York, 27th July, 1686.

Sir—I had the honour to receave two letters from you one dated the 6th and the other the 20th of June last and in them I have found very much satisfaction by the hopes of a good correspondence with a person of so great merit worth and repute spread abroad in the army in which I served. Believe it is much joy to have soe good a neighbor of soe excellent qualifications and temper and of a humour altogether differing from Monsieur de la Barre your predecessor who was so furious and hasty very much addicted to great words as if I had bin to have bin frighted by them. The Indians peradventure might justly offend him for they as you well remarke are not people of the greatest credit and reputation, but certainly I did not amiss in offering sincerely to compose the difference and I went expressly to Albany to do it and yet no suitable returns were made by him for it. I doubt not but your masters inclinations are very strongly bent to propagate the Christian Religion and I do assure you that my master had no less a share in so pious intentions; for my part I shall take all imaginable care that the Fathers who preach the Holy Gospell to those Indians over whom I have power bee not in the least ill treated and upon that very accompt have sent for one of each nation to come to me and then those beastly crimes you reproove shall be checked severely and all my endeavors used to suppress their filthy drunkennesse disorders, debauches, warring and quarrels and whatsoever doth obstruct the growth and enlargement of the Christian faith amongst those people.

I have heard that before ever the King your Master pretended to Cannida, the Indians so farr as the South Sea were under the English Dominion and always traded with Albany Maryland and Virginia, but that according to your desire with very good reason is wholly referred to our Masters, and I heartily pray that neither you nor myself give occasion of any of the least misunderstanding between them, but that a prosperous correspondence stricht amity and union may perpettually bee continued between those monarchs, The strictest care shall be taken concerning runaways from you and those who are here if you please to send for them shall bee all conveyed to you—but if there be any soldiers who have deserted, I desire you to give me the assurance that they shall not loose their lives, And now, Sir, I beg your pardon for giveing you the trouble of my particular affairs which is thus: when my Prince called me out of the French service twenty five thousand livres were due to me as was stated and certified to Mons[r] De Lenoy by the Intendant of Nancy—my stay was so short that I had no time to kisse the King's hands and petition for itt—a very great misfortune after so long service, for in the circumstances I was then in I served him faithfully to the uttermost of my power. After I quitted France I went to Tangier and having left that place sometime after came hither so that I never had time to represent my case to His Majesty which I request you to espouse for me that so by your means I may obtaine either all or at least some part of that which is due to me—The King I know had bin bountifull to all and I am confident hath too much generosity to see me suffer; however it happens I shall as heartily pray for his good health and happy success in all his undertakings as any one breathing and be ever ready to make all just acknowledgements to yourselfe for so great an obligation and favour; wishing heartily for a favorable occasion to demonstrate how profound an esteem I have for your person and meritts and give undenyable proofs that I am sincerely and with all respects

Sir

Your most humble and affectionate servant

THO[s] DONGAN

M. DE DENONVILLE TO GOV. DONGAN.

[Paris Doc. III.]

29 Sept. 1686.

I received by the Rev. Father de Lamberville, the elder, missionary among the Iroquois of the village of the Onontagués the letter which you took the trouble to write to me on the 27th July. I repeat, Sir, what I already had the honour to state to you that it will not be my fault that we shall not live in very good intelligence. I am willing to believe, Sir, that you will contribute thereunto on your side, and that you will put an end to all those causes that may exist for dissatisfaction at what is doing under your government by your traders and others whom you protect.

I do not believe, Sir, that the King your master approves of all the trouble you have taken in arming and soliciting by presents all the Iroquois Nation to wage war on us this year, neither the exhortations you have made them to plunder our Frenchmen who trade to places which up to the present time we have acquired long before New York was what it is.

You have proposed, Sir, to submit every thing to the decision of our Masters, yet your emissary to the Onnontagués, told all the nations in your name to pillage and to make war on us. This is so notorious a matter that it cannot be doubted, and it will be maintained before your emissary; whether he acted by your order, or at the suggestion of your merchants at Orange, it has been said and done. You are not ignorant of the expedition of your merchants against Michilimaquina. I ask you, Sir, what do you wish that I should think of all this, and if this behaviour accord with the letter which you did me the honour to write on the 27th July filled with courtesies and friendly expressions as well regarding Religion as the good understanding and friendship existing between our Masters which ought to be imitated in this country in token of our respect and obedience to them.

You had the civility to tell me that you would give me up all the deserters, who to escape the chastisement of their knaveries, take refuge with you; yet you, Sir, cannot be ignorant of those who are there, but as all these are for the major part bankrupts and thieves I trust they will finally give you reason to repent of having given them shelter, and that your merchants who employ them will be punished for having confided in rogues who will not be more faithful to them than they have been to us.

You know, Sir, they spare neither the Outaouas, our most antient allies, nor the other tribes among whom we have Preachers of the Gospel and with whose cruelties to our holy Missionaries, whom they have martyred, you are acquainted. Are all these reasons, Sir, not sufficiently conclusive to induce you to contribute to designs so pious as those of your Master? Think you, Sir, that Religion will progress whilst your Merchants supply, as they do, *Eau de Vie* in abundance which converts the savages, as you ought to know, into Demons and their cabins into counterparts and theatres of Hell.

I hope, Sir, you will reflect on all this, and that you will be so good as to contribute to that union which I desire, and you wish for.

Finally, Sir, you must be persuaded that I will contribute, willingly and with pleasure, my best to obtain for you the favor you desire from the King my master. I should have wished, Sir, that you had explained your case more clearly, and that you had placed in my hands the proofs or vouchers of your debt, so as to explain it to the King, for so many things pass through the hands of Messrs. his Majesty's Ministers that I fear M. de Lonnoy will not recollect your affair, which he cannot know except through the Intendant who was at Nancy, whose name you do not mention. I shall not fail, Sir, to endeavour to obtain for you some favor from the King my master for the services which you have rendered his majesty. I should wish, Sir, to have an opportunity, on some other more fitting occasion to prove that I am,

Sir,

Your very humble and very obedient Servant.

M. DE DENONVILLE'S MEMOIR

ON THE PRESENT STATE OF AFFAIRS IN CANADA AND THE NECESSITY OF MAKING WAR NEXT YEAR ON THE IROQUOIS.

[Paris Doc. III.]

Quebec the 8th 9ber 1686.

Our reputation is absolutely destroyed both among our friends and our enemies. It is no trifling thing, My lord, to reëstablish it in view of the expeuse and labor and the dreadful consequences of a war, absolutely necessary. But, my lord, when we are certain that it is God's business and the King's glory that are in question, and that all those to whom they are committed have head and heart occupied only with zeal to perform their duty so as to have nothing wherewith to reproach themselves, we labour untroubled, confident that Heaven will supply the defects of our understanding and abilities, more especially having you as our Protector near to King with whom all things are possible, his piety being the foundation and motive of all his undertakings.

I annex to this Memoir, the duplicate of the letter of June last in which I advised My lord of the expedition of the Iroquois against our allies the Hurons and Ottawas of Missilimakina in the Saguinan.1 I have learned since that the English had more to do with that expedition than even the Iroquois who struck the blow. Their intrigues, My lord, reached a point that without doubt it would be much better that they should have recourse to open acts of hostility by firing our settlements, than to do what they are doing through the Iroquois for our destruction.

1 The Country between Lakes Erie and Huron was thus called. Paris Doc. iii. 84.

I know, beyond a moment's doubt that Mr. Dongan has caused all the Five Iroquois Nations to be collected, this spring at Orange to tell them publicly, so as to stimulate them against us, that I want to declare war against them; that they must plunder our Frenchmen in the Bush which they can easily effect by making an incursion into the country, and for that purpose Mr. Dongan caused presents of arms and ammunition to be given them by the merchants, neither more nor less than if it were himself who was to make war. There is no artifice, therefore My lord, that he did not employ to persuade them of their destruction, unless they destroyed us.

Father de Lamberville, Jesuit Missionary at Onontagué, one of the five villages, being advised of the wicked designs of the English, set all his friends to work to avert the storm, and enjoining them to report everything to him, he obtained from them that they would not budge until he had seen me. During his absence Mr. Dongan sent an express to the Iroquois to notify them to march without delay and fall on the Colony, ordering Father de Lamberville's brother, who had remained as hostage to be brought to him, thinking to deprive us of all our missionaries among the Iroquois. At the same time, he sent emissaries among our savages at Montreal to debauch them and draw them to him, promising them Missionaries to instruct them, assuring them that he would prevent Brandy being conveyed to their villages. All these intrigues have given me no small exercise all summer to ward off this blow.

Mr. Dongan wrote me, and I answered him as a man may do who wishes to dissemble, and who cannot yet get angry, much less crush his foe. I thought it better to temporise and answer Mr. Dongan by eluding rather than exhibiting one's chagrin without having the power to injure his enemy. The letters which I rec[d] from him and my answers, copies of which I send, will advise you of my conduct in this conjuncture. Mr. Dongan, notwithstanding works secretly with all the artifices in the world, to debauch our Frenchmen and Indians. Col. Dongan's letters will sufficiently explain his pretensions which embrace no less than from the Lakes inclusive to the South Sea. Missilimackinac belongs to them. They have taken its elevation. They have been there treating with our Outawas and Huron Indians, who received them there very well on account of the excellent trade they made there in selling their goods for beaver which they purchase much dearer than we. Unfortunately we had at the time but very few French at Missilimackinac. M. de la Durantaye on arriving there would pursue the English to plunder them; the Hurons ran to escort them after saying many bad things of us. M. de la Durantaye did not overtake the English, who met on their road the Senecas going to meet them to escort them through lakes Erie and Ontario until they were beyond the risk of being attacked by us.

Thus you see, My lord, that the Senecas and the English understand each other charmingly, and are in perfect harmony and this alliance is made particularly with the army whom M. de la Barre went against, for at the time of his march the Senecas ran to Orange to find Colonel Dongan to beg him to take them under his protection, giving themselves over to him by a public Acte which was registered and sent to England, and, then, he caused poles with the arms of England to be planted in all their villages.

Nevertheless, previous to that time we had missionaries there, the first before any Englishman had an idea there were Senecas there. I annex to this letter am emoir of our Right to all that Country of which our registers ought to be full, but of which we can find no trace. I am told that M. Tallon had originals of the entries of possession (*prises de possessions*) of many discoveries made in this country, which our registers ought to contain. Doubtless he has given them to my late lord, your father.

Father de Lamberville having given me an account of all the Colonel's intrigues which tended to take the Hurons away from us and to draw off the Outawas, I entrusted him with presents to gain over the principal and most intriguing of the Iroquois to secure the friendship of the young men who were disposed to be out of humor with us. He arrived in very good season, for all the Nations, assured by Mr. Dongan that the good Father would not return, had assembled and were marching, but his return woke up the Father's party, who by means of secret, which are called here "under-ground" presents, dispelled the storm.

All the summer has been spent in comings and goings to get back the prisoners, the Outawas wishing to demand them of the Iroquois without my participation, according to the promises of the Senecas to restore them, provided I did not demand them. In fine the Hurons and the Outawas resolved to repair to Cataraqui, and the Onontagoés alone have given up their prisoners, the Senecas saying that theirs did not wish to return home. Father de Lamberville returned here in the latter part of September, he gave me an account of all his cares, and of all his troubles and fatigues. Whatever affection he may have for the mission where he has been stationed fifteen or sixteen years, every year in danger of being killed by the Iroquois, he admits himself that nothing is to be done for the mission unless that nation be humbled. This, My lord, is so true that the Iroquois have no other design than to destroy all our allies, one after the other, in order afterwards to annihilate us; and in that consists all the policy of Mr. Dongan and his Traders, who have no other object than to post themselves at Niagara, to block us; but until now they have not dared to touch that string with the Iroquois, who dread and hate their domination more than ours, loving them not, in truth, except on account of their cheap bargains.

Mr. Dongan caresses considerably those deserters of ours whom he requires to execute his designs for the destruction and ruin of our trade by promoting his own. This wakes up our restless spirits, and obliges me to manage them, until I shall be in a position to treat them more severely. You will notice, My lord, by a letter of the Colonel's how desirous he is for something from the King which he says is due to him. He is a very selfish man, who would assuredly govern himself thereby if you thought proper; but the fact is he is not the master of those merchants from whom he draws money.

Father de Lamberville has returned with orders from me to assemble all the Iroquois nations next spring at Catarqui to have a talk about our affairs. I am persuaded that scarcely any will come, but my chief design is to draw [them] thither, (the Jesuit Father remaining alone for he must this year send back his younger brother,) in order that he may have less trouble in withdrawing himself. This poor Father knows, however, nothing of our designs. He is a man of talent, and who says himself that matters cannot remain in their present state. I am very sorry to see him exposed, but if I withdraw him this year the storm without doubt will burst sooner on us, for they would be sure of our plans by his retiring.

I have advices, notwithstanding, that the Five Nations are making a large war party, supposed to be against the Oumiamis and other savages of the Bay *des Puans* who were attacked this year, one of their villages having been destroyed by the Iroquois; on receiving notice thereof the hunters of those tribes pursued the Iroquois party whom they overtook and fought with considerable vigor, having recovered several prisoners and killed many of the Iroquois, who without doubt pant for revenge. I sent them word, to be on their guard and to have their women and children removed to a distance when they will be required to march to join me. I say nothing to you of what they have done to the Illinois whom they spare not, having since two years committed vast destruction on them.

Nothing more, My lord, is required to convince you that we cannot hesitate, and that the Colony must be put down as lost if war is not waged next year; they destroy on all sides our allies who are on the point of turning their backs on us if we do not declare for them. The Iroquois plunder our canoes wherever they find them, and no longer observe appearances. Nevertheless, My lord, in the deranged state of the Colony, war is the most dangerous thing in the world; nothing can save us but the troops you will send and the redoubts which it is necessary for us to build. Yet I dare not begin to work at these, for if I make the least movement for these Redoubts, I will assuredly draw all the Iroquois down on us, before I am in a condition to attack them.

The copy I transmit of the orders I have issued for our next year's expedition will advise you of all the measures I have adopted to ensure the success of our plans. The distance is terrible and success is in the hands of God. If you will be pleased, My lord, to take the trouble to read all these orders with the Map which I send, you will perceive all my projects. I have overrated a little the number of the force I shall have with me, in order to give a little more character to our expedition. I cannot draw more than eight hundred militia, one hundred of the best of whom will be required to manage the fifty canoes for convoys. These will do nothing else than come and go during our expedition to transport provisions for our troops and for those whom we shall station during the winter at the Post which we must occupy either at Niagara or near the Senecas, to serve as a retreat for those of our Indians who will be desirous to harrass them during the winter and the following year. Without this nothing effectual will have been done to humble this Nation, for to be satisfied in driving them from their villages and then to retire, is not accomplishing any great thing, as they immediately return and re-establish themselves in their Villages.

As you, My lord, are perfectly acquainted with the ruinous condition of this Colony, you understand very well the deplorable consequences of this war which require that the settlements be contracted, and it is here we must anticipate many difficulties; for in truth the establishment of the Colony would have to be almost begun over again, and this it is which causes me repeat the demand that I have already made for regular troops to support our *habitans*, and to occupy the posts necessary to be guarded, without which I cannot preserve many points very requisite to be protected; among others Chambly, where I should like to station a strong post, because it is the most important pass to reach the English by lake Champlain. That post will moreover always be a subject of uneasiness to the Indians who would incline to cross the River Richelieu thence to our settlements on the River St. Francis; in addition to which, communicating as it does with that of la Prairie de la Madelaine, would secure, in some sort, all the country from Sorel unto la Prairie de la Madelaine. Reflect again, My lord, if you please, how important is that post of Bout de l'Isle de Mont Real, that of Chateaugué, that of la Chesnaye and that of l'Isle Jesus.

I say nothing, My lord, of all the other settlements that are isolated and without communication, which we must endeavor to secure from insult. These details, My lord, require considerable troops, which could not fail to greatly advance this country by laboring to draw (*resserer*) the Colony closer together and make it more compact, by means of forts around which clearances would be made.

All this, My lord, is no trifling work to be prepared. For what certainty can there be of destroying so powerful an enemy as that Nation which has assuredly two thousand men under arms independent of a large number of other tribes their allies, estimated at twelve hundred? The vast extent of forest into which they will retreat and where Indians alone can pursue them; the uncertainty of the strength of the Indians which we shall have with us; the difficulty of rendezvousing so far off—all these considerations ought to make us reflect on the means of sustaining ourselves in case we should not meet that success we may desire, and which cannot come without a manifest interposition of Heaven for the success of projects so scattered.

It is very certain that were I in a position to be able to send a strong detachment to the Mohawk Country by the River Richelieu whilst I was proceeding against the Senecas, not only should I create considerable alarm among the English which would keep them at home, but I would obtain a great advantage over the Iroquois by separating and pillaging them and laying waste their corn fields at both ends of the Iroquois towns. It would be very desirable that I could destroy all the corn in the same year, so that the one could no longer support the other; this would reduce them to great wretchedness and would put a burthen on the English, if they sought a refuge there for means to live. Had I a sufficiency of troops I should not fail to undertake that enterprise, but having only what I have, I must attack one after the other, and endeavor to raise another army, which it is impossible to effect at first. 'Tis true, were all done at once it would be much better, and promote our expedition and dishearten our enemies considerably.

I am very sorry, My lord, to witness all the expense necessary for the support of Fort Cataracouy, merely with a garrison of fifty men. It is very unfortunate that the lands thereabout are not better, so that it might support itself. I am not yet sufficiently well informed of the environs to be able to write you with sufficient accuracy all that could be effected there; notwithstanding it is of great consequence to preserve that Post at the entrance to the Lake, though the posts in this Country do not command the passages so completely that the Savages cannot avoid them, two or three leagues either above or below. Yet that Post, and one at Niagara would render us entire masters, and keep the Iroquois in great check and respect, and give us immense advantages in our trade with the Illinois and Ottawas; that road being shorter, and much less difficult than the one we take, in which there is an infinitude of portages and rapids, much more dangerous than those on the Cataracouy side.

The letters I wrote to Sieurs du Lhu and de la Durantaye, of which I sent you copies, will inform you of my orders to them to fortify the two passes leading to Michilimaquina. Sieur du Lhu is at that of the Detroit of Lake Erie, and Sieur de la Durantaye at that of the portage of Toronto. These two Posts will block the passage against the English, if they undertake to go again to Michilimaquina, and will serve as retreat to the Savages our allies, either while hunting or marching against the Iroquois.

I send you again, My lord, copy of the orders I have issued for the assembling, marching and repairing of our Savage allies to Niagara with Sieurs du Lhu and de la Durantaye. You will, also, see, My lord, the orders I have issued for marching the Illinois in the rear of the Iroquois. It looks very well on paper, but the business is yet to be executed. Many difficulties may be encountered as well in regard to the nature of the Savages who are little accustomed to obedience and the prosecution of a design during several months, which are required to reach the rear of the Senecas from their country. Chevalier Tonty, who came to see me at Montreal in the month of July last, has taken charge of all these matters. I gave him twenty good Canadians, with eight canoes loaded with one hundred and fifty muskets, which was all I could collect in the country. He carries powder and lead and other things for the trade. Had the guns you sent me arrived I should have given him a good number. He left at the end of August and calculates to arrive at Fort St. Louis[1] before the departure of the hunters. He could not assure me of the number of Savages he could bring with him, but I'm certain he will make great exertions to succeed in this affair in which he will participate largely if the Indians will allow themselves to be governed and led by him. I cannot sufficiently praise his zeal for the success of this enterprize. He is a lad of great enterprize and boldness, who undertakes considerable. He left Fort des Illinois last February to seek after M. de la Salle at the lower end of the Mississippi. He has been as far as the sea, where he learned nothing of M. de la Salle except that some Savages had seen him set sail and go towards the South. He returned on the receipt of this intelligence to Fort St. Louis des Illinois, and thence to Montreal, where he arrived in the beginning of July with two Illinois Chiefs, to whom I had made some presents, and to another who had not come. They promised me wonders. Nothing remains but the execution which is in the hands of God, for according to what I'm told of the temper of these Savages, a mere nothing sometimes is only necessary to cause them to change their minds. He will have about twenty good Canadians with him to march at the head of the Indians, which he hopes will encourage them. He will have to walk three hundred leagues over land, for those Savages are not accustomed to canoes (*ne sont pas gens de Canot.*)

1 Now Peoria, Ill.

I should have greatly desired to shorten my letters to you. But, My lord, as it is necesssary to inform you of the state of our affairs and to render you an account of my conduct, I thought I would send you all the orders as I had issued them, so that I might be corrected if I fail in any respect, being very anxious to satisfy you.

I receive letters from the most distant quarters; from the head of the River Mississippi, from the head of Lake Superior, from Lake des Lenemyngon[1] where they propose wonders to me by establishing posts for the Missions and for the Beavers which abound there. But in truth so long as the interior of the Colony is not consolidated and secured, nothing certain can be expected from all those distant posts where hitherto people have lived in great disorder and in a manner to convert our best Canadians into banditti. All these distant posts cannot maintain themselves except from the interior of the Colony, and by a secure communication with them from here. Whilst we have the Iroquois on our hands, can we be certain of anything? Solicited by the English they daily plunder our canoes and openly declare they will continue (to do so) being unwilling that we should carry ammunition to the Savages, their enemies and our allies.

The principal affair at present is the security of this Colony which is in evident danger of perishing whether the Iroquois be let alone or we make war without having a decided advantage over them, and however decided ours may be, the people separated as they are will always be in danger. Yet My lord, if you aid us with troops, war will be the least inconvenience, for if we do not wage it, I do not believe that the next year will pass away without the whole trade being absolutely lost; the savages, our friends, would revolt against us, and place themselves at the mercy of the Iroquois, more powerful because better armed, than any of them. The whole of the Hurons are waiting only for the moment to do it. Had I not by the care of Father de Lamberville fortunately avoided the war this year, not a single canoe would have come down from the forests without having been captured and plundered in the river of the Outtawas. We should have lost a great number of good men.

This, My lord, is a long narrative about the state of the affairs of the country with the Iroquois which absolutely require that we wage war without longer delay. Every person sees its necessity so clearly that those concur in it now, who had been hitherto the most opposed to it. I hope that on the sketch I give you of our wants, you will aid us both in men and other necessaries. In regard to troops, My lord, I had the honor to ask you for Regulars, for in truth the employment of people picked up anywhere is very unwise. It requires time to make them fit for service and on their arrival they will have to take arms in their hands and drill. If you propose to send us some it would be well to have them arrive about the end of May which is the season when the North West winds prevail in our River. For that reason, the ships ought to leave Rochelle in the month of March. Sieur Dambour, one of our best ship captains that come to Canada, can give good advice thereupon.

Our march cannot begin before the fifteenth of May, for we must let the sowing be finished, and the storms before that time are furious on our river and Lake Ontario. I say nothing of the risks to be incurred that the harvest will not be saved next year on account of the war, nor of the necessity of making store-houses. By sending us troops, many things will be done of which we dare not dream if you do not send any.

A few days since a man named Antoine L'Epinart, an old resident among the Dutch, at present among the English, came to Ville Marie on the Island of Montreal in search of a child he had boarding with the Jesuits. He reports that the English kept watch three months this summer, our deserters having told them that I would attack them for having armed the Iroquois against us. He also says that the Iroquois are drawing to them the Loups (Mohegans) and other tribes toward the Andastes, with whom they are forming alliances; he believed the Iroquois had evil intentions

1 Most probably, Lake Aleminipigon of the old maps; now L. St. Ann, north of Lake Superior.

towards us—that the English who had been to the Outtawas had been well received and invited to return among them with merchandize, and well nigh procured from the Iroquois the restitution of their prisoners, by which means they will be more attached to them than to us; that the Merchants at Orange had urgently entreated Colonel Dongan to request the Senecas to surrender the prisoners; that the Colonel had convoked a meeting of the Five Nations who went together to see him; that it is the general belief that the Colonel will obtain satisfaction of the Iroquois and thus the English will attract to them both the Outtawas and the Hurons and that their cheap bargains will ruin our trade. The said Antonie L'Epinart assures moreover, that there is a company of fifty men formed to go to Missilimakina; that their canoes were purchased, and that the low state of the waters had prevented them starting; that they waited only the rising of the rivers by the rain; and that the Senecas promised to escort them.

I have heard that Sieur du Lhu is arrived at the post at Detroit of Lake Erié, with fifty good men well armed, with munitions of war and provisions and all other necessaries sufficient to guarantee them against the severe cold and to render them comfortable during the whole winter on the spot where they will entrench themselves. M. de la Durantaye is collecting people to entrench himself at Michilimaquina and to occupy the other pass which the English may take by Taronto, the other entrance to Lake Huron. In this way our Englishmen will find somebody to speak to.

All this cannot be accomplished without considerable expense, but still we must maintain our honor and our prosperity.

The Oumeamies and other savages of the Bay des Puans have expressed much joy to me on learning that Sieur du Lhu was posted at Detroit, but I am very sorry to hear that Tonty has learned on the road that these same savages had quarrelled with the Illinois, which would prevent the Illinois attacking the rear of the Senecas, as we had projected. It would, in truth be an afflicting circumstance to see our allies devouring one another instead of uniting with us to destroy the common enemy. But it is useless to be vexed at it. Nothing remains but to be prepared for everything that may happen, and rely only on ourselves. If God gives us the advantage, the people will rouse to our aid.

My lord ought to place no reliance on the changeable disposition of a people without discipline, or any sort of subordination. The King must be the master in this country to effect any sort of good, and success cannot be secured without expense.

THE M. DE DENONVILLE.

M. DE DENONVILLE TO THE MINISTER.

[From the same.]

Quebec, 16th Nov. 1686.

My Lord,—Since my letters were written a very intelligent man whom I sent to Manat, who had conversed and had much intercourse with Colonel Dongan, reports to me that the said Colonel has despatched fifty citizens of Orange and Manat among whom are some Frenchmen, to winter with the Senecas whence they will depart, at the close of the winter, under the escort of the Senecas, for Michilimaquina, carrying with them the Huron prisoners to restore them on the part of the English Governor, who is desirous to prevail on the Outaouas, by the service which he renders them, to abandon our alliance in order to attach themselves to the English. They carry an abundance of merchandize thither to furnish it at a much lower rate than we.

This is not all. Colonel Dongan has given orders that one hundred and fifty other English should depart, accompanied by several Mohegan Indians to follow the first fifty Englishmen with goods. But this detachment is not to leave until spring. I believe there is no room to doubt but the design is to seize the post of Niagara. Were the English once established there, they must be driven off or we must bid adieu to the whole trade of the country.

* * * * * * * * * * *

The same man who came from Manat told me that within a short time fifty or sixty men, Hugenots, arrived there from the Islands of St. Christophers and Martinique, who are establishing themselves at Manat and its environs. I know that some have arrived at Boston from France. There again, are people to operate as Banditti.

Whilst writing this, My lord, further advice is come from Orange that Colonel Dongan sent to tell the fifty men who are to winter among the Senecas, not to leave until the arrival at the Senecas of the one hundred and fifty men which he is to despatch in the spring to support them. The reason of this order is that he has learned by Indians that the Sieur Du Lhut is posted at the Detroit of Lake Erié. If those men commanded with the savages attack that post, you perceive, my lord, that I have nothing more to manage with the English. Send me, if you please, orders on this point, for my disposition is to go straight to Orange, drive them into their fort, and burn the whole.

* * * * * * * * * * *

The English governor prompted at present by the cupidity of the merchants and by his avarice to drag money from them, pretends that all the country is his, and will trade thither though an Englishman has never been there. He gives passes under pretext of hunting, to his creatures, from whom one was taken at Michilimaquina, which I would have sent, had he who was bringing it, not upset in the water and been thereby drowned.

* * * * * * * * * * *

Whilst writing this letter here, My lord, I receive from Father de Lamberville confirmation of the news which I had the honor to communicate to you respecting Colonel Dongan. I send you what he writes me of the speech made by the said Colonel to the Iroquois assembled by his order at Manat. Be so good as to read it yourself my lord.[1]

COL. DONGAN TO M. DE DENONVILLE.

[Par. Doc. III.; Lond. Doc. V.]

1 Decem. 1686.

Sir—I had the honour to receiue your letter of the first of October 1686 and had sooner sent an answer, butt that I wanted a convenient opportunity to do itt, I find you was angry at the writing and therefore for fear it was ill turned into French for I have no great skill in your language, have sent a copy of it in English. I desire you to continue in your opinion that nothing shall bee wanting on my part that may contribute to a good and friendly correspondence, and that I will not protect either merchant or others that shall give any just occasion to suspect it. Bee assured, Sir, that I have not solicited nor bribed the Indians to arme and make warr against you, all the paines I have taken hath bin to keep those people in quiet who are so inclineable to warr that one word is enough for them. I have forbidden their joining (if they should be entreated) with any others

1 See postea, "Susquehanna Papers," for an extract from this speech.

against you neither have I ever allowed any to plunder. I have only permitted severall of Albany to trade amongst the remotest Indians with strict orders not to meddle with any of your people, and I hope they will finde the same civility from you—It being so farr from pillageing that I beleeve it as lawful for the English as French nations to trade there we being nearer by many leagues than you are—I desire you to send me word who it was that pretended to have my orders for the Indians to plunder and fight you; that I am altogether as ignorant of any enterprise made by the Indians out of this Government as I am of what you meane by "mihilmiqum" and neither have I acted any thing contrary to what I have written, but will stricktly endeavour to immitate the ammity and friendship between our masters—I have desired you to send for the deserters, I know not who they are but had rather such Rascalls and Bankrouts as you call them were amongst their own countrymen than this people, and will when you send word who they are, expell, not detain them and use all possible means to preuent your good wishes and hopes that our merchants may suffer by them—Tis true I ordered our Indians if they should meet with any of your people or ours on this side of the lake without a passe from you or me, that they should bring them to Albany and that as I thought by your own desire expressed in your letter, they being as you have very well remarked very ill people and such that usually tell lyes as well to Christians as Heathens, The Missionary Fathers, if they please but do me justice can give you an account how careful I have bin to preserve them, I have ordered our Indians strictly not to exercise any cruelty or insolence against them and have written to the King my master who hath as much zeal as any prince living to propagate the Christian faith and assure him how necessary it is to send hither some Fathers to preach the Gospell to the natives allyed to us and care would be then taken to dissuade them from their drunken debouches though certainly our Rum does as little hurt as your Brandy and in the opinion of Christians is much more wholesome: however to keep the Indians temperate and sober is a very good and Christian performance but to prohibit them all strong liquors seems a little hard and very turkish—What I wrote concerning what was due to me for my service in France was very true, Monsr Charnell, the Intendant at Nancy, adjusted and sent them to Monsr Lenoy signed by himself and me and I gave the copies of them to Monsr Pagaion living in the street of St Hon^e^ to putt them into the hands of Monsr Carillon Chaplaine to the Duchesse of Orleans, but, Sir, you need not to trouble yourself about itt for I intend to get it represented out of England and doubt not but the King your master who is so bountiful a prince will be so just as to pay what became my due by a great deal of fatigue and labour, however I humbly thank you for the civill obliging offers you make and doe assure you shall bee heartily glad of any occasion to requite them desiring you to believe I earnestly wish and contend for the union (you say) you desire and will contribute all in my power to promote and preserve it which is all the reflection I shall make on your letter being—

Sir, assuredly with all due respect your most humble

and affectionate

servant—T. DONGAN.

MEMOIR FOR THE MARQUIS OF SEIGNELAY,

REGARDING THE DANGERS THAT THREATEN CANADA, THE MEANS OF REMEDYING THEM, AND OF FIRMLY ESTABLISHING RELIGION, COMMERCE AND THE KING'S POWER IN NORTH AMERICA. JANUARY, 1687.

[Paris Doc. III.]

Canada is encompassed by many powerful English Colonies who labour incessantly to ruin it, by exciting all our savages, and drawing them away with their peltries for which the English give them a great deal more merchandize than the French, because they pay no duty to the King of England. This profit attracts towards the English, also, all our Bush rangers (*Coureurs de bois,*) and French libertines who carry their peltries to them, deserting our Colony and establishing themselves in those of the English who take great pains to attract them.

They advantageously employ those French deserters to bring the far savages to them who formerly brought their peltries into our Colony which wholly destroys its trade.

The English began by the most powerful and best disciplined [Indians] of all America. They have excited them entirely against us by the avowed protection they afford them, and the manifest usurpation they claim to the sovereignty of their country, which belongs beyond contradiction to the King for nearly a century without the English having up to this present time had any pretension to it.

They also employ the Iroquois to incite all our other Indians against us. They set them last year to attack the Hurons and the Outawas, our most ancient subjects; swept by surprise from them more than 75 prisoners among whom were some of their principal Chiefs, killed several others, and finally offered them peace and the restitution of their prisoners, if they would quit the French and acknowledge the English.

They sent the same Iroquois to attack the Illinois and the Miamis our allies who are in the neighborhood of Fort St. Louis, built by Monsr de la Salle on the Illinois River which empties into the River Colbert or Mississippi; massacred and burnt a great number of them and carried off many prisoners with threats of entire extermination if they would not unite with them against the French.

Colonel Dongan, Governor of New-York, has pushed this usurpation to the point of sending Englishmen to take possession, in the King of England's name, of the post of Mislimakinac which is a Strait communicating between lake Huron and lake des Illinois, and has even declared that all those lakes including the river St. Lawrence which serves as an outlet to them and on which our Colony is settled, belong to the English.

The Reverend Father Lamberville, a French Jesuit who has been 18 years a Missionary among the Iroquois in company with one of his brothers also a Jesuit, wrote on the first of November to Chevalier de Callieres, Governor of Montreal, who informed the Governor General that Colonel Dongan has assembled the Five Iroquois Nations at Manatte where he resides and declared to them as follows:

1. That he forbids them to go to Cataracouy or Fort Frontenac and to have any more intercourse with the French.

2. That he orders them to restore the prisoners they took from the Hurons and Outawacs, in order to attract them to himself.

3. That he sends thirty English to take possession of Missilimakinak and the lakes, rivers and adjoining lands and orders the Iroquois to escort them and to afford them physical assistance.

4. That he has sent to recall the Iroquois Christians belonging to the Mohawk tribe, who have ettled a long time ago at Saut St. Louis, adjoining the Island of Montreal, where they have been

established by us and converted by the care of our Reverend Jesuit Fathers, and that he would give them other land and an English Jesuit, to govern them.

5. That he wishes that they should have Missionaries only from him throughout the whole of the Five Iroquois Nations, and that they cause our French Jesuits to withdraw, who have been so long established there.

6. That if Monsieur de Denonville attacks them, he will have to do with him.

7. That he orders them to plunder all the French who will visit them; to bind them and bring them to him, and what they'll take from them shall be good prize.

The Iroquois.—He accompanied his orders with presents to the Five Iroquois Nations, and he despatched his thirty English, escorted by Iroquois, to make an establishment at Missilimakinak.

The Iroquois pillage our Frenchmen every where they meet them, and threaten to fire their settlements which are much exposed and unfortified.

These measures, and the discredit we are in among all the savages for having abandoned our allies in M. De la Barre's time, for having suffered them to be exterminated by the Iroquois and borne the insults of the latter, render war against them absolutely necessary to avert from us a General Rebellion of the Savages which would bring ruin on our trade and finally the extirpation of our Colony.

It is likewise necessary for the establishment of Religion which will never spread itself there, except by the destruction of the Iroquois; so that on the success of the war which the Governor-General of Canada proposes to commence against the Iroquois on the 15th of May next, depends either the Ruin of the Country and of Religion if he be not assisted, or the Establishment of Religion, Commerce and the King's Power over all North America if he be granted the aid he demands.

If the merit in the eyes of God, the Glory and utility which the King will derive from this succor be considered, it is easy to conclude that expense was never better employed since, independent of the Salvation of the quantity of Souls in that vast country to which His Majesty will contribute by establishing the Faith there, he will secure to himself an Empire of more than a thousand leagues in extent, from the mouth of the River Saint Lawrence to that of the River Mississippi in the Gulf of Mexico; a country discovered by the French alone, to which all other nations have no right, and from which we shall eventually derive great Commercial advantages, and a considerable augmentation of His Majesty's Revenues in those countries.

The Marquis de Denonville, whose zeal, industry, and capacity admit of no addition, requires a reinforcement of 1500 men to succeed in his enterprize. If less be granted him success is doubtful and a war is made to drag along, the continuation of which for many years will cost his Majesty more to sustain than would the immediate expense necessary to guaranty its success and prompt termination.

It is necessary to attack the Iroquois in two directions. The first and principal attack, through the Seneca Nation on the borders of Lake Ontario; the second, by the River Richelieu and Lake Champlain on the side of the Mohawk Nation. 3000 Frenchmen will be required for that purpose. Of those there are sixteen companies which make 800 men and 800 selected from the *habitans*, 100 of the best of which the Governor General destines to conduct 50 canoes which will go and come incessantly to convey provisions. Of these 3000 Frenchmen, of which he has only the half though he boasts of more for reputation's sake, because the other *habitans* are necessary to protect and cultivate the farms of the Colony, a part must be employed in guarding the posts of Fort Frontenac, Niagara, Toronto, Missilimackinak so as to secure the aid he expects from the Illinois and other Saviges, on whom however he cannot rely unless he will be able alone to defeat the Five Iroquois Nations.

The Iroquois force consists of two thousand picked warriors (*d'elite*) brave, active, more skilful in the use of the gun than our Europeans and all well armed; besides twelve hundred Mohegans

(*Loups*), another tribe in alliance with them as brave as they, not including the English who will supply them with officers to lead them, and to fortify them in their villages.

If they be not attacked all at once at the two points indicated, it is impossible to destroy them or to drive them from their retreat, but if encompassed on both sides, all their plantations of Indian corn will be destroyed, their villages burnt, their women, their children and old men captured and other warriors driven into the woods where they will be pursued and annihilated by the other savages.

After having defeated and dispersed them the winter must be spent in fortifying the post of Niagara, the most important in America, by means of which all the other nations will be shut out from the lakes whence all the peltries are obtained; it will be necessary to winter troops at this post and at others, to prevent the Iroquois returning and reëstablishing themselves there, and to people these beautiful countries with other savages who will have served under us during this war.

EXTRACT FROM A MEMOIR OF THE KING

TO SIEURS MARQUIS DE DENONVILLE AND DE CHAMPIGNY, DATED VERSAILLES, 30th MARCH, 1687.

[Paris Doc. III.]

* * * * * * * * * * *

His Majesty has no knowledge of the claim of Colonel D'Unguent for 25m lbs which he pretends to be due him in France; therefore he has nothing to say about it.

* * * * * * * * * * *

His Majesty has seen the Memoir that the said Sieur de Denonville has sent of the measures he has adopted and the orders he has given for the ensuing campaign. He approves of them and doubts not of success, and that it will be as favorable as can be expected having to do only with Savages who have no experience as to regular war, whilst, on the contrary, those he will be able to collect, being led by a man so capable and so experienced as he is, will be of great utility.

Finally, He expects to learn at the close of this year, the entire destruction of the greatest part of those Savages. And as a number of prisoners may be made, and His Majesty thinks he can make use of them in his Galleys, He desires him to manage so as to retain them until he have vessels for France; by the return of His Majesty's Ships which will convey the troops he can, even, send those which will have been captured before the departure of these ships.

COLL. DONGAN TO FATHER DE LAMBERVILLE.

[Lond. Doc. V.]

20 May. 1687,

Reverend Father—I have received yours of the tenth currant from the Onnondages and am heartily glad that you are in good health and as much as lyes in me you may bee assured I will do all my endeavors to protect you from the danger you apprehend from those people and all those others of your fraternity that continue in doing good service, I am sorry that our Indians are soe troublesome to the Indians of Canada but I am informed from Christians that it is the custom of those people, that what country they conquer belongs to them as their own, yet I lay no stress on that, but I am still in doubt whither that land where the Indians goes to warr belongs to our King or to the King of France, but in all probability if I bee truly informed it must depend on the King of England territories it lying west and by south of this place and your countryes lyes to the northward of us but that is no material reason for the Indians to disturbe the people of Canada and I will use my endeavour that they shall disturbe them no more but leave the decision of that to my master at home as I leave all other things which relates to any difference between us and the people of Canada and I am sure that Mon[sr] de Noville will do the same—

I have not spoke to the Indians as yet. Your messenger being in hast cannot give an account what they can say for themselves, but to continue a right understanding between the Government of Canada and this if any of the Indians will doe any thing to disturb the King of France's subjects, let the Governour sent to me and I will doe all the justice that is possible for me to do and if he will do the same it will be a meane to keep those people in, and to see both Governments in a good correspondence one with another. But I hear they pretend that they are affraid of the French but I hope that Mons[r] de Nonville will well weigh the business before he invades any of the King of England's subjects—I have no time to write to him at present but assure him of my humble service and that I will write to him before I goe, haveing no other businesse here in sending for the Indians but to check them for offering to disturbe the people of Canada

Reverend Father

I am your humble servant

(Signed) THO: DONGAN

I pray you to pray to God for me

M. DE DENONVILLE TO THE MINISTER.

[Paris Doc. III.]

8 June 1687.

I am informed that the English have given notice to the Senecas that I am going to attack them, and have obliged them to run after six hundred men of their tribe who were at war against the Miamis, our allies, to induce them to return to defend their country against us. Other war parties who had gone against the people towards Virginia have also returned through the same troubles. The consternation of our enemies thus costs Colonel Dongan very dear. I have learned that a party has come from Virginia who brought a dozen prisoners, Englishmen, whom they will also burn, and this is a matter about which Monsieur Dongan gives himself scarce any trouble.

COLL. DONGAN TO M. DENONVILLE.

[Lond. Doc. 5.]

11th June 1687.

Sir—The enclosed[1] came to my hands last night from England with orders to have it proclaimed which has accordingly bin done, what is there agreed upon I will observe to the least title and I doubt not but your Excell: will do the same and I hope bee so kinde as not desire or seek any correspondence with our Indians of this side of the Great Lake if they doe amisse to any of your Goverm^{t} and you make it known to me you shall have all justice done and if any of your people disturbe us I will have the same recourse to you for satisfaction as for those further Nations, I suppose that to trade with them is free and common to us all until the meets and bounds bee adjusted though truly the scituation of those partes bespeakes the King of England to have a greater right to them than the French King, they lying to the southward of us just on the back of other partes of our King's dominions and a very great way from you. I am informed by some of our Indians that your Excell: was pleased to desire them to meet you at Cadaraque; I could hardly believe it till I had a letter from Father Lamberville, wherein he informs me that 'tis true, I am also informed of your Fathers' endeavors dayly to carry away our Indians to Canada as you have already done a great many, you must pardon me if I tell you that that is not the right way to keepe faire correspondence—I have also been informed that you are told I have given to Indians orders to rob the French wherever they could meet them, that is as false as tis true that God is in heaven, what I have done was by your own desire which was that I should suffer none of Canada to come to Albany without they had your passe in complyance wherewith I ordered, both, the Indians and people of Albany that if they found any French or English on this side of the great Lake without either your passe or mine, they should seize them and bring them to Albany: I am now sorry that I did it since its not agreeable to you and has as I am informed hindered the comeing of a great many Beauers to this place—I shall therefore recall the orders. I am daily expecting Religious men from England which I intend to put amongst those five nations. I desire you would order Monsr de Lamberuille that soe long as he stays amongst those people he would meddle only with the affairs belonging to his function and that those of our Indians that are turned Catholiques and live in Canada may content themselves with their being alone without endeavouring to debauch others after them, if they do and I can catch any of them I shall handle them very severely. S^{r} setting aside the trust my master has reposed in me I should be as ready and willing to serve Monsr de Nonuille as any friend he has, I could wish with all my heart the wildernesse betwixt us were not soe great but that there were conveniences whereby we might see one another often, for I have as much respect for all the people of quality of your nation especially such as have serued in the armies as any man in the world can have: as for newes, the ships lately come from England say all things are at peace both there and in France and that both our Masters are in very good health and that the Emperour and the King of Poland are very vigorous against the Turques—

I am sir

Your most humble servant

(Signed) THO. DONGAN

S^{r} I send you some Oranges hearing they are a rarity in your partes, and would send more, but the bearer wants conueniency of Carriage—

1 Treaty of Neutrality.

FROM A PAPER SUPPOSED TO HAVE BEEN WRITTEN BY M. DE CALLIERES, DATED QUEBEC, 16 JULY, 1687.

[Paris Doc. III.]

I yesterday received a letter from M. de Denonville from Cataracouy of the 3rd of this month, informing me that he sends me fifty Iroquois taken near that place, to forward them to France in the King's Ships, conformably to his orders. I'll take advantage of the delay of the *Fourgon*, in which I shall have them embarked, and as the crew is too few to convey so many prisoners, very difficult to be guarded, I reinforce them by some passengers and sailors from a merchantman, the Catharine, which was wrecked last autumn near Tadoussac, and could not be got off.

M. DE DENONVILLE TO THE MINISTER.

ATTACK ON THE SENECAS; ERECTION OF FORT NIAGARA.

[Paris Doc. III.]

Ville Marie, 25 August, 1687.

The first thing with which I occupied myself on my arrival [at Irondequoit Bay] was to select a post easily to be fortified for securing our batteaux to the number of 200 and as many canoes. We cut 2000 palisades which we finished planting in the forenoon of the 12th of July.

I had brought with me Sieur d'Orvilliers as the fittest to receive the whole of Canada into his hands; for the loss of this post would be the assured loss of the whole country which obliged me to leave 440 men there.

On the 12th I departed at three o'clock in the evening with all our French and Indian allies and Christians having caused them to take 15 days provisions. We made only three leagues that day across the woods which are very open.

On the 13th about four o'clock in the afternoon, having passed through two dangerous defiles, we arrived at the third where we were vigorously attacked by 800 Senecas, 200 of whom fired, wishing to attack our rear whilst the remainder of their force would attack our front, but the resistance they met produced such a great consternation that they soon resolved to fly. All our troops were so overpowered by the extreme heat and the long journey we had made that we were obliged to bivouac on the field until the morrow. We witnessed the painful sight of the usual cruelties of the savages who cut the dead into quarters, as in slaughter houses, in order to put them into the pot; the greater number were opened while still warm that their blood might be drank. Our rascally Otaous distinguished themselves particularly by these barbarities and by their poltroonery, for they withdrew from the combat; the Hurons of Michilimaquina did very well, but our Christian Indians surpassed all and performed deeds of valour, especially our Iroquois of whom we durst not make sure having to fight against their relatives. The Illinois performed their duty well. We had five or six men killed on the spot, French and Indians, and about twenty wounded, among the first of whom was the Rev: Fath: Angleran, superintendent of the Otaous missions, by a very severe gunshot. It is a great misfortune to us that this wound will prevent him going back again, for he is a man of capacity, of great influence who has conducted everything at Michilimaquina well, and to whom the country owes vast obligations. For had it not been for him the Iroquois had been long since established at Michilimaquina.

We learned from some prisoners who had escaped from the Senecas that this action had cost them 45 men killed on the field, 25 of whom we had seen at the shambles; the others were seen buried by this deserter, and over 60 very severely wounded.

On the next day, 14th July, we marched to one of the large villages where we encamped. We found it burned and a fort quite nigh, abandoned; it was very advantageously situated on a hill.

I deemed it our best policy to employ ourselves laying waste the Indian corn which was in vast abundance in the fields, rather than follow a flying enemy to a distance and excite our troops to catch only some straggling fugitives.

We learned from deserters that the Senecas had gone to the English where they will not be allowed to want for anything necessary to make war on us. Since that time I have had no news of the enemy.

We remained at the four Seneca villages until the 24th; the two larger distant 4 leagues, and the others two. All that time was spent in destroying the corn which was in such great abundance that the loss, including old corn which was in *cache* which we burnt and that which was standing, was computed according to the estimate afterwards made, at 400 thousand minots of Indian corn.[1] These four villages must exceed 14 to 15 thousand souls. There was a vast quantity of hogs which were killed; a great many both of our Indians and French were attacked with a general rheum which put every one out of humor.

'Tis an unfortunate trade, my lord, to command savages who, after the first broken head ask only to return home carrying with them the scalp which they lift off like a leather cap. You cannot conceive the trouble I had to detain them until the corn was cut.

During the whole time we were in the Seneca country we did not see a single enemy, which caused me divers alarms lest they had been at our batteaux, but terror and consternation deterred them too much from effecting their first threats.

Returning to our batteaux I should have greatly wished to have been able to visit other villages, but the sickness, the extreme fatigue among all and the uneasiness of the savages who began to disband, determined me to proceed to Niagara to erect a fort there in their presence, and point out to them a sure asylum to encourage them to come this winter to war in small bodies.

I selected the angle of the Lake on the Seneca side of the river; it is the most beautiful, the most pleasing and the most advantageous site that is on the whole of this Lake, the Map and plan of which you will have if Sieur de Ville marie will take the trouble, for I tormented him considerably for it; I sent him expressly to Quebec that he may have nothing else to do.

This post being in a state of defence I left a hundred men there under the command of Sieur de Troyes who made the Northern expedition last year. He is a worthy fellow who richly deserves some share in the honour of your good graces and protection. He can be very useful to you in many things; he is prudent and intelligent, very willing, and has well served on land.

This post has caused much joy to all ou rfarther Indians, who having no place of retreat, scarcely dared to approach the enemy. They have made me great promises—especially our Illinois—to harass them this winter by a number of small parties.

M. de Tonty had returned with them designing to invite them to come. He could collect only very few savages because an alarm had been spread among them of a large body of Senecas having departed last fall on a war expedition against them, which fell through on the information Mr. Dongan gave the Senecas that I was about to attack them; yet, as this large force had marched six

1 A minot as equal to three bushels.

days, it was the cause that of six @ 700 savages on whom we relied, only 80 came, which was the reason of their having been obliged to come to the fort of Detroit to join Sieurs du L'hut and de la Durantaye not being able to take the Senecas in the rear.

On quitting Niagara I left M. de Vaudreuil there for a few days with the troops to cut fire wood, after having done what was necessary for lodgings. The inconvenience of this post is, that timber is at a distance from it. M. de Callières and I returned without delay with our *habitans* to issue the orders necessary for the interior of the Colony.

* * * * * * * * * * *

I have not yet told you, my lord, that the *habitans* who left the lower part of the Colony, will on their return to their homes, have made four hundred and sixty leagues from the 24 May to about the 17th or 18th of August. You will well conceive that, what with the two forts which it was necessary to build, the destruction of the enemy's corn and the thirty leagues of road we had, going and coming, to travel by land, they will not have been idle.

It was impossible for us to do any more than we accomplished, for provisions would have failed us had we made a longer delay. It is full 30 years that I have had the honour to serve, but I assure you, my lord, that I have seen nothing that comes near this in labour and fatigue.

* * * * * * * * * * *

You ordered me to send you the prisoners we took. You have perceived, my lord, it was impossible for us to make any among the Senecas, and even had we made any, we should have distributed them among the savages our allies and those who made the seizure in the neighbourhood of Fort Cataracouy who are themselves native Iroquois, but for the most part from villages north of Lake Ontario where there had been some fine and large which the Iroquois south of said Lake forced to join them; this began to swell their numbers and depopulate the northern border. It would be for our interest to repeople these villages because they would be more close allies, and under our control.

Among the prisoners there are some I cannot send you, being near relatives of our Christian Indians. Besides there are some of the Onnontagué village whom we must manage with a view to detach them from the Senecas, and to use them for purposes of negotiation if necessary. As I have not yet any news of the movements of the Iroquois, I should much like not to dispose of all these prisoners. Nevertheless, my lord, as you desire them, I shall content myself by retaining those only who will be of use to me and are guiltless of all the disorders of others. Yet, my lord, be so good as to keep them in a place from which they can be withdrawn, in case of need and we finally come to a general arrangement; I believe that would be a very useful thing. Regarding their women and children, I had them distributed through all our missions in the Colony. All the men, women and children had themselves baptised, testifying joy on that occasion. It remains to be seen if it be in good faith.

* * * * * * * * * * *

The copper of which I sent a sample to M. Arnou is found at the head (*au fond*) of Lake Superior. The body of the mine is not yet discovered. I have seen one of our voyageurs who assures me that he saw, 15 months ago, a lump 200 weight, as yellow as gold in a river which falls into Lake Superior. When heated, it is cut with an axe, but the superstitious Indians regarding this piece as a good Spirit would never permit him to take any of it.

ACTE OF THE TAKING POSSESSION OF THE COUNTRY OF THE IROQUOIS, CALLED SENECAS, 19 JULY 1687.

[Paris Doc. III.]

On the nineteenth of July, One thousand six hundred and eighty seven, the troops commanded by Messire Jacques René de Brisay Chevalier Signeur Marquis de Denonville and other places, Governor and Lieutenant General for the King throughout the whole of Canada and country of New France, in presence of Hector, Chevalier de Callière, Governor of Montreal in said country, Commandant of the camp under his orders, and of Philip de Rigaud, Chevalier de Vaudreuil, Commandant of the King's troops, which being drawn up in the order of battle, Charles Aubert Sieur de la Chenays citizen of Quebec, deputed by Messire Jean Bochart, Chevalier, Signeur de Champigny, Norvy, Verneuil and other places, Privy Councilor to the King, Intendant of Justice, Police and Finance, in all Northern France, presented himself at the head of the army, who stated and declared that on the requisition of the said Seigneur de Champigny, he took possession of the village of Totiakton, as he has done of the other three villages of Gannagaro, Gannondata and Gannongarae, and of a Fort half a league distant from the said village of Gannagaro, together with all the lands in their vicinity as many and how far soever they may extend, conquered in His Majesty's name, and to that end has planted in all the said Villages and Forts His said Majesty's Arms and has caused to be proclaimed in loud voice, *Vive le Roi*, after the said troops had beaten and routed eight hundred Iroquois Senecas, and laid waste, burnt and destroyed their provisions and cabins. Whereof and of what precedes, the said Sieur de la Chenays Aubert has required an Acte; granted to him by me Paul Dupuy Esq. Councilor of the King and his Attorney at the Provost's Court of Quebec: Done at the said Village of Totiakton, the largest of the Seneca Villages in presence of the Revd Father Vaillant, Jesuit, and of the Officers of the Troops and of the Militia Witnesses with me, the said King's Attorney undersigned, the day and year above mentioned, and have signed the Minute, Charles Aubert de la Chenays, J. René de Brisay Monsieur de Dénonville, Chevalier de Callière, Fleutelot de Romprey, de Desmeloizes, de Ramezay; Francois Vaillant of the Society of Jesus, de Grandville, de Longueil, Saint Paul and Dupuy.

TAKING POSSESSION OF NIAGARA BY MONSIEUR DE DENONVILLE.

[Paris Doc. III.]

Jacques René de Brissay Chevalier Seigneur Marquis de Denonville and other places, Governor and Lieutenant General for the King in the whole extent of Canada and Country of New France.

This day, the last of July of the year One Thousand Six hundred and Eighty seven, We declare to all whom it may concern, in presence of Hector, Chevalier de Gallières, Governor of Montreal in the said Country and Commandant of the Camp under our orders, and of Philippe Derigaud, Chevalier de Vaudreuil, Commanding the King's troops, being encamped with all the army at the post of Niagara, returning from our expedition against the Seneca villages, that being come to the camp of Niagara situate south of Lake Ontario west of the Senecas, twenty-five leagues above them, in the angle of land East of the mouth of the River of the same name which is the outlet of Lake

Erie, coming from Lakes Huron, Illinois, the Great Lake Superior and several others beyond the said Great Lake, to reiterate anew for, and in the name of the King, the taking Possession of the said Post of Niagara, several establishments having been formerly made there many years since by the King's order, and especially by Sieur De la Salle having spent several years two leagues above the Great Fall of Niagara where he had a Bark built which navigated several years Lakes Erie, Huron and Illinois, and of which the stocks (*les chantiers*) are still to be seen. MOREOVER the said Sieur De la Salle having erected quarters (*logemens*) with settlers at the said Niagara in the year one thousand six hundred and Sixty Eight which quarters were burned Twelve years ago by the Senecas, which is one of the causes of discontent that with many others have obliged us to wage war against them, and as we considered that the houses we have thought fit to rebuild could not remain secure during the war, did we not provide for them, WE have Resolved to construct a Fort there in which we have placed one hundred men of the King's troops to garrison the same under the command of Sieur de Troyes, one of the Veteran Captains of His Majesty's troops with a necessary number of Officers to command said soldiers.

This Acte has been executed in Our presence and in that of Monsieur Gaillard, Commissary on behalf of the King attached to the Army and subdelegate of Monsieur de Champigny, Intendant of Canada: which Acte We have signed with Our hand and sealed with Our Seal at Arms, and caused to be subscribed by Messrs de Callières and Vaudreuil and by Monsieur Gaillard and countersigned by Our Secretary. And they sign: J. RENÉ DE BRISSAY, Marquis de Denonville, le Chevalier de Callières, Chevalier de Vaudreuil, Gaillard; and lower down by Monseigneur Tophlin.

[From Council Min. V.]

ffort James Tuesday ye 19th July 1687. (O. S.)

Mr Brockholes Informed ye Council he is now come from Albany & Schenectadae with Instructions ffrom the Govern[r] to bring up with all convenient speed a Certain Number of Men & some Provisions.

The Instructions Read

Ordred that sixty men be raysed out of y[e] Citty & County of New York & sixty men out of Queens County that Warrants be forthwith made out to Major Willett to Raise the men in y[e] Queens County and to Coll. Bayard to raise y[e] men in y[e] Citty & County of New York. that an Expresse be Imēdiately sent to Major Willett with y[e] s[d] Warrant & that he & Coll. Bayard have their Complement of Men Well armed in ffort James on y[e] 22th Inst.

FROM MR. GRAHAM TO. MR. SPRAGG.

[London Doc. V.]

New York, 16 July 1687.

Sir—I am invited by your favours to give you by this occasion acknowledgments and also to acquainte you that Mr. Swinton departed this life the 3[d] currant, after that he had been violently seized with three fitts of an apoplexie. In the interval of his fitts he was very sencible but without apprehensions of death, however was prevailed with to make a will, by which has constituted Mr. Delavel his executor, his affairs are in great confusion and he judged to be indebted £300. besides what his engagements may be to you, his Excell: being at Albany. The Councill, sealed up the office in which state it now remains and will continue until His Excell's pleasure be known. Mr. Knight in the mean time does the service of the office. Last night I received a letter from his Excell: in which aduiseth that the French had assaulted the Senaquaes, and were worsted, report by other hands saying the French had 300 men killed, the certainty wants confirmation, however, its consequence is like to be very injurious to us, we having already very little trade, besides are likely to be ingaged in a bloody warr, whose events is uncertain, we are strangely surprised with the french proceedings, not knowing what moves them to invade his Majtys dominions, without giving notice, and so soon after the publication of the treaty af Commerce betwixt the two Crowns—*P* the next which will be Jacob Maurite His Excell: will give you a full account of his resolves, he having sent a messenger to the French which is not yet returned. Five days agoe, My Lord Effingham.... Sr Robert Parker arryved here from Virginia, he laments the Governours absence otherwise wer satisfied with his entertainments: all your friends are well, my wife kisseth your hands and joins with me in the request that you would give our duty to our Father, our service to Major Baxter, to whom please to excuse not writing, being strained with time, and accept of the assurance that I am

Sir

Your affectionate friend and most humble servant

JA GRAHAM.

INFORMATION GIVEN BY SEVERALL INDIANS TO THE GOVERNOR AT ALBANY, 6 AUG. 1687.

[Lond. Doc. V.]

The Govr of Canada last fall, sent word to the Sachems of all the Five Nations to come and speak with him at Cadarachqui this spring, which we acquainted His Excellency withall, but in pursuance to his Excellcys commands wee being the King of England subjects, thought ourselfs noways obliged to hearken to him, and therefore refused to go, and shortly after we heard by an Onondage Indian that had lived long at Cadarachqui, that the Govr of Canada had a design to warr upon us, for hee had seen a great deal of amunicion and iron Doubletts brought to Cadarachqui, and that a Frenchman at Cadarachqui told him, that they would warr with all the Five Nations, About ten days after wee got the news, that the Govr of Canada with his army was seen encampt att the side of the Lake with many Canoes about halfe way between Onnondage and Cadarachqui: upon which they sent a hundred men to the Lake side to spy; who see a Barke neer Irondequat the landing place a lyeing by and not at anker they sent four men in a Canoe to haile them, their orders from the Sachems being expressly not to doe the French any harme, and when they hailed them, the French answered in base language: Enustoganhorrio, squa, which is as much in their language as the Devil take you, whereupon they paddled for the shore, and told the rest of their companions, what answer they had, the hundred men went forthwith to the Castles, and told the Sachems, what they had seen who forthwith sent twenty men to spy what theire designe was, and they see another Barke come to the first, and while they were theire as scouts spied a great many of the Twichtwich Indians come by land, and had almost environed them before they were awarr of them: the twenty men seeing this, went up forthwith to the Castles and had much adoe to gett through, and the Sachems having sent out three Spyes, after the twenty, to see what the French would have, and before the three were come to the Lake side (it being about twenty miles from their Castles) the French Army out of Barks and Cannoes was landed, they seeing that, called to them and asked what they were intended to do, A Maquase answered out of the Army. You Blockheads, I'll tell you what I am come to doe, to warr upon you, and to morrow I will march up with my army to your Castles, and as soone as hee had spoke they fyred upon the three Ind[ns] butt they runn home and brought the news to the Sachems about the twilight, The Sachems upon this news concluded to convey their wives and children, and old men away, and beeing busy thereabouts all next day, most parte retiring to Cajouge, and the rest to a Lake to the Southward of there Castles in the meantime the French were as good as there words, and marched up halfe way between the landing place and the Castles and there encamped that night; As soon as the women and children were fled, their fired their own Castles and all the men being gon to convey them away except a hundred in a small Fort who had sent out Spyes and received information that the French were upon their march towards them. they sent forthwith messengers to them that were conveying the Women and Children and desired the assistance of as many of their young men as could conveniently bee spared to turn back and face the French and give battle: whereupon 350 turned back and joyned with the hundred, butt being all young men, were so eager to fall on, that the officers could not bring them in a posture to engage, they went out about halfe a league from the Castle, on a small hill, and there stayed for the French army, but the officers could not persuade them to be in order there neither, all being so fiery to engage, and having scoutts out, brought them intelligence, that they were approaching and how they marched, viz[t] the Right and left wing being Indians and the Body French, and when they came in sight of the Sennekes, the French not seeing them satt down to rest themselves and the Indians likewise; the Sennekes seeing this advance upon the left wing being Indians, the French seeing them stood to their arms and gave them first valley, and then the enemy Ind[ns] that were on the left wing; whereupon the Sennekes answered them with another, which occasioned soe much smoak that they could scarce see one another, wherefore they immediately runn in and came to hardy blows and putt the left wing to the flight, some went quite away and some fled to the reare of the French, and when that wing was broake, they charged and fyred upon the French and the other Indians. The French retired about 150 paces and stood still, the Sennekes continued the fight with their Hatchets, butt perceiving at last the French were too numerous and would not give ground, some of the sennekes begun to retreat, whereupon the French Indians cryed out, the Sinnekes run and the rest heareing that followed the first party that gave way and so gott off from another and in their retreat were followed about half an English mile, and if the Enemy had followed them further, the Sinnekes would have lost abundance of people because they carried off there wounded men and were resolved to stick to them, and not leave them.

The young Indian that was in the engagement relates that after the engagement was over, when the Sinnekes were gott upon a Hill, they see a party of Fresh French come up, the French called to them and bid them stand and fight, but the Sinnekes replyed, come out four hundred to our four hundred and wee have butt a hundred men and three hundred boyes, and wee will fight you hand to fist, The said Boy being asked, whether he see any of the French with Gorges about their necks, it was to hott, they were to numerous,

There was amongst the 450 Sinnekes five women, who engaged as well as the men, and were resolved not to leave their husbands but live and dye with them

A true copy examined p me

ROB[t] LIVINGSTON CL.

EXAMINATION OF INDIAN PRISONERS.

[Lond. Doc. V.]

31 August, 1687.

A few days after the French came and gave him all the Indians in the Christians Castle, each thirty bullets and a double handfull of powder, and bad them appeare att a French Gents house, neare Mont Royall: the Christian Indians being about one hundred and twenty or thirty strong, in meane time the French and other Nations of Indians all appeared at Mont Royall, and the second day after that the Govr himselfe; the number of the French being two thousand and of all the Indians one thousand. The army went all by water in about two hundred boates in each Boate some seaven and some ten menn, the rest went in Canoes, they were sometimes forced to draw the Boates with Cordes against the Trenches, the Provisions being part in the Boats and a great deal sent upp before at Kadraghke: they were going up from Mont Royall to Kadraghke three dayes, makeing verry short journeys; att Kadraghkie they rested three days from thence they went and lay att night upon an Island, the night after they lay at Cadranganhie next morning about nine the clock they saw ten Onnondages att Aranhage; the Govr gave orders not to meddle with them, upon that the Onnondages gave a greate shout and went their way, and the army went along the shore-side to a passage that goes to the Cayouges; the day following they saw a Brigantine at anker, and all the army went ashore and lay there that night. Some of the French went aboard the Brigantine where Arnout was, as this Examinant has heard; next day the army went along and att Jedandago, the Govr landed fifty men to discover the place and the rest went on to Ierondokat where at the same time they mett with the French that came from Twightwig and Dowaganha with their Indians, then the Govr ordered the Xtian Maquasse and some other Indians to bee putt in the middle of the army and stayed there three dayes till the Fort was finished, in the mean time four or five Indians came and asked what the matter was, and why the French came so strong in their Country, the French answered (by a Xtian Maquasse) wee come to meet you, the Sinnakes asked againe, and said, why doe you make a Fort, you should butt come on, for we intend to kill you all in a short time. The third day the army marched in the afternoon and came that night about half way between the Lake and Sinnakes Castle: next morning very early after prayers they marched on all the Indians being putt on the right side somewhat before the French, and we marched on till about noone, then the Indians would boyle their potts, but the Govr bid them march on, till they come upon a grate hill from whence the Govr sent three Dowaganhas to spye towards the Sinnakes Castle, who were out but a little time, and returning said that the Sinnakes were neare by and lay in the passage, upon which the Govr gave order that one hundred Indians should be chosen out and sent to discover the Sinnakes, who went but not farr before the army then the Govr sent out againe four Dowaganhas Indians and one Frenchman to discover, who went out, and stood in the path till the army came to them, and a little time after fouer hund^d Sinnakes appeared att the right side of the army, where the French Indians were and with greate cry or shout, fyred upon them without wounding one mann being too farr off, but the Sinnakes advancing came nearer by, and fyred againe, then the French Indians got some wounded, who fyred also upon the Sinnakes and wounded some of them, but the Sinnakes came so neare, and tooke an Indian out of the French army, and cutt off his hands, the rest firing stoutly upon one and the other, till the Douwaganhas and other French Indians fled without returning to the fight, but the Maquass came up againe and stood their ground till the whole body of the French, came firing all at once upon the Sinnakes, soe that the Sinnakes retreated, having got some dead and wounded in that firing; the Govr forbidd following of them having gott seven Frenchmen killed and many wounded and five dead Indians and several wounded; of the Sinnakes were killed sixteene and some wounded; forthwith the Govr gave orders that the army should fortify themselves at the same place where the Battle was and so stood there all that night. Next morning the whole army marched towards the Sinnakes Castle called Kohoseraghe, leaving their dead Frenchmen unburried but the Indians burried their dead, and carried all the wounded French and Indians with them to the aforesaid Castle, where one of the wounded men died at said Castle; they found itt all burned, then the Govr gave orders that the Christian Indians should cutt downe and destroy the Indians corne, which they refused: soe Frenchmen were sent and destroyed all that they could find. Afterwards the Govr sent four hundred men to another small castle neare by, to surround the same till the whole army should come, thinking the Sinnakes might be there, but found the same burned also, butt found a great deale of provisions which they destroyed, takeing only some beanes along with them, for they had provisions enough, every man carried some and the Boates were loaded at Jerondekott with corne and other necessaries, soe the army went to every place where the Castles were burnt and lay att every Castle one night destroying all the corne they could finde except some out fields, which the Xtian Indians would not show them, The Sinnekes made severall times small allarms, butt never attacked the French, since the first fight. From the last Sinnekes Castle, called Theodehacto, the army went back againe, by another way, as they came to Jerondekatt, being butt one night by the way, and were butt two dayes still there, then the Govr gave orders that the whole army should goe directly to Oneageragh but the Xtian Indians refused itt butt would returne to Kadaradkie, and soe went that way, the Govr forthwith followed them with seven Canoes, each seven menn, and stopt them saying, what is the matter that you leave us, itt is better that wee goe and returne together; but they would not, till one Smiths John stood up and spoke very loud, saying to the rest of the Xtian Indians, you hear what the Govr's will is, that wee should goe up with him, if wee doe not, he will force us to it; come, you are lusty men let us goe with him, soe they were persuaded, and returned back with the Govr, severall Canoes endeavoured yett to escape, butt were soe watched by the French, that they could not except two or three Canoes that stole away: soe were forced to goe with the French along the shore side of the Lake till they came to Oneagorah being two days by the way, where the French made a Fort and putt two great gunns and several Pattareras in it with four hundred men to bee there in Garrison, After they had been there five dayes, the rest of the army returned to Cadarachque and slept there one night, and left there some men, from whence they went to Mont Royall in two dayes, there this deponent left the Govr and the Christian Indians went to their Castles.

[From Council Min. V.]

Councill held at ffort James

Thurs day ye 18th of Aug^s. 1687. (O. S.)

Present His Excel^cy the Gover^r &c.

The account of the Expense that has been about the Seneckas & the ffrench, Read

Resolved that it be taken into Consideration that the Councill Do tomorrow give their oppions about a Method for Raising it,

Councill held at ffort James.

ffriday ye 19th Augst 1687

The Councill give their opions about Raising money to Defray ye expense about ye Indyans & ye ffrench.

Resolved that a penny in ye pound besides the former tax of a halfepenny in ye pound be raised out of ye Estates of the ffreholdrs Inhabitants of Kings County queens County Dukes County Dutchess County Countys of Richmond Orange Suffolk & Westchester & one halfepenny in ye pound out of ye Estates of ye Inhabitants & ffreeholdrs of ye Cittys & Countys of New York and Albany & County of Vlster and the mony be brought in to ye Kings Collector at ye Custome house on or before ye first day of May next.

Ordered that two bills be Drawn up for the same Accordingly

Councill held at ffort James.

Saturday August ye 20th 1687

The Bill for Raiseing a penny in ye pound out of ye Estates of ye ffreeholdrs & Inhabitants of ye Kings Queens Dukes & Dutcheses Countys the Countys of Richmond Orange westchester & Suffolk, Read and approved Passed and Signed by ye Governr & Councill

---

MR. SCHUYLER TO GOV. DONGAN.

[London Doc. V.]

2 Sept. 1687.

May it please your Excellency

Last night Anthy Lesjinard & Jean Rosi arrived here from Canada, have been twenty days upon the way, have letters from [for?] your Excell: have therefore dispatched Anthoy with 2 Indians down, his compagnion being sick, could not goe—

The news your Excell: will hear of Antho. neverthelesse have thought fitt to examine his compagnion, who is an honest man, tells us these following news, of which your Excell: may discourse Antho about at large—

1 That he heard of father Valiant that the French will not release our people, Except that your Excell: will promise not to supply the Sinnokes with ammunition or any other assistance—

2 That Antho told him he heard one of the Fathers say, if the Sinnekes got any of there people prisoners would exchange our people for them, man for man.

3 That they had now a great advantage of your Excell: and of the Indians also, having so many of our people and of the Indians prisoners—

4 He heard the Jesuits say that Cryn and the rest of the Christian Indians, were no ways inclined to engage in the war if the Maquas, Oneydes and Onnondages were concern'd, because their brethren sisters, uncles ants ettc were there; and therefore all means was used to engage said three nations to sit still, for he see 5 Onnondae Christian Indians dispatched with belts and presents to the Onnondages 26 days agoe, to persuade them not to warr—

5 The French were not minded to warr with any of the Indians, except the Sinnekes, and would make a peace with them also if they would deliver to them 10 or 12 of the best Sachims children for hostage and then they would appoint them places where they should hunt: and so gett them wholly to their disposition—

6 The Governour of Canida sent for all the Bosslopers that were at Ottowawa and ordered them to come only with their arms and meet him at Cadarachqua which they did, being about 300 men under the command of three French Captns and left their Bevers in the Jesuits house at Dionondade, and so marched with the Governour of Canida to the Sinnekes, in the mean time a fortunate fyer

takes the house and burns them all to the number of 20,000 Bevers, when the news came to Mon-Royal the Bosslopers were like to go distracted—

7 He heard by beat of Drumm proclaimed throu Mon Royall that as soon as the peace was made with the Sinnekes the Ottowawa trade should be farm'd out, which displeased the Bosslopers much and said, that if that was done they were all ruined—

8 Many of the Bosslopers were inclined to come here not being minded to fight against the Sinnekes, but dare not come for fear of the Indians by the way—

9 Itt was generally beleev'd that the Sinnekes would come to Canida and begg for peace, because there corn was destroyed, and if they were supplyed by them of Albany they would come hither in the winter and plunder this place, having 1500 pare of snow shoes ready made, and if they found that we gave the Sinnakes any the least assistance, they would not let the Childe in the cradle live—

10 He heard further of a Merchant that if we would supply the Sinnekes they would send our people away all severall ways, some to Spain, some to Portugall some to the Islands, and it was no more than the English had done to Monsr Pere whom they kept 18 months in close prison at London.

11 The French all acknowledge the Sinnekes fought very well, and if their number had been greater it would have gone hard with the French for the new men were not used to the Sinnekes hoop and hollow. all the officers falling down closse upon the ground, for the Officers jeared on another about it att Mont Royall—

This is what Jean Rosie Antho Lespinard's compagnion doth relate being an inhabitant of this towne, and a verry honest man, although a frenchman, they were kept 5 weeks in arrest after they came to Canida upon a pretence that there passe was false, for could not beleive your Excellcy was here butt gone home haveing such advice from the French ambassadour he prays your Excell: would consider the pains and trouble and the loss of time that has been att waiting for an answer from the French Governour; we have put down these articles that your Excell: may examine Antho about them (since he knows nothing of this) because he was extream familiar with the Governr and all there great men there: We have the news of Keman that the Indians have taken 8 men 1 woman and 8 crownes or scalpes, and kild neer upon 20 more at the place where the Barks are, the particulars your Excell: will have in R Levingstone's letter—We find that the selling of strong Liquor to the Indians is a great hindrance to all designs they take in hand. lay a drinking continually at Skinechtady, if your Excell: would be pleased to prohibit itt for two or three months would do very well: We remain

Your Excellency
most humble and most
obedient servant

Pr SCHUYLER.

COLL. DONGAN TO THE LORD PRESIDENT.

[London Doc. V.]

Sept. 8 1687

My Lord—I gave your Lodp an acct in my last letter that I had Intelligence the French were come on this side of the Lake, to make war with the Sennekes

I send the Bearer Judge Palmer to give his Maty an account of their Invading his territories without any manner of Provocation if your Lodp will please to read his Instructions you will find a true accompt of their Proceedings

The Senekas desired assistance of men but I put them off by giving them powder, lead, arms, and other things, fitting & necessary for them & also by making such Propositions as I thought would please them being unwilling actually to ingage the French until I knew his Maty's pleasure.

I must needs say of ye French without being partiall that they are very unjust, to enter the King's territories in a hostile manner after the offers I made them.

I know their Pretence will be, that our Indians have wronged them, but it is not soe, for the Beaver trade is the sole end of their Designs, whatever Colour they give to their actions which is only hindered by the Five Nations of Indians on this side of the Lake who have submitted themselves & their lands to the King's subjection. Those Five Nations are very brave & the awe & Dread of all ye Indians in these Parts of America, and are a better defence to us, than if they were so many Christians.

The claim the French can make, to the father Indians, or any on this side ye Lake is no other than what they may have to Japan which is that some of their Priests have resided amongst them.

Peace or Warr, it will be very necessary to send over men & to build those Forts, I have mentioned in my Instructions to Judge Palmer, for the French are encroaching as fast as they can, and a little thing can prevent now what will cost a great expense of Blood & money hereafter. My Lord there are people enough in Ireland who had pretences to Estates there & are no advantage to the country & may live here very happy. I do not doubt if his Maty think fitt to employ my Nephew he will bring over as many as the King will find convenient to send who will be no charge to his Maty after they are landed, Provided all Connecticut & East & West Jersey be added to this Government & to add anything of Connecticut to Boston is the most unproportionable thing in the world they having already a hundred times more Land, Riches & People than this province & yet the charge of this Governm^t^ more than that.

GOVERNOR DONGAN'S INSTRUCTIONS TO CAPT. PALMER.

[Lond. Doc. V.]

8th Sept. 1687.

You are to inform his Maty that in May last I had letters from Albany & Informacons of Indians that came from Canada, That the Governor of Canada went from Monte Royall with a great many French and Indyans in Boats and Canno's towards Cadaraque with an Intention to come on this side of the lake & war against the Sennekes upon Receipt of which I called the Council & the letters & Information were read upon which the Councill thought convenient to give what assistance possibly we could to our Indians, and to that intent I, Major Brockhells yourself & other gentlemen went up to Albany where there was from time to time such orders and Instructions sent & given to the Indians as was thought fitt for their security.

The French Pretence for Coming into the King's Territories & warring with our Indians is that they war with the further nation of Indians who lye on the back of Maryland, Virginia, & Carolina, which is only a feigned pretence for that I have sent sev^ll^ Letters to Monsr La Bar who was Governor of Canada to signify that if our Indians had done them any injury they should make them all reasonable satisfaction, but that would not satisfy, for he came to Cayonhage where the Indians would have me build a Fort & there made a Peace with the Indians so that what the

Indians had done before this Gov[t] came was concluded and agreed thereby tho they had not done any thing to the French but what was in Pursuance of his own orders.

And as to their Warring with the farther Indyans that is more hurtfull to us than the French they being inclined to trade with us rather than them which by their Warring is hindered & in my opinion the Christians ought not to meddle with the Indians warring one with another it being the ruin of themselves. And as for this present Governor of Canada Mons. de Nonville he has no ground for what he does, for I have from time to time offered to do him Justice for any ill the Indians should committ and sent a messenger this spring to him for that purpose; to take away all pretence whatsoever & also sent him word that those five nations on our side of the lake had delivered themselves & their Lands under the subjection of our King & that I had caused the King's arms to be sett upon all their Castles.

But their reason for this Warr is that the Indyans would not submitt & joyn themselves to the French who have used all other meanes to effect it & those failing have caused this attempt so that we find they have a further design which is by the Ruin of those Indians to engross both the trade & Country wholly to themselves, and to that intent the French King has sent over upwards of 3000 men besides what came this last spring and alsoe has built a Fort at a place called Shamblee and another at Monte Royall and another at Trois Riviers one at Catarque at the other side of the Lake and this spring an other on our side of the Lake at a place called Onyegra where I had thought to have built one it being the place where all our Traders & Beaver Hunters must pass.

So that they are resolved to Ruin all those Indians & if they compass their design it will be of very ill consequence to all his Mat[ys] subjects in those parts of America for they are a better Bullwark against the French and the other Indians than so many Christians, & if the French have all that they pretend to have discovered of these Parts, the King of England will not have 100 miles from the sea any where, for the people of Canada are poor & live only on the Beaver & Peltry and the King's subjects here living plentifully have not regarded making discoveries into the country until of late being encouraged by me one Roseboon had leave in the year 1685 to go with some young men as farr as the Ottawawe & Twiswicks, where they were well rec[d] & invited to come every year, and they desired that the Sinnekas being their enemies would open a path for them that they might come to Albany.

But a little after their being there a party of our Indians being out attacked a Castle of theirs, took 5 or 600 prisoners and brought them away to their own country, which when I heard of I ordered the Indians to deliver to Roseboom & to one Major McGregory a Scots gent[n] (who went with 60 of the young men of Albany, and some of Albany Indians a Beaver trading to those further nations) as many of those prisoners as were willing to return home, the Gov[r] of Canada hearing of their going that way sent 200 French & 3 or 400 Indians to intercept them, has taken them Prisoners taken their goods from them & what they further design to do with them is not yet known.

And for this Government which is too poor of itself to help our Indians without adding Connecticut & East & West Jersey in case the war continues without the assistance of our Neighbors & some men out of Europe will be wholly impossible, for we are the least government & the poorest & yet are at the greatest charges & we find this year that the Revenue is very much diminished for in other years we are used to Ship off for England 35 or 40,000 Beavers besides Peltry & this year only 9,000 and some hundreds peltry in all.

The Council to show their readiness to serve the King have passed two acts for raising 1[d] p[r] lb at New York, Isopus & Albany, these three places being the only support of the Government & $1\frac{1}{2}$[d] on Long Island & the rest of the Government who do not advance the King's Revenue neither by Excise nor Customs 150[lb] P ann:

To secure the Beaver and Peltry Trade & the Kings right to the Country: It's mine and the Councils opinion (alsoe to have an awe over our Indians & make them firm to us) to build a Fort at

Corlars Lake; to secure us that way from the Incursion of either French, or Indians, another at Cayonhage upon the great Lake, and another at Onyegra & two or three little other Forts between Schonectade & the Lake to secure our people going & coming

This cannot possibly be done without 4 or 500 men out of Europe, & in case Connecticut & the two Jerseys be added to this Government, with some help from Pennsylvania, & the three lower Countys it may be effected without any charge to the King, and will be a great security to all these parts of America

If the metes & bounds could be adjusted at home it would be very convenient, provided always that the Country were first well discovered by us in which the French at present have much the advantage. And it is very unreasonable that the French who lye so much to the Northward of us sh[d] extend themselves soe far to the Southward & Westward on the Backside of his Maty[s] Plantacōns when they have so vast a quantity of land Lying Directly behind y[e] dominions they now possess, to the Northward & Northwest as far as the South sea

Whether Peace or War it is necessary that the Forts should be built, & that religious men live amongst the Indians.

I have that influence over our Indians, that I am sure they will not war on any Indians living amongst His Maty[s] subjects.

The monies that are now to be raised is for defraying the charge of Arms, Powder, Lead & other presents given to the Indians this summer as also to make some preparations against the Spring in Case of Necessity.

Whatsoever is his Maty[s] pleasure I desire that My Lord Sunderland, will by the first conveniency either by the way of Maryland, Virginia or Boston let me know and send me orders, how I shall proceed in this affair,

You are so well acquainted with all that has passed in this Government, concerning this affair with the French, and my constant Endeavors to preserve a good correspondence with them, that what I have here omitted I desire you will take care to inform his Maty.

Thos Dongan

Dated the 8th
September 1687

M. DE DENONVILLE TO GOV. DONGAN.

[Paris Doc. III.; Lond. Doc. V.]

August 22, 1687.

Sir—The respect I entertain for the King your Master and the orders I have from the King to live in harmony with His Britannic Majesty's Subjects induce me, Sir, to address you this letter on the present state of affairs, so as not to have any thing to reproach myself with.

On seeing, Sir, the letter you were at the trouble to write me on my arrival in this government I persuaded myself by your frank discourse that we should live in the greatest harmony and best understanding in the world, but the event has well proved that your intentions did not at all accord with your fine words.

You recollect, Sir, that you positively asked me in that same letter to refer the difference about boundaries to the decision of our Masters; letters more recently received from you fully convince me that you received that which I wrote you in reply to your first to shew you that I willingly left that decision to our Masters. Nevertheless, Sir, whilst you were expressing these civilities to me you were giving orders and sending passes to despatch canoes to trade at Missilimaquina where an Englishman had never set his foot and where we, the French, are established more than 60 years. I shall say nothing of the tricks and intrigues resorted to by your people and by your orders to induce all the Savage tribes domiciled with the French to revolt against us. I tell you nothing, either, of all your intrigues to engage the Iroquois to declare war against us. Your Traders at Orange have made noise enough about it, and your presents of munitions of war made, with this view, last year and this, are convictions sufficiently conclusive not to entertain a doubt of it, even were there not proofs at hand of your wicked designs against the subjects of the King whose bread you have eaten long enough and by whom you have been sufficiently well entertained to cause you to have more regard for His Majesty, though you had not all the orders from his Brittannic Majesty that you have to live well with all the subjects of the King, his antient friend.

What have you not done, Sir, to prevent the Senecas surrendering to me the Outaouas and Huron prisoners of Missillimaquina whom they treacherously captured last year, and how many going and comings have there not been to the Senecas on your part and that of your traders who do nothing but by your orders, to prevent the restitution of the said prisoners who were solicited at the village of the Onontagues to give me satisfaction.

I avow to you, Sir, that I should never have expected such proceedings on your part, which without doubt will not please the King your Master, who will never approve your so strenuously opposing by threats of chastisement the Iroquois coming to me, when I invited them to visit me to arrange with them the causes of discontent that I had on account of their violences. Three years ago, Sir, you made use of them to wage war against the French and their allies, you took great pains to give them, for that purpose, more lead, powder and arms than they asked. You did more, Sir; for you promised them reinforcements of men to sustain them against the King's subjects; quite recently, Sir, you would have again pushed your ill will further by sending two Parties, commanded by men carrying your orders, to Missilimaquina to expel us from there and put you into possession, contrary to the word you have given not to undertake anything before the arrangement of their Majesties, our Masters.

You have, Sir, still surpassed all that; for after the pains you had taken to prevent the Iroquois assembling at Catarocouy where I expected to meet them to settle all our differences and receive from them the satisfaction they should have afforded me, as well in regard to the Huron and Outaouas prisoners they would have given up to me had you not opposed it, as for the pillagings and robberies that they have committed on us, and all the insults they daily offer our missionaries, as well those they may have actually among them as those they have expelled after an infinite amount of ill treatment during 20 years they lived in their villages; after you, Sir, having, I say, so little regard for the interests of the King's subjects and the good of Religion whose progress you thus prevent, you have, Sir, quite recently contravened the last treaty entered into between our masters, a copy of which you have received with orders to observe it, and of which you have also sent me copy. Read it well, Sir, if you please, and you will there remark how strongly their Majesties have it at heart to preserve their subjects in good union and understanding, so that their Majesties understand that the enemies of one are the enemies of the other. If the avarice of your merchants influenced you less than the desire to execute the orders of the King your master, doubtless, Sir, I should already have had proofs of your good disposition to execute the said treaty, according to which you ought not to afford either refuge or protection to the savages, enemies of the French Colony, much less assist them with ammunition to wage war against it. Nevertheless, I assert positively that you have, since the publication of said treaty of neutrality, contravened it in this particular, since nothing is done in your government save by your orders.

After that, judge, Sir, what just grounds I have to complain of, and be on my guard against, you.

On my return from the campaign which I had just made against the Senecas, I received the letter that you took the trouble to write me, Sir, on the 11th (20th) June of this year. You send me copy of the Treaty of Neutrality entered into between our masters of which I also transmitted you a copy as I had recd it from the King and it was published in this country. Nothing more is required therein, Sir, than to have it fully and literally executed as well on your part as on mine. To do that you must discontinue protecting the enemies of the Colony and cease to receive them among you, and to furnish them with munitions as you have done. You must, also, observe the promise you gave me at the time of my arrival, that you would leave the decision of the limits to our masters. You must, likewise, not undertake any expedition against us in any of our establishments, the greatest portions of which were before Orange (Albany) was what it is, or any of Manate were acquainted with the Iroquois and the Ouatouas.

When you arrived at your present government, did you not find, Sir, in the whole of the five Iroquois villages, all our Missionaries sent by the King almost the entire of whom the heretic merchants have caused to be expelled even in your time, which is not honorable to your government. It is only three years since the greater number have been forced to leave; the fathers Lambreville alone bore up against the insults and ill treatment they received through the solicitations of your traders. Is it not true, Sir, that you panted only to induce them to abandon their mission? You recollect, Sir, that you took the trouble to send under a guise of duty so late as last year to solicit them by urgent discourses to retire under the pretext that I wished to declare war against the village of the Onnontagués. What certainty had you of it, Sir, if it were not your charge and prohibitions you had given them, against giving me up the prisoners I demanded of them, and they surrendered to me? You foresaw the war I would make because you wished me to make it against them and because you obliged me to wage that against the Senecas. In this way, Sir, it is very easy to foresee what occurs.

I admire, Sir, the passage of your last letter of the 11th June of this year in which you state that the King of England your Master has juster title than the King to the Posts we occupy, and the foundation of your reasoning is that they are situate to the South of you, just on the border of one portion of your dominion (*domination.*) In refutation of your sorry reasonings, Sir, it is only necessary to tell you that you are very badly acquainted with the Map of the country and know less the points of the compass where those Posts are relative to the situation of Menade, (New York.) It is only necessary to ask you again what length of time we occupy those Posts and who discovered them—You or we? Again, who is in possession of them? After that, read the 5th article of the treaty of Neutrality and you will see, if you were justified in giving orders to establish your trade by force of arms at Missilimaquina. As I send you a copy of your letter with the answer to each article, I need not repeat here what is embraced in that answer. Suffice it to say this in conclusion, that I retain your officer Mr. Gregory here and all your orders for your pretended expedition, who were taken within the Posts occupied by the King. My first design was to send them back to you but as I know that you entertain and give aid and comfort to the Iroquois Savages contrary to the Treaty of Neutrality of the 16th Novr 1686 agreed to by our Masters, causing them to be supplied with all munitions necessary to wage war against us, I have determined, in spite of myself, to retain all your people until you have complied with the Intentions of the King your Master and executed said Treaty, being obliged to regard you as the King's enemy whilst you entertain his enemies and contravene the treaties entered into between the King of England and the King my Master.

All that I can tell you for certain, Sir, is, that your conduct will be the rule of mine, and that it will remain with yourself that the said Treaty be thoroughly executed. I must obey my Master and

I have much respect and veneration for one of the greatest Kings in the world, the protector of the Church. You pretend that the Iroquois are under your dominion. To this I in no wise agree, but it is a question on which our Masters will determine. But whether they be or be not, from the moment that they are our enemies you ought to be opposed to them and be their enemies, and if you comfort them, directly or indirectly, I must regard you as an enemy of the Colony and I shall be justified in subjecting the prisoners I have belonging to your government to the same treatment that the enemies of the Colony will observe towards us.

Hereupon, Sir, I will expect news from you as well as the fitting assurances you will please give me that I may be certain you do not employ the Iroquois to wage war on us by giving them protection.

Rely on me Sir. Let us attach ourselves closely to the execution of our Masters' intentions; let us seek after their example to promote Religion and serve it; let us live in good understanding according to their desires. I repeat the protest, Sir, it remains only with you. But do not imagine that I am a man to suffer others to play me tricks.

I send you back Antoine Lespinard, bearer of your passport and letter. I shall await your final resolution on the restitution of your prisoners whom I wish much to give up to you, on condition that you execute the treaty of Neutrality in all its extent and that you furnish me with proper guarantees therefor.

Your very humble & very obt Servt

THE M. DE DENONVILLE.

[From Council Min. V.]

Council held at ffort James,

Monday the ffifth of September 1687.

Present His Excelcy the Governr &c

Proposed that Some Course may be taken about Major McGregorie & his Company who are prisoners in Cannada.

Resolved that a lettr be sent by a ffitt person to ye Governor of Cannada about that and the othr injurys he has done his Majties subjects of this government

Councill held at ffort James,

Wednesday, ye Seaventh day of Septemb. 1681.

Present His Excelcy the Governr &c

It being now plaine that ye ffrench are Resolved to Do all the Prejudice they can to the Kings Subjects of this Government It is for ye preventon thereof

Ordred that ye people of ye City and County of Albany Do Cutt Pallasadoes and by ye five and twentienth day of March naxt Cart them to ye sd Citty and ye towne of Schanechtade to fortifye those places in ye Spring That in ye meantime they Keep a careful Watch there and that this ordr be sent to ye Justices of ye Peace of ye sd County who are to take Care that it Be put in Execution.

That ye Mayor of Albany send ordrs to ye North Indyans to Keep thirty or forty Indyans allways towards Corlaers lake. That the sd Mayor if he be in Albany send a belt of Wampum to Each of the five Nations with ordrs that ye Christian Indyans who Come from Caunada to them be sent Hithr to his Ex^{y} ye Govern^{r} and to encourage ye Indyans to look out Carefully letting them Know the Govern^{r} will be up early there ye next Spring

Ordered that a Proclamacôn be Drawn up Prohibiting ye Bringing any Indyan Corne or Pease Out of ye Countys of Albany and Vlster until further Ord^{rs}

Ordered that Peiter Schuyler take examinacôns of ye antientest traders In Albany how many yeares Agon they or any others first traded with ye Indyans y^{t} had the Straws or Pipes thro' their noses and the ffarther Indyans.

GOV. DONGAN TO M. DE DENONVILLE.

[Par. Doc. III.; Lond. Doc. V.]

8th Sept. 1687.

Sir—Yours of the 21st of August last I have received and am sorry that Monsr de Nonville has so soon forgot the orders he had received from his master to live well with the King of England's subjects. but I find the air of Canada has strange effects on all the Governour's boddys, for I no sooner came into this province than Monsr de la Barr desired my assistance to warr against the Sinnekes, upon which I went to Albany and sent for the fiue nacôns to come to me, and when they came was very angry with them for offering to doe any thing to the French that might disturb their hunting, or otherwise, on which they answered me that they had not don anything to the French, but what Monsr de la Barr ordered them, which was that if they mett with any French hunting without his passe to take what they had from them, notwithstanding if any of their people which were abroad had don any injury they knew not of, they assured me they would give satisfaction. I send him word of all this, and assured him satisffaction, butt notwithstanding, he comes in a hostile manner on this side of the lake to a place called Kayonhaga, and there by the means of the Onnondages made a peace with the Sinnekes, sô if they have committed any fault before that, it was all concluded there, but I appeal to any rational man whatever whether it was fitt for any Govern^{r} of Canada to treate or make any peace with his Majesty's subjects withont the advice and knowledge of the Governour of the Province they lived under, butt I find the designe to ruine those five nations (Since you cannot with bribes or other means gain them to be of your party), is of a longer date than three or foure yeares. since Monsr Denonuille follows the same steps his predecessors trod in, tho' he proposed to himselfe so fair a beginning, I am sure he will not make so good an end for no sooner was Monsr Denonuille in possession of his government butt he began to build a great many boates and cannoes, and putt a great deal of provisions and stores in the Cataraque at which our Indians on this side of the lake were much alarmed and came to me, to know the meaneing of itt. upon which I sent to you by the way of Mons^{s} Lamberville to know what you intended by all these preparations, your answer was, as Monsr Denonville may remember that the winters being long, and you resolving to have a good number of men at Cataraque, you accordingly made provision for them, and if I had not really believed what you writt to be be true I might have bin in as much readinesse to have gone on the other side of the lake as Monsr de Nonuille was to come on this. Now sir, I will not answer your hayty way of expressions in your own stile butt will plainly let you know the matter of fact as it is; if S^{r} you [will] please to peruse those letters I from time to time sent you, you will find that I still couetted nothing more than to preserue that friendshipp which is between our masters, and aught to be between their subjects here, and as you well remarke, is according to their commands, and pray, Sir, which is itt of us both that hath taken the way to unty that knott of friendshipp—Mons[r] de Nonuille invadeing the King of England's territorys, in a hostill manner, (though his reception has not been according to his expectation) is soe plaine a matter of fact that it is undenayable whether you did it designedly, to make a misunderstanding or noe, I cannot tell, if you did I hope itt will take noe effect but that our masters at home notwithstanding all your trained souldiers and greate officers come from Europe will suffer us poor planters and farmers, his Majesties subjects in these parts of America, to do ourselves justice on you for the injuryes and spoyle you have committed on them, and I assure you Sir if my master gives leave I will be as soon [with you] at Quebeck as you shall be att Albany. as for Major M[c]Gregorie and those others you took prisoners they had no passe from me to go to Missillimaquine butt a pass to go to the Ottowawas, where I thought it might be as free for us to trade as for you, and as for giving them any commission or instructions to disturb your people I assure you do me wrong, and if you please to read his instructions you will find there I give express orders to the contrary and for your pretences to sixty yeares possession, 'tis impossible for they and the Indians who wear pipes thro' their noses, traded with Albany long before the French settled att Montreall, butt in case it weare as you alledge, which I have not the least reason to believe, you could only have prohibited their trading in that place and let them goe to some other nation—

It is verry true I offered you to leave the decision to our masters at home, in case of any difference, and pray Sir lett me know in what I in the least have acted to the contrary; you tell me I hindered the five nations on this side the lake, who have subjected themselues, their countrys, and conquests under the King of England to go to you at Cattaraque: Itts very true I did so and thought itt very unjust in you to desire their comeing to you—for the King of England did not send me here to suffer you, to give laws to his subjects of this Government—you also alleage that I have given orders to those Indians to pillage and warr upon your people—sure Sir, you forget what you desired of me; if you will please to reflect on one of your owne letters, in which you acquainted me, that many of your people run away into this Government, and desired that I would take and send back any should be found upon this side the lake without your passe, upon which I ordered those of Albany and also the Indians, to seize and secure all persons whatever, as well french as English, they should finde on this side of the lake without your pass or mine—truly Sir, I ought severely to be rebukt for this, itt having been the hindrance of many thousands of beavers comeing to Albany: further you blame me for hindring the Sinakees deliuering up the Ottawawa prisoners to you, this I did with good reason—for what pretence could you have to make your applications to them and not to me, neverthelesse I ordered Major M[c]Gregory to carry them to the Otttawaways and if your claim be only to Missilimaquina what cause had you to hinder Magregory to go to the Ottawawas—

What you allege concerning my assisting the Sinnakees with arms, and amunition to warr against you, was neuer giuen by me until the sixt of August last, when understanding of your unjust proceedings in invadeing the King, My Masters territorys, in a hostill manner I then gave them powder lead and armes; and united the five nations together to defend that part of our King's dominions from your injurious invasion. And as for offering them men in, that you doe me wrong, our men being all biusy then att their haruest, and I leave itt to your judgment whether there was any occasion when only foure hundred of them engaged with your whole army.—You tell me in case I assist the Indyans you will esteme me an enemy to your colony—Sir, give me leave to lett you know, you are a farr greater enemy to your Colony than I am, itt haueing always been my endeavour to keepe those Indyans from warring with you, who in your protecting their enemys that have killed and Robbed them in their hunting and otherwise, and that not once but several times have given them great provocations, butt you have taken away to spill a great deale of Christian blood without gaining the point you aim att, and for you who have taken the King's subjects prisoners, in a time of peace and taken their goods from them without any just grounds for so doing, how can I expect but that you will use them as you threaten; You say also in your letter, that the King of England has no right to the five nations on this side of the lake. I would willingly know if so, whose subjects they are in your opinion, You tell me of your haveing had Missionaryes among them, it is a very charitable act, but I suppose and am very well assured that gives no just right or title to the Government of the Country—Father Bryare writes to a Gent: there that the King of China never goes any where without two Jessuits with him: I wonder why you make not the like pretence to that kingdome: you also say you had many Missionaryes among them att my comeing to this Government, in that you have been missinformed for I never heard of any, but the two Lamberuills who were at Onondages, and were protected by me from the Insolencys of the Indians, as they desired of me, and as by letters in which they gave me thanks appears, but when they understood your intentions they thought fit to goe without takeing leave: butt their sending there was as I afterwards found, for some other end than propagating the Christian Religion as was apparent by some letters of theirs directed to Canada, which happened to come to my hands—

Now you have mist of your unjust pretensions—you are willing to refer all things to our Masters, I will endevor to protect his Majesty's subjects here from your unjust invasions until I hear from the King my master who is the greatest and most glorious monarch that ever sat on a throne and would do as much to propagate the Chistain faith as any Prince that liues and is as tender of wronging the subjects of any Potentate whatever, as he is of suffering his owne to be injured—

Itt is very true that I have eat a great deale of the bread of France and have in requittal complyed with my obligations in doing what I ought and would prefer the service of the French king before any, except my owne, and have a great deal of respect for all the people of quality, of your nation which engages me to aduise Mons[r] Denonuille to send home all the Christians and Indians prisoners the King of England's subjects you unjustly do deteine, this I thought fitt to answer to your reflecting and provoking letter.

a true coppy.

GOV. DONGAN TO THE LORD PRESIDENT.

[Lond. Doc. V.]

New York Sept. 12. 1687.

My Lord—Since writing my other Letter some messages have come to my hands from Albany of their apprehensions of the French, which obliges me to carry up thither two hundred men, besides the Garrison & go and stay there this winter, and to get together five or six hundred of the five nations about Albany & Schonectade which will be a great charge but I see no remedy for it.

My Lord it is a great misfortune for this Governm[t] that there are so few of his Mat[ys] natural born subjects, the greater part being Dutch, who if occasion were, I fear would not be very fitt for service. I am sending to the further Indians to try if I can make a Peace between them & the Sennekes and also to the Christian Indians about Canada who have a mind to come I will do what is possible for me to save the Government against the French til I have further orders from your Lodp Judge Palmer has more papers to show your Lodp that came from Albany, by those he carries with him your Lodp may perceive the grounds I have for my proceedings

I am your Lodps most obed[t]

and Humble Serv[t]

THO DONGAN

[Council Min. V.]

Councill Held at ffort James;

ffriday the Ninth of Septembr 1687.

Present His Excy the Governor &c.

Informacon being given to his Excy and some of the Members of ye Board that ye ffrench at Canada are providing fifteen hundred pair of Snowshews,

Ordered that ye Mayor and Magistrates of Albany send orders to the five Nations to bring Down their Wives Children and old men least ye ffrench come uppon them in the Winter and none to stay in the Castles but ye young men. That they who come be settled some at Cats Kill Levingstons land and along ye River where they can find Conveniency to be neer us to assist them if they should want and that they send Downe with them all ye Indian Corne that can be spared by ye Young Men who are to stay in ye Castles.

Councill held at ffort James.

Sonday, the 11th of Septembr, 1687.

Present his Excy the Governr &c.

Letters from Albany giveing account that the people there are in great Consternation thro apprehension that ye ffrench will come down uppon them this Winter.

Resolved that every tenth man of all ye Militia troups & Companys within the Province Except those that were out ye last yeare a whaling be drawn out to go up thither.

M. DE DENONVILLE TO GOV. DONGAN.

[Paris Doc. III.; Lond. Doc. V.]

Kebec, 2 Octob. 1687.

Sir—On arriving in this town I recd a letter from the King copy of which I send, so that you may see, Sir, how much His Majesty has at heart that we should live on good terms. This has induced me to await your reply to the letters I had the honour to write you by Antoine Lespinard regarding the complaints I made to you of the infraction yourself and your officers at Orange have committed and continue to commit of the Treaty of Peace and Union entered into between the Kings, our Masters.

Though I have quite recently again cause to complain of you and your officers since you have a short time since hired a party of sixty Mohawks to come and make a foray in the country of New France, which is a truth so well known that it cannot be doubted, yet, Sir, in conformity with my Master's orders and in response to the intentions of His Majesty whose will I follow, directing me to do all in my power to contribute to the union that our Masters desire should exist between us, I have determined to send you back Mr. Gregory and all those whom you despatched under his orders, being very happy to evince to you thereby the desire I have to live well with you and to avoid every subject of quarrel, which will be very easy if you wish to remain within the rules prescribed by our Masters. . . . .

As it is very necessary to the maintenance of good correspondence between us according to our

Masters' intentions, that I be informed of your last resolutions; in order to afford you an opportunity to communicate with me I retain here only those named Captain Loquerman, the son of Arian, Abraham Squelar (Schuyler) and Jean Blaquer whom I shall take care will want for nothing until I have replies from you to justify me in not doubting that we shall live hereafter in union and good understanding.

[Council Min. V.]

Councill held at ffort James;

tuesday the 13th day of March 168$\frac{7}{8}$.

Present the Members of the Council.

Major Baxter now come ffrom Albany Informing that he is Instructed by His Excelcy The Governour to propose to this board that they Consider what y^{e} amount of the Extraordinary Charge of the Expedicôn ag^{t} y^{e} ffrench will be this year and what will be ye best & easyest means for defraying It in pursuance whereof Computacôn being made the Charge of the new Raised forces with ye Incidentall Charges thereon Is Computed to bee about Eight thousand Pound and finding ye last tax of one penny halfe penny per pound will not amount to above Twelve hundred pound of which many of the Inhabitants are not able to pay their own proportion, it is the opinion of this board that this Goverment alone is no way able to bear so great a burden, Whereuppon It is Resolved that a lett^{r} be sent to his Excelcy proposeing this Board's Opinion that It will be Convenient proposalls be sent to the Neighbouring Collonyes to send Commissiones thither to treat and make some settlement for defraying the Charges of the said Expedition as will be Esteemed most Easy and Convenient.

Council Held at ffort James;

Monday the thirtyeth day of Aprill 1688.

Present His Excellcy the Govern^{r} &c.

Account of Disbursements made by Robert Levingston at Albany by His Excelcy^{s} Ord^{rs} ffor ye Maintenance of his Majties fforces there and for sundry Guefts & p^{r}sents made to ye Indyans and Releife of ye ffrench Prisoners, ffrom ye 11th August 1687 to ye first day of June 1688 amounting to Two thousand sixty seaven pound six shillings and four pence read.

Council held at ffort James

Monday ye third day of May 1688.

Present His Excelcy the Govern^{r} &c.

Resolved upon Debate had thereof that the taxes lately made will not Raise money sufficient to bear ye p'sent necessary Charge of the Govern^{t} and that a new Levy of £2556. 4s. be made to be paid by all the Inhabitants and ffreeholders in ye Province in money to his Maj^{ties} Collector at ye Custome house in New York before ye first day of Novemb^{r} next in manner following vizt

	s d
The City & County of New Yorke to pay	£434 : 10 : 00
County of Westchester	185 : 15 : 00
Citty and County of Albany	240 : 00 : 00
County of Richmond	185 : 15 : 00

	£ : s : d
County of Ulster	408 : 00 : 00
Kings County	308 : 08 : 00
Queens County	308 : 08 : 00
County of Suffolk	434 : 10 : 00
Dukes County	040 : 00 : 00
County of Orange	010 : 00 : 00

. Ordered that ye Attorney Generall Draw upp an Act for ye s^d^ tax accordingly.

An establishment to be Allowed to the Officers and Soldiers who hath been att Albany upon the present Expedicón vizt

The Major ten Shillings Curr^tt^ Money of this Province

	Per Diem		Per Diem
The Captn of horse	£0.10.0	The Capt off ffoott	£0.8.0
The Liev^t^ d^o^	0. 7.0	The Liev^t^	0.4.0
The Cornett	0. 6.0	The Ensigne	0.3.0
The Quartermaster	0. 5.0	The Sergeant	0.1.6
The Corporall	0. 2.0	The Corporall	0.1.0
The Trumpiter	0. 2.0	The Drumbeater	0.1.0
The Troopers	0. 1.6	The rest of the private men	0.0.8

[Lond. Doc. IX.]

In the year 1687 when the French at Canada were making preparations to attack the Five Nations of Indians belonging to New York, Coll. Dongan then Govr there sent some of the forces of the Countrey to Albany, & went himselfe to sustain the Indians against the French, towards the charges of wch Expedition a Country Rate and other taxes were laid by the Gov^t^ and Councill in New York amounting to £3813.6.4 whereof Peter (Livingston) alledges £1129.3.6 to remain yet unpaid in the severall Countyes.—*Statement of Mr. Livingston's Case, &c. Sept.* 1695.

CONDITION IN WHICH FORT NIAGARA WAS LEFT IN 1688.

[Paris Doc. IV.]

On the fifteenth day of September of the Year One thousand, Six hundred and Eighty and Eight, in the forenoon, Sieur Desbergères Captain of one of the companies of the Detachment of the Marine, Commandant of Fort Niagara having assembled all the officers, the Rev : Fath^r^ Millet of the Society of Jesus Missionary, and others, to communicate to them the orders he received from the Marquis de Denonville Governor and Lieutenant General for the King in the whole extent of New France and Country of Canada, dated the 6th of July of the present year, wherein he is ordered to demolish the fortification of the said Fort, with the exception of the cabins and quarters, which will be found standing (*en nature*) ; We, Chevalier de La Motthe, Lieutenant of a detached company of the Marine, and Major of said Fort, have made a Proces Verbal, by order of said Commandant, containing a memorandum of the condition in which we leave said quarters which will remain entire, to maintain the possessian His Majesty and the French have for a long time had in this Niagara district.

Firstly :—

We leave in the centre of the Square a large, framed, wooden Cross, eighteen feet in height, on the arms of which are inscribed in large letters, these words :—

REGN· VINC· ✠ IMP·CHRS·

which was erected on last Good Friday by all the officers and solemnly blessed by the Rev. Fath^r Millet.

Item, a Cabin in which the Commandant lodged, containing a good chimney, a door and two windows furnished with their hinges, fastenings and locks, which cabin is covered with forty-four deal boards and about six other boards arranged inside into a sort of bedstead.

Item, in the immediate vicinity of said Cabin is another cabin with two rooms having each its chimney; ceiled (*lambrisés*) with boards and in each a little window and three bedsteads, the door furnished with its hinges and fastenings; the said cabin is covered with fifty deal boards and there are sixty like boards on each side.

Item, right in front is the Rev. Fath^r Millet's Cabin furnished with its chimney, windows and sashes; with shelves, a bedstead and four boards arranged inside, with a door furnished with its fastenings and hinges, the which is of twenty-four boards.

Item, another Cabin, opposite the Cross, in which there is a chimney, board ceiling and three bedsteads, covered with forty-two boards, with three like boards on one side of said cabin, there is a window with its sash and a door furnished with its hinges and fastening.

Item, another Cabin with a chimney, and a small window with its sash and a door; covered with thirty deal boards; there are three bedsteads inside.

Item, a bake house furnished with its oven and chimney, partly covered with boards and the remainder with hurdles and clay; also an apartment at the end of said Bakery containing two chimneys: There are in said Bakery a window and door furnished with its hinges and fastenings.

Item, another large and extensive framed building having a double door furnished with nails, hinges and fastenings, with three small windows; the said apartment is without a chimney; 'tis floored with twelve plank (*madriers*) and about twelve boards are arranged inside; without, 'tis clapboarded with eighty-two plank.[1]

Item, a large storehouse covered with one hundred and thirty boards, surrounded by pillars, eight feet high, in which there are many pieces of wood serving as small joists, and partly floored with several unequal plank. There is a window and a sliding sash.

Item, above the scarp of the ditch a Well with its cover.

All which apartments are in the same condition in which they were last winter, and consequently inhabitable. Which all the Witnesses, namely, the Rev. Fath^r Millet of the Society of Jesus, Missionary; Sieur Desbergéres, Captain and Commander; Sieurs Le la Motthe, La Rabelle, Demuratre, de Clerin and Sieurs de Gemerais, Chevalier de Tregay all lieutenants and officers, and Mahuet Pilot of the Bark the General, now in the Roadsted, certify to have seen and visited all the said apartments and have therefore signed the Minute and Original of these presents :—PIERRE MILLET of the Soc^y of Jesus, DESBERGERES, le Chevalier DE LA MOTTHE, DE LA RABELLE MURAT, DE GLEZIN, de la GEMESAIS, Commander de TSEGIMO, and MAHUET.

1 This most probably was the Chapel.

VIII.

NAMES

OF THE

Male Inhabitants of Ulster County,

1689.

A ROOL OF THE NAMES AND SURNAMES

OF THEM THAT HAUE TAKIN THE OATH OF ALLEGIANCE IN Y^e^ COUNTY OF VLST^r^, BY ORD^r^ OF HIS EXCELY: Y^e^ GOUERNOR; Y^e^ FFIRST DAY OF SEPTEMB^r^ ANNO Q^e^: DOMINI 1689—

Cap^n^ : Hennery Beekman
Cap^n^ Matthis Matthison
Left: Abraham Haesbrock
Lowies Bouier
John Hendricks
Albert Johnson V: Steenwicke
Marten Hoffeman
William Van ffredingborch
Lowranc. Van der Bush
Wessell Tenbrock
John Boorehanc
John Willianson Hogetilen
Gerritt Arsin
Tunis Elison
John ffocken
William DeMy^r^s:
Johanas Schencke
William De Lamontanij
John Johnson Van Osternhoudt
Jochijam Hendricks
Harrama Hendricks
Pett^r^: Johnson
Claes Claes Sluitt^r^
Powlas Powlas
Thomas Quick
Nicolas Anthony
Johanas Wincop
Jost Jansin
Jacob Arsin
Matthies Slecht
John Middag
Hendrick Cornelis Bogard
Gisbort Albortsa
Gerrit Van ffleitt
Cornelius Slecht
John Haesbrock
Cornelius Sweitts
Burgar Mind^r^son
Hendrick Albertsa
Abraham ffranckford
William Danswick
Moses Depuis
William Hoogtilin
Gerritt Wincoop
Symon Cool
Isaac Dibois
Benj^a^ Provorist
Jesely Valleij
Andries Laffever
Pett^r^: Dovo
Abraham Deboijs
Moses Laconta
Petter Hellibrandts
Symon Laffever
Sander Roesinkranc
Cornelis Cool
Arrie ffrance
John Osternhoudt Juno^r^:
Hendrick Traphager
Jacob Decker
Roloff Hendricks
Cornelis VerNoij
Hendrick Van Wien
Hiuge ffreri Senior
Hiuge ffreri Junior
Pett^r^: Cornelis
Gerritt Johnson
Anthony Criupill
Abraham Carrmar
Pett^e^ Winniy

Jacob Cool
Abraham Rutton
Abl Westfalin
Abraham Lamiater
Pett[r]: Jacobs
Isack Van ffredinborch
Gerrit Cornelis
Jacob Lamiater
Arrian Tunis
Claes Westfalin
John Cottin
Johannas Westfalin
Thomas Johnson
Hendrick Johnson Van Bush
Andries Petters
Gerritt Jansa Decker
Lendart Cool
Cornelis ffinehoudt
Tunis Jacobs
Jacob Schutt
Leury Jacobs
John Elting
Rollof Swartwout
Dirrick Westbrock
Agbert Hendricks
Sam[l]: Berrey
Lambert Heybertsin
Hendrick Claes
Brown Hendricks
Harrama Pier
John David
John Blanchard
Cornelis Gerritts
John Smedis
Barrant Cuinst
Hellebrandt Lazer
Johanas Bush
Pietter Lhommedien
August Jay
John Rulland
William Traphager Juno[r]
Jochyam Van Ama
Aimi canchi
Jacob Besteyansa
Abraham Larew
Matthis Blanzan Junio[r]
John Lazier
John Pett[r]son
John Josten
Wallraven DeMont Junio[r]
Johanas Traphager
Hendrick in the ffeelt
Petter Criupill
Gerrit Gisborts
Hendrick Hendricks
John Gerrittsa of new Church
Hendrick Arreyn
John Van ffleitt
Claes Tunis
Andries Dewitt
Jacob Van Etta
John Schutt
John Dewitt
Hendrick Johnson
Thomas Swardtwout
John Van Etta
Anthony Swartwoudt
John Jacosa Stoll
Heybert Lambertsa
William Jacobs
David Deboyes
Sallomon Deboyes
Evert Wincoope
Johanas Westbrock
John Peteet
Rutt Jores
Heibort Sealand
Jury Tunies
John Broerson Decker
Roulof Johnson
John Matthies
Heymon Roos
John Roos
Arrie Roos
Petter Pettersin
Gerritt Agbortsin
Claes Roosinffelt
Jno Evedin
Cornelis Lambertsin
Thomas Harramansa
Johanas Dehogos
Moses Cantine
Isack Deboyes
Cornelis Mastin

James Bonamiz
Dirrick Hendricks
John Gerrittsa
James Cordaback
Powlas Powlason Junor
John Williamson ye Duitcher
William Schutt
Cornelis Tacke
John Johnson Poast
Petter Demarr
Privie go Doon
Lowies Deboyes Senior
Jacob Deboyes
John Euertsa
Coinradt Elvendorop
Cornelis Petterson
Barrant Jacobs
Marinos Van Acar
Claes Lazier
Barrant Coll
Symon Westfallin
Arrent Jacobs
Artt martenson Doorn
Cornelis Bogardos
Arrent Van Dick

These ffowing persons were present when ye Oath was A givin. but Did Reffeuse to take it Vizt

Antony Tilba
Thomas Van der Marrick
Joseph ffocker
Jacob Horne

These ffollowing persons Did nott appeare Vizt

John Archer
Livie Larrow
Maghell De Mott
Euert Pelce
Symon Pelce
Terrick Claes Dewitt
Wallraven Demont Senior
Dirrick Schepmous
Matthis Tennick
Claes Tunis
Gisbert Crum
Arre Gerritt Van ffleitt
Dirrick Van ffleitt
Jno: Lodtman
Jury Lodtman
Hellebrandt Lodtman
Jacob Brown Alis ye Noorman
Warnar Hornebeak
John Lowrance
Symon Larow
Cornelis Hogoboom
Cornelis ye Duitcher
Gombart Powlasin
Jno: Meueson. Alis Jn De pape
William Wallaffish
Jno Pollin
Antony Bussalin
Gerritt Aylberts
Dirrick Keizer

THOMAS CHAMBERS.

IX.

PAPERS

RELATING TO THE

Invasion of New-York and Burning of Schenectady

BY

THE FRENCH.

1690.

PROJECT OF THE CHEVALIER DE CALLIERES,

GOVERNOR OF MONTREAL AND COMMANDING BY COMMISSION THE TROOPS AND MILITIA OF CANADA, REGARDING THE PRESENT STATE OF AFFAIRS OF THAT COUNTRY. JANUARY, 1689.

[Paris Doc. IV.]

To Monseigneur, the Marquis of Seignelay.

As the recent Revolution in England will change the face of American affairs it becomes necessary to adopt entirely new measures to secure Canada against the great dangers with which it is threatened.

Chevalier Andros, now Governor General of New England and New York, having already declared in his letters to M. de Denonville that he took all the Iroquois under his protection as subjects of the Crown of England and having prevented them returning to M. de Denonville to make peace with us, there is no longer reason to hope for its conclusion through the English nor for the alienation of the Iroquois from the close union which exists with those in consequence of the great advantages they derive from thence, the like to which we cannot offer for divers reasons.

Chevalier Andros is a prosestant as well as the whole English Colony so that there is no reason to hope that he will remain faithful to the King of England [James II.] and we must expect that he will not only urge the Iroquois to continue the war against us but that he will even add Englishmen to them to lead them and seize the posts of Niagara, Michilimakinak and others proper to render him Master of all the Indians our allies, according to the project they have long since formed, and which they began to execute when we declared war against the Iroquois and when we captured 70 Englishmen who were going to take possession of Michilimakinak, one of the most important posts of Canada; our entrêpot for the Fur Trade and the residence of the Superior of the Rev: Jesuit Fathers, Missionaries among our Savages, and which belongs incontestably to us.

It is to be expected, then, that they are about to endeavor to invest all Canada and raise all the Savages against us, in order to deprive us wholly of every sort of Trade and draw it all to themselves by means of the cheap bargains of merchandize they can give them, nearly a half less than our Frenchmen can afford theirs, for reasons which will be, elsewhere, explained, and thus become masters of all the peltries; a trade which sustains Canada and constitutes one of the chief benefits that France derives from that Colony.

No sooner will the English have ruined our Trade with the Savages than uniting with them they will be in a position to fall on us, burn and sack our settlements, scattered along the River St. Lawrence to Quebec, without our being able to prevent them, having no fortress capable of arresting them.

Things being thus disposed, the only means to avoid this misfortune is to anticipate it by the expedition which will be hereafter explained and which I offer to execute forthwith, if it please His Majesty to confide its direction to me on account of the particular knowledge I have acquired of the affairs of that country during five years that I had the honor to serve His Majesty and to command his troops and military there, after twenty years service in the army.

The plan is, to go straight to Orange (Albany) the most advanced town of New-York, one hundred leagues from Montreal, which I would undertake to carry, and to proceed thence to seize Manathe, the capital of that Colony situated on the seaside; on condition of being furnished with supplies necessary for the success of the expedition.

I demand for that only the troops at present maintained by His Majesty in Canada if it be pleasing to him to fill them up by a reinforcement of soldiers which they require in consequence of sickness that has produced the deaths of many among them.

These troops number 35 companies which at 50 men each ought to give 1750. Yet at the review made when I left, there were found only about 1300, so that 450 soldiers are still required to complete them; thus it would be necessary that His Majesty should please to order the levy of at least 400 men, and to have them enlisted as quick as possible in order that they may be embarked in the first vessels.

The use I propose to make of these 1700 men is to take "the pick" (*l'elite*) of them to the number of 1400 and to adjoin to them the elite of the Militia to the number of 600, so as to carry these 2000 men necessary on this expedition; leaving the 300 remaining soldiers to guard the principal outposts at the head of our Colony in order to prevent the Iroquois seizing and burning them whilst we should be in the field.

I propose embarking these 2000 men, with the supplies necessary for their subsistence in a sufficient number of canoes and flat Batteaux which we already employed in the two last Campaigns against the Iroquois.

My design is, to lead them by the Richelieu River into Lake Champlain as far as a Carrying Place which is within three leagues of the Albany River that runs to Orange.[1] I shall conceal this expedition, which must be kept very secret, by saying that the King has commanded me to proceed at the head of His troops and Militia to the Iroquois Country to dictate Peace to them on the conditions it has pleased His Majesty to grant them without the interference of the English, inasmuch as the Iroquois are his true subjects; without letting any one know our intention of attacking the English until we have arrived at the point whence I shall send to tell the Iroquois, by some of their Nation, that I am not come to wage war against them but only to reduce the English, who have caused our division, and to re-establish the good friendship that formerly existed between us; therefore they had better avoid coming to their aid if they wish not to be treated with the greatest rigor, the said English being unable to protect them from the force I lead against them, and that I shall turn against the said Iroquois, if they dare assist them.

As the Batteaux cannot proceed further than the Carrying Place, my intention is to erect there a small log fort (*un petit fort de pieux terrassés*) which I shall have built in three days, and to leave 200 men in it to guard the Batteaux; thence march direct to Orange, embarking our supplies on the River in canoes which we shall bring and which can be convoyed by land, we marching with the troops along the river as an escort.

I calculate to seize in passing some English Villages and Settlements where I shall find provisions and other conveniences for attacking the town of Orange.

That town is about as large as Montreal, surrounded by picquets at one end of which is an Earthen Fort defended by palisades and consisting of four small bastions. There is a garrison of 150 men of three companies in the fort and some pieces of Cannon. Said town of Orange may contain about 150 houses and 300 inhabitants capable of bearing arms, the majority of whom are Dutch and some French Refugees with some English.

After having invested the Town and summoned it to surrender with promise not to pillage if it capitulate, I propose in case of resistance to cut or burn the palisades, in order to afford an opening,

1 This "Carrying Place" or portage is now traversed by that section of the Champlain Canal extending from Fort Ann to Sandy Hill.

and enter there sword in hand and seize the fort. These being only about 14 feet high can be easily escaladed by means of the conveniences we shall find, when Masters of the town, or by blowing in the gate with a few petards or two small field pieces which may be of use to me and I shall find means of conveying there, if his Ma[ty] will please to have them furnished at La Rochelle to take with me, and some grenades and other munitions, a list of which I shall hand in separately, and which will be deducted from the funds His Majesty destines for Canada so as not to increase the expenditure of preceding years.

After I shall have become Master of the town and fort of Orange, which I expect to achieve before the English can afford it any succor, my intention is to leave a garrison of 200 men in the fort with sufficient supplies which I shall find in the City, and to disarm all the Inhabitants, granting at His Majesty's pleasure pardon to the French deserters and inhabitants I shall find there, so as to oblige them to follow me.

I shall seize all the barks, batteaux and canoes that are at Orange, to embark my force on the river which is navigable down to Manathe, and I shall embark with the troops the necessary provisions and ammunition, and some pieces of Cannon, to be taken from Fort Orange to serve in the attack on Manathe, [New-York.]

This place consists of a town composed of about 200 houses and can put about 400 inhabitants under arms. They are divided into four Companies of Infantry of 50 men each, and three Companies of Cavalry of the same number, the horses being very common in that country. This town is not enclosed, being situated on a Peninsula at the mouth of the river that falls into a Bay forming a fine harbour. It is defended by a Fort faced with stone having four Bastions with several pieces of cannon, commanding the Port on one side and the town on the other.

I contemplate first carrying the town by assault, it being all open, and making use of the houses nearest the Fort to approach the latter; forming a battery of the Cannon I shall have brought from Orange and of that I may find in the stores of the town, where the vessels arm and disarm.

It is necessary for the success of this Expedition that H. M. give orders to two of the ships of War destined this year to escort the merchantmen who go to Canada and Acadie or the fishermen who go for Cod to the Great Bank, to come after having convoyed the merchants, towards the end of August, into the Gulf of Manathe and cruize there during the month of September, as well to prevent succor from Europe which may arrive from England or Boston, as to enter the port when I on my arrival shall give the signal agreed upon, so as to aid us in capturing the Fort which they may cannonade from aboard their ships whilst I attack it on land. They can in case of necessity even land some marines (to replace the 400 men I shall have left on the road guarding Orange and the Batteaux); also some pieces of Cannon if we require them. They might reimbark and return to France in the month of October after the capture of the Fort and carry the intelligence thereof.

After we should have become masters of the town and fort of Manathe I shall cause the Inhabitants to be disarmed and send my Canadians back by the Albany river to Orange on their way to their batteaux and on their return home. I should winter at Manathe with all the troops I would have brought with me except the 200 soldiers left to guard Orange; and as I shall have nothing to fear from the land side, being master of the rivers, I would work through the winter to strengthen myself against attacks of the English whilst waiting until H M. should be pleased to send what may be necessary to secure this important conquest.

It would render H. M. absolute Master of the whole of Iroquois who derive from this Colony all the arms and ammunition with which they make war on us. This will afford the means to disarm them whenever considered necessary, and thereby impose on them such laws as H. M. may please; the town of Boston, the capital of New England being too far from them to afford any aid.

Having mastered the Iroquois we shall have equal control of all the other Savages who will come without hesitation and bring us all their peltries. This will cause the trade of our Colony to flourish; will considerably augment H. M.'s revenues and eventually diminish the expences he is obliged to incur for the preservation of Canada.

It will firmly establish the Christian Religion as well among the Iroquois as among the other Savages to whom we shall be able to speak as Masters when they are encircled on the side of Canada as well as of New York. It will secure and facilitate the Cod fishery which is carried on along our Coasts of la Cadie and on the Great Bank. It will give H. M. one of the finest harbours in America which can be entered during almost all seasons of the year in less than one month of very easy navigation; whilst that from France to Quebec cannot be prosecuted except in summer on account of the Ice which closes the River St. Lawrence, itself long and perilous.

It may be objected to this plan, that the Colony of Orange and Manathe may remain faithful to the King of England, and in this case it would not be apropos to attack it and draw down an open war with that English Colony to the prejudice of the Treaty of Neutrality concluded between the two nations.

It may be answered to this, that the colony of Manathe and Orange, being the same as that formerly called New Netherland which the English took from the Dutch, and the greater part of which is still of this latter nation and all Protestants, it is not to be doubted but that they would receive the orders of the Prince of Orange and even force their Governor, did he not consent, to acknowledge him, and therefore we must look on as certain a war between that Colony and us, and not give it the time to push its intrigues with the Savages to ruin us by means of them, if we do not anticipate them. And in case that, contrary to all appearances, they remain faithful to the King of England during the general rebellion of the English, we might, if H. M. thought proper, being on terms with that King, confide to him the secret of this expedition, draw from him an order to the Commandant of Orange and of Manathe to surrender these places into H. M.'s hands, who would keep them for him and prevent the Rebels becoming masters of them, so as to have an opportunity to treat them as rebels did they not obey that order, being besides this, in a position to force them to it, on condition of negotiating eventually with the King for that Colony, which is the only means of securing Canada, firmly establishing Religion, Trade and the King's authority throughout all North America. If the favourable opportunity which presents of becoming master of that Colony be neglected, it may surely be calculated that, through its intrigues with the Iroquois and other Savages, it will destroy Canada in a little time; whose ruin will entail that of the establishment at Hudson's bay, the beaver and other peltry trade; that of Acadia, the local fishery, and that of Newfoundland; and if we be forced to abandon Canada, it will, hereafter, in consequence of the frequent chasing of our fishermen by English vessels, render very difficult and dangerous for H. M.'s subjects the Codfishery on the Great Bank, which produces several millions to France, and is one of the most profitable investments that we have.

MEMOIR OF INSTRUCTIONS TO COUNT DE FRONTENAC

RESPECTING THE EXPEDITION AGAINST NEW-YORK. 7TH JUNE, 1689.

[Paris Doc. IV.]

The King, having examined the proposition made him by Sieur Chevalier de Callières Bonnevue of Montreal to attack New-York with his Majesty's troops in Canada and a number of the militia of that country, has the more willingly assented to it as he knows that the English inhabiting that quarter have resolved since the last year to excite the Iroquois Nation, His Majesty's subjects, and force them to wage war against the French, having furnished them for that purpose with arms and ammunition, and endeavored in every way, even to the prejudice of the King of England's orders and the faith of Treaties to usurp the trade of the French in the country in possession of which they have been from all time.

To accomplish this project His Majesty has given orders to Sieur Begon to prepare the munitions necessary for the expedition and has caused two of his ships of war to be equipped in the port of Rochefort under the command of Sieur de la Caffiniere whom he has ordered to follow exactly the directions which said Sieur de Frontenac will give him regarding this expedition.

He will set out with all diligence to embark at Rochelle in one of the ships and sail without loss of time for the entrance of the gulf of St. Lawrence and Campseaux bay, where he will embark in the best of the merchantmen that will follow and repair to Quebec. * * *

Therefore on his arrival at Quebec he will take advantage of the state in which he will find things, to complete the suitable arrangements for departing with batteaux, canoes, and all the equipage necessary for this expedition with the Chevalier de Callières who will command the troops under his orders.

He will despatch by land or water as he shall deem most certain, orders and instructions to Sieur de la Caffiniere, to the place he will have designated, as to what he shall have to do, in order to repair to Manathe, he making use of the cypher which shall have been furnished him.

He will order him to sail directly and without undertaking any thing along his course, follow the coast of Acadie (where he will leave in passing what he shall have for the said coast of Acadie) down to Manathe, and order him to anchor as safely as possible and to observe well the quarter where he will make his landing when said Sieur de Frontenac shall have arrived there.

He will give orders to the Sieur de la Caffiniere to sieze the vessels he will find in the bay of the said Manathe, without exposing himself to any accident that may render him unable to cooperate in that enterprize.

As it is impossible to fix on a certain rendezvous for the arrival of said vessels at Manathe at the same time that the Sieur de Frontenac will arrive there with the troops, without alarming those at that place, the two vessels of war must go right into the bay, more especially as the attack on the frontier post of New-York will give warning to those of Manatha; and the vessels thus arriving before the land forces, will cause a diversion.

* * * * * * * * * * *

The said Sieur de Frontenac having informed himself of the route he is to take, of which he will make more particular enquiries on the spot, as regard the convenience, security and expedition of the troops, His Majesty will not enter into further detail on this subject, nor on the attack on Orange and Manatte nor on anything that relates thereto. He will solely recommend him to act as much as possible, in such a manner as that those of Orange may not be advised of his march, so that he may surprise this first post and cut in below Orange to secure the number of vessels he may require to descend on Manathe, and place things in such order as not to be uneasy when he shall depart for and be established at, the said Manathe. For this purpose he ought to leave a confidential officer at Orange with such detachment as he will find necessary to be left there, with orders to be on his guard and to fortify himself, and obtain all information possible for the success of the expedition against Manathe. He will also cause all the inhabitants to be disarmed and their effects to be seized, giving them to hope every good treatment with which they can flatter themselves until he entertains no further apprehensions; then His Majesty desires that what is hereinafter prescribed to him, may be executed.

He wishes particular care to be taken to prevent any plunder of provisions, merchandize, ammunition, property, cattle, utensils and principal household furniture; and as his object must be to place Forts Orange and Manathe in a state of defence, and to support the Frenchmen who will have remained there, he will not only victual the forts for the longest time possible but collect there all he can of provisions, and in default of a sufficient quantity of magazines in said forts, he will lock them up in the towns, taking care not to touch those which he should deposit in said forts except when obliged.

His Majesty does not wish any suspected inhabitants be left in that Colony. His intention also is that an exact inventory be made in the settlements and plantations by Commissary Gaillard (whom his Majesty wishes him to take with him,) of all cattle, grain, merchandize, furniture, effects and utensils he may find in each of the said settlements; that he select from among the inhabitants of Canada and the officers and soldiers of the troops those who will be found qualified to maintain and improve them, and that he furnish these with farms in his Majesty's name leaving them of the provisions that will be found there, as much as shall be necessary to support them until they have produced some; and he will examine one with another, those to whom he will think proper to grant said farms, so as to distribute the greater number in proportion to their skill and strength, observing to associate several in the same settlement when he shall deem such necessary. He will inform his Majesty of all he shall have done in this regard by sending him the enumeration of all that he shall have left in each such settlement, and furnish his opinion of the quit rents which they will be in a condition to pay him. After having settled on what he shall judge absolutely necessary to leave to those to whom he will have given these farms, he will place in store all the surplus, such as grain, whale oil and all sorts of merchandize and other principal effects of which also inventories shall be made to be equally sent to his Majesty.

He will examine into the means of distributing said property so that from what he will acquire there his Majesty may order, on his advice, the gratuities he shall judge fitting to bestow on said militia, the army and navy officers, soldiers and sailors who shall have distinguished themselves and given individual marks of that satisfaction which he expects from their zeal and industry on this occasion.

If he find among the inhabitants of New-York, whether English or Dutch, any Catholics on whose fidelity he can rely, he may leave them in their habitations after making them take the oath of allegiance to his Majesty, provided there be not too many of them and they do not excite any suspicion, having regard, in that, only to what will best promote the preservation and advantage of the Colony and its security at the same time as well as that of the French.

He may likewise retain, if he think proper, mechanics and other working people necessary to cultivate the land and work at fortifications in the capacity of prisoners, distributing them among the French inhabitants who may require them, until matters being in a state of entire security, they may be restored to liberty.

The officers and principal inhabitants, from whom ransom can be exacted, must be detained in prison.

Respecting all other foreigners, men, women and children, His Majesty deems it proper that they should be put out of the Colony and sent to New England, Pennsylvania and to such other quarters as shall be considered expedient, either by land or sea, together or in divisions—all according as he shall find will best secure their dispersion and prevent them, by reunion, affording enemies an opportunity to get up expeditions against the Colony.

He will send to France the French Refugees whom he will find there, particularly those of the pretended Reformed religion. When he will have captured the fort and conquered that Colony he must think particularly of his return to Canada to convey thither the Militia and Soldiers he shall deem necessary for the King's service, according to the disposition in which he shall find things both as regards the Iroquois as well on the side of Canada as on that of New York, and in proportion to what troops he will calculate necessary to be left to guard the forts and country.

And as nothing appears more important, after his expedition, than to take advantage of the season to return to Canada, he must, in case he cannot execute all that is above contained, confide its execution to Sieur Chevalier de Callières, giving him orders conformable and according to what he shall consider most fitting the King's service; His Majesty having determined to confer on the said Chevalier de Callières the Government of New York, and of the town and fort of Manathe in particular, under the authority of His Majesty's Lieutenant General in New France.

He will select, before leaving, the officers and soldiers he will deem proper to leave at New York and put over the posts those officers best qualified to maintain and fortify them.

In case he find, after having provided sufficient troops for New York and concluded on the number of soldiers necessary for His Majesty's service in Canada, that he has a superabundance, he can send some to France in the King's Ships, and retain thirty-five to forty men to be sent eventually to Acadia.

His Majesty is very glad to observe to him on this head, that he must regulate himself, as regards the number of men he will leave in New York, by the means of subsistence there and the necessity of guarding the country; and he will also consider that his return to Canada will be more convenient for those he will have to convey back there, when they will not be more numerous.

In case, contrary to all appearance, the season be too far advanced to admit his return to Canada during the remainder of the Fall, he will give advice of his expedition and sojourn there until the Spring, and he will employ himself during winter in securing his conquest and waging war on the enemy.

However that be, he ought if he be obliged to remain, either personally or through Chevalier de Callières, if that be convenient, profit by circumstances to conclude a solid and advantageous peace with the Iroquois, whom he will, doubtless find disposed to sue for it, being deprived of aid from and communication with the English.

In order to deprive the English of the facility of undertaking land expeditions against New York from New England, His Majesty desires that the English Settlements adjoining Manathe and further off if necessary, be destroyed; and that the more distant be put under contribution.

He will send an exact report of all the observations he will be able to make regarding the trade of the new inhabitants of New-York, the security of the navigation thence to France, the communication with Canada, so that His Majesty may give him on those points the necessary orders to derive from that conquest all the advantages to be expected from it. But should this expedition contrary to all appearances, and for reasons which His Majesty cannot foresee, not be executed, he will convey his orders to the said Sieur de la Caffinière to make war against the English, and to range along the Coasts of New England and New York to capture there as many prizes as possible, and to remain there until he have no more provisions than are necessary for his return to France.

AN ACCOUNT

OF THE MOST REMARKABLE OCCURRENCES IN CANADA FROM THE DEPARTURE OF THE VESSELS, FROM THE MONTH OF NOVEMBER 1689 TO THE MONTH OF NOVEMBER 1690. BY MONS. DE MONSEIGNAT, COMPTROLLER GENERAL OF THE MARINE IN CANADA.

[Paris Doc. IV.]

[EXTRACT.] The orders received by M. le Comte (de Frontenac) to commence hostilities against New England and New York, which had declared for the Prince of Orange, afforded him considerable pleasure, and were very necessary for the country. He allowed no more time to elapse before carrying them into execution than was required to send off some despatches to France—immediately after which he determined to organize three different detachments, to attack those rebels at all points at the same moment, and to punish them at various places for having afforded protection to our enemies, the Mohawks. The first party was to rendezvous at Montreal, and proceed towards Orange; the second at Three Rivers, and to make a descent on New York, at some place between Boston and Orange;1 and the third was to depart from Quebec, and gain the seaboard between Boston and Pentagouet, verging towards Acadia. They all succeeded perfectly well, and I shall communicate to you the details. * * * * * * * *

The detachment which formed at Montreal, may have been composed of about two hundred and ten men, namely: eighty savages from the *Sault* and from *La Montagne;* sixteen Algonquins; and the remainder Frenchmen—all under the command of the Sieur Le Moyne de Sainte Helene, and Lieutenant Daillebout de Mantet, both of whom are Canadians. The Sieurs le Moyne d'Iberville and Repentigny de Montesson commanded under these. The best qualified Frenchmen were, the Sieurs de Bonrepos and de La Brosse, Calvinist officers, the Sieur la Moyne de Blainville, Le Bert du Chêne, and la Marque de Montigny, who all served as volunteers. They took their departure from Montreal at the commencement of February.

After having marched for the course of five or six days, they called a council to determine the route they should follow, and the point they should attack.

The Indians demanded of the French what was their intention. Messieurs de Sainte Helene and Mantet replied that they had left in the hope of attacking Orange, if possible, as it is the Capital of New York and a place of considerable importance, though they had no orders to that effect, but generally to act according as they should judge on the spot of their chances of success, without running too much risk. This appeared to the savages somewhat rash. They represented the difficulties and the weakness of the party for so bold an undertaking. There was even one among them who, his mind filled with the recollections of the disasters which he had witnessed last year, enquired of our Frenchmen, "since when had they become so desperate?" In reply to their raillery, 'twas answered that it was our intention, now, to regain the honor of which our misfortunes had deprived us, and the sole means to accomplish that was to carry Orange, or to perish in so glorious an enterprise.

As the Indians, who had an intimate acquaintance with the localities, and more experience than the French, could not be brought to agree with the latter, it was determined to postpone coming to a conclusion until the party should arrive at the spot where the two routes separate—the one leading to Orange, and the other to Corlear (Schenectady). In the course of the journey, which occupied eight days, the Frenchmen judged proper to diverge towards Corlear, according to the advice of the

1 This detachment entered New Hampshire, where they burned a place called Salmon Falls.

Indians; and this road was taken without calling a new council. Nine days more elapsed before they arrived, having experienced inconceivable difficulties, and having been obliged to march up to their knees in water, and to break the ice with their feet in order to find solid footing.

They arrived within two leagues of Corlear about four o'clock in the evening, and were harangued by the great Mohawk chief of the Iroquois from the Sault. He urged on all to perform their duty, and to lose all recollections of their fatigue, in the hope of taking ample revenge for the injuries they had received from the Iroquois at the solicitation of the English, and of washing them out in the blood of the traitors. This savage was without contradiction the most considerable of his tribe—an honest man—as full of spirit, prudence and generosity as it was possible, and capable at the same time of the grandest undertakings. Shortly after four Squaws were discovered in a wigwam who gave every information necessary for the attack on the town. The fire found in their hut served to warm those who were benumbed, and they continued their route, having previously detached Giguieres, a Canadian, with nine Indians, on the look out. They discovered no one, and returned to join the main body within one league of Corlear.

At eleven of the clock that night, they came within sight of the town, resolved to defer the assault until two o'clock of the morning. But the excessive cold admitted of no further delay.

The town of Corlear forms a sort of oblong with only two gates—one opposite the road we had taken; the other leading to Orange, which is only six leagues distant. Messieurs de Sainte Helene and de Mantet were to enter at the first which the squaws pointed out, and which in fact was found wide open. Messieurs d'Iberville and de Montesson took the left with another detachment, in order to make themselves masters of that leading to Orange. But they could not discover it, and returned to join the remainder of the party. A profound silence was every where observed, until the two commanders, who separated, at their entrance into the town for the purpose of encircling it, had met at the other extremity.

The signal of attack was given Indian fashion, and the entire force rushed on simultaneously. M. de Mantet placed himself at the head of a detachment, and reached a small fort where the garrison was under arms. The gate was burst in after a good deal of difficulty, the whole set on fire, and all who defended the place slaughtered.

The sack of the town began a moment before the attack on the fort. Few houses made any resistance. M. de Montigny discovered some which he attempted to carry sword in hand, having tried the musket in vain. He received two thrusts of a spear—one in the body and the other in the arm. But M. de Sainte Helene having come to his aid, effected an entrance, and put every one who defended the place to the sword. The Massacre lasted two hours. The remainder of the night was spent in placing sentinels, and in taking some repose.

The house belonging to the Minister was ordered to be saved, so as to take him alive to obtain information from him; but as it was not known it was not spared any more than the others. He was slain and his papers burnt before he could be recognized.

At daybreak the same men were sent to the dwelling of Mr. Coudre [Sander], who was Major of the place, and who lived at the other side of the river. He was not willing to surrender, and began to put himself on the defensive with his servants and some Indians; but as it was resolved not to do him any harm, in consequence of the good treatment that the French had formerly experienced at his hands, M. d'Iberville and the great Mohawk proceeded thither alone, promised him quarter for himself, his people, and his property, whereupon he laid down his arms, on parole, entertaining them in his fort, and returned with them to see the commandants of the town.

In order to occupy the savages, who would otherwise have taken to drink and thus rendered themselves unable for defence, the houses had already been set on fire. None were spared in the town but one house belonging to Coudre, and that of a widow who had six children, whither M. de

Montigny had been carried when wounded. All the rest were consumed. The lives of between fifty and sixty persons, old men, women and children were spared, they having escaped the first fury of the attack. Some twenty Mohawks were also spared, in order to show them that it was the English and not they against whom the grudge was entertained. The loss on this occasion in houses, cattle and grain, amounts to more than four hundred thousand livres. There were upwards of eighty well built and well furnished houses in the town.

The return march commenced with thirty prisoners. The wounded, who were to be carried, and the plunder, with which all the Indians and some Frenchmen were loaded, caused considerable inconvenience. Fifty good horses were brought away. Sixteen only of these reached Montreal. The remainder were killed for food on the road.

Sixty leagues from Corlear the Indians began to hunt, and the French not being able to wait for them, being short of provisions, continued their route, having detached Messieures d'Iberville and Du Chesne with two savages before them to Montreal. On the same day, some Frenchmen, who doubtless were very much fatigued, lost their way. Fearful that they should be obliged to keep up with the main body, and believing themselves in safety having eighty Indians in their rear, they were found missing from the camp. They were waited for next day until eleven o'clock, but in vain, and no account has since been received of them.

Two hours after, forty men more left the main body without acquainting the commander, continued their route by themselves, and arrived within two leagues of Montreal one day ahead, so that there were not more than fifty or sixty men together. The evening on which they should arrive at Montreal, being extremely fatigued from fasting and bad roads, the rear fell away from M. de Sainte Helene, who was in front with an Indian guide, and who could not find a place suitable for camping nearer than three or four leagues of the spot where he expected to halt. He was not rejoined by M. de Mantet and the others until far advanced in the night. Seven have not been found. Next day on parade, about ten o'clock in the forenoon, a soldier arrived who announced that they had been attacked by fourteen or fifteen savages, and that six had been killed. The party proceeded somewat afflicted at this accident, and arrived at Montreal at 3 o'clock, p. m.

Such, Madame, is the account of what passed at the taking of Corlear. The French lost but twenty-one men, namely four Indians and seventeen Frenchmen. Only one Indian and one Frenchman were killed at the capture of the town. The others were lost on the road.

[From Mortgage Book B, in County Clk's Office, Albany.]

Albany ye 9th day of Februaro $16\frac{89}{90}$
Die Sabbathi.

This morning about 5 o'Clock ye alarm was brought here by Symon Schermerhoorn who was shott threw his Thigh yt ye french and Indians had murthered ye People of Skinnechtady; haveing got into ye Towne about 11 or 12 a Clock there being no Watch Kept (ye Inhabitants being so negligent & Refractory) and yt he had much adoe to Escape they being very numerous. They fyred severall times at him at last throw his Thigh and wounded his horse and was come over Canatagione[1] to bring ye news.

The allarm being given all People Repared to there Post ye fort fyred severall gunns to give ye alarm to ye farmers but few heard there being such an Extream Snow above Knee Deep Severall ye

1 Now Niscayuna.

People haveing Escaped ye Cruelty of ye french and those Indians came Running here & told us ye Village was a fyre and yt they had much adoe to Escape for all ye streets were full of french and Indians, & yt many People were murthered and yt ye enemy were marching hither which news was Continually Confirmed till afternoon Letters were sent forthwith to Sopus for ye assistance of a hundred men an Expresse sent to Skachkook but by reason of ye highwater—deep snow & yse could not Proceed, notice was given to all ye farmers of Kinderhook Claverak &ca of ye sad news, Some horse men sent out to Discover ye Enemies force and there march but were forced to Return ye snow being so Deep yet some were sent out again who got thither, Laurence ye Indian with ye Maquase yt were in Town were sent out also to Skinnechtady to Dispatch posts to ye Maquase Castles for all ye Indians to come doune, but unhappily sad Indians comeing to Skinnechtady were soe much amazed to see so many People murthered and Destroyed that they omitted ye sending up to ye Maquase Castles according to there Engagement, While ye Enemy was at N. Scotia a man came to Ensign Joh: Sander Glen and said he would goe to ye Maquase Castles and warn ye Maquase to come doune who was ordered to goe in all haste and comeing to ye Upper Plantations went for fear along with some of ye oyr Inhabitants into ye Woods and never went to ye Maquase Castles, this night we gott a letter from Skinnechtady Informing us yt the Enemy yt had done yt Mischieffe there were about one hundred and fifty or 200 men but that there were 1400 men in all; One army for Albany & anoyr for Sopus which hindered much ye marching of any force out of ye City fearing yt ye enemy might watch such an opportunity.

The 10th day of February.

Present. Pr Schuyler Mayr D. Wessels Recr, J. Bleecker, C. Bull, Capt Staets, Ald. Shaick, Ald Ryckman, Joh. Cuyler, Ens. Bennett.

Resolved yt Capt Jonathan Bull be sent wth 5 men out of each Compy to Skinnechtady to bury ye dead there & if ye Indians be come doune to joyn with them & Pursue ye Enemy.

Instructions for Capt Jonathan Bull.

You are to goe wth all Convanient speed with - - - - - - men to Skinnechtady & there Bury ye dead which are Killed by ye Enemy and give such succor and Relieffe to ye Poor People left alive at Skinnechtady as yu can, and if there be any considerable number of friendly Indians at Skinnechtady yu are wth all speed to Pursue & follow after the french and Indian Enemy & them Spoyle and Destroy what in yu Lyes and use all means Imaginable to Rescue ye Prisoners which they have Carried along with them.

You are to take Especial Care to have always Spyes and Skouts out on both sides of ye Path where yu March yr Men and to be as Carefull as Possible for ambushes of ye Enemy and to keep yr men in good order and Discipline

LIST OF YE PEOPLE KILD AND DESTROYED

BY YE FRENCH OF CANIDA AND THERE INDIANS AT SKINNECHTADY TWENTY MILES TO YE WESTWARD OF ALBANY BETWEEN SATURDAY AND SUNDAY YE 9th DAY OF FEBRUARY 16$\frac{89}{90}$.

Myndert Wemp killd		1
Jan van Eps and his Sonne & 2 of his Children kild		4
a negro of dito Van Eps		1
Serjt Church of Capt Bull's Compy		1
Barent Jansse Killd and Burnd his Sonne Kild		2
Ands Arentse Bratt shott and Burnt & also his childn		2
Mary Viele wife of Dowe Aukes & her 2 children killd		3
and his Negro Woman Francyn		1
Mary Alolff Wife of Cornelis Viele Junr Shott		1
Sweer Teunise Shott & burnt his wife kild & burnt	all in one house	2
Antje Janz daughter of Jan Spoor kild & burnt		1
Item 4 Negroes of ye said Sweer Teunise ye same death		4
Enos Talmidge Leift of Capt Bull kild & burnt		1
Hend Meese Vrooman & Bartholomeus Vrooman kild & burnt		2
Item 2 Negroes of Hend Meese ye same death		2
Gerrit Marcellis and his Wife & childe kiled		3
Robt Alexander souldr of Capt Bulls Shott		1
Robt hesseling shott		1
Sander ye sonne of gysbert gerritse kild and burnt		1
Jan Roeloffse de goyer burnt in ye house		1
Ralph grant a souldier in ye fort shott		1
David Christoffelse & his wife wth 4 Children all burnt in there house		6
Joris Aertse shott and burnt Wm Pieterse kild		2
Joh: Potman kild his wife kild & her scalp taken off		2
Dome Petrus Tassemaker ye Minister kild & burnt in his house		1
Frans harmense kild		1
Engel the wife of Adam Vroman shot & burnt her childe the brains dashed out against ye wall		2
Reynier Schaets and his sonne kild		2
Daniel Andries & George 2 souldiers of Capt Bull		2
a french girl Prisoner among ye Mohogs kild		1
A Maquase Indian kild		1
Johannes ye sonne of Symon Skermerhoorn		1
3 Negroes of Symon Skermerhoorn		3
In all		60

LYST OF YE PERSONES WHICH YE FRENCH AND THERE INDIANS HAVE TAKEN PRISONERS ATT SKINNECHTADY AND CARIED TO CANIDA YE 9th DAY OF FEBRUARY $16\frac{89}{90}$

Johannes Teller and his negroe - - - - - - - -	2
John Wemp sonne of Myndt Wemp & 2 negroes - - - - - -	3
Symon, Abraham, Philip, Dyrck & Claes Groot all 5 sonnes of Symon Groot - -	5
Jan Baptist sonne of Jan Van Epps - - - - - - - -	1
Albert & Johannes Vedder, sonnes of harme Vedder - - - - -	2
Isaak Cornelise Switts & his Eldest Sonne - - - - - - -	2
a negroe of Barent Janse - - - - - - - - -	1
Arnout ye sonne of Arnout Corn: Viele ye Interpr - - - - - -	1
Stephen ye sonne of Gysbert Gerritse - - - - - - -	1
Lawrence sonne of Claes Lawrence Purmurent - - - - - -	1
Arnout sonne of Paulyn Janse - - - - - - - -	1
Barent ye sonne of Adam Vroman & ye neger - - - - - -	2
Claes sonne of Franse Harmense - - - - - - - -	1
Stephen adopted sonne of Geertje Bouts - - - - - - -	1
John Webb a souldier Belonging to Capt Bull - - - - - -	1
David Burt belonging to ye same Compe - - - - - - -	1
Joseph Marks of ye same Compe . - - - - - - -	1
In all - - - -	27

THE WAY HOW YE BLOODY FRENCH AND INDIANS COMMITTED THIS TRAGEDY WAS THUS.

After they were gott into ye Toune without being discovered (no watch or guard being kept, notwithstanding several gentn of Albany no longer than three days before were up there to Persuade ym to it.) The french and ye Indians besett each house and after they had murthered ye People they burnt all ye houses and barns Cattle &ca Except 5 @ 6: which were saved by Capt Sander to whom they were kinde as they had particular orders so to be by reason of ye many kindnesse shewne by his wife to ye french Prisoners.

Albany, ye 22 day of february $16\frac{89}{90}$.

Symon Van Ness and Andries Barents who went out ye first wth ye Maquaese returning told; they had Pursued ye Enemy to ye great Lake & would have overtaken them had they not been spyed by some of ye Enemy Indians that went out to looke for 2 Negroe boys, yt were Runn away from them, & yt ye Indians & Christians were all Tyred when they came to ye Croune Point neer ye Lake; some went further till they came to where ye Ise was Smoth; where the french had with horses that they carried from Skinnectady & Skeets and Yse Spurs, made all the way they could over ye Lake in so much that our People could gain nothing upon them; whereas at first they went 2 of there days journeys in one; neverthelesse Laurence ye Maquase and about 140 Mohoggs & River Indians are gone in Pursuite of them, and will follow them quite to Canida.

JACOB LEISLER TO MARYLAND.

[From Vol. in Sec's Office, endorsed "Duke of York's Charter, Laws, Papers &c. in Leisler's time. I."]

March 4, 1689 (O. S.) In fort William.

To our great griefe I must acquaint you of the sad and deplorable massacre which happened at skenectady near Albany by the french and their Indians the 19th of ffebruary last betwixt Saturnday & Sunday at eleven of the clock in the night 200 men fell upon them & most barbarously murdered sixty two men women & children & burnt the place left but 5 or 6 houses unburned carried away captive 27 the rest escaped many of which being about 25 persons much damnified by the french women withe chyld ript up, children alive thrown into the flames, some their heads dashed ag^t the doors & windows all occasioned by their neglect of their not watching, deryving to obey under the command of the Commission of Sir Edmond, the s^d commander being onley spared withall which belongs to him a safeguard being sett in his house & he himselfe to release the prisoners he desired last Nov'ber a certaine number of rebellious people at Albany calling themselves the convention & ruling by the arbitrary Comission of Sir Edmond & encouraged and supported by some of the wicked creatures of Sir Edmond, desired from me assistance of men gunes ammunition & money being afraied of the french to whom we have sent 52 men 50^lbs match 950^lbs pouder, boulits etc wch arryving there ag^t their expectatione would not receive them, & were left there by the Inhabitants desire, the s^d rebells with their fort keept the Inhabitants under a faire. I have sent up this Winter & commissioned one Captn with 25 men to Joine with our confederate Indians to warre ag^t the french at Canada, who were hindered by the s^d rebells, who proclaimed upon paine of being punished for rebells if they mett above four men soe they were prevented to goe, we would else have discovered the enemy & prevented that disaster

---

fort William March 4th 1689

Honorable Sir Governor of Boston:

Yours of the 8th instant by Mr Pembroke I received & I returne yow many thanks for the care I perceive yow have had for our packet, Since your last wee have received the sad and miserable newes from Skenectedy neere Albany whereof wee understand is laid to your woeful account it is such newes as wee feared long since, Alace what could there be expected of a certaine number of rebellious people that remained rulling under that arbitrary Commissions of sir Edmund at Albany within this province, and encouraged and supported by Connecticoatt by ordering their forces sent thither to observe the directions of the s^d rebells named a Conventione, being well assured the same is supported more especially by that waylerous John Allan the Secretary of that Collony.

THE SAME TO THE BISHOP OF SALISBURY, 31 March 1690.

[London Doc. VII.]

May it please your Lordship—The foregoing being sent via Boston p^r the agents for New England which we hope are safely arrived ere this date, we take leave to add, that [to] a certain village named Schanectede 24 miles to the northward of Albany on Saturday the 9th of Febr. last about 11 a clock at night, came 200 French and Indians near 100 each and attacqued the same while it snowed thick, barbarously destroying the Inhabitants all being dutch; they murthered 60 persons, and bore away with them 27 prisoners, wounding some others so that there remain but about one sixth part of them having their cattel, goods and provisions destroyed and arrested from them, the remnant sheltering themselves at Albany, where there is provision made for them from New Yorke. Being alarmed by the daily expectations of the French and Indians advancing towards us with a considerable number of 2500 french besides their Indians at Mont-Real, endeavouring to obtaine upon the allyed Indians with us, vizt The Macquaes, Oneydauns, Onnondades, Cayougaes, Sinnekaes, and Mehekanders who have espoused our cause, we have appointed persons to meet them at Albany in few dayes to consult our best way to intercept the Ennemies march; The Macquaes having given us a proofe of their fidelity and courage by pursuing those who destroyed Schenechtede even near their own home, taking and slaying twenty five of them who lagged in the reare, and promise to raise more than 1000 men of theirs to joyne with 400 of ours which we have near raysed for that intent, keeping the passe upon the lake with a Company of Indians and Christians in number about 50. that upon the enemyes approach, we may be timely notice, lying about 150 miles northward of Albany which we have fortified, to the best of our power and capacytyes, the fort having 13 canon, 10 Barrells of powder and 60 men in garrison with other habiliments; the towne palasadoes round and making breast works within, but want canon.

ROBT LIVINGSTON TO SIR EDMUND ANDROS.

Hartford, 14 April 1690.

May it Please y^r Excell^y—I was in hopes Yo^r Excel: should have heard ye newes of ye destroying Skinnechtady by ye French and Indians before your departure y^t your Excel. might ye more hastned their motion at Whitehall for our Settlement. On ye 9th of Feby last a Comp^y of 250 French and Indians came upon y^t place when they were all asleep about 11 a Clock at night, and killed and destroyed 60 men women and children, carryed 27 men and boys prisoners and burnt ye towne except 6 or 7 houses which are saved by Capt. Sander, whom they did not touch, having expresse command to meddle wth none of his relations for his wife's sake, who had always been kinde to ye French prisoners. The people of that Towne were so bygotted to Leysler that they would not obey any of ye Magistrates neither would they entertain ye souldiers sent thither by y^t Convention of all; nothing but men sent from Leysler would do theire turn.

Thus had Leysler perperted y^t poor people by his seditious letters now founde all bloody upon Skinnechtady streets, with the notions of a free trade, boalting &c. and thus they are destroyed; they would not watch, and where Capt. Sander commanded, there they threatened to burn him upon ye fire, if he came upon the garde. We were much alarm^d at Albany; we sent ye Maquase y^t were at hand out, and to ye Maquase Castles; but ye Messenger being so timorous did not proceed; so y^t it was 3 days before we could get ye Maquase downe to pursue them, who being joyned with our men, follow'd them to the Great Lake, where ye Yse being good and ye French haveing robb'd sundrey horses, put ther plunder upon sleds and so over ye Lake: however ye Indians pursued and gott 10, and afterwargs 5, and killed 3. Who being examined relate, y^t ye French design to attacke Albany early in ye Spring, haveing 120 batoes 100 birch canoes and 12 light morter peeces and severall other engines ready, and are to come with 1500 men. . . . . Poor Sharpe is lame being wounded with a great gunn y^t split when ye alarm came [to Albany] of Skinnechtady.

JACOB LEISLER TO THE GOVERNOUR OF BARBADOES.

[From Vol. endorsed, Letters in Leisler's time &c.]

Ao 1690: 17 May in fort William.

Honorable Sir—The French of Cannada with their Indianes committed six bloody masacres in this province three, & in New England three, they have destroyed Skanectady a village 20 miles from Albany, murdered sixty three men women and children, carried captive 27: & have committed the greatest tyranny imaginable, rypt up women with chyld throwed children alive into the flame, dasht others ag^t door post till their brains stuck to it, another murder of eleaven people, and one or two committed since last fall, we send fifty men up to guard that place, but a certaine number of people there maintaining the cômissions from Sir Edmond Andross & Coll. Dongan deryving from the authority of the late King James would not accept them there, but keept the fort by virture of the s^d Commission & would not suffer any of them to goe & guard s^d Village being the frontier but send of their people there, by which meanes from treachery cowardice and carelesnes that too unfortunate and to be lamented accident hes hapened there, the river being frozen that noe forces could be sent up the winter, the well meaned people, lodged our souldiers who kept guard in the City whereof the french & Indian (in number of 200 men) had advise the Indianes would not goe there & so altered the designe, and that place was by that meanes spared our Indians pursued them kild & took 25 frenchmen who gave us an account of severall troops out in a designe in the Spring with 2500 french besides their Indianes.

MR. VAN CORTLANDT TO S^R ED. ANDROSS.

[Lond. Doc. VII.]

19 May, 1690.

May it please your Excellency,

* * * The French and Indians have againe, since your Excell^cy's departure, destroyed some people to the Eastward of Boston, have also burned Scheneghtade killed 60 people and tooke 28 young men and boys prisoners: About 150 Indians and 50 young men off Albany followed the French overtooke them upon the lake killed some and tooke 15 Frenchmen, which the Indians have killed in their castles; the french Indians have killed eight or ten people att Conestagione,

which has made the whole country in an alarm, and the people leave their plantations. Most of the Albany Wood men are att New-Yorke. Arent Schuyler went with eight Indians to Chambly, killed 2 and tooke 1 Frenchman prisoner.

MR. LIVINGSTON TO [CAPT. NICHOLSON.]

[London Doc. VII.]

7th June. 1690.

Honble Sir,—We of Albany stood out the longest till were deserted by all New-England, and while I was sent by the Convention of Albany to procure assistance from the neighbouring colonies, Leisler sends up one Jacob Milborne, formerly a servant to a man in Hartford, but now a fitt tool for his turn with 160 men, who gott the fort surrendered to him, after I had maintained the garrison, and all publick charge to the 12th of March, turn'd out all the Souldiers but 12 or 13, which they tooke in again, and so kept there for some weeks. This Jacob Millborne, John de Bruine and Johannes Provoost, under the dominion of New-York commiss^rs^ spending their time with drinking and quaffing, while the French Indians comes and cutts off the people at Canastagione and above Synectady, and never one of them catcht. We have all Leisler's seditious letters secured which was the occasion of the destruction of Synechtady, miraculously found in the streets, all embrued wth blood the morning after massacre was committed, so that we want nothing but a Govern^r^ to call him to account.

X.

CIVIL LIST

OF THE

Province of New-York.

1693.

A LIST OF ALL THE OFFICERS

EMPLOYED IN CIVIL OFFICES IN THE PROVINCE OF NEW-YORKE IN AMERICA THE 20th OF APRIL 1693, AND OF THEIR SALLARIES.

[Lond. Doc. IX.]

Patent Officers.

	Sallarys.
His Excellency Benjamin Fletcher Esqr Capt^t Gen^ll and Governour in Chiefe of the Province of New-York and Territories depending thereon in America and Vice-Admirall of the same £600 sterling att 30 p^r cent advance is . . .	780 00 00
Matthew Clarkson Esqr Sec^ry allowed him for Paper pen and ink p^r annum . .	30 00 00
Chidley Brook Esqr Coll^r and Receiver Genn^ll p^r ann. £200—£30 Sterl p^r cent advance	260 00 00

Members of Council.

Fred. Phillips, Stephen Courtlandt, Nich Bayard, Will. Smith, Gab: Monveille, Chid. Brook, Wm Nicolls — Esqrs.

Thos Willett, Willm Pinhorne, Peter Schuyler, John Lawrence, John Youngs, Caleb Heathcote — Esq^rs.

James Grayham, Esqr Attorney Gen^ll	
David Jamison Clerk of the Councill, allowed per annum	50 00 00
Dan. Honan Accomptant-Gen^ll p^r anñ:	60 00 00
Jarvis Marshall Doorkeeper and Messenger of ye Councill	30 00 00

Justices of the Supreme Court of Judicature having the power of Kings Bench, Comôn Pleas and Exchequer.

William Smith Esq Chiefe Justice per annum	130 00 00
William Pinhorne, Esq. 2^d Justice per annum	100 00 00

(Allowed for riding the circuit.)

Steph Courtlandt
Chid Brooke — Esq^rs Justices
John Lawrence

The Secretary is the Clerk of this Court.

Custome House Officers.

Robt Livingston Sub Collector att Albany per annum	£50 00 00
Wm Shaw, Gauger att Albany p^r ann:	8 00 00
Thos Munsey Surveyor att New-York p ann	40 00 00

James Evetts Waiter	30 00 00
Emanuel Young waiter	30 00 00
The Guager at New York paid by ye cask	
Allowed to Godfredus Dellius for teaching and converting the Indians p^r^ ann .	60 00 00
To the Interpretess Helene to interprete for ye Five Nations p^r^ annum . .	20 00 00
Allowed for their Maties Barge one Coxwain p^r^ ann : and eight oars att 50^s^ each, £20	30 00 00
Allowed to a printer p^r^ ann	40 00 00
Clerk of the Assembly allowed 12^s^ p^r^ diem during ye Sessions	
Door Keeper and Messenger 4^s^ p^r^ diem during ye Sessions	
Allowed the Honble N. Blaithwayte 5 p^r^ cent out the Revenue as Auditor Generall	
	£1738 00 00

In the Citty of New Yorke

Abraham Depeyster Esq. Mayor and Clerk of the Mercate

James Graham Esqr Recorder

Standley Handcock Esqr High Sheriff

William Sharpas Towne Clerke

The Aldermen, Collectors, Assessors and Constables are elective.

In the Citty of Albany

Peter Schuyler Esq Mayor

Dirck Wessels Esq Recorder

Robt Livingston Esq Town Clerk

John Apell Esqr Sherriffe

The Aldermen, Collectors, Assessors and Constables elective.

The Mayor's Court hath the Power of the Comôn Pleas.

In each County there is a Court of Comôn Pleas whereof the first in the Commission of the Peace is Judge, and is to be assisted with any two of the three next in the commission of the Peace.

The Mayor and Aldermen are Justices of the Peace and have power to hold Quarter Sessions in the Cittys of N. York & Albany.

Justices of the Peace

In the County of Albany to joyne the May^or^ Record^r^ and Aldermen in the Quarter Sessions.

Eghbert Theunisse, Killian Van Ranslaer, Martin Gerritse, Dirck Theunisse } Esq^rs^

Nicholas Rispe, Sanders Glenn, Peter Vosburgh, Gerryt Theunisse } Esq^rs^

Justices in Westchester County

Caleb Heathcote Esqr Judge of Common Pleas.

Joseph Theale, William Barnes, Daniel Strange } Esq^rs^

James Mott, John Hunt, Wm Chadderton, Thomas Pinkney } Esq^s^

Benjamin Collier Esqr Sheriffe.

Joseph Lee Clerk of the County

Collectors Assessors and Constables elective

Justices in the County of Richmond

Ellis Duxbury Esqr Judge of the Comôn Pleas

Abraham Cannor
Abraham Lakeman
Dennis Theunisse
John Shadwell } Esq^{rs}

John Stillwell Esqr Sheriff

Justices in the County of Ulster

Thomas Garton Esqr Judge of the Comôn Pleas

Henry Beeckman
Dirck Shepmers
Wessell Tenbrook
Abraham Haasbrough } Esq^{rs}

Nicholas Antonio Esqr Sherriffe

Justices in Suffolk County

Isaac Arnold Esqr Judge of ye Comôn Pleas.

John Howell
Samuell Mulford
Richd Smith
William Barker
Matthew Howell
Ebenetus Platt
Thomas Mapes } Esq^{rs}

Josiah Hobbart Esqr Sheriffe

Justices in Queens County

Thomas Hix Esqr Judge of the Common Pleas

Richard Cornwall
Ellias Doughty
Dan. Whitehead
John Smith
Tho. Stevensant } Esq^{rs}

John Harrison Esqr Sherriffe

Andrew Gibb Clerke

Justices in the Kings County

Stephen Courtlandt Judge of y^{e} Common Pleas

Roeloffe Martinse
Nicholas Stillwell
Joseph Hogeman
Henry Filkin

Esq^{rs}

Dirk Huyle
John Theunisse
Peter Cortiliau
Stoffell Probasco

Esq^{rs}

Gerryt Strycker Esqr Sherriff

Dukes County consisting of Nantuckett and Martins Vineyard claimed by Sr William Phipps, the case of Martins Vineyard laid before their Ma'ties.

Orange County not above twenty families, for the present under the care of New York

Dutchess County haveing very few inhabitants committed to the care of the county of Ulster

Surveyors of Highways, Collectors, Assessors and Constables, are elective throughout the whole Province

An Account of all Establishmts of Jurisdiction within this Province.

Single Justice—Every Justice of the Peace hath power to determine any suite or controversy to the value of forty shillings.

Quarter Sessions—The Justices of the Peace in Quarter Sessions have all such powers and authorities as are granted in a Commission of ye Peace in England.

County Court—The County Court or Common Pleas hath cognizance of civil Accôns to any value, excepting what concerns title of land, and noe Accôn can be removed from this court if the damage be under twenty pounds.

Mayor and Aldermen—The Court of Mayor and Aldermen hath the same power with the County Courts.

Supreme Court—The Supreme Court hath the powers of Kings Bench, Common Pleas & Exchequer in England, & noe accôn can be removed from this court if under £100.

Chancery—The Governour and Councill are a court of Chancery and have the powers of the Chancery in England, from whose sentence or decree nothing can be removed under £300.

Prerogative Court—The Governour discharges the place of Ordinary in granting Administracôns and proveing Wills &c. The Secretary is Register. The Governr is about to appoint Delegates in the remoter parts of the Government, with Supervisors for looking after intestates estates & provideing for orphans

Court Marshall—The Governr hath established a Court Martiall att Albany whereof Major Richd Ingoldesby is President & Robert Livingston Judge Advocate who with the other cômissionated Captains att Albany have power to exercise Martiall Law, being a frontier Garrison and in actuall warr.

Admiralty—Their Majesties reserve the appointment of a Judge, Register, and Marshall

M. Clarkson, Secry.

A STATE OF THE MILLITIA

IN THEIR MAJESTIES PROVINCE OF NEW YORK IN AMERICA, APRIL 1693.

[Lond. Doc. IX.]

	Men.
The Millitia of the City and County of New Yorke & Orange, commanded by Coll: Abraham Depeyster, being Eight Companys of foot, and one Troop of Horse, consisting of	477
The Millitia of Queens County in ye Island of Nassaw, commanded by Coll. Thomas Willett being nine Companys Foot, and one Troop of Horse, consisting of	580
The Millitia of Suffolke County in the Island of Nassaw, commanded by Coll: John Young being nine companys of Foot, consisting of	533
The Millitia of Kings County in ye Island of Nassaw, commanded by Coll: Stephanus Van Cortland, being six Companys of Foot and one Troop of Horse, consisting of	319
The Millitia of the county of Albany comânded by Major Peter Schuyler being five companys of Foot and one Troop of Horse, now formed into Dragoons by the Governr, consisting of	359

The Millitia of Ulster and Dutchess Countys comânded by Lieut Coll. Beeckman being four Companys of Foot and one Troop of Horse now made Dragoons, consisting of - -	277
The Millitia of the County of Westchester, comânded by Coll. Caleb Heathcott, being six Companys of Foot, consisting of - - - - - - - - - - - -	283
The Millitia of the County of Richmond commanded by Capt Andrew Cannon being two Companys of Foot, consisting of - - - - - - - - - - -	104
In all -	2932

BEN. FLETCHER

XI.

PAPERS

RELATING TO

Count de Frontenac's Expedition

AGAINST

THE ONONDAGOES.

1696.

FRONTENAC'S EXPEDITION, 1696.

[Council Min. VII.]

At a Council held at his Maties ffort in New Yorke the 9th of July 1696.

Present His Excellency Benjamin Fletcher &c

ffred Phillips Steph. Cortlandt Nich: Bayard	Esq^{rs}	Gab Monvielle Peter Schuyler John Lawrence	Esq^{rs}

His Excell: did communicate intelligence from Albany with the examination of a ffrench prisoner wherein appears there is great preparacôn in Canida and a resolution of the Govern^r of Canida to reduce the five Nations this summer that all the men between fifteen & fifty in Canida are ordered to be in readiness and that all the ffrench Indians and Ottawawaes are together & that they are to joyn the Dawaganhaes

His excell. offered his opinion to march up 400 men to the Castle of Onondage to encourage and confirme the Indians.

The Council do approve thereof, but affirm the impossibility for want of money which is not to be had our neighbours having denyed assistance the Revenue lessened much by the decay of trade and great backwardness in bringing in the taxes

At a Council held at his Ma^{tys} ffort in New Yorke the 27th of July 1696.

Present His Excellency Benjamin Fletcher &c.

ffred Phillips Steph: Cortlandt Gab Monvielle	Esq^{rs}	John Lawrence Caleb Heathcote	Esq^{rs}

His Excell: did communicate a letter from Mr. Allyn of Connecticutt giving account of two ffrench men taken prisoners neere the heads of their rivers and that they report there is 1000 ffrench & 2000 Indians marched against the five Nations.

Also a letter from Coll. Ingoldesby with a belt from Onondage bringing intelligence of a great body of ffrench & Indians on this side Mount Reall on their march towards them 12 dayes aggo.

His Excell: desired the advice of the Council what is to be done offering his readynesse to march immediately to the frontiers in person and his opinion it were convenient to march up men for the frontiers that a body may be spared to go to Onondage to cover them and show our zeal for their preservacôn which will give them encouragement.

It is the opinion of the Council that there being no assistance of men from the neighbouring Colonies and a small summe of money sent from Virginia and Maryland to assist in the many great charges this Province is put to upon the alarms of the enemy it being harvest time and many of the South of the Province already listed to recruit the Companyes it will be very grevious to take the people from their labour and hardly possible there is likewise no money to answer the charge thereof

Do therefore advise that a letter be wrote to the Indians to give them encouragement and to acquaint them the King of England has sent them some presents & desire them to be watchfull.

At a Council held at his Ma^{tys} ffort in New Yorke the 31st day of July 1696.

Present his Excell: Benjamin Fletcher etc

ffred Philips Steph: Cortlandt Nich Bayard	Esq^{rs}	Gab Monvielle Caleb Heathcote	Esq^{rs}

His Excell: did communicate to the Council intelligence from the frontiers that the enemy are upon their march that the Indians of the five Nations have sent to call for assistance of Christian force and did expresse his readynesse to go to Albany.

His Excell: did desire their opinion what is to be done being there's no money in the Coffers

It is the opinion of the Council that there may be men found upon the frontiers that upon encouragement will march to the Indian Country if there were a fund to answer the charge thereof

His Excell. did declare his readynesse to go provided they will finde money to answer the necessary charge thereof

Coll Cortlandt proferred his personall credit for £200 towards the expedicôn

Coll Bayard offers the same ffred Phillips offers the same Lt Coll. Monvielle the same Coll Heathcote the same

His Excell: did recommend to them to procure the credit each for £200 forthwith.

FRONTENAC'S EXPEDITION AGAINST THE ONONDAGA INDIANS. 1696.

[Paris Doc. V.]

The Count is already advised, by despatches at the departure of last year's ships, of the preparations for a considerable expedition against the Iroquois and principally against the Onnontagues which is the chief nation, where the councils of the other five are held, the most devoted to the English, and the most strenuously opposed to the negociations for peace of preceding years. It became of importance to crush them, and it appeared to many more advantageous to do so during winter inasmuch as it was certain, said they, to find in the Village at least all the women and children who being destroyed or captured would draw down ruin on the warriors or oblige them to surrender to us.

The necessary preparations for this expedition were begun last autumn, but the large amount of snow produced a change of design, the rather as it was impossible to transport the Militia (*habitans*) from the south shore and the Island of Orleans to the government of Quebec, the river having been absolutely impassible from the sailing of the vessels to the commencement of this year.

This it was that caused the adoption of the resolution to proceed by the Mohawk country with whatever troops could be collected capable of travelling on the snow with the militia of Three Rivers and Montreal and Indians, which had always been the plan of Monsieur the Count de Frontenac who foresaw the difficulty of executing the other project during winter. But this design also aborted, because we were informed that a Mohawk prisoner who escaped from us, had communicated our intention, and that this Nation, united with the English of Orange, awaited us with resolute determination, which, however, would not have prevented us going in quest of them had the continuance of the season permitted a large body to make so long a march and to carry munitions and the supplies necessary for subsisting there.

* * * * * * * * *

The intelligence which we stated that M. le Compte de Frontenac received from the Ottawas obliged us to interrupt what we had commenced of the preparations for the Onnontagué voyage. Every thing was put in order during his short stay at Montreal. He departed for la Chine where the army arrived on the 4th July; ten Ottawa savages arrived there the same day, and coming from the vicinity of the Onnontagués they roved a long time around the village without having been able to make any prisoners, and finding themselves pursued by a considerable party, took refuge in fort Frontenac. They thanked Monsieur le Comte for not having deceived them, and for having saved their lives by furnishing them at that fort with something to eat and particularly, to smoke.

On the information given them by Sieur Dejordis, a Calvanist Captain, who commanded that fort, of the march of M. le Comte, they said they were going to meet him, and that they expected to accompany him.

Provisions having been furnished to the indians, the whole army proceeded to encamp on the 6th at Isle Perrot. Next day it was ranged in the order of battle, which it was intended should be observed during the entire march.

The savages, to the number of 500, were so divided that the greater portion were always in the van which was composed of two battalions of troops consisting each of two hundred men. They were followed by several detached batteaux of militia, bearing supplies and the baggage of M. le Comte, Messrs de Callieres, de Vaudreuil, and de Ramezay.

Monsieur de Callieres commanded the vanguard, having two large batteaux on board which were two brass pieces mounted, also mortars for grenades, fire works and other necessary ammunition, with the Commissary of Artillery.

Monsieur le Comte de Frontenac followed the vanguard surrounded by the canoes of his Staff, Sieur Levasseur, Engineer, and several volunteers. The four battalions of militia, stronger than those of the soldiers, composed the main body. Monsieur de Ramezay, Governor of Three Rivers, commanded the entire militia. The rearguard, commanded by Monsieur de Vaudreuil, consisted only of two battalions of troops and the remainder of the savages who brought up the rear.

Sieurs de la Durantaye, de May, de Grays et Dumesnil veteran captains commanded the four battalions of troops; sieur de Subercase acted as Major General and there was an adjutant (*Aide Major*) to each battalion of troops and militia; sieur de Saint Martin, a Calvinist captain, commanded the Quebec battalion, sieur de Grandville, Lieutenant, that of Beaupré; sieur le Grandpré, Major of Three Rivers, was at the head of the militia of that government, and sieur Deschambaux, King's attorney at Montreal, commanded the battalion of that place. No officers remained in the country except those whom infirmity prevented undertaking such a voyage; and with difficulty were any found for the requisite garrisons.

Sieur de Maricourt, Captain, led the savages of the Sault and the Abenakis who formed one corps; sieur Gardeur de Beauvaire, Lieutenant of those of the Mountain and of the Lorette Hurons, and sieur de Beaucourt also Lieutenant, commanded the Algonquins, Socoquois, Nipissirmens, and and the few there were of Ottawas, who constituted another corps.

The order of battle was not deranged during the march, and the troops which formed the van on one day, retired on the morrow to the rear. As there were nearly thirty leagues of Rapids to be passed the march was very tedious; it is, therefore, inconceivable what difficulty was encountered in making the portages, being obliged often several times in one day to discharge from the batteaux the greater part of the freight.

Those who have no knowledge of the country, cannot understand what we call *Cascades* and *Sautts.* Falls from seven to eight feet high are often met, and there fifty men find difficulty enough in dragging a batteau, and in places less troublesome they are under the necessity of getting into the water up to, and sometimes beyond the waist, it being impossible to stem the current even with the lightest canoes by aid of poles and paddles.

A part of the army encamped, on the day of departure, above the chute called Le Buisson; the rest followed in file next day and the rain obliged them to bivouac there.

On the 9th the Cedars rapid was passed; on the 10th the army divided in two to ascend that of Coteau du lac, a part to the north and a part to the south. The same thing was repeated next morning, and a junction was re-formed at the entrance of Lake St. Francis, which is over seven leagues long, and which was passed under sail and in full battle array.

Our Indian scouts reported at night that they had seen some ascending and descending trails. A detachment of savages and a few Frenchmen was formed to march some leagues ahead of the main body and to prevent ambuscades.

On the 12th before decamping, nine Abenakis joined Monsieur le Comte de Frontenac. Messieurs l'Intendant and the King's lieutenant at Quebec remarked in their letters that these savages said that they had learned that the English intended coming to Quebec. These false reports, which are but too prevalent in these parts, did not interrupt the continuance of the march, and the camp was formed at the foot of the Long Sault.

However long and difficult, it was all passed on the 13th. On the 14th they came to the foot of the Rapide Plat. Sieur de Mantesh, Lieutenant, was detached with fifty Frenchmen and savages to make the necessary discoveries.

On the 15th they arrived at the rapid *des Galets;* the 16th after having repaired several batteaux, they could not make any more than three leagues beyond the place called *la Galette* where the bad navigation terminated.

At those places where portages were required to be made, several detachments marched on land to cover those who drew (the batteaux.) On the 17th the rain prevented a long march.

On the 18th they proceeded to within 4 leagues of the fort [Frontenac.] They made more than twelve leagues that day, and arrived there the next day, noon; so that of 70 leagues, the distance from Montreal to this fort, they were only four days passing through the smooth water, crossing Lake St. Francis included, and thirty ascending the Rapids which do not comprise half the distance.

* * * * * * * * *

On the 26th they took their departure, and encamped at Deer island, (Ile aux chevreuils,) the scouts marching continually ahead of the army. Sieur de Luth, captain, was left in the fort as commandant with a garrison of 40 men and masons and carpenters necessary for the buildings which he was recommended to hasten. There remained only 26 sick in the fort, most of whom were wounded in the legs ascending the rapids.

On the 27th they got to within three leagues of *Riviere de la Famine,* [Black River,] and on the 28th at the mouth of that of Onontagué, our scouts reported having seen the trails of nine men.

29th. As this river is extremely narrow, 50 scouts were detached on each side, and the army proceeded only according to their reports. Some had seen the trails of thirty to forty men, and the others a canoe which had been only recently abandoned. But two leagues could be made this day, and three the next. M. le Comte and M. de Vaudreuil with the troops and a battalion of militia occupied the northern, and Messrs. de Callieres and de Ramezay with the remainder passed on the southern side. It would be useless to attempt describiug the rapids of this river; the difficulties could not be understood, since by marching from morning until night five leagues only could be made in two days.

30th. The portage of all the batteaux, canoes and baggage commenced, it being impossible to pass the Falls otherwise. M. le Comte de Frontenac, who expected to pass on foot like the others, was borne in his canoe by fifty savages singing and uttering yells of joy. The battalions who could not make this Carrying place passed it the day following. Four leagues were travelled, the road being better.

On the first of August, half the army was detached beyond the river which goes to Oneida (*Onnejoust*), and made more than five leagues in roads up to the knee. M. de Vaudreuil and the majority of the officers were at their head. This precaution was the more necessary as at a place called *Le Rigolds*, the river is not more than half a pistol shot wide, to the mouth of Lake Genenta.[1] Nothing was met during this day's march except the description of our army drawn on bark, after the manner of the Savages, and two bundles of cut rushes which signified that 1434 men accompanied us. We passed the Lake in the order of battle. Monsier de Callières who commanded that day on the left, that being the side of the enemy, made a large circuit under pretence of debarking on that side, whilst M. de Vaudreuil with the right wing hugged the shore to clear what he could encounter all around of the enemy. The vigorous manner this landing was made, sword in hand, convinced us that had the enemy been met they would not have long stood their ground. M. de Vaudreuil's detachment made a circuit of half a league and anchored at the place where M. de Callières waited. The entire body landed.

The scouts did not cease marching; they reported having seen trails proceeding from the village of the Onnontagués to Cayuga (*Oyogouis*) and Oneida (*Onejoust*), which induced them to believe that the women and children withdrew thither, and that the Warriors of these two villages came to aid their brethren.

A strong light was seen the same night in the direction of the village, which caused the supposition that they had burned it; it was even supposed that they fired cannon.

The Fort was completed next morning, the 3d. An Ottawa Savage, named the Cat, returned from scouting. He had gone some days previously with a Seneca taken last winter, whose life had been spared. They at first discovered two women whom they had neglected to capture, and they subsequently seized a man who was bathing with his wife. The Ottawa wished to bind him, but the Seneca opposed it, and released him under the pretext that he would bring in others, which began to make the Outaouac distrust him, but he had still more reason to do so when the Seneca quit him, saying that he wished to eat some new corn, and having wandered aside for that purpose, he uttered the ordinary warning cry to direct some young Onnontagués who pursued the Outaouacs, the swiftness of whose legs saved him. Half a league was made that day.

Sieur Marquis de Crissaffy, captain, was left in the fort with Sieur Desbergères, also captain, and some other officers and 140 militia men and soldiers to guard the batteaux, canoes, provisions and other heavy baggage, which could not be transported; their loss would have absolutely caused that of the whole army, and though every one wished to share the glory which M. le Compte was expected to reap, he thought he could not leave too good officers at this post. The other Seneca, the comrade of him to whom we have just alluded, deserted the night of the same day to advise his nation of the danger which mënaced the Iroquois. Inconceivable difficulty was experienced in moving the cannon and the remainder of the artillery equipments over marshes and two pretty considerable rivers which it was necessary to traverse, being obliged to carry them on their carriages and parapets, which occupied a very great number of the militia.

We camped at the place called The Salt Springs, which in truth they are. They produce enough of salt to make us wish that they were near Quebec; the cod fishery would be very easy then in Canada.

1 La Rigolle is that part of the Oswego River between Lake Onondaga and the Mouth of the Seneca River.

The 4th. The order of battle was formed at sunrise; the army being divided into two lines.

The first was commanded by M. de Callières who kept on the enemy's left; his centre consisted of two battalions of militia and the two battalions of troops composed the wings, the artillery being in the middle preceded by the two centre battalions. The greater portion of the Indians of the first line had been thrown on the right wing, as they desired. From time to time forlorn hopes of the most active savages and Frenchmen were deployed to discover and receive the first fire.

The second line was commanded by M. de Vaudreuil who placed himself on the right wing. It was composed of an equal number of battalions of militia and soldiers.

M. le Compte preceded by the cannon was borne, on a chair, (*fauteuil*,) between the two lines, in a position to place himself when he thought proper at the head, through the interval of the two battalions of militia of the first line.

Each battalion was only two deep, and showed a very great front. M. le Compte had around him his guard, his staff, and the canoe and batteaux men.

They united during the march at some places at which it was very difficult to pass the cannon hrough defiles, and over streams of some magnitude where the order of battle was broken, so that we were from sunrise till night in getting to the location of the village after a number of wheelings (*quarts de conversion*) and other evolutions sufficiently difficult to execute in the woods. But the activity of Sieur Subercaze, major, supplied every requisite. Ten other men would not have accomplished all that he performed alone, and though he was assisted by good adjutants (*aides major*) he considered it nevertheless his duty to be everywhere. This campaign furnished him with an opportunity to signalize his activity and his zeal on several occasions, but as this is the principal, mention of it cannot be avoided. Never did a man execute with more promptitude the prudent orders he received from his general.

If we did not fear being considered rather a panegyrist than a historian, we should speak as we ought of the conduct of Messrs de Callières, de Vaudreuil, Ramezay and other principal officers; but the confidence which the king reposes in them is a sufficient guarantee that he deems them worthy the posts they fill in this country, and it is unnecessary to enlarge in their praise to demonstrate that they are truly so. His choice alone justifies it.

The cabins of the Indians and the triple palisade which encircled their fort were found entirely burnt. It has since been learned that it was in a sufficiently strong state of defence. It was an oblong flanked by four regular bastions. The two rows of pickets which touched each other, were of the thickness of an ordinary mast; and at six feet distance outside stood another palisade of much smaller dimensions, but from 40 to 50 feet high.

If the flight of the savages saved the army the trouble of forcing their fortifications by trenches, as was resolved upon having all the necessary tools, it robbed them of the glory of utterly destroying them; but it must not be expected that the Indians will ever stand against a considerable opposing force. The expense which this expedition entailed ought not however to be regretted.

There were some alarms the night after arriving, and a soldier on duty at an outpost was wounded by our people.

On the 5th arrived two squaws and a child of the Mountain near Montreal, who had been a long time prisoners. They told us that they had escaped five days ago with the other women and children who were removed on the rumor of our approach. Another old woman was captured in the woods, and being unable to follow our soldiers broke her skull. In the afternoon a Frenchman, a prisoner among the Oneidas, arrived with a savage. They brought a belt from that Nation whereby they solicited peace from M. Le Comte de Frontenac. He immediately sent them back, and promised peace on condition that they should establish themselves with their families among us, assuring them that they should receive land and wherewithal to sow it. He added if their wives and children were not ready, they should bring five of their most influential Chiefs as hostages, and that they should be soon followed by the army to oblige them by force to execute the conditions imposed on them.

On the next day, the 7th, a young Frenchman, seven years a prisoner among the Onnontagués arrived in the camp. He had escaped with those who had come into the outposts the night preceding. He reported that they had retired with their families twenty leagues from their fort, having scouts always around them in order to fly farther off if pursued. He added that it is probable a great number would perish having been in such a hurry to fly that they took away scarcely any corn, caches of which they hastily made, and that they began to fall short. Almost all these caches were discovered. The grain and the rest of the booty consisting of pots, guns, axes, stuffs, wampum belts, and some peltries were plundered by our Frenchmen and Savages. The destruction of the Indian corn was commenced the same day, and was continued the two following days. The grain was so forward that the stalks were very easily cut by the sword and sabre without the least fear that any could sprout again. Not a single head remained. The fields stretched from a league and a half to two leagues from the fort: The destruction was complete. A lame girl was found concealed under a tree, and her life was spared.

An old man, also captured, did not experience the same fate. M. le Comte's intention, after he had interrogated him, was to spare his life on account of his great age, but the savages who had taken him and to whom he was given were so excited that it was not deemed prudent to dissuade them from the desire they felt to burn him. He had, no doubt, prepared himself during his long life to die with firmness, however cruel the tortures he should have to endure. Not the slightest complaint escaped his lips. On the contrary he exhorted those who tormented him to remember his death, so as to display the same courage when those of his nation would take vengeance on them; and when a savage, weary of his harangues, gave him some cuts of a knife, "I thank thee," he cried, "but thou oughtst to complete my death by fire. Learn, French dogs! and ye, savages! their allies—that ye are the dogs of dogs. Remember what ye ought to do, when you will be in the same position that I am." Similar sentiments will be found perhaps to flow rather from ferociousness, than true valour; but there are heroes among barbarians as well as among the most polished nations, and what would be brutality in us may pass for valour with an Iroquois.

The 9th M. de Vaudreuil returned from Oneida at eight o'clock in the morning. He departed on the morning of the 6th, with a detachment of six to seven hundred of the most active men of the whole army, soldiers, militia and Indians. He had, under him, Sieurs de Louvigny and de Linvillieres, Captain; Desjordis and Dauberville, Calvinist Captains; Soulange and de Sabrevois, lieutenants of foot, and several other subaltern officers. Sieur de Villedenay, also lieutenant, acted as his Aid de Camp.

As it was necessary to use great expedition, they did not march in as exact order as the army had done; M. de Vaudreuil contented himself throwing the scouts some quarter of a league in advance; and on the wings, between the scouts and the main body he placed a detached corps of 50, a forlorn hope commanded in turn by a lieutenant. They arrived on the same day before sundown within a league of the village; they would have pushed even farther if the convenience of encamping on the bank of a beautiful river had not invited them to halt. They were at the first dawn in sight of the village and as they were about to enter the fields of Indian corn, they met the Deputies of all that Nation.

They requested M. de Vaudreuil to halt, fearing that our savages would spoil their crops, assuring him that they would execute in good faith the orders which M. le Comte had given to their first delegate.

M. de Vaudreuil determined also on his side to obey punctually those which he had received, told them it was useless for them to think of preserving their grain, as, according to the word of their Father they should not want for any when retired among us; that, therefore, he should cut all down;

that their fort and cabins would not, either, be spared, having every thing ready for their reception.

He found in the village but 25 @ 40 persons, almost all having fled at the sight of the detachment, but the most influential chiefs had remained. M. de Vaudreuil consented that two or three men should follow these fugitives to try to bring them back.

On entering this village a young French woman was found a prisoner, just arrived from the Mohawk. She reported that that Nation and the English to the number of 300, were preparing to attack us. A Mohawk who had deserted from the Sault last year, the same who had given information of the proposed attack against his Nation; was captured roving around the village. He said he came there intending to surrender himself to us, which it was pretended to believe. An eye was kept on him, notwithstanding. He confirmed the report of the young French woman.

Another savage, also of the same Nation, but who had been captured with a party of our people of the Sault, where he resided, assured M. de Vaudreuil that the English and Mohawks had indeed set out to come; that many of the former had moved out from Orange, but that they had contented themselves with remaining outside some hours in line, and had returned; that the consternation was pretty general among the one and the other.

This last intelligence caused M. de Vaudreuil's detachment as much regret as the first had given them joy. It was received with a thousand yells of satisfaction, particularly by the Abenakis who said they had need neither of knives nor hatchets to beat the English; that it was idle to waste powder on such a set.

M. de Vaudreuil resolved to await them in the wood without shutting himself up in the fort. He left on the 9th between nine and ten o'clock in the morning after having seen it burned and the corn entirely cut. He camped the same night about two leagues from Onnontagué. The celerity of his movements cannot be too much praised, since he occupied only three days in going, coming and executing all he had to do, although from one village to the other was fourteen good leagues in the woods with continual mountains and a multitude of rivers and large streams to be crossed. He was therefore not expected so soon, and M. le Comte was agreeably surprized to see him return in so short a time with 35 Oneidas, among whom were as we have said, the principal Chiefs of the nation, and four of our French, prisoners.

But we are accustomed in Canada to see him perform so many gallant actions, and he has the King's service so much at heart that those acquainted with him will not be surprized at this, however extraordinary it be.

The Mohawk deserter was burnt before the departure of the army who camped that same day midway from the fort where the batteaux were left; some savages having remained behind in the hope of finding more plunder received the fire of a small party; three of them were killed without the enemy daring to advance near enough to take their scalps.

The fort was reached on the 10th and destroyed. The army encamped on the 11th below the Portage, and on the 12th at 10 o'clock in the morning at the mouth of the river, on Lake Frontenac. It was time to quit that river, and if the waters had been as low as they ordinarily are in the month of August a portion of the batteaux should have been, of necessity, abandoned. A very violent gale from the West retained the army until the 14th and though it was not altogether calm, ten leagues were made that day under sail, though we did not leave until noon.

The navigation is pretty dangerous for canoes and batteaux; the waves extraordinarily high, and the landing very difficult, there being numerous shoals in some places and in others headlands against which the sea breaks at a stupendous height. We camped in a river where the wind was less violent, and arrived next day, the 15th, at Fort Frontenac.

On the 16th, the militia and soldiers were occupied in conveying fire-wood to the fort and in cutting and transporting what was necessary for the requisite planks and boards. The masons who had been left there had erected during the Count's absence a building of 120 feet, along one of the curtains, not so high on that side as the parapet. The wood work is attached, and there is a range of loop holes along the upper loft as in the remainder of the fort. This long building contains a chapel, the officers' quarters, a bakery and the stores which are at present filled with provisions for the subsistence of the troops for more than eight months, exclusive of refreshments and what will be required for the Indians who may pass there. The two pieces of cannon, one of which was employed in the campaign and a quantity of grenades were left there. The army sojourned there the 17th; encamped on the 18th at La Galette and on the 19th on Lake St. Francis.

On the same day, the enemy attacked some canoes of our people, who had found means to precede us. One of our party was drowned, one wounded; the enemy lost three men and could not be captured by a detachment which was sent in pursuit.

On the 20th we arrived at Montreal. Some batteaux upset in the rapids and three militiamen were drowned. We were obliged to make good to the others the arms and baggage that the boat lost by upsetting.

We might extend the narrative of this campaign to a greater length, but as we should be obliged to use terms little known to those unacquainted with Canada, we considered this slight sketch would suffice.

It might have been more advantageous to His Majesty's arms, and more glorious to Count de Frontenac, had the Onnontagués followed their first plan; it would have, no doubt, cost the lives of some brave men, as the Iroquois do not fight with impunity. There might have been, perhaps, six to seven hundred men in their fort including those who had come to their aid, and scarcely any would have escaped; but their loss cannot fail to be considerable. After M. Denonville's [departure from] the Seneca country, we know the difficulty that nation had to subsist for several years. The Iroquois were powerful, and are diminished since; assistance from the English, especially provisions, comes in less abundantly; wheat is worth twenty francs the *minot* [three bushels] at Orange; the pound of powder, a *pistole;* lead and other merchandise are, in truth, cheaper than with us.

The Mohawks have very little Indian corn; the Oneidas are ruined, and it is not known whether the Senecas will not remember the high price the Onnontagués set on provisions at the time of their discomfiture, when they were obliged to give most valuable belts for supplies. There remain then only the Cayugas who can succor their neighbors, and we cannot say if they alone are sufficient for that purpose. Their hunting and fishing will, without doubt be interrupted by the different small parties now in the field. In fine, it is certain, by continuing the war as at its commencement, and as Count de Frontenac determined, the Iroquois will be reduced to the necessity of dying of hunger, or accepting peace on the conditions we may think proper to impose on them; and if the almost invincible obstinacy they seem to have to wage it with us continue, we will not despair to bring them to it, if this blow, struck without the participation of our allies from above, and which they did not believe could be undertaken without them, could force them to make as great efforts on their side as we have made on ours; it will be easy to urge them to it as long as the French remain at Missilimakinac and at other posts, but when the fatal moment of their return arrives, their absence will put an absolute termination to the little good will the former may feel towards us, when they shall see themselves abandoned. Possibly they will be greatly cooled down this autumn, seeing neither powder nor balls, nor goods coming to them. How can they be persuaded to wage war without furnishing them with the means; how can the destruction of the Iroquois be completed without their aid, if they withdraw from us and retire into the woods?

Count de Frontenac learned on his arrival, that an Onnontagué who had been captured at the fort above the island of Montreal [killed] himself in prison.

On the 22d August, thirteen Algonquins brought in two Mohawk scalps, and one woman and two girls prisoners. Seven savages from the Sault and the Mountain who had been detached to Oneida with Monsr de Vaudreuil, brought in a prisoner of the same Nation, who was burned at Montreal. Some small parties of the enemy appeared along the south shore, but they made no attack, and the harvest has been saved very quietly.

COLL. FLETCHER TO THE LORDS OF THE LATE COMMITTEE DATED THE 22D AUG. 1696.

[Lond. Doc. X.]

May it please your Lordships.

On the 2nd instant I had intelligence the Governor of Canida was in our Indian Country with 1000 French and 2000 Indians, and that the people of Albany were in some consternation lest the Indians of the Five Nations should joyne with them and fall down upon Schenectady and Albany. He surprized one Castle at Oneyde which he burnt and destroyed the Indian corne. The Onondages sent away their old men, women and children to the southward, the young men tarryed 'till they perceived the French were too numerous for them, then burnt their Fort and retreated, leaving their corne to be destroyed. It is reported by some prisoners that did escape, that an Indian brought tydings to Count Frontenac, that I was on my march from Albany with a great army as numerous as the trees of the woods, which hastened his retreat, the Cayounges and Sinnekes are no[t] hurt, I wrot to Connecticut for their quota and to the Governour of the Jerseys for men to meet me at Albany, but all my endeavours could not obtain a man from them

It is resolved in Council here for His Majtys service that the Oneydes and Onondages be supply'd with corne the ensuing yeare which will add to the charges of this Province.

I have herewith transmitted to your Lordps a copy of my proceeding at Albany on this occasion, I have delayed the giving them the present from His Majty until such time I can get them all together, and having received advice from the Rt Honble the Lords of His Majtys Privy Council of a designe the French have upon some part of America, I hastened to Yorke, for in a month or six weeks time the winds are esteemed a defence to this coast.

AN ACCOUNT OF THE LATE EXPEDITION TO ALBANY IN THE MONTH OF AUGUST 1696.

[Lond. Doc. X.]

July 31. His Excelly Benjamin Fletcher had certain intelligence that the French were on their march against the Indians of the Five Nations.

Sunday Augst the 2d. Intelligence came that the French were in the Indian Countrey and that the inhabitants of Albany were apprehensive of their marching against that garrison. At the same time came a letter from the Rt Honble the Lords of his Matys Privy Council advising of preparacons made by the French against some part of America. His Excell. the same day did recommend to the Council to cause the guns and batterys to be put in order and about noone took his departure for Albany.

On the 7th of Augst his Excell arrived at Albany and called a Council of such gentl. and officers as were upon the frontiers.

[Council Min. Vol. VII.]

At a Council held at Albany the 7th day of August 1696.

Present. His Excellency Benjamin Fletcher &c.

Col. Nich. Bayard of the Council	Coll. Richd Ingoldesby
Majr Peter Schuyler of the Council	Capt James Weems
Matth : Clarkson Secy	Capt William Hyde
Lt Coll. Charles Lodwick	Capt. Peter Matthews
Mr. Dellius the Minister to the Indians	Evert Banker Esqr
	Dirck Wessells, Esq.

His Excell the Governor said :—

Gentl. As soon as I had certaine notice from you that the enemy were marched into the Countrey of our Indian friends, and by the number of their forces did seeme to threaten this place & Schenectady, I made all the haste I could to yor assistance, loosing no more time but while I wrott to Connecticutt & the Jerseys for such supplys of men as I conceived necessary upon this occasion by this letter which I received at the same time (with those from Albany) from the Lords of His Matyes Council in England, you will see that I could not reasonably draw forces from New Yorke nor be well spared from that place myself; yet by advice of his Matyes Council there I am come up with a part of my own Company and desire yor advice what is most proper to be done for the King's service and yr own safetyes and for the secureing the Indians in their fidelity and renewing the covenant chain : this we are to consider, that time may not be lost and the Countrey not burthened by an unnecessary charge.

His Excell. further proposed sending thirty men of his own Company now brought up with him with a detachment of twenty out of each of the three Companyes here, into the Indian Countrey to cover the retreate of our Indians and secure them from their fears.

The Council were of Opinion the French being retreated it would be an unnecessary charge. And offered their advice that the Sachems of the Oneydes should be sent for (who are here) and their losse condoled, which was accordingly done.

The Council are of opinion that the members of Council present with the officers of the Companyes and principal inhabitants of this place should meet & consult with the chiefe Indians now in town about the propperest methods for bringing back those Indians that are fledd, and settling them firm again in the covenant chain, and make report what they have done therein to His Excellency. Which His Excell. did approve of & order accordingly

May it please yor Excell.

In obedience to yor Excell. order of the 7th instant we underwritten have mett & considered about the properest methods for bringing both those Indian Nations vizt the Onondages and Oneydes that are fled, and renewing with them and the rest of the Five Nations the Covenant Chain, and having thereupon sounded the opinions of the Sachims of the Maquaes and Oneydos Nations and severall of their chiefe men now at Albany, do humbly offer as our opinions that since we are informed that it is now twelve dayes ago the French army left the Indian Countrey and that the Senekes and Cayouges are still undisturbed in their own country that the Onnondage Nation upon the approach of the enemy have set their own Castle on fire and all fledd to be out of the enemy's reach, that the Oneydes Nation have in like manner left their Castle and great part of them already are come in here to Albany for reliefe in their wants of provision and ammunicôn &c. and that the Maquaes Nation or great part of them are in the like manner come in hither, We cannot perceive that it can be any great service to send any great body of men now to the Upper Nations, who are seated at that distance from hence, neither can any men be well spared from Albany, here being only three establisht companyes in garrison with a detachment of yo[r] Excell. own Company now brought with you, besides a few inhabitants; which we judge to be little enough for the defence of the place: but we humbly suppose that its of absolute necessity that small partyes be frequently sent out to clear the coast from such small troops that may come to annoy the adjacent farmers in getting in their harvest; and lastly with submission we are of opinion that the best method to reduce the Indians that are fled & to unite them with the rest to this government as formerly in renewing the Covenant chain, is,—

First, that trusty and faithfull Indians be procured and sent to the Senekes and Cayouges in their Castles and to the Onondages that are fledd, with instruccôns to acquaint them that his Excell. the Governor upon the first news of the French invading their Countrey came to Albany from New Yorke in order for their assistance and reliefe.

2. That upon his Excell. comeing hither hehad intelligence the enemy was already departed out of our Indian Countrey.

3. That it is hardly possible to have a meeting with all the brethren of the Five Nations now to consult with them what may be propper for the common good and to present them with those things which are sent to them from his Excell: great Master the King of Great Brittaine.

4. That therefore yo[r] Excell: do appoint the brethren to meet you thereunto at Albany this day two months, but if it should so happen that by reason of the Onnondages being fledd the brethren could not then meet in a body at that time the Onondages and Senekes and Cayouges will consult and pitch upon the time, and to give yo[r] Excellency timely notice thereof to the end the brethren of the Maquaes and Oneydes may be acquainted therewith accordingly, Dated the 8th of August in Albany 1696.

NICH BAYARD

G. DELLIUS EVERT BANCKER

DIRCK WESSELS P[r] SCHUYLER.

Copy of a Commission left by his Excell.

Benjamin Fletcher, Capt. Gen[l] & Govern[r] in Chiefe of his Ma[tyes] Province of New-Yorke, &c. to Peter Schuyler Esq. one of his Ma[tyes] Council for the s[d] Province, Mr. Godfrey Dellius Minister at Albany and places adjacent, Maj[r] Dirck Wessels and the May[r] of the city for the time being. I doe by virtue of the power and authority to me given by his Ma[tys] Letters Patents under the Greate Seale of England, hereby impower you or any two of you to treat conferr and consult with the Five Indian Nations of the Maquaes Oneydes Onondages and Sinnekes who have hitherto been faithful to my Master his Majesty of Great Brittain, France & Ireland &[c]. and to hold a correspondence with them pursuant to such instruccôns as you shall from time to time receive from me, so as by y[r] endeavours they may be confirmed in their fidelity and allegiance. And from time to time you are hereby required to give a constant and minute account of all yo[r] proceedings to me & his Ma[tyes] Council for the province of New-Yorke, and I doe hereby supersede vacate make null any former warr[t] or commission granted in this behalfe. Given under my hand and seal att Albany the tenth day of August in the 8th year of his Ma[tyes] reigne Anno Dmi 1696.

BEN. FLETCHER.

(Copy) *The Instructions.*

Instruccôns for Major Peter Schuyler one of his M[atyes] Council for the Province of New-Yorke, Mr. Godfrey Dellius Maj[r] Dirck Wessels and the May[r] of Albany for the time being, commissionated by me in my absence to conferr with the Five Indian Nations for his Ma[tyes] service pursuant to the s[d] Commission.

To send out trusty and faithful Indians with one or two Christians that understand the Indian Language to the Castles of the Sinnekes Cayouges and Onnondages who are fled, to acquaint them that upon the first news I had of the French Invasion I came up to their reliefe and assistance.

That att my arrivall at Albany I had Intelligence the French were retreated out of their country.

That I am desirous to have a meeting with the Five Nations at Albany to consult with them what may be proper for their common good and safety, and present them with such things as are sent from my Great Master the King.

And that I desire to meet them the Eleventh day of October next, but if it should so happen there be reason of their seperacôn and flight the brethren cannot meet in a body at that time, the Onnondages, Sennekes, and Cayouges being the uppermost Nations do consult and appoint a time and give me notice thereof, to the end the brethren of the Maquaes and Oneydes be acquainted therewith that the meeting may not faile.

That if any of the Sachims come down in my absence you hear and answer their propositions as you shall finde most to conduce to his Ma^tyes service and the safety of the Province.

That by all opportunityes you give a minute account of these affairs to me and his Ma^tyes Council for this Province and from time to time follow such further directions and instruccôns as you shall receive from us.

And it is hereby further directed by & with the advice of those of his Ma^tyes Council here present that the sume of One Hundred pounds be lodged in the hands of Mr Dellius towards the defraying the necessary charges of these persons thus employed for his Ma^tyes service of which he is hereby obliged to give a particular account to me and for his Ma^tyes Council at New Yorke or to the Governour and Council for the time being. Given under my hand and seale at Albany the tenth day of August in the eighth year of his Ma^tyes reigne Anno Domini 1696.

BEN FLETCHER

Signed DAVID JAMISON Cl. Concilij.

[Council Min. VII.]

Att a Council held at his Matyes ffort in New Yorke the 18th of August 1696

Present His Excell: Benjamin Fletcher &c.

Steph Cortlandt Nich: Bayard Gabr Monvielle	Esq^rs	John Lawrence Caleb Heathcote	Esq^rs

Resolved the Indians of the two Nations of Onnondage and Oneyde whose Corn is destroyed by the enemy be supplyed the ensuing winter at the charge of this Government.

Ordered no Indian Corne be brought down the river from Albany Vlster and Dutchesse Countyes untill the Indians be supplyed this ensueing winter and that the Commissioners appointed to treate with the Indians in his Excell: absence do purchase soe much corne as is necessary for them.

LETTER FROM COLL. FLETCHER TO Mr. BLAITHWAYTE, DATED THE 18th SEPTR 1696.

[London Doc. X.]

Sir—I am not willing to take up much of your time by my scurvy scribblings; having said all that occurs to my thoughts in this hasty call from the Five Indian Nations, who have been driven by the French from their wooden castles and are returned; they desire to see me at Albany in a short warning and I am now ready to step on board. The French Count of Canada has made but a very silly business of it after three years preparations afrighting a few naked Indians only; by this he shews them his strength and his mercy, being this summer recruited from France, he told all he took prisoners, his business was to bring them under the protection of his Master but not to destroy them. Our Chiefe Sachims would not be persuaded to stay and treate, but seeing his force, they fled, and are return'd. I hope to revitt them in their allegiance, by the presents sent from His Majty and an addition sent from this Province; but yet I want the most congent argument; a good body of men.

A JOURNALL

OF WHAT PASSED IN THE EXPEDITION OF HIS EXCELL. COLL. BENJAMIN FLETCHER CAPTAINE GENERALL AND GOVERNOR IN CHIEFE OF THE PROVINCE OF NEW YORKE &C. TO ALBANY TO RENEW THE COVENANT CHAIN WITH THE FIVE CANTON NATIONS OF INDIANS, THE MOHAQUES, ONEYDES, ONONDAGES, CAYOUGES AND SENNEKES.

Sept. 17, 1696. On Thursday after sunsett his Excell: imbarqued at Greenwich: on Tuesday morning arrived at Albany.

22. This day his Excell. viewed the fortifications of the city and gave orders to ye Mayr and Aldermen for such reparacôns as were found needfull in the blockhouse platformes and stockadoes.

27th Sunday afternoone the Sachims of Oneyde and Onnondage arrived at Albany, in the evening they supped with his Excel. giving great expression of ye joy and satisfaccôn they had in meeting his Excell.

28th His Excell sent Capt James Weems to view the garrison at Schenectady and bring report to His Excell what necessary repairs are wanting which was performed accordingly.

This day the Sachims of the other three Nations arrived and desired time to rest themselves till tomorrow.

29th His Excell. called the Sachims together and spake.

At a Meeting of the Sachims of the Five Nations at Albany the 29th of September, 1696
Present His Excell Coll Benjamin Fletcher &c

Coll. Nicholas Bayard }
William Pinhorne Esq } of the Council
Majr Peter Schuyler }
Matthew Clarkson Esq Secretary.
The Mayr Recorder & Aldermen of Albany &c

His excell said :—

Brethren, It is an inexpressible satisfaction to me that I see you here. I do heartily condole the losse our brethren the Onondages and Oneydes have susteined by the late eruption of the French army from Canida.

Upon the first certaine intelligence I had, I came up in person with [what] I could hastily gather for your assistance.

And I am now here and present you the Onondages and Oneydes these two belts of Wampum as a confirmacôn of my sincerity and these kettles to repair your losse in that kinde.

Brethren

Two months agoe I received at New Yorke the first intelligence that the French had made an insult upon your country. I forthwith came up as I said before to yor reliefe and assistance. I had an account before I did reach Albany from some of your people that the French army were retreated and marched back towards Canida. I then sent expresses desiring you all to meet me at this place. Some time after I received yo[r] answer that you would meet me about this time at Albany; and I am now come up a second time this summer in order to renew the Covenant Chain and to consult with the brethren what is most proper and may be most conducing to the common good and safety of the whole House.

I do acquaint you from my most illustrious Master the King of Great Brittaine, France and Ireland, that he will always extend his gracious protecôn to you and as a seal of it his Majesty has commanded me to deliver you these presents to keep bright the Covenant Chain from all rust and to strengthen it in behalfe of all his Majesty's Subjects, not only of this Province, but those also of New England, Connecticut, the Jerseys, Pennsylvania, Maryland and Virginia.

A list of the Presents sent from the King's Most Excellent Majesty and given to the Indians (viz[t])

24 blew coats
24 laced hatts
24 p[r] shoes with buckles
24 shirts
22 dozen hose
30 gunn barrills and locks
30 brasse kettles
1 barrell powder
400 weight of lead
1000 flints
1 grose of tobacco pipes, wood and tinn
2 grose of knives
6 pound of vermillion

Prime cost in England of the above goods £200 sterling.

A list of presents added by the government of New York.

1 piece of duffils
2 cask of Swan shott
7 barrills powder
14 large kettles
7 pieces of white hamills for shirts
100 hatchetts
54½ lbs tobacco in roll
2 grose pipes
Wampum £3. 9.
28 gallons rumm

All which cost in New York money, ...	£169	5	4½
For provision to the Indians and repairing their arms	130	19	7
Cash for Messengers, Indian Scouts for intelligence of the Enemyes motion p[d] by Mr. Dellius, Mr. Barker, Maj[r] Schuyler & Major Wessells	100	00	0
From England £200 stg in New York money is	260	00	0
In all	£660	4	11½

At a Meeting of the Sachems of the Five Nations at Albany the first of October 1696.

Present

His Excell. Coll. Benjamin Fletcher, &c.
Coll. Nicholas Bayard
William Pinhorne Esq[r]
Major Peter Schuyler
Matth: Clarkson, Esq[r] Sec[y].
The May[r] Aldermen of Albany &c

Sanonguirese a Sachim of the Mohaques was Speaker

Brother Cayenquiragoe

We returne you thanks for what you have said the day before yesterday in condoling of our losse, and for the kettles which you gave us to boyle our victuals in the room of those that are lost by the enemy as also for the two Belts of Wampum given us as a token of your sincerity, by which our hearts are mightily rejoiced and lifted up in this our poor condition.

Brother Cayenquiragoe

We are exceedingly rejoiced that the great King over the Seas has sent to us in this our low condition, by which our hearts are lifted up, we were ready to sink in a miserable perishing Condition and this makes us revive again. He laid down six Beaver Skins.

Brother Cayenquiragoe

We come to desire you to acquaint the Great King that the enemy has brought us to a very low condition and have destroyed five of our Castles; one is now left, and if that be destroyed we know not what to do; we know not what shall become of us next; pray let the Great King know this.

Brother Cayenquiragoe

We desire that since the Great King of England &c. has Canoes of Seaventy gunns a piece and many forces, you may acquaint him that it is a great pity we should be so plagued with soe small an enemy as the French and Indians of Canida. We are not able of ourselves to destroy them.

We are become a small people and much lessened by the warr. If the people of Virginia, Maryland, Pensilvania, the Jerseys, Connecticut and New-England who have all put their hand to the Covenant Chain will joyn with the inhabitants of this place we are ready to go and root out the French and all our enemyes out of Canida. He then laid down a bundle of six Beaver skins, and on the outside thereof a draft of the river of Canida with the chiefe places thereof marked to show the smallnesse of the enemy and how seated upon Canida river; which they desire may be sent over and shown to the Great King.

Quebecq
Montreal
Troy rivier

Brother Cayenquiragoe

We again thank you for the Message you have brought us from the Great King.

And we pray you to send again to him for us with all vigour and speed, and to lay before the King what we have here said, faile not in writing, faile not to let the King know it. We give these five Beavers to the man that writes, to pay for paper, penn and ink.

Brother Cayenquiragoe

We desire you to acquaint the Great King as before, that we are a small people and he has a great people and many canoes with great gunns, we desire you to write to him to know whether he will send them to destroy Canida or not against the next time the trees grow green; and if he will not send forces to destroy Canada then to send us word thereof that we may make peace for ourselves forever, or for sometime.

And we earnestly pray you will desire the Great King to send us an answer by the next time the trees grow green. He laid down a bundle of six beavers.

At a meeting of the Sachims of the Five Nations at Albany Octob 2d 1696.

Present His Excell. Coll. Benjamin Fletcher, &c.

Coll. Nich. Bayard
William Pinhorne Esq. } of the Council
Major Peter Schuyler,
Matth: Clarkson Esq. Secy.
The Mayr Recorder & Aldermen of Albany &c

Dackashhata a Sachem of the Sennekes was Speaker

Brother Cayenquiragoe

We come to condole the losse you daily receive having daily alarms of skulking partyes of the enemy doing mischiefe. Then laid down a belt of Wampum.

Brother Cayenquiragoe

I am come with the whole House to consider what tends to the comôn good of the whole House

Brother Cayenquiragoe

We come here to quicken the fire, and renew the Covenant chain.

Brother Cayenquiragoe

We come to renew the Covenant chain with all the brethren of New England, Connecticutt, New Yorke, the Jerseys, Pensilvania, Maryland and Virginia that they may partake of the warmth of the fire.

Brother Cayenquiragoe

We recommend to all that are in the Covenant Chain to be vigorous and keep it up.

Brother Cayenquiragoe

When all is said I drincke to all yor healths & then I deliver you the cupp.

Brother Cayenquiragoe.

There has been a cloud and we come to remove it, as the Sun in the morning removes the darknesse of the night.

Brother Cayenquiragoe.

The tree of safety and welfare planted here we confirme it.

Brother Cayenquiragoe.

As the tree is planted here and confirmed, so we make fast all the roots and branches of it, all the brethren of the Five Nations and the brethren of Virginia, Maryland, Pensilvania, the Jerseys, New Yorke, Connecticutt & New England.

Brother Cayenquiragoe.

We wish we may rest in quietness under that tree. We fill it with new leaves, and wish all that are in the Covenant chain may have the benefite to sitt down quiett under its shaddow.

Brother Cayenquiragoe

I do hereby renew the covenant chain with all that have put their hands in it Virginia, Maryland, Pensilvania the Jerseys, New Yorke Connecticutt & New England

Brother Cayenquiragoe.

We renew the covenant chain in behalfe of the whole House, the Mohaques, Oneydes, Onondages Cayouges & Sinnekes

Brother Cayenquiragoe.

We have lately had the losse of two Castles by the enemy, we have concluded to do our best to assist them and we desire Cayenquiragoe will doe the same.

Brother Cayenquiragoe

We wish the Cannoes may go to and again in safety that the Great King may know what we have here said and that we may have an answer. We now have made our word good: here is the cup. Then laid down some small bundles of beaver saying—it is but small, but [it] is as it were saved out of the fire.

His Excell; stood up and said—

Brethren

I have heard what you have said, and have here renewed the Covenant Chain with all the Five Nations, the Mohaques, Oneydas, Onnondages, Cayouges & Sinnekes in behalf of the Brethren of this Province, Virginia, Maryland, Pensilvania, the Jerseys, Connecticutt & New England and I assure the Five Nations of His Maties proteccôn. I have provided for you some victuals and drink to drink the King's health, and in confirmacôn thereof that it may last as long as the Sun & Moon endures I give this Belt Wampum.

The principle Sachim of the Mohaques called—Ohee.

The whole Assembly answered Heeeeee Hogh.

The principal of Oneyde called—Ohee.

The whole Assembly answered Heeeeee Hogh.

The principal Sachim of Onnondage called Ohee.

The whole Assembly answered Heeeeee Hogh.

The principal Sachim of Cayouge called Ohee.

The whole Assembly answered Heeeeee Hogh

The principal Sachim of Sinneke called—Ohee

The whole Assembly answered Heeeeee Hogh

In the evening His Excellency did appoint the principal Sachims to meet him at a private conference next morning.

At a private Meeting of the Sachims of the Five Nations at Albany the 3d Oct: 1696.

Present His Excell. Coll. Benjamin Fletcher &c

Coll. Nich. Bayard
William Pinhorne Esq. } of the Council
Major Peter Schuyler
Matthew Clarkson Esq: Sect.

His Excellency said:—

Brethren

It was proposed by the Speaker of the Five Nations the first day that I should write to my Great Master the King of England &c concerning the warr that is between the Five Nations and the French & Indians of Canida and that I should gett an answer from the Great King to you the brethren next spring.

Brethren

I must assure you its utterly impossible in so short a time to send over to my Great Master and to receive an answer for reasons which I shall now give you.

The way over the great sea is long, the danger and hazards are many, and in the winter season many storms and contrary winds.

Brethren,

I do promise you to use all the speedyest means with the first opportunity to write to the Great King and to gett you an answer which I am sure will be to yor content and satisfaction and so soon as it comes I shall communicate it to you

Brethren.

In the mean time I have appointed Maj[r] Schuyler M[r] Dellius Major Wessels and the Mayor of the Citty of Albany, to receive yo[r] propositions upon any occasion that may happen in my absence.

Bretheren

I do heartily wish you home well to yo[r] own castles and that you may look out and be carefull not to be surprized; you can never be too watchfull. I now take my leave of you and give each of you a kegg of rumm for a dram to comfort you in the way home, and a coat to keep you warm in the winter. I shall see you again (God willing) next summer or sooner if yo[r] affairs call, if it please God to continue my health.

The Sachims offer to make some propositions.

Sanongurese Sachim of the Mohagues Speaker.

Brother Cayenquiragoe

We have been a long time in the Covenant Chain with the brethren of New-Yorke, in which afterwards at sundry times the brethren of Virginia Maryland Pensilvania, the Jerseys, Connecticutt and New England came and linked themselves. They like'd the chain of peace, but where are they now; they do not like to take part with us in the war. They are all asleep; they came not to our assistance against the enemy; their hands hung down straight, and their arms are lame; we see none minde the warr but the brethren of New Yorke.

We are now down upon one knee, but we are not quite down upon the ground; lett the Great King of England send the great Cannoes with seaventy gunns each, and let the brethren of Virginia, Maryland, Pensilvania, the Jerseys, Connecticutt & New England awake, and we will stand up straight againe upon our feet; our heart is yet stout and good; we doubt not but to destroy the enemy. Then laid down a Belt of Wampum.

Brother Cayenquiragoe.

We again desire you to write to the Great King and to gett us an answer against the next time the trees become green and that there be no delay. Let it not be said to us the cannoes are lost under water, or that the wind has carried them into another country, or the like excuse, but let us have the answer against the trees grow green, without faile, for we are in great need of it. Then laid down a Bever Skin.

To which His Excell: made answer.

Brethren. I shall be faithfull and exact to my promise to you. I shall send to the Great King my Master by the first opportunity and be careful in sending you the Great King's answer, as I told you before; but I cannot be positive to a time when the voyage depends upon winde and weather which are soe uncertaine. I wish you well to yo[r] castles.

The principal Sachim of the Mohaques called—Ohee

The whole number of Sachims answered Heeeeee Hogh &c.

EXTRACT OF GOV. FLETCHER'S SPEECH

AT THE OPENING OF 4th SESS. 5th PROV: ASSEMBLY 16 OCT: 1696.

[Council Min. VII.]

Mr Speaker I am to acquaint you I have been necessitated twice this summer by advice and consent of the Council to visite Albany the ffrench Governor of Canida marched with so considerable a force into the Indian Countrey of Onnondage and Oneyde that I could not suppose his design would end there but expected that he would with that strength attempt Albany where I was ready to adjust my duty in defence of the place he contented himselfe with a poor insult over our naked Indians and retired Yet he destroyed the Castles and corne of those two Nations who must perish this winter if not relieved by us.

You all know they have been true to His Matyes interest in joyning with this Province against our common Enemy the ffrench and unlesse encouraged may be compelled by poverty to make their peace with them.

XII.

New-York Army List.

1700.

LIST OF THE OFFICERS OF THE MILITIA OF THE PROVINCE OF NEW-YORKE, 1700.

[London Doc. XIII.]

A Table of the Number of the severall Regiments in ye Province of New-York.

County of Suffolk - - - - - - -	614
Queen's County - - - - - - -	601
King's County - - - - - - -	280
Richmond County 2 Compas - - - - -	152
City & County of New York - - - - -	684
County of West Chester - - - - - -	155
Ulster and Dutchess County - - - - -	325
City and County of Albany - - - - -	371
Totall - - -	3182 men

Province of New Yorke.

List of ye present officers of ye Militia in his Matys Province of New York in America commissionated by his Excel. Richd Earle of Bellomont, Capt Generall & Govr in Chief in & over his Matys said Province &c. viz:

Of ye Regiment of Militia of ye County of Suffolk on ye Island Nassaw

Isaac Arnold - - - -	Colonel	Field Officers.
Henry Pierson - - - -	Lieut Col	
Matthew Howel - - - -	Majr	

The several Compas in ye said Regimt

The Foot Compa in the town of Brookhaven

Sam Smith - - - -	Captain	Comon Officers
Richd Floyd - - - -	Lieut	
Joseph Tucker - - - -	Ensigne	

Of the Foot Compa in ye town of Huntington

Thos Wicks - - - -	Capt	C. O.
Jon Woods - - - -	Lieut	
Epenetus Plat - - - -	Lieut	

Of ye Foot Compa in ye town of Southampton

Abra Howell - - - -	Capt	C. O.
Joseph Fordham - - - -	Lieut	
Isaac Halsey - - - -	Ensigne	

Of another Comp^a in ye said Town

-	Capt	}	C. O.
Jo^n Lupton	Lieut.		
Joseph Moore	Ensigne		

Of another Comp^a in ye said Town

Tho. Stephens	Capt	C. O.
Joseph Pierson	Lieut	
Jerem. Scot	Ensigne	

Of ye Foot Comp^a in ye Town of Southold

Tho Young	Capt.	C. O.
Sam Glover	Lieut	
Rich. Brown	Ensigne	

Of another Foot Comp^a in ye said Town

Jonathan Harlon Capt^t ——— Griffin Lieu^t

——— Emens Ensign

Of another Foot Comp^a in ye said Town

Thos Mapas Capt Joshua Harlow Lieu^t

Jo^n Booth Ensigne

Of another Foot Comp^a in ye town of East Hampton

—— Capt; —— Lieut; —— Ensigne;

Of another Foot Comp^a in ye said Town

John Wheeler Capt, Enoch Fitchin Lieut,

Corn. Conchling Ensigne

This Regiment consists of six hundred and fourteen men

Of the Regim^t of Militia in Queens County on ye said Island

	Colonel	Field Officers
John Jackson	Lieut Col	
	Maj^r	

Of the Foot comp^a in the town of Jamaica

Hope Carpenter	Capt.	Com^on Officers
Benjn Thurston	Lieut.	
Richd Oldfield	Ensigne	

Of another Foot comp^a in ye said town

Sam. Carpenter	Capt.	C. O.
Joseph Smith	Lieut.	
Dan Smith	Ensigne	

Of the Foot Comp^a in ye town of New Town

Content Titus	Capt.	C. O.
Sam. Ketcham	Lieut.	
Sam. Morrell	Ensigne	

Of another Foot Comp^a in ye said Town.

Robt Coe	Capt.	C. O.
Jo^n Berian	Lieut.	
Jonathan Coe	Ensigne	

Of the Foot Comp^a in ye Town of Hampstead

Jerem. Smith - - - - Capt.

Richd Hubbs . . .	Lieut.
Isaac Smith . . .	Ensigne,

Of another Foot Comp^{a} in ye said Town

Joseph Smith . . .	Capt.
. . .	Lieut.
Thos Gildersleeve . . .	Ensigne.

Of another Foot Comp^{a} in ye said Town

Tho. Treadwell . . .	Capt,
Jon. Pine	Lieut,
Jo^{n} Forster . . .	Ensigne,

Of the Foot Comp^{a} in ye Town of Flushing

Robert Hinchman . . .	Capt,
——— Harrington . .	Lieut,
Daniel Wright . . .	Ensigne,

Of the Foot Comp^{a} in ye town of Oysterbay

Robt Coles	Capt.
Josia Latten . . .	Lieut
Nath : Coles Junr . . .	Ensigne

Of the Troope of Horse in ye said Regm^{t}

John Lawrence . . .	Capt.
Jonath : Smith . . .	Lieut
Daniel Lawrence . . .	Cornet
Jo^{n} Finne	Quartermaster

The Regiment consists of six hundred & one men,

Of the Regiment of Militia in King's County on ye said Island,

Stephen Cortlandt . . .	Colonel	Field Officers
Gerardus Beekman . .	Lieut^{t} Col.	
Corn : Van Brunt . . .	Maj^{r}	

Of the Foot Comp^{a} in the town of Amersfort,

Jo^{n} Terhermon . . .	Capt.
Peter Mansford . . .	Lieut,
Corn Van Voorhuyen . .	Ensigne

Of the Foot Comp^{a} in ye Town of Gravesend.

John Lake	Capt.
Chr : Bemoyn . . .	Lieut,
Albert Coerten . . .	Ensigne,

Of the Foot Comp^{a} in the town of Brookland,

Joris Hansen . . .	Capt,
Daniel Repalie . . .	Lieut,
Teunis Repalie . . .	Ensigne.

Of the Foot Comp^{a} in ye town of New Uytregt.

John Van Dyke . . .	Capt.
Joost Van Brunt . . .	Lieut.
Matys Smake . . .	Ensigne.

Of the Foot Comp^{a} in ye town of Midwout

Arie Van de Bilt . . .	Capt,

Symon Hansen	Lieut,	
Isaac Hegeman	Ensigne.	

Of the Foot Comp^a in ye town of Boswick

Peter Pra	Capt,	
Michill Parmyter	Lieut,	
Jochem Vouchnewen	Ensigne.	

Of the Troop of Horse in ye said Regiment

Dan. Polhemius	Capt.	
Roeloft Verkirk	Lieut,	
Jerominus Remse	Cornet	
Gysbert Bayard	Quarter Master	

This Regiment consists of two hundred & eighty men.

Of the Militia in the County of Richmond.

Of the Foot Comp^a in the said County.

Tho. Stilwell	Capt,	
Tho. Morgane Nice Teunisse	Lieuts^s	

Of another Comp^e in ye said County

Andrew Carmon	Capt	
John Stilwell Jaque Poilton	Lieuts^s	

The said two Comp^{as} in the said County consists of one hundred & fifty two men.

Of the Regim^t of Militia in ye City and County of New York

Abra: De Peyster	Colonel	Field Officers
Wm Mervet	Lieut. Col.	
Jo^n Henry De Bruyn	Maj^r	

Of a Foot Comp^a in ye said city.

Robt. Walters	Capt,	Com^{on} Officers
Andrew Teller	Lieut	
Jo^n Hardinbrooke	Ensigne,	

Of another Foot Comp^a in ye said City

David Provost	Capt,	C. O.
Wm Churcher	Lieut,	
Absa: Brasier	Ensigne	

Of one other Foot Comp^a in ye said City.

Leonard Lewis	Capt,	C. O.
Jacob Vander Speigle	Lieut,	
Isaac Governeur	Ensigne,	

Of one other Troop Comp^a in ye said City.

Isaac De Keimer	Capt	
Steph Richards	Lieut	
Nicho. Blank,	Ensigne	

Of one other Foot Comp^a in ye said Citty

Cornelius De Peyster	Capt,	
Roger Baker	Lieut	
Corn: Lodge	Ensigne	

Of one other Foot Compa in ye said Citty

John Theobalds . . . . Capt
Peter De Melt . . . . Leiut
Isaac Brasier . . . . Ensigne

Of another Foot Compa in ye said Citty

Evert Byvanck . . . . Capt,
John Vander Speigel . . . Leiut,
Jon Tiebout . . . . Ensigne.

Of one other Foot Compa in ye said City

Martin Clock . . . . Capt,
Tho Fornuier . . . . Leiut,
Hend : Breevort . . . . Ensigne,

Of the Troop of Horse in ye said Regimt

John De Peyster Capt, Jon Outman Cornet
Jon Hoghland Leiut, Evert Van de Water Quarter master

This Regiment consists of six hundred & eighty five men.

Of the Regiment of Militia in ye County of West Chester.

. . .	Colonel	Field Officers	
. . .	Lieut. Col.		
Augt Graham . .	Majr		

Of a Foot Compa in the town of East Chester.

John Drake . . .	Capt,	C. O.
Joseph Drake . . .	Lieut,	
Henry Tower . . .	Ensigne	

Of a Foot Compa in ye town of New Rochell,

Oliver Besley . . . . Capt,
Isaac Merier . . . . Leiut,
Pierre Vasleau . . . . Ensigne

Of a Foot Compa in ye town of Mamarioneck.

James Mott . . . . . Captain
Robert Lauting . . . . Leiut,
Tho : Ives . . . . . Ensigne

This Regiment consists of one hundred fifty five men.

Of the Regiment of Militia in ye Counties of Ulster & Dutchess.

. . .	Colonel	Field Officers
Jacob Rutsen . . .	Lieut Col	
. . .	Majr	

Of a foot Compa in ye said Countys.

Matthias Mattyson . .	Captain	Comon Officers
Evert Bogardus . . .	Leiut.	
Tennis Tappen . . .	Ensigne,	

Of another Foot Compa in ye sd Countys.

Abso : Hasbrooke . . Captain
Moses Quantaine . . Lieut,
Lewis Bavea . . . Ensigne.

Of an other Foot Comp[a] in y[e] said Countys.

George Middagh . . .	Capt,
Gysbert Kroom	Lieut,
Alex, Rosebrans . . .	Ensigne.

Of another foot Comp[a] in y[e] said Countys,

Aria Rose, ...	Captain
John Rose	Lieut.
Aria Gerrutse	Ensigne

Of another Foot Comp[a] in y[e] said Countys.

Jocham Schoonmaker . . .	Captain
John Van Camp . . .	Lieut
Jacob Decker	Ensigne

Of another Foot Comp[a] in y[e] said Countys.

Coenrod Elmendorp . . .	Captain
Mattyse Sleight . .	Lieut
Garret Wyncoop . . .	Ensigne

Of another Foot Comp[a] in y[e] said Countys

Baltus Van Cleet . . .	Captain
Hendrick Kipp . . .	Lieut
John Ter Bus	Ensigne

Of the Troop of Horse in y[e] said Regiment

Egbert Schoonmaker	Captain	Abra: Gasbert	Cornet
Corn: Decker	Lieut.	Mattys Jansen	Quartermaster

This Regiment consists of Three hundred five & twenty men.

Of the Regiment of Militia in y[e] City & County of Albany.

Peter Schuyler . . .	Colonel	Field Officers
. . .	Lieut. Col.	
Dyrck Wessels	Maj[r]	

Of a Foot Company in the city of Albany.

Johannes Bleeker . . .	Captain	Com[n] Officers
Johannes Roseboom . . .	Lieut	
Abra: Cuyler . . .	Ensigne	

Of another Foot Comp[a] in y[e] said city

Albert Rykman . . .	Captain
Wessel ten Broek . . .	Lieut.
Johannes Thomasse . . .	Ensigne

Of another Foot Comp[a] in the said County.

Martin Cornelisse . . .	Captain
Andris Douw	Lieut.
Andris Koyman . . .	Ensigne.

Of another Foot Comp[a] in the said County

Gerrit Teunisse . . .	Captain
Jonas Douw Jochem Lamerse . . .	Lieut[s]
Volckart V. Hoesem Abra: Hanse . .	Ensignes

Of a Foot Comp^{a} in ye town of Schenectady

Johannes Sanderse Glen . .	Captain
Adam Woman [Vrooman?] . .	Lieut.
Harman V. Slyke . . .	Ensigne.

Of the Troope of Horse in ye said Regiment

Kilian van Renslaer . . .	Captain
Johannes Schuyler . . .	Lieut.
Bennone V. Corlaer . . .	Cornet
Anthony Bries . . .	Quartermaster

This Regiment consists of Three hundred seaventy one men.

(Indorsed) "No 13. New Yorke. List of the officers of the Militia in the Province of New Yorke
"Referred to in ye E of Bellomonts lrê of y^{e} 28 Novr 1700 Recd 18 Feb Read 1700$\frac{0}{1}$

XIII.

CENSUS

OF THE

Counties of Orange, Dutches & Albany.

1702, 1714, 1720.

LIST OF THE INHABITANTS IN THE COUNTY OF ORANGE. 1702.

Males from 16 To 60.	Males men Above 60:	ffemales women	Males Childeren	ffemales children	Males Negros	ffemales Negros	Males negros Children	ffemales Negros Children
	William Merritt	Margry His Wijff			4 Men	1 Women	1 Child	2 Gerls
Daniel D. Clerque		Geretje His Wijff	1 Child	1 Mayd	1 Men	1 Women	1 Child	1 Gerl
Jacob d Clerque								
Abram Heraingh								
Thomis Van Howtten		Trijintje His Wijffe	1 Child	6 Mayds		1 Women	1 Child	
Roloff Van Howtten								
Claes Van Howtten								
Hendrick Geritssen		Mary His Wijfe	3 Children					
John Hendrickssen								
Herman Hendrickssen.								
Geridt Hendricssen								
Lambert Arianssen		Margrit His Wiffe	2 Childeren	4 gerells				1 gerell
Geridt Lambertzen								
Lowe Reynerssen	Reyn Janzen	Lysbeth His Wijffe	1 Child	1 gerell				1 gerrell
Thonis Taelman		Brechtie His Wyffe		3 gerells	2 Men			
		Dirckje A Widow				1 Women		
Caspar Janssen		May His Wyffe	3 Childeren					
Johan Classen		Trijntje His Wyffe		3 gerells			1 Child	
Johanns Gerissen		Cathrin His Wiffe	6 Childeren	2 gerells				
Jacob Cool		Barbara His Wiffe	2 Childeren	2 gerells				
Coenrat Hanssen		Leuntje His Wiffe	1 Child	1 gerell				
Reijnier Mijnerssen		Mary His Wiffe		1 gerell			1 Child	
Dirck Straat		Tryntje His Wiffe	1 Child	1 gerell	4		1 Child	
Cornelis Hearingh		Cathe His Wiffe	1 Child	4 gerls	1 Men			
Cosyn Hearingh		Mary His Wiffe	2 Children	2 gerls		1 Women		
Jacob Flierboom		Marij His Wiffe		1 gerll				
Samuel Conklijn		Hanna His Wiffe	1 Child	3 gerels	1 Men			
Abram Blauvelt		Gritje His Wiffe	4 Children	3 gerlls				
John: Waard		Gritje His Wiffe		3 gerlls				
Isaac Gerissen		Mary His Wiffe	1 Child					
Pieter Hearingh		Gritje His Wiffe	1 Child	5 gerlls	1 men			
Jeremiah Ceniff		Anna His Wiffe	3 Children	3 gerlls				
John D'puy		Janneke His Wiffe	3 Childeren	3 gerlls				
John: d'fries		Ariantje His Wiffe	2 Children	2 gerlls				
Gerritt Huijbrechtz								
John: Meijer		Antje A Wedow	2 Children	3 gerlls	1 Men			1 Gerll
Poulus Tjurckssen								
John: Hey		Trijntje A Wedow		2 Gerlls				
Melchert Casperssen		Gertruyt His Wife	2 Children	2 Gerlls				
Jeurian Melgertssen								
John: Perre		Sara His Wiffe	1 Child	3 Gerells				
Jemes Weller		Bethe His Wiffe	3 Children					
Isaac Brett		Magdalen His Wiffe		1 Gerlls				
Will: Juell		Sara His Wiffe	2 Children	4 Gerlls				
Will Juell Juner								
	floris Crom	Lyne His Wiffe	1 Child	2 Gerells				
Willem Crom		Geritje His Wiffe	1 Child					
Ariam Crom								
Gysbert Crom								
Albert Mimelay		Meenske His Wiffe		5 Gerlls	1 Men		1 Child	
Cornlis Coeper		Altje His Wiffe	4 Children	7 Gerlls	1 Men	2 Women		
		Sara Crab Widow	2 Children	1 Gerll				
Edward Mek								
	frans Wey	Indian w: His Wiffe						
	Dirck Storm	Mery His Wife						
Coms to 49 men	Coms to 5 men	Coms to 40 Wiffe	Coms to 57 C'ilder:	Coms to 84 gerlls	Coms to 13 men	Coms to 7 Women	Coms to 7 Childes	Coms to 6 gerels

In the Countij Orange the 16th Day of Junij 1702. This ji a Trew ACount off all the Males and ffemales off Men Women and Childeren

WITNESS OUWER HAND . . . . WILL MERRETT
DANIEL DE KLERCK

Pr: Order of the Justices
the paes
D. STORM CI:

Dit is TR het marck van

THEUNIS ROELOFFZEN VAN HOWTEN
CORNELIS CLASEN

} Justices.

[Endorsed] This is a Trieuw Account of the County Orange.

A LIST OF THE INHABITANTS AND SLAVES IN THE COUNTY OF DUTCHES. 1714.

The Severall places or Districts in the County where Inhabiting.	Number of Male persons above sixty years of age.	Numbers of male persons from sixteen to sixty years of age.	Numbers of male persons under sixteen.	Numbers of ffemales above sixty.	Numbers of ffemales from sixty to sixteen.	Numbers of ffemales under sixteen.	Numbers of male slaves from sixteen and above.	Numbers of male slaves under sixteen.	Numbers of female slaves from sixteen and above.	Numbers of female slaves under sixteen.
Jacob Kip	...	2	4	...	...	4	...	1	1	
Jacob Plowgh	...	1	...	...	1	2				
Matieis Stegt	...	1	1	...	1	1				
Evert Van Wagenen	...	1	3	...	...	2	1			
Whilliam Ostrander	...	1	1	...	1	2				
Lowrans Ostrout	...	1	2	...	1	2				
Peter Palmater	...	1	2	...	1	3				
Maghell Pallmatir	1	2	1	...	1	2	1	...	1	
William Tetsort	1	2	...	...	2	1				
Hendrick Pells	...	1	2	...	2	1				
Peter Vely	...	1	1	...	1	2				
John Kip	...	1	5	...	1	1				
Elena Van De Bogart	...	4	1	...	4	1				
John De Grave	...	1	2	...	1	2				
Lenard Lewis	...	3	3	...	5	2	1			
Bartolumus Hogenboom	...	1	1	...	1					
Baltus Van Kleek	1	2	1	...	1	...	...	2	1	2
Frans Le Roy	...	1	3	...	2	2	...	1	1	1
Barent Van Kleck	...	2	3	...	1	1				
John Ostrom	2	3	2	...	2	1				
Harmen Rinders	...	1	3	...	1	1				
Meindert Van Den Bogart	...	1	3	...	1	1				
Johanes Van Kleck	...	1	2	...	2	1				
Lenar Le Roy	...	1	2	...	1	2				
Swart Van Wagenen	...	1	3	...	1	1				
Henry Van Der Burgh	...	1	...	...	2	3	2	1	1	
Elias Van Bunchoten	...	1	2	...	1	1				
Thomas Sanders	...	1	2	...	2	2				
Cattine Lasink Wedo	1	1	2	...	...	1				
Peter Lasink	...	1	4	...	1					
———ey Scouten	...	3	3	...	2	1				
Mellen Springsteen	1	...	2	...	1	2				1
Johnes Terbots	...	2	2	...	1	3				
John Beuys	...	1	1	...	3	2				
Abram Beuys	...	1	...	...	1					
Garatt Van Vleit	...	2	1	...	4	1				
William Outen	1	...	...		...					
Andreis Daivedes	...	1	3	...	1	2				
Frans De Langen	...	1	4	...	1					
Aret Masten	...	1	1	...	1	3				
James Husey	...	2	2	...	3	1				
Roger Brett	...	1	3	...	1	1	1	1	1	
Peter De Boycs	...	1	5	...	2	1				
Isaack Hendricks	...	1	1	...	1	1				
John Breines	...	1	...	...	1	1				
Jeurey Sprinsten	...	1	4	...	1	1				
Peck De Wit	...	1	2	...	2	3	1			
Adaam Van alsted	...	1	1	...	2					
Cellitie kool	...	1	2	...	2					
Harmen knickerbacker	1	1	2	...	2					
Johanis Dyckman Seinjer	...	1	...	...	1	1	1			
Jacob Hoghtelingh	...	1	2	...	1	3				
Dirck Wesselse	1	2	...	1	2	...	2	1	2	
Willem Schot	...	1	...	...	3	3				
Jacob Vosburgh	...	5	...	...	3	1	1			
Tunis Pieterse	...	2	2	...	3	2				
henderick bretsiert	...	1								
Roelif Duijtser	...	1	3	...	2	1	1			
Johannis Spoor Junjoor	1	1	5	...	1	1				
Abraham Vosburgh	...	1	3	...	1	2				
Abraham Van Dusen	...	1	2	...	1	4				
Willem Wijt	...	1	1	...	1	3				
Louwerens knickerbacker	...	1	2	...	1					
henderck Sissum	...	1	...	...	1	1				
Aenderis Gerdener	...	2	1	...	1	1				
Gysbert oosterhout	...	1	...	...	1	6				
Johannis Dyckman Junjor	...	1	...	...	1	1				
	11	89	120	1	97	98	12	6	7	4

A LIST OF THE FFREEHOLDERS OF THE CITY AND COUNTY OF ALBANY. 1720.

first ward

Evert Wendell
Jno Dunbar
Harmanis Wendell
Peter Van Brugh
Johannis Schuyler
Antoney Van Schaick
Mindert Schuyler
Antoney Vanschaick Snor
Robert Livingston Junr
Tho: Williams
Coonrodt Tennyck
Joseph Yates Junr
Jacob Roseboom
Jacob Staats
John Rosie
Wm: Hogan
Johannis Van Alen
Jacob Lansen
Baltis Van Bentheusen
Harmanis Ryckman
Fred. Mindertsen
Daniell Kelly
Johannis Vandenbergh
Joseph Vansante
Joseph Yeats Snor
Winant Vanderpoel
John Kidney
Mindert Lansen
Obediah Cooper
Johannis Vansante
Matthews Flantsburgh
Tobias Ryckman
Peter Ryckman
Wm. Hilton
Johannis De Garmoe
Claes Van Woort
Henry Holland
John Collins
Hend: Halenbeek
Peter Gramoe
Johannis Ratclif
Luykas Hooghkirck
Hendrick Oothout
Nicolas Winegaert
Cornelis Vandyke
Johannis Lansen
Luykas Winegaert
Ryert Gerritse
Gose Van Schaick
Barent Egbertsen
Bastian Visser
Antoney Bregardes
Thomas Wendell
Johannis Tenbroeck
Antoney Coster
Danl Flantsburgh
Johannis Beekman
Johannis Wendell Junr
Antoney Van Schaick Junr
Phillip Livingston
Jacob Beekman
Revr'nd Thomas Barclay
David Grewsbeck
Stephanis Grewsbeck

2d Ward.

Johannis Cuyler
Nicos: Bleeker
Abram: Cuyler
Warner Van Ivera
Reyner Mindertsen
Barent Sanders
Wm: Grewsbeck
Guisbert Marselis
Herpert Jacobsen
Arent Pruyn
Johannis Mingeall
Johannis Hansen
Seibolet Brigardes
David Van Dyke
Johannis Vinhagen
Abram Kip
Cornelis Schermerhorn
Hendrick Tennyck
Johannis Beekman Snor
Gerrit Lansen

Issack Kip
Nanning Visser
Hendrick Roseboom
Mindert Roseboom
Andries Nach
Jan: Janse Bleeker
Johannis Bleeker
Christofell Yeats
Phillip Wendell
Jan Lansen
Gerrit Roseboom
Cornelis Van Scherline
Johans: Evertse Wendell
Abram: Lansen
Johannis Roseboom
John Hogan
Johannis Visser
Benj. Egbertsen
Johannis Grewsbeck
Claes Funda
Wm: Jacobsen

3d Ward.

Isaac Funda
Samuell Babington
Gerrit Van Ness
Albert Ryckman
Cornelis Borghaert
Jacob Borghaert
Johannis Hun
Phillip Van Vechten
Lenord Gansivoort
Jan: Evertsen
Evert Janse
Jacob Evertse
Jno: Solomonse
Hendrick Hansen
Abram: Schuyler
Derrick Brat
Johannis Van Ostrande
Johannis Evertsen
Tunis Egbertsen
Derrick Tenbroeck
David Schuyler
Winant Vandenbergh
Takel Derrickse
Johannis Backer
Thomas Long
John Gerritse
Elbert Gerritse
Isaac Borghaert
Cornelis Maasse
Jan Maasse
Barnt Brat
Jacob Borghaert Junr
Jacob Visser
Jacobus Luykasse Winegaert
Johannis Pruyn
Wessell Tenbroeck
Peter Winne
Jacob Muller
Johannis Muller
Samll: Pruyn
Reuben Ven Vechten
Cornlis Switzs
Guisbert Vandenbergh
Teirck Harminse Visser
Tunis Brat
Peter Walderom
Rutger Bleeker
Harpert Vandeusen

COUNTY OF ALBANY VIZ.

Schonectady.

Jonathan Stevens
William Coppernoll
Claes Franse
Teirck Franse
Yellous Fonda
Adam Vroman
Phillip Schuyler
David Lewis
Mindert Guisling
Peter Quacumbus
Abram Meebe
Benj. Van Vlack
Marte Powlisse
Harma Van Slyck
Sanders Gelon
Evert Van Eps
Arent Van Petten
John Weemp
Simon Switzs
Jacob Switzs
Mindert Weemp
Arent Brat

Hendrick Vrooman Junr
Harmanis Vedder
Dow Aukus
Johannis Mindertsen
Adam : Smith
Abram Trueax
Rob : Yeats
Abram : Lythall
Assweris Marselis
Abram: Groot
Hendrick Vroman Snor
Wouter Vroman
Jno. Baptist Van Epps
Derrick Brat
Jan Barentse Wemp
Barent Vroman
Jan Vroman
Gerrit van Brackell
Arent Danilse
Simon Vroman
Lawrence Chase
Cornlis Vander Volgen
Abram De Grave
Daniell Danielse
Cornelis Pootman
Sam: Hagadoring
Guisbert Van Brakell
Volkert Simonse
Jacob Schermerhorn
Jacobus Vandyke
Helmes Vedder
Arnout De Grave
Johannis Teller
Albert Vedder
Derrick Groot
Gerrit Simonse
Yealous Van Vost
Victore Pootman
Jan Delemont
Caleb Beck
Nicolas Schuyler
Johannis Gelen
Jacob Gelen
Jesse De Grave
Carle Hanse Toll
Daniell Toll
William Marrinas
Arent Schermerhorn
Esays Swaert
Johannis Vroman
Andries De Grave
Joseph Clament
John Bumstead
Harma Phillipse
Jereme Thickstone
Jacob Van Olinda
Arent Vedder
Peter Vroman
Daniel Janse
Peter Danielse
Jan Danielse
Jan Meebe
Johannis Peek
Jacobus Peek
Claes Van Petten
Cornelis Van Slyck
Marte Van Slyck
Cornelis Feele
Arnout Brat Junr
Johannis Vedder
Tunis Vander Volgen
Claes Van Petten
Andries Van Petten
Jan Schermerhorn
Wouter Swaert
Arent Pootman

Kenderhook and part Mannor of Livingston Viz.

Jochim Van Valkenburgh
Isaac Fansborough
Casper Rouse
Peter Van Alen
Lamert Huyck
Burger Huyck
Johannis Huyck
Derrick Gardineer
Peter Van Slyck
Jno: Gardineer
Evert Wieler
Derrick Goes
Peter Fausburgh
Peter Van buren
Jno: Goes
Mattias Goes
Luykas Van Alen

Jacobus Van Alen
Evert Van Alen
Johannis Vandeusen
Cornelis Schermerhorn
Johannis Van Alen
Gerrit Dingmans .
Bartlemeus Van Valkenburgh
Thomas Van Alstine
Coonrodt Burgaret
Stephanis Van Alen
John Burgaret
Abram: Van Alstine
Lawrence Van Schauk
Elias Van Schauk
Jurie Klaime
Guisbert Scherp
Lawrence Scherp
Hendrick Clawe
Lamert Valkenburgh
Melgert Vanderpoel
Lenord Conine

The north part of the Mannor of Livingston:

Robert Livingston Esqr
Peter Coole
Killian Winne
Jan Emnerick Plees
Hans Sihans
Claes Bruise
Jonat: Rees
Coonrodt Ham
Coonrodt Schureman
Johannis Pulver
Bastian Spikerman
Nicolas Smith
Baltis Auspah
Jno: Wm: Simon
Hanse Jurie Prooper
Abram Luyke
Droer Decker
Jurie Decker
Nicolas Witbeck
Johannis Uldrigh
ffitz: Muzigh
Coonrod Kelder
David Hooper
Gabriell Broose
Solomon Schutt
Jacob Stover
Johannis Roseman
Nicos: Styker

Claverack

Tobias Tenbroeck
Cornelis Mulder
Cornelis Esselstine
Jeremias Mulder
Derrick Hogoboom
Cornelis Huyck
Isaac Vandeusen
Jno: Hoose
George Sidnem
Richard Moor
John Hardyck
Hendr: Van Salsbergen
Jacob Van Hoosem
Kasper Van Hoosem
Jan Van Hoosem
Saml Tenbroeck
Peter Hogoboom
Rob: Van Deusen
Casper Conine
Frank Hardyke
Johannis Van Hoosen
John Bout
Wm: Halenbeck
Johannis Coole
John Rees
Wm: Rees
Johannis Scherp
Andries Rees
Ghondia Lamafire
Hendrick Whitbeck
Jurie Fretts
Hendrick Lodowick
Jacob Eswin
Jurie Jan
Cloude Lamatere
Nicos: Vanduse *Cats Kills*

Coxhacky and Cats Kills

Mindert Schut
Wessell Tenbroeck
Wm: Lefferrese
Helme Janse
Saml Van Vechten
Gerrit Van berghen

Marte Van berghen
Frank Salisbury
Jno Brunk
Minkas Van Schauk
John Albertse
Arent Van Schauk
Michael Collier
Cornelis Van Wormer
Johannis Halenbeek
Casper Halenbeek
Jan Van Loan
Albert Van Loan
Jno: Van Loan Junr
Abram: Provoost
Jacob Halenbeek
Jno: Casperse
Coonrodt Hotlen
Philip Conine
Jno: Vanhoosem
Lenord Brunk
Peter Brunk
Isaac Spoor

Canastigonie

Jno: Quacumbus
Jno: ffoort
Jacob Pearse
Derrick Brat
Maes Rycksen
Evert Rycksen
Gerrit Rycksen
Nicholas Van Vranken
Lapion Kanfort
Cornelis Christianse
Eldert Timonse
Jno: Quackenboes Junr
Peter Ouderkerk
Jacob Cluit
John Cluit
Frederick Cluit
Saml: Creeger
Derrick Takelsen
Mattias Boose Snor
Johannis Christiansa

Half Moon.

Jacobus Van Schoonhoven
Evert Van Ness
Daniell Fort
Corn'ls Vanburen
Cornelis Van Ness
Isaac Ouderkerk
Lavinus Harminse
Tunis Harminse
Winant Vanderbergh
Roolif Gerritse
Hendrick Roolifse
Jno: De Voe
Daniell Van Olinda
Eldert Ouderkerk
Cornelis Vandenbergh

Schaatkooke

Saml Doxie
Curset Fether
Johannis Knickerbacker
Derrick Van Vechten
Johannis De Wandelaer
Simon Danielse
Martin Delamon
Lewis Fele
Daniell: Ketlyne
Peter Winne
Adrian Quacumbus
Abram Fort

Colloney Renselaers Wyck

Wouter Barheyt
Johannis Vaulkenburgh
Jno: Barheyt
Isaac Van Alstine
Jacob Schermerhorn
Jacob Schermerhorn Junr
Johns: Ouderkerk
Claes Gardineer
Andries Gardinier
Hend: Valkenburgh
Jacob Valkenburgh
Andries Huyck
Maes Van Buren
Corn'lis Van Vechten
Jonat: Witbeek
Martin Vanburen
Barent Geritse
Jan Witbeck
Jonas Dow
Andries Dow
Folcort Dow

Jno : Van Vechten
Gerrit Lansen
Volcort Van Vechten
Melgert Vandeuse
Rut Vandeuse
Tho : Witbeek
Luykas Witbeek
Solomon Van Vechten
Cap : Hendrick Van Renselaer
Philip Foreest
Martin Van Alstine
Albert Roolifse
Marte Van Alstine Junr
Jno : Funda
Derrick Vanderhyden
Gerrit Vandenbergh
Albert Brat
Cornelis Van Alstine
Johns : Wendell
Jan : Van Alstyne
Adrian Oothout
Peter Coyeman
Barent Staats
Andries Coyeman
Samuell Coyeman
Jno : Witbeek
Coonrod Hooghteeling
Storm Backer
Jno : Backer
Hendrick Van Wyen

Wm : Van Alen
Daniell Winne
Gerrit Van Wie
Jan Van Wie
Gerrit Vandenbergh
Hendr : Dow
Albert Slingerlant
Evert Banker
Wouter Vanderse
Killian Vanderse
Johannis Appel
Peter Husyele
Derrick Hagodorn
Andries Brat
Storm Brat
Ome Legrange
Johns : Legrange
Johannis Simonse
Nicos : Grewsbeek
Jno : Oothout
Mindert Marselis
Jacob Lansen
Abram Ouderkerk
Peter Schuyler Esqr
Abram Wendell
William Ketlyne
Frans Pryn
Jaac Falkenburgh
Claes Bovie
Phillip Wendell

Pursuant to an Order of Court of Judicature held for the Province of New York on the Eleventh Day of June 1720, Directed to Gerrit Vanschaick high Sheriff of the City and County of Albany; A Returne of the free holders of the said City and County.

GERRET VANSCHAIJCK Sheriff

XIV.

CADWALLADER COLDEN

ON

The Lands of New-York.

1732.

STATE OF THE LANDS IN THE PROVINCE OF NEW YORK IN 1732,

BY CADWALLADER COLDEN, SURVEYOR GENERAL.

[Colden Manuscripts, N. Y. Historical Society.]

In obedience to your Excellency's Commands, I now lay before you the State of the Lands in this Province, in the best manner I am capable of, by a plain Narrative of such facts as have come to my knowledge.

It may be necessary in the first place to observe, that the Kings Commissioners, who were sent in the year 1664 to reduce this Country to the Kings obedience (it being then in the possession of the Dutch) issued a Proclamation wherein they *Promised and Declared, that whosoever of what Nation soever will upon the Knowledge of this Proclamation, acknowledge and testify themselves to submit to his Majesties Government, as good subjects ought to do, shall be protected by his Laws and Justice, and peacibly enjoy what ever Gods blessing and their own industry hath furnished them with, and all other privilidges with English Subjects* And by the third article of Surrender, agree'd to with the Dutch Govr it is stipulated that *All People shall continue free Denizens, and enjoy lands, houses, goods, ships wheresoever they are within the County, and dispose of them as they please.* And by the eleventh Article *The Dutch here shall enjoy their own customs concerning inheritances.*

In pursuance of which the Inhabitants took out Confermations of their Lands and tenements under the hand and seal of Coll Nicholls the first English Governor under the Duke of York in which their Title under the Dutch is recited, and the form of these Confirmations appear to be every where the same.

Govr Nicholls likewise granted unimproved Lands, to any that were willing to settle and improve them and these first grants were made without any previous survey, or without reciting any certain Boundaries, but only to contain for example 100, 200 or 300 Acres adjoining to such another mans Land, or to a certain Hill or River, or Rivulet

The Reddendum in these first Grants varied from time to time. At first it was *Paying the usual Rents of New Plantations*, what that was is now a dispute, but perhaps it may still be ascertained by living Evidences and sometimes their is added as a condition of the Grant, that the Grantee *shall do and perform such acts and things as shall be appointed By his Royal Highness or his Deputy.*

In about a years time the form of the Reddendum was changed as follows *Paying such duties as shall be constituted and ordained by his Royal Highness and his heirs or such Govr or Gov^rs as shall from time to time be appointed or set over them.* It is probable people were not willing to axcept of Grants upon such precarious terms and therefore we find this form soon after changed into the folling, Paying such duties and acknowledgements as now are or hereafter shall be constituted and established by the Laws of this Government.

What Laws were then in being or afterwards enacted I know not tho° perhaps they are still among the Records; but it is to be observed, that the Legislative authority was then assumed by the Govr and Council without the assent or concurrence of the Representatives of the People and the Laws then made are now in disuse. And for this Reason, none of these Lands pay now any Quitrent, tho' their number be large, being, as I compute, not less than a Thousand: but I take into this computation all those grants in recording whereof the Clerks have omitted all that part of the grant which is commonly called the Habendum and Reddendum. The reason of which neglect, I suppose to be that they were all in the same words with a few that are Recorded at length in the beginning, for so much is recorded as wherein they can differ, when the Habendum and Reddendum is the same viz The Motives to the Grant, the bounds to the thing granted, and the Grantees name and designation.

Before I proceed further, It will be likewise necessary to observe that the greatest part of Long Island, Viz all that part which lies opposite to Connecticut, was settled from Connecticut, and claimed by the Inhabitants under the Connecticut Title, to which in pursuance of the Proclamation above mentioned some regard is had. For the first, or at least the principle Grants of Lands upon this Island, are made in Townships according to the custom of Connecticut, & to the Freeholders and Inhabitants which supposes a previous Title some I know, think that these Grants of Townships are not Grants of the Soil, but only for the Good Government of these parts of the Country, as I remember it is expressly mentioned in the Patents for the Townships of Southampton and Southold and perhaps it is so in others likewise, and the Governours who granted these Town Patents continued to grant the Soil, within the limits of these Townships, as some of the succeeding Governours did likewise, However most of all the Lands within these Townships are held by Grants from Trustees, or Common Council of these Towns upon the General Town rights only. If these Town Patents should not be valid, as to the whole Soil contained within their limits yet they may operate as a confirmation of the particular rights and possessions of those who are called freeholders in the said Grants. These Town Patents are generally upon small yearly acknowledgements—

Notwithstanding that the Gov^rs under the Duke of York, took these extraordinary methods to secure their Masters Authority, and interest, they made some Grants of Large Tracts of Land, upon trifling Quitrents but as these are very few in Comparison of what happened afterwards what observations I have to make on this head will come in more properly in another place.

Sir Edmond Andross the third English Govr of New York, as he seems to have had the interest of his Master and of the People he Governed as much at heart as any Govr that has at any time been set over this Province so he was very carefull in Granting of Lands: All lands to be Granted were Surveyed before the Grant and bounded in the Grant according to the Survey. The Quitrents were likewise fixed by the Grant, generally at the rate of one Bushel each hundred acres tho' some times at a higher rate and sometimes the rent was less, probably as the value of the land was represented. And as these grants are the most profitable to the Lords of the soil, so are they to the Tenant, they being free of all those disputes about their Boundaries which have in a great measure rendered some others useless to the grantees. Sr Edward has left but a few exceptions to be made to this general account given of his care of his Masters Interest. Coll Dungan who succeeded him, followed his steps in the Granting of Lands, but the exceptions to the General Good Rule are both more numerous and more considerable than in Sr Edmonds administration.

While Coll Dungan was Govr the Duke of York became King by which the property of the Soil and the Quitrents became annexed to the crown, and have continued so ever since, but as the Revolution happened soon afterwards, there is nothing material to be observed 'till after that time.

After the Revolution the Grants of Lands to all ran in the Kings name, whereas before that they were made in the Gov^rs name that granted the Land, and this method of Granting in the Gov^rs name was continued after the Duke of York became King, as it was before.

Coll Slaughter the first Governor after the Revolution, found the Country in such confusion and lived so short a while that I think only one Patent passed in his time for Lands. But Coll Fletcher who succeeded him, made amends by the liberal hand with which he gave away Lands. The most extraordinary favors of former Gov^rs were but petty Grants in comparison of his He was a generous man, and gave the Kings Lands by parcels of upwards of One hundred thousand Acres to a man, and to some particular favourites four or five times that quantity, but the King was not pleased with him, as I am told, and he was recalled in disgrace. This lavishing away of lands probably was one reason for

The Earl of Bellamont, who succeeded, having orders to use all legal means for breaking extravagant grants of Land, joined with the assembly in vacating several of the extravagant Grants made by Coll Fletcher but as this act was carried thro' with Spirit of party in the assembly, it passed with much less impartiality than might have been expected from the Justice of the Legislature. For some of the most extravagant Grants were passed over, while some others were declared extravagant and vacated, that no way deserved that Character. However this act has considerably encreased his Majestys Quitrents for of these tracts which were then vacated, and which by their patents were to pay altogether five beaver skins, one otter skin one fat Buck and twenty shillings the lands since that time regranted within the bounds of the said patents pay near four hundred pounds yearly at the rate of 2^s^ 6^d^ per hundred acres, notwithstanding that a great part of these lands still remain ungranted. The Earl of Bellamont's administration was short he being removed by Death before he could compleat the designs he had in view

After his death the administration fell into Capt Nafans hands, then Lieu^t^ Govr. It appears that the Grants made in his time pass'd in a hurry, without any previous Survey, but upon very uncertain informations of the natural Boundaries, which the Grantees took in their Grants, so that some of them are become a sort of ambulatory Grants. The Pateentees claiming, by virtue of the same Grant, sometimes in One part of the Country, and sometimes in another, as they are driven from one place to another by others claiming the same lands with more certainty. In other grants we find the same persons joined in several Grants with others, which Grants were intended for different Tracts and in appearance seem to be so, and yet by their present claims they take in the same Lands within the bounds of their several grants.

The Earl of Bellamont was succeeded, after Queen Anns ascension to the throne by her Cousin the Lord Cornbury. The Grants of large tracts upon trifling quitrents, that were made during his Lordships administration at least equalled those of all his predecessors put together. Indeed his Lordship's inclinations were so evident to everybody at that time that two Gentlemen (as I am well assured) had agreed with his Lordship for a Grant of all the lands in the Province, at a Lump, which were not at that time granted, and that the only thing which prevented the passing of that grant was, that those Gent^n^ apprehended that the Grant would of itself appear so extravagant and would create so many enemies, that they would not be able to hold it. During the Lord Cornbury's administration an act was likewise passed, repealing the act above mentioned for vacating the extravagant Grants of Land by Coll Fletcher. The vacating Act passed not long before King Williams Death, and lay in the offices in England without any notice taken of it, till after the Lord Cornbury was removed from his Government; then the vacating Act was confirmed and the Act repealing it was repeal'd by the Queen and at the same time new instructions were given to the Govr, by which the Quitrent was directed not to be less than 2^s^ 6^d^ each hundred acres, and previous surveys were ordered to be made before the Grant should pass, which have effectually prevented the above mentioned abuses.

I shall now proceed to some more particular account of the great Grants of Lands, I mean of such as contain fifty thousand Acres and upwards to a Million of acres, for if I be not very much misinformed, there is more than one that contain that quantity.

No quantity of Land or number of Acres, for the most part, are mentioned in any of these Grants, nor is it possible to discover the Quantity, by inspection of the Patents, as it may be done in those Grants which are founded on a previous Survey and where any quantity is expressed, it seems to be done more with design to hide the real quantity (if their present claims be truly conformable to their original bounds) than to set forth the truth, for I have heard of one instance at least, where the patent Grants 300 acres, and the patentee now claims upwards of sixty thousand acres within the bounds of his Grant. Others suspecting that such disproportion, between the real quantity and the quantity express'd in the Grant, might invalidate the Grant, got the quantity of land to be expressed in the following manner, Containing for example, One thousand acres of profitable Land, besides wood Land, and waste and yet, when these Lands were Granted, perhaps there was not ten acres that was not wood Land, or One Acre that at the time of the Grant yielded any profit or one acre that by improvement might not be made profitable. Others guard against this exception to their Grant, by adding to the quantity of Land expressed in the Grant these words, *Be it more or less*, or some such words, and by virtue of these they not only claim a small quantity more than is expressed in the patent, but claim twice as much, and often ten times as much, and sometimes above one hundred times the quantity of Land that is expressed in the Grant, but as I said before, generally no quantity of Land is expressed in the Large Grants

There being no previous Survey to the Grants, their Boundaries are generally expressed with much uncertainty, by the Indian names of Brooks, Rivulets, Hills, Ponds, Falls of water &c which were and still are known to very few Christians, and which adds to this uncertainty is, that such names as are in these Grants taken to be the proper name of a Brook, Hill, or Fall of water &c in the Indian Language signifies only a Large Brook or broad Brook, or small Brk or high Hill, or only a Hill or fall of water in general, so that the Indians shew many places by the same name Brooks and Rivers have different names withe the Indians, at different places and often change their names, they taking their names often from the abode of some Indian near the place where it is so called. This has given room to some to explain and enlarge their Grants according to their own inclinations by putting the names mentioned in their grants to what place or part of the Country they please, of which I can give some particular instances where the claims of some have increased many miles, in a few years, and this they commonly do, by taking some Indians, in a Publick manner, to shew such places as they name to them, and it is too well known that an Indian will shew any place by any name you please, for the small reward of a Blanket or Bottle of Rum; and the names as I observed, being common names in the Indian language, and not proper ones as they are understood to be in English, gives more room to these Frauds.

Several of the great Tracts lying on Hudson's River are bounded by that River, on the East or West sides and on the North and South sides by Brooks or Streams of Water which, when the Country was not well known, were supposed to run nearly perpendicular to the River, as they do for some distance from their mouths, whereas many of these Brooks run nearly parallel to the River and sometimes in a course almost directly opposite to the River. This has created great confusion with the adjoining patents, and frequently Contradictions in the boundaries, as they are expresssed in the same patent.

Sometimes the Grant is of the Land that belonged to such an Indian by name or is bounded by such an Indians lands, but to prove that any particular spot belonged to any particular Indian, or to show the bounds of any particular Indian, I believe is beyond human skill, so as to make it evident to any indifferent man.

I shall next recite what have been the consequences of these large Grants, It is evident that thereby the King has been deprived of almost all his Quitrents, which it appears by the powers given to the Govrs to grant Lands, the King design'd to reserve. But the consequence I think, has been much worse as to the improvement of the country for tho this Country was settled many years before Pennsylvania, and some of the Neighboring Collonies, and has many advantages over them, as to the situation and conveniencies of Trade, it is not near so well cultivated, nor are there near such a number of Inhabitants, as in the others, in proportion to the quantity of Land; and it is chiefly if not only where these large Grants are made where the Country remains uncultivated—tho they contain some of the best of the lands, and the most conveniently situated. And every year the Young people go from this Province, and purchase Land in the Neighboring Colonies, while much better and every way more convenient Lands lie useless to the King and Country The reason of this is that the Grantees themselves are not, nor ever were in a Capacity to improve such large Tracts and other People will not become their Vassals or Tenants for one great reason as peoples (the better sort especially) leaving their native Country, was to avoid the dependence on landlords, and to enjoy lands in fee to descend to their posterity that their children may reap the benefit of their labor and Industry. There is the more reason for this because the first purchase of unimproved Land is but a trifle to the charge of improving them.

It may perhaps deserve the consideration of those who are more capable of Political foresight than I am, whether, if these large Grants take place, as they are designed and become great Lordships with large dependencies and revenues, whether this will secure or indanger the Dependancy of the Colonies on their Mother Country. I think few instances can be given where great changes were brought to effect, in any state but when they were headed by Rich and powerful men; any other commotions generally produced only some short lived disorders and confusions

Now that I have done with what is more peculiarly my business the Historical part of this representation, yet, as your Excellency did me the Honour likewise to ask my opinion of what Remedy may be most proper and effectual, I flatter myself that the giving my opinion at large in writing will be most agreeable to your Excellency's commands.

What at first Sight occurs in the vacating or breaking these Grants by due course of Law, and indeed there seems in common justice to be room enough for it but (to the purely Legal part, as it is an art or science I pretend to no skill in it) It is evident that in many of these the Governor who granted them was deceived as to the quantity; but that the King was deceived in all of them. The Govr who granted these large tracts, if they knew their extent, were guilty of a notorious breach of trust, and as it cannot be supposed, that they did this merely in the gayety of their heart, they must have had some temptation, and this must be supposed to proceed from those that received the Benefit of it. That therefore the Grantees are equally guilty with the Govr in deceiving the King, and likewise of defrauding all the adventurers or settlers in the Colony of their equal chance of obtaining the most improvable and convenient lands, and of preventing the improvement and settling of the Colony for which purpose only the Lands are supposed to be Granted. These things supposed, I can make no doubt of a remedy in the common course of the Law, but notwithstanding of this I apprehend, that it will be accompanied with so many difficulties, that it will be better to think of some other. For all attempts, of those in the administration upon the properties of the subjects, are looked upon with an evil eye and as dangerous, and will be more so in this country, where perhaps few grants in America are made with such skill and care that some flaw may not be found in them by a strict and legal search, so that every man will be apt to look upon any attempt of this kind, as in some measure his own case, and those that are really concerned will use all their Art to stir up the people to make it a Country Quarrel. To prevent this it may be proposed, to give an absolute confirmation of all the Grants excepting such as are truly extravagant. But it will be difficult how to define or determine the Grants that are truly such without making the exceptions too general or too particular, by naming the particular Grants to be excepted.

The following proposal seems to me to be more practicable, viz to abolish all the present rents, by an act of the Legislature, and in lieu of them to establish the Quitrents of all passed grants at 2^s 6^d per hundred acres, with an absolute Confirmation of all Grants upon their paying the said Quitrents.

This would effectually restore the Quitrents, and would as effectually destroy all the Gr^{ts} which are truly extravagant. I mean such as the Proprietors cannot improve in any reasonable time for as this rent would be very heavy where the Tracts exceed twenty or thirty thousand acres, the Patentees would gladly surrender their Grants, to free themselves from this Burden, but at the same time it would be just to preserve to them their improved Lands under proper restrictions of not rendering useless any part of what is not delivered up.

The Quitrents would in this case be sufficient to support the Government, and if they were applied to that purpose, I believe would give a general satisfaction, because it would be as equal a Taxation as could well be contrived, and the taxes would not, as they do now, fall only upon the improvements and the industry of the people. It wou'^{d} likewise absolutely remove the complaints of the Merchants, so that it would generally please all sorts, excepting the owners of the large Tracts—And I humbly conceive it for the Kings interest and of all those in the Administration to consent to this because the Quitrents are of no use besides paying the Salary of the Receiver and Auditor, and that Gentlemans estate would be thought to be ill managed, when it only paid his Steward and his Clerks wages. Besides when the revenue shall be fixed in this manner it will be much easier to obtain extraordinary supplies when they shall be wanted, and it will likewise be much easier for the People to pay them.

The chief objection, which I can conceive, that will be made to this is that if a perpetual revenue be Granted, then the Gov^{rs} will be free'd from that dependance on the People, and check on their behaviour that is necessary in all well ballanced Governments and which is the only check which the poor people have in America and that without such check the people of the Plantations may become a prey to Rapacious Tyrannical Gov^{rs} or other officers, tho the people do not doubt of their obtaining relief from the King and his Ministers, yet that relief is at such a distance, and must be attended with so much charge, that few private persons can have any benefit by it, and may often prove ineffectual by being too late even when many join in the complaint. Therefore unless some effectual solid check be given to the people, in lieu of what they have at present, by granting the Revenue for a short time, it cannot be expected that ever they will consent to a perpetual Revenue of any kind, or that they will be easy under it.

Now I have laid before your Excellency in the best manner I can within the bounds I think it necessary to confine myself, the most material things concerning the Grants of Lands, as far as relates to the King, the people of the Province, and the Grantees. If the remedy for the abuses set forth be thought practicable, no doubt your Excellency will easily obtain an Instruction, such as the Earl of Bellamont had to propose to the Assembly to find some proper means for establishing the Quitrents generally over all the lands in Province at the same rate and for promoting the improvements and settling of the Country, for that otherwise the King will take such legal methods, as shall be thought proper for vacating extravagant Grants, and receiving his Quitrents. And if there be a permission given at the same time to apply the Quitrents to the support of Government and absolutely to confirm all past Grants, I believe an Assembly may conform with the Instructions, under such restrictions as shall be thought necessary checks on the officers—

In order to compute what the Quitrents would immediately yield I make the following calculation—

Long Island is computed to be 150 miles long, and Albany to be the same number of miles distant from New-York, I suppose Long Island to be eight miles wide, one place with another, and that 10 miles on each side Hudson's River would immediately pay rent, this amount to—2,688,000 Acres, which at 2^{s} 6^{d} the hundred will yield £3350, and if the Cities of New York and Albany pay a reasonable Quitrent for their house lots the whole Quitrent will immediately amount to 4000 pounds yearly, which is more than the Assembly has at any time given for the support of Govern^{t}

It may be objected that the length of Long Island and distance to Albany may be less than what is vulgarly computed: That New Jersey extends 20 miles on one side Hudson's River: and that some Mountainous places, within my computation will yield no quitrent in this age but if it be considered that Staten Island is not within the Computation that the settlements extend 30 miles beyond Albany, and that many settlements are twenty miles from the river and some thirty miles, it will be granted the Quitrents will at least amount to the sum above mentioned.

In the last place it may be objected, that the Kings Ministers design the Quitrents for other uses, but if it be considered of what consequence it is to free the Kings Officers of that immediate dependance on the humours of an Assembly, they are now under for their daily support, I believe it will be thought more for His Majesty's service to apply the Quitrents to the support of the Administration in this Province, than to the uses the Quitrents have been hitherto applied.

NOTE.—Appended to the copy of the preceding, in possession of the N. Y. Historical Society, is the following memorandum, in the hand-writing of Lieut. Governor COLDEN:—

MAY 6th, 1752.

It is now twenty years since I delivered the above Memorial to Col. Cosby, soon after his arrival. I question whether ever he read it. I have reason to think he gave it to the person in whom he then confided who had no inclination to forward the purposes of it. It had no other effect than to be prejudical to myself.

The computations of what the lands would have at that time produced at 2^{s} 6^{d} p^{r} hundred acres I believe were made within bounds. The settlements are greatly increased since that time more than in fifty years before it so that I make no doubt they will produce six thousand pounds a year, taking in a reasonable Quitrent for the house lots in the Cities of New-York and Albany.

I forgot to mention that it appears from the Records that numbers of house lots were granted under the yearly Quitrents of one shilling two shillings &c or some such small rent which I believe is now never paid.

XV.

PAPERS

RELATING TO

The Susquehannah River.

1683—1757.

[From the Dutch Records entitled "Proceedings of the Justices of the Peace from 1680 to 1685," in the County Clerk's Office, Albany.]

Extraordinary Meeting holden in Albany
on the 7 *Septemb*r 1683.

Present—Marte Gerritse, Cornelis Van Dyck, Dirck Wessels, Joh: Provoost, J. Janse Bleker.

Two Cayugas, Aekontjaeken and Kakejaegoeke by name, and a susquehanne being questioned in the Court house relative to the situation of the Susquehanne River which Mr. Wm Haig and Mr. James Graham, Gov: Wm Penn's Agents, propose to purchase, Report as follows:—

That it is one day's journey from the Mohawk Castles to the Lake whence the Susquehanne River rises, and then 10 day's journey from the River to the Susquehanne Castles—in all 11 days:

One day and a half's journey by land from Oneida to the kill which falls into the Susquehanne River, and one day from the kill unto the Susquehaune River, and then 7 days unto the Susquehanne Castle—in all 9½ days' journey:

Half a days journey by land and one by Water from Onnondage before we arrive at the River, and then 6 days from the River:

From Cayuga one day and a half by Land and by water before arriving at the River and then 5 days from the River:

From Sinnekes' four Castles 3 days by Land and two days by water ere arriving at the River and then 5 days from the River—in all 10 days which is very easy, they conveying their packs in Canoes from the River—

The Indians demand wherefore such particular information relative to the Susquehanne River is sought after from them, and whether people are about to come there? The Indians are asked if it would be agreeable to them if folks should settle there? The Indians answer, that they would be very glad if people came to settle there, as it is nigher than this place and more convenient to transport themselves and packs by water inasmuch as they must bring every thing hither on their backs; say further, that people must go from here and dwell there. Those there should be pleased on that account—they will come to trade there.

N. B. The ascending the Susquehannah River is one week longer than the descending.

A Map of the Susquehannah River is sent to the Governour with this letter:—

Albany 8*th* *of Sep*r 1683.

Right Honble—We have according to your honrs Commands taken Informacôn both off Christians and Indians concerning ye situation of Susquehannes River, and how near it Lyes to ye severall Nations off Indians Westwards, that Live in his R: highnesse Territories and from whence ye trade is brought to these Parts, and after that we caused Twoo Cajouges Indians and a Susquehanne Indian demonstrate to us all ye Rivers and Creeks Relating thereunto, doe finde, that they that settle upon said River will be much nearer to ye Indians than this Place, and consequently y Indians more Inclinable to goe there, where ye accommodation of a River is to be had, then come by Land here, as the said Indians did expresse, soe yt by that meanss your honr may easily conjeecture, how advantageous it will be to his Royall highnesse Intrest, and since your honr was desyreous to know our opinions of y^e bussinesse, wee cannot juge, but that it will be Prejudiciall to his Royall highnesse Government but y^e Expedient that it is to be found for Preventing y^e same, is Left to your $hono^r$ Consideracôn Wee have ordered our Secretary to draw a draught of y^e River, and how y^e $fores^d$ five Nations of Indians Lie, as near as y^e $fores^d$ Indians could demonstrate, which wee are apt to beleeve is not much amisse, and have sent it here Inclosed, we shall p^r y^e first conveniency expect your hon^{rs} Comânds how to act and Proceed in y^e Bussinesse. In y^e meantime shall break off and Remain

Your hon^{rs} most humble &
most obedient Servants
Y^e COMMISSARIES OF ALBANY $\&c^a$

THE MAGISTRATES OF ALBANY TO GOV. DONGAN.

Right hon^{ble}

Last night Arnout y^e Interpreter arrived here from y^e Indians Westward and brings us news y^t y^e four Nations vizt Cajouges, Onnondages, Oneydes & Maquase are upon there way hither and may be expected her to-morrow, Wee are credibly Inform'd of there willingnesse to dispose of ye Susquehanne River, being verry glad to hear off Christians intending to come and Live there, it being much nearer them then this Place and much easier to get thither with there beever, The River being navigable w^t Canoes till hard by there Castles, soe y^t if Wm Penn buys said River, it will tend to ye utter Ruine off ye Bev^r Trade, as ye Indians themselfs doe acknowledge and Consequently to ye great Prejudice off his Royall highnesse Revenue's and his whole Territoryes in general, all which we doe humbly offer to your hon^{rs} serious Consideracôn, Wee presume that there hath not any thing Ever been mooved or agitated from y^e first settling of these parts, more Prejudiciall to his Royall highnesse Intrest, and y^e Inhabitants of this his $govern^t$ then this businesse of y^e Susquehanne River, The french its true have endevoured to take away our trade, by Peace mealls but this will cutt it all off at once; The day after your hon^r departed, wee sent a draught of y^e River and how near there Castles lie to it, drawne by our $Secr^r$ as near as y^e Indians could deskribe, a copy Whereof we have kept here, and Arnout y^e Interpreter says that he is also informed by diverse Indians, that y^e Castles are situate as near y^e Susquehanne River as y^e draught demonstrates, if not nearer; and in his Private discourse with them, did Perceive there joy of People comeing to live there; Wee did expect an $answ^r$ of our Letter w^t y^e Last Sloops with absolute orders concerning this bussinesse, In the meantime shall Putt a Stopp to all Proceedings till wee have Rec^d your hon^{rs} Commands wch we hope will be to deny y^e treaty in this point. This goes by an Expresse sent by Mr Haig We suppose to Mr Graham to come up and Prosecute businesse; In y^e meantime shall use our uttmost Endeavours in our Stations both for Our Masters hon^r and y^e Interest and y^e Welfare off his Territories, whilst wee subscribe ourselfs

Your hon^{rs} most humble
& Devoted Servants Y^e
Commissaries of Albany $\&c^a$

Albany 24 $Sept^r$ 1683

Mr Haig did not send y^e Canoo yesterday, expecting Possibly to hear first off y^e Indians arrivall who are now all att Skinnecttady.

PROPOSALS

OFFERED BY THE CAYUGA AND ONONDAGE SACHEMS TO THE W. COMMISSARIES OF ALBANY, COLONIE RENSELAERSWYCK &C. IN THE COURT HOUSE OF ALBANY THE 26th SEPTEMBER, 1683.

[From Dutch Record C. No. 3, in County Clerk's Office, Albany.]

Present—Marte Gerritse, Corn: Van Dyck, Dirck Wessells, J. Provoost, P. Winne, Hend: Van Ness, J. Janse Bleker, R. Pretty, Sheriffe, P. Livingston, Sec.

Brothers. We are rejoiced to see the Brethren here who Represent Corlaer, We were yesterday together and heard the Great Penn, (meaning the agent of Governr Penn) speak about the Land lying on the Susquehanne River, but saw none of the Commissaries, nor Corlaer's order.

I have slept but little through the night though I constantly tried, and think that the Land cannot be sold without Corlaer's order, for we transferred it to this Government four years ago. Therefore we shall do nothing in the Sale without Corlear (meaning the Gov. Genl) or his order or those who Represent him.

The aforesaid Land belongs to us, Cayugas and Onondages, alone; the other three Nations vizt the Sinnekes, Oneydes and Maquaas have nothing to do with it.

We have not only conveyed, but given it, four years ago, to Corlaer, that is the Gov. Genl, to rule over it, and we now Convey and Transport it again and give it to the Gov. Genl or those who now Represent him; and in confirmation hereof we have signed and sealed these Presents. Dated as above.

This is the mark of
Thaowe ⊙ ratt Sachem of Cayuga [L. S.]
This is [mark] the mark of Corrachjundie of Cayuga [L. S.]
This is the + mark of Ochquari okichke of Cayuga [L. S.]

Me present
Ro: Livingston Secr

Albany the 26 *Septr* 1683.

Present as before.

ANSWER TO THE PROPOSALS OF THE CAYUGAS AND ONNONDAGES.

We have heard your Proposals and thankfully accept for Corlaer the conveyance of the Susquehanne River, with the Land situate thereupon and have seen that you have adhered to your word of over four years since, and in confirmation of your gift and conveyance of the Land aforesaid have signed and sealed it. We, therefore, give you a half piece of Duffels, Two Blankets, Two Guns, Three kettles, Four Coats, Fifty lbs. of Lead and Five and twenty lbs. of powder.

Meanwhile we shall communicate this to His Excell: the Gov: Genl. of whose good disposition towards you, you need not doubt, who will compensate you therefor when occasion permits.

Whereupon the Sakamakers have signed and sealed their gift and conveyance as is to be seen on the other side, and have accepted in full satisfaction, the aforesaid presents.

Albany in the Court house as above.

CORNELIS VAN DYCK
DIRCK WESSELS
JAN JANZ BLEECKER
PIETER WINNE.

[Council Min. V.]

At a Council held at ffort James in New-York, Octob^{r}. [1683.]

Psent — The Governo^{r}
Capt. A. Brockholls
M^{r}. ffr. Fflypsen
J. Spragge — M^{r}. S. V. Cortland

The Indians being asked if they were only for the Maquas, they answered, yes; and came from the three castles of the Maquas

* * * * * * * * * * *

Speech of the Sachem Odianah.

That ossoone as they received the Message, they came hither and are very gladd to be so well received and that his Mat'y hath so great a kindness for them; os for the Indians that are gone to Canada, they are very gladd his hono^{r} speaks of it and they will endeavor to get them back again and they desire the Governor's assistance in it that they may goe hand in hand to promote it, and they doubt not to get them back againe.

That when they were sent for hither they did not know what might be proposed to them; and for Corlear's proposition to make peace with the Indians they war against, they say that ossone as they com home they shall have a Generall meeting of all the Castles and will tell them what is here proposed and doubt not but it shall be effected; for the former Governor said the same and they obeyed and made peace and why should it not be allso at this time performed, for they have been always obedient to this governm^{t} that his Hono^{r} having told them to have an eye to the ffrenchmen, they give his Hono^{r} their thanks, & will allways have an eye open to those people, and they desire if anything happen to be informed for they are and have been allways belonging to this Governm^{t}. and we expect no favo^{r} from the ffrench, but will put themselves under his Hono^{s} protection. That the Governor haveing wondred why they bring so little Beaver and formerly did bring so much, that it may be the Governo^{r} thinks they carry it to some other Governm^{t} they answer no they do not They never had so firm a friendshipp with any, os with this Government but the true reason is they haveing a warre with other Indians, those Indians would not dare to come on their hunting places; but now they are all in peace; the Indians catch away the Beaver so fast that ther be but very few left; his Hono^{r} haveing told them they should harbour no ffrench but the Jesuits and each of them a man, they answer they will never suffer any straggling ffrenchmen amongst them, but those Jesuits who are very good men and very quiett; and yet if his Hono^{r} shall please, they will send them away allso; and that none hath any land from them and they are resolved never to sell or give them any or any others except the people of this Governm^{t} that they were sent for by the Govern^{r} of Canada who told them that they should make a peace with all the Indians and that the Govern^{r} took their axe and threw it into the water, but did not bury it because if it had been buried it might have been taken up again; and that nothing shall com to their ears but they will acquaint this Govern^{t} with it, and expect the same from this Government.

They allso say the Govern^{r} of Canada promised them to have free passage upon all the Rivers and Creeks and said they should suffer al other Indians to have the same & the Govern^{r} took them os his children and told them they should be all of the ffrench Religion.

That all this land is under the Governm^{t} of his R^{ll} High^{ss} that there has been som Strangers at Albany to buy the Susquehannah River, but they have considered and will not sell it to them except by the particular leave of his Hono^{r}.

The Governr desired them to make up the differences amongst themselves about Susquehanna River in a civil and peaceable way, that being don to send word to the Governor, and that then he will give them fuller orders about it.

At a Council held April 29th, 1684.

P'sent — The Governor
Mr Luças Santen
J. Spragg. — Coll Lewis Morris.

Mr. Willm Welch said Governr Penn had a desire to treat wth the Indians of Susquehannah River by the consent of the Governor of New-York.

Mr. Lloyd said that Governr Penn complained of ye unkind usages and sinister dealings of the people of Albany who caused him to be put to a vast expence in bringing down the Indians and the desire of Governr Penn was that hath already bin expended may be valued and som consideration had to the loss of time and monies.

Governor Dongan replyed that as for the charges Mr Penn had bin at he had nothing to say to it, that they of Albany have suspition it is only to get away their trade and that Mr Penn hath land allready more than he can people these many yeares that the Indians have long since given over their land to fhis Govermt and advised them to write over to the Duke about it.

Mr Lloy & Mr Welch desired a letter from the Governor to the Indians wch was not granted.

FATHER LAMBERVILLE TO M. DE LA BARRE.

[Paris Doc. II.]

February 10, 1684.

The man named Oreouaké of Cayuga told me also that he would go to Montreal to see you. 'Tis he who caused Father de Carheil to withdraw and who treacherously brought the six Tionnontates to Cayuga. He is extremely proud. Sorennoa and he are the two most considerable Captains of Cayuga. It was of this Oreouaké that the English of Albany (formerly Orange) made use to prevent Sieur Penn purchasing the Country of the Andastognés who have been conquered by the Iroquois and the English of Marilande.

ABSTRACT OF THE PROPOSALLS OF THE ONOUNDAGES AND CAYOUGES SACHEMS AT NEW YORK, 2. August 1684.

[Lond. Doc. IV.]

That the English will protect them from the French otherwise they shall loose all the Beaver and hunting.

That they have put themselves and their lands under the Protection of the King and have given Susquehannah River to the Government of New York of which they desire it may be a Branch, and under which they will shelter themselves from the French.

That Penn's people may not settle under the Susquehannah River.

They have putt themselves under the King and give two Deer Skins for the King to write upon them, and put a great read Seale to them, that they put all their lands under His Ma^{ty} and under no other Government than New Yorke.

They desire these proposalls may be sent to the King with a Belt of Wampum peeg and another small Belt for the Duke of York.

And they give Col. Dungan a Beaver to send over this Proposall.

And my Lord Effingham is desired to take notice that Penn's agents would have bought the Susquehanna River of them, but they would not, but fastened it to the government of New York.

That being a free people uniting themselves to the English, it may be in their power to give their land to what Sachim they please.

PROPOSITION OR ORATION

OF THE ONONDAGOES AND CAYOUGES SACHIMS MADE IN THE TOWN HALL ALBANY BEFORE THE RIGHT HON^{ble} THE LORD HOWARD OF EFFINGHAM, GOVERNOR OF VIRGINIA AND COL. THOMAS DUNGAN GOV^{r} OF NEW YORK UPON THE 2^{d} DAY OF AUGUST 1684.

[Lond. Doc. V.]

Brother Corlaer

Your Sachim is a great Sachim and we are but a small people, When the English came to Manhattans that is N. York, Aragiske which is now called Virginia, and to Jaquokranogare now called Maryland, they were but a small people and we a great people, and finding they were good people we gave them land and treated them civilly, and now since you are a great people and we but a small, you will protect us from the French, which if you do not, we shall losse all our hunting and Bevers, The French will have all the Bevers, and are angry with us for bringing any to you.

Brethren. Wee have putt all our land and our selfs under the Protection of the great Duke of York, the brother of your great Sachim; We have given the Susquehanne River which we wonn with the sword to this Government and desire that it may be a branch of that great tree that grows here, Whose topp reaches to the Sunn, under whose branches we shall shelter our selves from the French or any other people, and our fire burn in your houses and your fire burns with us, and we desire that it always may be so, and will not that any of your Penns people shall settle upon the Susquehanne River; for all our folks or soldiers are like Wolfs in the Woods, as you Sachim of Virginia know, We having no other land to leave to our wives & Children.

Wee have put ourselves under the Great Sachim Charles that lives over the Great Lake, and we do give you Two White Drest Deer Skins to be sent to the Great Sachim Charles That he may write upon them, and put a great Redd Seale to them, Thatt we do putt the Susquehanne River above the Washinta or falls and all the rest of our land under the Great Duke of York and to nobody else, Our brethren his Servants were as fathers to our Wives and Children, and did give us Bread when we were in need of it, and we will neither joyn our selves nor our Land to any other Governm^{t} then to this, and this Proposition we desire that Corlaer the Govern^{r} may send over to your Great Sachim Charles that dwells over the Great Lake with this Belt of Wampum Peeg, and another Smaller Belt for the Duke of York his brother, and we give a Bever to the Corlaer to send over this Proposition.

And you great Man of Virginia, meaning the Lord Effingham Govern^{r} of Virginia, we let you know that Great Penn did speak to us here in Corlaer's house by his agents, and desired to buy the Susquehanne River, but we would not hearken to him nor come under His Government, and therefore desire you to be witness of what we now do and that we have already done and lett your friend that lives over the Great lake know that we are a ffree people uniting our selves to what Sachem we please, and do give you one beavor skinn.

This is a true Copy Translated, compared and Revised *P* me

ROB[t] LIVINGSTON.

SIR JOHN WERDEN TO COL. DONGAN.

[From same, Vol. IV.]

St. James's, 27th August, 1684.

[EXTRACT.] Touching Susquehannah River or lands abo[t] it or trade in it, w[ch] the Indians convey to you or invite you to, we think you will doe well to preserve yo[r] interest there as much as possible that soe nothing more may goe away to M[r] Penn or ether New Jerseys. For it is apparent they are apt enough to stretch their privileges as well as the people of New England have been, who never probably will be reduced to reason by prosecution of the Quo Warranto w[ch] is brought ag[st] y[m]

[Council Minutes V.]

At a Council August the 30th 1686

P'sent the Govern[r] M[r]. S. V. Cortlandt M[r] N. Bayard, Maj. Ger. Baxter J. Spragge Arnold Interpreter.

The Govern[r] gave presents to the Indians for w[ch] they thanked him after their manner, and he said to them

Brethren * * * * * * * *

I allso desire that neither ffrench nor English go & liue at the Susquehannah River; nor hunt nor trade amongst the Brethren without my passe and seale, the impression of which I will give them but if they doe that the Brethren bring them to Albany and deliver them at the Town house when care shall be taken for punishing them (except the priests and one man wth each or either of them) allthough any of them should be married to an Indian squa; they being only spies upon the Brethren.

At a Council Septemb 1st 1686.

P'sent the Gov. M[r] Steph. v. Cortlandt M[r] N. Bayard, Maior G. Baxter J Spragge

The Indians of the fiue Nations returned the following answer

The Cayouges & Oneydes answered first & said

Brother Corlear We are come hither at New York by y[r] order although the appointed place is at Albany.

We have understood your propositions that we are no more Brothers but looked upon as Children of wch we are gladd.

And what concerns the sending the prisoners back againe which the Cayouges and Oneydes have no hand in taking them; that concerns the Sinequas

What your Hono^r hath said about the Indians that are at Canada we will do our utmost endeauo^r to bring them from thence & do desire that y^r Hono^r would write a letter to them, wch will have more influence upon them then our bare words

Concerning the Indians going to Cadaracqua that doth not concern us but the Onnondagos.

What yor Hono^r hath said of the Christian hunters & the traders that may come upon the Susquehañah River to hunt or trade w^thout your passe; that we should take their goods from them & bring their persons to Albany, we dare not meddle therewith; for a man whose goods is taken from him will defend himself wch may create trouble or warre, and therefor we deliver the seales to y^r Hono^r againe. * * * * * * *

The Maquas stood up and said

We desire that y^r Hono^r will order that lande & a priest may be at Saraghtoge; for they will be most Maquas that return from Canada; and for the reasons given your Hono^r by the Cayouges & Oneydes we allso deliver your Hono^r the Seals againe—upon that they gaue a present

The Onondages stood up and said in Answer

Brother Corlear * * * * We are affraid the seals given us put us in a new trouble; therefore we deliver them to your Honour againe, that we may liue wholly in peace.

The Sinnequas said

We came first to Albany Although we liue the furthest off, and do find Corlear to be a good brother to us, therefore did not delay.

I shall speak first of the Seales; We know the ffrench by their Coats and the other Christians by their habitts & if we should take their goods from them, it would create trouble or warre & therefor deliver the same againe.

EXTRACT OF A LETTER FROM GOV DONGAN TO M. DE DENONVILLE, DATED 31 Octbr 1687.

[Lond. Doc. VI.]

Sir, I doe not take the King my Master's right to the five nations on this side of the lake from Monsr de la Barr, but from our records which demonstrates that these five nations has been in a free and brotherly correspondence from the first Settlement of this towne, and further they have submitted themselves, there country and conquests to the Dutch in their time and to the Kinge of England since this Colonie came under His Majes^ties obedience, so that the King haveing given a Pattent to Mr Wm Penn of a tract of land in which there conquest land uppon the Susquehana River was included in the grant, Since all this they came to me in the presents of the Lord Effingham now Govr of Virginia presentinge two dorst [dressed ?] Deerskins desiringe me to send them to the Kinge that a red broad seale might be affixed to them, that, that part of Susquehanna river might be annexed to this Collony haveing some of their friends livinge there.

THE HUMBLE ADDRESS

OF THE GOVERNOUR AND COUNCILL OF YOUR MAJESTY'S PROUINCE OF NEW YORKE AND DEPENDENCYS.
[6 AUG. 1691.]

[Lond. Doc. VIII.]

Most Gracious Sovereigne

May it please Yo[r] Most Excell[t] Maj[ty]

There being nothing so dear unto us as the prosperity of your Majesty the increase of your empire and the safety of your people planted in these remote parts of America, We therefore in all humble manner find it is our duty to represent unto your most sacred Majesty the State and Condicôn of this your Majesty's Province, that by a view thereof Your Majesty may be truly informed of the advantages accruing to your Majesty and also of the great detriment and prejudice that threatens your Majesty's interest by the pretences of our Neighbours and the strength of the French your Majesty's declared enemys.

Therefore Most Excel[t] Sovereigne

This your Maj[tys] Province was first settled and planted in the year of our Lord 1619, by the States Generall of the United Provinces, who did extend the line of their dominion from this your Majesty's Citty of New Yorke to the Eastward so farr as Connecticut River and to the Westward along the Coast beyond the Delaware River, and to the Northward up Hudson's river so farr as Schenectady and from thence to the Lakes of Canada, and from thence to the Westward so farr as the Sinnekes land or the Indian hunting reacheth. Since which time in the year of our Lord 1664, King Charles the Second did subdue and reduce to the allegiance of your Majesty's Crowne all the Inhabitants and Territorys within the limits aforesaid; all which was granted by King Charles the Second unto His Royall Highness James Duke of Yorke in the same year together with the governm[t] of all that tract of land to the Westward of Delaware River unto Maryland.

His Royall Highness was pleased out of the premises to grant a certain tract of land unto the Right Honorable John Lord Barclay, and Sir George Carterett limited and bounded by Hudson and Delaware River, as per the Deed of Conveyance relation being thereunto had may more fully appeare; the remaining part continued in his Royall Highness possession untill the yeare of our Lord 1682, William Penn procured a Patent from King Charles the Second for land to the Westward of Delaware River, now called Pensilvania, as per said pattent doth more largely appeare.

His Royall Highness was also pleased to grant unto the said William Penn, New Castle upon Delaware River and twelve miles round about and afterwards he made another grant unto him of all the land to the Southward of New Castle.

Now, may it please your Majesty, all that been reserved out of the Territorys and dominion aforesaid is only Long Island and some other small Islands adjacent, New York, Zopus, Albany and the limitts thereof; for the preserving of which the Crowne hath been at great charge, and for the support of your Maj[ties] governm[t] there is now in Generall Assembly a revenue established upon the trade thereof which is managed in manner following.

New Yorke is the Metropolis, is scituate upon a barren island bounded by Hudson's River and the East River that runs into the Sound, and hath nothing to support it but trade, which chiefly flows from flower and bread they make of the Corne the West end of Long Island and Zopus produceth; which is sent to the West Indies, and there is brought in returne from thence amongst other things a liquor called Rumm, the duty whereof considerably encreaseth your Majesties revenue.

Zopus is a place upon Hudson's River, 80 miles distant from New Yorke; consists of five small towns whose inhabitants manage husbandry and have not above 3000 acres of manureable land; all the rest being hills and mountains, not possible to be cultivated.

Albany lyes upon the same River distant from New Yorke 144 miles, only settled for Indian trade; its commerce extends itself as far as the Lakes of Canada and the Sinnekes Country in which is the Susquehannah River; their chiefe dependance is upon their traffick with the 5 Nations called Sinnekes Cayeugoes Oneydes Onondages and Maquase; which Indians in the time of the Dutch did surrender themselves and their lands to the obedience & protecôn of Albany, and upon that place's reduccôn to your Majesties Crowne of England they continued confirming the same successively to all the Governours of this Province, and hath now ratifyed and confirmed the same unto your Majesty; so that all that tract of land from the Westermost extent of the Sinnekes Country unto Albany, hath been appropriated and did absolutely belong unto the Inhabitants of Albany upwards of fourty yeares; The Indian inhabitants have always reckoned themselves subjects to your Majesties Crowne, and are not willing to submitt or have any trade or Commerce with any of your Majesty's subjects but those att Albany, your Majesty's forts of New Yorke and Albany had always an absolute dominion over all the Indian Nations adjacent to this Province but especially of all those to the Westward; and they were accustomed annually to bring tribute to your Majesty's forts, acknowledging the same, but of late years the neighbouring Colonys have obstructed them which we conceive highly injurious to your Majesty's interest and that this royalty is not conveyed by any of the afore recited grants.

Long Island is pleasantly situated and well planted but brings little gain unto your Majesty, the East end being chiefly settled by New England people who have erected five towns. Their improvements are most in pasturage and whaleing. What is produced from their industry is frequently carried to Boston and notwithstanding of the many strict rules and laws made to confine them to this place they interlope that the revenue there is not able to defray the expense of looking after it. The middle of the Island [is] altogether barren; the West end chiefly employed in tillage, which in a great measure supplys the traffiq of New Yorke.

All the rest of the Province, West Chester, Staten Island and Martin's Vineyard excepted, consist of barren mountains hills not improveable by humane industry.

Now May it please Your Maj[ty]:

The revenue that is established in this Province is in such a nature that if the encroachm[ts] and pretences of our neighbours be removed, it will not only be sufficient to defray the charge of your Maj[ties] Governm[t] but also bring in profitt into your Maj[ties] Coffers.

East Jersey is scituate on Hudsons River over against Long Island Staten Island and New York, and they pretend by the aforementioned grant to be a free place and to have free ports to trade as they please, which if admitted must certainly destroy yo[r] Maj[ties] interest and revenue here; for what merchant will come to New York and trade and pay to yo[r] Maj[ty] 2 and 10 p cent with the excise and yo[r] Maj[ties] duties settled here, if they can at 2 or 3 miles distance over against the same place go and be free from any duty or imposition whatever.

Connecticut lyes to the eastward of us & pretends to the like freedome as East Jersey, and doth in the same degree threaten y[r] Majestys interest with the like inconveniency and prejudice. Therefore may it please our Maj[ty] if Connecticut East and West Jersey be not annexed to your Majesty's Government of this Province it will be alltogether impossible to raise such a revenue to yo[r] Majesty here as will be sufficient to defray the charge of the government, and the annexing thereof cannot be injurious to the proprietors, but on the contrary advantageous to them, for it will ease them of the charge of governm[t] which hath allways exceeded the quitt Rents accrueing to them; whereas if they were annexed the profits would be freed from that charge, retain their propertys and putt the Quitt Rents clear in their pocquets.

These inconveniences of Connecticut East and West Jersey are not only prejudiciall to yo[r] Maj[tys] interest, but also the pretences of William Penn Esq[r] to the 3 lower Countrys on Delaware River and to the Susquehanna River are equally if not more injurious to your Maj[ty] and particularly in this respect Susquehanna River is scituate in the middle of the Sinnekes Country which they gave unto your Majesty's Crowne and hath belonged as an appendix to this your Maj[ties] Governm[t] many years before Mr Penn had his pattent. Notwithstanding thereof Mr Penn endevors to disturb your Majesty in the peaceable and quiett possession of the premises; endeavoring to tempt the Indians to sell it again to him, by that means not only to dispossess your Majesty of your antient rights, but also to pervert and draw away the trade of the Indians to his Province; which will be an irreparable loss to your Majesty, all the Nations with whom Albany hath their trade liveing at the head of Susquehanna River. So the revenue of 10 p[r] Cent, the impost upon powder, lead, alum and furrs, quite lost, and if Mr Penn should attain his pretences to the Susquehanna River, it will not only destroy the best branch of your Maj[ties] revenue, but it will likewise depopulate your Province, the inhabitants of Albany haveing only seated themselves there and addicted their minds to the Indian language and the misteries of the said trade with purpose to manage it, that if it should be diverted from that channell they must follow it, haveing no other way or art to gett a livelyhood.

The 3 Lower Countrys were planted at the charge and expence of this your Maj[tys] citty of New Yorke and chiefly to encrease and preserve the navigacôn of this port, being recommended to imploy their industry in planting of tobacco, which being a bulky commodity gave great encouragement to shipping as well as it brings great profitt to yor Maj[ty] Since we have mett with obstruccôns from that place by the pretences of Mr Penn, we have not been able to load so many ships as formerly; all that yor Majesties province produceth suitable for Europe being only furrs, which are of great value and in small bulk, gives little encouragement to navigation. We were also accustomed to have considerable parcells of peltry from said Countrys, which go now another way without paying yo[r] Majesty any thing, and that which is a heavier presture upon us, they constrain us a penny p[r] pound for the tobacco brought here, and send it to Pensilvania, a distinct Province, without paying any thing; by that means diverting the trade of this port to Pensilvania; by all which your Majesty may perceive that the pretences of M[r] Penn to the Susquehanna River are very injurious to your Maj[ties] right and revenue; so that some care must be taken if your Maj[ty] sees cause shall remain a distinct governmen[t] that his line doth encroach upon your Majesties right noe further upon the Susquehanna River then the fall thereof; otherwise its scituation being so near the Sinnekes Indians, if planted by him, must of necessity divert the whole trade of Albany.

May it please Your Most Excel[t] Maj[ty].

This is the state of your Majesties Province with relation to our neighbours your Majesty's subject. There is likewise the French formerly under the pretence of propagating the Christian faith amongst the Indians, did thereby very much incroach upon yo[r] Majesties right on this side of the lake, and particularly did draw away many of our Indians into Canada, under the notion of supplying them with priests to instruct them in the Christian religion; by which means they lessened our hunting much, and has so weakened the Maquase nation that they are not capable to do yo[r] Majesty the service as formerly. Besides they are so affected to the French Yo Maj[ties] enemys that while they are in being we cann have no safety. Since the war the French priests have retired from their castles, and the Dutch Minister at Albany hath been very successfull in converting many of them to the true religion, in which they are very devout and desirous to have a ministry settled amongst them for their pious comfort and instruccôn. This would be of great advantage to your Majesty not only in the increase of your revenue but also to endear the Indians to us, that they would continue to be the preservacôn of this and the rest of your Majesty's adjacent Colonys; these Nations being the strongest and most terrible among the Indians are the only bulwarke and wall of defence both against other Indians and the French pretences, which we are daily threatened with, being informed that they intend with a considerable force of themselves and the Ottawaes Indians to descend upon Albany and take it, which is not at present able (if attaqued) to resist, neither is the whole Province as now narrowed, capable to secure that post, which hath occasioned an applicacôn to our neighbours for assistance, but positively denyed: the particulars whereof are more plainly expressed in letters to the Secretary of State and Plantacôns: by all which yor Maj^ty^ may judge of the present state of this Province, and of the incônveniencys that dayly attend it.

Now may it please your most Excell^t^ Maj^ty^.

The premises considered we humbly presume and represent unto y^r^ most sacred Majesty that there can be nothing in America more conducive to yor Maj^ties^ subjects upon this continent then that Connecticut, East and West Jersey, Pensilvania and 3 Lower Countys be reannexed to this y^r^ Maj^ties^ Province which then will be a governm^t^ of sufficient extent; our late annexing to Boston haueing been evidently ruinous and destructive to these parts and may be other waies prejudicial to yor Maj^ties^ interest for these reasons. Your Maj^ty^ hath already by the unanimous consent of the people, a revenue established of greater value than is any where else in yor Maj^tys^ Plantacôns and whoever are joyned to this Province submit to the Establishm^t^; whereas it will be difficult to settle the like among our neighbours, and if settled, remain distinct governments they are so weak as not capable to defend themselves, and the revenue will be eat up in looking after it, that they cannot be profitable to your Maj^ty^. Whereas if they be annexed the charge will be no more to you^r^ Maj^ty^ than now without them, and their conjunction must at least increase the Revenue 3 fold, besides will make this province not only capable to defend themselves but to anoy if not subdue the enemy

May it please your Majesty; the small quantity of stores Govern^r^ Sloughter brought over are mostly disposed of in the severall small forts of Albany and Schenectady &^c^ so that now we must begg the favor of a fresh supply.

All which is humbly submitted

Rich^d^: Ingoldsby
Fred: Phillips
Stev: Cortlandt
Nich: Bayard
Gab: Monviell
Chid: Brook
Will: Nicolls.

A true Copy
M. Clarkson *Secy.*

REMARKS

UPON THE OBSERVATIONS OF THE PROPRIETORS OF PENSILVANIA ON A PARAGRAPH OF SIR WILLIAM JOHNSON'S LETTER TO THE RIGHT HONOURABLE THE LORDS OF TRADE AND PLANTATIONS BEARING DATE THE 10TH OF SEPTEMBER 1757.

[Lond. Doc. XXXIV.]

1757 22d Sept The whole paragraph of the above letter which gave birth to the observation is as follows:—

"I think I have before now hinted to your Lordships my opinion that the Hostilities which Pensilvania in particular has suffered from some of the Indians living on the Susquehannah did in some measure arise from the large purchase made by that Government two years ago at Albany. I have more reason every day from talking with the Indians to be confirmed in this Suspicion. I am inclined to believe that this purchase was publicly consented to at Albany, *some* of the Six Nations are disgusted at it, and others repent their consenting to it, and that part of them do underhand connive at the Disturbance between the Susquehannah Indians and the Province of Pensilvania whose raising forces and building Forts on the Susquehana, tho' it hath very plausible pretences is at the bottom bad policy and really intended to secure Lands which it would be more for the true interest of the community to give up at least for the present. I conceive the most effectual method of producing tranquility to that province would be a voluntary and open surrender of that Deed of Sale, fix with the Indians in the best manner they can the Bounds for their Settlements and make them Guarantees to it.

" The Proprietors are pleased to introduce their observations with a challenge to Sir William Johnson and all the World to shew any one Instance of their Conduct that has given dissatisfaction to the Six Nations and which they say those Nations will readily acknowledge in any free Conference."

Tho' the real Intent of the above paragraph from Sir William Johnson's letter was, and its obvious meaning is, to assign a cause to which he suspected the Indians' Hostilities in Pensilvania were in a great measure owing. Yet upon Sir William Johnson saying he was inclined to believe &ca The Proprietors are pleased to sound this unprovoked challenge, which thô to answer as well as to have given is departing from the main argument, Yet Sir William Johnson begs leave to say something in answer to it.

First, He will now presume to assert that from many Private conversations he hath hadd with severall of the Chiefs of the Six Nations, they are not satisfied with the conduct of the Government of Pensilvania in General, nor with the aforesaid purchase in particular.

Secondly, He will adduce some facts public and upon Record in support of the above assertion.

At the Treaty of Lancaster in the year 1744 the Six Nations complained to Governour Thomas that the Connoge Indians had not been satisfied for their Lands. The Gouvernour promised redress. In the yeare 1749 the Six Nations renewed the aforesaid Complaint to Governor Hamilton.

(NB. It doth not appear upon Record that the Connoge Indians are to this day satisfied.)

In the year 1750 Connageriwa a Sachim of the Six Nations living on the Ohio came at the head of a Deputation from thence to Mr. Croghan's house, and told Mr. Peters he was sent down from Ohio to enquire about the purchase they had heard the Governour had made on the East side of the Susquehannah the year before, from the Onondaga Council and said they were entitled to part of the goods paid for those Lands as well as the Onondaga Council, but they had received no part.

That they were come down to desire the Gouvernour to purchase no more Lands without giving them notice and desired the Gouvernour might send that Belt of Wampum to the Onondaga Council and let them know what the Ohio Indians had said on this head. Gave a large belt.

The Indians of the Six Nations who were settled on the Ohio were so dissatisfied with the Albany purchase made by the Proprietary Agents and saw such bad consequences arising from it that they left the Ohio and returned to their own Country.

In a Speech of the Six Nations at a publick meeting with Sir William Johnson on the 3d July 1755 They said

Brother, You desire us to unite and live together and draw all our allies near us, but we shall have no land left either for ourselves or them, for your people when they buy a small piece of land of us, by stealing they make it large. We desire such things may not be done and that your people may not be suffered to buy any more of our lands. Sometimes its bought of two men, who are not the proper owners of it. The land which reaches down from Oswego to Schahandowana (Wyoming) we beg may not be settled by Christians. The Governour of Pensilvania bought a whole track and only paid for half, and desire you will let him know that we will not part with the other half but keep it. These things makes us constantly uneasie in our minds, and we desire you will take care that we may keep our land for ourselves.

At a Meeting between Governour Denny George Croghan Esqr Sir William Johnson's Deputy, and sundrey Six Nations and other Indians held at Lancaster in May 1757, a coppy of the proceedings of which lays before the Board of Trade. There is a speech of the Six Nations bearing date Thursday 19th May from the whole letter and speech of which it appears that the Six Nations have been, and are very far from that satisfaction of mind, with the conduct of the Province of Pensilvania which the Proprietors boast of and found their challenge upon.

The Proprietors are further pleased to add to their challenge this assertion, that the Six Nations will readily acknowledge the truth of it in any free conference.

As the truth of this assertion can depend only upon a Contingent event, Sir William Johnson begs leave to be of a very different opinion, and from a variety of circumstances is well perswaded the Six Nations never will be reconciled to the conduct of the Proprietors, their Deputies and Agents unless the deed of the Albany purchase be surrendered and the claims founded thereupon in a great measure given up.

The Proprietors say they cannot conceive that the last purchase made of land to the Westward of Susquehanna could possibly be the Cause of the hostilities committed by the Indians living on that River &ca.

Sir William Johnson gave it as his opinion that the hostilities which Pensilvania had suffered from some of the Indians living on the Susquehanna did in some measure arise from the large purchase made by the Governour two years ago.

This is the point to be proved and more than this it is apprehended will be proved by the following Quotations from authentick Records & Papers.

" Before the year 1742 the Delaware Indians complained that they were defrauded out of some lands or not paid for them.

" It is well known that the purchase made at Albany in 1754 gave a great uneasiness to the Susquehanna Indians and from the time the County Surveyor began to survey Juniatta, and up the Susquehana: The Delewars, Shawanese and Nanticokes then settled on the River began to remove farther back, some to Tirjahoga some to Ohio.

" The Ohio Indians at a Meeting with Mr Wiser (the Pensilvania Interpreter) at Aughwick, after the defeat of Colo Washington asked Mr Wiser how those lands came to be sold. He said in answer that the Six Nations had only made over their right of sale, and taken an earnest piece, and that when the lands came to be settled, that they should receive a consideration for them. At the same time John Schecelany, a Delaware Indian, burned some houses that were built on Penns creek (below Shamokin on the West side) and said there should be no plantations made on their hunting grounds, and all the Indians at Shamokin seemed very uneasie, and indeed obliged the Surveyor to come away, and quit surveying."

In the Spring of 1756. Gouvernour Morris sent several messages with Belts and strings of Wampum by an Onondaga Indian to the Five Nations, amongst which is the following just and remarkable Confession.

" That he found by woful experience that making purchases of Lands was the cause of much blood having been shed, he was determined therefore to buy no more."

As a Confirmation of Sir William Johnsons said opinion he refers himself to the following extract from Margaret Williams deposition who was a prisoner amongst the Delaware Indians, sworn before him the 8th day of September 1756.

" The said Margaret says she often heard the Indians say and declare most solemnly they never would leave off killing the English as long as there was an Englishman living on their lands that they were determined to drive them all off their lands, naming Minisinck almost to the North River East, (in the provinces of New York & Jersey) also Bethlehem and the lands in parallel to it West which the English cheated them out of."

In further support of his opinion Sir William Johnson refers himself to the Treaty Governour Denny held with Tedinscung the Delaware Chief at Easton last autumn, and which is before the Board of Trade

Sir William Johnson also refers himself to the Extract from a Speech of the Six Nations to Govr Denny and Mr Croghan (before mentioned in these Remarks) in answer to their earnest call upon the Six Nations to assign if they knew the Cause of the hostilities and Discontents of the Susquehana Indians.

The Indian proceedings this Summer which past at Easton between Governo^r^ Denny, Mr Croghan & the sundry Indians therein mentioned, & which Sir William Johnson transmits herewith to the Right Honorable the Lords of Trade puts beyond dispute and demonstrates the Truth of what Sir William Johnson gave as his opinion in his aforesaid letter to the Lords of Trade and he apprehends it doth very fully evidence the conclusions of belief he then drew from that opinion.

Lastly Sir William Johnson refers himself to the following Extract from the Examination of John Morris of Lancaster County, who was taken by, and made his escape from, the Delaware Indians sworn before him 27th August 1757.

The Examinant says he often heard the Delawares say that the reason of their quarrelling with and killing the English in that part of the country was on account of their lands which the people of Pensilvania Government cheated them out of, and drove them from their settlement at Shamokin by crowding upon them, and by that means spoiled their hunting and that the people of Minisinck used to make the Indians always drunk whenever they traded with them and then cheated them out of their furs and skins, also wronged them with regard to their lands. This he has heard from many of the chief and oldest men amongst them both in the English and Delaware Language which he sufficiently understands

The Proprietors say, that as the Six Nations are not well satisfied with the sale of those lands on the Ohio, they are willing to waive that part of the Treaty provided &c^a^.

As Sir William Johnson has never seen the deed of sale for the Albany purchase, he cannot to his knowledge tell how far the purchase extends, but he hath in his possession a Report of several Indian Transactions, relative to the Government of Pensilvania signed by George Croghan Esqr who was for several years employed as an Indian Agent by that Government, in which Report Mr Croghan says as follows:—

"I never understood from any of the Six Nations that they deemed the Lands west of the Susquehana as a purchase, but rather as a deed of Trust and rec^d^ 1000 Dollars as an Earnest Price and looked on it that when the lands came to be settled they should receive the Consideration and the Commissioners who were sent from Pensilvania to make that purchase at Albany in 1754, vizt Mr Norris & Mr Peters, with the Interpreter Mr Wiser, have repeatedly acknowledged to me, *that the Land West of Allegany Mountains cross to Lake Erie was included in the deed of* 1754, *that it was neither purchased nor paid for, and which will appear by a private Conference in Mr. Peter's hand at the time of signing.*"

Certainly the proprietors are not apprized of the fact here asserted, or they would not have made an offer to relinquish Land they have never purchased, nor allowed it to have been put in a deed of sale.

In answer to Sir William Johnson's opinion about the Government of Pensilvania raising Forces and building Forts on the Susquehanna River

"The Proprietors say this Insinuation is without any sort of Foundation, as it never would have been attempted had not the Chiefs of the Indians living on the Susquehannah and Dalaware River on their own Motion entirely desired they should be built at Shamokin and near Wyoming for their own security.

"In this the Proprietors must certainly be misinformed for none of the Indians on Susquehanna or Delaware ever requested any Forts to be built there. Indeed after the defeat of General Braddock, Scarayade, Cayseuntenego, and two or three more Ohio Indians who had left their country on the first approach of the French in the year 1753 did desire the Government of Pensilv[a] to build a Fort at Shamokin, in order to protect their interest with the Susquehanna Indians, but the request of those four or five dispossessed Indians can never be fairly construed as an authority of application from the Six Nations, or any other Bodies of Indians. However this request for a Fort was not complied with at that time."

In a Message which Sir William Johnson received the 23[d] May 1756 from the Onondaga Indians they say as follows:—

"Tell our Brother farther that since we took the hatchet out of the hands of the Delaware and Shawanese they have told us there is an army of the English coming against them, (they mean the Provincial Troops of Pensilvania under Colonel Clapham) and that they think it unreasonable and unnatural for us to hold them in our arms, and preventing them defending themselves when People are just on their backs to destroy them.

"We are informed the English are building a Fort at Shamokin. We can't comprehend the method of making War which is made use of by our Brethren the English. When we go to war our manner is to destroy a Nation and there's an End of it. But the English chiefly regard building Forts which looks as if their only scheme was *to take possession of the lands.*"

Here is an evident Proof of the jealousy which the Pensilvania levies and Fort building occasioned and a strong hint of the Ends intended by them, as it stood in the minds of the Indians.

Sir William Johnson well knowing how extremely tender the Indians in general are, with regard to Forts, near to their country or hunting grounds and naturally judging a Body of Armed Men, to support as it were the building of those, at a time, and in places where he had many reasons to believe the neighbouring Indians (as it hath since fully appeared) were dissatisfied with the Government on the score of Lands, and Encroaching by their purchases on their hunting grounds, and crowding too near upon them by their extended settlements he judged this conduct in the Government of Pensilvania was impolitick, and he must beg leave to be still of the same opinion, and as he looked upon those proceedings to be contrary to the true interest of the Community, he did suspect they were pushed forward upon other motives.

And to conclude, unless the Province of Pensilvania is both able and willing to maintaln their land pretensions by force of Arms against the Indians, Sir William Johnson hath not altered his opinion but doth with yet stronger degree of conviction than formerly, humbly offer his conception of the matter in the same words as before. Namely, "that the most effectual method of producing tranquility to that Province would be a Voluntary and open Surrender of that Deed of Sale, to fix with the Indians in the best manner they can, the bounds for their settlements, and make them Guaranties to it."

NOTE—See further on this subject, *The Susquehannah Title Stated and Examined in a Series of Numbers first published in the Western Star and now Re-published,* &c Catskill; by Mackay Croswell. 1796.

XVI.

PAPERS

RELATING TO THE

Early Settlement at Ogdensburgh,

NEW-YORK.

1749.

ESTABLISHMENT OF A MISSION IN THE NEIGHBORHOOD OF FORT FRONTENAC. APRIL, 1750.

[Paris Doc. X.]

A large number of the Iroquois Savages having declared their willingness to embrace Christianity, it has been proposed to establish a Mission in the neighborhood of Fort Frontenac. Abbé Picquet, a zealous Missionary in whom the nations have evinced much confidence has taken charge of it, and of testing, as much as possible what reliance is to be placed on the disposition of the Indians.[1]

Nevertheless, as Mr. de la Gallisonnière had remarked in the month of October, one thousand seven hundred and forty eight, that too much dependence ought not to be placed on them, Mr. de la Jonquière was written to on the fourth of May one thousand seven hundred and forty nine, that he should neglect nothing for the formation of this establishment, because if it at all succeeded it would not be difficult to give the Indians to understand that the only means they had to relieve themselves of the pretensions of the English to their lands is the destruction of Choueguen which they founded solely with a view to bridle these Nations; but it was necessary to be prudent and circumspect to induce the Savages to undertake it.

31st 8ber 1749. Mr. de la Jonquière sends a plan drawn by Sieur de Lery of the ground selected by the Abbé Picquet for his mission and a letter from that Abbé containing a Relation of his voyage and the situation of the place.

He says he left the fourth of May last year with twenty-five Frenchmen and four Iroquois Indians; he arrived the thirtieth at the River *de la Presentation*, called Soegatzy. The land there is the finest in Canada. There is Oak timber in abundance, and trees of a prodigious size and height, but it will be necessary, for the defence of the settlement, to fell them without permission. Picquet reserved sufficient on the land he had cleared to build a bark.

He then set about building a storehouse to secure his effects; he, next, had erected a small fort of pickets and he will have a small house constructed which will serve as a bastion.

Sieur Picquet had a special interview with the Indians; they were satisfied with all he had done; and assured him they were willing to follow his advice and to immediately establish their village. To accomplish this, they are gone to regulate their affairs and have promised to return with their provisions.

The situation of this post is very advantageous; it is on the borders of the River *de la Presentation*, at the head of all the rapids, on the west side of a beautiful basin formed by that river, capable of easily holding forty or fifty barks.

In all parts of it there has been found at least two fathoms and a half of water and often four fathoms. This basin is so located that no wind scarcely can prevent its being entered. The bank is very low in a level country the point of which runs far out. The passage across is hardly a quarter

1 The following Extract from Paris Doc. X., furnishes the date of the Abbe Picquet's departure to establish his colony on the Oswegatchie River:—"30 Sept. 1748. The Abbe Picquet departs from Quebec for Fort Frontenac; he is to look in the neighborhood of that Fort, for a location best adapted for a village for the Iroquois of the Five Nations who propose to embrace Christianity."

of a league, and all the canoes going up or down, cannot pass elsewhere. A fort on this point would be impregnable; it would be impossible to approach, and nothing commands it. The east side is more elevated, and runs by a gradual inclination into an Amphitheatre. A beautiful town could hereafter be built there.

This post is, moreover, so much the more advantageous as the English and Iroquois can easily descend to Montreal by the River *de la Presentation* which has its source in a lake bordering on the Mohawks and Corlar. If they take possession of this River they will block the passage to Fort Frontenac and more easily assist Choueguen. Whereas by means of a Fort at the Point, it would be easy to have a force there in case of need to despatch to Choueguen and to intercept the English and Indians who may want to penetrate into the Colony, and the voyage to Missilimakinac could be made in safety.

Moreover, this establishment is only thirty-five leagues from Montreal; twenty-five from Fort Frontenac and thirty three from Choueguen;[1] a distance sufficient to remove the Indians from the disorders which the proximity of Forts and Towns ordinarily engenders among them. It is convenient for the reception of the Lake Ontario, and more distant, Indians.

Abbé Picquet's views are to accustom these Indians to raise Cows, Hogs and Poultry; there are beautiful prairies, acorns and wild oats.

On the other hand it can be so regulated that the batteaux carrying goods to the posts, may stop at *La Presentation*. The cost of freight would become smaller; men could be found to convey those batteaux @ fifteen to twenty livres instead of forty-five and fifty livres which are given for the whole voyage. Other batteaux of *La Presentation* would convey them farther on, and the first would take in return plank, boards and other timber, abundant there. This timber would not come to more than twelve @ fifteen livres, whilst they are purchased at sixty-eight livres at Montreal and sometimes more. Eventually this post will be able to supply Fort Frontenac with provisions which will save the King considerable expense.

The Abbé Picquet adds in his letter, that he examined in his voyage the nature of the rapids of the Fort Frontenac river, very important to secure to us the possession of Lake Ontario, on which the English have an eye. The most dangerous of those rapids, in number fourteen, are the *Trou* (the Hole) and the *Buisson* (the Thicket). Abbé Picquet points out a mode of rendering this River navigable; and to meet the expense he proposes a tax of ten livres on each canoe sent up and an *ecu* (fifty cents) on each of the crew, which according to him will produce three thousand livres, a sum sufficient for the workmen.

Messrs. de la Jonquière and Bigot remark that they find this establishment necessary as well as the erection of a saw mill, as it will diminish the expense in the purchase of timber; but as regards the Rapids they will verify them in order to ascertain if in fact the river can be rendered navigable and they will send an estimate of the works.

They have caused five cannon of two pound calibre to be sent to Abbé Picquet for his little fort so as to give confidence to his Indians and to persuade them that they will be in security there.

M. de la Jonquière in particular says, he will see if the proprietors of batteaux would contribute to the expense necessary to be incurred for the Rapids; but he asks that convicts from the galleys or people out of work (*gens inutiles*) be sent every year to him to cultivate the ground. He is in want of men, and the few he has exact high wages.

1st 8ber, 1749. Mr. Bigot also sends a special memoir of the expense incurred by Abbé Picquet for improvements (*defrichemens*) amounting to three thousand four hundred and eighty five livres

1 Ogdensburgh is 105 miles from Montreal; 60 from Kingston, Can., and about 90 from Oswego. The distances laid down in the Text are very accurate, considering the time and the circumstances.

ten sous.[1] Provisions were also furnished him for himself and workmen, and this settlement is only commenced. M. de la Jonquière cannot dispense with sending an officer there and some soldiers. Sieur de la Morandière, Engineer, is to be sent there this winter to draw out a plan of quarters for these soldiers and a store for provisions. If there be not a garrison at that post, a considerable foreign trade will be carried on there.

7th 9ber 1749. Since all these letters M. de la Jonquière has written another in which he states that M. de Longueuil informed him that a band of Savages believed to be Mohawks had attacked Sieur Picquet's Mission on the twenty-sixth of October last—that Sieur de Vassau, commandant of Fort Frontenac, had sent a detechment thither which could not prevent the burning of two vessels loaded with hay and the palisades of the fort. Abbé Picquet's house alone was saved.

The loss by this fire is considerable. It would have been greater were it not for four Abenakis who furnished on this occasion a proof of their fidelity. The man named Pedreaux had half the hand carried away. His arm had to be cut off. One of the Abenakis received the discharge of a gun the ball of which remained in his blanket.

M. de Longueuil has provided everything necessary. M. de la Jonquiére gave him orders to have a detachment of ten soldiers sent there, and he will take measures, next spring, to secure that post. M. de la Jonquière adds that the Savages were instigated to this attack by the English. The Iroquois who were on a complimentary visit at Montreal were surprized at it and assured M. de Longueuil that it could only be Colonel Amson [Johnson ?] who could have induced them. He omitted nothing to persuade those same Iroquois to undertake this expedition and to prevent them going to compliment the Governor, having offered them Belts which they refused.

COL. JOHNSON TO GOV. CLINTON, 18 AUG. 1750.

[Lond. Doc. XXIX.]

The next thing of consequence he (an Indian Sachem) told me was, that he had heard from several Indians that the Governor had given orders to the Priest who is now settled below Cadaraqui to use all means possible to induce the five Nations to settle there, for which end they have a large magazine of all kinds of clothing fitted for Indians as also Arms, Ammunition Provision &c which they distribute very liberally.

THE SAME TO THE BOARD OF TRADE, 28 AUG. 1756.

[Lond. Doc. XXXIII.]

The Onnondagas and Oneides are in the neighbourhood of Swegatchie a French settlement on the River St. Lawrence, whither numbers of those two Nations have of late years been debauched and gone to live. Tho' our Indians do not now resort to those places as frequently and familiarly as

1 Equal to $653.23.

they formerly did, yet some among them do occasionally visit there, when the French and the Indians in their interest poison the minds of ours with stories not only to the disadvantage of our good intentions towards them, but endeavour to frighten them with pompous accounts of the superior prowess and martial abilities of the French.

BIOGRAPHICAL SKETCH OF THE REV. ABBE PICQUET.

[Abridged from Lettres Edifiantes et Curieuses, XIV.]

Francois Picquet, doctor of the Sorbonne, King's Missionary and Prefect Apostolic to Canada was born at Bourg in Breese on the 6th December, 1708 . . . As early as the seventeenth year of his age, he successfully commenced the functions of a missionary in his country and at twenty years the Bishop of Sinope, Suffragan of the Diocese of Lyon, gave him, by a flattering exception, permission to preach in all the parishes of Breese and Franche-Comté which depended on his diocese. The enthusiasm of his new state rendered him desirous to go to Rome, but the Archbishop of Lyons advised him to study theology at Paris. He followed this advice and entered the Congregation of Saint Sulpice. The direction of the new converts was soon proposed to him ; but the activity of his zeal induced him to seek a wider field, and led him beyond the seas in 1733, to the Missions of North America where he remained thirty years, and where his constitution debilitated by labor, acquired a force and vigor which secured for him a robust health to the end of his life.

M. Picquet was among the first to foresee the war which sprung up about 1742 between the English and the French. He prepared himself for it a long time beforehand. He began by drawing to his Mission (at the Lake of the Two Mountains) all the French scattered in the vicinity, to strengthen themselves and afford more liberty to the savages. These furnished all the necessary detachments; they were continually on the frontiers to spy the enemy's movements. M. Picquet learned, by one of these detachments that the English were making warlike preparations at Sarasto [Saratoga ?] and were pushing their settlements up to Lake St. Sacrement.[1] He informed the General of the circumstance and proposed to him to send a body of troops there at least to intimidate the enemy, if we could do no more. The expedition was formed. M. Picquet accompanied M. Marin who commanded this detachment. They burnt the fort, the Lydius establishments,[2] several saw mills, the planks, boards and other building timber, the stock of supplies, provisions, the herds of cattle along nearly fifteen leagues of settlement and made one hundred and forty five prisoners without having lost a single Frenchman or without having any even wounded.[3] This expedition alone prevented the English undertaking anything at that side during the war.

Peace having been re-established in 1748, our Missionary occupied himself with the means of remedying, for the future, the inconveniences which he had witnessed. The road he saw taken by the Savages and other parties of the enemy sent by the English against us, caused him to select a

1 "I am building a Fort at this Lake which the French call Lake St. Sacrement, but I have given it the name of Lake *George*, not only n honour to his Majesty but to ascertain his undoubted dominion here." *Sir William Johnson to the Board of Trade, Sept. 3d,* 1755. *Lond. Doc.* xxxii., 178.

2 Now Fort Edward, Washington County.

3 "I received an account on the 19th inst., by express from Albany, that a party of French and their Indians had cut off a settlement in this Province called Saraghtoge, about fifty miles from Albany, and that about twenty houses with a Fort (which the publick would not repair) were burned to ashes, thirty persons killed and scalped and about sixty taken prisoners. *Gov. Clinton to the Board,* 30 *Nov.* 1745. *Lond. Doc.* xxvii., 187, 235.

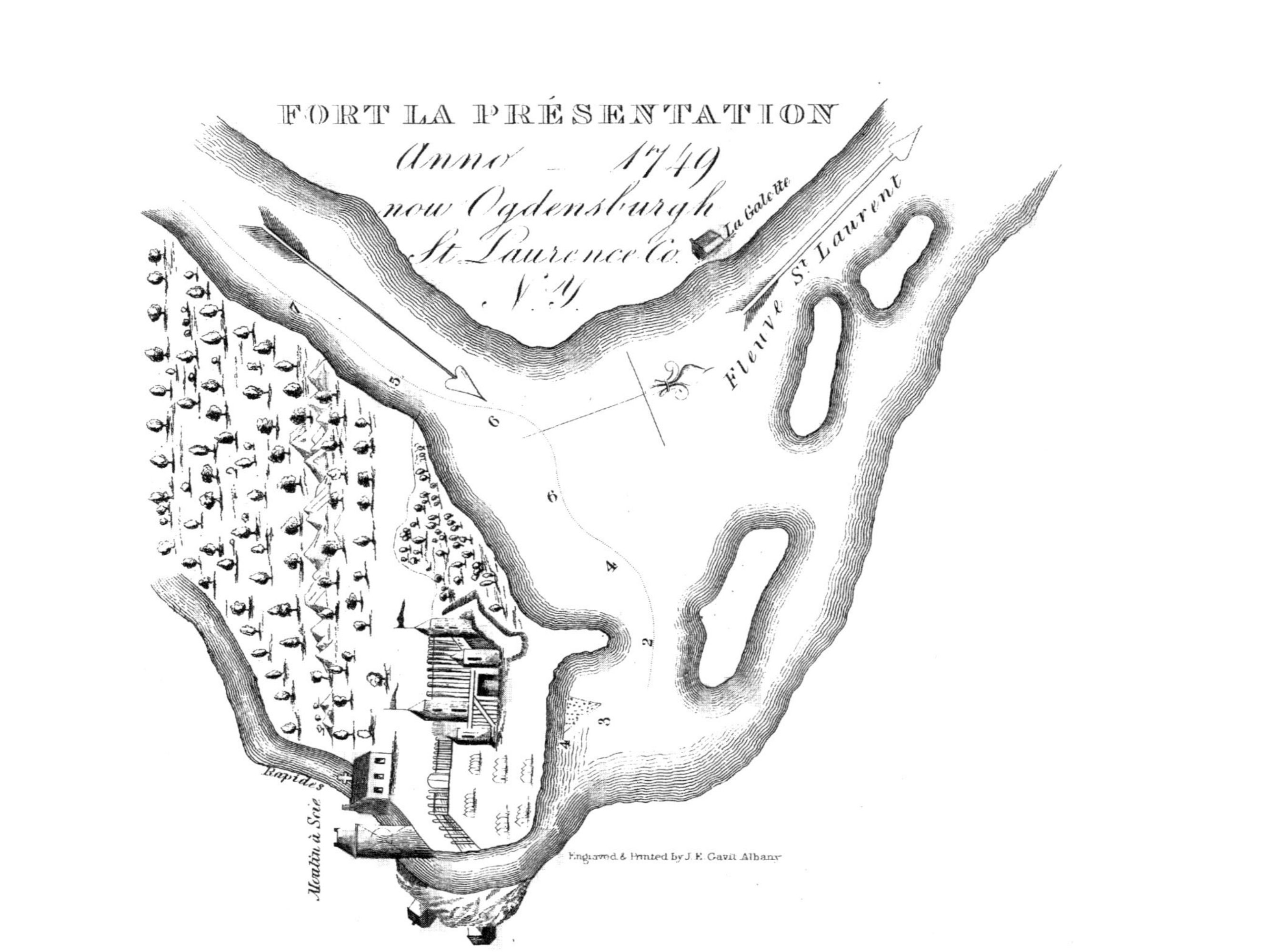
FORT LA PRÉSENTATION
Anno — 1749
now Ogdensburgh
St. Laurence Co.
N.Y.
La Galette
Fleuve St Laurent
Rapides
Moulin à Scie
Engraved & Printed by J. E. Gavit Albany

post which could, hereafter, intercept the passage of the English. He proposed to M. de la Galissonière to make a settlement of the Mission of *La Presentation*, near Lake Ontario, an establishment which succeeded beyond his hopes, and has been the most useful of all those of Canada.

Mr. Rouillé, Minister of the Marine wrote on the 4th may 1749; "A large number of Iroquois having declared that they were desirous of embracing Christianity, it has been proposed to establish a Mission towards Fort Frontenac in order to attract the greatest number possible thither. It is Abbé Picquet, a zealous Missionary and in whom these Nations seem to have confidence, who has been entrusted with this negotiation. He was to have gone last year, to select a suitable site for the establishment of the Mission, and verify as precisely as was possible what can be depended upon relative to the disposition of these same nations. In a letter of the 5th October last, M. de la Gallisonnière stated that though an entire confidence cannot be placed in those they have manifested, it is notwithstanding of so much importance to succeed in dividing them, that nothing must be neglected that can contribute to it. It is for this reason that His Majesty desires you shall prosecute the design of the proposed settlement. If it could attain a certain success, it would not be difficult then to make the savages understand that the only means of extricating themselves from the pretensions of the English to them and their lands, is to destroy Choueguen,[1] so as to deprive them thereby of a Post which they established chiefly with a view to control their tribes. This destruction is of such great importance, both as regards our possessions and the attachment of the savages and their Trade, that it is proper to use every means to engage the Iroquois to undertake it. This is actually the only means that can be employed, but you must feel that it requires much prudence and circumspection."

Mr. Picquet eminently possessed the qualities requisite to effect the removal of the English from our neighborhood. Therefore the General, the Intendant, and the Bishop deferred absolutely to him in the selection of a settlement for this new Mission, and despite the efforts of those who had opposite interests, he was entrusted with the undertaking.

The Fort of *La Presentation* is situated at 302 deg. 40 min. Longitude, and at 44 deg. 50 minutes Latitude on the Presentation River, which the Indians name *Soegasti*, thirty leagues above Mont-Real; fifteen leagues from Lake Ontario or Lake Frontenac, which with Lake Champlain gives rise to the River St. Laurence; 15 leagues west of the source of the River Hudson which falls into the sea at New-York. Fort Frontenac had been built near there in 1671, to arrest the incursions of the English and the Iroquois; the bay served as a port for the Mercantile and Military Marine which had been formed there on that sort of sea where the tempests are as frequent and as dangerous as on the ocean. But the Post of *La Presentation* appeared still more important, because the harbour is very good, the river freezes there rarely, the barks can leave with northern, eastern and southern winds, the lands are excellent, and that quarter can be fortified most advantageously.

Besides, that Mission was adapted by its situation to reconcile to us the Iroquois savages of the Five Nations who inhabit between Virginia and Lake Ontario. The Marquis of Beauharnois and afterwards M. de la Jonquière, Governor General of New France, were very desirous that we should occupy it, especially at a time when English jealousy irritated by a war of many years, sought to alienate from us the tribes of Canada.

This establishment was as if the key of the Colony, because the English, French and Upper Canada savages could not pass elsewhere than under the cannon of Fort Presentation when coming down from the South; the Iroquois to the South and the Micissagués to the North were within its reach. Thus it eventually succeeded in collecting them together from over a distance of one hundred leagues. The officers, interpreters and traders, notwithstanding, then regarded that establishment as chimerical. Envy and opposition had effected its failure had it not been for the firmness of the Abbè

1 Oswego.

Picquet supported by that of the Administration. This establishment served to protect, aid, and comfort the posts already erected on Lake Ontario. The Barks and Canoes for the Transportation of the King's effects could be constructed there at a third less expense than elsewhere because timber is in greater quantity and more accessible, especially when M. Picquet had had a saw mill erected there for preparing and manufacturing the timber. In fine he could establish a very important settlement for the French Colonists and a point of reunion for Europeans and savages, where they would find themselves very convenient to the hunting and fishing in the upper part of Canada.

M. Picquet left with a detachment of soldiers, mechanics and some savages. He placed himself at first in as great security as possible against the insults of the enemy, which availed him ever since. On the 20th October 1749, he had built a Fort of palisades, a house, a barn, a stable, a redoubt and an oven. He had lands cleared for the savages. His improvements were estimated as thirty to forty thousand *livres*, but he introduced as much judgment as economy. He animated the workmen and they laboured from three o'clock in the morning until nine at night. As for himself his disinterestedness was extreme. He received at that time neither allowance nor presents; he supported himself by his industry and credit. From the King he had but one ration of two pounds of bread and one half pound of pork, which made the savages say, when they brought him a Buck and some Partridges, "We doubt not, Father, but that there have been disagreeable expostulations in your stomach, because you have had nothing but pork to eat. Here's something to put your affairs in order." The hunters furnished him wherewithal to support the Frenchmen, and to treat the Generals occasionally. The savages brought him trout weighing as many as eighty pounds.

When the Court had granted him a pension he employed it only for the benefit of his establishment. At first, he had six heads of families in 1749, eighty-seven the year following, and three hundred and ninety six in 1751. All these were of the most antient and most influential families, so that this Mission was, from that time sufficiently powerful to attach the Five Nations to us, amounting to twenty-five thousand inhabitants, and he reckoned as many as three thousand in his Colony. By attaching the Iroquois Cantons to France and establishing them fully in our interest, we were certain of having nothing to fear from the other savage tribes and thus a limit could be put to the ambition of the English. Mr. Picquet took considerable advantage of the peace to increase that settlement, and he carried it in less than four years to the most desirable perfection, despite of the contradictions that he had to combat against; the obstacles he had to surmount; the jibes and unbecoming jokes which he was obliged to bear; but his happiness and glory suffered nothing therefrom. People saw with astonishment several villages start up almost at once; a convenient, habitable and pleasantly situated fort; vast clearances covered almost at the same time with the finest maize. More than five hundred families, still all infidels, who congregated there, soon rendered this settlement the most beautiful, the most charming and the most abundant of the Colony. Depending on it were La Presentation, La Galette, Seugatzi, L'isle au Galop, and L'isle Picquet in the River St. Lawrence. There were in the Fort, seven small stone guns and eleven four to six pounders.

The most distinguished of the Iroquois families were distributed at La Presentation in three villages: that which adjoined the French fort contained, in 1754, forty-nine bark cabins some of which were from sixty to eighty feet long and accommodated three to four families. The place pleased them on account of the abundance of hunting and fishing. This Mission could no doubt be increased, but cleared land sufficient to allow all the families to plant and to aid them to subsist would be necessary and each Tribe should have a separate location. . . . . . The Bishop of Quebec wishing to witness and assure himself personally of the wonders related to him of the establishment at *La Presentation* went thither in 1749, accompanied by some officers, royal interpreters, Priests from other Missions and several other clergymen, and spent ten days examining and causing the

Catechumens to be examined. He himself baptized one hundred and thirty-two, and did not cease during his sojourn, blessing Heaven for the progress of Religion among these Infidels.

Scarcely were they baptized when M. Picket determined to give them a form of Government. He established a Council of Twelve Ancients; chose the most influential among the Five Nations; brought them to Mont Real where at the hands of the Marquis Du Quesne they took the Oath of Allegiance to the King to the great astonishment of the whole Colony where no person dared to hope for such an event.

In the month of June 1751, M. Picquet made a voyage around Lake Ontario with a King's Canoe and one of Bark in which he had five trusty Savages, with the design of attracting some Indian families to the new settlement of La Presentation. There is a memoir, among his papers on the subject, from which it is proposed to give an extract.

He visited Fort Frontenac or *Cataracoui*, situate twelve leagues west of La Presentation. He found no Indians there though it was formerly the rendezvous of the Five Nations. The bread and milk, there, were bad; they had not even brandy there to staunch a wound. Arrived at a point of Lake Ontario called Kaoi, he found a runaway there from Virginia. . . . . At the Bay of Quinteé he visited the site of the antient Mission which M. Dollieres de Kleus and Abbé D'Urfé, priests of the Saint Sulpice Seminary had established there. The quarter is beautiful but the land is not good. He visited Fort Toronto, seventy leagues from Fort Frontenac, at the West end of Lake Ontario. He found good Bread and good Wine there, and every thing requisite for the trade, whilst they were in want of these at all the other posts. He found Mississagues there who flocked around him; they spoke first of the happiness their young people, the women and children would feel if the King would be as good to them as to the Iroquois for whom he procured Missionaries. They complained that instead of building a church, they had constructed only a canteen for them. M. Picquet did not allow them to finish and answered them that they had been treated according to their fancy; that they had never evinced the least zeal for religion; that their conduct was much opposed to it; that the Iroquois on the contrary had manifested their love for Christianity, but as he had no order to attract them to his Mission, he avoided a more lengthy explanation.

He passed thence to Niagara. He examined the situation of that fort, not having any savages to whom he could speak. It is well located for defence not being commanded from any point. The view extends to a great distance; they have the advantage of the landing of all the canoes and barks which land and are in safety there. But the rain was washing the soil away by degrees, notwithstanding the vast expence which the King incurred to sustain it. M. Picquet was of opinion that the space between the land and the wharf might be filled in so as to support it, and make a glacis there. This place was important as a Trading post and as securing possession of the Carrying place, Niagara and Lake Ontario.

From Niagara, M. Picquet went to the Carrying place which is six leagues from that Post. He visited on the same day the famous Fall of Niagara by which the four Great Canada lakes discharge themselves into Lake Ontario. This Cascade is as prodigious by its height and the quantity of water which falls there, as by the variety of its falls which are to the number of six principal ones divided by a small island, leaving three to the North and three to the South. They produce of themselves a singular symmetry and wonderful effect. He measured the height of one of those falls from the south side, and he found it about one hundred and forty feet.[1] The establishment at this Carrying place, the most important in a commercial point of a view was the worst stocked. The Indians, who came there in great numbers, were in the best disposition to trade, but not finding what they wanted, they went to Chouoguen or Choëguen [Oswego] at the mouth of the river of the same name. M.

1 These are French feet. The falls on the American side are 164 feet high—Burr's Atlas, Introd. p. 31.

Picquet counted there as many as fifty canoes. There was notwithstanding at Niagara a Trading House where the Commandant and Trader lodged, but it was too small, and the King's property was not safe there.

M. Picquet negotiated with the Senecas who promised to repair to his Mission and gave him twelve children as hostages, saying to him that their parents had nothing dearer to them and followed him immediately, as well as the Chief of the Little Rapid with all his family. . . . . He set out with all those Savages to return to Fort Niagara. M. Chabert de Joncaire would not abandon him. At each place where they encountered camps, cabins and entrepots, they were saluted with musquetry by the Indians who never ceased testifying their consideration for the Missionary. M. Picquet took the lead with the Savages of the hills; Messrs Joncaire and Rigouille following with the recruits. He embarked with thirty-nine Savages in his large canoe and was received on arriving at the fort with the greatest ceremony, even with the discharge of cannon which greatly pleased the Indians. On the morrow he assembled the Senecas, for the first time, in the chapel of the Fort for religious services.

M. Picquet returned along the south coast of Lake Ontario. Alongside of Choëguen, a young Seneca met her Uncle who was coming from his village with his wife and children. This young girl spoke so well to her Uncle, though she had but little knowledge of Religion that he promised to repair to La Presentation early the following spring, and that he hoped to gain over also seven other cabins of Senecas of which he was chief. Twenty-five leagues from Niagara he visited the River Gascouchagou[1] where he met a number of Rattlesnakes. The young Indians jumped into the midst of them and killed forty-two without having been bitten by any.

He next visited the Falls of this River. The first which appear in sight in ascending resemble much the great Cascade at Saint Cloud, except that they have not been ornamented and do not seem so high, but they possess natural beauties which render them very curious. The second, a quarter of a mile higher, are less considerable, yet are remarkable. The third, also a quarter of a league higher, has beauties truly admirable by its curtains and falls which form also, as at Niagara, a charming proportion and variety. They may be one hundred and some feet high.[2] In the intervals between the falls, there are a hundred little cascades which present likewise a curious spectacle; and if the altitudes of each chute were joined together, and they made but one as at Niagara, the height would, perhaps, be four hundred feet; but there is four times less water than at the Niagara Fall which will cause the latter to pass, for ever, as a Wonder perhaps unique in the World.

The English to throw disorder into this new levy sent a good deal of brandy. Some savages did, in fact get drunk whom M. Picquet could not bring along. He therefore desired much that Choëguen were destroyed and the English prevented rebuilding it; and in order that we should be absolutely masters of the south side of Lake Ontario, he proposed erecting a Fort near there at the bay of the Cayugas[3] which would make a very good harbour and furnish very fine anchorage. No place is better adapted for a Fort.

He examined attentively the Fort of Choëguen, a post the most pernicious to France that the English could erect. It was commanded almost from all sides and could be very easily approached in time of war It was a two story very low building; decked like a ship and surmounted on the top by a gallery; the whole was surrounded by a stone wall, flanked only with two bastions at the side towards the nearest hill. Two batteries each of three twelve pounders, would have been more than sufficient to reduce that establishment to ashes. It was prejudicial to us by the facility it af-

1 The Genesee River. In Berlin's Map of *Partie Occidentale de la Nouvelle France*, 1755 (No. 992 W. C. State Lib.) it is described as a "River unknown to Geographers, filled with Rapids and Waterfalls."

2 The highest fall on the river is 105 feet.

3 Sodus bay.

forded the English of communicating with all the tribes of Canada still more than by the trade carried on there as well by the French of the Colony as by the savages: for Choëguen was supplied with merchandize adapted only to the French, at least as much as with what suited to the savages, a circumstance that indicated an illicit trade. Had the Minister's orders been executed, the Choëguen trade at least with the savages of Upper Canada would be almost ruined. But it was necessary to supply Niagara, especially the Portage, rather than Toronto. The difference between the two first of these posts and the last is, that three or four hundred canoes could come loaded with furs to the Portage, and that no canoes could go to Toronto except those which cannot pass before Niagara and to Fort Frontenac, such as the Otaois of the head of the Lake (*Fond du Lac*) and the Mississagues; so that Toronto could not but diminish the trade of these two antient posts, which would have been sufficient to stop all the savages had the stores been furnished with goods to their liking. There was a wish to imitate the English in the trifles they sold the savages such as silver bracelets etc. The Indians compared & weighed them, as the storekeeper at Niagara stated, and the Choëguen bracelets which were found as heavy, of a purer silver and more elegant did not cost them two beavers, whilst those at the King's post wanted to sell them for ten beavers. Thus we were discredited, and this silver ware remained a pure loss in the King's stores. French brandy was preferred to the English, but that did not prevent the Indians going to Choëguen. To destroy the Trade the King's posts ought to have been supplied with the same goods as Choëguen and at the same price. The French ought also have been forbidden to send the domiciliated Indians thither: but that would have been very difficult.

Mr. Picquet next returned to Frontenac. Never was a reception more imposing. The Nipissings and Algonquins who were going to war with M. de Bellestre, drew up in a line of their own accord above Fort Frontenac where three standards were hoisted. They fired several volleys of musketry and cheered incessantly. They were answered in the same style from all the little craft of bark. M. de Verchere and M. de la Valtrie caused the guns of the Fort to be discharged at the same time, and the Indians transported with joy at the honors paid them also kept up a continual fire with shouts and acclamations which made every one rejoice. The commandants and officers received our Missionary at the landing. No sooner had he debarked than all the Algonquins and Nipissings of the Lake came to embrace him, saying that they had been told that the English had arrested him, and had that news been confirmed they would soon have themselves relieved him. Finally when he returned to La Presentation, he was received with that affection, that tenderness which children would experience in recovering a father whom they had lost.

War was no sooner declared in 1754 than the new children of God, of the King and of M Picquet, thought only of giving fresh proofs of their fidelity and valor, as those of the Lake of the Two Mountains had done in the war preceding. The generals were indebted to M. Picquet for the destruction of all the Forts as well on the river Corlac (Corlear) as on that of Choëguen. His Indians distinguished themselves especially at Fort George on Lake Ontario where the warriors of La Presentation alone with their bark canoes destroyed the English fleet commanded by Capt. Beccan who was made prisoner with a number of others and that in sight of the French army, commanded by M. de Villiers who was at the Isle Galop. The war parties which departed and returned continually, filled the Mission with so many prisoners that their numbers frequently surpassed that of the warriors, rendering it necessary to empty the villages and send them to Head-quarters. In fine a number of other expeditions of which M. Picquet was the principal author have procured the promotion of several officers. . . . . . . He frequently found himself in the vanguard when the King's troops were ordered to attack the enemy. He distinguished himself particularly in the expeditions of Sarasto (Saratoga), Lake Champlain, Pointe a la Chevelure (Crown Point), the Cascades, Carillon (Ticonderoga) Choëguen (Oswego), River Corlac

(Mohawk), Isle au Galop etc. The posts he established for the King protected the colony pending the entire war. M. du Quesne said that the Abbé Picquet was worth more than ten regiments.

In the month of May 1756 M. de Vaudreuil got M. Picquet to depute the Chiefs of his Missions to the Five Nations of Senecas, Cayugas, Onontagués, Tuscaroras and Oneidas to attach them more and more to the French. The English had surprised and killed their nephews in the three villages of the *Loups* (Mohegans ?) M. de Vaudreuil requested him to form parties which could succeed each other in disquieting and harassing the English. In 1758 he destroyed the English forts on the banks of Corlac, but at length the battle of the 13 Sept. 1759, in which the Marquis of Montcalm was killed, brought ruin on Quebec and that of Canada followed. When he saw all thus lost, M. Picquet terminated his long and laborious career by his retreat on the 8th May 1760, with the advice and consent of the General, the Bishop and Intendant, in order not to fall into the hands of the English. He had determined never to swear allegiance to another power.

He passed to Michilimachina between Lake Huron and Lake Michigan; proceeded thus by way of Upper Canada to the Illinois country & Louisiana, and sojourned twenty two months at New Orleans. On his return to France, he passed several years in Paris. A hernia which afflicted him a long time, having become aggravated, finally caused his death at Verjon on the 15th July 1781. In his life time he was complimented with the title of "Apostle of the Iroquois."

NOTE.—Fort la Presentation, with the River, under the names of *Wegatchi*, *Swegatchi*, *Oswegatchi*, will be found laid down in the following Maps and Charts, vizt

A map of that part of America which was the principal seat of War in 1756, published in the Gentleman's Magazine for 1757, Vol. xxvii.;

An Exact Chart of the River St. Lawrence from Fort Frontenac to the Island of Anticosti by Thos Jeffereys, London 1775; with the River St. Lawrence from Quebec to Lake Ontario copied from D'Anvill's Map of 1755;

Sauthier's Map of the Inhabited parts of Canada and Frontiers of New York, &c. London 1777;

Sauthier's Map of the Province of New York, Lond. 1779 and in Carte Generale des (14) Etats Unis de l'Amerique Septentrionale renfernant quelques Provinces Angloises adjacentes, being No. 30 in Atlas of Maps on America in State Lib.

Reference to this settlement will be also found in Gent. Mag. xxiv, 593. It is sometimes, though corruptly, called Fort Patterson.

XVII.

PAPERS

RELATING TO THE

First Settlement and Capture of Fort Oswego.

1727—1756.

FIRST SETTLEMENT OF THE ENGLISH IN WESTERN NEW-YORK.

[Lond. Doc. XXII.]

Gov. Burnet to the Board of Trade.

NEW YORK, Oct. 16, 1721.

That I might improve their (the Indians') present good humor to the best advantage I have employed the five hundred pounds granted this year by the Assembly chiefly to the erecting and encouraging a settlement at Tirandaquet a Creek on the Lake Ontario about sixty miles on this side Niagara[1] whither there are now actually gone a company of ten persons with the approbation of our Indians and with the assurance of a sufficent number of themselves to live with them and be a guard to them against any surprise, and because the late President of the Council Peter Schuyler's son [2] first offered his service to go at the head of this expedition I readily accepted him and have made him several presents to Equip him and given him a handsome allowance for his own salary and a Commission of Captain over the rest that are or may be there with him and Agent to treat with the Indians from me for purchasing Land and other things which I the rather did that I might shew that I had no personal dislike to the family.

This Company have undertaken to remain on this Settlement and that never above two shall be absent at once, and tho' these have the sole encouragement at present out of the public money yet there is nothing that hinders as many more to go and settle there or any where else on their own account as please.

This place is indisputably in the Indians possession and lies very convenient for all the far Indians to come on account of Trade from which the French at Niagara will not easily hinder them because first it must be soon known and is against the Treaty and besides they may easily slip by them in canoes and get to this place before the French can catch them in the pursuit if they should attempt to hinder them.

This, my Lords is the beginning of a great Trade that may be maintained with all the Indians upon the Lakes and the cheapness of all our goods except Powder above the French will by degrees draw all that Trade to us which can not better appear than by the French having found it worth while to buy our Goods at Albany to sell again to the Indians. Wherefore to break that Practice more effectually I have placed a sufficient guard of Soldiers on the Carrying Place to Canada and built a small Blockhouse there[3] with the remainder of the five hundred pounds before mentioned.

As to Niagara I did write to the Governor of Canada to complain of all the unwarrantable steps he has taken and among others of his erecting a Blockhouse at Niagara before the Treaty of Limits had settled who it belong to

I received his answer at Albany in which he flatly denies most of the Facts I complain of.

But as to Niagara he pretends possession for above fifty years first taken by Mr de la Sale

1 Irondequoit bay, Monroe Co. 2. Major Abraham Schuyler.

3. Now Fort Edward, originally Fort Lydius, Washington Co.

EXTRACTS FROM FRENCH LETTERS.

[Paris Doc. VII.]

Letter, dated 22 *May*, 1725. M. the Marquis of Vaudreuil writes that he received advice the 8th December that the English and the Dutch had projected an establishment at the mouth of the River Chouaguan on the borders of Lake Ontario and very near the post we have at Niagara.

The news of this establishment on soil always considered as belonging to France, appeared to him the more important as he felt the difficulty of preserving the post of Niagara where there is no fort, should the English once fortify Chouaguen; and that in losing Niagara the Colony is lost and at the same time all the trade with the upper Country Indians, who go the more willingly to the English since they obtain goods there much cheaper and get as much brandy as they like, which we cannot absolutely dispense furnishing the upper country Indians, though with prudence, if it be desirable to prevent them carrying their furs and surrendering themselves to the English.

M. de Longueuil wrote in the month of February that the Iroquois of the Sault had appointed four of their chiefs and one of the Lake of the Two Mountains to go to Orange to represent to the Dutch that they would not suffer their settling at Chouaguen and that they would declare war against them if they established themselves there.

He repaired on the ice to Montreal on the 12 March where he received the confirmation of the news of the English, and learned that they and the Dutch had started with a great many canoes for Lake Ontario to make a settlement at the mouth of the River Choueguen in concert with the Iroquois; that he was afraid he could not prevent it if they be supported by those Indians, to a war with whom he knows, the King does not intend to expose himself.

The Indians of the Sault returned from Orange dissatisfied with their reception. He immediately despatched M. de Longueuil to the Iroquois and thence to Choueguen. He commanded him to induce the savages not to suffer this Establishment, and in case he could not prevail on them to oppose it openly, to persuade them to remain neuter and to suggest to them at the same time, that it is their interest to maintain us at Niagara or to consent to our building a more solid and secure house than the one that is here.

In regard to the English he ordered M. de Longueuil, should he find them settled at Choueguen, to summon them to withdraw from their lands until the boundaries were regulated, failing which he should adopt proper measures to constrain them.

Letter dated 10 *June* 1725. M. de Longueuil writes to him (M. Begon) from Fort Frontenac the ninth of May that there was no Trading Post as yet at Choueguen.

Letter dated 31 *October*, 1725. Messrs de Longueuil & Begon send particulars of said Sieur de Longueuil's voyage. He found 100 English at the portage of the River, four leagues from Lake Ontario, with more than 60 canoes; that they made him exhibit his passport and showed him an order from the Governor of New-York not to allow any Frenchmen to go by without a passport.

M. de Longueuil took occasion to reproach the Iroquois Chiefs who were present that they were no longer masters of their lands. This succeeded; they blew out against the English; told them they would bear with them no longer, having permitted them to come to trade. They even promised him they should remain neuter in case of war against the English.

He next repaired to Onontague, an Iroquois Village and there found the Deputies of the other four Iroquois Villages who were waiting for him there. He made them consent to the construction of 2 barks and the erection of a stone house at Niagara, of which he took the plan which they send with an estimate amounting to 29,295 livres (=$5,592.)

Nota. The two barks were built in 1726.

The House (Niagara) was commenced the same year and finished in 1726.

Nota. Sieur Chaussegross, engineer, writes that he erected this House on the same spot where an antient Fort had been built by order of M. d'Enonville former Governor and Lieutenant General of Few France in 1686.

25 *July*, 1726. (M. de Longueuil writes that) he has given orders to Chevalier de Longueuil his son who commanded there (at Niagara) not to return until the English and Dutch retire from Chouguen where they have been all summer to the number of 300 men, and should he meet their canoes on the lake, to plunder them.

18 *Sept* 1726. M the Marquis of Beauharnois sends an extract of a letter from Chevalier de Longueuil dated Niagara the 5th of 7ber 1726, in which he states that there are no more English at Choueguen, along the Lake nor in the River and if he meet any of them in the Lake he'll plunder them.

GOV. BURNET TO THE BOARD OF TRADE.

[Lond. Doc. XXIII.]

New York May 9th 1727.

I have this Spring sent up workmen to build a stone house of strength at a place called Oswego, at the mouth of the Onondage River where our principal trade with the far Nations is carried on. I have obtained the consent of the Six Nations to build it, and having intelligence that a party of French of ninety men were going up towards Niagara I suspected that they might have orders to interrupt this work, and therefore I have sent up a detachment of Sixty Souldiers with a Captain and two Lieutenants, to protect the building from any disturbance that any French or Indians may offer to it. There are besides about two hundred traders now at the same place, who are all armed as Militia, and ready to join in defence of the Building and their Trade, in case they are attacked; The French can have no just pretence for doing it, but their lately building a Fort at Niagara, contrary to the last Treaty makes me think it necessary for us to be on our guard against any attempts they may make.

When the house is finished it will be sufficiently strong against an attack with small arms, which is all that can be brought thither, and I intend to keep an Officer and twenty men always in Garrison there, which will be of the greatest use to keep our Indians true to us, it being near the centre of all the Six Nations, & lying most conveniently to receive all the far Indians who come to trade with us.

My Lord Bellomont formerly intended to build a Fort by King William's order near this place, and it went so far that even plate and furniture for a chapple there, were sent over from England. but the Design was laid by upon his Death, and has never been resumed since 'till now.[1]

The Assembly provided three hundred pounds last fall for this service, of which I then acquainted Your Lordships, but I have been obliged to lay out more than double that value upon my own credit, to furnish necessaries and provisions, and hire workmen, & make Battoes to carry up the men, for it is all Water carriage from our outmost Town called Schenectady to this place, which is about two hundred miles, except five miles, where they must draw their Battoes over Land, which is easily enough done, and this makes the communication much more convenient than by Land.

1 Smith Hist. N. Y. Ed. 1828, i. 253, represents the erection of the above Fort as having been begun in 1722; an error which has been copied by McAuley, Dunlap and others who have followed him without enquiry. Gov. Burnet's despatch and the preceding Docs., correct the mistake and furnish the precise date.

I hope the Assembly will supply this Deficiency when they meet, but I was so convinced of the benefit of the undertaking that I was resolved not to let it fail for want of a present supply of money.

I am with great Respect,
My Lords, Your Lordships most dutifull and
most obliged humble servant

W. BURNET.

GOV. BURNET TO THE BOARD OF TRADE.

[Lond. Doc. XXIII.]

New York 29th June 1727.

EXTRACT.—The province is much obliged to your Lordships for representing the French building a Fort at Niagara, and in order to obtain Redress The same fort which I have been building at the mouth of the Onnondage's River called Oswego this Spring, goes on successfully hitherto, and without any interruption from the French or their Indians, and with the full consent and approbation of our own Indians.

The Detachment of Souldiers which I sent to up arrived safely there the beginning of this month, so that it is not likely that any attempt will now be made to hinder it, and I depend upon its being of the best use of anything that has ever been undertaken on that side either to preserve our own Indians in our Interest, or to promote and fix a constant Trade with the remote Indians.

GOVERNOR OF CANADA TO THE GOV. OF NEW-YORK.

[Paris Doc. VII.; Lond. Doc. XXIII.]

July 20th, 1727.

Sir—I am very well persuaded that you have been informed that the King my master has done me the honor to name me Governour and his Lieutenant General in all New France, and that you have likewise been so of my arrival to this country.

I find myself, Sir, in a juncture when the close union that subsists between our Sovereigns ought to flatter me with the hopes of the like between you and me. But I cannot avoid observing to you my surprise at the permission which you have given to the English Merchants to carry on a trade at the River of Oswego, and that you have ordered a Redoubt with Galleries (*Machicoulies*) and full of Loop holes and other works belonging to fortification, to be built at the mouth of that River, in which you have placed a Garrison of Regular Troops.

I have been, Sir, the more astonished at it, since you should have considered your Undertaking as a thing capable of disturbing the Union of the two Crowns; You cannot be ignorant of the possession during a very considerable time, which the King my Master has of all the Lands of Canada, of which those of the lake Ontario and the adjacent Lands make a part, and in which he has built Forts and made other Settlements in different places as are those of Denonville at the Entrance of the River of Niagara, that of Frontenac, another called La Famine, that which is called the Fort des Sables, another at the Bay of the Cayougas at Oswego, &c., without any opposition, they having been one and all of them possessed by the French, who alone have had a right, and have had the possession of carrying on the Trade there.

I look, Sir, upon the Settlements that you are beginning and pretending to make at the Entrance of the Lake Ontario into the River of Oswego, the fortifications that you have made there, and the Garrison that you have posted there, as a manifest infraction of the Treaty of Utrecht, it being expressly settled by that Treaty, that the subjects of each Crown shall not molest nor encroach upon one another, 'till the Limits have been fixed by Commissaries, to be named for that purpose.

This it is, Sir, which determines me at present to send away M. De la Chassaigne Governour of the Town of trois Rivieres, with an Officer, to deliver this letter to you, and to inform you of my Intentions.

I send away at the same time a Major to summon the Officer who commands at Oswego, to retire with his Garrison and other persons who are there, to demolish the fortifications and other works, and to evacuate entirely that post and to retire home.

The Court of France which I have the honour to inform of it this moment, will have Room to look upon this undertaking as an act of hostility on your part, and I dont doubt but you will give attention to the justice of my Demand.

I desire you to honour me with a positive answer which I expect without delay by the return of these Gentlemen, I am persuaded that on your side you will do nothing that may trouble the harmony that prevails among our two Crowns, and that you will not act against their true Interests.

I should be extremely pleased, Sir, if you would give me some occasion to show you particularly the sentiments of Respect with which I have the honour to be, Sir,

Your most humble and
most obed[nt] servant

At Montreal, BEAUCHARNOIS.
this 20th July 1727.

P. S. M. De la Chassaigne who did not at first intend to carry with him any but the Officer of whom I had the honour to inform you in my Letter, has since desired me to let him have the four Gentlemen named in the Passport which I have ordered to be made out for him. I dont doubt, Sir, but you will have the same Regard for them as for the King's Officer who goes along with them.

COPY OF THE SUMMONS

TO THE COMMANDANT OF THE FORT BUILT BY THE ENGLISH ON THE SHORE OF LAKE ONTARIO AT THE MOUTH OF THE RIVER CHOUEGUEN TO WITHDRAW WITH THE GARRISON OF SAID FORT, SERVED BY M[r] BEGON MAJOR OF THE TOWN AND CASTLE OF QUEBEC ON BEHALF OF THE MARQUIS OF BEAUHARNOIS, GOVERNOR GENERAL IN CANADA.

[Paris Doc. VII.]

His Lordship the Marquis of Beauharnois appointed by His Most Christian Majesty Governour General in and over Canada and the whole Dependencies of New France, being informed of your Governour's enterprise at the Mouth of Choueguen River, where he ordered a Stone Redoubt to be built on the shore of Lake Ontario where the French only have traded, and of which they have been possessors for a very great while, and considering that Enterprise as a plain Contravention to the Treaty of Utrecht, which mentions that the subjects of the two Crowns shall not intrench upon one anothers Land, 'till the Decision of the Limits by the Judges delegated to that End, has sent me with orders to summon you to draw out at furthest within a fortnight the Garrison of this place with arms, munitions and other effects belonging to the people of Albany or other places, to cast down the block house and all pieces of work you raised up contrary to all law, leaving you if you think fit to establish yourselves at Lake Thechiroguen, or the Oneida River where you formerly traded and to leave the mouth of this river free, as it has always been, to the French, failing which his Lordship the Marquis of Beauharnois will take measures against you and against your unjust usurpation as he will think fit.

(Signed) BEGON.

Montreal the 14th of July 1727.

COPY OF THE PROCES VERBAL OF THE SERVICE OF SAID SUMMONS.

[Paris Doc. VII.]

THIS DAY the first of August 1727, we the undersigned, Knight of the Military Order of St. Louis, Major of the Town, Castle and Government of Quebec, having in execution of the orders to us given by the Marquis of Beauharnois Governor and Lieutenant General for the King in all New France, arrived before the Fort built by the English on the borders of Lake Ontario, at the mouth of the River Choueguen, sent to advise Mr. Bancker Commanding the Garrison of our arrival and had him informed, at the same time, that we came on the part of the Governor General Commanding in Chief over all New France, to summon him to withdraw at least within fifteen days the garrison of said fort, with the arms, ammunition and other effects belonging to individuals at Orange and other places, and to demolish said fort and other work he had there constructed.

He sent to invite us on shore and came to meet us on the bank of said river Choueguen, accompanied by two officers of the garrison, he conducted us into the fort with much courtesy and after service on the said Commandant in the usual manner of the said summons which we left him in writing in French and in English, he answered us that he was on his land and in his house; that he had been sent thither by his General Government to build the said fort there with the consent of the Six Nations and even under valid contracts with them; that if we wished, he would cause the Chiefs of the Onondaga Indians then on the spot, to come who would inform us of it; whom we refused to hear being unwilling to have any discussion with them. After which he added, that he was but a subordinate officer like ourselves, and consequently equally obliged to follow the orders of his General; that we had an order in writing from the Marquis of Beauharnois; it would be necessary for him to have one also from Mr. Burnet, his General, so as to be able to furnish his reply; whereupon we asked to have his refusal in writing, but having communicated to us that a little time would be necessary to consider of it, and if we wished he would leave us at liberty to walk wherever we pleased; and having kept us waiting about three quarters of an hour and consulted with his officers, he persisted in his original sentiments and said that he had as much right to summon the Commandant of Niagara; finally he should send the summons to his Governor General, promising to give an answer so soon as he should receive orders. Done at Choueguen the 1st August 1727.

(Signed) BEGON.[1]

1. In Lond. Doc. XXIII. are papers purporting to be Translations of the two preceding Doc's, but they are essentially imperfect and incorrect.

GOV. BURNET TO THE GOVERNOR OF CANADA.

[Lond. Doc. XXIII.]

New York, 8th August, 1727.

Sir—I have received the letter which you have done me the honour to write to me, and which was delivered to me by Mr. De la Chassaigne. You have done me a singular pleasure in taking this occasion to make me acquainted with a person of so distinguished merit, and in sending along with them Gentlemen who do honour to their country. I could have wished that these marks of your good will had not been attended with a proceeding so little suitable to them.

You perceive, Sir, that I would complain of the sudden and peremptory summons that you have sent to my Officer posted at Oswego; and which was brought to me by an express, before the arri val of M^r De la Chassaigne.

I should think, Sir, that you might have waited for my reasons in answer to what you were pleased to write to me, before you took so Extraordinary a step, and that in giving so short a time, that my Officer could not possibly receive my orders before it expired.

I agree with you, sir, that the close union that prevails between our Sovereigns ought naturally to produce the like between you and me, and it shall never be through my fault if it does not subsist in all its extent. It was, Sir, with the same intention that I made my complaint in the modestest manner I could to Mr. De Longueuil, then Commander in Chief in Canada, of a Fort that had been built at Niagara and tho' I received no answer from him by the bearer of my letter and at last received one that was not at all satisfactory, I contented myself with writing to our Court about it, whence I am informed that our Ambassadors at the Court of France, has orders to represent this undertaking as contrary to the treaty of Utrecht.

This, Sir, was all that I did upon that occasion. I did not send any summons to Niagara, I did not make any warlike preparations to interrupt the work, and I did not stir up the Five Nations to make use of force to demolish it, which I might have done easily enough, since at the very time I received Mr. de Longueuil's letter, they were all come to complain to me of this undertaking, as the justest cause of uneasiness that could have been given them. I won't tire you with repeating all that I writ to Mr. de Longueuil upon that subject which he has no doubt shown to you.

I come now, Sir, to the subject of your Letter, there are two things which you complain of, first of the trade at Oswego, secondly of the Redoubt as you call it, and of the Garrison that is in it; as for the Trade I cannot understand how you could be surprised at it, since we have carried on a trade there regularly for more than five years running without opposition, and I have reason to wonder how you can call that an Infraction of the Treaty of Utrecht, since it is expressly stipulated in that very 15th Article which you cite, That on both sides the subjects of each Crown shall enjoy full liberty of going and coming on account of Trade.

Going and coming must imply (as appears clearly by what goes before) among all the American subjects or allies or friends of Great Britain and of France. It is upon this, Sir, that we pretend to have an equal right with you of trading thro' all the Lakes and all the Contiuent, and that incontestably, by virtue of the Terms of the Treaty.

It follows therein that also the Natives of those Countries shall with the same liberty resort as they please to the British and French Colonies, for promoting a trade on one side or the other, without any Molestation or hindrance either on the part of the British subjects or the French.

I cited to you before the Right which we have to carry on a Trade every where among the Indians. In these last words is contained the Right which all the Indians have to come and trade with us, and I leave it to you to reflect sincerely upon the conduct of the People of Canada, and to consider whether they have not done all they could and do not continue still to hinder the Indians from coming to trade with us. But as for our Right to carry a Trade every where among the Indians, one cannot find expressions more contrary to the terms of the Treaty than those in your letter, where you name several places occupied by the French, who alone, say you, have had the Right and been in possession of trading there.

You will oblige extremely if you will shew me how to reconcile that with a full liberty on both sides of going and coming on account of trade which the subjects of both crowns shall enjoy. But if you say that formerly it was as you pretend, that will signify nothing, since at present the Treaty alone onght to regulate the matters.

I hope, Sir, I have said enough upon the first subject of Complaint which relates to the Trade, for to shew you the right we have to it, and to make you sensible that the future regulation of Limits, can never make any alteration in the general liberty which there is of trade.

I come now to the second subject of Complaint which relates to the Redoubt and Garrison at Oswego. It is true, Sir, that I have ordered a Stone house to be built there, with some contrivances to hinder its being Surprized, and that I have posted some Souldiers in it, but that which gave me the first thought of it, was the fortified and much larger house which the French have built at Niagara, upon the lands of the Five Nations, as it appears even by the Confession of M. de Longueuil, in his letter to me of the 16th of August 1726, for he pretends that the Five Nations had agreed to it by an unanimous consent. If that Post was not upon their Land, but upon Land that belongs incontestably to the French, I believe, Sir, that you would be very far from asking their consent to do what you had a mind to do there.

It has been always the same case with all the posts you mention and which besides had been abandoned many years before the Treaty of Utrecht, except Fort Frontenac only, which is on the other side of the Lake. It is certain that the French never built any of them but by the permission of the Five Nations, and always on pretence that they were only to be houses for the conveniency of Trade with them and without ever pretending to claim the Property of those places: And you seem, Sir, to allow almost as much yourself for you say, That His Most Christian Majesty had ordered Forts and other Establishments to be built in different places, &c., without any opposition. What has been built without opposition can never be looked on as a conquest, as Mr. De la Chassaigne would maintain, and I should be very glad to learn by what Treaty or Agreement the five Nations ever yielded to you any of their lands, On the contrary those Nations have always maintained that the Lands on both sides of the Lake Ontario are theirs and will always maintain it.

I can't comprehend what use the Article of the Treaty to which you allude, can be to you, and I can't find the words in the Treaty as you have cited them, nor even the sense entirely agreeable to them. You call the post which we have settled at Oswego a manifest infraction of the Treaty of Utrecht, it being mentioned expressly in the Treaty that the Subjects of one and the other Crown shall not molest nor encroach upon one another, 'till the Limits shall be regulated by Commissaries to be named by them for that purpose. I dont know, Sir, what copy of the Treaty you make use of, but for my part, I have compar d the French translation which I have quoted, with the Original Latin, which is printed at London by Royal Authority and have found it entirely agreeable to it.

The words we are now upon are these as follows, The Subjects of France inhabiting Canada and others, shall hereafter give no hindrance or Molestation to the five Nations or Cantons of Indians, subject to the Dominion of Great Britain, nor to the other Natives of America who are friends to the same, in like manner the subjects of Great Britain shall behave themselves peaceably towards the Americans, who are subjects or friends to France.

This is the first part at full length of what you refer to; second part is at the end of the Article in these words, But it [is] to be exactly and distinctly settled by Commissaries, who are and who ought to be accounted the Subjects and friends of Britain or of France.

Upon reading all this together it is impossible to imagine that the last clause of this Article can relate to the Five Nations, as if Commissaries were yet to determine whether they are our subjects or yours, as Mr. de Longueuil writ to me that they were neither.

This would be directly opposite to the first part of the same Article which declares them expressly subject to the Dominion of Great Britain. But as there is mention made of other Americans Allies of Great Britain and of American Subjects or friends to France, without naming them, it as clear as daylight that the Commissaries are only to determine about these last.

You have now, Sir, my reasons for acting as I have done, and of which I have given an account to the Court at the same time that I represented the affair of Niagara. I expect every day a compleat answer upon both these points, & I think myself obliged, notwithstanding all the reasons which M. De la Chassaigne has given me to the contrary, to maintain the post of Oswego, till I receive new orders from the King my Master.

You may, Sir, make such complaints hereupon as you judge proper, as you have informed me that you have already made some, and at the same time you will not think it strange that on my part I inform the Court, in what manner you have summoned the King's Officer posted at Oswego, without waiting for any Explanation from me upon it. This is a step which the King my Master may perhaps be offended at, and which His Most Christian Majesty may perhaps think fit to disown.

I am very sorry, Sir to find myself under a necessity to have sentiments so opposite to yours. I should be glad to see all these differences end in a good understanding, & that you would honour me with your friendship, and it is with a great deal of respect that I have the honour to be, Sir, Your most humble

and most obedient Servant.

GOV. BURNET TO THE BOARD OF TRADE.

[Lond. Doc. XXIII.]

New York, 24th August, 1727.

I had News that the Fort which I have been building this Spring at Oswego, at the mouth of the Onnondages River, was upon the point of being finished, when at the same time I learnt by an Express that the Governour of Canada had sent a summons to the said Fort to have it demolished and abandoned in 15 days, copies whereof in French & English both as they were delivered to the commanding officer there, are herewith transmitted. Soon after my receiving this Summons arrived here the Governour of trois rivieres in Canada, who is next in rank to the Governour of Montreal, as he is to the Governour General of Canada. This Gentleman with his attendants was sent by the Governour of Canada to deliver a letter from him to me, and to persuade me to abandon this Fort for the present and to leave it to be afterwards settled between the two Crowns, who had the Right to that place. I agreed to leave it to be decided between the two Crowns as he proposed but in the mean time thought myself obliged to hold and maintain it.

I have enclosed copies of the Governour of Canada's letter to me in French and my answer to him in the same language, together with my own translation of both letters, wherein Your

Lordships will find the whole argument stated on both sides. There is no variation between the French & English but what was necessary to be made according to the different Translations of the Treaty from the Original Latin, but I think my argument holds equally in either translation and as strongly in the Latin as in either.

Your Lordships know very well how backward the French have been to name Commissaries, and in the mean time if they are permitted they would seize upon everything. But this new house at Oswego will make a stand that will embolden our Five nations, & will not easily be taken without great Cannon, the wall being four foot thick of good large stone, and it is represented to me that the French cannot bring large cannon against it, since they have no way but to come up from Montreal to the Lake against a Violent stream, all full of Rifts & Falls & Shallows, where they are forced to set up with poles most part of the way in light Canoes, or Battoes, & if they had cannon to carry, it is thought they could not set them along, and by land it is all over precipices and mountains, and Rivers to cross on both sides of the great river, so that it is not believed practicable for them to bring battering Cannon any way. The French have a Fort on the Lake at Cadaraqui, where the biggest Guns they have are patereros, that one man can carry about in his arms. So that probably they could bring no bigger thither.

I have had a report from some New England captives lately redeemed from Canada that the Governour of Canada was preparing 400 French & 800 Indians to attack this Fort. But there is reason to believe that this is more given out to intimidate us than really intended, and when I charged the Governour of trois Rivieres with it he utterly denyed it, but I thought I had ground enough to hint at it by way of Reproach in my letter tho' without asserting it positively. However if they should come we are provided with a double Garrison at Oswego, provisions for six months and powder and Ball sufficient for their Defence, and I have sent proper persons among our five nations with presents to them to engage them to stand by us, and not to suffer any Indians to molest us upon their Lands, as we shall be ready to defend ourselves against the French, so that I am in good hopes to be able to hold this place, in case we are attacked, and I hope Your Lordships will support me in taking these measures for securing our right to the five nations against the Encroachments and Pretensions of the French, and represent the whole affair to His Majesty, both of the French building at Niagara, contrary to the treaty of Utrecht, and of their disturbing our undoubted right of Trading and building upon the land of the five Nations at Oswego.

EXTRACT FROM THE PARTICULARS

OF THE VOYAGE OF M. DE LA CHAUVIGNELIE, OFFICER, INTERPRETER OF THE FIVE IROQUOIS NATIONS, SENT BY ORDER OF THE GENERAL WITH A MESSAGE TO THE NONTAGUES (ONONDAGAS). 1728.

[Paris Doc. VIII.]

Three leagues from Choueguan I sent three Wampum belts to notify the Nontagué Chiefs to meet me on business which brought me among them; and with three other belts I invited the four other Iroquois Nations their allies to repair to the Nontagués to hear the message of their Father of which I was the bearer to them.

On the arrival of the Nontagués at my tent, they told me on the part of the Commandant of Choueguen, that as I was passing his place on public business, I must fire the first salute and lower my flag. This proposition surprised me; my people would persuade me to do so. I therefore suddenly stood up and said to them—Ye know such is not the intention of your Father Onontio whose message I carry. A young fool in the canoe of those of the Lake said to me aloud, that he would fire and salute the fort. I replied to him, Indian fashion, that he lied and that I should not suffer it, being unwilling either to witness or be accomplice to such a folly; that I was surprised he had so soon forgotten the words of his father Onontio whose intentions I had communicated to him during our voyage; that I had no manner of business with him who was Commandant of the house at Choueguen.

They returned to said fort and reported to me that the Commandant insisted on what they had first communicated to me. I asked them whose was the land over which I wished to pass? This question caused them to droop their heads and they remained in pensive silence. It was not until I told them that I wanted a decisive and substantial answer, that they replied—The ground over which I wished to walk was theirs. I then said to them, since it was their property I, as a child of their father Onontio and bearer of his message to them, wished a clear road and that all the branches overhanging the river, be cut away so that my flag might pass without being obliged to remove it from where their Father Onontio had placed it; and that I should not fire a salute until others had saluted me. Willingly or unwillingly they approved and we proceeded.

When I arrived opposite the house of Chouguen we found, at the Mouth of the river a canoe with people of the Sault who were returning from war. This obliged us to land to give our folks an opportunity to learn the news and to cause the Prisoners to dance, as is the custom among the tribes. During this interval the Commandant of Choueguen sent for six of the principal Chiefs including me. My Chiefs invited me to follow them. I answered that I had no business at that house; they were masters to go since they wished it; I should keep my tent with the young men. Tegarioguen wished to remain with me; I persuaded him to accompany the others, so that I may learn from him what transpired. He is, moreover, a man on whom I have great reliance. They, therefore, set out for the fort. In the interval of their visit three cannon were fired the meaning of which I did not understand. On their return I learned that it was to honor the Toasts. They began by—The King of England; The Commandant of the Fort, and The General of the French of Canada. These are the terms they made use of. Here is what was said to them by the Commandant of the Fort.

Brothers, I never failed to assist the people of your Nation and you in particular when you pass by my house and come to see me. I will always act so towards you. I invite you to peace and tranquillity between you and us.

He gave them three pots of Rum, a large piece of Pork and a bushel of peas which they brought to the Camp. I found them in a state of great Drunkenness, except Tegarioguen. He assured that the Choueguen Sachem had been charmed to see them and that he gave them milk to drink to their Brother's health. But the excitement they were in led them, notwithstanding all the entreaties I could make, to finish what liquor they brought. This delayed me three days before the Fort, they being drunk so that I was unable to do any thing. I was not free from uneasiness having only Tegarioguen for support, if I were insulted.

When the Chiefs of the Lake of the Two Mountains and of Sault St. Louis returned to my tent, the Nontagué Chiefs came to summon me, on the part of the Commandant of the Fort, to strike my flag which I had hoisted over my Tent, inasmuch as I was under the guns of the Fort. I always answered Indian fashion; I knew no flag but that of their Father Onontio which I carried, and it should not be lowered until I was tied. Contrary to the custom of lowering it at sundown, it remained flying night and day the whole of the time I was constrained to remain at that post.

On the day of our departure it was again the same tune. I must absolutely fire first and strike my flag. This I would not do; therefore no salute on the one side nor the other, and we set out to proceed. A Nontagué Chief carrying a British flag in his hand, called out to me to embark. I forbid my people to do so, telling them I would not march under an English flag, and they heard me. I told them we should start when the English flag was no longer to be seen, which we did. I reproached the Nontagués with their weakness and the little respect they paid their Father and his Flag since they dared not pass Choueguen without a British flag. They answered—You're right, Father; but you know we have every thing to manage here. I replied—Under their Father's flag, there was nothing to be feared. And forthwith they furled the British flag which has not made its appearance since.

GOV. CLARKE TO THE COMMANDER AT OSWEGO.

[Lond. Doc. XXV.]

New York Nov'r 1st 1736.

Sir—I am truly sorry to hear so many complaints of your conduct at Oswego. I hope for better things, but am now in fear, if some better care be not taken, that the Garrison will all desert or perish for want of provision of which I am told there is no manner of Oconemy, it behooves you, Sir, to be very circumspect, and I earnestly recommend to you, to keep good dissipline, and to take care of the provissions and of the security of the house and garrison.

Mr Beauharnois complained to me of your Commanding a French Canoe a shore, which was passing by, I assured him I wo'd enquire into it, and I hope you will be able to acquit yourself of what he lays to your charge.

I desire you will be very vigilant and guard carefully against all surprizes of the Indians or others, Capt: Dick will convey this to you to whom you ought to give an account of your Garrison by all opportunity's as he is the Commanding Officer on the Frontiers. Sr &c

Capt. Congreve. G. C.

[Journ. of General Ass.]

Die Sabatii May 23. 1741.

Resolved, That there be allowed a sum not exceeding the sum of *Six Hundred Pounds*, to and for erecting a sufficient stone Wall, at a proper Distance, round the Trading House at *Oswego*, either in a Triangular or Quadrangular Form, as the Ground will best admit of, with a Bastion or Block House in each Corner, to flank the Curtains, which are to be single for the Accommodation of Men, if need be.

MR. CLARKE TO THE BOARD.

[Lond. Doc. XXVI.]

New York Aug: the 20th 1742.

My Lords—If the loss of Oswego (which I much fear will fall into the hands of the French on the first rupture) does not stagger the best resolutions of the Six Nations, who at present fear more than they love the French; that Fortress, or rather Trading house, for it is no better, is in a very defenceless condition, the Garrison consists but of a Lieutenant, Sergeant, Corporal and 20 men it is and has been without Ammunition, the Assembly refusing to be at the expense, as well as to make provision for victualling a larger Garrison; it is true they have given money to build a wall round the house, but the Director of the works, instead of laying the stones in lime and sand, as by the Act he was to do, is laying them in clay;[1] it is, as it is managed a jobb calculated rather to put money in the Pockets of those who have the management of the business, than for any real service to the publick; tho' it is a thing of the utmost importance, as the loss of it will certainly be followed by the loss of the furr trade, and very probably may by a defection of the Six Nations, the consequence whereof your Lordpps know perfectly well.

GOV. CLARK'S REPORT

ON THE STATE OF THE BRITISH PROVINCES WITH RESPECT TO THE FRENCH WHO SURROUND THEM. 1743.

[Lond. Doc. XXVII.]

Tho' it has been my duty to consult in a more particular manner the welfare of the Province; which I have had the honour to Govern some years, yet I never took myself to be thereby discharged from carrying my thoughts to things of a more extensive nature, especially to such whereon the peace & happiness of the Plantations, and the Trade of England, if not the very being of His Majesty's Dominion on this continent depend, I have often reflected on the progress that our natural Enemies the French have made in their settlements on the back of us, Chiefly since the peace of Utrecht, the vast increase of their Indian Trade, the interruption of ours by the power which their communication between Canada and Messassippi, (by means of the Lake Cadaraque or Ontario) gives them over all the Indian Nations, living on that, and all the other Lakes, which disembogue into Cadaraqui, and from thence into the River St. Lawrence, & by what means that communication may be cut off, & those Indian Nations brought to an absolute dependence on His Majesties Provinces, who will thereby be possesst of a very great additional Trade, and (which is principally to be considered) be for ever secured from the annoyance of the French, and may without danger or interruptions extend their settlements as far back as they please.

The French had lately three, and have now two sailing vessells, each of about 50 or 60 Tons, on the Lake Cadaraqui: On the North East end whereof, near the entrance into the River of St. Lawrence, they have a small stone Fort called Frontenac, with a Garrison of about thirty or thirty five

1 "He pretended that there was not Limestone to be gotten and without giving himself much trouble to search went on his own way."—Lond. Doc. xxvii. 3. The wall above alluded to, cost when finished £630.11.11¼ Cury.—Journal of N. Y. Assemb. 1744.

men, and on the Southwest End, near the fall of Niagara, another with the like garrison, a trading house under the cover of it, and are now building there one or two more trading houses. In those vessells they carry the Soldiers, Artillery, Ammunition and Provision to the Forts, and transport to & fro the goods they sell to & buy from the Indians: It is through this Lake they pass from Canada to Messasipi, & from thence back again to Canada: By means only of their Mastery on that Lake it is that, they have acquired, and still hold their power over all the Indian Nations, from Canada to Messasippi, except only the Indians who are next adjoining to our Provinces, and have all along been dependent on them, (of which the Five Nations or Cantons are the most considerable) and in all those they have of late gotten too great an influence, especially among the five Nations whose youth being of a martial spirit, they intice (contrary to the Public Engagements of those Nations) to join them in their Expeditions against the Indian Nations, subject to His Majesty, and depending on the Governments of Virginia, the two Carolina's & Georgia, who have it in their power (by their situation, if their strength were equal, as it would be, were they united and resolved) to interrupt the march of the French from Niagra to Messasippi: this the French know full well, and fearing that they may sometime or other confederate against them for that purpose, they seldom fail once a year, to attack one of those Nations while they are disjoined, thereby to exterpate, or bring them over to their Interest, and they have gone but too great a length towards it, none of those Nations daring now to give them any interruption & thinking themselves happy when they are not annoyed by the French. We have a trading House and a Garrison of 20 men in it at Oswego, almost opposite to Fort Frontenac, which in our present situation will inevitably fall into the hands of the French, on the first opening of a War, & with it the Five Nations, the only Barrier against the French to all the Provinces from this to Georgia, for tho' they now intice some of their youth to join them in their hostile marches, yet the Body of those Nations oppose it all they can, & live in a good intelligence with us, professing to observe inviolably their original Allyance, (or Covenant Chain as they phrase it) which has subsisted ever since we first settled this Country, yet if Oswego be taken, (as nothing can hinder it while the French are masters of the Lake) the Five Nations will, and must of course, submit to our Enemy, who will oblige them to assist in all their expeditions: In which Event every one of our Provinces may be so attacked, that the Planters will be obliged for the security of their Persons to quit their settlements, retire into the Towns, wherever they are, or under the cover of Forts, of which we have very few on the whole Continent, or, what is worse, leave the Country to seek a living elsewhere, the consequences whereof to England are but too obvious, & this the Enemy will more easily do, as they have a line of Forts from Canada to Messasippi.

As a remedy for these Evils, which are almost as great as can befall the Nation, I propose that a Regiment of eight hundred men be sent from England (or if half the number of private men be sent, the other half I believe may be raised here) with an Engineer, Artillery, and Ammunition, & posted in the Sineca's Country on the Lake Cadaraqui, at a proper Harbour for building of Vessells their being more than one of sufficient depth of Water, That the Harbour be fortified and Barracks erected for the men. That there be then built two or three Vessells of superior force to those of the French, on board whereof a few sailors, & a sufficient number of soldiers being put with proper Officers, we may take, sink or otherwise destroy the French Vessells, and then easily take their Forts on the Lake, & for ever hinder them from building more on those shores, or any Vessells on the Lake, nor, (if they should build any in the River St. Lawrence) can they carry them against that rapid stream into the Lake. The consequences whereof will be of the greatest moment. All our Colonies from this to Georgia, will be secure from the incursions of the French in time of War. The Indians depending on the Governments of Virginia, Carolina and Georgia, who are now almost every year attacked by the French, and their Indians will live unmolested; All the Indian Nations living on or near the Lakes, and all those over whom the French at present have a very great power, will no sooner hear of our conquests, than they will submit to, & trade altogether with us, The Five Nations will no longer be divided by French Intrigues, but will be absolutely at our Devotion, and the Trade & Influence of our Enemy will be confined to the Cold Country of Canada, which will scarce be worth keeping, and to the Banks of the River Messasippi, Nay, no sooner will the Five Nations see us masters on the Lake, than they will assist us to take the two Forts of Frontenac, & Niagra, for they are now complaisant to the French only through Fear, knowing them to be a treacherous & enterprising people. It was I presume to think, a very great Oversight, to suffer the French to build those two Forts, & I am persuaded if it had been strongly & rightly represented by the Governors of this & the other Provinces a stop would have been put to it. Those Forts being built on the Lands of the Five Nations (whose native and conquered countries encompass the Lake on the shore whereon they are built) who by the 15th Article of the Treaty of Utrecht are explicitly acknowledged to be subject to the dominion of Great Britain, I am sensible that by the same article it is stipulated that both the English & French, shall have a free Intercourse for Trade with all the Indians & the Indians with them, let them enjoy it, (when we are Masters of the Lake) in the like manner that ours is now carried on, vizt By Canoes and small rowing Boats, but I am pretty sure that when the French yoke is taken off their necks, the Indians will no longer trade with them, for the English Manufactures are much better, and they prefer them to French goods, but supposing that they should still trade with them, it will be in a much smaller proportion than they now do, & besides they cannot then march in any numbers to disturb our Provinces, or the Indians, now & of old depending on them. An Event of the highest importance, nor can Canada supply Messasippi, or Messasippi Canada, with forces or merchandize in time of need: Before the French begun to build the Fort at Niagra, which is about 20 years ago, they cajoled some few of the young fellows of the Five Nations, to give them permission to build a trading House there, but so soon as it reached the ears of the Sachims or Rulers of those Nations, they resented it, acquainted the Governor of this Province, that the French had begun to build, & offered to join any force he should send to demolish the works, and to drive the French from thence, but this was unhappily neglected: incouraged by their success there, they did, about twelve years ago, erect another Fort, and much stronger (on the lands likewise of the Five Nations) at a place called the Crown Point, about 160 miles from Albany between that & Canada. In that part of the Country, where the Senecas chiefly dwell, & where I propose our Vessells should be built, and the Regiment quartered, the Climate is temperate, and the lands exceeding Fertile, so that in three years time from their going thither, provisions of all kinds (sufficient for the Regiment & Vessells) may be raised, Except only Beef, which will require a year or two more, in the mean time cattle may be drove thither from the County of Albany, with as much ease as they are now to the Garrison at Oswego, and no sooner will the Regiment march towards it, than farmers will go thither under their cover to settle in that Country, being sure both of protection, & of a market for what they raise, The Five Nations being acknowledged by the Treaty of Utrecht to be subject to the Dominion of Great Britain, & the Lake lying in their Country, it being surrounded by their Lands, I humbly submit it, whether we have not a Right even before a Rupture to assume the Dominion thereof, and to destroy the Forts the French have built in the Country of those Cantons, especially if we have their concurrence, of which & of their assistance too, I make no doubt, when they see the Regiment among them.

When we have thus vindicated our Right and established our Dominion on the Lake, the Regiment may then be employed in the reduction of the Fort at the Crown Point, wherein, if there be need, we may I believe have assistance from the Provinces of Massachusetts Bay and New Hampshire, who have settlements not far from thence, and who claim the lands adjoining to it, & one of them even that whereon the Fort is built.

If this or something else (of which I own I can think of nothing so effectual) be not soon done to put a stop to the French Encroachments farewell to the English Colonies and to that most valuable Trade of the Nation.

If it ever be thought advisable to attempt again to take Canada, the dispossessing the French of their mastery on the Lake & of the Fort at the Crown point, will greatly facilitate the Enterprize, but before we begin that work I presume to think we ought to take Cape Breton, a Place well fortifyed, & from whence the French can annoy our Fishery at Newfoundland, and guard their own navigation to and from Canada. That place is such a Thorn in the sides of the New England people, that it is very probable a large body of men may be raised there to assist in any such design, and if proper officers are sent from England in the summer to exercise them, they may by the ensuing spring be well disciplined, as all their youth are expert in the use of fire arms, from the unrestrained liberty of Fowling, which obtains in all the Provinces, & I conceive the spring is the most proper season to attack the place, before the Men of War & Fishing Vessells come from France, for in the Winter they have few men except the Garrisons, & Boston being a proper Fort for our Fleet to harbour in the Winter, we may block up the Harbour of Breton before the Ships from France can come upon the coast.

New York 1743.

GOV. CLINTON TO THE N. Y. ASSEMBLY.

[Journals of Gen. Assembly.]

Die Lunæ Aug. 20, 1744.

Gentlemen, From the Examination herewith laid before You, it must be inferred, that the Province has suffered Considerable damage this summer, by the precipitate Retreat of our *Indian* Traders from Oswego, upon Notice of the *French* War; most of them you will find, left the Place immediately upon the Alarm, sold what they could of their Goods, to those few of their Brethren, that had Sense, Courage and Resolution to stay behind, and brought the Remainder back with them. You will judge what a Baulk and Discouragement, this Instance of Pusilanimity has occasioned to those Number of *Indians*, of the far Nations, who have rarely come to Trade with us; but perhaps finding the *French*, had no Goods to supply them at *Niagara*, resolved to proceed to *Oswego*, where some of them found the place was basely deserted by most of the People, and no Goods to exchange for their Furs; upon Information whereof, many other *Indian* Canoes were turned back before they reached that place.

How mean an Opinion, must the Savages entertain of us, when they find our People so easily frightened, as it were with a Shadow, and that the great Gains, which are constantly reaped by this Advantageous Traffick, are not sufficient to excite a Resolution in our Traders, to stand to the Defence of this Fortress, the Loss of which, would determine that Trade, and it is to be feared the *Indians* too, in favour of our natural Enemies the *French*; how fatal such an event would prove to this Colony in particular, and the *British* Interest upon the Continent in general, may be easily foreseen.

The pernicious Consequences which must inevitably flow from this sort of Demeanour, I persuade myself, you will think deserving of your serious Attention, and that you will put this most profitable Branch of our Trade, into such a Method for the Future, as may encourage and invite the most distant Nations to come yearly to trade at that Mart; when by the Wisdom and Justice of the

Legislature, Matters are so regulated for the future, that the *Indians* may be assured, that not only their Occasions, will always be plentifully supplied there with Goods, the best of their kind, but also at the most reasonable Rates; touching which last Article the Six Nations have made frequent complaints; by these Measures, we shall establish such a Credit amongst our own, and the remotest *Indians*, that it will not be in the power of the *French* to rival us in that Point.

[Paris Doc. X.]

April 4, 1748. Nanangousy, Chief of the Iroquois at the Sault has returned from Choüeguen where he has been to spy. He reports that outside Fort Choueguen there is but one Trader's house; that there was a great number of Dutch and Palatine traders at the place called Theyaoguin who were preparing to come and make a considerable trade at Choueguen, and that there was nothing at that fort to betoken any expedition on the part of the English among the 5 Nations.

[Council Minutes XXV.]

Fort George, New York, 23 April, 1755.

The Governor acquainted the Board that among the other measures concerted at Alexandria, the Fort at Oswego, as a Post of great Importance, is to be strengthened by a detachment of all the effective Men belonging to the two independent Companies at Albany, and two Companies from S[r] William Pepperel's Regim[t] who are to throw up Intrenchments and make Such additional Works as may be thought wanting for its Security. That he signified to the General [Braddock] that the Province would not he apprehended, supply Provisions for so many men, unless the Expense might be taken out of the Fund of £5000 granted for Transportation and Refreshment of the King's troops, and for other extraordinary services Necessary for the Use and Security of the Colony, in the present Juncture; and that if he was willing it Should be taken out of that Fund, he would advise with the Council upon it, on his Return. To which General Braddock had agreed. And thereupon the Governor desired the opinion of the Board.

The Board were of Opinion His Honour might draw out of that Fund for Six Months Provisions for those troops and for One hundred Battoes and a sufficient number of Steersmen, to be employed in transporting them and their Provisions & Stores. And also for Pickaxes, Spades, Shovells and other necessaries for making Intrenchments, if such proper Implements could not be supplied out of the King's Stores here.

M. DE VAUDREUIL TO THE MINISTER.

[Paris Doc. 11.]

Quebec, 10 July, 1756.

My lord,—I had the honour to inform you by my letter of the 2d inst. that the English were deploying a large force towards Chouaguen; that they had built some 10 gun brigs there and two descriptions of galleys;[1] that a body of 3000 men were also assembling at Fort Necessity about 40 leagues from Fort Duquesne and that its vanguard of 700 men had already arrived there.

1 The *first* English vessel on Lake Ontario was a little schooner of 40 feet keel with 14 sweeps or oars and 12 swivels. She was launched n 28th June, 1755.

We had confirmation of this news from reliable Indians of different villages and they gave us assurances sufficiently convincing not to allow us to doubt it. They even added, as a matter of certainty that 4000 men were going to Choueguen; that the five nations were spread on the wings of this army; that the English would seize Niagara and Fort Frontenac, and moreover that they had constructed 600 batteaux at Orange; that they were still busy at a great many others; that there were, likewise, 5000 men encamped outside Orange covering two leagues of Country; that this army was to march against Fort St. Frederic [Crown Point] and finally advance on our settlements on this Continent. I am, my lord, about to send some reinforcements to this last fort, but this diversion will not cause me to change my design on Lake Ontario which I had the honour to communicate to you. The preservation of Niagara is what interests us the most; if our enemies became masters of it and keep Chouaguen, the Upper Countries would be lost to us, and besides, we should have no more communication with the river Oyo.

THE SAME TO THE SAME.

Montreal 24 July 1755.

However great the evil [the backward state of Canada and the low state of its finances] I must remedy it and in carrying out my views and my zeal in this regard, I must not lose sight of my design against Chouaguen, since on the success of this depends the tranquility of the Colony.

The expedition against Chouaguen which had at all times been easy, is to-day unfortunately very difficult and that, I cannot help repeating, because the English experienced no opposition in their undertaking and preparations. The quiet state of the Colony had, even rendered them so haughty that having arrived at the degree of perfection they aspired to, they boldly raised the mask, and were daring enough, in the beginning of June, to send three balls through the King's Flag flying from a batteau of an Officer who was conducting a detachment to the *Belle Riviere.*

They have actually two and perhaps three flat bottomed gun brigs with sweeps, which cruise from day to day, on Lake Ontario. They are about to launch others for similar purposes. I have advices of the 20th of this month stating that those two barks have been with several Batteaux as far as beyond Quinté where the English landed, and that it is certain they will go to Niagara.

Chouaguen is no longer a Trading house; it is regularly fortified and suitably furnished with pieces of artillery. There is a second Fort equally provided with cannon. The Woods that surrounded Chouaguen and militated against its defence, no longer exist. They have rendered its approaches difficult.[1]

They are in strength there and become stronger every moment by the troops that arrive from Orange. Yet, My Lord, I act with confidence, and dare flatter myself to have Chouaguen razed.

The army will be composed of about 4300 men 2000 of whom will be regular troops, 1800 Canadians and 500 domiciliated Indians. I perceive with joy that the one and the other greatly exert

1 "When it was determined that the Army at Oswego should go into winter quarters, they began a new fort upon a hill on the east side of the river about 470 yards from the old one; it is 800 feet circumference, and will command the harbour; it is built of logs from 20 to 30 inches thick; the wall is 14 feet high and is encompassed by a ditch 14 feet broad and ten deep; it is to contain barracks for 300 men, and to mount 16 guns. On the other side of the river, west from the old fort, another new fort is erecting; this is 170 feet square, the rampart is of Earth and Stone, 20 feet thick and 12 feet high, besides the parapet; this is also encompassed with a ditch 14 feet broad and 10 feet deep, and is to contain barracks for 200 men. An hospital of framed work, 150 feet by 30, is already built, which may serve as a barrack for 200 men; and another barrack is preparing of 150 feet by 24.—*Account of American affairs in 1755, in Gentleman's Magazine,* xxvi. 6.

themselves to accomplish my wishes. This army will be furnished with portable cannon and munitions of war and implements generally requisite for a seige. Since the 12th instant the troops file off by brigades for Fort Frontenac. I expect the remainder of the army will have left Montreal by the 10th of next month; and that all my forces will be collected at Fort Frontenac by the 25th of the same month, unless the weather be unfavorable.

I should have been highly gratified, My Lord, to march at the head of the army, persuaded of the effect my zeal for the Kings service and my country would have produced on the Canadian soldiers and more particularly the Savages. But Fort St. Frederick [Crown Point] being equally menaced, my presence is necessary at Montreal.

Baron Dieskaw will command this army. I confer daily with him and see with pleasure that he ardently desires to accomplish my views.

As for the five Nations I reckon not on their aid, but I do not despair of their neutrality. From the hour of its foundation, Chouaguen is the rendezvous of the different Indian tribes. It is from Chouaguan proceed all the Belts and messages that the English scatter among the Far Nations. It was always at Chouaguen that the English held Councils with the Indians and by means of presents, principally of intoxicating liquors, persuaded them to assassinate the French. In fine, Chouaguen is, consequently, the direct cause of all the troubles that have supervened in the Colony, and of the infinitude of expences these have entailed on the King. From the destruction of Chouaguen will follow:

On the one hand the complete attachment of all the upper country Indians; on the other, a considerable diminution in the expenditure incurred at present by the King for the Colony. Should the Five Nations take sides with the English, they would abandon them the moment Chouaguen was no more. The Indian tribes having no longer a resource with the English to obtain intoxicating liquors, I shall insensibly destroy the trade in Brandy at certain posts, so destructive to the prosperity of the service and of commerce. These same tribes acknowledging and from that moment unable to have any other communication except with the French, the prodigious quantity of Beaver and Peltry which went to the English will return to the trade of France.

I request you, My Lord, to be assured of my punctuality in obeying all that is prescribed by my instructions and that I shall do everything in my power to signalize my zeal for the King's service.

With the most profound respect, I am, My Lord,

Your very humble and very Obedient Servant

VAUDREUIL.

THE SAME TO THE SAME.

[Paris Doc. XII.]

Montreal 2 Feb. 1756.

Chouaguen is now in a state of defence; it would be impossible to undertake besieging it unless with a strong army and considerable artillery. The English have three forts there, each of which has cannon and bombs. The garrison consists of 600 men who are constantly on the alert. I know less of the situation of Chouguen through the reports of prisoners and deserters, than through a reconnoissance I caused to be made of it this winter by two small parties I sent thither.

The first of these parties brought me two prisoners, the second commanded by M Mo de Louvigny, Ensign has completely fulfilled its mission. That officer remained several days in the neighborhood of Chouaguen and did, himself, examine everything. He could not burn the barks because they were under the cannon of the Fort and well guarded. He made two prisoners, and on his return rendered 60 @ 80 batteaux unfit for service.

[From Council Minutes XXV.]

At a Council held at Fort George in the City of New-York on Wednesday the 21 day of April 1756.

His Excellency (Gov. Hardy) communicated a Letter from Sir William Johnson of the 16[h] Inst, advising that he had just rec[d] a letter from Colonel Bradstreet in which he writes " This moment arrived two Indians of the Onondaga's to give Notice that Oswego was surrounded four days since by a considerable Number of French and Indians from Cadaraqui and Niagara. That they had heard the Cannon of Oswego for half a day after they left their Castle, and that the General Rendezvous of the Enemy was about twelve Miles from Oswego.

That upon the receipt of Col. Bradstreet's Letter he had determined to set off with what Militia he could get together immediately, and to order the rest to follow him to the German Flats, and in his way to take the two Mohawk Castles with him. That he hath been informed of the Weak state of the Forts Edward and William Henry and that the Garrisons apprehended an attack, and had therefore ordered the Militia to March to the Relief of these Forts on Notice of the approach of an Enemy.

His Excellency informed the Council that he had upon former Intelligence which he had received of the danger the Garrison of Oswego was exposed to, wrote to the Commanding Officers of the King's Troops at Albany and Schenectady, representing the great importance of that Post, and the bad consequences the loss of it must be attended with, and therefore that he hop'd they would march the Troops or such part of them as they should find necessary for the relief of that place.

The Council declared His Excellency had taken all the measures in his power on this Occasion.

[N. Y. Mercury May 31. 1756.]

Oswego May 17. 1756.

I arrived here three days ago, after a Tedious Time occasioned by the large Train I was with, consisting of 200 Whale Boats, and 200 Battoes, excepting two Whale Boats, and two Battoes that were lost at the Falls, twelve Miles from hence, & four Men drowned in them. On my arrival I heard, that a few days before, a Party of Indians came on some ship Carpenters cutting Timber not 300 yards from the Town; & before a Party could be turned out, Killed and carried off Twelve: They were pursued by the Party, but they could not get sight of them : Our People found one Killed, which they Scalped, & threw his Body in the River, besides several Blankets shot thro,' Knives, Muskets &c. by which 'tis thought some more of the Enemy have been Killed. About eight o'Clock this Day we heard a firing up the River which we took to be an attack on one Lieut Blair, who went up this Morning to the Reefs, with 24 Men, two miles off, for a Guard to the Battoes at that Place; upon which Numbers of People, with a few Mohawks run from the Town that Way. The firing still continued; and soon after a man came in with an Indian Scalp, and brought Word, that Blair's Party was attacked by a Party of French & Indians, himself and one Soldier killed: Upon which upwards of 500 Battoe Men were sent different Ways into the Woods. We soon further heard, that a brave Mohawk, who went out on the Alarm, with some Battoe Men, was Killed by a French Indian, after he (the French Indian) had received a Wound in the Thigh, the Mohawk attempting to take him alive, and by that means he lost his Life; but a Battoe man that stood next to him soon despatched the French Indian, and Scalped him; another they found dead, which they Scalped also; two more they are certain are killed, as they saw them drawn off. Lieut. Blair, though a Young Gentleman not more than 18 or 19, behaved like a brave Soldier; for being wounded the first Fire, he begged his Men to TREE ALL, and fight on, for he was a dead Man, and that they might soon expect assistance; Soon after he received another Ball in his Throat, when he immediately fell. The Sergeant, with the Men, bravely maintained their Ground, till they were relieved by Numbers, on whose Approach, the Enemy soon made off, and the Woods being now green, our People stood no chance in following them. Another Soldier is mortally wounded, one slightly, and a Ship Carpenter, who went out without any Fire Arms some Time after the Attack, was shot in the Leg, the Bone not hurt. Our People have brought in several Blankets, Knives, Small Arms &c. by which we hope they have had a warm Reception. They had not time to Scalp our Dead. Lieut. Blair, the Mohawk & Soldier were interred this afternoon, with all the Honors of War.

We are busy getting the Vessels here ready for the Lake, and hope to be out in Eight Days. As yet, little is done to the new Ones, and will not, till we are reinforced, that we may have a Strong Guard to cover our Men in the Woods. At the Falls, (12 miles from hence) a good Stockaded Fort is building, to defend that Pass. Plenty of fresh Beef and Fish, the latter of which, in three Hawls of a Seine, filled a Battoe, so hope soon to have a very healthy Garrison.

[From the same, 14 June 1756.]

The Names of the Carpenters & Sawyers that were Killed & Missing at Oswego about a Month since, are, Edmond Banton, John Mitchell, Henry Jackson & Philip Philips of New York; the three former Killed & Scalped, & the latter Missing; John Jordan, Samuel Mash & Lewis Dunham of Brunswick, the two former Killed, the latter Missing; Michael Murray, Killed; James Grant, John English & Charles Carter, of Philadelphia, the two former Killed, & the latter Missing; James Flanagan missing, one Soldier Killed and another Shot in the Knee.

[From the same, June 28 1756.]

By Several Letters received from Albany we have the following Intelligence from Oswego viz[t] That on the 16th Instant, about 4 o'clock in the Morning, a Party of 3 or 400 French & Indians. attacked the Forts Oswego and Ontario and Killed & Scalped five of the Battoe Guard, sent from Fort Ontario on that side of the River: That they took one Prisoner, mortally wounded another, and slightly wounded a third, but were repulsed, and not without considerable Loss, as the Cannon play'd upon them for an Hour and a Half; that they went quite off about Eleven o'Clock: That two Whale Boats were sent to make Discoveries on the French Shore, the Same Day, and after rowing about 11 miles, they saw a Smoak, and about 100 Yards farther, a man running from the Shore into the

Woods; that they immediately fired a Volley from the Boats, when the Smoak was put out, & about ten Minutes after, upwards of 1000 French and Indians appeared upon the Beech, and drew up in a Line three deep, reaching almost a Mile, and gave the Bcats a Volley, some of their Shots droping within 5 yards of them: That they fired about five Minutes, when the Boat gave them another Fire, three Huzza's & row'd off, and returned to Oswego about 5 o'Clock: That the three Vessels were returned from a Cruize of about two weeks, but have made no Discoveries; And that another, and more formidable Attack was hourly Expected.

Albany June 27. 1756.

Friday last Harkamers Son came down from Oswego, with Letters from Col. Merser, for General Shirley: He says, there had been a smart Skirmish at Fort Ontario; that a Body of about a thousand French and Indians had attacked the Fort, but were beat off by Colonel Schuyler, and those that were in Garrison there, after an engagement of two Hours; that Col. Schuyler lost 26. Men and the Regulars, 6.

EARLY NAVAL OPERATIONS ON LAKE ONTARIO.

[From the same.]

His Majesty's Sloop, Oswego;
Oswego, July 2d, 1756.

I have been out with Commodore Bradley on two cruises. On the first we were out twelve days, endeavoring to get to Niagara, but the wind blowing constantly from the westward were forced to return, having made no discovery but what related to a further knowledge of the Lake. Last Wednesday, seven nights, we sailed on a second cruise, and the Sunday following, at day dawn, as we were steering a course for Oswego, (having promised Col. Mercer to return off the harbor in four days,) we saw four sail of French vessels, from whom we were glad to make all the sail we could. As I make no doubt this affair will be variously represented at New York, I shall give an impartial account of the same, which is as follows: At half past two, A. M., we saw two sail standing towards us from the N. W., on which we immediately made the signal for the Ontario to chase, and got all ready for action, wore ship, and stood for them. At three quarters past three, we saw two more sail from the same quarter. At this time, one of the two vessels, which proved to be the Commodore, fired two guns to leeward and hoisted a French flag at his foretop mast head, which we took for a signal for the two sternmost vessels to make sail and join, as he and the next to him directly hauled on the wind, and clewed up their main top sails. At 5 o'clock, being then about one and a half miles from them, we found they were all four schooners, and the two whose distance I have just mentioned, very large vessels with several guns of a side. The other two appeared as large, but of what force we could not see, they being farther off. On which, Capt. Lafory came on board and a council being called, it was thought most prudent to avoid an engagement, the enemy being far superior to us, and the utmost consequence our welfare was to Oswego. Our force consisted: first, the Oswego, Com. Bradley, with only 4 pounders, 1 three pounder, and 45 seamen and soldiers; the Ontario, Capt. Lafory, with 4 four pounders, 1 three pounder, and 45 seamen and soldiers; a small schooner not bigger than a four cord boat, under the command of Mr. Farmer, with 6 swivels, and 13 seamen and soldiers. At half past five, wore and made the best of our way to Oswego. On which the enemy gave chase, and had the French Commodore behaved at the time as he ought, he must have brought us to action very soon and taken us: but he was unwilling to attack without his little fleet close together, and in chasing fired single shot at us; to do which, he was obliged to luff up in the wind, having no bow chase, by which means he lost every time, twice his length. At 7 o'clock, he being little better than half a mile off, first luffed up in the wind, then clapt his helm hard a-weather, wore round, and fired his broadside at Capt. Lafory, astern of us, and left off chase—none of which, or those before, did any execution. At our first making off, we found Mr. Farmer to drop astern very fast, on which the Commodore hailed the Ontario to tell him to bare up more large. The two sternmost schooners gave chase to him, and soon after saw him haul up to the northward, for what reason we know not, and the two vessels in chase of him firing at him, which guns by the report they made were heavy. We soon after lost sight of him and the chase and at 11 o'clock heard firing again. At three P. M. we got into Oswego.

The new brigantine and sloop are to be launched to-morrow; the Snow in ten or twelve days. But we are greatly disappointed in guns for them, for Col. Bradstreet arrived here yesterday with 600 battoes, and with him came only sixteen carriage guns and sixteen swivels, whereas the Brigantine only should mount sixteen carriage guns. However, we shall get some small guns from the Fort the sloop, and directly go and look for *Monsieur*, who I am afraid will not give us the opportunity of speaking with him, as they had been to Niagara and I suppose have carried provisions sufficient for the garrison.

We are yet much troubled by scalping parties—large bodies lying within six or seven miles of us, and as our garrison is not sufficient to dislodge them, they do us much damage. We are obliged to have large parties to cover the carpenters: others to clear the woods around the garrison—that it would be imprudent to attempt it till we are stronger. For these ten days past we have quitted the Fort on the hill, on the Oswego side, it not being tenable; but as some troops (about 200) are come up with Col Bradstreet, we expect it to be immediately put in a posture of defence. Provisions we abound in, but now the cry is *Men!* So believe we shall rest on the defensive this summer and winter. What is the occasion, time may discover; and may the enemies of our country meet their just deserts is my sincere wish.

M. DE VAUDREUIL TO THE MINISTER.

[Paris Doc. XII.]

Montreal, 5 July, 1756.

My lord,—English vessels have appeared several times on Lake Ontario; our's occupied with the freight to Niagara, could not chase them. Nevertheless, our two barks returning from Niagara on the 26th of June perceived across the Bay of Quintée some coming towards them. We gave them chase, all our sails set, but the enemy immediately sheered off. He was pursued so close that he was obliged to abandon his sloop, which was his third vessel. We left this to our two barks; our two Corsairs continued in pursuit of the enemy who seeing himself gained on cut his boat loose and threw a number of other things overboard. In vain we fired our chasers after him he made no response, taken up altogether in pushing himself ahead, and the wind having fallen he gained on our Corsairs by means of the quantity of sail he carried. Having chased him into Chouaguen we tacked to overhaul the sloop our barks had missed. She struck at once. This prize is about 20 tons, armed with 6 patereros, 12 muskets, 6 sailors and 8 soldiers.

On the 25th June, as our two Corsairs were cruising between the Islands of Couis and the Galops, one of them being near the Bay of Niagara,[1] got intelligence of a schooner returning to Chouaguen. He gave chase and found himself in doubling a point quite close on Chouaguen. The Schooner had time to enter the River, were it not for which she would not have escaped this Corsair.

This, My lord, is what the movements and exploits of our little Navy of Lake Ontario is at present reduced to.

I am with most profound respect, My Lord,

Your very humble and very ob[t] Servant,

VAUDREUIL.

ACTION BETWEEN THE FRENCH AND ENGLISH.

[N. Y. Mercury, July 19.]

Albany, 13 July, 1756.

On Monday Colonel Bradstreet arrived here from Oswego. On the 3d, about 3 o'Clock in the Afternoon, nine Miles on this side that place, having about 300 Battoemen with him, in their Battoes, he was attacked from the North side of the River by about 700 of the Enemy, of which 200 were Regulars, the Rest Canadians and Indians. Col. Bradstreet, who at that time was near the Front of his Party, proceeded with six Men to a small Island near the Enemy, and ordered a few more to follow him there, to keep back the Enemy from fording the River, till the rest of his Men could land on the South side of it. He had no sooner landed with the Six men, but he was attacked by Twenty of the Enemy, whom his party beat back, kept Possession of the Island and were joined by six more Battoemen. They were then attacked by about 40 of the Enemy, who stood their Ground very well, and wounded eight out of the Twelve; yet as our People never fired, without each killing his Man, the Enemy gave Way. The Party on the Island were then increased to about Twenty, besides the Wounded, and were again attacked by 70 of the Enemy, whom our Folks also beat back a third time. This Affair on the Island lasted near an Hour, and had given the Rest of the Battoemen Time to land on the South side of the River and those on the Island perceiving the Enemy were coming to surround them with their whole strength, retired to the South side of the River, and were followed by the Enemy. Our People made a feint Flight until the chief of the Enemy had forded the River, then faced about, and push'd the Enemy back into the River, where they killed great numbers of them; the Rest took to their Heels; and were so closely pursued, that they left all their Packs, Blankets & Provisions behind, and many of them their Guns. About forty of our People are killed & missing & 24 slightly wounded. The number of the Enemy killed is not Exactly known, as most of them fell in the River, but it must be at least triple the Number of Ours. Col. Bradstreet has brought two prisoners with him.

1 Incorrectly written for *Neaoure* or Hungry Bay, Jefferson Co., at the entrance of which are the Galop Islands. On the opposite or north side are the Islands of Couis, near the bay of Kenti. They are to be seen in Sauthier's Map 1777, 1779.

English Plan of the Forts ONTARIO & OSWEGO with part of the River Onondago and Lake Ontario 1756.

From Gentleman's Magazine 1757.

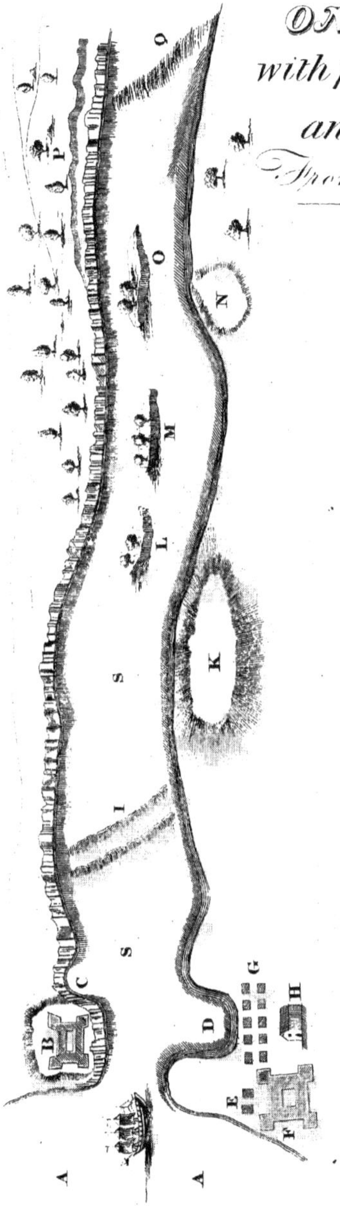

REFERENCE TO THE PLAN

A. Lake Ontario. B Fort Ontario.
C A small harbour for whale boats.
D Harbour for Ships.
E Ship carpenters houses.
F Fort Oswego. G Oswego Town.
H A new guard room.
I Oswego rift. K A large hill.
L An Island.
M A small Island. — Here Col. Broadstreet beat off 40 French with six men only. This was the first skirmish July 3rd 1756.
N A large swamp here they had the second skirmish where Broad street first with 40 men beat off 200 and after with 400 routed 660.
O An Island. P A carrying place.
Q The great Oswego Falls.
S Onondago River.

Places	Distance from Oswego	
Ontario Fort	2 English Miles	
Oswego Rift	3	ditto.
Whale boat harbour	1½	ditto.
Hill K	4½	ditto.
Island L	8	ditto.
Island M	9	ditto.
Swamp N	10½	ditto.
Island O	11	ditto.
Oswego Falls	13	ditto.
Carrying place	12½	ditto.

[From the same, July 26, 1756.]

Since our last, many letters are come to Town from Albany, all confirming the Account we had of the Defeat of the French and Indians by the Battoemen under the command of Col. Bradstreet and all doing Honour to the active, brave and circumspect Behaviour of that Gentleman, during the whole affair. They also all agree in this, That after the repulse of the Enemy in their three several Attacks on the Island, it was discovered that the Enemy in great Numbers were passing from the North to the South side of the River, at a Ford about a mile above, on which Col. Bradstreet immediately marched with 250 men, to meet them. He found that the Enemy to the number of about 400 had possessed themselves of a thick Pine Swamp, on which he attacked them in their own way, behind Trees, but finding that to little purpose, while the Enemy remained covered, he prevailed on his Men to rush in upon them, which had so good an effect that the Enemy were soon dispossessed of the swamp, but still made a running Fight from Tree to Tree. In this manner they were pushed backwards for near two Miles, when having the River in their Rear, they were obliged to cross, which they did in a Manner most terrible to themselves. It was either to drown or be shot: Destruction stared them in the Face on all sides, and it soon laid hold of them, for the Battoemen having now a fair View of them, took them down fast; and here it was that the Enemy sustained their greatest Loss. One of the Prisoners taken in this pursuit, informed Colonel Bradstreet, that one of our Indians had, during the Engagement, deserted to the Enemy, and informed them of our Disposition, on which a Party of the Enemy was ordered to cross the River, a little higher up, and to come down upon our Flanks or Rear. Col. Bradstreet marched up to the Place described by the Prisoner, and fell in with a few of them straggling before the Rest; but the whole party soon took to their Heels, and with the utmost Precipitation and Confusion, repassed the River, some leaving behind them their Arms, others their Blankets, and many Indian Implements of War. The first attack of the Enemy was made about 3 O'Clock, the Action ended about 6 in the Evening. A Scouting Party was then sent out on the North side of the River, to see if any of the Enemy were remaining, but found that they were gone off, and that in the utmost Haste and Confusion, for they had left behind them their Packs, Blankets, and Provisions. About half an hour after the Action ended, Capt. Patten, with one Hundred Grenadiers of the 50th Regt joined the Battoemen. The former being on their March from Onondago to Oswego, about 4 Miles from the place of Action, heard the Fire, and made all the Haste they could to come up, but they came a little too late. However with this Reinforcement it was determined to pursue the Enemy to their Camp about 12 Miles off, if they could, by the next Morning, have 200 Men more from the Garrison of Oswego, and acccordingly an Express was dispatched to Col. Mercer for that Purpose, who sent the 200 Men requested; but unluckily a Storm of Rain came on so hard as to render it impossible to keep the' Men's Ammunition dry. It continued raining till next day, and then it was judged too late to attempt the pursuit.

A further Account of the Action on the 3d of July last.

[From the same, Aug. 2, 1756.]

You have doubtless before this Time, had the agreeable News of the Defeat of the French by the Battoemen on the Onondaga River.—Capt. Bradstreet's Conduct was much to his honour, and will be very advantageous to the English operations in the present Campaign.—His success against the Enemy shews us the Wisdom, of taking large numbers of Battoemen into the service—But for this

Expedient, we should have been unable to keep the Passage open to Oswego; and unless our Provisions, stores, &c. had been sent to that Garrison, in large Squadrons of Battoes, all other attempts to support it, would have been ineffectual; for notwithstanding our Interest in the Six Nations, we have undoubted Accounts, that 1200 of the Enemy have lain undiscovered in their Country, not far from Oswego ever since May last.

When Capt. Bradstreet left Oswego, he gave strict Orders, that the several Divisions of the Battoemen, should keep close together. But such an irregular Body, could not be easily kept to good order, and therefore they were at some Distance from each other, when the Enemy attacked them.—Our Success was owing to Capt. Bradstreet's taking Possession of the Island, for by this means he prevented the Enemy from fording the River, and gave the Battoemen who were fired upon time to rally and collect themselves on the opposite shore.—When Capt. Bradstreet gained the Island, he had not above Eight Men with him, and these repulsed about 30 of the Enemy. Upon this he was joined by six more Battoemen, and was attacked a second Time by a party of 40 French, whom he also compelled to give Way.—Capt. Bradstreet was after that, reinforced by six others, and a Party of above 70 of the Enemy then fell upon him, and by pouring in cross Fires, wounded 12 of his Men; but after some Time, the French were forced to retire a third Time.

A large Body of about 400, being then observed to advance upon the North Side of the River, about a Mile higher, Capt, Bradstreet imagined, that they intended to ford the River, and surround him. On this he quitted the Island, and with 250 Men, Marched up the South Side of the River, to prevent it, but the Enemy had not only forded it, but taken Possession of a Pine Swamp on that Side, before he came up. Doctor Kirkland, who was returning from Oswego, in Company with Capt. Bradstreets command, had now gathered together 200 Battoemen, with Design to reinforce him; but Capt. Bradstreet sent him Orders to keep his Post, to cover the Battoes which were behind; and directed that Capt. Butler should Command the farthest Division of Battoes down the River, and post them in the most proper place upon the same Duty.

When Capt. Bradstreet came to the Swamp, an Engagement began in the Indian manner, which lasted above an hour; Capt. Bradstreet then animating his Men, entered the swamp, and forced the Enemy out of it into the River, where many of them were slain. . . . Another Party was at that Time, attempting to ford the River when Capt. Bradstreet came up with them, and after he fell in with them, the whole Body was routed.

Not long after this last Action, a Company of Grenadiers belonging to General SHIRLEY's Regiment, which was upon the March from Onondaga to Oswego, joined our Battoemen; aud the next Morning 200 Men came to them from the Garrison. Capt. Bradstreet now proposed, to have gone in quest of the main Body of the French, but was prevented by excessive Rains.

We lost in these Actions about 20 Men, and 24 were wounded. What the loss of the Enemy was is uncertain.—All conjecture that above 100 were killed.—This we know, that about 80 Firelocks were brought to Schenectady: Seventy-four Men more were found by a Party, that afterwards went out from Oswego to patrole the Woods; and many doubtless were lost in the River. The Enemy fled in the utmost Disorder; for some Traders were passing by the Place of Action a few Days after, were hailed from the Shore by 20 Frenchmen, who being without provisions and unable to find their Camp, were stroling about the Woods, upon the Banks of the River in great Distress, and begged to be taken up and carried to Oswego.—The Traders being in Number but about Half a Dozen, were fearful of taking more than one of them in, and him they delivered to the Garrison.

This Repulse will doubtless check the Incursions of the French, shake their Indian Interest, strengthen our own, and secure our future Convoys in their Passage to Oswego.—Capt. Bradstreet's Gallantry and Conduct are justly Commended.—The former, in his Defence of the Island, and the attack at the Swamp; and the latter in his prudent Disposition of the Remainder of the Battoemen,

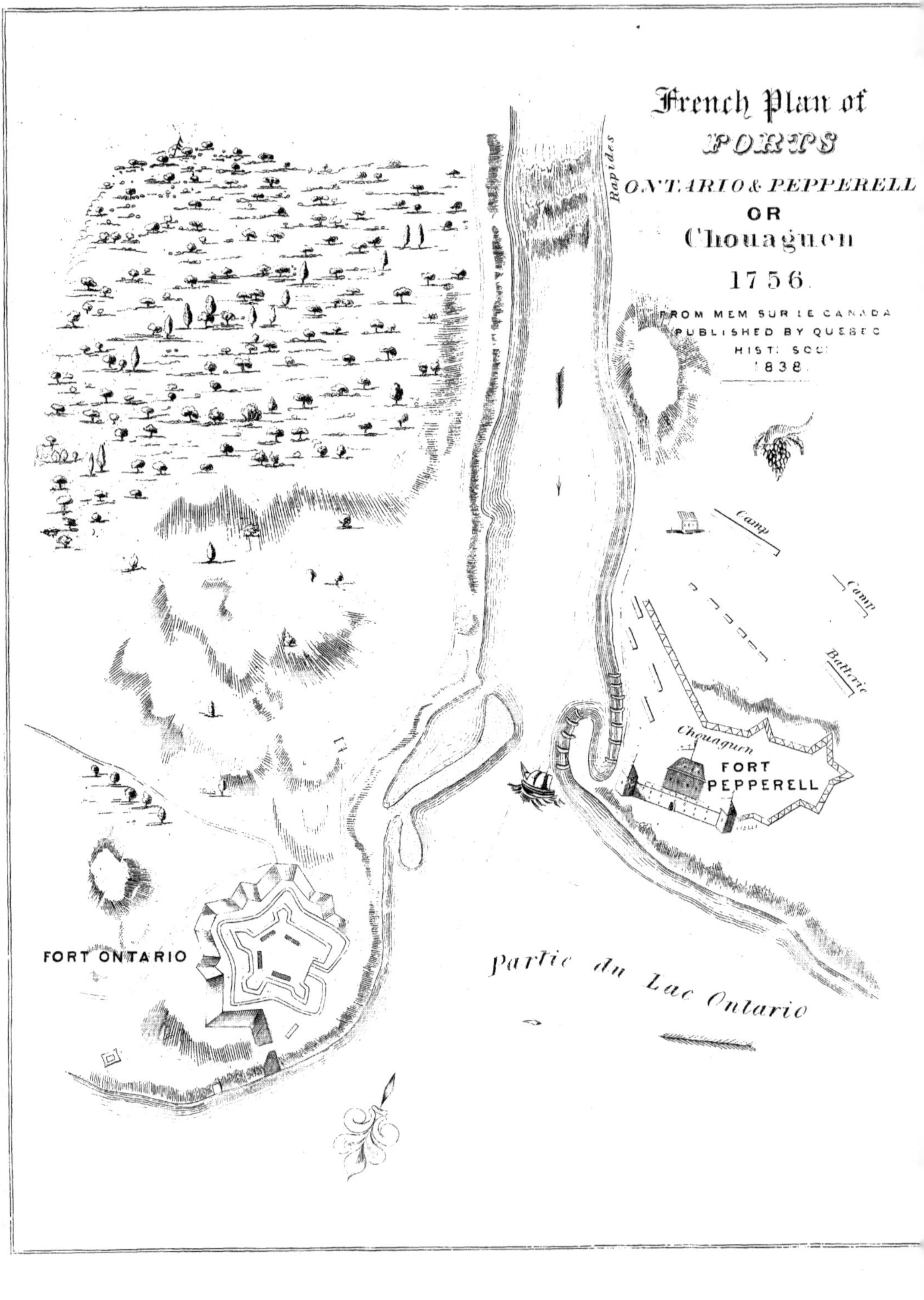

French Plan of FORTS ONTARIO & PEPPERELL OR Chouaguen 1756.

FROM MEM SUR LE CANADA
PUBLISHED BY QUEBEC
HIST: SOC:
1838.

Rapides

Camp

Camp

Batterie

Chouaguen

FORT PEPPERELL

FORT ONTARIO

Partie du Lac Ontario

for secúring his Rear, and preventing the Enemy from Surrounding his whole Party.—Nor did he receive any Help from our Indians.—The whole Number he had with him, was only Twelve.—Nine of these (such is the State of our Interest with them!) could not be brought to engage.—One went immediately over to the French, and informed them of our Numbers & Disposition. An Oneida Indian fought bravely thro' the whole Dispute but another Indian escaped to the Onondaga Castle, and spread a Report that Capt. Bradstreet was killed, & all his Battoemen defeated.—I hope we shall in the ensuing campaign, fully avenge the loss we sustained on the banks of Monaungahela

---

DESCRIPTION OF OSWEGO, 1756.

[Paris Doc. XII.]

Fort Ontario is situate at the right[1] of the River in the middle of a very high plateau. It consists of a square of 30 toises [180 feet] a side, the faces of which, broken in the centre, are flanked by a redan placed at the point of the break. It is constructed of pickets 18 inches in diameter smooth on both sides, very well joined the one to the other and rising 8 @ 9 feet from the ground.

The ditch that encircles the fort, is 18 feet wide by 8 deep. The excavated earth had been thrown up *en glacis* on the counterscap with a very steep slope over the berm [covered way]. Loop holes and embrasures are formed in the pickets on a level with the earth thrown up on the berm and a scaffolding of carpenter's work extends all around so as to fire from above. It has eight guns and 4 mortars with double grenades.

The old Fort Chouaguen, situate on the left [or west] bank of the River, consists of a house with galleries (*machecoulis*) with loop holes on the ground floor and principal story, the walls of which are three feet thick and encompassed at a distance of three toises [18 feet] by another wall 4 feet thick and 10 high, loopholed and flanked by two large square towers. It has likewise a trench encircling, on the land side, the Fort where the enemy had placed 18 pieces of cannon and 15 mortars and howitzers.

Fort George is situate 300 toises beyond that of Choauguen on a hill that commanded it. It is of pickets and badly enough entrenched with earth on two sides.

JOURNAL OF THE SIEGE OF CHOUAGUEN.

COMMENCED THE 11th AUGUST 1756, AND CONCLUDED THE 14th AT NIGHT; BY THE MARQUIS OF MONTCALM.

[Paris Doc. XII.]

On the arrival of the French Troops in Canada in the month of May, every disposition having been made for the Campaign, the Marquis of Vaudreuil Governor General of New France detached a body of Colonial Troops and Militia towards the St. John River to harrass the English and receive

1 That is, the East Bank.

the remains of the Acadians driven from their Settlements, of whom those who had not been transplanted to the more distant English Colonies were wandering in the woods. Another detachment of observation of about 500 men was in the direction of Fort Lydius. The Queen's battalion and that of Languedoc were encamped in front of Fort Carillon. Barn was destined for Niagara; Guyenne for Frontenac, and Sieur de Villiers Captain of a Colonial Troop, hung on the enemy and watched his movements towards the river Chouaguen, with a corps of 700 men, Canadians and Indians. The defence of Fort du Quesne and the Belle Riviere (Ohio) was confided to a somewhat considerable party of Canadians and Savages, and Sieur Dumas, Commandant in that Quarter, had orders to retain with him all the Indians of the Upper Country whose rendezvous was at Presque isle, in case his posts were threatened; if not to send a part of them to Montreal.

Reinforcements having arrived from France, Royal Rousillon was sent to Lake St Sacrement and La Sarre to Frontenac with the two French Engineers, also arrived this year, to the order of Sieur Colonel Bourlamaque, to erect new fortifications at that place, or rather an entrenched Camp which would have placed them beyond insult. Chevalier de Levis, Brigadier, was destined to command on Lake St. Sacrement, and the Marquis de Montcalm, Field Marshal, to proceed to the quarter which may apparently be most threatened by the enemy.

Thus every thing seemed arranged for defence in different parts; on Lake Ontario, Lake St. Sacrement, and the Belle Riviere. Some parties only of Canadians and Indians succeeded each other without intermission on the English frontiers exposed to their ravages, and they laid waste more especially Pensilvania, Virginia and Maryland.

Toward mid-June it clearly appeared from the report of the Indians sent out as scouts; from the depositions of several prisoners; from the vast preparations made at Albany and Fort Lydius, that the English had offensive intentions in the direction of the Point of Lake St. Sacrement. Upon this intelligence, the Marquis de Montcalm proposed a diversion towards Lake Ontario, for the purpose of attracting a portion of the enemy's forces thither, and consequently relieving La Pointe. This diversion was to be made, however, in such a way that the defensive could be changed into offensive, according to circumstances.

The Marquis de Vaudreuil had never lost sight of the siege of Chouaguen, a post most important by its situation at the Mouth of the River of that name on Lake Ontario, the key of the Upper Country by its communication with the Five Nations, Albany and the River Hudson; defended by three forts—Fort Ontario on the right bank of the River, Forts George and Chouaguen on the left bank, as well as a species of Crown work, in earth serving as an intrenched Camp, having also a good port and a well sheltered harbour. But this siege so important to the Colony did not seem feasible this Campaign, the season being already far advanced, the preparation which this expedition required, being very great, the distance considerable and transportation not being accomplished except with difficulties and endless delays across a country having no other roads but rivers, filled with falls and rapids, and lakes rendered frequently impassable to batteaux in consequence of the violence of the waves.

Sieur Bigot, Intendant of Canada, arrived at this conjuncture at Montreal; took upon himself the collection of munitions of war of all sorts, and of provisions—the despatch of convoys and their uninterrupted supply. The diversion towards Chouaguen was then determined on with the design to besiege it, if the condition of that place, or the carelessness of the enemy permitted.

Sieur de Rigaud de Vaudreuil, Governor of Three Rivers, was accordingly sent with a fresh body of Colonial troops and Indians to assume command of Sieur de Villiers Camp, established at Niaouré bay about 15 leagues from Chouaguen; Sieur de Bourlamaque received orders to commence at Fort Frontenac whatever preparations he may deem necessary; Sieur Decombles, Engineer, to proceed with a detachment of Canadians and Savages to reconnoiter Chouaguen; and to conceal the project from the enemy, the Marquis de Montcalm departed 27th June with Chevalier de Levis for Fort Carillon. The defensive positions to be adopted in this quarter; the fortifications erecting at Carillon; the movements of the enemy at Fort Lydius and Albany; all these reasons justified the Marquis of Montcalm's presence at Lake St Sacrement. This General remained there only long enough to make the necessary arrangements and put the English on the wrong scent. He placed the defence of that frontier in the hands of Chevalier de Levis with a corps of 3000 men; returned on the 15th July to Montreal where he arrived on the 19th; received there his last Instructions and set out again on the 21st and arrived at Frontenac on the 29th. Bearn's battalion had already received orders to repair thither from Niagara, and Sieur Mercier Commander of Artillery had arrived there two days before.

Having made those preparations inseparable from a new expedition in this country, which consequently presents difficulties unknown in Europe, and provided every thing necessary to secure a retreat in case superior forces rendered this inevitable, orders were given to two barks—one of 12, and the other of 16 guns—to cruize in the latitude of Chouaguen. A corps of Scouts, Canadians and Indians, were sent on the road between the latter place and Albany, to intercept Runners.

The Marquis de Montcalm left Frontenac on the 4th August with the first division of the army consisting of De la Sarre's and De Guyenne's battallions and four pieces of cannon.[2] He arrived on the 6th at the Bay of Niaouré, which the Marquis de Vaudreuil had designated as the rendezvous of all the Troops, and where the second division composed of Bearn's battallion, of the Militia, of 80 batteaux of Artillery and provisions arrived on the 8th. The number of troops destined for the expedition was nearly 3000 men—to wit, de la Sarre's, Guyenne's and Bearn's battallions amounting to only 1300 men; the remainder, soldiers of the Colony, Militiamen and Indians.

Sieur de Rigaud's corps, destined as the vanguard, set out on the same day to advance to a cove called, *L'anse aux Cabanes* (Wigwam Cove)[3] within three leagues of Chouaguen. The first division having arrived there on the 10th at two o'clock in the morning, the vanguard proceeded four hours afterwards across the woods to another Cove situated half a league from Chouaguen to cover the debarcation of the artillery and troops. The first division reached the same Cove at midnight. A battery from Lake Ontario was forthwith erected there and the troops bivouacked during the night at the head of the batteaux.

On the 11th, at break of day the Canadians and Indians advanced to within a quarter of a league of, and invested Fort Ontario, situated, as we have stated, on the right bank of the River Chouaguen. Sieur Decombles, sent at 3 o'clock in the morning to make arrangements for this siege and the attack was killed, returning from his reconnoissance, by one of our savages [a Nipissing] who escorted him and who took him in the dark, for an Englishman—a mishap which was rendered of the greatest consequence to us from the circumstance of carrying on a siege in America with one Engineer only, that remained. Sieur Desandronius the surviving Engineer, ran a road through the woods, partly through swamps explored the evening before, for the purpose of conducting the artillery across. This road, commenced at 11 o'clock in the morning was finished at night and thoroughly completed next morning. The camp was established at the same time, the right resting on Lake Ontario covered by the same battery that protected our batteaux from attack; the left on an impassable swamp.

1 Supposed to be a part of the celebrated Irish Brigade, then in the French service, and mentioned in the Deposition of a French Deserter, post p. 324; Bearn's Battalion was between 400 and 500 men.

2 Another account says—"Orders came for the Regiment of La Sarre to proceed to the Bay of Niaouré. . . . We proceeded on the 29th to encamp at l'Isle aux Aillo and arrived at the rendezvous on the 30th. . . . We had orders to send back our batteaux to Frontenac for Guyenne's and Bearn's Regiment and the Artillery."

3 Now, Sandy Creek Bay. "We marched all the night of the 9th and 10th, (says another account) when we joined Mr. Rigaud at Wigwam Cove. The army bivouacked at the Rivière aux Sables," now Sandy Creek, Oswego co.

The precaution of marching only at night and of entering rivers when halting by which we were concealed, had till then hid our advance from the enemy. It was announced to them only that same day by the Indians who went even to the foot of the fort to fire. Three armed barks which sailed at noon from the River Chouaguen came cruising in front of the Camp, discharged some pieces of artillery, but the fire from our battery forced them to sheer off. Since then, they cruised only at a considerable distance.

On the 12th at day break Bearn's Regiment arrived with the batteaux of artillery and provisions. These batteaux were forthwith unloaded in presence of the English barks which cruised in front of the Camp. The battery on the beach was increased—the park of artillery and the depot of provisions established, and Sieur Pouchot, Captain in Bearn's Regiment, who had successfully begun a fortification at Niagara, received orders to act as Engineer during the siege. Arrangements were made to open the trenches that very night; Sieur de Bourlamaque superintended them. Six pickets of workmen, fifty men each, were under orders for that night; two companies of grenadiers and three pickets to support them.

Notwithstanding the greatest possible diligence, the work at this trench could not be begun until midnight. It was rather a parallel of about 100 toises[1], the front opened at 90 toises from the ditch of the fort through ground embarrassed by obstructions and stumps of trees. This parallel finished at five o'clock in the morning was completed by the day labourers who cut the lines of communication and commenced erecting batteries. The enemy's fire which had been very brisk since the break of day ceased about eleven o'clock at night, and it was perceived that the garrison evacuated Fort Ontario and passed over to that of Chouaguen at the opposite side of the river. They abandoned in retiring 8 pieces of cannon and four mortars. The fort having been immediately occupied by the grenadiers of the trench, the workmen were commanded to continue the communication of the parallel to the river side where at nightfall was commenced a large battery placed so as to batter Fort Chouaguen, the road from that fort to Fort George, and take the entrenched camp in the rear. Twenty pieces of cannon were conveyed during the night in men's arms, a labour which occupied the whole army, with the exception of the picquets and the camp guard.

On the 14th, at daylight, the Marquis of Montcalm ordered Sieur de Rigaud to ford the river to the other side with the Canadians and Indians, to occupy the woods and harrass the communication with Fort George where the enemy appeared making considerable preparations.[2] At six o'Clock we had nine pieces ready to bear, and though the fire of the besieged, up to that time was more brisk than our's, they hoisted the White Flag at ten o'Clock and sent two officers to demand a Capitulation. The celerity of our operations in a soil which they considered impracticable, the erection of our batteries completed with so much rapidity, the idea these works gave them of the number of the French troops, the movement of the corps detached from the other side of the river, the dread of the savages, the death of Colonel Mercer, commandant of Chouaguen who was killed at eight o'Clock in the Morning,[3] doubtless determined the besieged to a step which we had not dared to expect so soon.

The Marquis de Montcalm sent Sieur de Bougainville, one of his aids de camp as a hostage and to propose articles of Capitulation which were to the effect that the garrison should render themselves prisoners of war and that the French troops should forthwith take possession of the Forts. The ar-

1. A toise is a French measure of six feet.

2. "Sieur Rigaud executed this order forthwith. Though there was considerable water in that River, and the current was very rapid, he threw himself in and crossed over with the Canadians and Indians; some swimming, others in the water up to the waist or to the neck and arrived at their destination without the fire of the enemy having been able to stop a single Canadian or Savage."—*Another account.*

3. This officer was gazetted, 7th Oct. 1754, Lieut. Col. of Sir Wm. Pepperells, or the 2nd American, Regt. He had been previously on half pay.

ticles having been accepted by the Commandent Sieur Littlealles, commanding Shirley's Regiment[1] and sent to the Marquis of Montcalm, Sieur de la Paur, Aidemajor to Guienne's Regiment (acting Major General) was sent to revise them; and Sieur de Bourlamaque named Commander of Forts George and Chouaguen took possession of these with two companies of Grenadiers and the Pickets from the trenches. He was entrusted with the destruction of said Forts and the removal of the artillery, Munitions of war and the provisions found there.

There were, on our side only about thirty men killed or wounded; on that of the English about 150, including several soldiers who wishing to escape across the woods fell into the hands of the Indians. The number of prisoners was nearly 1700 men; to wit Shirley's and Pepperel's regiments, arrived from old England and who were at the battle of Fontenoy, a detachment of Schuylers regiment, Militia of the Country, about 80 officers, among whom were two artillery, two engineers, and 12 navy officers. We captured also 7 vessels of war; one of 18 guns, one of 14, one of 10, one of 8, three mounted with patereros, 200 barges or batteaux, 7 pieces of bronze, 48 of iron, 14 mortars, 5 howitzers, 47 patereros, a quantity of bullets, bombs, balls, powder and a considerable pile of provisions.

On the 21st all having been demolished, the prisoners, artillery and supplies being removed, the army re-imbarked and repaired in three divisions to the Bay of Niaouré whence the several corps proceeded to their respective destinations. The savages having, with the Marquis of Montcalm's permission, departed successively after the seige, This general had previous to the expedition bound the Nations the one to the other by a Wampum belt which he had presented them in His Majesty's name according to the custom of the Country.

So much munition of war and provisions found at Chouaguen—the fleet which secured the command on Lake Ontario to the English—the additional reinforcements they expected from day to day—all announced designs on their part against our posts, Frontenac and Niagara, the execution of which was calculated on this Autumn, and the danger of which the Colony, very fortunately, had not to incur.[2]

[For another *French* account of the taking of Oswego, see Gentleman's Magazine, Vol. xxvi. 508.]

ARTICLES OF CAPITULATION,

GRANTED TO THE ENGLISH TROOPS COMMANDED BY JOHN LITTLEHALES, COMMANDING SAID TROOPS AND THE FORTS CHOUAGUEN, BY M. LE MARQUIS DE MONTCALM, FIELD MARSHAL OF THE KINGS ARMIES, GENERAL OF HIS TROOPS IN NEW FRANCE.

Article the first.

It has been agreed that the English troops shall surrender themselves prisoners of War; that the Officers and soldiers shall be allowed to preserve their effects.

1. John Littlehales was appointed Major of Shirley's (or the 1st American) Reg't also on 7th Oct. 1754. He had been previously on half pay.

2. "The Abbe Picquet . . . . came to Chouaguen to plant a Cross there, on which was affixed *In hoc signo vincunt*; and along side, a pole with the Kings arms and this inscription—*Manibus date lelia plenis*."—*Additional account.*

That the said Forts shall be given up at two o'Clock in the afternoon with generally all the effects, munitions of war, provisions, Barks, Rigging and other property in general whatsoever, without any injury being done thereto by their troops.

Article the second.

That all their arms shall be deposited in a store at the moment one half the troops are embarked to cross the river; that a number of French troops are passed over by the return to take possession of the Fort and that the remainder of the troops shall retire at the same time.

The Flags and Drums shall likewise be deposited in said Stores with the Officers' arms.

A new Inventory shall be made of the property in the stores and of the artillery, powder, bullets, provisions, barks and rigging conformably to the returns made to me.

The Officers shall in passing, each take away their effects with them.

The 14th at 11 o'Clock in the morning.

(Signed) JOHN LITTLEHALES Lt Colonel and Commandant.

The said articles are granted in His most Christian Majesty's name according to the power which I have from M. the Marquis de Vaudreuil, his Governour and Lieutenant General in New France.

Signed, MONTCALM.

Return of Effects found in the Fort and sent to Frontenac, the pillage not included.

7 cast cannon of the calibre of 19. 14. & 12.
48 of iron of 9. 6. 5. & 3.
1 cast mortar, 9 inches 4 lines.
13 others of Iron of 6 inches & of 3 inches.
44 patereros.
23 thousand of powder.
8 thousand of Lead in balls and shot.
2950 bullets of divers calibres.
150 Bombs of 9 inches and 300 of six.
1476 grenadoes.
730 grenadier's muskets.
340 Grape shot (*Raisins.*)
12 pairs of iron wheels for naval carriages.

Vessels Captured on Lake Ontario.

1 Snow of 18 guns; 1 brigantine of sixteen; 1 sloop of ten; one battoe of 10; one of eight & two stone guns; 1 skiff mounted with 8 patereros & one skiff in the stocks, burnt; 200 barges & batteaux.

Provisions found in this Fort.

704 barrels filled with biscuit.
1386 barrels of pork & beef
712 barrels of flour.
200 sacks of ditto.
11 barrels of Rice
7 barrels of Salt.
1 garret full of Vegetables
1 other piled with flour
32 live oxen
15 hogs
3 boxes of silver & the military chest containing 18,000lb
A quantity of liquors and wines.

ADDITIONAL PARTICULARS.

Our artillery thundered on their camp and at the moment we were thinking only of our destruction we were about to witness the glorious termination of our labours I had seven men of my picquet killed or wounded within an hour and a half and I had still the whole day before me when we heard the *Rappel* and saw the White Flag hoisted on the turret of their embattled house. Cries of *Vive le Roy* informed the French of the fact. The loss of their commander; that of the officer of artillery; the tears of their wives; the terror of those who saw their husbands exposed to the same danger; induced them to surrender. We made 1640 prisoners, 120 of whom were Women, five Standards,[1] 120 fire eaters (cannon) and six large Barks. Their Stores were provided with every thing to maintain our army during the next Campaign. The loss of the king of England is estimated at 20,000,000. The least superstitious attribute our success to Providence. They could, in truth Sir, hold out much longer. We have lost, notwithstanding, 80 men, and our little army had been swamped if that valour so justly attributed to the troops of Old England had extended to their Colonies. Our's is now more flourishing than ever; trade entirely re-established; lake Ontario our's without any opposition. We can hardly recover from our astonishment. The bulwark (*le boulevard*) of New England was originally but the house of an individual whom the Iroquois had permitted to build; of this the King took possession some years afterwards for purposes of Trade. He increased it with all the works which we demolished. Their loss, Sir, is incredible. The Canadians and Indians have had a very considerable slice of the cake; the latter perpetrated there a multitude of horrors and assassinated more than 100 persons included in the capitulation, without our being able to prevent them or having the right to remonstrate with them. This species of animal I look upon as mad dogs; when they are intoxicated they are uncontrolled.

THE EXAMINATION OF MONS^R^ BELESTRE

A FRENCH ENSIGN TAKEN BEFORE THE HON^BLE^ EDMUND ATKYN ESQ HIS MAJESTYS AGENT FOR, AND SUPERINTENDENT OF INDIAN AFFAIRS, IN THE SOUTHERN DEPARTMENT; IN PRESENCE OF COL. WASHINGTON AND GEORGE CROGHAN ESR^R^ DEP^Y^ TO SIR W^M^ JOHNSON.

[Lond. Doc. XXXIV.]

He says he is a native of Canada and served Monsr Vaudreuil, that he came last from Fort Duquesne with a party of 40 Indians and 12 White men, 3 of whom were officers. . . . . That only 100 of the Garrison at Fort Duquesne are quartered within the Fort the rest lodging in barracks without. That the train of Artillery taken from General Braddock was sent down after his defeat to Niagara, and that it was the same train the French had used at the taking of Oswego.[2]

1 The Marquis de Vaudreuil caused to be deposited in the Churches of Montreal, Quebec and Three Rivers, with the usual ceremonies, the four Standards of Shirley's and Pepperel's regular troops and that of Schuyler's Regiment of Militia —*Another Account*.

2 The same day the French invested the place with about 5000 men and 32 pieces of Cannon, from 12 to 18 pounders besides several large brass mortars and hoyets (among which artillery was part of Genl. Braddock's.)—*Journal of the Seige of Oswego; Gentleman's Mag.* xxvii. 76.

[Council Min. XXV.]

At a Council held at Fort George in the City of New York on Friday the 27th day of April 1756.

His Excellency communicated to the Council the Intelligence he had received from the Rt Honble the Earl of Loudon, by Express, of the Enemy's having laid seige to Oswego, of their having taken the Fort on the East side of the River, and that it was apprehended they were or would soon be Masters of the other works there, with all the stores and Naval Armament.

Also a Letter from his Lordship of the 21st inst in which his Lordship desires that his Excellency seeing the situation of Things, and Knowing so well the Consequences of such a situation would send him such aid as he may see necessary and may be in his power to do.

EXTRACT OF A LETTER FROM ALBANY, DATED AUG. 30.

[N. Y. Mercury.]

Last night a Letter came to Town from Onide Carrying Place, where was come an Indian from Oswego, who informed, that the French had carried every Thing from thence and demolished the Place; that they had carried away three or four Officers, the Carpenters and Sailors to Frontenac, the Remainder they killed, cut off their Heads, and posted them on Stakes along the Lake Side. It is said Col. L——e scandalously surrendered the Fort, no more than 7 Men killed in the whole, among whom was Col. Mercier. *Commodore B——y also behaved scandalously, not firing one Gun from his Vessels on the Enemy. I cannot conceive (if true) why this Barbarity was Committed, unless our Men repented their Shameful Surrender, or there must have been a Quarrel between the French and Indians.

The accounts received from Albany since our last, concerning Oswego, are more favourable, than those that have been inserted heretofore; for we are Assured from good Authority, that some white people are returned to Albany, who were despatched to Oswego, in order to reconnoitre the Woods, and, if possible, to get a View of the Place, who report that they lay two Nights there, where every thing that could be of service to the French was carried away, and the Forts and Houses entirely demolished, that no signs of Murder or Massacre was to be seen, and that they found only three Graves, which were very handsomely made up, and one in particular, which they imagined was Col. Mercer's.

'Tis also said, That a Negro Fellow, who made his Escape, after the Garrison of Oswego was taken, is lying sick at Onida Castle, and says, that immediately after Col. Mercer was killed, the Place was given up to the French, by Order of Lieutenant Colonel Littlehill; that the Number of the Besiegers were but little superior to those of the Besieged; and that the Enemy had no other Cannon, than those they got at Fort Ontario.

A Letter from Oneida Carrying Place dated August 18 says—That John Gall who belong'd to one of the Vessels on the Lake, and made his Escape reports, That on the 11th instant the Row Galley went out on a Cruise, and return'd in 10 Minutes, first giving a Signal that he had discovered the Enemy: Upon which the two other Sloops with Part of the Regiments on board immediately went out, and in about a Mile from the Fort discovered the Enemy's Camp. The 12th the Enemy engaged

MS. Note in the Mercury.—If an enemy should stand on the brink of the hill no gun pointed could reach him from the vessels.

Ontario Fort, with Small Arms only, the Fort returning the Fire very smartly with their Cannon and Small Arms, all that Day and Night following. The 13th a Council of War was held at the old Stone Fort, and two Shells and one Ball thrown, which was a Signal for the Troops to quit Ontario Fort and join those at the old Fort, the opposite side of the River, where Col. Mercer was, which they immediately did: That at Night the Enemy hove up a Fachine Battery and Entrenchment on the Edge of the Bank, opposite the old Fort. The 14th in the Morning the Enemy began their fire on the old Fort, which was warmly returned till Col. Mercer was killed by a Cannon Ball as he was in the Camp encouraging the Men about 11 o'Clock: That the Fire continued very hot about an Hour after, when Lieutenant Cook with a Flag of Truce was sent to the Enemy; and upon their return all the Indians came in with him. That Orders were immediately given for every Man on board the Vessells to lay down their Arms take 1 Blanket and 2 Shirts and march Prisoners into the old Fort. That Shirley's & Pepperell's Regiments were ordered to march to Fort Ontario, to be sent Prisoners to Frontenac (500 Indians being to guard them) in the Vessels which they took from us in our Harbour, being 2 Sloops 6 Guns each, besides Swivels, and 2 Hoies; 2 Schooners, one of them with Swivels; and a Brig lately built, with 14 Carriage Guns, and the same number of Swivels: That Col. Schuyler and his Regiment were carried away Prisoners also. That by the best accounts he could collect there were but five men Killed besides Col. Mercer.

SIR CHARLES HARDY TO THE BOARD.

[Lond. Doc. XXXIII.]

Fort George, N. York, Sep 5th 1756.

My Lords—I enclose for your Lordshipps information the Declaration sent me from Albany of the Soldiers who were originally Deserters from the French, & had taken on in Generals Shirley & Peperells Regiments this paper did not come to me from any publick authority, as Lord Loudoun could not then have time to copy papers. One of the Sailors that belonged to the Ontario Captn Lafory, I have seen he gives this information that to the best of his memory on the morning of the 10th of August a small Schooner was sent from Oswego to make discovery, that she returned off the Harbour again in about two hours, informing them that they had discovered a large incampment of the enemy about three miles to the Eastward of Oswego, upon this information Captns Lafory & Deane sailed in two sloops to attempt cannonading the Camp, before they could reach the shore where the enemy lay they were fired upon with Cannon very briskly, that four shot struck the Ontario, three of them stuck in her side, which they cut out found them to be balls of twelve pound weight with the Kings broad arrow on them, that they did not think it adviseable to make any further attempt, but returned to Oswego, & sail'd again the next morning as [and?] observed the encampment as before. By this time the enemy had marched Bodys of their Forces and attacked Fort Ontario with Musquetry which they continued for two days, when the English Garrison abandoned it, first spiking their small Cannon threw their Powder into a well, and retired into the old Fort, soon after the enemy drew up their Cannon to Fort Ontario in number 8 or 9 and cannonaded the old Fort, which continued for 24 hours when Lieut. Col. Littlehales, who succeeded to the command upon Lieut Coll Mercers being killed sent out an Officer and Drum with a white Flag, soon after the surrender took place, & the French possession of the Fort, that the Garrison were made prisoners of War & well used, that the vessels which were all in Port, was soon after taken possession of by the French. during the siege was killed Lieut Coll. Mercer Captn Hind of the Train of Artillery, and eight or nine private men, and one Engineer wounded, he further says that the Enemy's force was reported to be three thousand Regulars & a great number of Indians, These two accounts, tho' not materially different are greatly so from an account sent me from Gen: Willi's Camp. An Onondaga Sachem came to them the 25th in the evening with strings of Wampum and declared.* That two of their young men that had been sent to Oswego returned to their Castle & reported that Oswego was not taken till six days before, that the enemy had put the whole to the sword, except 150, sailors carpenters & artificers included, That they had demolished the works and evacuated the place, carrying away the shipping Guns ammunition &c, That they had laid the Dead in Banks with their heads in the Water, and scattered a great quantity of Provisions about the Place. That they told the Indians upon their leaving the place, You see we do not want to seize your Lands, only to drive the English away whom we are much obliged to for supplying us with Artillery & Tools which we were in want of to take their Forts, the Sachem added that those that gave us the former accounts were deserters who went away before the affair was decided,

These are all the particulars I can furnish your Lordpps with with respect to the loss of Oswego.

Declaration of a Soldier in Shirley's Regiment.

Albany, Aug the 21, 1756. Past 8 o'clock.

The following account is given by 5 other men who had deserted from the French and were in Generals Shirley & Pepperel's Regiments and escaped with the Declarant.

Claude Frederic Hutenac of Major Genl Shirley's Regt declares that on Monday the 9th of Augt a Prow Galley went out of the harbour of Oswego, and discovered the French Camp about a mile from Fort Ontario, the next day two sloops sailed out of the Harbour who were fired upon from that camp & brought in two of the Bullets one of them an eighteenth and the other a twelve Pounder. That on Wednesday & Thursday the enemy continued to fire with Small Arms only from the tops of the Trees & behind bushes upon a rising ground which commands Fort Ontario,which is no more than stockaded with a ditch of 14 feet wide and 10 deep but not quite finished. That on Thursday night the enemy opened Trenches within Pistol shot of the Fort, & on Friday the 13th between one & two in the afternoon, the whole Garrison consisting of 300 men of Pepperells commanded by Captn Barford of that Regiment haveing first spiked their Cannon consisting of two Six Pounders and six four Pounders—abandoned their fort and embarked aboard Whale Boats and got into the old Fort Oswego, without suffering any loss, that during the time they remained in Fort Ontario, they had only 3 men killed & Ensign Ting of Major Genls Pepperells Regiment, wounded, that they neither wanted ammunition or Provisions, & that the enemy never fired any cannon at this Fort. That soon after they arrived in the old Fort Oswego, Lieut Coll Mercer marched Pepperell's Regiment with 100 of Shirley's to reinforce Coll Schuyler who with his men were posted at a small unfinished redoubt upon a rising Ground about 600 yards to the Westward of old Fort Oswegoe, this Post had been deserted for some months past, and made use of only in keeping Cattle, this detachment was employed that afternoon cutting down the bushes near that fort and making fascines, That on Saturday morning early the 14th the French opened a Fascine Battery of 5 Pieces of Cannon before the Gate of Fort Ontario, & played upon the old Fort Oswego, across the mouth of the Harbor, that the Garrison on their side continued to fire above 4 hours with 12 Guns and 4 Mortars whereof one of the latter burst, that between 8 & 9 o'clock that morning Coll Mercer was killed at the Battery upon which the command devolving upon Lieut. Coll. Littlehales, he sent for Coll Schuyler & the detachment from the Redoubt who on their marching to the old Oswego Fort had two men killed upon Coll Schuyler's arrival a council of War consisting of the Field Officers & Captains was called and presently thereafter orders was given to cease firing, upon which Lieu[tt] Montcreif of Shirleys and an officer of Pepperells with a Sergeant & Drum went out of the Works with a White Flagg in order to cross over at the mouth of the Harbour, upon which this Declarant said to Colonel Littlehales that if you are to give up the Fort you must suffer me who am a deserter from the French to make the Best of my way, because they will have no mercy upon me, the Colonel replyed that he expected to march out with the Honors of Warr, & consequently he the Declarant would be safe, not trusting to this, he with seven more who had formerly deserted from the French had leave to make their escape, but before they got quite clear they saw the French from the opposite side of the Harbour getting into Boats, and amongst them some cloathed in Red faced with Green which he imagines belongs to the Irish Brigade, that about 30 of the Garrison of old Fort Oswego were killed and wounded, and that no officer was killed except Lieut. Coll. Mercer, nor any wounded but Lieut de la Cour of the Artillery. That the Enemys battery was raised so high that their shott plunged in amongst them and the only cover they had towards the side of the Lake upon which the Enemys Battery chiefly pointed, were from Barrels of Pork placed by way of parapet, with embrasures through. That one Saturday morning the 14th a Party of the French forded the River about Cannon shot from the olk Fort who remained in the Woods without coming near the works. That there was no sortie made from any of the Forts and that all the vessels were in the Port when the Place was given up. That from the report of the Seamen who saw the French Camp they judged them to be about 4000 regulars, besides Canadians & Indians. That the Garrison of Oswego consisted of about 400 of Shirley 300 of Pepperels, and 150 of Schuyler's besides the seamen, carpenters and other artificers who worked the Guns & did the other dutys in the works. The 4 men of Shirley's Regiment who are all deserters from the French declare that there was 8 months pay due to them when the enemy appeared, they were then paid up six months. The two men of Pepperels who are also deserters from the French declare they have received no pay for 9 months past. That last winter there was only 140 men fit for duty of both Regiments with 20 of the independent companys. That their provision was extremely bad and only received half allowance, and that even at that they had resolved to quit the place without a supply had speedily arrived.[1]

EXTRACT OF A LETTER FROM PORTSMOUTH, DATED FEB. 13, 1757.

[From N. Y. Mercury.]

Inclosed you have a List of Several Carpenters, Sailors and other Artificers that were taken with me at Oswego, and are now here; some of them were retaken going to France, and others were sent here from Canada. Some of them are on board the Royal Anne, and some in the Hospital; all in good Health, and are to be sent home by the first opportunity.

1 For another *English* account of the Surrender of Oswego, see Gentleman's Magazine, vol. xxvii, 75. A Writer in the London Monthly Review, vol. xvii, 174, accuses the Merchants of England of opposing the important settlement at Oswego from interested motives as a company of them had engrossed the whole trade of supplying the Colony, as was pretended, with goods for the Indian Trade; which goods they sold wholesale to the French instead of retailing them to the English or the Indians.

Joseph Gleddon, William Drewry, Henry Cosdrop, Samuel Spenser, Thomas Lyneal, Daniel Chadwell, James Dawson, Joshua Sprigs, Alexander Ogleby, Philip Peak, William Robinson, Edward Clannon, Joseph Petterson, Zebulon Drew, James Wilson, John Lum, Samuel Forgison, Samuel Edmunson, David Evans, Thomas Meloney, Cornelius Scantling, Rufus Church, Samuel Moot, Neal Walkinson, Thos Hogin, Benj. Bachoon, James Cavenagh, John Wood, Dan. Carpenter, Benj. Summer, Jonas Wright, Sam. Miles, Samuel Noe, William Davenport, Thomas Godard, Peter Wright, Brier Goddard, John Tarlox, James Wilson, Richard Brincroff, Robert Watts, Arthur Donaldson, Joseph January, Peter Goodman, William Hunter, William Mullett, Matthew Thompson, Will. Taylor, Jacob Fedrick, Matthew Bayly, Robert Hart, David Williams, Daniel Noroway, William Kemp, Severn Anderson, James Gibson.

[From same. Oct. 24 1757.]

In the packet came Passenger also, a seaman named Edward Mariner who was taken at Oswego. He, in Company with Mr John Walters, of this Place, Robert Isburn & son, of Philadelphia; Capt Rusco, Lieutenants Bickers and Prince, with Ensign Ogden, of the New Jersey Provincial Forces, and about 299 more, sailed from Quebeck the 18th of July last, in a Cartel, and arrived at Plymouth, in 28 days after: . . . . . He informs us that the brave Colonel Peter Schuyler was in good Health, and the great support of many English Prisoners, without whose assistance several of them would have been reduced to the greatest extremities. Captain [Jasper] Farmer [of the Artillery] Son of Mr Jasper Farmer, of this City, Merchant, was likewise at Quebeck, when our Informant came away, with several others whose names he could not recollect; and as Provisions were very scarce when he left that, 'twas said the remainder of the Prisoners were to be sent to Old France in the Fall.

Note—Further particulars of the operations before Oswego may be found in the London Magazine for the years 1756—1759.

XVIII.

PAPERS

RELATING TO THE

Oneida Country and Mohawk Valley.

1756, 1757.

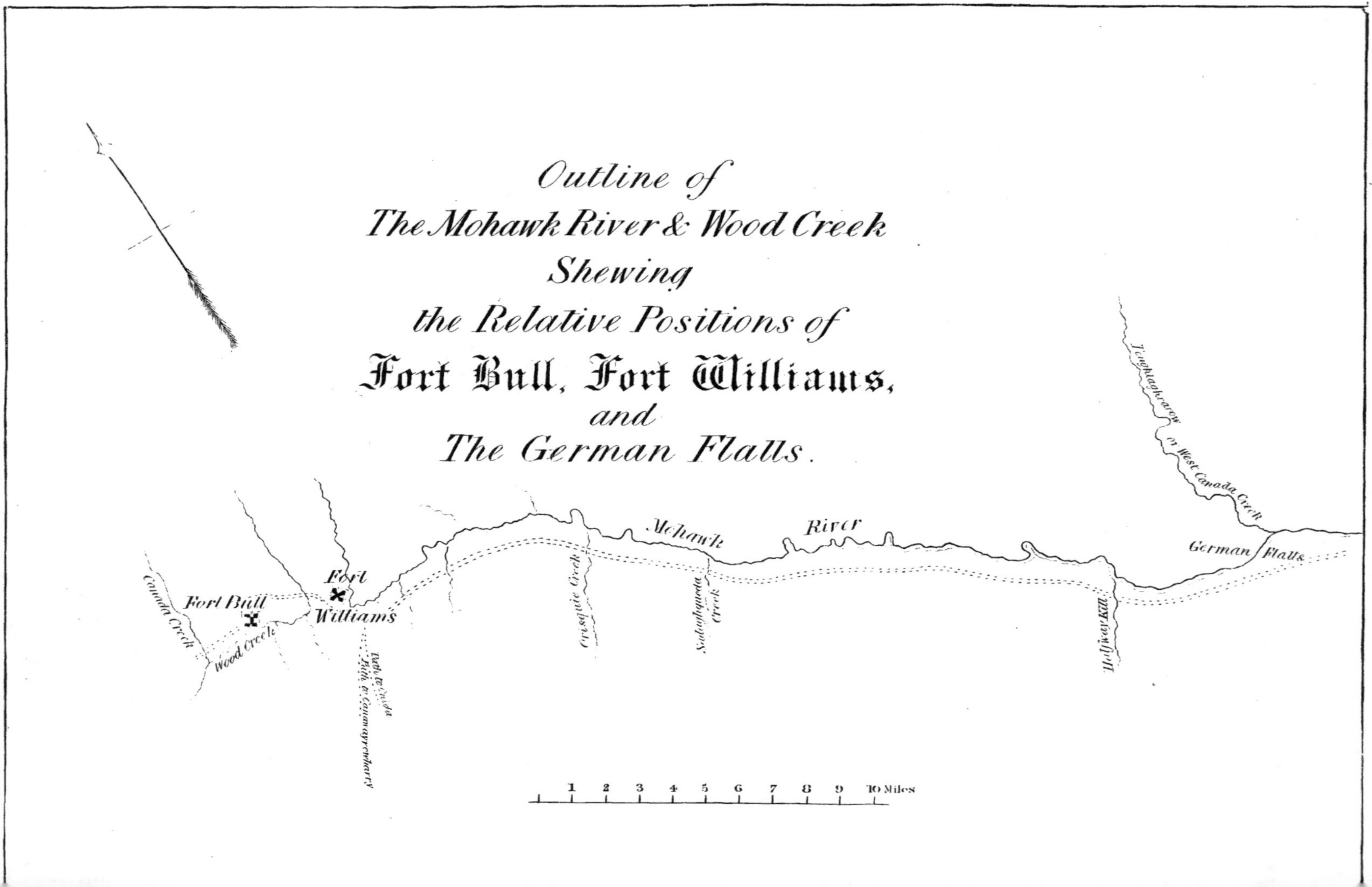

Outline of
The Mohawk River & Wood Creek
Shewing
the Relative Positions of
Fort Bull, Fort Williams,
and
The German Flatts.

Canada Creek
Fort Bull
Wood Creek
Fort Williams
Path to Onida
Path to Canawayrowharry
Crisquie Creek
Sadaghqueda Creek
Mohawk River
Halfway Kill
German Flatts
Tenghtaghrarow or West Canada Creek

1 2 3 4 5 6 7 8 9 10 Miles

CAPTURE OF FORT BULL,[1] BY MR. DE LERY.

[Paris Doc. XXV.]

On the 27 March 1756 at four o'clock in the morning, the detachments commanded by M. de Lery, Lieutenant of the Colonial troops, commenced their march, very much weakened by the fatigue they experienced during fifteen days since they left Montreal, for they were two days entirely out of provisions.[2] At half past five they arrived at the road to the Carrying place, and the scouts in advance brought in two Englishmen who were coming from the fort nearest to Chouaguin, whom M. de Lery caused to be informed that he should have their brains knocked out by the Indians if he perceived that they endeavored to conceal the truth, and if they communicated it to him, he should use all his efforts to extricate them from their hands.

These prisoners stated that the Fort, this side of Chouaguin, was called Bull, having a garrison of 60 soldiers, commanded by a lieutenant, that there was in this fort a considerable quantity of munitions of war and provisions; that the fort was constructed of heavy pickets, 15 to 18 feet above ground, doubled inside to a man's height, and was nearly of the shape of a star; that it had no cannon, but a number of grenadoes which Colonel Johnson had sent on intelligence being communicated to him by the Indians of our march; that the Commandant of this Fort was called Bull; that 15 batteaux were to leave in the evening for Chouaguin; that at the moment sleighs were arriving with 9 batteaux loads; that the fort on the Corlaer side, at the head of the Carrying Place was of much larger pickets and well planked, having four pieces of Cannon and a garrison of 150 men, commanded by Captain Williams, whose name the fort bore; that they did not know if there were any provisions in the fort not having been in it.[3]

At 10 o'clock the savages captured 10 men who were conducting the sleighs loaded with provisions. These confirmed what the prisoners had stated and added that 100 men arrived at 8 o'clock on the preceding evening, who were said to be followed by a large force.

Monsieur de Lery whilst occupying himself in distributing among his detachment the provisions found in the sleighs, was informed that a Negro who accompanied the loads had escaped taking the

1 This Fort is referred to in a Report of a Committee appointed to explore the Western Waters in the State of New-York.——Albany, Barber and Southwick, 1792. It is laid down in Sauthier's Map, as fort *Bute*. Its situation was about two miles west of Rome. See Outline Map annexed.

2 He left on the 17th March on the ice, passed by La Presentation (Ogdensburgh) and proceeded across the country and along the mountains, by paths known only to the savages to within a short distance of one of those Forts called Bull. *Mem. sur les aff. du Canada dep.* 1749 *jusq.* 1760. Published by Hist. Soc. Quebec, 1838.

3 The necessity of fortifying this Pass was pointed out, for the first time, in October 1736, by a number of Indian Traders who petitioned the Assembly to erect a fort at "the Carrying Place at the upper end of the Mohawk River." When Fort Williams was erected has not been ascertained. There was a Fort *William* in the Mohawk Country as early as 1745-6, but whether it be identical with Fort *Williams* is undetermined. The latter stood until 1756, when it was destroyed by Gen'l Webb on his famous flight from Wood creek immediately after the fall of Oswego. It was succeeded in 1758 by Fort Stanwix, and finally by the present city of Rome, Oneida county.

road to Fort Williams; whereupon not doubting but they would have intimation of him at that fort, he acquainted M. de Montigny, his second, of his determination to attack Fort Bull, the prisoners having assured him that the greater part of the provisions and stores were there. Each officer received immediate orders to form his brigade and M de Lery told the savages that he was about to attack the Bull but they represented to him that now they had provisions to carry the detachment to La Presentation—English meat that the Master of Life had bestowed on them, without costing a man—to risk another affair would be to go contrary to His will: if he desired absolutely to perish he was master of his frenchmen. The Commander replied that he did not wish to expose them and asked them only for two Indians to guide his expedition which they with difficulty granted. Some twenty determined afterwards to follow him being encouraged by some drams of brandy. The Algonquins, Nepissings and those Iroquois who were unwilling to follow him, accepted the proposition made by M de Lery to guard the road and the 12 prisoners. They assured the Commander that he may make the attack; they would take possession of the road and watch the movements of the English at Fort Williams.

The detachment having commenced their march along the high road, the soldiers having their bayonets fixed, M deLery gave orders, when within 15 acres of the fort, to move strait forward without firing a shot, and seize the guard on entering the fort. He was still 5 acres off when he heard the whoop of the savages, notwithstanding the prohibition he had issued. He instantly ordered an advance double quick in order to carry the gate of the Fort, but the enemy had time to close it. Six Indians only followed the French: the others pursued six Englishmen who unable to reach the fort threw themselves into the bush.

M. de Lery set some men to cut down the gate, and caused the Commandant to be summoned to surrender, promising quarter to him and all his garrison; to which he only answered by a fire of musketry and by throwing a quantity of grenades. Our soldiers and Canadians who ran full speed the moment the Indians whooped, got possession of the portholes; through these they fired on such of the English as they could get a sight of. Great efforts were made to batter down the gate which was finally cut in pieces in about an hour. Then the whole detachment with a cry of *Vive le Roi* rushed into the Fort and put every one to the sword they could lay hands on. One woman and a few soldiers only were fortunate enough to escape the fury of our troops. Some pretend that only one prisoner was made during this action.[1]

The Commandant and Officers repaired to the stores and caused their men to use diligence in throwing the barrels of powder into the river, but one of the Magazines having caught fire and M. de Lery considering that he could not extinguish it without incurring the risk of having the people blown up who should be employed there, gave orders to retire as quick as possible. There was hardly time to do this when the fire communicated to the powder which blew up at three points. The explosion was so violent that a soldier of Guyenne and an Iroquois of ths Sault were wounded by the debris of the fort though they were already at a distance. The Indian especially is in danger of losing his life by the wound.[2]

A detachment was, however, sent to look after the baggage that remained on the road and shortly after an Indian came to notify M de Lery that the English were making a sortie. This caused him to rally his forces and placing himself on the bank of the creek he had the bombs, grenades, bullets

1 "Except five persons they put every soul they found to the sword." *A faithful Narrative of the dangers, sufferings and deliverances of Robert Eastman, and his captivity among the Indians of North America.* Annual Reg. Vol. I. Anno, 1758. This Eastburn was taken prisoner by the French on this occasion and removed to a town called "Oswegotchy."

2 He was scarcely four *arpens* off when the fire communicating to the rest of the powder blew up the fort. The buildings were carried away and whatever remained was in an instant in a blaze. The shock was so violent and the commotion so great, that his troop, seized with terror, fell on their knees. *Mem. Sur les aff. du Canada.*

and all the ammunition that could be found, thrown notwithstanding into the water. He had the 15 batteaux staved in, and then set out to meet the sortie of which he had been informed. But he learned on the road that the Indians had repulsed it after having killed 17 men. This sortie was from Fort Williams on the intelligence carried thither by the Negro. The Indians who, unwilling to attack Fort Bull, took charge of the road, acquitted themselves so well that this detachment quickly retreated with a loss of 17 men. The Indians coming some hours after to congratulate M de Lery on his fortunate success failed not to make the most of their advantage.

A chief asked him if he proposed attacking the other fort; which was nothing more than a boast on his part. M de Lery replied he would proceed forthwith if the Indians would follow him. This reply drove this Chief off and all those of his party prepared to follow. Our troops did the same and encamped in the wood three quarters of a league from the fort. The fort Bull prisoners were examined and we learned that Colonel Johnson having been informed of our march had sent notice to all the posts, regarding it, however, as impossible in consequence of the rigor of the season. Fort Bull is situate near a small creek that falls into that of Chouaguin about four miles from the fort. Fort Williams is near the River Mohawk which falls into that of Corlar. The carrying place from one Fort to the other is about four miles long over a pretty level country though swampy in some places.

M de Lery's detachment was 15 officers, 2 Cadets, 10 soldiers of the Queen's Regiment, 17 of Guyenne's, 22 of Bearn's, 27 of the Colony; in all 93 soldiers; 166 Canadians, 33 Iroquois from the Lake of Two Mountains, 33 from La Presentation, 18 from Sault St. Louis, 3 from St. Bigin, 3 Abenakis of Missiskoui, 2 Algonquins, and 11 Nipissings. Total 362 men, 265 of whom attacked the fort. A soldier of the Colony and an Indian from La Presentation were killed. A soldier of the Queen's, 2 Canadians and 2 Iroquois were wounded.

It is estimated that more than 40 thousand weight of powder was burned or thrown into the creek with a number of Bombs, grenades, and balls of different calibre. A great deal of salted provisions, bread, butter, chocolate, sugar and other provisions were likewise thrown into the water. The stores were filled with clothes and other effects which were pillaged; the remainder burnt. This day cost the English 90 men of whom 30 are prisoners. Our detachment killed or captured 30 horses.[1]

[N. Y. Mercury April 5, 1756.]

By an Express that arrived here on Friday last, from Albany, we are told that a number of French & Indians had attacked Lieutenant Bull, and 30 men, that were posted at the upper End of the Great Carrying place; that he, & some of his People were killed, and a small store and Provisions in it burnt; & that they were in Pain for some of their Battoes, which they feared were cut off by the enemy.

1 After this exploit they retired to the woods and formed their main body which consisted of 400 French and 300 Indians commanded by one of the principal gentlemen of Quebec; as soon as they got together, they threw themselves on their knees and returned thanks to God for their victory; an example says Eastburn well worthy of imitation. They continued their march through the woods about four miles, and then it being dark, and several Indians being drunk, they encamped. . . . They encamped and rested much in the same manner the night following; and the next morning, Sunday the 28th, they rose very early and retreated hastily towards Canada, for fear of General Johnson who as they were informed was on his march against them. . . . After a march of seven days they arrived at Lake Ontario where they were met by some French batteaus with a large supply of provisions, of which they had been so much in want that they had subsisted during some part of the march upon horse flesh, and had even devoured a porcupine without any other dressing than sufficed just to scorch off the hair and quills. Eastburn, after a tedious voyage with part of this company, arrived at Oswegotchy an Indian town.—*Eastburn's Narrative.*

Those who may not have access to the Vol. of the Annual Reg. containing this Nar. will find it reprinted in London's Coll. of Ind. Narratives, Carlisle, Pa., 1811, Vol. ii; Incidents of Border Life, Chambersburgh, Pa., 1839; also in Drake's Tragedies of the Wilderness, Boston, 1841.

[From the same, April 12.]

What we have been able to collect from some Letters and Verbal Information is as follows, viz[t].

That about the 18th March [O. S.] a large Body of French & Indians attacked, and cut off 16 of our Battoes, near the Carrying Place, and either killed or captivated the greatest Part of the People ; that as soon as the Officer that commanded about 35 men that were posted there, heard the firing, he detached a party to their Assistance, and as they did not return agreeable to his Expectation, he sent another Detachment, which so weakened the Garrison, that a Number of the Enemy that lay in Ambush, rushed in, put them all to the sword, blew up the Powder, & destroyed the Garrison, whilst the rest of the Enemy were engaged with our people, whom they killed or carried off, as only one was arrived at Fort Williams, the 20th of March, as will appear by the following Letter.

Extract of a Letter from Fort Williams, dated the 20th *March* 1756.

These may serve to inform you, that we arrived here safe, Yesterday about Eleven o'Clock. The People that were transporting Lansing's Provisions, were attacked between this and the Marsh by a Body of French and Indians, and are all, but one that got in here, either killed or taken Prisoners; their names you have underneath. The Fort at Wood Creek is burnt down, and none of Lansing's Men, or the Red Coats are as yet come in. Just now the Commissary arrived from Oswego, and informs us, that the 20 Battoes sent there by Capt Williams, were safe arrived to their great joy; and that the People in Garrison were pretty hearty. All Lansing's Provisions are destroyed, as well as the Powder that was in the Garrison, the People laid in Heaps and burnt. John Davids, Henry Dawson, James Tock, George Roberson, John Tuyle, John Griefey, John Pain, and Closs Marseillis, went down Wood Creek last Wednesday, whether they are taken or not, we cannot tell. We believe John Davis got safe to Oswego, as the Commissary met him on the other side of the Lake. Philip Lansing and John Van Alle, are safe here yet, with the rest of their Men. Just now 70 of our Indians are came in, and acquaints us, that by the Tracts of the Enemy, they imagined there was at least 500 of them. The names of the Persons, Residents in and about Albany, and supposed to be killed, are as follows, viz[t]. John, Jacob, and Andries Kidnee, John Vanderheyden, Jacobus Sickles, Wolker Dawson, Anthony Brandt, Peter Griffins, Cornelius Sprong, three Servants & five Negroes.

FRENCH DESCENT ON THE GERMAN FLATTS.

[Paris Doc. XIII.]

Summary of M. de Belletre's Expedition, the 28th *November,* 1757

M. de Belletre with his detachment of about 300 Men, Marines, Canadians and Indians, arrived notwithstanding all the obstacles of the season and the greatest scarcity of provisions, at the river *à la Famine* [Black river,] where he met seven or eight Nontaguès who on a message reported to them in the General's name, expressed delight in uniting with him.

He continued his route and after inexpressible fatigues and suffering reached the vicinity of the Oneida Castle whither he sent four influential Indians as bearers of the General's Word.

He continued his march as far as the River Corlaer and had the satisfaction of examining five English forts abandoned by command for that erected since the reduction of Chouaguen, on the site of Old Fort Bull.

The Indians, informed that there was a garrison of 350 men in a fort named Kouari situate on the said river about a quarter of a league from the Village of the Palatines[1] did not fail to exhibit fear, but M. de Belletre having told them that their Father did not despatch a picked detachment, so well selected, except to make a blow of some interest, they recovered their courage and evinced a lively ardor, except some young Warriors and aged men who gave in already fatigued by a weary march,

The four Savages sent to the Oneidas returned with the six warriors of that tribe who joined our detachment, and told M de Belletre that they had no other will than that of their Father.

On the 11th November at three o'clock in the afternoon M. de Belletre, preceded as was his custom by the scouts crossed the River Corlaer [Mohawk] with his detachment partly swimming, partly in the water up to the neck. He encamped at night fall in the woods a league and a half from the first of the five forts that covered the Palatine Settlements.

The 12th at three o'clock in the morning he gave his detachment the order of March and attack so as to surround the said five forts and the entire Palatine Village, consisting of sixty houses.

Though M. de Belletre knew that the English got notice the day preceding, yet that the courage of the Indians may not receive the least check and to show them he would not rashly expose them, he liberated an Indian of the Five Nations whom he had until then detained under suspicion. But this Savage could not injure M. de Belletre because he commenced at the same time to attack the five forts and the Palatines' houses.

At sight of the first fort he decided to take it by assault. The enemy kept up the most active fire of musketry but the intrepidity with which M. de Belletre, with all the Officers and Canadians of his detachment advanced, coupled with the war whoop of the Indians, terrified the English to the degree that the Mayor of the Village of the Palatines, who commanded the said Fort, opened the doors and asked for quarter.

M. de Belletre lost no time in repairing to the second, the third, the fourth and fifth which were not less intimidated than the first by his intrepidity and the cries of the Indians. They all surrendered at discretion, and were entirely burnt.

During this time a party of Canadians and Indians ravaged and burnt the said 60 houses of the Palatines, their barns and other out buildings as well as the Water Mill.

In all these expeditions about 40 English perished—killed or drowned. The number of prisoners is nearly 150 men, women and children, among whom is the Mayor of the Village, the Surgeon and some Militia Officers. We had not a man killed; but M. de Lorimer, officer, was wounded in the right side by a ball, and three or four Savages slightly.

The damage inflicted on the enemy is estimated according to the representations of the English themselves, To wit

In grain of all sorts, a much larger quantity than the Island of Montreal has produced in years of abundance.

The same of hogs.

1 This fort, to which so much reference is made in a subsequent paper describing the Valley of the Mohawk, was situate on the South side of the Mohawk River, nearly opposite the mouth of the West Canada Creek, in what is now the Town of German Flatts. It is alluded to by Lt. Gov. Delancey (see post p. 334) as "Fort Hareniger," and is now known as Fort *Herkimer*. The settlement destroyed by the French was on the opposite, or North side of the Mohawk.

3000 horned cattle.

3000 sheep.

All these articles were to have been sent in a few days to Corlaer (Schenectady.)

1500 horses, 300 of which were taken by the Indians and the greater number consumed for the support of the detachment.

The property in furniture, wearing apparel, merchandize and liquor might form a capital of 1,500,000 livres. The Mayor of the Village alone has lost 400,000.

The French and Indians have acquired as rich a booty as they could carry off. They have in specie more than 100,000 livres. One Indian alone has as much as 30,000. There was likewise plundered a quantity of Wampum, silver-bracelets &c, scarlet cloth and other Merchandize which may form a capital of 80,000 more.

All this damage could not be done short of 48 hours. M. de Belletre made provision to be always able to resist the enemy, who as has been observed, were to the number of 350 men in the said Fort Kouari, about a quarter of a league from the field of battle.

In fact, on the 13th at 7 o'clock in the morning, 50 Englishmen accompanied by some Mohawks, left the said Fort, but as soon as they were perceived our Frenchmen and Indians went to meet them double quick, and forced them to swim across the river after receiving several discharges of Musketry. The number that perished cannot be estimated. At noon the same day, M. de Belletre gave orders to his detachment to commence their return march.

On the 15th he sent an Oneida, who is much attached to the General, with some Chiefs from the Sault and St. Francis to bear a message to the Oneidas by which he communicated to them the success he experienced; invited them to persevere in their good Sentiments and not to fear the English. Our Oneida delegate rejoined M. Belletre at the River *Au Sable* [Sandy Creek Jeffer. Co.] and told him that the Five Nations had sent three Belts to the Oneida Villages of which they wished him to take charge as a present to the General. By these they demand assistance to resist the English being about to experience their resentment inasmuch as they refused to allow four of their Chiefs to enter Fort Kouari having fired several shots at them. This had obliged the Oneidas to withdraw their women and children from the Lake side, hoping their Father will protect them.

MR. DE LANCY TO THE BOARD OF TRADE.

[Lond. Doc. XXXIV.]

New York 5 January, 1658.

It may be proper to acquaint your Lordships that we had the misfortune on the 12th November to lose a valuable settlement on the North side of the Mohawks river opposite to Fort Hareniger, called the German Flatts, the loss is estimated at twenty thousand pounds this money, it is as fertile a piece of ground as any perhaps in the world the settlers were generally rich and had good buildings on their lands, some of the inhabitants were slain, about 100 carried into captivity, their houses and barns with the crops destroyed by Fire. This was done by a party of about three hundred Canadians & Indians; the people there thought themselves in great security and though advertised of the approach of the enemy, they neglected the advices they received and so fell an easy prey.

MR. DAINE TO THE MINISTER.

[Paris Doc. XIV.]

Quebec, 19 May, 1756.

Annexed are two little Relations or Summaries of what has occured of most interest since the departure of the ships last year. The damage inflicted on the English in horned cattle, sheep and horses has been greatly exaggerated in the Relation of M. de Bellestre's expedition of the 28th November 1757. It must be diminished at least a good half. It is still more exaggerated in regard to furniture, wearing apparel, merchandize and liquors which are carried up to fifteen hundred thousand livres, as well as the loss of the Palatine's village in Indian corn.

M. DE VAUDREUIL TO THE MINISTER.

[Paris Doc. XV.]

Montreal, 28 June, 1758.

M. de Bellestre's success last autumn in destroying the village of the Palatines and carrying the forts that covered it would have been actually, My lord, a great aid to the Colony, had it been possible to remove the considerable portion of provisions of all sorts found in that village. I had particularly provided for this by the orders I gave that officer. But circumstances were not sufficiently favorable to execute them.

1st. M. de Bellestre being much exposed to be pursued and perhaps cut off by a force infinitely superior to his own was under the absolute necessity of using the greatest activity in his operations, success depending essentially thereon. He was consequently unable to restrain the attack of his detachment. This was made by one party with all possible vigor whilst others were busy firing the houses, barns etca.

2. The 500 horses, lost by the enemy in this affair, were not exactly captured. The greater part were killed or wounded, and M. de Belletre brought with him but a very small number which was a great resource to him to support his detachment on his return.

3d. Had he all those horses and all the provisions at his disposal he could not absolutely have profited by them, either because it was prudent for him to hasten his retreat, or because the transportation of the provisions had been utterly impossible, both on account of the difficulty of the roads and rivers to be passed and the impossibility of feeding the horses.

A SUMMARY NARRATIVE

OF THE CONDUCT OF THE ONEIDA INDIANS (LIVING AT THE UPPER TOWN) PREVIOUS TO THE ATTACK OF THE FRENCH AND THEIR INDIANS UPON THE NORTH SIDE OF THE GERMAN FLATS IN THE PROVINCE OF NEW-YORK, IN NOVEMBER, 1757.[1]

A few days after this Massacre and desolation had been perpetrated, Sir William Johnson despatched Geo. Croghan, Esq; Deputy agent, with Mr Montour, the Indian interpreter, to the German Flats, where he understood several of the Oneida and Tuscarora Indians were assembled, in order to call upon those Indians to Explain themselves why they had not given more timely notice to the Germans of the designs and approach of the Enemy; it having been reported, that no intelligence had been given by the Indians, until the same morning the attack was made; and as these Indians might naturally be supposed, from their situation and other circumstances, to have had earlier knowledge of the Enemy's design and march.

Before Mr Croghan could get up to the German Flats, the aforesaid Indians were on their road homewards, but he was informed the Chief Sachem of the Upper Oneida Town, with a Tuscarora Sachem and another Oneida Indian, were still about four miles from Fort Harkeman: upon which he sent a messenger to acquaint them, that he was at the said fort.

The aforesaid Indians returned, and on the 30th November at Fort Harkeman, *Conaghquieson*, the Chief Oneida Sachem, made the following speech to Mr Croghan, having first called in one Rudolph Shumaker, Hanjost Harkman, and several other Germans, who understood the Indian language, and desired them to sit down and hear what he was going to say.

Conaghquieson then proceeded and said:

'*Brother*,

'I can't help telling you that we were very much surprised to hear that our brethern the English suspect and charge us with not giving them timely notice of the designs of the French, as it is well known we have not neglected to give them every piece of intelligence that came to our knowledge.

'*Brother*,

'About fifteen days before the affair happened, we sent the Germans word, that some Swegatchi Indians told us, the French were determined to destroy the German Flats, and desired them to be on their guard. About six days after that we had a further account from Swegatchi, that the French were preparing to march.

'I then came down to the German Flats, and in a meeting with the Germans, told them what we had heard, and desired them to collect themselves together in a body, at their fort,* and secure their women, children, and effects, and make the best defence they could; and at the same time told them to write what I had said to our brother Warraghiyagey (meaning Sir William Johnson†) but they paid not the least regard to what I told them; and laughed at me, slapping their hands on their buttocks, saying they did not value the Enemy: Upon which I returned home and sent one of our people to the lake, (meaning the Oneida Lake) to find out whether the Enemy were coming or not; after he had staid there two days, the Enemy arrived at the Carrying-Place, and sent word to the Castle at the Lake, that they were there; and told them what they were going to do; but charged them not to let us at the Upper Castle know anything of their design. As soon as the man I sent

1 Lyman C. Draper, Esq., of Phila., has had the politeness to communicate this "Narrative."

* A Stockaded work round the church, and a block-house, with a ditch, and a parapet pallisadoed, thrown up by Sir William Johnson a year ago, upon an alarm then given.

† They never sent this intelligence to Sir William.

there heard this, he came on to us with the account that night; and as soon as we received it we sent a belt of Wampum to confirm the truth thereof, to the Flats, which came here the day before the enemy made their attack: but the people would not give credit to the account even then, or they might have saved their lives.* This is the truth, and those Germans here present know it to be so.'

The aforesaid Germans did acknowledge it to be so; and that they had such intelligence.

GEORGE CROGHAN.

EXTRACT OF A LETTER FROM ALBANY,

DATED THE 13th INSTANT, BEING A RELATION OF THE MURDER COMMITTED AT THE GERMAN FLATTS, NEAR FORT HERCHAMER, BY 80 INDIANS AND 4 FRENCHMEN.

[N. Y. Mercury, May 22, 1758,]

About 12 o'Clock, on Monday the 30th of April last an Oneida Indian acquainted Captain Herchamer that a Party of 80 Indians and four Frenchmen, were nigh his fort, and would certainly come down and attack the settlements that Day, and advised Capt Harchamer to go into the Fort and take as many of the Inhabitants with him, as he could collect. About 3 o'Clock, most Part of the Inhabitants, having Notice from Capt Herchamer, left their Houses and assembled at the Fort; four Families, that fled from Henderson's Purchase in the spring for fear of the Enemy, could not get in, and had in their Houses two Indian Traders, of the name of Clock, and six Waggoners that were carrying Capt. Gage's Baggage to the Fort. At 4 o'Clock, all of a sudden, the Houses were attacked and the Waggoners being surprized, run up stairs, the better to defend themselves. The Indians immediately rushed into the House, and killed and scalped all that were below; some of the Indians attempted the stairs, but they were knocked down by the Waggoners; they then fired up thro' the Loft, and soon were joined by more Indians who fired many shot quite thro' the House, and proposed to set it on fire, which intimidated John Ehel, a Waggoner, to such a degree, that he leap'd out at a window, thinking to make his Escape, but was soon killed; the other five defended themselves with great Intrepidity, having killed one Indian, until they were relieved by a Party of Rangers, who came to their assistance, and after exchanging a few Shot the Indians fled, seeing our People have the advantage of a Log Fence. . . . Capt. Herchamer says he saw four or five of the Indians drop, but were carried off.—In the above affair, 33 of the Inhabitants were killed, & Lieut. Hair, of the Rangers, received a slight Wound in the Breast. . . . Next day some Oneidas came down to Trade, and met the Enemy going off, who told them they had 6 of their Company killed, and 9 Wounded. Next Morning a Woman came into the Fort that had been scalped, besides having her Nose almost cut off, with a wound in her Breast, and another in her side. She is likely to recover, related all that happened till she was scalped, and says there was Onondado Indians amongst them.

* The Indians who brought this belt of Wampum finding the Germans still incredulous, the next morning, just before the attack began, laid hold on the German Minister, and in a manner forced him over to the other side of the river; by which means he and some who followed him escaped the fate of their brethren.

DESCRIPTION OF THE COUNTRY BETWEEN OSWEGO AND ALBANY—1757.

[Paris Doc. XIII.]

ITINERARY from the Mouth of the river Chouegen (Oswego) in Lake Ontario to Lake Oneida, then up Vilcrick (Wood creek) to the summit level which is the source of the river of the Mohawks, or *des Agnies*, by which we can descend to Corlar or Chenectedi whence Albany or Orange can be reached.

The entrance of the River Chouegen is easy; the harbour is formed of a cove. The English had a fort on each side of this River by which this entrance was defended.

From Chouegen to the Great fall is an ascent of four leagues. In this space the navigation is intricate, the river rapid and encumbered by large rocks. Good pilots, familiar with the shoals, are requisite to be able to pass through it. Batteaus must be unloaded at the Great fall where a portage occurs of about 40 to 50 paces. The batteaus are dragged along the ground.* It is estimated to be about four leagues from the Fall to the mouth of the River of the Five Nations, [river Seneca] which mouth is called the Three Rivers;[1] its navigation is good. About a quarter of a league before coming to the Three Rivers there is, however, a current where precaution is requisite.

From the Three Rivers to Lake Oneida is computed at 8 leagues; the navigation is good; the river is about 60 paces wide; it is at all times passable with loaded vessels. This river is the outlet of Lake Oneida. There is neither fall nor rapid at its entrance.

Lake Oneida is twelve leagues long by about one league wide. Its navigation is beautiful and practicable at all times, unless there be a strong contrary wind. It is best on the right of the lake which is the north side.

From Lake Oneida we enter the River Vilcrick,† which empties into that Lake, & ascend nine leagues to Fort Bull. This river is full of sinuosities, narrow and sometimes embarrassed with trees fallen from both banks. Its navigation is difficult when the water is low. It is, however, passable at all times with an ordinary batteau load of 14 to 1500 weight. When the waters of this stream are low, an ordinary batteau load cannot go by the river further than within a league of Fort Bull. It becomes necessary then to unload and make a carrying place of the remainder by a road constructed to the Fort, or to send back the batteaux for the other half load.

Fort Bull which was burnt in 1756 by a detachment under the orders of M. de Lery, was situated on the right bank of this River near its source on the height of land.

From Fort Bull to Fort Williams is estimated to be one league and a quarter.[2] This is the Carrying place across the height of land. The English had constructed a road there over which all the carriages passed. They were obliged to bridge a portion of it, extending from Fort Bull to a small stream near which a fort had been begun though not finished; it was to be intermediate between the two Forts, having been located precisely on the Summit level.

* *Note in the original.*—From Chouegen to Fort Bull is estimated to be about 36 leagues. The ordinary batteau load is only 14 to 1500 weight. It takes five days to ascend the River from Chouegen to Fort Bull and three and a half from Fort Bull to Chouegen. The river of the Five Nations [Seneca Riv.] rises in little lakes near which, about six leagues from its entrance into the River Chouegen, the Indians of the Five Nations reside. That river divides into two branches. That from the Right rises in the Lake of the Senecas and Cayugas; that from the left beyond the Lake of the Ononontagués.

1 The Junction of the rivers Oneida and Seneca with the Oswego is still known as the Three Rivers, and the Point of land, as the Three Rivers Point. It is sometimes confounded with the Three Rivers in Canada, as appears by a note in Stone's Life of Brant, i, 216.

† *Note in the original.*—The River of the Killed Fish [now Fish Creek] flows also into this Lake; the English used it formerly; they abandoned it because there was a Portage, and have preferred Vilcrick which they have cleared.

2 For locations of these Forts, see ante p. 329; also Outline Map.

Fort Williams was situated on the right bank of the River Mohawk or *des Agniés*, near the rise of that river on the height of land. It was abandoned and destroyed by the English after the capture of Chouegen.

Leaving Chouegen there is a road over which the English used to drive cattle & horses. This road follows the border of the left bank of the River Chouegen. The Five Nations river is passed at a fall near its entrance into the River Chouegen, after which the road proceeds along the edge of the right bank of the Five Nation's river to the Village of the *Onnontagués* whence it proceeds across the country to the village of the Caskarorins [Tuscaroras ?] and the Oneidas* whence we can go to Forts Bull and Williams; also to fort Kouary without being obliged to pass the said two forts. The path or road taken by M de Belhêtre in his expedition against the village of the Palatines may be also used. He went from the mouth of the Famine River [now Sacketts Harbor] ten leagues below Chouegen; ascending this river for the distance of four leagues, and leaving it on the left followed the path leading to Oneida Lake on his right, and came to the Summit level at Fort Williams.

The Country through which he passed is fine; there being but few mountains. The soil is soft only in the latter part of the season. He forded three rivers the waters of which were very high during the four days that he was going from the River Famine to Fort Williams, a distance estimated at 24 to 30 leagues.

From Fort Williams the Mohawk river is navigable. Batteaux carry the same load as in the river Vilcrick to the portage at the Little Falls, which is about two leagues below the village of the Palatines and Fort Kouari.

From Fort Williams to Fort Kouari,[1] situated on the right bank of the Mohawk river, is estimated to be 12 leagues. The road follows the right bank of the river which is the south side.

Leaving Fort Williams there is a road that unites with that by which horses and cattle pass from Fort Kouari and Chouagen. This road is bad for about four leagues after leaving Fort Williams. The Country is marshy. Carriages (*les trains*) travel it in winter and during the summer, and it can be easily passed on horseback at all times, though in some places, there is a great deal of mud. After these four leagues, carts can easily go as far as Fort Kouari. Having traveled three leagues on this road which is five leagues from Fort Kouari, we come to the forks of two roads one of which, to the left, leads to the Palatines' village by fording the Mohawk river.

Continuing along the high road, which is on the right bank of the River Mohawk, to go to Fort Kouari, a creek is met that must be forded. Here was a grist mill that has been burnt. One league before reaching Fort Kouari another small stream is encountered over which there is a bridge. This stream is fordable almost at all seasons. There was, also, a saw mill on this creek which has been burnt.

Fort Kouari is situate on the right side of the Mohawk river, on a small hill on the edge of that river's bank. It is a large three story stone house with port holes (*crénelée*) at each story, and likewise in the basement for the purpose of cross firing. There are some small pieces above. The house is covered with plank and shingles. It was built as a store and depot for Choueguen. It is surrounded by a ditch at a distance of about 30 feet. This ditch is six feet deep and seven wide. The crown of the ditch inside is planted with palisades in an oblique form; they are well jointed the one to the other. Behind these there is a parapet of earth so as to be able to fire over the pali-

* *Note in the original.*—The road goes to the great Oneida Village, about two leagues from the Lake. A picket Fort with four bastions, had been constructed in this Village by the English. It was destroyed by the Oneidas in observance of their promise given at a council held between them & the Marquis de Vaudreuil. Each of its sides might have been one hundred paces. There is a second Oneida Village, called the little village, situated on the bank of the lake. There is no fort in the latter.

1. For location of Fort Kouari see ante p. 333.

sades. The four angles of this parapet which is at the back of the ditch, form as it were, four little bastions that reciprocally flank each other. On the West side there is a house apart from the large one. It backs against the parapet of the palisades and serves as a barrack and guard house. There are two doors to the large building; the one at the North is a small swing door. It is used only in going to the river for water. At this side of the house there is no ditch; only palisades fixed in boards set against the brow of the right bank of the river to support the earth. The large door of the house is on the south side; it is folding but not ironed. To go outside the palisades and ditch through this large door, you must leave the house to the left and turn to the Eastward where there is a passage. The ditch has not been excavated. The earth serves as a bridge and road. There are palisades to the right and left, on both sides of the way the whole width of the ditch. Outside the ditch there is a folding gate. There is no other barrier nor chevaux-de frise in front. The nearest house outside the fort is about 150 paces. Opposite this fort in the river is a small cultivated island which can be reached at low water by fording.

From Fort Kouari to that of Cannatchocary is four leagues. Some twenty houses are located at a distance one from another, within the space of one league from this road, which is through a flat country. After making this league we go up a mountain that occupies two hours to ascend and descend. The country throughout the whole of this space is covered with wood. After descending, two houses somewhat distant the one from the other are in the league which is still to be travelled to get to Cannatchocari.

The Inhabitants of this Country are Palatines or Germans. They form a Company with some who dwell above the Fall[1] on the other side of the River which is the left bank. This company consists of about 80 men. The road from one to the other of these two forts is good for all sorts of carriages.

Fort Cannatchocari is situated at the side of the Mohawk River on the right bank. It is a square of four bastions of upright pickets joined together with lintels. They are fifteen feet high, about one foot square with port holes inserted from distance to distance with a stage all around to fire from.

This Fort is one hundred paces on each side. It is not surrounded by a ditch. There are some small pieces of cannon at each of its bastions, and a house at each curtain to serve as a store and barrack. Five or six families of Mohawk Indians reside outside the fort.

From Fort Cannatchocari to Fort Hunter is about 12 *leagues;* the road is pretty good; carriages pass over it; it continues along the banks of the Mohawk river. About a hundred houses, at a greater or less distance from one another are found within this length of road. There are some situated also about half a league in the interior. The inhabitants of this section are Germans who compose a company of about 100 men each.

Fort Hunter is situated on the borders of the Mohawk river, and is of the same form as that of Cannatchocari, with the exception that it is twice as large. There is likewise a house at each curtain. The cannon at each bastion are from 7 to 9 pounders. The pickets of this Fort are higher than those of Cannatchocari. There is a church or temple in the middle of the Fort; in the interior of the fort are also some thirty cabins of Mohawk Indians, which is the most considerable village. This fort, like that of Cannatchocari, has no ditch; there's only a large swing door at the entrance.

Leaving Fort Hunter a creek[2] is passed at the mouth of which the fort is located. It can be forded, and crossed in batteaux in summer and on the ice in winter. There are some houses outside under the protection of the Fort in which the country people seek shelter when they fear or learn that an Indian or French war party is in the field.

From Fort Hunter to Chenectedi or Corlar is seven leagues. The public carriage way continues along the right bank of the Mohawk river. About 20 to 30 houses are found within this distance separated the one from the other from about a quarter to half a league. The Inhabitants of this section are

1 Little Falls. 2 Schoharie Creek.

Dutch. They form a company with some other inhabitants of the left bank of the Mohawk river, about 100 men strong.

Chenectedi or Corlar, situated on the bank of the Mohawk river, is a village of about 300 houses. It is surrounded by upright pickets, flanked from distance to distance. Entering this village by the gate on the Fort Hunter side, there is a fort to the right which forms a species of citadel in the interior of the village itself. It is a square, flanked with four bastions or demi bastions, and is constructed half of masonry and half of timbers piled one over the other above the masonry. It is capable of holding 2 or 300 men. There are some pieces of cannon as a battery on the rampart. It is not encircled by a ditch. The entrance is through a large swing gate raised like a drawbridge. By penetrating the village in attacking it at another point, the fire from the fort can be avoided.

The greatest portion of the Inhabitants of Chenectedi are Dutch.

*From Chenectedi to Albany or Orange is estimated to be 6 or 7 leagues.** The road is excellent for all sorts of carriages; the soil sandy and the country covered with open timber. There are only a few hills. A league and half from Chenectedi, there is a house on the road which is a tavern. A league and half farther on, that is to say half way, another house is met which is also a tavern.

Orange is situate on the right bank of the river Orange, otherwise called Hudson. It is not fortified on the forest side except by an enclosure of walls, or pickets, without a ditch, which is flanked at certain distances; the river defends the entrance on the other side. It is calculated to be smaller than the enclosure of the town of Montreal. In the interior of Orange there is a fort, a sort of citadel, capable of containing 300 men; here are some cannon.

This is all that relates to the Right bank of the Mohawk river. Let us pass to the left bank, which is the North side of that river, departing likewise from near its source at Fort Williams, [Rome.]

Leaving Fort Williams by the left bank of the river Mohawk, the village of the Palatines is estimated to be 12 leagues. The Mohawk river is fordable near Fort Williams whence a path leads to the interior, half a league from the shore, parallel with the river whose borders are so marshy that nothing but hay can be had there.

This path leads over hills and small mountains and can be traveled only afoot or on horseback. Eight leagues must be traversed by this path before reaching the forks of the high road that comes from the other side, or right bank of the river. After having traveled this high road a quarter of an hour, a small creek is found, called *Rassedot.*[1] It can be forded. There were two houses on the left flank of this creek, which were burnt, and nothing remains of them but the ruins. Having passed this creek, the high road is followed for a distance of four leagues to the village of the Palatines. All sorts of vehicles travel this road.

The Palatine Village† was situated on the left bank of the Mohawk river, not directly opposite Fort Kouari but about half a quarter of a league above it. You go from this village to the fort by batteau; the river can even be forded in several places.

The Palatine Village which consisted of thirty houses has been entirely destroyed and burnt by a detachment under M. de Belhetre's orders. The inhabitants of this village formed a company of 100 men bearing arms. They reckoned there 300 persons, men, women and children, 102 of whom were made prisoners and the remainder fled to Fort Kouari, except a few who were killed whilst fording the river.

From the Palatine Village to the Little Falls, still continuing along the left bank of the river, is estimated about three leagues. In this distance there had been eight houses which have been aban-

**Note in the Orig.*—The total distance from Chouegen to Orange is 78 *a* 79 leagues.

1 This Creek is on the Kass farm in the town of Schuyler, Herkimer Co. It was called by the Indians, Raxetoth Creek.

† *Note in Orig.*—It requires a day to descend the river with batteaux from Fort Bull to the Palatine Village and three to return; and to go down from the Palatine village to Corlar requires [a day?] and a day and a half to return.

doned. The inhabitants of these houses compose a company with those of Fort Kouari at the opposite side of the river.

The portage at the Little Falls is a quarter of a league, and is passed with carts. There is a road on both sides of the river, but that on the left bank is preferable, being better.

From the portage at the Little Falls, continuing along the left bank of the river, there is only a foot path which is traveled with difficulty on horseback. Three leagues must be made over this path to arrive at the Canada creek where we meet the high road that passes from the termination of the Little Falls portage, along the right bank of the Mohawk river, where there is a ford above Fort Cannatchocari, opposite the mouth of the Canada Creek. There is also a ferry boat at this place to put carts across when the river is high.

After fording Canada Creek, we continue along the left bank of the Mohawk river and high road which is passable for carts for 12 leagues to Col Johnson's mansion. In the whole of this distance the soil is very good. About 500 houses are erected, at a distance one from the other. The greatest number of those on the bank of the river are built of stone. Those at a greater distance from the river in the interior are about half a league off; they are new Settlements, built of wood.

There is not a fort in the whole of this distance of 12 leagues; There is but one farmer's house built of stone that is somewhat fortified and surrounded with pickets. It is situate on the bank of the river three leagues from where the Canada Creek empties into the Mohawk river.

The inhabitants of this Country are Germans. They form four companies of 100 men each.

Col. Johnson's mansion is situate on the border of the left bank of the River Mohawk; is is three stories high; built of stone, with port holes (*creneleés*) and a parapet and flanked with four bastions on which are some small guns. In the same yard, on both sides of the Mansion, there are two small houses; that on the right of the entrance in a Store, and that on the left is designed for workmen, negroes and other domestics. The yard gate is a heavy swing gate well ironed, it is on the Mohawk river side; from this gate to the river there is about 200 paces of level ground. The high road passes there. A small rivulet coming from the north empties itself into the Mohawk river, about 200 paces below the enclosure of the yard.[1] On this stream there is a Mill about 50 paces distance from the house; below the Mill is the miller's house where grain and flour are stored, and on the other side of the creek 100 paces from the mill, is a barn in which cattle and fodder are kept. One hundred and fifty paces from Colonel Johnson's Mansion at the North side, on the left bank of the little creek, is a little hill on which is a small house with port holes where is ordinarily kept a guard of honour of some twenty men, which serves also as an advanced post.

From Colonel Johnson's house to Chenectedi is counted seven leagues; the road is good; all sorts of vehicles pass over it. About twenty houses are found from point to point on this road.

The Mohawk river can be forded during summer, a league and a quarter west of Chenectedi. Opposite Chenectedi the traverse is usually in a ferry boat and batteaux.

The inhabitants of this country are Dutchmen. They form a Company of about 100 men with those on the opposite side of the river below Fort Hunter.

Going from Chenectedi to the mouth of the Mohawk river where it discharges into that of Orange, there is a Great Fall (Cohoes) which prevents the passage of batteaus, so that every thing on the river going from Chenectedi to Orange, passes over the high road that leads there direct.

From Orange to New York is counted 50 to 60 leagues. Barks from New York ascend to Orange. There is also a high road from one to the other of these towns, on the left bank of the river. The country is thickly inhabited on both sides of the river. The inhabitants of Orange are, also, mostly Dutch like those of Chenectedi.

1 This Creek (I am informed by Fisher Putman, Esq. P. M. of Tribes Hill,) goes now by the name of Old Fort Creek. Its original Indian name, he adds, was Kayadarosseros.

From Orange to Boston is considered about 60 leagues. The road thither is across the country. From Boston to New York is reckoned the same distance following the road along the seaside.

New York, situate on the left bank of the Orange River, near its mouth at the sea, is located on a tongue of land forming a peninsula. It is fortified only on the land side. Opposite New York is a large Island (Long Island) very well inhabited and very wealthy. All sorts of vessels of war and Merchantmen anchor between the town and that Island.

NOTA. In the whole Country of the River Corlar there are nine Companies of Militia under the Command of Colonel Johnson; eight only remain, that of the Village of the Palatines being no longer in existence, the greater portion having been defeated by M. de Belhetre's detachment. Colonel Johnson assembles these companies when he has news of any expedition which may concern the Mohawk river.

In the latter part of April 1757, on receiving intelligence by the savages that there was a strong detachment ascending the river St. Lawrence and entering Lake Ontario, he assembled these Companies and went to the Village of the Palatines where he was joined by another body of 11 @ 1200 men sent him by the commandant of Orange; this formed in all a force of 2000 men. He entrenched himself at the head of the Palatine Village where he remained in Camp fifteen days, and did not retire until he received intelligence that the French detachment seen on the River St. Lawrence had passed by and taken the route to the Belle Rivière (Ohio.)

This was the detachment of 500 men that had been sent last year to reinforce Belle Riviére, and had left Montreal in the latter days of the month of April.

XIX.

PAPERS

RELATING TO

The French Seigniories on Lake Champlain.

THE BOARD OF TRADE AND PLANTATIONS TO LT. GOV. COLDEN. 13 JULY 1764.

[Lond. Doc. XXXVII.]

Monsieur Michel Chartier de Lotbinière, heretofore an officer in the French King's Service in Canada has presented to us a Memorial desiring the confirmation of two Concessions in America, the one called D'Alainville, four leagues and upwards in front, part upon Lake George and part upon Crown Point River, and extending in depth five leagues to the West, granted by the Marquis de Vaudreuil in 1758; the other situated opposite to Crown Point, having the same extent in Front & extending in depth five leagues to the East, purchased of Mons[r] Hocquart in 1762, to whom it is alleged to have been granted in 1743 and 1745.

As this Gentleman's case appears to us to require particular consideration, we have wrote to the Governor of Quebec for authentick copies of these grants from the Records, in order that we may be enabled to make a representation to His Majesty thereupon, and in the meanwhile we think proper to direct that no grants whatever be made under the authority of the Government of New-York of any part of the lands comprehended within the limits of these Concessions. So we bid you heartily farewell, and are, Sir

Your very loving friends

HILLSBOROUGH
GEO. RICE
BAMBER GASCOYNE
J. DYSON.

Whitehall, July 13.
1764

EXPLANATIONS

ON MY TWO SEIGNIORIES OF ALLAINVILLE AND HOCQUART AT THE HEAD OF LAKE CHAMPLAIN AND DETAIL OF MY PROCEEDINGS AS WELL IN LONDON AS IN THIS COUNTRY ON THE SUBJECT, BY M. DE LOTBINIERE. MONTREAL 20 SEPT. 1771.

[From MSS. in Sec. of State's Off. Alby.]

The situation of Alainville is designated so clearly in my affidavit annexed in perfect conformity to the Deed granted to me, that it appears useless to add anything thereto.

Though that of Hocquart is indicated in the two Deeds of Concession of which I annex copies, yet to obviate doubts which may arise on the subject, I shall give the details which have been furnished to me of that Seigniory. Its front commences on the south side about 15 or 18 *arpens* above a tract bordering on the Lake, in front (*en face*) of Fort Crown-point, from two to three hundred arpens square in superfices reserved by the original proprietor to himself as an Inalienable Domain, which is separated from the lands conceded to divers *Censitaries* (Tenants) by a marsh formed by a stream that empties there. This front extends thence four leagues* on a direct line drawn towards the North at each extremity of which ought to be run two perpendiculars of a length sufficient to give the totality of the Seigniory five leagues in depth. Moreover it must be observed that in my quality of first Grantee in that quarter, I must be satisfied according to my titles before any other presenting his claims can claim the smallest trifle.

As to the validity of my titles at the time of the Reduction of the country, let but a single glance be directed to these two Seigniories; the frequent clearances to be seen there which cannot have yet disappeared; the various settlements the wrecks of which at least cannot have been swept away by the misfortunes inseparable from a period of War; these will prove incontestably that nothing can oppose their entire effect. Nothing, then, remains but to detail my proceedings in regard to them.

Shortly after my arrival in London, in June, 1763, after having presented myself to the Secretary of State for the department, to the Lords and others to whom I was recommended, I was told that the Provinces were making great exertions to deprive us, if they could, of our properties on Lake Champlain and neighborhood, and that the Ministry much importuned by them appeared to be undecided. I explained; they endeavored to reassure me but not with that positive answer I should desire. Not wishing to expose myself to any difficulty with any one, I decided to wait patiently. Meanwhile, the Earl of Shelburne, the President of the Board of Trade and Plantations, offered to present me to the King. I observed to him that in my quality as immediate Vassal of the King for all the Fiefs which I held, depending from His Majesty, it appeared to me that I ought to begin by rendering him my Fealty & Homage and I prayed him to have me received at once. He replied, that could not be as yet, some previous arrangement being necessary. I since offered myself; I was always put off under the same pretext.

At the moment so to speak, when his Lordship was promising me entire satisfaction regarding the object of my sojourn, he suddenly resigned and was succeeded by My lord Hills-borough. I renewed all my original proceedings with the new President who appeared to listen to me with complaisance and feel perfectly the Equity of my case but would decide nothing, doubtless until he saw every thing established elsewhere in a perfect equilibrium. Being advised not to content myself with talking but to hand in a Memorial which could fix the attention of the Office on the subject of my demand, I presented, in March 1764 the one below, (Letter A.) Every day I visited all the Lords of this office who individually gave me to hope a prompt conclusion but who when assembled decided nothing. Finally, seeing each of them prepared to retire to the country, I represented with all the force I was master of to Milord the Earl of Hills-borough the injustice I had already sustained by so long a sojourn, and if he left London without my being informed of my lot, I was irremediably ruined not only by the heavy loans I was obliged to contract, but by perceiving myself arrested in all my affairs which it was moreover of the last importance to me to prosecute. He then told me, for the first time, that he had over three months ago addressed several questions to the King's Attorney General, without the decision of which nothing could be determined for me. I requested that he would allow me to use his name to urge an answer, and he permitted me. I forthwith prepared the Memorial to be seen below, (under Letter B.) which I presented next morning to the said Attorney General, and in the evening I addressed him the note copy of which is under Letter C. I was informed ten or twelve days after, that his answer had reached the Bureau. On the first day of July I was sent for to the office when Milord the Earl of Hills-borough informed me, in presence of all the Lords assembled and on their part: "That I might return home as soon as I pleased without entertaining the least uneasiness regarding my two Seigniories beyond the limits of the Government of

* *Note in orig.*—The league of Canada is 84 *arpens:* the *arpent,* 30 toises; the *toise* 6 feet royal of Paris.

Quebec. By means of the orders they should transmit to the Governour of New York to which Province His Majesty had been pleased quite recently to annex those parts not settled by His Proclamation of the 7th October last, they should instruct him not to concede any land either in my Seigniories or their vicinity, until their situation was perfectly understood; that I may be assured that in whatever part of the King's obedience any of my property may be situate, I should possess and enjoy them equally as those included within the limits of the Government of Quebec"—and terminated with the most gracious compliments for Mde. de Lotbiniere and the rest of my family. These orders have been addressed and arrived at the time in the Province: The letter which Lieutenant Governour Cadwallader Colden did me the honour to write me on the 11th of September 1765, proves it beyond dispute.

Since my arrival in this Country I have done every thing in my power, as well with the said Sieur Colden as with Sir Henry Moore, to whom I presented on Lake Champlain my original titles. I constantly endeavored to interest in my behalf all those with whom I was acquainted, residents of the said Province, who have been so good as to act, from time to time, near the said Government. I experienced the same attention here and in London, since my departure, so that it is impossible to conceive in me any, even the smallest, neglect as regards these two Seigniories, which at present are the sole certain portion of my existence, abridged in all the rest by a forced prosecution of my proceedings in their regard, and unable to enjoy them since the peace. MONTREAL, the 20th September, One thousand seven hundred and seventy one.

(*A.*)

MEMOIR OF TWO SEIGNIORIES AT THE HEAD OF LAKE CHAMPLAIN.

To the Right Honble the Lords Commissioners of Trade and Plantations, the following Memorial of Michael Chartier de Lotbiniere &c.

Sheweth, That he is proprietor of two Fiefs and Seigniories which are held from the King; the one under the name of *Alainville* four leagues and over in front, partly on Lake St Sacrement, (now lake George) and partly on the River St Frederic (Crown point River) with a depth of five leagues towards the West which was granted to him the 15th November 1758 by the Marquis of Vaudreuil the then Governor General in Canada, (copy of said Concession annexed) on which he had made divers establishments that have been successively ruined by the English armies.

The other of a nearly equal front opposite St Frederic (Crown point) extending northwardly along the River and Lake by a depth five leagues East, which he acquired 7 April last from Sieur Hocquart Councillor of State and Intendant of the Naval forces at Brest to whom the aforesaid was granted by two Patents of Concession the 20 April 1743, and 1 April 1745, of which the major part of the settlements have been, in like manner, destroyed in the last war.[1]

The Memorialist being assured that the said two Fiefs are not included within the new Government of Quebec formed from a part of Canada, and not being unable to discover from the Kings Proclamation of the 7th October last, which establishes the boundaries of said New Government,

1 The first of these Seigniories was in the present County of Essex, N. Y.; the other, on the opposite side of Lake Champlain, embraced the present towns of Panton, Addison and Bridport, in Addison Co., Vt., and will be found laid down in the English Map of Lake Champlain annexed.

nor elsewhere, to what other part the two Seigniories in question, at present belong, he prays your Lordships to instruct the government to which they are at present annexed, to have him acknowledged there as Proprietor of said Estates; to cause him to enjoy the same without delay, in the same manner that he or his predecessors have or ought to enjoy them, in order that he may be in a position to replace the inhabitants there who were already located there; that he may as soon as possible make there the settlements he proposes and improve said Seigniories in the most useful manner, and according as he may judge most proper.

LONDON, 6 May, 1764.

(*B.*)

To Sir Fletcher Norton, King's Attorney General.

The affair in question at present which alone detains me here over a year in consequence of difficulties which I perceived to arise on my arrival in this country that I could not even suspect before; by which the Attorney General is at this moment interrupted, is already decided in a very clear manner both by the general Capitulation granted to Canada on the 8th September, 1760, and by the Treaty of Peace which followed it.

The first formally states that all those who have property in that Country shall be maintained as heretofore in the possession of such property as well as of their rights, privileges and prerogatives. The Treaty of Peace since concluded confirms in regard to the King's New Subjects in that quarter what had been granted by the Capitulation, and permits all others, within the space of eighteen months from the day of the Ratification of the Treaty, freely to sell what they possess in the said Country. The question then resolves itself, as far as I am concerned, to enquiring, If I am to be considered a subject of the King and if in that capacity, I am to possess what already belonged to me and what I have since acquired.

Without requiring to enumerate the proofs I have given of a special attachment to my new Country, the sole fact of having acquired new possessions in that Country ceded to the Crown of Great Britain, instead of endeavoring to sell those I already had there, manifests the dispositions I entertained to attach myself and mine forever to it, and consequently I cannot but be comprehended under the denomination of Kings Subjects granted to those of Canada by the Treaty.

After having spent eleven consecutive months in fruitless expenses and proceedings I finally succeeded in appearing four weeks ago before a meeting of the Lords Commissioners of Plantations, when Milord Hillsborough, President of that department, put divers questions and objections to me.

That on which he appeared to me most to dwell was that the two Seigniories in question being situated on Lake Champlain, to which His Britannic Majesty had formed pretensions, he did not consider that the Title I derived from His Most Christian Majesty ought to insure me their property. My answer was, that without seeking to discover whether these pretensions were founded or not (a question which it did not become me to agitate,) I presumed to assure him, at least, that they were recent, much more so than the titles which Insured me the property of these estates; that, moreover, I did not imagine that His Most Christian Majesty, who has had uninterrupted possession of the Country up to the moment of the conquest in 1759, ought at any time allow himself to be stopped by a single pretension, in the desire he had to grant a part of it, as long as it was in his power, to those of his subjects whom he desired to reward. In fine, supposing everything in the position predicated, 'twas certain that I was possessor of these Estates in good faith; that they cost me much money and trouble; that no individual could come forward of right, to question my property in them; that the King alone opposes to me pretensions which can tend only to establish his right of Sovereignty over that portion before the entire cession of the Country, and not to despoil one of His subjects in whose favour every thing speaks at this moment, and to whom justice cannot be refused.

If this chapter of pretensions is examined in its entire breadth where will it not lead to? And if the argument that is derived from it be considered invincible, who can assure himself of an inch of land in any country whatsoever as soon as it is conquered? And if treaties which assure the subject the property of his Estates, cannot serve as a barrier, on what is he to stand, and what hereafter is to be done to preserve them.

The Attorney General, who perceives all the consequences of such a principle; who feels how essential and just it is to preserve to every one his right, is requested to give the Lords Commissioners of Plantations to understand that however laudable may be their zeal for the maintainance of the rights of the Crown, it is carried too far when it unnecessarily tends to the ruin of a private Individual. However, if they consider for reasons they doubtless foresee, that His Majesty cannot depart from the original pretensions He has formed to the country, and that my Titles received may affect them, I am too much attached to His Majesty's Interests to object to any new Titles He shall please to grant me *Gratis* for the whole of the same objects, and which reintegrate me in all my rights. I would supplicate him merely to observe my present situation which does not admit of my remaining any longer in London, and to order that I be despatched with the greatest possible promptness. This 15th June 1764.

GRANT IN FAVOUR OF M. HOCQUART OF A TRACT OF LAND ON LAKE CHAMPLAIN, 1743.

This day, twentieth of April One thousand seven hundred and forty three, the King being at Versailles, desirous to treat Sieur Hocquart Intendant of New France graciously and to bestow on him a mark of the satisfaction he entertains of his services, His Majesty has granted to him by tenure of Fief and Seigniory, a tract about one league in front by five leagues in depth, situate in the said Colony on Lake Champlain opposite Fort St. Frederic, bounded on the West by said Lake, east by unconceded lands, North by a line drawn East and West, and South by a line parallel to this, which two lines form the division of lands to be conceded at a quit rent (*en censives*) in His Majesty's name & for His profit, for the perpetual enjoyment by the said Sieur Hocquart his heirs & assigns of said Tract by tenure of fief and Siegniory, with High, Middle and Low Justice, and Right of Hunting, Fishing and Trading with Indians throughout the extent of said Seigniory without being obliged by reason of this, to pay to His Majesty nor to his Successors, Kings, any duty money as an indemnity whereof, whatever sum it may amount to, His Majesty hath made him a grant and release; On condition to render Fealty and Homage at the Castle of St. Louis Quebec from which the said Fief will be holden and the other customary services, according to the custom of Paris observed in the said country, and that the appeals from the Court which will be established there shall be to the Royal Court (*Justice Royale*) of Montreal; on condition also of preserving and causing to be preserved by the Tenants the Timber of all descriptions adapted for the construction of His Majesty's ships; of informing His Majesty of all Mines or Minerals, if any be found in said Concession; to improve it and to hold & cause to be held fire & light there by the Tenants, in default whereof it shall be reunited to His Majesty's Domain; of allowing roads necessary for public convenience and allowing also the beaches free to all Fishermen, except those they may require for their fishing; and in case His Majesty may have use, hereafter, of any portions of said Tract, to erect thereupon Forts, Batteries, Arsenals, Magazines & other public Works, He can take them as well as the trees necessary for said public Works, and the fire wood necessary for the Garrisons of said Forts, without being holden to any compensation: His Majesty willing that the said Concession be subject to the conditions above enumerated without any exception; and In testimony of His Will, He has ordered me to issue the present Brevet which shall be enregistered at the Office of the Superior Council of Quebec, to have such application there as shall appertain, and which he has willed to sign with his hand to be countersigned by me His councillor Secretary of State and of His Commands and Finances. Signed, LOUIS. and lower down, *Phelippeaux.* Below, the present Brevet has been enregistered in the Registers of the Superior Council of New France, By the King's Attorney General according to the *Arret* of the day, by us, Councillor Secretary of the King, Chief Greffier of said Council, undersigned. At Quebec the 7th October 1743 Signed, DAINE.

[Here follows another Deed, dated 1st April 1745, to the same person of an additional Tract in Seigniory, three leagues in front on Lake Champlain, by five in depth, extending from the North bounds of the former grant, subject to the same burthens and conditions; and a Deed of Sale of the entire "Seigniory Hocquart" to M. Michel Chartier, Seigneur of Lotbiniere &c for the sum of Nine Thousand *livres*—bearing date Paris 7th April. 1763.]

SITUATION OF THE SEIGNIORY OF ALAINVILLE;

ACCORDING TO M. DE LOTBINIERE'S AFFIDAVIT.

I, undersigned, affirm and declare on oath that the Seigniory of Alainville, four leagues and more in front by five leagues in depth to the West, commences at *La Pointe des habitans* (one league and a half or thereabouts, above the Fort at Pointe a la Chevelure, and on the same side of the River) and that it terminates at *Pointe du Bivac* [Bivouac point] of M. de Contrecour's Camp, the lower point above l'Isle au Mouton near the entrance of the Lake St. Sacrement; that the said Seigniory belongs to me in virtue of the Grant which the Marquis de Vaudreuil made to me dated 15th November of the year One thousand seven hundred & fifty Eight; that this deed of Concession was left, in the original by me in July 1764 with Mr Pownall Secretary of the Board of Trade and the Colonies to be registered in said Office; that Sr Henry Guinaud, my agent in London informed me by letter that the Title deeds deposited by the Honble Mr. Cholmondely on my behalf & by me at the said office had been returned to him all registered.

GOV. MOORE TO THE BOARD OF PLANTATIONS.

[Lond. Doc. XXXIX.]

New York, 7 Nov. 1766.

My Lords—I had the honour of informing your Lordpps in a former letter that I proposed to settle the Boundary line between this Province and Quebec as soon as I could conveniently leave this City, and it was not long before I had an opportunity of doing it, for upon the arrival of Brigadier Carleton from England, I set out in company with him for Lake Champlain, and after encountering with many difficulties occasioned by the badness of the weather, we fixed the limits on the River Sorell about two miles and a half below windmill Point, which is further to the Northward than we imagined to find it from the observations which were said to be made there by the French some few years agoe; upon our arrival at Windwill Point, several French Gentlemen came to us, there from Quebec, as well to pay their compliments to Brigr Carleton, as to request of me the confirmation of their Rights to those Seigneiories, which on our observations should be found in the Southward of the 45th degree, and which were granted to them before the conquest of Canada. To this demand I could make no other answer than, that His Majesty had by his instructions to me laid down such rules for the granting of lands in this Provce that I could not deviate from them without incurring his displeasure, and that the power of confirming what they now requested of me, was not at present lodged in my hands, as I was particularly restrained from granting to any one person more than one thousand acres, whereas they demand confirmation of Grants, some of which consisted of Tracts containing 100,000 acres and others of 150,000 acres; I further informed them that no land was granted in this Provce to any of His Majtys subjects without their paying a quit-rent of two shillings & sixpence sterling to the Crown for each hundred acres, & desired to know if they expected to have their grants confirmed, without paying any such quit-rent; to which they answered in the affirmative, and requested that I would not grant any lands on the Lake till I had laid their claims before His Majestys Ministers. On the other hand the reduced Officers, and disbanded soldiers, many of whom are now in actual Possession of large Tracts of those Lands, are greatly alarmed at these Claims, and desire to be protected in the Grants made to them by Lieut Govr Colden, as they have vested their whole fortunes in the settlements already begun on them, and must be reduced to beggary, on being dispossessed. I had the honor of informing Mr. Secretary Conway, soon after my arrival at New York from England that Lieut Govr Colden had declined showing me his correspondence with the Secretary of State's Office, & the Board of Trade, which I was desirous of seeing, so that if any orders relative to the French claims have been transmitted they have not yet come to my hands. Your Lordpps will see at one view how great a prejudice to the settlement of the Provce the present uncertain tenure must occasion, for several other persons who have obtained His Majtys sign manual for large Tracts are desirous of taking them up on the sides of Lake Champlain, and have already gone so far, as to make actual surveys of the Lands, but are now discouraged from proceeding farther, lest after a great expense incurred they might be turned out of possession. I was in hopes that I should have been able to have sent over to your Lordpps by this opportunity an actual survey of the Lake taken by a skillful hand, in which all the French claims were to be distinguished, with the number of acres which each of them contained, and likewise the grants made to the Officers and Soldiers, under the great seal of this Provce in consequence of His Majtys Proclamation which would have showed at one view how far they interfere with each other. The Deputy Surveyor of Canada, who attended me the whole time I was employed in fixing the line of division between the Provinces, promised to furnish me with an exact draught of all the Seigneuries on the Lake, time enough to transmit to your Lordpps by the Packet, but I have not heard from him since my return hither. As this is a matter of very great importance to a considerable number of persons in this Province, whose whole fortunes are vested in these Lands, they have requested me to take the earliest opportunity of laying the state of their case before your Lordpps and to set forth the distressed situation in which they are at present, that His Majestys pleasure might be known on this head. During my absence from hence, two Packets arrived but as I was at too great a distance, they had sailed again before I heard of their arrival, which I hope will appologize for my not having acknowledged sooner the honor of your Lordpps letter of the 11th July, and the receipt of the queries sent by the same opportunity, which shall be answered with all expedition and in the fullest manner from the best Intelligence I am capable of procuring.

I have the honor to be, ettc.

H. Moore.

LORD HILLSBOROUGH TO SIR H. MOORE.

[Lond. Doc. XLI.]

Whitehall Feb. 25th 1768.

Your letter to Lord Shelburne No. 5. which relates to the Claims of His Mâtys Canadian Subjects, to lands on that part of Lake Champlain which is now a part of the Colony of New York, has been referred to the Lords of Trade, & their Lordships having made a Report to His Mâty thereupon, It is His Mâtys Resolution upon the fullest consideration not to allow any claims made upon the grounds of ancient grants from the Government of Canada, to Lands which were never acknowledged to belong of right to the Crown of France.

His Mâty has the most tender Regard to the Rights of His new subjects, & is desirous of giving every proper Testimony of His Attention to their Interests and Welfare, & therefore it is his Mâtys Pleasure, that they should not be disturbed in the peaceable possession of any Tracts so circumstanced, which they may have actually settled & improved, provided they consent to establish their Title by Grants under the seal of the Province of New York, upon the usual Conditions of Quit Rent & Improvement.

LORD HILLSBOROUGH TO SIR H. MOORE.

[N. Y. Council Minutes XXVI.; Lond. Doc. XLI.]

Whitehall 13th August 1768.

I have only in command from His Majesty to send you the inclosed order of His Majesty in Council confirming the Boundary Line betweenn New York & Quebec, as agreed upon and fixed by yourself and Governor Carleton, for the due execution of which Order under the several Limitations and Restrictions contained in it, His Majesty has the fullest Reliance on your Zeal for and Attention to His Service.

[N. Y. Council Minutes XXVI.]

At the Court at St. James the 12th day of August 1768.

Present

The Kings Most Excellent Majesty.

Duke of Grafton
Duke of Rutland
Duke of Queensbury
Marquis of Granby
Earl of Litchfield
Earl of Hillsborough
Earl of Shelburne
Viscount Weymouth
Viscount Falmouth
Viscount Barrington
Viscount Villiers
Lord North
James Stuart Mackenzie Esq
Thomas Harley Esq[r]
Sir Edward Hawke

Whereas there was this Day read at the Board a Report from the Right Honorable the Lords of the Committee of Council for Plantation Affairs dated the 9th of this Instant, upon considering a Report made by the Lords Commissioners for Trade and Plantations, upon an Extract of a Letter from Sir Henry Moore Governor of New York to the Earl of Shelburne dated the 16th of January last, relative to the settling the Boundary Line between that Province and Quebec: By which Report it appears that it having been mutually agreed upon between Sir Henry Moore and the Commander in Chief of the Province of Quebec, at a meeting for that purpose appointed, that the Line of Division between these Provinces should be fixed at the forty-fifth Degree of North Latitude, conformable to the Limits laid down in his Majesty's Proclamation of October 1763, and it having been ascertained and determined by proper Observations where the said line would pass; it is therefore proposed that these Proceedings above stated should be confirmed by His Majesty—His Majesty taking the said Report into Consideration was pleased with the Advice of His privy Council, to approve thereof, and doth hereby confirm the said Proceedings above stated, and order that the said Line of Division be run out and continued as far as each Province respectively extends, Provided that nothing hereinbefore contained, shall extend to affect the Properties of his Majesty's new Subjects, having Possessions under proper titles, on those parts of the Lands on the South side of this Line, the Dominion of which was not disputed on the part of the Crown of Great Britain; And Provided also, that this Determination shall not operate wholly to deprive his Majesty's New subjects of such Concessions on the South side of the said Line, on which they may have made actual Settlement and Improvement, although the Lands may have been disputed by the Crown of Great Britain; but that such Possessors shall be entitled to so much of the said Concessions, as shall be proportioned to their Improvements, at the rate of fifty Acres for every three Acres of Improvement, provided they take out Grants for the same under the Seal of the Province of New York, subject to the usual Quit rents, and provided also that the Grant to no one person shall exceed twenty thousand Acres, and the Governors or Commanders in Chief of his Majesty's said Provinces of New-York and Quebec for the Time being, and all others whom it may concern, are to take Notice of his Majesty's Pleasure hereby signifyed and govern themselves accordingly.

STEPH: COTTRELL.

SIR H. MOORE TO LORD HILLSBOROUGH.

[Lond. Doc. XLI.]

Fort George, Oct. 25th 1768.

Since my writing the foregoing Letter, I have had an opportunity of laying the order before his Majesty's Council, who are under some difficulties in regard to the construction of the first proviso therein mentioned viz: "Provided that nothing herein contained shall extend to affect the Properties of His Majesty's new subjects having possessions under proper titles on those parts of the Lands, on the south side of this Line the Dominion of which was not disputed on the part of the Crown of Great Britain." No line of jurisdiction having ever been settled between this Province & Quebec 'till that which was fixed by General Carleton & myself and approved of by His Majesty, each of the Provinces have endeavored to extend their claims as far as they possibly could. The English to the River St. Lawrence, and the French to the Southward of Lake George: The consequence of which has been that the lands on both sides of Lake Champlain have been granted to the English & French by their respective Governors, as will appear by the Map which I had the honour of transmitting to England & mentioned in my letter No. 6, to the Earl of Shelburne dated 22d of February 1767, & in my letter to the Lords of Trade dated 4th April 1767. Your Lordship will see by these different claims what the difficulties are which we labour under at present, for [there is] no particular boundary Line fairly drawn between the Provinces, the English claim supported by that which was made before them by the Dutch extended as far as the forty fifth Degree of Latitude. This Line was supposed by the French to be more to the Southward than we found it on observation, & several of their grants in those parts are covered by those since made by Mr. Colden to the reduced officers and soldiers under His Majesty's Proclamation. This will of course open such a scene of litigation, as I am afraid will defeat the expectations of forwarding the settlements in that part of the Country, to prevent which it is our humble request that His Majestys pleasure might be known how far to the southward of the 45th Degree any French grants are to be allowed for they have no settlements to claim under (which I am informed was an absolute condition of their Grant, as they have paid no Qnit-Rent) and the Quantity of Land in most of their Grants far exceeds that which his Majesty has been pleased to allow to those mentioned in the 2d proviso which was not to exceed 20,000 acres to each Person where an actual settlement had been.

ADDITIONAL INSTRUCTION

TO OUR TRUSTY AND WELL BELOVED SIR HENRY MOORE BARONET, OUR CAPTAIN GENERAL AND GOVERNOR IN CHIEF OF OUR PROVINCE OF NEW YORK AND THE TERRITORIES DEPENDING THEREON IN AMERICA. GIVEN, &C. DATED 5 JULY 1769.

[N. Y. Council Minutes XXVI; Lond. Doc. XLII.]

Whereas sundry persons, proprietors under titles derived from the Crown of France when that Crown was in possession of Canada, of lands on that part of Lake Champlain now lying within our Province of New-York have humbly represented unto Us that several parts of the said lands so claimed have already been granted to other persons by Letters Patent under the Seal of Our said

Province of New-York, and have therefore humbly prayed that a proceeding so prejudicial to their rights and pretensions may receive Our Royal disapprobation; and whereas it appears both just & equitable that the claims of persons under such titles as aforesaid should not be affected without the fullest examination thereof. It is therefore Our Will and Pleasure & you are hereby directed & required in no case to make any grants of lands so claimed, as aforesaid, upon Lake Champlain to the northward of Crown Point, within Our Province of New York, until the petitions & proposals for grants of any part or parts of such lands shall have been transmitted to one of Our principal Secretaries of State, in order to be laid before Us, & until Our approbation thereof shall have signified to you Our said Governor or to the Commander in Chief of Our said Province for the time being.

[N. Y. Council Minutes XXVI.]

At a Council held at Fort George in the City of New York
on Wednesday the fourteenth day of August, 1771.

Present His Excellency William Tryon Esq[r] Capt. Genl. &c.

M[r] Watts	M[r] Morris	M[r] Cruger	M[r] White
M[r] De Lancey	M[r] Smith	M[r] Wallace	M[r] Axtell

It is Ordered by his Excellency with the advice of the Council that a Proclamation issue Notifying to all Persons holding or laying Claim under Titles derived from the Government of France, while in Possession of Canada, to any Lands upon Lake Champlain Northward of Crown Point, and to the Southward of the forty fifth Degree of Northern Latitude, to transmit unto the Secretary's Office of this Province within three months from the Date thereof, Authentic Exemplifications of the Original Grants, together with satisfactory Evidence of the situation of the Lands therein mentioned, and of the Solidity of the Titles of the Claimants thereof at the time of the Surrender of Canada to the Crown of Great Britain; to the End that the Government of this Province, by being duly apprized thereof, may be enabled to give the Claims under such French Grants, the attention they shall appear to Merit.

[N. Y. Council Min. XXVI.]

In Council; Wednesday, 18 Dec[r] 1771.

Present His Excellency William Tryon Esq. Capt. Gen'l &c.

M[r] Horsmanden	M[r] DeLancey	M[r] Smith	M[r] White
M[r] Watts	M[r] Apthorp	M[r] Cruger	M[r] Axtell

His Excellency communicated to the Board a Letter of the 30th of October from Lieutenant Governor Cramahe of the Province of Quebec enclosing several papers relative to the French Claims to Lands on Lake Champlain and acquainting his Excellency that he shall by the next Post furnish him with all the Information he has collected relative to the French Grants on that Lake.

His Excellency also communicated to the Board another Letter from Lieutenant Governor Cramahe, dated Quebec Novr 11th acquainting his Excellency that in consequence of his Letter of the 17th August,[1] he ordered the public Register deposited with the Secretary of the Province to be very exactly searched, and Transmitted him by Mr Marr two Abstracts containing the Grantees Names, those of the new Proprietors that have come to their knowledge, the Dates of the Grants as well as of the Ratifications, and their extent as entered upon those Registers, as well of the Lands granted en Seigneurie as of those granted by the King en Roture—Also Copies under the Great Seal of the Province of all the Kings Edicts and Declarations relative to Grants of Lands which had Force of Law there, that his Excellency might be enabled to Judge of the Justice of such Claims—That by these it appears that the Governor and Intendant, or in Case of their Death or Absence those who executed their respective offices, had the power of granting Lands to be ratified by the King within Twelve Months, and that they likewise were the sole Judges in case of a reunion to the Demesne, where the Grantees had not complyed with the Conditions of their Grants, which however never took place till after a Solemn Hearing upon a legal Process before those Officers at the instance of the King's Attorney General—That among the Papers transmitted under the Great Seal of the Province is a Sentence of Reunion of Several Grants upon Lake Champlain dated 10th May 1741 by the then Governor Beauharnois and Intendant Hocquart, since which time there does not appear upon the Registers, altho' very complete, a single reunion of any Grant in those Parts; & therefore that all Grants precedent thereto, and not comprehended therein, are thereby confirmed—and after several observations respecting two Grants to Monsieur Foucault purchased by General Murray; On the Title of Mademoiselle de Ramzay—On the Grant of Monsieur De Beaujeu Villemonde—And the two Grants to Monsieur Hocquart, purchased by Monsieur de Lotbiniere, further acquainting his Excellency that the Canadian Grantees, Trust his Excellency will be pleased to consider the Possession of their Estates with all the Immunities thereunto annexed, was secured to them by the capitulation of Montreal, and the Treaty of Paris—That the King's Old Subjects who under the Faith thereof became considerable purchasers of their Estates, Hope and doubt not his Excellency will pay a due attention to their just Rights, and that all expect so serious a matter of so much Consequence to themselves and Families, will be carefully weighed and sufficient Time given them to adduce such proofs as in Honour and Justice may be required of them.

In Council; Thursday 31st day of Decembr 1771.

Present His Excellency Govr Tyron and the other Members of Council as last mentioned, except Mr Apthorp absent, and Mr Wallace who is present.

His Excellency laid before the Board the following Writings and Papers which had been transmitted from the Province of Quebec in pursuance of the late Proclamation relating to the French Claims to Lands within this Government, on the banks of Lake Champlain.

1st. An Exemplification under the Seal of Quebec of the Order of the French King authorizing the Grant of Lands in Canada dated 20th May 1676.

2dly. An Exemplification of his Arret in Council directing that the Lands Granted be cultivated by the Inhabitants, dated 6th July, 1711.

1 Forwarding Proclamation mentioned in the preceding entry, dated, 14 Augt. 1771.

3dly. An Exemplification of the French King's Declaration concerning the Grants in Canada, dated 17th July 1743, & an Explanatory Order dated 19th June 1748.

4thly. An Exemplification of an Arret in Council of the 15th March 1732.

5thly. Of an Ordinance of the Governor and Intendant of 10th May 1741, for a Reunion of divers Seigniories to the Demesnes of the French Crown.

6thly. Certificate from the French List of the Lands Granted en Seigneurie on Lake Champlain North of Crown Point dated Quebec 28th October 1771, and signed George Alsop Clerk of the Enrolments.

7thly. A like Certificate of the Lands granted en Roture or in Soccage to the Southward of the 45th degree of North Latitude.

8thly. Copies of the Concession and Ratification to Daniel Lienard de Beaujeu Junr of the 6th of March 1752 and 1st June 1763 mentioned in the said List of Seigniories & Certified under the hand of said Geo. Alsop.

9thly. Copies certified in like manner of the Concession and Ratification to Antoine Bedout mentioned in said List of Seigneuries.

10thly. Copies under a like Certificate of the Concession and Ratification in the said List to Nicholas Berré Le Vasseur.

11th. Copies Certified in like manner of the Concession and Ratification in the said List to Francis Daine.

12th. Copies of a Concession by the King to Monsieur Giles Hoquart Intendant, dated 20th April 1743, and of a like Concession to the same on 1st April 1745, and of a Contract and Sale thereof certified by Pierre Meziere and Pierre Panet, Notaries, who are Certified to be Notaries at Quebec by John Collins a Justice of the Peace 21st September, 1771.

13th. Copy of a Memorial to the Lieutenant Governor of Quebec by Lewis Lienard de Beaujeu de Villemonde dated 15th October 1771. representing that he had a Grant of a Seigneurie dated 20th July 1755 but that the Ratification was lost in 1756 and praying his Intercession with the Governor of New-York for further Time to produce it than is prescribed by the New York Proclamation of August last.

14th. A Copy of a Notarial Certificate of the Sale of the Seigneurie mentioned in the said List to be Granted to Pierre Raimbault made by his heirs to Benjamin Price and others Certified by the said George Alsop 15 August 1771.

15th. A Map of the French Grants on Lake Champlain from Fort Chambly to Crown Point Surveyed by Mr Anger dated 10th October 1748 and signed de Lery.

16th. Mr. Cramahe's Letter to His Excellency dated 11th Decr 1771.

Upon which his Excellency desired the opinion of the Council on the Measures proper to be pursued as well with Respect to the Lands granted upon Lake Champlain, as to the new applications for Patents in that part of the Country, and it was thereupon Ordered that the said Writings be referred to the Gentlemen of the Council, or any five of them.

ORDINANCE

OF THE GOVERNOR AND INTENDANT OF NEW FRANCE REUNITING TO HIS MAJESTY'S DOMAIN ALL SEIGNIORIES NOT IMPROVED. 10 MAY 1741.

[MSS. relating to French Claims, &c., in Sec's Off.]

Charles Marquis de Beauharnois &c.
Gilles Hocquart &c.

At the Superior Council of Quebec, Between the King's Attorney General. Pltff in his suit of the 20 Feby last on the one side; And Sieurs . . . Pean, Major of the town and Castle of Quebec . . . St Vincent Ensign of Foot, De Beauvais Junr., De Contrecour Capt. of Infantry; De Contrecour Junr. Ensign, and La Perriere Capt of sd. Troops . . . Lafontaine, Councillor in sd. Superior Council . . . Roebert Kings Store Keeper at Montreal . . . All the above named Grantees of Lands on . . . . Lake Champlain Defts and cited the sixth and eleventh of March last and the ninth of the present month: and Sieurs Douville . . . . . . and De la Gauchetiere Defts and defaulters through lack of appearance either personally or by attorney on the summons which was served on them the eleventh of said Month of March by the Huissier Decoste, on the other side.1

Having seen the suit of the King's Attorney General demanding for reasons therein contained, that We would be pleased to permit him to cause to be summoned the said Sieurs above mentioned to be and appear before us at the Castle St Louis of Quebec within the delays of the ordonnance to direct and order, that they having failed to have cultivated & improved the lands granted to them in Seigniory and to have placed and settled inhabitants thereon according to the terms of the Arrets of the King's Council of State of sixth July 1711. and fifteenth of March 1732 and within the time specified therein, they shall remain and be reunited to His Majesty's Domain in this country; The answers of the said Defend^ts^. present by which . . . . Sieur Pean states that he could not find any farmer, up to this time, to place on his Seigniory, that if he should find any he is ready to furnish them with axes and picks, for clearing, with one year's provisions; that he will continue to look for them; that he will do his best to find some and that he intends to form a demesne there. . . . . Another answer of Sieur Estebe appearing as above, by which he says that Sieur St. Vincent is actually detached as Commander of the post of Ouyatanois, that he already made several grants on his Seigniory, namely to a habitant of the Cote de Beaupré; that the said Sieur St. Vincent told him before his departure that he intended immediately establishing a demesne there, the said Sieur Estebe requesting moreover in his name, that a sufficient delay be granted him, in consequence of said Sieur St Vincent's absence on the King's service. . . . . A writing without date intituled a Summary Remonstrance furnished to Us by the Sieurs de Contrecour, Father & Son, & La Perrier covenanting by the said Sieur Pean, in which they set forth among other things that they had done everything to settle their grants; that it was impossible to find individuals willing to accept lands though they offered them some on very advantageous terms and were willing to give even Three hundred livres to engage the said individuals; that the said Contrecour, Senr. has rendered Fealty & Hommage for said Seigniory and that he, as well as said Sieurs La Perrier & Contrecoeur, Junior has been subjected to various expenses; that they intend, moreover, to do all in their power to find farmers to settle said Seigniories and they hope to succeed therein; requesting Us that we would please to grant them a delay on the offers which they make to conform themselves herein to his Majesty's intentions. . . . Another writing of Sieur La Fontaine not dated, and signed by him . . . whereby he offers with our permission to go this summer on the Grant with three men to build there, and begin clearances and to give to those whom we will find willing to settle there, Grain and even money, asking from them no rent, in order to obtain from them by the allurement of this gift what he cannot obtain from them by force;

1. So much of this Record only is given as applies to Grants on Lake Champlain and south of Line 45.

a writing of Sieur Roebert . . . also not dated in which he says that at the time his Grant was made him, he set M. Janvrin Dufresne, sworn Surveyor, with six men to measure, survey and define the said Grant who occupied forty days in their voyage & that this expense amounted to Seven hundred *livres* ten *sous*, according to the certificate of said Dufresne which he presents, and that he has neglected nothing to induce some young farmers to go and settle there by procuring for them great advantages and many facilities, concluding for these reasons We may grant him delay to allow him to satisfy His Majesty's intentions; Seeing likewise His Majesty ordinances dated 6 July 1711 and 15th March, 1732, and his orders addressed to Us last year wherein He orders Us very expressly to proceed with the reunion to His Domain of the Lands formerly and recently Granted in default of the proprietors thereof having fulfilled the conditions set forth in their deeds: We grounding ourselves on the requisition of the King's Attorney General HAVE REUNITED AND DO REUNITE to His Majesty's Domain the Lands following, to wit:

That granted on the 10th of April of the year 1733 to Sieur Pean two leagues or two leagues & a half in front by three in depth along the River Chambly and Lake Champlain together with the River Chazy included therein and Isle à la Motte; . . . that granted to Sieur St. Vincent on 12th April 1733 two leagues in front by three leagues in depth on Lake Champlain;[1] Another to Sieur de Beauvais on 20th July 1734 two leagues in front by three leagues in depth on Lake Champlain together with the peninsula which is found to be in front of said land; Another conceded on 7th July of the same year 1734 to Sieur Contrecour *fils*, on the borders of Lake Champlain beginning at the mouth of the *Riviere aux Loutres* [Otter River] one league and a half above and one league and a half below, making two leagues in front by three in depth together with so much of said *Riviere aux Loutres* as is found included therein with three Islands or Islets which are in front of said Concession and depend thereon; another granted to Sieur de la Perriere on the border of Lake Champlain beginning at the Mouth of the River Ouynouski one league above and one league below making two leagues front by three leagues in depth with the extent of said River which will be found comprehended therein together with the Islands and Battures adjacent; . . .. that granted the 5th April 1733 to Sieur Lafontaine being five quarters of a league in front on the River Chambly by the depth that may be found to the Bay of Missiskouy;[2] that conceded on the 13th June 1737 to Sieur Roebert, three leagues front by two leagues in depth on the West side of Lake Champlain, taking, in going down, one league below the River Boquet and in going up two leagues and a half above said River [3] Wherefore WE have declared all the Grantees above named deprived of all rights and property over these Lands, and yet having in no wise regard to the representations made by any of the said Defendts We reserve to Ourselves, under His Majesty's good pleasure, to grant new Patents of the same lands to those of the Defendants who shall prove within a year to Us, that they have seriously and by real outlays and labour improved a notable portion of said Lands, or placed Settlers thereupon during the course of this year, such time having elapsed, by virtue and Execution of these presents and without others being necessary the said Lands shall be conceded to whom and as it shall appertain: We grant default against Sieur Douville . . . . and for benefit, We have declared the present Judgment Common, for the lands equally conceded to them, to wit, to Sieur Douville, that granted to him the eighth October 1736 two leagues front by three leagues deep on the East side of Lake Champlain . . . . and finally that granted to Sieur La Gauchetiere the 20th of April of the year 1733 of two leagues front by three leagues deep on said Lake Champlain.[4] We order &c. Done at the Castle of St. Louis of Quebec the tenth May 1741. Signed Beauharnois & Hocquart; Countersigned and Sealed.

For Copy. HOCQUART.

1 Now the town of Champlain, Clinton Co. 2 Qu.? Town of Alburg, Vt. 3 Now the town of Essex and greater part of the town of Wellsborough, Essex county, N. Y. 4. Now the town of Chazy, Clinton county, N. Y.

GRANT OF THE SEIGNIORY BEDOU, ON THE RIVER CHAZY. 1 Nov. 1752.

[From the same.]

The Marquis Duquesne &c.
Francis Bigot &c.

On the Petition to us presented by Sieur Bedou, Councellor in the Superior Council of Quebec to the effect that We would be pleased to grant him a Tract two leagues or two leagues and a half front by three leagues in depth along the River Chambly and Lake Champlain with the River Chazy included therein, the front of said Tract to extend from the bounds of the Seigniory recently conceded to Sieur de Beaujeau to a league from the mouth of the River Chazy on the South side, with the part of the River Chazy which will be found within the extent of said land; which will be bounded by a line North and South passing by the mouth of said River Chazy, by three leagues in depth, and besides, all the said land which will be found beyond the said line on the River Chambly and Lake Champlain and Isle a la Mothe that is opposite in the said Lake, which Tract was heretofore granted to the late M. Pean in his life time Major of Quebec and reunited to the Kings Domain by an Ordinance of Mess[rs] de Beauharnois & Hocquart dated 10 May 1741. All by tenure of Fief and Seigniory with Right of High, Middle and low Justice, rights of Hunting, Fishing and the Indian trade as well in front of, as within said Tract. We in virtue of the power granted to us by his Majesty have given granted and conceded to said Sieur Bedou the said Tract of land as and in the manner it is above described, which shall be bounded on the North and South by two lines drawn East & West in front by the River Chambly and Lake Champlain, and in depth three leagues joining the nonconceded lands by a line drawn North & South parallel to that which shall pass the mouth of the River Chazy and, besides, the Island called *a la Mothe* which is opposite to the said Tract in Lake Champlain, to possess it by himself his heirs and assigns in perpetuity and for ever by the tenure of Fief & Seigniory with High Middle and Low Justice, with privileges of Fishing, Hunting and the Indian Trade throughout the whole extent of said Tract, on condition of rendering Fealty & Homage at the Castle of St Louis of Quebec from which he will hold with the usual duties and charges according to the custom of Paris followed in this Country, of preserving & causing to be preserved by his Tenants the Oak timber fit for building King's Ships, of giving His Majesty all Mines Minerals &c.

[The remainder of this Patent is in terms similar to that already inserted p. 351. The grant was ratified by the King of France 18th June 1753. The Seigniory was afterward made over by the proprietor on 2d May 1754 to Daniel Lienard Sieur de Beaujeu, who had a Seigniory adjoining inmediately North.]

TO HIS EXCELLENCY HECTOR THEOPHILE CRAMAHE ESQR.

LIEUTENANT GOVERNOUR AND COMMANDER IN CHIEF OF THE PROVINCES OF QUEBEC, &C. &C.

Respectfully Sheweth—Louis Lienard de Beaujeu de Villemonde Chevalier de St. Louis, covenanting for him & in his name Francois Joseph Cugnet Seigneur de St Etienne, who has the honour most respectfully to represent to your Excellency that there was granted to him on the 20 July 1755 by Mess[rs] de Vaudreuil and Bigot Governor General and Intendant, in compensation of his Military

Services, the Concession of a Seigniory, situated on Lake Champlain part of which is found by the new Line to be within the Province of New York, extending from the bounds of the Seigniory granted and conceded in 1744 to Guillaume Estebe proceeding Eastward to the River *Senerinduc* the said River included, forming about four leagues front by as many in depth, together with the Isles & Islets which might happen to be in front of the said tract. And as it is the Petitioner's interest to preserve the said Seigniory which is the only property remaining to him after the losses he has experienced by the misfortunes of the War, he has recourse to your Excellency's Clemency and asks of him the favor to be so good as to interest himself in his behalf with His Excellency the Governour of New York who has been so good as to admit the Canadians to represent to him their Titles to the said grants, in the Gracious disposition in which he is to do them Justice, in order to obtain a longer delay than he has granted by his Proclamation of the 20th August last to represent His Most Christian Majesty's Ratification of said Grant, copy of which he has ordered from his brother at Paris, and which he will only receive in the course of next year, that Ratification having been lost in the Brigatine *les Deux Frères*, Capt. Dufycharest captured by the English in 1756; and to be able also to shew that it was impossible for him to have kept fire & light there at the time, and as prescribed by said Deed of Concession, because being a Military Man he left in the same year 1756 to command a Post in the Upper Country by the orders of the Governor General, an absence which has rendered him not only unable to improve and establish his said Seigniory and to have fire and light kept there according to the terms of his title but even to solicit the Intendant to apply to the Court of France for Copy of the Ratification of his Grant the original of which had been lost; and he has not been able since the Definitive Treaty of Peace, to establish said Seigniory, it being notorious that he has not returned to this Province until the month of August 1769. And in fine he could not send the title of his Concession to New York to be there enregistered since his arrival in this Province, on account of the considerable expense that Envoy would have occasioned him. He dares flatter himself that you will be favorable to him and he will not cease to offer his prayers to Heaven for your Excellency's preservation.

QUEBEC 15th Octobr 1771.

DEED OF SALE OF THE SEIGNIORY OF LAMANAUDIERE

ON THE EAST SIDE OF LAKE CHAMPLAIN, 27th SEPTEMBER 1766.

[From the same.]

Before the undersigned Notaries residing in the City of Montreal in the Province of Quebec, appeared Sieur Jean Marie Raimbault and Dame Louise De Montigny his Wife whom he duely authorized, and Demoiselle Lse Raimbault his daughter of age, living at the *Cote de la Montagne* near this City of Montreal acting as well for themselves as for Sieur Claude Raimbault their brother absent from this Province for whom they render themselves guaranty & security; Who have by these Presents voluntarily sold, ceded and transported from now and forever, promised & promising jointly as well in their names as in those of their Executors, Administrators, Heirs and Assigns to guarantee from all Troubles, Grants, Doweries, Debts, Mortgages and other Burthens in general whatsoever, except solely the Troubles and Hindrances which may be caused on the part of Governments, unto Benjamin Price Esq. Daniel Robertson Esq. and John Livingston Esqr the said Sieurs Robertson &

Livingston purchasers, present at and accepting as well for themselves as for said Sieur Price, their Executors Administrators & Assigns, a Seigniory called *La Manaudiere* situated on Lake Champlain on the East Side, containing four leagues front by five leagues deep, the said four Leagues commencing in descending the Lake, from the Bounds of the Seigniory granted to Sieur La Perriere on the sixth of July One thousand seven hundred and thirty four, in which is included the River called *A la Mouelle*, with the Isles, Islets, and Battures adjacent, with the Privilege of High, Low and Middle Justice, Rights of Hunting, Fishing and Indian Trade and the Rights and Prerogatives annexed to said Seigniory without any Exception whatsoever, nothing being reserved nor retarded by the said Sellers to whom the said Seigniory belongs as sole heirs of the late M. Pierre Raimbault their Father in his life time Lieut: General for his Most Christian Majesty of the Jurisdiction of this City, to which said Sieur Raimbault the said Seigniory belonged by Grant to him made by His said Most Christian Majesty according to the Patent of Ratification of the thirtieth of April One thousand seven hundred & thirty seven duly enregistered at the Superior Council of Quebec, formal conveyance whereof the said Sellers promise to immediately give the said Purchasers: The Present Sale made on condition that the said Purchasers pay from this day and render to the Domain of His Majesty, our Most Sovereign Lord the King of Great Britain all the Rights and Duties for which the said Seigniory is bound to Him; and besides give the price and sum of Ninety Thousand *livres* current Money of this Province half of which in gold and silver Specie and the other half in Merchandize at the prices current in this City, which the said Sellers acknowledge and Confess to have now received from the said Purchasers; The said Sieurs Robertson & Livingston Declaring that three fourths of the said Seigniory will belong to them and the other fourth will belong to said Seur Benjamin Price—in consequence whereof the said Sellers consent that said Purchasers enjoy, do with, and dispose of, the said Seigniory and its Dependancies, as to them will seem good and enter therein in good Seizin and infeoffment. For thus &c. Promising &c. Obliging &c. Renouncing &c. Done and Executed in the said Montreal in the Year One Thousand seven hundred & sixty six, the twenty seventh of September after noon; and the Sellers have Signed and Sealed these Presents with the said Sieurs Robertson & Livingston, acting for the said Sieur Price, after reading being done.

Signed { RAIMBAULT (LS.)
LOUISE MONTIGNY RAIMBAULT (LS.)
LOUISE RAIMBAULT (LS.)
JOHN LIVINGSTON (LS.)
DAN'L ROBERTSON (LS.)

Signed, Sealed & delivered in presence of

Signed { PRE PANET
FR. SIMONNET } Nots

Quebec, 27. July 1767.

Received from Benjamin Price, Daniel Robertson and John Livingstone Esquire the sum of Twelve Pounds, Lawful Money of this Province for the *Droit de Quint* or Mutation fine for the Seigniory called *La Manaudiere* situate on the East side of Lake Champlain, joining on a Seigniory granted to M La Perriere by the French King 6 July 1764, purchased by them of Jean Marie Raimbault, Louise Montigny his Wife & Louise Raimbault of Montreal as specified in the Contract of Sale, signed by the parties the 27th of September last, having remitted to the said Purchasers one Third, pursuant to the Ancient Custom of this Colony, and by which I have put the same Benjamin Price, Daniel Robertson and John Livingston Esquires in good Possession and Seizing of the said Seigniory, they having for that effect paid the fine due to His Majesty.

Signed THOMAS MILLS, Rr GENl.

The above and foregoing are true Copies of a deed of Sale of the Seigniory called La Manaudière[1] and of the Receipt for the Droit de Quint, as taken from the French Register Letter E. pages 313 & 358. in my office.

Given under my hand at Quebec this
15th August 1771.

GEO. ALLSOPP Dy Regr
& Clk of Enrolments.

[N. Y. Council Minutes, XXVI.]

At a Council held at Fort George in the city of New York,
on Monday the sixth day of January 1772.

Present His Excellency William Tryon Esq. Captain General &ca

Mr Watts	Mr Morris	Mr Cruger	Mr White
Mr Apthorp	Mr Smith	Mr Wallace	Mr Axtell

Mr. Smith from the Committee to whom by Order of the 31st ultimo was referred the Papers relative to the French claims to Lands on Lake Champlain presented to His Excellency the Committee's Report thereupon, which being Read was on the Question being put agreed to and approved of, and Ordered to be entered in the Minutes and is as follows:

REPORT OF THE COMMITTEE ON THE SUBJECT OF THE FRENCH CLAIMS TO LANDS ON LAKE CHAMPLAIN.

May it please your Excellency:

The Committee to whom were referred the several Writings lately transmitted (in pursuance of your Proclamation) from the Province of Quebec relative to the French Claims to Lands within this Government humbly Report

That soon after his Majesty was pleased by his Royal Proclamation of the 7th October 1763 to declare the 45th Degree of Northern Latitude to be the Boundary between this and the Province of Quebec, divers Tracts of Land were granted under the Great seal of this Province to the Northward of Crown Point on both sides of Lake Champlain, and chiefly to the reduced Officers and Soldiers claiming his Majesty's Bounty Graciously promised by that Proclamation.

That Sir Henry Moore and Mr Carlton the Governors of the two Provinces fixed the place of the Latitude of 45, by actual observation near the North end of the Lake in the Month of September 1767, and that on the 12th August 1768 his Majesty was pleased to declare his Approbation in Privy Council, and to direct in favour of his New Canadian Subjects that nothing in the Order of that Date contained should affect the property of such as had possessions under proper Titles in Lands on the South side of the Line, the Dominion of which was not disputed on the part of the Crown of Great Britain; And that the said Determination should not operate wholly to deprive them of such Concessions on the South side of said Line, whereon they had made actual settlements and Improvements, altho' the said Line might have been disputed by the Crown of Great Britain, but proportioned to their Improvements at the Rate of 50 acres for every three that were improv-

1. The present Town of Burlington, Vt., is situated on part of the above Seigniory.

ed, with the Provisoe that Grants should be sued out under the seal of New-York, Subject to the usual Quit Rents, and that a Grant to one person should not exceed 20,000 acres.

The Committee have examined the Council Books and cannot discover that the Government of Quebec ever gave the least Intimation to this Province of any French Grants upon Lake Champlain, neither before nor after the said Order of August 1768 until excited thereunto by your Excellency's late proclamation, nor is there an Entry to be found of any Notification of such Claim by Private persons, nor even of an application for any grant or Confirmation under this Government for Lands Granted in Canada before the surrender of that Country.

The Committee therefore conceive that it was a natural and reasonable presumption either that there were no such French Grants or that the Grantees and their Assigns considered them as invalid and perhaps forfeited to the French Crown before the Conquest or that they declined the acceptance of British Confirmations subject to Quit Rents and new Patent Charges, intending to set themselves up as sufficient under the Capitulation Articles in the Courts of Law, upon the supposition that they were within the Ancient Dominions of the Crown of France, and agreeable thereto this Government began again to Grant Lands in that Quarter, and continued the practice until Your Excellency was pleased to communicate to the Council his Majestys 50th Instruction prohibiting Patents for Lands to the Northward of Crown Point, claimed under French Titles, and if the late Grants of this Province are detrimental to those Claimants, the Committee are of Opinion that the Blame falls upon themselves, as it is owing to their neglecting to give the Information naturally to be expected, if they intended to submit to and take advantage of the Royal order of the 12th August 1768.

The Committee observe that among the Papers now transmitted from Quebec, there are no French Concessions and Ratifications for any of the Lands mentioned in the List of those said to be Granted en Roture, nor for several of those in the List of the Seigneuries, besides those specified in M[r] Cramahe's Letter to your Excellency, nor is there a single petition sent or preferred by either of those Claimants for a Confirmation under this Province of any of their Grants, which is the more extraordinary as Your Excellency's Proclamation required a full exhibition of their Titles, and the Crown is greatly interested in the Question concerning the Validity of the French Claims in the Articles both of Quit Rents and Escheats, their pretentions extending not only to a vast Quantity of Land, but to Lands the more valuable for their Contiguity to the Forts and Passes, and the Navigable Waters of the Lake: and from the whole we conjecture that this Conduct is owing to their adopting an Opinion which deserves a serious attention to wit:

That the Lands they Claim are situated to the Northward of the Antient British Claim, and that consequently they can maintain a Title under the Surrender without the aid of the Crown, and free from the usual Reservations, Restrictions, Conditions, and Quit Rents.

With respect therefore to the Lands Southward of Crown Point, and to those to the Northward of that Fort, not within the Limits of the French Grants, we are of Opinion that your Excellency may issue Patents for them as Lands to which the 50th Article of the Royal Instructions has clearly no relation.

Nor do we think that Article ought to be considered to prohibit the Grant of those Tracts to which no French Concessions or Ratifications appear to be transmitted from Quebec, nor any Excuse assigned for not laying them before this Government pursuant to the late Proclamation, it being very plain from the Instruction that it was intended to restrain only new Patents for Lands before claimed by Titles derived from the French King, and prior to the Surrender o Canada and as clear that it was the indispensable Duty of all such Claimants in justice to the Crown to give due Notice of their Claims.

But in due deference to his Majesty's authority, we advise as to the Lands to the Northward of Crown Point, and included by the Concessions & Ratifications lately notified to this Government, that all Petitions for them or any part of them be sent Home, together with Copies of the French Grants for His Majesty's Royal consideration.

Several points of Enquiry will arise upon those Grants, concerning which the Committee chuse not to decide, on account of their singular Importance and Delicacy.

1st. Whether a Title, if good under the French Government will by the Surrender be valid by our Laws, without the Royal Confirmation; or in other Words whether the Capitulation gives more to the French Grantee, than an Equitable Right to be preferred before others in the Application for a new Grant?

2ndly. Whether those Lands were not forfeited to the Crown of France by the Conditions in the Grants before the Surrender, and so became thereby transferred to his Majesty? And

3rdly. Whether they were not within the antient British Claim and consequently never Grantable by the Crown of France?

And upon this last Question the Committee beg leave to remark that the British Claim of Dominion before the last War, extended to the Southerly Bank of the River St. Lawrence, and by Treaty to all the Country of the Six Nations in particular, of which the controverted Grants are a part, and we find that so early as the 3rd of September, 1696, a patent did pass to Godfrey Dellius, under the Seal of this Province, for Lands including some of those now claimed under the Canadian Grants, greatly to the Northward of Crown Point, of which the French were not possessed till nearly forty years afterwards, to wit about the year 1731, and whether it is imputable to the Consciousness in the French of their want of Title or to any other Cause, the Committee cant help observing to your Excellency that in Fact very few Settlements or Improvements were found upon any of those Canadian Grants, except about the French Forts at or since the Conclusion of the last Peace; the Country near Lake Champlain, but for the late Settlements under this Colony, being in general in a wild and uncultivated State.

And as it may be of essential Moment to the reduced Officers and soldiers and others who have seated themselves in that District that his Majesty be fully informed of the numerous Patents that have passed the Seal of this Colony since the acquisition of Canada, we recommend it to your Excellency to order the Surveyor General to frame a Map exhibiting the French Grants and English Patents to the Northward of Crown Point, to be laid before his Majesty with all convenient speed, with a List of the Patentees and an account of the Quantity of Land contained in their Patents and the Quitrents they are chargeable with. And for the security and satisfaction of the French Grantees, we also advise that in the Interim the several papers referred to us, be filed in the Secretary's Office, and a Copy of this Report and the Order to be made thereon transmitted to the Commander in Chief of Quebec. All which is nevertheless msot humbly submitted by your Excellency's

Most obedt humble servants,

By order of the Committee,

Wm SMITH, Chairman.

Council Chamber at
Fort George, in New York.
January 6th 1772.

And thereupon It is ordered by his Excellency the Governor with the advice of the Council, that the Surveyor General of this Province do frame a Map exhibiting the French Grants, and the Patents which have passed the seal of this Colony to the Northward of Crown Point, in order to be laid before his Majesty, with a List of the Patentees, and an account of the Quantity of land, contained in their Patents, and the Quit rents they are chargeable with. That the several papers referred to in the Report of the Committee be filed in the Secretary's office, and that a Copy of the said Report and of this Order be prepared in order to be transmitted to the Commander in Chief of Quebec.

GOVR TRYON TO LORD HILLSBOROUGH.

[Lond. Doc. XLIII.]

New York, 1. Septr. 1772.

My Lord—I have had the honor to receive your Lordship's dispatches Nos 11, 12 & 13.

It is a matter of real concern to me to learn the consideration of the Canada Claims has not undergone a final decision. Upon a more strict examination of the claims of the French grantees to lands within this Governt I cannot be persuaded that the last Treaty of peace, or the articles of the Capitulation at the surrender of Canada gives any valid title to such claims. The territory southwards of St. Lawrence River has been always acknowledged the property of the Five Nations, subjects or allies of Great Brittain, & as the French settlements, as well as grants within that district were made, not under the sanction of Cession, purchase or conquest, but by intrusion, the justice of the Title of those claimants seems to rest on His Majtys generosity which will operate no doubt as powerfully in the behalf of those Officers & Soldiers, who now hold a great part of those disputed lands under grants from this provce in consequence of His Majesty's proclamation in 1763.

LORD DARTMOUTH TO GOVR TRYON.

[Lond. Doc. XLIII.]

Whitehall 4 Novr 1772.

The State of the French Claims on Lake Champlain appears to me, as far as I am at present informed to be a consideration of great difficulty and delicacy, and by no means of a nature to admit of an hasty decision. Those Claims are now before the Board of Trade in consequence of a reference from the privy Council, and I will not fail from what you say of the State of the Colony, as well in respect to those Claims as to the increasing disorders & confusion on the Eastern Frontiers in general, to press an immediate attention to both these important considerations.

The whole of this very important business will, I am persuaded, be discussed by the Lords of Trade with that impartiality that has always distinguished their conduct; I shall therefore avoid saying any thing more upon that subject or upon the Canadian Claims further, than, that I think it proper to observe that the proposition in your letter N° 43, that all the territory on the south side of the River St. Lawrence was the property of the five Nations, and therefore that every Canadian Grant on that side of the River, was an encroachment on the British possessions, does not appear to me, from any information I have been able to collect, to be maintainable on any fair ground of argument; an observation which I think I am called upon to state to you, lest by my silence on that subject I should appear to acquiesce in a proposition that, if adopted in the extent you state it, would strip one half of the King's new subjects of their ancient possessions and must spread an alarm that may have very fatal consequences to the King's interest.

I am, etc.

DARTMOUTH.

MINUTE OF MR. EDMUND BURKE ATTENDING THE BOARD OF TRADE.

Thursday Nov[r] 12th 1772

At a meeting of His Majesty's Comm[rs] for Trade & Plantations Present, Mr Gascoyne, Lord Greville Lord Garlies; The Earl of Dartmouth, one of His Majesty's Principal Secretaries of State, attending

Mr. Edmund Burke attended & moved their Lordships that he might be heard by his Council, as well in behalf of the Province of New York as of sundry persons, Proprietors of Lands within the said Province, under grants from the Governor and Council thereof, against the confirmation by the Crown, of any grants made by the French King or the Government of Canada—within the limits of the said Province of New York.

Their Lordships upon consideration of M[r] Burke's motion, agreed that he should be heard by his Counsel, as he was desired, so soon as his Councel should be prepared, to acquaint the Secretary therewith, in order that an early day might be fixed for the further consideration of this business.

Ordered that the Secretary do acquaint Mons[r] Lotbiniere who now attends to solicit the Confirmation of two seigneuries on Lake Champlain, of which he claims the possession, with Mr. Burke's application to be heard by counsel, and that he will also be at liberty to be heard by his Counsel in support of his pretensions if he thinks fit.

GREVILLE.

GOV[R] TRYON TO LORD DARTMOUTH. EXTRACT.

New York 5 January 1773

The opinion I presumed to give your Lordship respecting the Canadian Claims, was grounded on the following facts, which if I am rightly informed are capable of satisfactory proof. I hope considering the importance of the subject, to be excused in submitting them to your Lord[pps] consideration.

The Dutch, who first settled this Colony, claimed the whole of Connecticut River and Lake Champlain, and all the Country to the Southward of the River St. Lawrence down to Delaware River; this appears from many ancient Maps, and particularly from Blair's and Ogilby's, which I have had an opportunity of seeing. In 1664, King Charles the Second granted this country to the Duke of York, expressly comprehending all the Lands from the west side of Connecticut River.

On a late actual survey by Commiss[rs] from this & Quebec Govern[t], the head of that River is found to lie several miles to the Northward of the Latitude of forty five degrees, lately established by his Majesty as the boundary between this Colony and Quebec.

A west line therefore from the head of Connecticut River (which will comprehend Lake Champlain) has been always deemed the ancient boundary of New York, according to the Royal Grant; nor has it been abridged but in two instances. His Maj[tys] proclamation limiting the extent of Quebec, and an agreement confirmed by the Crown with Connecticut. Every Act and Commission subsequent to King Charles's grant, describes the Province in General words—"The Province of New York and the territories depending thereupon" and supposes its limits to be notorious, & properly established by that grant. On this principle the Judicatories, here have grounded their determinations, in suits between the New York Patentees, and the N. Hampshire claimants. The original Colony of New Hampshire as it was granted by the Council of Plymouth, & confirmed by the Crown about the year 1635, lay altogether on the East side of Connecticut River, which it did not reach by 20 miles. As it was new modelled & enlarged by the Commission to Govr Benning Wentworth in 1742, no distance from the sea, or station is given: but it is, bounded to the west by the King's other Govern^s and could not comprehend the Lands on the west side of the Connecticut River which were already a part of New York, as established by the Grant of the Crown abovementioned. Hence on the footing of original Right, our Courts determined, that the New Hampshire Grants were void for want of a legal authority in that Govern^t. They considered his Maj^{ys} order in Privy Council in 1764, as a confirmation of a prior Right, & not as having altered or enlarged the ancient Jurisdiction.

I am now cautious to give an opinion on the propriety of this decision, but barely mention the principles as they have been represented to me for your Lordp's information.

Whether the Dominions of the French in Canada interfered with the bounds of this Colony as anciently established by King Charles the Second, remains to be considered. All the Country to the Southward of the River St. Lawrence originally belonged to the five Nations or Iroquois, and as such, it is described in the above mentioned and other ancient Maps, & particularly Lake Champlain is there called "*Mere des Iroquois*," Sorel River which leads from the Lake into the River St. Lawrence "*Rivier des Iroquois*," and the Tract on the East side of the Lake, Irocoisia.

So early as the year 1683, the Five Nations by Treaty with the Govr of New York, submitted to the Sovereignty & protection of Great Brittain, and have ever since been considered as subjects, & their Country as part of the dominions of the Crown.

By the Treaty of Utrecht, the French King expressly recognized the Sovereignty of Great Brittain over those Nations.

Godfrey Dellius's purchase from the Mohocks, & grant under the Seal of New York in the year 1696, is esteemed a memorable proof of the Right of this Province, under the Crown, to the Lands on Lake Champlain. It comprehends a large Tract extending from Soraghtoga along Hudson's River, the Wood Creek, & Lake Champlain, on the East side upwards of twenty miles, to the northward of Crown Point; & it is thought a circumstance of no small importance, that this Grant was repealed by the Legislature in the year 1699, as an extravagant favour to one subject; which act would have been a nullity if that territory had not been within the jurisdiction of this Province.

Altho' the Canadians by their Savage depredations had long obstructed the settlement of this Frontier part of the Colony, it was not till the year 1731, that, in profound peace, they took possession of Lake Champlain & ordered Fort St. Frederick at Crown [point]; & afterwards another Fort at Ticonderoga. This was regarded as an act of hostility, and as such complained of & resented; and the Colonies before the late war, to disappoint so dangerous a project, raised money and Troops to erect Fortifications on His Majesty's lands, at, or near Crown Point. The operations became more general, and the success of His Maj^{tys} arms, rendered it unnecessary.

The French had endeavored to fortify their encroachments by Negociations; in 1756 their Ambassador insisted as a condition of the Convention then proposed that Great Brittain should relinquish her claim to the south side of the River St. Lawrence, and the lakes which discharge themselves into that River; a demand which was peremptorily rejected, and put an end to the conference. I depend, My Lord on Entiv's history of the late war for the truth of this Fact. If it is well founded, it seems to show in a strong point of light the sense of the Crown at that Crisis, respecting the territory under consideration.

If it was necessary, My Lord, to add prior instances of the encroachments of the Canadians, I would beg leave to refer yonr Lord^p to Governor Burnet's Speeches to the General Assembly of this Province in 1725, 1726 & 1727, and the resolutions of that house, stated in their Journals, deposited in the Plantation Office, on the subject of those encroachments. That Govr in his speech of the 30th Septr 1727, has these remarkable words: "I have the satisfaction to inform you, that your Agent has been very active in sollicitiug the affairs of this Prov^ce, and particularly that he has succeeded in obtaining, that pressing instances might be made at the Court of France, against the Stone House built at Niagara," ettc. This shows that the Govern^t at home so early as that period viewed this measure of the French as an encroachment on the limits of this Colony.

I assure your Lord^p that I had no idea that the decision of this controversy could affect the ancient possessions of any of his Mat^ys new subjects. Unacquainted with their settlements on, and near the south side of the River St. Lawrence, I carried my views no further than the Province over which I preside: and which, as it is now limited does not include the whole of Lake Champlain.

I have frequently been informed, by those on whom I thought I could depend, that when the French, on the approach of Sir Jeffry Amherst in 1759, abandoned Crown Point, there were found no ancient possessions, nor any improvements, worthy of consideration on either side of the Lake. The Chief were in the environs of the Fort, and seemed intended meerly for the accommodation of the Garrisons, and I have reason to believe, that even at this day, there are very few, if any, to the Southward of the latitude forty five, except what have been made since the peace, by British subjects under the grants of this Colony. I had the honor of transmitting to the Earl of Hillsborough a paper on this subject drawn up by Council here, at the request of the reduced officers, to whom & the disbanded Soldiers a very considerable part of the Country on the East side of Lake Champlain, hath been granted in obedience to his Maj^tys Royal proclamation. The proof of several material facts, which influenced my opinion, are there stated, and to which I beg leave to refer your Lord^p.

LORD DARTMOUTH TO GOV^R. TRYON.

Whitehall 3 March 1773

With regard to the grants heretofore made by the Governors of Canada adjacent to Lake Champlain, and by the Govr of New Hampshire to the west of Connecticut River, I do not conceive that the titles of the present claimants or possessors ought to have been discussed or determined upon any argument or reason drawn from a consideration of what were or were not the ancient Limits of the Colony of New York. Had the soil and jurisdiction within the Prov^ce of New York been vested in proprietaries as in Maryland, Pennsylvania, Massachusets Bay, or other Charter Govern^s it would have been a different question: but when both the soil and jurisdiction are in the Crown, it is I conceive, entirely in the breast of the Crown, to limit that jurisdiction and to dispose of the property in the soil in such manner as shall be thought most fit: and after what had passed, and the restrictions which had been given respecting the claims, as well on Lake Champlain, as in the district to the westward of the Connecticut River, by which the King had reserved to himself the consideration of those claims, I must still have the misfortune to think that no steps ought to have been taken to the prejudice of the claimants under the original Titles. At the same time confident of your integrity and impressed with the most favorable sentiments of your conduct, so far as rests upon the Intention, I will not fail to do the fullest justice to the explanation of it, contained in your letters upon this subject, and there is no one of your friends, that will be more forward than myself to bear testimony of the sense of your zeal for the King's service, or more ready to concur in any proposition, that may induce the conferring on you such marks of the King's Favor, as shall be judged adequate to your great merit.

I am Sir your most obed^t humble serv^t

DARTMOUTH.

EDMUND BURKE ESQ[R]

TO THE SECRETARY—15 JUNE 1773.

Sir—I am honoured with your letter of the 14th wishing to be informed, on whose behalf, and on what question, I desire to have Counsel heard against the Canadian Grants on Lake Champlain. You will be so good as to acquaint their Lordpps that I would have Counsel heard on behalf of the grantees under New York Governt who are composed in a great measure of half-pay Officers, that have received grants, agreeably to his Majesty's proclamation. And I am instructed to take care of the interests of these Grantees, not only so far as they are concerned, but also so far as the territorial rights of the Province may be affected by the French claims.

I beg leave to be heard by Counsel (if their Lordpps should not expressly confine the Counsel) to all such matters, as they, or the parties shall advise as proper and effectual towards invalidating the said French Grants, and establishing the rights of the New York Grantees.

I am with great regard Sir

Your most obedt and humble servt

EDM: BURKE.

EXTRACT FROM A REPORT

OF A COMMITTEE OF COUNCIL OF THE PROVINCE OF QUEBEC RELATIVE TO COMPLETING THE BOUNDARY LINE BETWEEN THAT PROVINCE AND NEW YORK, DATED QUEBEC, AUGt 4, 1773.

[Council Minutes XXVI.]

We think . . . Your Honour may safely give the necessary Directions for going on with the service immediatly under the following Reservations, which we consider as the only expedient for Resolving the many Difficulties which have occurred, and without which we must find ourselves under the necessity of deferring the Proceedings till another year.

That every thing shall remain between the two Provinces exactly in the same situation as well with regard to Jurisdiction as Property after the Line is run, as it does now until his Majesty's Pleasure upon that subject shall be known.

That his Excellency the Governor of New York will engage not to pass any new Grant or Grants of Land to the southward of the Line, the property of which is now or has at any Time been claimed under any Title from the Crown of France.

That we do not by our Consent to the running of the Line give up or in any manner recede or depart from any Right or Claim to Lands to the Southward of the Line which have at any time been or now are disputed between the two Provinces, but that the whole shall be submitted to his Majesty's Pleasure without Prejudice or advantage of any kind to be taken of this Instance, which we are willing to show, tho' at some Hazard, of our Desire of a good Correspondence at all times with the Province of New York.

GOV. TRYON TO LT. GOV. CRAMAHE.

Quebec 4th August 1773.

Sir, I am honoured with your Letter of this Day with the Report of the Council of your Government on the subject Matter of my Letters to you of the 5th and 25th July.

It is with singular pleasure I can inform you I accept of and assent to the Terms contained in the Reservations of the said Report; at the same time I assure you it never has been nor is my Wish or Design to take any Advantage either over the Jurisdiction of the Government of Quebec, or of French claims lying within the Government of New York; but am determined to wait the declaration of the Royal Mind concerning the Premises; I own I do not apprehend Hazard in paying Obedience to the King's Proclamation of 1763, and carrying into execution the reciprocal obligations of both governments.

THE BOARD OF TRADE TO THE COMMITTEE OF THE PRIVY COUNCIL. 25 MAY, 1775.

[Lond. Doc. XLV.]

My Lords; Pursuant to your Lordships order dated the 17th day of June 1772, we have taken into our consideration the Petition of Michel Chartier de Lotbiniere, Chevalier and styling himself Seigneur de Alainville and d'Hocquart, setting forth amongst other things that he has been deprived and dispossessed of his two Lordships of d'Alainville and d'Hocquart situated at the head of Lake Champlain in a most advantageous position and consisting of the best and richest land in the Province of New York to which they were annexed eighteen months after the Treaty of Peace and humbly praying for the reasons therein contained that they [he ?] may be reinstated in the full enjoyment of his said two Lordships in the same manner as when under the Government of France and that he may be reimbursed the expense he has been at in endeavoring to obtain redress therein and to be indemnified for having been kept out of his Estate and property for so long a time as well as for the damage his said Estates may have sustained. Whereupon we beg leave to Report to your Lordships:—

That the Petition of Monsr de Lotbiniere refers to two Tracts of Land under very different circumstances.

With regard to that Tract which is claimed by the Petitioner under a Title derived from a purchase made by him of Monsr d'Hocquart in April 1763 after the conclusion of the Peace with France, it consists of two Seigneuries which amongst several other Seigneuries were granted by the Most Christian King, or under his authority by the Governor of Canada upon Lake Champlain after France had in violation of the Rights of the Crown of Great Britain usurped the possession of the lake and the circumjacent Country and forcibly maintained that possession by erecting in the year 1731 a Fortress at Crown Point.

It appears by the most authentic evidence upon the Books of our office that Lake Champlain and the circumjacent Country were at all times claimed by the Five Nations of Indians as part of their Possessions and that by agreement with them the Land on both sides the Lake to a very great extent was granted by the Govrs of New York to British Subjects long before any possession appears to have been taken by the Crown of France which having by the express Stipulation of the fifteenth

Article of the Treaty of Utrecht acknowledged the Sovereignty of the Crown of Great Britain over the Five Nations had upon every principle of Justice and Equity precluded itself from any claim to the possession of any part of their Territory.

Upon these Grounds it was that erecting a Fort at Crown Point in 1731 was then, and ever after complained of as an Incroachment on the British Territories and a violation of Our Rights and so carefull were the Ministers of this Country to preserve those Rights that when in consequence of the Treaty of Aix la Chapelle Commissaries were in the Year 1750 appointed to settle with Commissaries on the part of France the limits of each others possessions in North America, they were instructed to insist that France had no right to any possession on the South side of the River St. Lawrence.

Under these circumstances therefore and for as much as we are clearly of opinion that the Stipulations of the Treaty of Paris, by which Canadian property is reserved doth both in the letter and spirit of them refer only to the property and possession of the Canadians in Canada of which we insist that the Country upon Lake Champlain was no part. we cannot recommend to Your Lordships to advise his Majesty to Comply with what is requested by the Petitioner or to do any Act which may in any respect admit a right in the Crown of France to have made those Grants under which the possessions upon Lake Champlain are now claimed either by Canadian Subjects or others deriving that Claim under purchases from them : We do not, however, mean by any opinion of Ours to prejudice their Claims in any suit they may bring for establishing those claims by due course of Law and we submit under any circumstances of the Case the question in dispute between these Claimants and the possessors under New York Grants cannot be properly decided by his Majesty in Council, unless upon any appeal from such Courts as have constitutionally the cognizance of such matters.

On the other hand when we consider that many of his Majesty's subjects trusting to the validity of the Canadian Titles have become proprietors of those Seigneuries under purchases for valuable considerations We cannot but be of opinion that the making Grants under the Seal of New York of any part of those Seigniories was an unjust and unwarrantable proceeding, That the claimants therefore ought to be quieted in the possession of at least those parts which remain yet ungranted by such order as his Majesty's Law Servants shall think more effectual for that purpose that the Governor of New York should receive the most positive orders not to make any further Grants whatever of any part of the Lands within the limits of any of those Seigneuries and that a suitable compensation should be made to the Claimants for what has already been taken away by giving them gratuitous Grants, equivalent in quantity, in other parts of his Majesty's Provinces of Quebec or New York.

With regard to the other Tract claimed by the petitioner under the description of the concession of d'Alainville, when we consider its situation to the South of Crown Point, that it is stated to have been Granted to him at a time when his Majesty's armies had penetrated intc, and occasionally possessed themselves of the Country and that independent of these objections there is no evidence of the Grants having been ratified by the Crown of France, or registered within the Colony, we cannot recommend to Your Lordships to advise His Majesty to give any countenance thereto; But the Petitioner, if he thinks he has a good title, should be left to establish that Title by due course of law in such mode as he shall be advised to pursue for that purpose.

Having said thus much upon the merits of the Petition itself, in so far as it regards the validity of the Petitioner's title to the Lands he claims we think it necessary in Justice to the Noble Lord, that presided at this Board in the year 1764 to take some notice of what is alledged therein, in respect to the declaration said to have been made by his Lordship to the effect of what is stated by the petitioner; and to observe that admitting that his Lordship had, in conversation with the petitioner made use of the expressions he states, they could only refer to possessions and property in general any where, to which he could shew a legal title; and as an evidence of this meaning we beg leave to lay before your Lordships the annexed Extract of a Letter to the Lieutenant Governor of New York written in consequence of the petitioners application and subscribed by the Earl of Hillsborough which is so far from admitting a Title in the petitioner to those Lands which he claims in particular that it expressly reserves any discussion upon that question until the evidence of the legality of the Title should be more authentically adduced and in the mean time with equal Justice & humanity forbids any further Grants being made within the limits of the Seigneuries claimed by the Petitioner.

We are my Lords
Your Lordships Most Obedient and
Most humble Servants
DARTMOUTH
SOAME JENYNS
BAMBER GASCOYNE
WHITSHED KEENE
GREVILLE

Whitehall
May 25. 1775.

THE BOARD OF TRADE TO THE COMMITTEE OF THE PRIVY COUNCIL FEB. 13TH 1776.

[Lond. Doc. XLVI.]

My Lords—Pursuant to your Lordships Order of the 21st. Dec. last We have taken into our consideration the Matters therein contained respecting the case of Michel Chartiere de Lotbiniere stiling himself Signeur d'Alainville and de Hocquart and the reasonableness of making some adequate compensation to him for his pretensions to the said Lordships of Alainville and de Hocquart by recommending him to His Majesty for a grant of Land in some one of his Majesty's American Provinces in consideration of his said pretensions as well as of the losses and expenses in which he has been involved by the proceedings of His Majesty's Governors of New York in Granting away Lands within the aforementioned Lordships in express disobedience to orders received from hence whereupon we beg leave to Report to your Lordships.

That before we state Our opinion of what may be a reasonable compensation to M. Lotbiniere in the matter referred We must observe that although his claims extend to both the Lordships of Alainville and Hocquart yet upon a review of our proceeding in his Case we cannot for the reasons set forth in Our report to your Lordships of the 25th of May last see any such foundation in his pretensions to Alainville as can warrant the advising any compensation whatever to be made to him for his interest in that Lordship so that whatever we have to recommend will be grounded solely on his claim to the Lordship of Hocquart and the consideration of the losses and expenses in which [he] has been involved by the proceedings of the Governor of New York.

The Lordship of Hocquart is described as lying on the East side of Lake Champlain extending four leagues in front and five leagues in Depth and may be computed to contain about 115,000 acres of Land.

By the proceedings of the Council of New York on the 2nd day of Septr. 1771 it appears that almost the whole of this Lordship was granted away under the Seal of New York principally to officers and soldiers according to His Majesty's proclamation of the 7th Oct. 1773 [1763 ?]

As the greatest part therefore and probably the best in quality of those lands has been thus granted away we think that the most equitable way of making compensation to M. Lotbiniere will [be] for his Majesty to direct the Governor of Quebec to make a new Grant to M. Lotbiniere of other Lands within that Colony equivalent as nearly as may be in point of extent and in the advantages of Soil and Situation to that of Hocquart to be held upon the like terms and considerations as Lands are now held by his Majesty's other Canadian Subjects; provided that upon his being put in possession of this Grant he shall cause a full and ample surrender to be made of all his right and title to the aforesaid Lordship of Hocquart so that the present occupants who chiefly consist of Officers and Soldiers disbanded at the conclusion of the last war may be quieted & secured in their possessions.

At the same time that we state this as what we think will be a liberal compensation to M. Lotbiniere, we should have been glad to have informed your Lordships that he had acquiesced in the same sentiments but as he has declined giving his attendance at Our Board though invited thereto we submit the whole to your Lordships with this observation that if M. Lotbiniere shall not think proper to accept the proposed compensation it will then remain for him to pursue his claim or Claims by due Course of Law in such manner as he shall be advised.

We are my Lords your Lordships

Most obedient and humble servants

SOAME JENYNS
W. JALLIFFE
WHITSHED KEENE
C. F. GREVILLE.

WHITEHALL Feb. 13, 1776

XX.

Boundary Line Between the Whites and Indians.

1765.

DEED EXECUTED AT FORT STANWIX NOV. 5. 1768.

ESTABLISHING A BOUNDARY LINE BETWEEN THE WHITES AND INDIANS, OF THE NORTHERN COLONIES.

[Lond. Doc. XLI.]

To all to whom, These presents shall come or may concern. We the Sachems & Chiefs of the Six Confederate Nations, & of the Shawaneese, Delawares, Mingoes of Ohio & other Dependant Tribes on behalf of ourselves & of the rest of our Several Nations the Chiefs & Warriors of whom are now here convened, by Sir William Johnson Baronet His Majesty's Superintendent of our affairs send Greeting. Whereas His Majesty was graciously pleased to propose to us in the year one thousand seven hundred & sixty five that a Boundary Line should be fixed between the English and Us to ascertain & establish our Limitts and prevent those intrusions & encroachments of which we had so long and loudly complained & to put a stop to the many fraudulent advantages which had been so often taken of us in Land affairs, which Boundary appearing to us a wise and good measure we did then agree to a part of a line & promised to settle the whole finally when so ever Sir William Johnson should be fully empowered to treat with us for that purpose. And Whereas his said Majesty has at length given Sir William Johnson orders to compleat the said Boundary Line between the Provinces and Indians in conformity to which orders Sir William Johnson has convened the Chiefs and Warriors of our respective Nations who are the true & absolute Proprietors of the Lands in question and who are here now to a very considerable Number. And Whereas many uneasynesses & doubts have arisen amongst us which have given rise to an apprehension that the Line may not be strictly observed on the part of the English in which case matters may be worse than before which apprehension together with the dependant state of some of our Tribes & other circumstances which retarded the Settlement & became the subject of some Debate Sir William Johnson has at length so far satisfied us upon, as to induce us to come to an agreement concerning the Line which is now brought to a conclusion the whole being fully explained to us in a large Assembly of our People before Sir William Johnson and in the presence of His Excellency the Governor of New Jersey the Commissioners from the Provinces of Virginia and Pensilvania & sundry other Gentlemen by which Line so agreed upon, a considerable Tract of Country along several Provinces is by us ceded to His said Majesty which we are induced to & do hereby ratify and confirm to His said Majesty from the expectation and confidence we place in His royal Goodness that he will graciously comply with our humble requests as the same are expressed in the speech of the several Nations addressed to His Majesty through Sir William Johnson on Tuesday the first of the Present Month of November wherein we have declared our expectation of the continuance of His Majesty's favour & our desire that our ancient Engagements be observed & our affairs attended to by the officer who has the management thereof enabling him to discharge all these matters properly for our Interest. That the Lands occupied by the Mohocks around their villages as well as by any other Nation affected by this our cession may effectually remain to them & to their Posterity & that any engagements regarding property which they may now be under may be prosecuted & our present Grants deemed Valid on our parts with the several other humble requests contained in our said speech And Whereas at the settling of the said Line it appeared that the Line described by His Majesty's order was not extended to the Northward of Oswegy or to the

Southward of Great Kanhawa river We have agreed to & continued the Line to the Northward on a supposition that it was omitted by reason of our not having come to any determination concerning its course at the Congress held in one thousand seven hundred & sixty five and in as much as the Line to the Northward became the most necessary of any for preventing encroachments at our very Towns & Residences We have given the line more favorably to Pensylvania for the reasons & considerations mentioned in the Treaty, we have likewise continued it South to Cherokee River because the same is & we do declare it to be our true Bounds with the Southern Indians & that we have an undoubted right to the Country as far South as that River which makes the cession to His Majesty much more advantageous than that proposed. Now therefore Know Ye that we the Sachems & Chiefs aforementioned Native Indians or Proprietors of the Lands herein after described for & in behalf of ourselves & the whole of our Confederacy for the considerations hereinbefore mentioned and also for and in consideration of a valuable Present of the several Articles in use amongst Indians which together with a large sum of money amount in the whole to the sum of Ten thousand four Hundred and sixty pounds seven shillings & three pence sterling to Us now delivered & paid by Sir William Johnson Baronet His Majesty's sole agent and superintendent of Indian affairs for the Northern department of America in the name and on behalf of our Sovereign Lord George the third by the Grace of God of Great Britain France & Ireland King Defender of the Faith the receipt whereof we do hereby acknowledge. We the said Indians HAVE for us and our Heirs & Successors granted bargained sold released & confirmed & by these presents DO grant bargain sell release and confirm unto our said Sovereign Lord King George the Third ALL that Tract of Land situate in North America at the Back of the British Settlements bounded by a Line which we have now agreed upon & do hereby establish as the Boundary between us & the British Colonies in America beginning at the mouth of Cherokee or Hogohege River where it emptys into the River Ohio & running from thence upwards along the South side of said River to Kittanning which is above Fort Pitt from thence by a direct Line to the nearest Fork of the west branch of Susquehanna thence through the Allegany Mountains along the south side of the said West Branch until it comes opposite to the mouth of a creek called Tiadaghton thence across the West Branch along the South Side of that Creek & along the North Side of Burnetts Hills to a Creek called Awandae thence down the same to the East Branch of Sasquehanna & across the same and up the East side of that River to Oswegy from thence East to Delawar River and up that River to opposite where Tianaderha falls into Sasquehanna thence to Tianaderha & up the West side of the West Branch to the head thereof & thence by a direct Line to Canada Creek where it emptys into the Wood Creek at the West of the Carrying Place beyond Fort Stanwix & extending Eastward from every part of the said Line as far as the Lands formerly purchased so as to comprehend the whole of the Lands between the said Line & the purchased Lands or settlements, except what is within the Province of Pennsylvania, together with all the Hereditaments and appurtenances to the same belonging or appertaining in the fullest and most ample manner and all the Estate Right Title Interest Property Possession Benefit claim and Demand either in Law or Equity of each and every of us of in or to the same or any part thereof To HAVE AND TO HOLD the whole Lands and Premises hereby granted bargained sold released and confirmed as aforesaid with the Hereditaments and appurtenances thereunto belonging under the Reservations made in the Treaty unto our said Sovereign Lord King George the Third his Heirs & Successors to and for his and their own proper use & behoof for ever. IN WITNESS whereof We the Chiefs of the Confederacy have hereunto set our marks and Seals at Fort Stanwix the fifth day of November one thousand seven hundred and sixty eight in the ninth year of His Majesty's Reign.

By the Mohawks.

Tyorhansere als Abraham  [L S] for the Oneidas.

Canaghaguiesan [L S]

for the Tuscaroras.

Seguareesera. + [L S]

for the Onondagas.

Otsinoghiyata als Bunt [L S]

for the Cayugas.

Tegaaia [L S]

for the Senecas.

Gaustrax [L S]

Sealed and delivered and the consideration paid in the presence of

Wm Franklin Governor of New Jersey
Fre. Smyth Chief Justice of New Jersey
Thomas Walker Commissioner for Virginia
Richard Peters } of the Council
James Tilghman } of Pensylvania

The above Deed was executed in my presence at Fort Stanwix the day and year above Written

W. Johnson.

XXI.

PAPERS

RELATING TO

The City of New-York.

FIRST APPLICATION FOR A MUNICIPAL FORM OF GOVERNMENT.

[Holland Doc. Vol. IV.]

To the Noble, High and Mighty Lords
the Lords States General of the United Netherlands,
our Most Illustrious Sovereigns.

GRACIOUS LORDS,—This Province of New Netherland having been reduced, in the course of time to a very sad and utterly ruinous condition, in consequence, as we presume, of firstly, An unsuitable government; secondly, Scantiness of privileges and exemptions; thirdly, Heavy burthens of imposts, exactions and such like; fourthly, Long continued war; fifthly, The wreck of the Princess; sixthly, The multitude of Traders and fewness of Boors and farm servants; seventhly, Great scarcity in general; eightly and lastly, The insufferable arrogance of the Natives and Indians arising from the paucity of our numbers etc. and having long waited in vain, though we have petitioned and sought for aid redress and assistance from the Lords Directors, in the highest degree necessary for them and for us; We, therefore, unable to delay any longer, being reduced to the lowest ebb, have determined to fly for refuge to their High Mightinesses, our gracious Sovereigns and the Fathers of this Province, most humbly praying and beseeching them to look with merciful eyes on this their Province and that their High Mightinesses would be pleased to order and correct matters so that dangers may be removed, troubles terminated, and population and prosperity promoted, as their High Mightinesses in their renowned wisdom shall be determined, We, with humble reverence only deeming it good and necessary to petition their High Mightinesses for the following Points as of advantage for this Province:—

Firstly, We supplicate and beseech their High Mightinesses to people New Netherland so that it may support sustain and defend itself against Indians and others who might trouble and invade it; for if this should fail, that country will not only fall into the uttermost ruin, but also become easily appropriated by our Neighbors; and those who already dwell there will be forced to use all possible means to return and save themselves from misery, or to submit to foreign Nations. All which, according to our humble understanding, is to be remedied

1st. When their High Mightinesses shall be pleased to take this Province under their own gracious safeguard, and to allow their Fatherly affection for this Land to be promulgated and made manifest, throughout the United Netherlands, by their own accorded privileges. Many would, then, be attracted towards this country, whilst, on the contrary every one is discouraged by the Company's harsh proceedings and want of means.

2nd. Were their High Mightinesses pleased to equip some ships for a few years, for the free conveyance and transportation of people principally Boors and farm servants with their poverty hither, together with some necessary maintenance until the poor people had obtained something *in esse*, their High Mightinesses would not only relieve many incumbered men, but also expect from God, through their intercession, luck, blessing and prosperity.

3rd. If their High Mightinesses would please to order all vessels proceeding and trading toward these northern parts of America, to call first at tne Manhattans in New Netherland, and bring with them as many persons as they can seasonably procure and conveniently carry, at suitably fixed rates, many proprietors would, no doubt, emigrate within a short time to New Netherland.

Secondly, We humbly solicit permanent privileges and exemptions which promote population and prosperity & which in our opinion consist in

1st. Suitable BURGHER Government, such as their High Mightinesses shall consider adapted to this Province and resembling somewhat the Laudable government of our Fatherland.

2nd. Freedom from duties, tenths and imposts which at the first beginning are useless and oppressive, until the country is peopled and somewhat firmly established.

3rd. That the Returns in Tobacco shipped hence, be free from all duties, which would not only afford great encouragement to the planters who convert the forest into farms but be better also for their servants who could thus be accommodated with all sorts of necessaries.

4th. Also, permission to export, sell, & barter grain, timber work, and all other wares and merchandize the produce of the country every way and every where their High Mightinesses have allies and have granted to the Netherlanders the privilege of resort and trade.

5th. That their High Mightinesses would be pleased to accord privileges and freedoms for the encouragement of the inhabitants in favor of the fisheries, which many suppose were good and profitable heretofore, and would hereafter be of great consequence.

Thirdly, We humbly beseech their High Mightinesses to be pleased to determine and so to establish and order the Boundaries of this Province, that all causes of difference, disunion and trouble may be cut off and prevented; that their High Mightinesses subjects may live and dwell in peace and quietness, and enjoy their liberty as well in trade and commerce as in intercourse and settled limits. 2d. That their High Mightinesses would be pleased to preserve us in peace with the neighbouring Republics, Colonies and others their High Mightinesses allies, so that we may pursue without let or hindrance, under proper regulations from their High Mightinesses, the trade of our country as well along the coast from Terra Nova to Cape Florida as to the West Indies and to Europe whenever our Lord GOD shall be pleased to permit; and 3d. to make manifest to the incredulous their High Mightinesses earnest support of this Province, we respcctfully request that their H. M. would be pleased to quarter here a company or two of soldiers, for the defence of those residing at a distance and the establishment of New Plantations and Colonies, until by our progress, we shall dread neither Indians or other enemies, but even shall be able to prevent their mischievous designs.

All this have we concluded with humble reverence to propose according to our limited knowledge and understanding, earnestly supplicating their High Mightinesses, for the love of New Netherland which now lies at its extremity, as is to be seen at length in our annexed Remonstrance, to be pleased to direct their attention thereto according to their wise and provident council, and to interpret most favorably this our presumption.

We pray and hope that the name of New Netherland and the conversion of the Heathen which ought to be hastened, shall move their H. M. hereunto. Expecting, therefore, a happy deliverance we commend their H. M's persons and deliberations to the protection of the Almighty, and remain their H. M's humble and obedient servants. Written in the name and on the behalf of the Commonalty of New Netherland, the Six and Twentieth of July, in the Year of Our Lord JESUS CHRIST, One Thousand, Six hundred, Nine & Forty, in New Amsterdam on the Island Manhattans in New Netherland. (Signed,)

ADRIAEN VAN DER DONCK,	OLOFF STEVENS,
AUGUSTIN HERMAN,	MICHAEL JANSEN,
ARNOLDUS VAN HARDENBERCH,	THOMAS HALL,
JACOB VAN COUWENHOVEN,	ELBERT ELBERTZEN,
GOVERT LOOCKERMANS,	JAN EVERTSEN BOUT,

HENDRICK HENDRICKSEN KIP.

PROVISIONAL ORDER

FOR THE GOVERNMENT, PRESERVATION AND PEOPLING OF NEW NETHERLAND. ANNO. 1650.—[*Extract.*]

[Holland Doc. V.]

Art. X. The request for freedoms and exemptions shall be more fully examined, together with the considerations moved thereupon.

XVII. And within the city of New Amsterdam shall be erected a BURGHER Government, consisting of a Sheriff, two Burgomasters, and five Schepens.

XVIII. In the meanwhile shall the Nine men continue for three years longer, and have Jurisdiction over Small Causes arising between Man and Man, to decide definitely such as do not exceed the sum of Fifty Guilders, and on higher, with the privilege of appeal.[1]

THE DIRECTORS OF THE WEST INDIA COMPANY

TO THE DIRECTOR AND COUNCIL OF NEW NETHERLAND; DATED AMSTERDAM, THE 4th APRIL 1652.

[Dutch Records, Letter Q. 1648—1664.]

" We have already connived as much as possible at the many Impertinences of some Restless spirits in the hope that they might be shamed at our discreetness and benevolence, but perceiving that all Kindnesses do not avail, we must, therefore, have recourse to God, to Nature and the Law. We accordingly hereby charge and command your Honors, whenever you shall certainly discover any Clandestine Meetings, Conventicles or machinations against our States' government or that of our Country, that you proceed against such malignants in proportion to their crimes, with this precaution however, that we in no wise require that any one should have it in his power to complain, with reason or cause, that he was injured through private malice, which is far from our intention.

" We remark in many Representations, though of Malversants that some hide themselves under this cloak, though we must believe and even see, that they have not, in reality, so suffered ; yet to stop the mouth of all the world, we have resolved, on your Honors' proposition, to permit you hereby, to erect there a Court of Justice (*een banck van Justitie*) formed, as much as possible, after the custom of this City : to which end printed copies relative to all the Law Courts and their whole government are sent herewith. And we presume that it will be sufficient at first to choose one Sheriff,[2] two Burgomasters and five Schepens, from all of whose judgments an appeal shall lie to the Supreme Council, where definite judgment shall be decreed.

" In the Election of the aforesaid persons every attention must be paid to honest and respectable individuals who we hope can be found among the Burghers ; and especially do we wish that those promoted thereto be, as much as possible, persons of this Nation, who we suppose will give the most satisfaction to the Burghers and Inhabitants.

1 The above " order " will be found entire in O'Callaghans Hist. of N. Netherland, Vol. 2. p. 132, but so much of it only is given here as applies to the first establishment of a Municipal form of government, in the present city of New York.

2 In a Duplicate of the above Despatch, the words " een Schout " (a Sheriff,) are crossed over with ink, tho' not of the same color as that in which the original was written. New Amsterdam did not have a City Sheriff until 1660.

INSTRUCTION FOR THE SHERIFF OF NEW AMSTERDAM

[Dutch Records; Letter V. 1652—1663.]

1. In the first place, the Sheriff shall, as the Director General and Council's guardian of the law in the district of the city of New Amsterdam, preserve, protect and maintain to the best of his knowledge and ability, the preëminences and immunities of the privileged West India Company, in as far as these have been delegated by previous Instruction to the Board of Burgomasters and Schepens; without any dissimulation, or regard for any private favor or displeasure.

2. In the quality aforesaid, he shall convoke the meetings of Burgomasters and Schepens and preside thereat, also propose all matters which shall be brought there for deliberation, collect the Votes, and resolve according to the plurality thereof.

3. He shall, ex officio, prosecute all contraveners, defrauders and transgressors, of any Placards, Laws, Statutes and Ordinances which are already made and published or shall hereafter be enacted and made public, as far as those are amenable before the Court of Burgomasters and Schepens, and with this understanding that, having entered his suit against the aforesaid Contraveners, he shall immediately rise, and await the judgment of Burgomasters and Schepens who being prepared shall also, on his motion, pronounce the same.

4. And in order that he may well and regularly institute his complaint, the Sheriff, before entering his action or arresting any person, shall pertinently inform himself of the crime of which he shall accuse him, without his being empowered to arrest any one, on the aforesaid information, unless the offence be committed in his presence.

5. He shall take all his information in the presence of two members of the Board of Burgomasters and Schepens if the case shall permit it, or otherwise in the presence of two discreet persons who, with the Secretary or his deputy shall sign the aforesaid informations.

6. Which aforesaid Secretary with the Court Messenger are expressly commanded to assist and be serving unto the Sheriff in whatever relates to their respective offices.

7. He shall take care in collecting and preparing informations to act impartially, and to bring the truth as clear and naked as possible to light, noting to that end, all circumstances which in any way deserve consideration, and appertain to the case.

8. Item. The aforesaid Sheriff, on learning or being informed that any persons have injured each other or quarrelled, shall have power to command the said individuals, either personally or by the court messenger, or his deputy to observe the peace, and to forbid them committing any assault, on pain of arbitrary correction at the discretion of the Burgomasters and Schepens.

9. He shall not have power to compound with any person for their committed offences except with the knowledge of the Burgomasters and Schepens.

10. He shall take care that all Judgments pronounced by the Burgomasters and Schepens, and which are not appealed from, shall be executed conformably to the above mentioned Instruction given to the same, according to the stile and custom of Fatherland and especially the city of Amsterdam.

11. In like manner, that authentic copies of all the Judgments Orders, Actes and Resolutions to be adopted by the aforesaid Burgomasters and Schepens shall be communicated once every year, to the Director General and Council of New Netherland.

12. And in case he receive any information or statement of any offences which from their nature, or on account of the offending person are not subject to his complaint, he shall be bound forthwith to communicate the same to the Fiscal (Attorney Genl) without taking any information himself, much less arresting the offender, unless in actual aggression to prevent greater mischief, or hinder flight in consequence of the enormity of the crime.

13. Which being done, he shall, as before, surrender without any delay the apprehended person with the information taken to the Fiscal, to be proceeded against by him in due form as circumstances demand.

14. In order that the aforesaid Sheriff shall be the more encouraged hereunto, he shall enjoy &c. This must be fixed in the country yonder, with advice.

15. Should the Sheriff violate any of these Articles he shall be prosecuted on the complaint of the Fiscal before the Director and Council, to be punished according to the nature of the case.

NICOLLS' CHARTER. 1665.

[Book of General Entries 1.]

The Governo^rs Revocation of ye fforme of Government of New Yorke und^r ye style of Burgomast^r & Schepens.

By virtue of his Maties Letters Pattents bearing date the 12th day of March in the 16th year of his Maties Reigne, Granted to His Royall Highnesse, James Duke of Yorke wherein full and absolute power is given and granted to his Royall Highnesse or his Deputyes to Constitute, appoint, revoke and discharge all Officers both Civill & military, as also to alter & change all Names and styles fformes or Ceremonyes of Governm^t: To the End that His Mat^ies Royall Pleasure may be observed & for the more Orderly establishment of his Maties Royall authority, as near as may bee Agreeable to the Lawes and Customes of his Maties Realme of England; upon mature deliberacion & advice, I have thought it necessary to Revoke & discharge, and by these P'sents in his Maties Name, do revoke and discharge the fforme and Ceremony of Government of this his Maties Towne of New Yorke, under the name or names, style or styles of Scout, Burgomasters & Schepens; As also, that for the future Administracon of Justice by the Lawes established in these the Territoryes of his Royall Highnesse wherein the welfares of all the Inhabitants and the Preservacon of all their due Rights and Privileges, Graunted by the Articles of this Towne upon Surrender under his Maties Obedience are concluded; I do further declare, That by a particular Commission, such persons shall be authorized to put the Lawes in Execucon, in whose abilityes prudence & good affection to his Maties Service and ye Peace and happiness of this Governm^t I have especial reason to put Confidence, which persons so constituted and appointed, shall be knowne and call'd by the Name & Style of Mayor Aldermen & Sherriffe, according to the Custome of England in other his Maties Corporacons: Given under my hand & Seale at ffort James in New Yorke, this 12th day of June 1665.

Richard Nicolls.

The Mayor and Aldermen's Commission.

Whereas upon mature deliberation and advice, I have found it necessary to discharge the fforme of Governm^t late in practice w^thin this his Maties Towne of New Yorke, under the name and style of Scout, Burgomasters and Schepens, which are not knowne or customary in any of his Maties Dominions; To the end that the course of Justice for the future may be legally, equally and impartially administered to all his Maties Subjects as well Inhabitants as Strangers; Know all Men by these

Presents, That I Richard Nicolls, Deputy Governr to his Royall Highnesse, the Duke of York, by virtue of his Matties Letters Pattents, bearing date the 12th day of March in ye 16th yeare of his Maties Reigne, Do ordaine, constitute and declare, that the Inhabitants of New Yorke, New Harlem, wth all other his Maties Subjects Inhabitants upon this Island, commonly called & knowne by the Name of the Manhattans Island, are and shall bee for ever accounted, nominated and established as one Body Politique and Corporate under the Governmt of a Mayor, Aldermen and Sheriffe, and I do by these P'sents constitute and appoint for one whole year, commencing from the date hereof, and ending the 12th day of June wch shall be in the yeare of our Lord 1666; Mr Thomas Willett to bee Mayor, Mr Thomas Delavall, Mr Oloffe Stuyvesant, Mr. John Brugges, Mr Cornelius Van Ruyven & Mr John Lawrence to bee Aldermen, & Mr Allard Anthony to be Sheriffe; Giving & Granting to them the said Mayor and Aldermen, or any four of them, whereof the said Mayor or his Deputy, shall bee alwayes one, and upon Equall division of voyces, to have always the casting and decisive voyce, full power and authoritye to Rule & Governe as well all the Inhabitants of this Corporacon, as any Strangers, according to the Generall Lawes of this Governmt and such peculiar Lawes as are, or shall be thought convenient & necessary for the good and Welfare of this his Maties Corporacon; as also to appoint such under officers, as they shall judge necessary, for the orderly execution of Justice; and I do hereby strictly charge and command all persons to obey & execute, from time to time, all such warrants, orders & Constitutions as shall be made by the said Mayor and Aldermen as they will answer the Contrary at their utmost Perills; And for the due administracon of Justice, according to the fforme and manner prescribed in this Commission, by the Mayor, Aldermen & Sheriffe, These Presents shall bee to them, and every of them, a sufficient Warrant and discharge in that behalfe; Given under my hand and seale at ffort James in New Yorke this 12th day of June 1665.

Rich Nicolls

BENCKES AND EVERTSEN'S CHARTER. 1673.

[New Orange. Rec.]

The Commanders and Honble Council of War in the service of their High Mightinesses the Lords States General of the United Netherlands and his Serene Highness the Lord Prince of Orange etc., Health!

Whereas We have deemed it necessary, for the advantage and prosperity of Our City New Orange, recently restored to the Obedience of the said High and Mighty Lord States General of the United Netherlands and his Serene Highness the Lord Prince of Orange, to Reduce the form of Government of this City to its previous character of Schout, Burgomasters and Schepens as is practised in all the Cities of our Fatherland, to the end that Justice may be maintained and administered to all good Inhabitants without Respect or Regard to Persons; Therefore We, by virtue of our Commission, in the names and on behalf of the High and Mighty Lords States General of the United Netherlands and his Serene Highness the Lord Prince of Orange, have elected from the Nomination exhibited by those in office as Regents of this City for the term of one current year,

As Schout	Anthony de Millt.
As Burgomasters	Johannes Van Brugen, Johannes de Peyster, Egedius Luyck.
As Schepens	Willem Beekman, Jeronimus Ebbying, Jacob Kip, Lowrens Vander Spiegel, Geleyn Verplanck.

Which abovenamed Schout Burgomasters and Schepens are hereby authorized and empowered to govern the Inhabitants of this City, both Burghers & Strangers, conformably to the Laws and Statutes of our Fatherland, and make therein such orders as they shall find advantageous and proper to this City [*Here the paper is destroyed.*] And the Inhabitants of this City are well and strictly ordered and enjoined to respect & honour the above named Regents in their respective qualities, as all Loyal and Faithful Subjects are bound to do. Done ffortress Willem Hendrick, this 17th August A° 1673

(Was Signed)

JACOB BENCKES — CORNELIUS EVERTSEN, the Younger

NICOLAAS BOES — A. COLVE.

A F. VAN ZEYLL.

INSTRUCTIONS FOR THE UNDER SHERIFF AND SCHEPENS

OF THE SUBURBS (BUYTEN LUYDEN) BETWEEN HAERLEM AND THE FRESH WATER; DATED THE 14th OF NOVEMBER, 1673.

[New Orange Record.]

Firstly. The Under Sheriff shall preside at all the meetings but when he officiates for himself as a party, or on behalf of justice, he shall on such occasions rise up and absent himself from the Bench, and in this case have neither an advisory much less a casting vote, but the oldest Schepen shall preside in his place.

2nd, The Under Sheriff and Schepens are authorized to pronounce definitive judgment, without appeal, in suits for debt between man and man &c. arising within their District to the amount of fl. 100 Seawan currency; also in minor criminal cases such as fighting, striking, scolding & such like, but in all cases exceeding said sum of fl. 100, the aggrieved person may appeal to the Honble Court here.

3dly. Whenever any cases come before the court in which any of the Schepens are interested as parties, in such cases they shall rise up and absent themselves from the Bench as is hereinbefore directed in the first article of the Under sheriff.

4thly. All Inhabitants within the aforesaid District shall be citable before the said Under Sheriff and Schepens who shall hold their court as often as necessary.

5thly. The said Under Sheriff and Schepens shall be obliged strictly to observe and punctually to execute all such placards and orders as shall from time to time be directed to them from the Worshipful Court here.

6thly. Whereas We are informed of the great ravages the Wolf commits on the small cattle, therefore to animate and encourage the proprietors who will go out and shoot the same, We have resolved to authorize the Under Sheriff and Schepens to give public notice that whoever shall exhibit a Wolf to them which hath been shot on this Island on this side Haarlem shall be promptly paid therefor by them; For a Wolf fl. 20. and for a She Wolf fl. 30 Seawan or the value thereof which said Under Sheriff and Shepens shall by their messenger levy from those who keep any cattle, large or small, within their district, on said Island, each of whom shall, according to the number of cattle, be bound to contribute & pay thereto whatever he shall be taxed thereupon by the Under Sheriff and Schepens.

7thly. Whoever shall fail to pay his fine on the first, second and third notice in the name of the Under Sheriff and Schepens, shall be proceeded against with prompt execution by the Under Sheriff.

8thly. Whoever shall allow execution to issue, must pay in addition five stivers on each guilder which he owes for the behoof of the Under Sheriff for the trouble of the Execution.

9thly. Whereas 'tis necessary that the Pound shall be properly kept, the Under Sheriff & Schepens are therefore authorized and ordered to attend that the same be maintained conjointly by those who have lands there; and further make such orders regarding the impounding of cattle as they shall find for the advantage of Agriculture, which orders each and every are required promptly to observe as if they were made by Ourselves.

10thly. Said Under Sheriff and Schepens shall take good heed in the suits brought before them strict justice to administer according to the best of their knowledge, without distinction or respect of persons, or any partiality; and further, the Under Sheriff shall as much as possible prevent and check all disputes and quarrels that may arise within his District.

11thly. The Under Sheriff and Schepens shall, as often as they deem necessary, give publick Notice that any person who causes or allows trees to fall in a common wagon road shall again remove the same, branches and all, from the road, before the going down of the Sun subsequent to the falling of the tree, and make the road passable—or in default thereof and in case a fine be imposed therefor by the Under Sheriff or his order, he shall pay for each tree found across the highway, a fine of fl. 20. to be applied, one half for the Under Sheriff & the other half for the informer; and the person fined shall, notwithstanding, this be bound to remove the tree instantly from the road.

12thly. If any one exhibit any indisposition towards the order of the Under Sheriff and Schepens, and come before the Court here, and the matter be discovered well founded, he shall pay double the imposed fine.

13thly. The choice of all Inferior officers (the Secretary alone excepted) shall be henceforward made by the said Under Sheriff and Schepens, & they shall be confirmed in their respective Qualities after being approved by the Worshipl Court here.

14thly. If any thing further be necessary for Agriculture, or should there be any obscurity or omission or want of clearness in these Instructions, the Under Sheriff and Schepens shall on occasion, communicate the fact to the Bench.

And finally, said Under Sheriff and Schepens shall, 14 days before the Expiration of the Year, apply to the Honble Court here to receive its order regarding the new Nomination of the Under Sheriff & Schepens. THUS done in the City Hall of this City, at the Court of the Schout, Burgomasters & Schepens.

COLVES CHARTER, 1674.

[New Orange Rec.]

Provisional Instruction for the Schout, Burgomasters and Schepens of the City of New Orange.

1st. The Schout and Magistrates, each in his quality shall take care that the Reformed Christian Religion conformable to the Synod of Dordrecht shall be maintained, without suffering any other Sects attempting any thing contrary thereto.

2. The Schout shall be present at all Meetings and preside there, unless the Honble Heer Governour or some person appointed by him be present who then shall preside, when the Schout shall rank next below the youngest acting Burgomaster. But whensoever the Schout acts as Prosecutor on behalf of Justice or otherwise, having made his complaint, he shall then rise up and absent himself from the Bench during the deciding of the case.

3. All Matters appertaining to the Police, Security, and Peace of the Inhabitants, also to Justice between man and man, shall be determined by final Judgment by the Schout, Burgomasters and Schepens aforesaid to the amount of Fifty Beavers and under, but in all cases exceeding that sum, each one shall be at liberty to appeal to the Heer Governour General & Council here.

4. All Criminal offences which shall be committed within this City and the Jurisdiction thereof shall be amenable to the Judicature of said Schout, Burgomasters and Schepens who shall have power to judge and sentence the same even unto DEATH inclusive; provided that on condition, that no sentence of corporal punishment shall be executed unless the approval of the Heer Governour General and Council shall be first sought and obtained therefor.

5. The Court shall be convoked by the President Burgomaster who shall, the night before, make the same known to Capt. Willem Knyff, (who is hereby provisionally qualified and authorized to be present at and preside over the Court in the name and on the behalf of the H[r] Governour,) and so forth to the remaining Schout, Burgomasters and Schepens.

6. All motions shall be put by the first Burgomaster, whose proposition being made and submitted for consideration, the Commissioner there presiding in the name of the H[r] Governour, shall first vote there, and so afterwards the remaining Magistrates each according to his rank; and the votes being collected, it shall then be concluded according to plurality; But if it happen that the votes are equal, the President shall then have power to decide by his vote, in which case those of the contrary opinion as well as those of the minority may Register their opinions on the Minutes, but not publish the same in any manner out of the Court on pain of arbitrary Correction.

7. The Burgomaster shall change Rank every half year, wherein the oldest shall first occupy the Place of President and the next shall follow him; but during this current year the change shall take place every 4 months, since three Burgomasters are appointed for this year.

8. The Schout, Burgomasters and Schepens shall hold their Session and Court Meeting as often as the same shall be necessary, on condition of previously appointing regular days therefor.

9. The Schout, Burgomasters and Schepens shall have power to enact, and with the approbation of the H[r] Governour to publish and affix some Statutes, Ordinances and Placards for the Peace, Quiet and Advantage of this City and the inhabitants thereof within their district, provided that the same do not in any-wise conflict, but agree, as much as possible, with the Laws and Statutes of our Fatherland.

10. Said Schout, Burgomasters and Schepens shall be bound rigidly to observe and cause to be observed the Placards and Ordinances of the Chief Magistracy, and not to suffer any thing to be done contrary thereto, but proceed against the Contraveners according to the tenor thereof; and further promptly execute such orders as the Heer Governour General shall send them from time to time.

11. The Schout, Burgomasters & Schepens shall be also bound to acknowledge their High Mightinesses the Lords States General of the United Netherlands and his Serene Highness the Lord Prince of Orange as their Sovereign Rulers, and to maintain their High Jurisdiction, Right and Domain in this Country.

12. The election of all inferior officers and servants in the employ of said Schout, Burgomasters and Schepens shall, with the sole exception of the Secretary, be made and confirmed by themselves.

13. The Schout shall execute all judgments of the Burgomasters and Schepens, without relaxing any, unless with the advice of the Court, also take good care that the jurisdiction under his authority shall be cleansed of all Vagabonds, Whorehouses, Gambling houses and such impurities.

14. The Schout shall receive all fines imposed during his time, provided they do not exceed yearly the sum of Twelve hundred Guilders Seawant value, which having received he shall enjoy

the just half of all the other fines, on condition that he presume neither directly nor indirectly to compound with any criminals, but leave them to the judgment of the Magistrates.

15. The Schout, Burgomasters and Schepens aforesaid shall convoke an Assembly on the 11th day of the month of August, being eight days before the Election of new Magistrates, and in presence of the Commissioners to be qualified for that purpose by the Honble Governr General, nominate a double number of the best qualified honorable and wealthy persons, and only such as are of the Reformed Christian Religion, or at least well affected towards it, as Schout, Burgomasters and Schepens aforesaid, which nomination shall be handed and presented folded and sealed, on the same day, to his Honor; from which nomination the Election shall then be made by his Honor on the 17th day of the Month of August, with continuation of some of the old Magistrates, in case his Honor shall deem the same necessary. Done, Ffort Willem Hendrick the 15th January 1674.

By Order of the Honble Heer
Governr General of
New Netherland,

(Was Signed) N. BAYARD, Secrety

CENSUS OF THE CITY OF NEW-XORK.

[ABOUT THE YEAR 1703.]

EAST WARD.

MASTERS OF FAMILYS	Males from 16 to 60	females	Male Children	female Children	Male Negros	female Negros	Male Negro Children	female Negro Children	all above 60
Ebenezr Wilson	3	4	1	3	1	1			
Mr Leuis		1	4	2		1			
Mr Everson		2	2		1				
Mrs Vantyle		1	1	1					
Mr Haris	2	1		1		2	3	1	
Thoms Dyer	1								
Mrs Smith		3	4						
Garot Haier	2	2	2						
Frances Coderos		2	1	3		1			
John Lasly	1	1							
Thomas Evens	1	1	1						
Hendrick	1	3							
Peter Vantilbry	2	1	1			1			
Frances Wessells	2	2		5	5				
Mrs Basset		1	1	2					
Capt Novered		1	2	1		1			
John Morthouse	1								
Beverly Latham	1	1	3	1					
Mrs Rabi	1	2	2						
Capt Morris	1	1		3	1	2	1		
Peter Mountu	1	3	1						
Hendrick Mayr	1	1	2						
John Stephens	1	1	2	3					
Capt Tudor	2	5	2	4		1	1		
Stuen Volo	1	2	1	3					
Fany ye Doctr	1	3		1					
Abraham Brazier	1	1	1	1					
Mr Sinkeler	2	1	0	1	1	1	1	1	
Mr Lees	2	1				2			
Capt Forkell	1	1	1	2		1	1	3	
Peter Thouet	1	2					1	1	
James pencer		1		2					
Margrett Briges		1							
Doctr Defany	1	1		2					
Mr Sellwood	1								
Widd Brown		2	1						
Mr Cholwell	1	1	2	1		2	1		
John Ledham	1	1	1	1					
Andrew Gravenrod	1	1	2	3	1	1			
William Apell	1	1							
James Blower	1	1							
John Vanderspeygel	2	1	1	3				1	
John Bures	1	1		1		1			
Mrs Blackgrove		1	3	1	2	2	2	1	
Mrs Byner	2	2			1	1		1	
Doctr Peters	1	1		1					
John Devi	1	1	2	3		1			
Mr Burger	2	1	3	2	2	1			
John Brockman	1	1		1					
John Bason	1	1	1						
John Dyer	1	2	1	1					
Capt Borditt	2	1	2		1				
Capt Baker	1							1	
James Emmett	1	2	3		1	1			
Samson Boutons	4		2	1					
James Bouloro	1	1							
Evert Pelts	1	1		3					
Mr Carter		2							
Joseph Isacks	1	1	1	3	1				
John Theobalds	1		2	3	2	1			
Mr Rinderson	1	1		1	1	1			
Widd Smith		1	3		1				
Leend Hewsen	1		1	2	1	1			
Benj Druelef	3	1	2		1	1	1		
Mr Waters	1	1	2	1		2			

MASTERS OF FAMILYS	Males from 16 to 60	females	Male Children	female Children	Male Negros	female Negros	Male Negro Children	female Negro Children	all above 60
Mr Lysoner	1			2		2			1
Mr Hardinburg	1	1	3	2	1	1			
Paul Myler	1	1	3			1			
Capt Vancrouger	1	1	1	1				1	
Mrs Colbery		1		2		1		1	
John Marteris	1		1						
Georg Stanton	2	1	2	2	4	2	2		
Daniel Janden	2	1	3	1					
Abraham Vanhorn	1	1		1	1	1	1		
Abraham Abranson		2	2	1			1		
Andries Abrahamse	1	1		1					
Derick Adolph	1	1	3						
John Manbruitts	1	1	1	1					
Garott Van Caver	1	1	1	1		1			
Hogland	1	1	1	4	2	1		1	
Mr Read	1	1	1	1		1			
Mr Monsett	1	2	2	1					
Thomas Caroll	1	2	2	1		1			
Widd Petersebants	1	2	1	2			1		
Aaron Bloom	1	2	2	4		1	1		
Mr Toy	1	1	1						
Georg Maynard	1	1							
Abraham Wandell	1	2							
John Tomson	1	2	2	3					
Benj Barns	1	1							
Capt Cragror	1	2		2		1			
Wm Nasroses		1	1	4					
Wm Schickles		1		3					
Nicholas Dauly	1	1	1						
Caston Lusen	1	1		1					
Johnas Longstrauts	1	1	2	1					
Abraham Molts	1	1		1					
Capt Trevett	1	2							
Georg Elesworth	1	1	4	2	2				
Colonl Depyster	1	2	1	3	5	2		2	
Georg Dunken	1	1	1	1		2			
Widd Decay		1	3	2	1	1	1		
Meyer Merett	1	2		3					
Capt Shelly	1	2			1	1	1		
Peter Morrayn	1	1		6	1				
Thomas Adams	1	0	2	1					
Widd Kidd		2							
Widd Vanbroug		1			1				
Widd Proost		1	2	4	2				
Jacobus Vanderspegle	1	1	4	3		1			
Doct Stets	1		2	7		1			
Elyes Now	1	3	2	2	1				
Widd Van Vous		1	1	2	1	1	2		
John Davi	1	1	2				1		
Abraham Johns	2				1	1			
Simon Bonan	1	1							
Widd Vanbusing		1			1				
Widd Adolph	1	3	1				1		
Thoms Child	1	1	1		2	1	1	1	
Saml Phillips	1	1	1		1				
Amon Bonan	1		1			1			
Johanes D. Wandler	1		1	4					
Joseph Smith	1	2	4						
Johanes Dohneare	1	1	1	4	1	1	2	1	
John Godfry	1	1	1	1		1			
Barnardus Smith	1	1	1	1		0			
Elyes Rambert	1	1	4						
Jacob Bratt	1	1		2	1				
Peter Rous	1		2	1					
Widd Jordan		1	2	4	1	1	1		
Thomas Sanderson	1	1	1	1			1		
Michell									
Denes Rishey	1	1	2						
Andrew Larrance	1	1	5	1					
Agustous Loukes	1		1		1			1	
Cornelius Joussos	1	1	3						
John Poulee	1	2	4						
Mr Funnell	1	1	3			2	1		
Mr D Romer	1	1	2		1		1	1	
Capt Peneson	1	1	1		1				
James Turse	1	1	2	1					
James Turse									

MASTERS OF FAMILYS.	Males from 16 to 60	Females	Male Children	female Children	Male Negros	female Negros	Male Negro Children	female Negro Children	all above 60
Michael Slevett	2	2		1		1			
Peter Baunt	1	1	1	1					
Widd Ellworth		1	1	2					
Capt Wilson	1	1	3	2	1				
Boult Leire	1	1							
Benj Bill	1	1	1	1		1			
Danl Fargoe	1			1					
Danl Devous	1	1	2	1					
Arthr Williams	1	1		2					
Georg Brass	1	1	4	2					
Wm Elcworth	1	1	1	3					
Joshuah David.	1	1	4	1					
Widd Vandewater		1	2	1					
Cornelius Bolson	1	1	1						
Danl Mynard	1	1	1	1					
John Mambroits	1	1	1	1					
Mr Cromlin	1			1					
Lucas Tinhoven	1	1		2					
Johanes Urielant	1	1		1					
Pete Newcurk	1	1	0	5	0	2			
Gabriell Ludlow	1	1	1	5	1	1			
Canny Flower	1	1	1	2					
Mr Slay	1	1	2	2					
Wm Bikman	0	0	0	1	2	1			1
James Debross	1	0	0	0	1				
Wm Anderson	1	1	2	0	2	0	1		
Peter Rightman	1	1	3	2					
Capt Tuder	1	1	1	4	0	1			
Wm Fardnandus	1	1							
Hendrick Carkman	1	1	1	1	0	1			
John Lastly	1	1	1						
Widd Vontylborough	0	1	1	2					
Wm Pell	1	1	1	3					
Thoms Huck	2	0	0	0	1				
Widd Peterow	0	1	3	3	1				
Robert Pudenton	1	2							
Wm Shackerly	1	1	0	1	1				
Mr Huddleston	1	1	2	1	0	2			
Nichol Debower	1	1	1	1					
Johanes Depayster	1	1	1	3	1	2	0	2	
Wm White	1	1	1						
Widd Nanclaft	0	1		3		1	1	1	
Abraham Moll	1	1		1					
Levenus Deuind	1	1					1		
Richd Sackett	1	1	2	2	3	1			
Elener Eleworth	1		2	3	2	1			
Soffell Seeworth					1	1			1
Isaac Dinell	1	1	4	1					
Isaac Ferbergin	1	1	4						
Johanes Jooston	1	1	2						
Widd Lees		1		1					
Mrs Mussett	1	1							
Wm Naseros	1	1	1	4					
Loud Leuis	1	1	2	5	1	1	1		
Thomas Roberts	1								
Roger Britt	1								
Thoms Hams	1	1							
Robt Walls	1								
Giddeon Vergeren	1	0					1		
Evert Dicken									
John Nanfan	1				1				
Claud Bouden									
Hendrick Vandespegle	1								
Mr Gleencross	1	1							
Dan Thwaictes	1	1		2					
Widd Petrer Bond		2		2			1		
Charl Bakeman	1								
Johanes Banker	1								
Harma Louricar	1	1	1						
Jos Carlsee									2
Simeon Shumoine	1	0	2	2					

SOUTH WARD.

MASTERS OF FAMILYS.	Males from 16 to 60	females	Male Children	female Children	Male Negros	female Negros	Male Negro Children	female Negro Children	all above 60
Danill Roberts	3	1							
Mr Ling	2	0	0	0	0	3			
John & Elias Petram	2	1	4	2	1	1	0	1	
Hendrick Kellison	1	1	3	0	0	0	0	0	
Archibald Morris	1	1	0	1	0				
Jurian Bush	1	1	1	2					
Victor Bicker	1	2	0	1					
Elizabeth Eliot	0	1							
Sarah Scouton	1	2	1	4					
Saml Sokane	1	2	1	3					
Jacobus Cornelius	1	1	1	2	0	0	0	1	
Peter Wessels	1	1	3	1	0	1			
Jacobus Morrisgreen	1	1	0	1	1				
William Syms	1	1	0	3					1
John Wattson	0	1	1	1	1				1
William Haywood	2	1	2	2				1	1
John Canoon	2	1	0	1			1		
Thomas Elison	1	4	1	3					
Widdow Bush	1	2	1	1					1
William Kage	1	2	0			1			
Widdow Wessells	2	3							
William Jackson	4	1	1	1	1	1			
Johannes Van Geser	2	3							
Willelmus Neuenhousen	1	2						1	
William Taylor	1	1	3	1	2	1			
Michael Hardin	2	3						1	
Thomas Hardin	2	1	1	2	0	1			
Anna Smith	0	1	1			1			
Mr Shaepass	1	1	0	1	1	1			1
Capt Debrouts					0				3
Madam Duboise	0	3							
Cornelius Depeyster	1	2	1	3	0	1	1		
Widdow ffrouse		2	3	1					
Thomas Roberts	1	1	2	3	3	1			
John Elison	2	1	3	0	1	2	1		
Isaac Depeyster	1	1	3	3				3	
Widdow Howard		3		1				4	1
Nicholas Tinoven	1	1				1	1	1	
Mr Davenport	2	1					1		
Giles Gaudenoa		1						1	1
Widdow Stokes	1	1		1					
Robert Elison	1	2				2			
Andreas Maer	2	2	2	1		1			
Benjamin Winecope	2	1	1						
Widdow Stukey	1	2	2						
Madm Weaver		2	1	2	1	2		1	
Thomas Ives	2	1			1	1			
Derick Ten Eyck	3	1	2		12	1			
John Penoe	1	3							
Thos Gleaves	1	1	3	2	2	2	1		
Pasco	1	1					1	1	
Mr Cosens	1	1	2	2		2	1		
Andrew Law	2	3	2						
Widdow Bassett		1	2	1					
William Lloyd		1	2						
Adrian Man	4	01	3	1					
Widdow Lysenner	0	2		1					
Mr Van Dam	2	2	3	2	3	2	1		
Widdow Cloper	2	1	1	1				1	
John Pitt	1	1	1	1					
Robert Deintant	1	1		1					
Widdow Dikey		2	1	7	4	1	1	1	
Widdow van Scarck		6	1	2	1	1	1	1	
Capt Corbutt	3	3		2	2	2			
Delancena Jew	1	1	1	1		1		1	
Anthony Farmer	1	1	1	2		1	1	2	
Gilbert Vanimbrough	1	1	1	3	1				
Abraham Vanderell	1	1							
Lawrence Heading	1	2						1	
Widdow Symouse Janson		1							1
Widdow Hallgrave	0	1	0	1					
Widdow Phillips		1	1		1	2	2	1	
Stephen Richards	1	2	1	2		1			
Mr Rossoll	1	1	2	1		1	1		
Widdew Seiler		1	1		3	1	1		

MASTERS OF FAMILYS.	Males from 16 to 60	females	Male Children	female Children	Male Negros	female Negros	Male Negro Children	female Negro Children	all above 60
John Wansart	1	1						1	
Herman Rutgese	2	1		1	2				
Widdow Nespot	1	1		1					
Widdow Deforest	1	1	2	5					
Justus Jay	1	2		3	1				
Widdow Brown		1	1	3					
Peter Myir	1	1	1	4					
Widdow Doweher	1	1	1	2					
John Kingstone	1	1							
Nicholas Lorteen	1	1							
Capt Matthews		1	3	2		1	1		
Johannes Johnson	1	1	2	2					
John Petraaslot	1	1	1	1					
James Many	1	3							
Samll Burges		1		3		1			
Mr Cooper	1	2	2	2			1	1	
Johannes Vanrost	1	1	2	3			1		
Mr Vangoson	1	2	1						
Mr Vangoson	1	2	1	1					
Capt Tinoven	1	1				1	1	1	
Christophr Hogland	1	1	2						
Widdow van plank		3	2	3		1			
Johannes Vanderhiled	1	1	1		1	1			
Widdow Keisted		2	5	1	1				
Andreas Breestad	2	4	4	2	2	1			
Widdow Deshamp	1	2	1			4		2	
Mr Antill	1	1	2	2		2		2	
Wilellmus Navensusen	2	2						1	
Francis Vincent	2	1	1	2	1	1	1		
Peter Kip	1	1	1				1		
Gre Robertson		2							
Jacob Maurice	2	1	1		1				
Gerrett Vesey	1	1	1	3	1				
Widdow Bush	1	2							
Johannes Craft	1	1							
Samll Beckman	1	1	2	4					
Mr Honan	1	2		1		1			
Widdow Cortland	2	2		3	5	2	1	1	
Widdow Keisteed	1	1		1				1	
Hendrick Mester	1	1							
Abraham Webrana	1	1	2						
Edward Blagg	1		1			2			
Capt ffinch	1	1		2					

NORTH WARD.

MASTERS OF FAMILYS.	Males from 16 to 60	females	Male Children	female Children	Male Negros	female Negros	Male Negro Children	female Negro Children	all above 60
Isaac Stoutenbrough	1	1	2	0					1
Lydiah Rose	0	3	1						
Johannes Veckden	1	1	1	2					
Gerrard Grans	1	1	4	1					
Jeemz Lie	1	1		1					
Freerick Bloom	1	1	2	1					
Wm Ockton	1	1							
Gerret De Boogh	1	1	1						
Mangell Ransen	1	1	2	2	2				1
Danl Domskon	1	1	1	1					
Jacob Van Direse	1	1	1	3					
Eleazer Bogert	1	1	4						
Joriz Breger	1	1	2						
Jasbuz Boz	1	1	2		1				
Johannes Bogert	1	1		0					
Wm Waderson	1	2							
Johannes Proovoos	1	1		1					
Joseph Waderson	1	1	2	3					
Henry Coleman	1	1		1	1				
Philip Bellenz	1	1		1					
Joseph Bresser	1	1		1					
Ratie Vanderbeeck		1	2						
Johannes Bant	1	1	2						
Jacob Balck	1	1	0	1					
Saml Marten	1	1							
Jo Dicker	1	1		2					
John Terree	1	1		1					
Kuijbert Vandenberg	1	1		3					
John Bentell		3							
Joseph Paling	1	1	1	3	1	2			
Mr Evert	1	1	0	3	0	1			
Jacob Swart	1	1	2	1					

MASTERS OF FAMILYS.	Males from 16 to 60	females	Male Children	female Children	Male Negros	female Negros	Male Negro Children	female Negro Children	all above 60
Bartholomew Vonol	1	1	1						
Edwd Lock	1	1	2	1					
Marre Quick		1	1						
Isaac Juter	1	1	2	1					
Mr Floran	1	1	0	1					
Danl Travore	1	1	1						
Mr Ritvire	1	1							
Henderick Drimiez	1	1	1	1					
Derick Ritenbogert	1	1	1	1					
Abraham Vanaren	1	1	2	2	1	1	1	1	1
Jan Karelse	1	1		1					
Janetie degraus		2	0	1					
Hermen degraus	1	1	3	2					
Andrew Douwe	1	1		2					
Aijs Van Velsen	1	1	2	2					
Yochem Lotyer	1	1	2	1					
Mr Hooper		1	0	2					
Hendrick Oostrom									
Yan Heslook	1	1		1					
Jan Beadre	1	1	2						
Christian Lowrier	1	1	2						
Annetie Lowrier		1							
Wm Visser	1	1	2	4	1				
Robt Milre									2
Stoffel Pelz	1	1	2	2	1	1	1		
Aijme Vandyck	1	1	2	2					
Peter Van Waggele	1	1		2	1				
Susanna Tocter		1		1					
Evert Bressen	1	1	2	5					
Johannes P Cavice	1	1		1					
Hanz Kierstede	1	1	2	1					
Wyburgh Vanbos		1		1					
Direck Slick	1	1	2	1					
Enoch Kill	1	1							
Danl Barteloo	1	1		2					
Reyere Martese	1	1	2	1					
Abraham Vandurse	1	1	3	2					
Danl Walderon	1	1		5					
Morott		1	0	2					
Tam Pell	1	1		2					
Alexander Lam	1	1	2	4					
Wm Attell	1	1	2	3					
Mrs Ameker									1
Peter Burger	1	1	2	2					
Wm Mandriese	1	1	1	1					
Onerre Obee		5							
Catherine Kip		1	4	4	2	2		1	
Wm Vaneckt	1	1	3	1					
Isaack Kip	1	2	5	1	2	2			
Orseltie Vandyck		2	1						
Jacob Boele	1	1	4	1	0	1	2	1	
Engletre Mol		1	1	2					
Wm Rooseboom	1	1		3					
Abraham Vangeldere	1	1	1	3					
Yoost Heyresse	1	1	3						
Antre Vanoorstrant		1	2	2	1				
Johannes Kenne	1								
Nicholas Delaplyne									1
Jacob Carrebill	1	1							
Wier Boergeran	1	1	1						
Abraham Keteltaz	1	1	1	1					
Antiene Yellerton		1	2	1					
Benj Proovoost	1	0	5	6					
Denis Sweetman	1	1	1						
Hendrick Boz	1	1	3	1					
Garret Lansen	1	1	2	3					
Annetie Henne		1		1					
Mr Vandrick		1		1					
Abraham Kip	1	1	1	1	1	1	1	1	
ffrans Vandyck	1	1	3						
Robert Podventon	1								
Aaron Vanvlarden	1	1	4	1					
John Van strijp	1	1							
Hathman Wessels	1	1		1					
Peter Yaaokse	1	1	2	1	1	1			
Mattyz Boeckout	1	1							
Peter Saryo	1	1	1	1					

MASTERS OF FAMILYS.	Males from 10 to 60	females	Male children	female Children	Male Negros	female Negros	Male Negro Children	fem 'le Negro Children	all above 60
Yan Sivvere	1								
Yan Hille	1	2	3	3					
Yan Yonz	1								
Stijntie Yoris		1							
Anenez Tiebout	1	1	3	2					
Wm Yorster	1	1	3	2					
Wm Provoost	1	1	2	2					
Mr Kinning		1	7	1					
Catharina Selecoat		1							
Fillet Sweer	1	1							
Wm Pell	1	1	2	3					
Cornelia Vandervoers	1	1							
Yan Meet	1	1	4	2					
Barent Vantilburgh	1		1	1					
Wm Stenton	1	1	0	2					
Loo Witten	1	1		2					
Nieste Vienne		2	1			1			
Yan Devenne	1	1		1	1				
Cornelia Maruz		1	2	3					
Doreman Stor	1	1			1				
Mrs Lindslee		1							
Swerez Hendricks	2			1					
David Hoesaert	1	1	2	1					
Ante Burgers	0	1	3	3					
Ysack Brat	1	1		2					
Elsie Sippie		3	4						
Yohanniz Vandewater	1	2	2						
Nelte Plaurere	2	2	1	4					1
Garret Hallaer	1	1		1	1				
Hardmen Holduz	1								
Solomon Vanderboogh	1	1	3						
Allebertuz Ringo	1	1	3	2					
Vansent Tielo	1	1	2	3					
Hester Montaine		1	3	1					
David Christeaense	2	1	1	2					
Yan Keoeck	1	1	5	1	1	1			
Sarebz Loeter	1	4	1	1					
Mrs Stevez		2			4	1			2
Anderiez Marschalock	1	2	5	1					
Yacob Bennett	1	2	3	1					
Wm Bogaert	1	1	1	1					
Yan Vanhorn	1	1							
Aennez Yniek	1	1	2	2		1			
Garret Wouterse	1	1	1	1					
Hatie Provoost		1	2	4	2				
Martie Vandeheyden	0	1	1	1					
Barent Lool	1	1	2	2					
Yannez Laegerau	1	1		1	1				
Garret Onckelback	1	1	1	2					
Yan Vantilburgh	1	1							
Saml Lockeriest	1	1	3		1	1			1
Barnarduz Smit	1	1	9	1					
Yan Pieterze Boz									2
Caterina Boots									1
Barnarduz Hardebroer	1		1	4	1				
Corneliz Loris	1	1	4		1				
Peter Boz	1	1	1	2					
Mrs Monvel		1	1			2			
Garret Burger	1	1	2	2					
Yan Herrick	1	1	0	2					
Garret Wynanse	1	1							
Lavie Vandmirse		1	2	2					
Sijmon Breeste	1	1	2	3	1				
Yannetre Wande Watte		1							
Am Reijt	1	1	1	1					
Yacob deportee	1	1	2	1					
Yan Narbree	1	1	1						
Yohannez Vantiburgh	1	1	2						
Yan Konce	1								
Mrs Boseit		1							
Wessell Eversee	1	1	2	2					
Bettie Rammesen		2	1						

WEST WARD.

MASTERS OF FAMILYS	Males from 16 to 60	females	Male Children	female Children	Male Negros	female Negros	Male Negro Children	female Negro Children	all above 60
Peter Bayard	1	1		2		1			
Garret Vantright	0	2		1					1
Cornelius Lodge	1	1		1					
Wm Smith Aldermn	1	1			2	1	4	2	
Ball: Bayard	4	1			1	1	3	1	1
Matt: De Hart	2	2	1	2					
Jacob Vansune	1	2					1		
Catherine Rolegome		2			1			1	
Charles Denisoe	1	1				1			
Robt Darkins	2	2	1	1	1	2			
Derus Vandinbrough	1	1	1	1	2	1			
Bar: Laroox	2	1	3	3	0	1			
John Barbarie	2	1	3	3	0	3			
James Colett	1	1	4						
John Dublett		2							1
Peter Munvil	1	1				1			
Isaac De Boogh	1	1							
Peter Pieret	2	2	1	2	11	1	1	1	
Mrs Rumboll		3	0			1	0	2	0
Evert Van Howk	1	1	3	2					
Robt White	1	1	1	2					
Margrett Hudson		1	1	1					
Catherine White		2		2					
Wm Walch	1	2	3						
Johan: Van Gelder	1	1	5	2					
Isaac Anderson	1	1	3	1		1			
John Hutchins	1	1				2	1		
Susannah Wells		1	1	1					
Deborah Symcom				1					1
Cornelius Clopper	1	1	1	2					
And: Faucout	1	1							
Augustus Grassett	1	1				1			
Jacobus Berry	1	1	1	2			1		
Coll: Peartree	1	1	1		2	2	1	1	
Urian Blank	1								
Mary Blank		1		1					
Robt Edwards	1	1		2					
Rebekah Adams		1	1	1					
George Williams	1	1							
Wm Stoks	1	1	1	1					
Francis Bocketts	1	1	2	2					
Tobias Stoutenbrough	2	2	4		1	1			
Agnes Davis		1		2					
Daniel Ebbetts	2	1							
Eliz: Plumley		2	1			1			
Samp: ˢhilton Braughton	2	4			1				
Han: Tenijck	2	3	1	1					
Robt Anderson	1	1	1						
Peter Johnson	1	1			1				
Abra: Masiear	1	1	3	2	1	1			
John Anen	1	2		2					
Wm Arison	1	1		2	1	1			
David Mackdugell	1	1	1						
Isaac Garners	1	1	1						
Will: Shullwood	1	1		1					
Laynard D Graw	1	3	4	2					
Jores Riersie	1	2	4	4	2		1		
John Cure	1	1		1					
Archibald Reed	1	1							
Hanna Tinbrook	2	1	1						
Andrew Lamarue	1	1	1	1					
Michael Harring	1			1					
Edwd Burley	1	1	1						
Lieft Buckley		1		4					
Rinear Risoe	2	2	1	1					
Walter D Boise	1	1		1		1			
Garret Cosyn	1	1	1	1					
Pietr Parmyter	1	2	1	1					
Alberts Laynderts									1
Pual Tuk		1							1
Peter Marks	1	1							
Armanus Van Geldr	1	1	2	3					
Phill: Doley	1	1	1						
Jno D Le ffountaine	1	1	3	2					
Jacob Kuwning	1	1	1	2					

MASTERS OF FAMILYS	Males from 16 to 60	females	Male Children	female Children	Male Negros	female Negros	Male Negro Children	female negro Children	all above 60
Joseph Wright	1	1		1					
Peter Willtrans Roome	1	1	4	4					
Wm Moss	1	2	2	2					
Nicholas Blachford	1	1							
Will: Robinson	1	1							
Mary Collum		1		2	1				
Garret Blank		1	2	2	1				
Margaret Van D: Schuyer		1							
Peter Do	1	1	4	2					
John French	1	2		3					
Mary Harks		2							
Edmund Thomas	1	1	1						
Francis Cowenhoaf	2								
Margrett Markner		4							
John Swere	1	1	2	1					
Eliz: Collier		1							
Cor: Garretts	1	1	1	1					
John Harris	1	1	1	1	1				
Alford Suerts	1	1	1	4	1	1	3		
Will: Hagers	1	1	2						
Walter Hagers	1	1		1					
Johannes Ebon	2	1	2	2					
Garret Ketteltass									
James Beard									
Cornelius Quick	1	1	4	2		1			
Jacob Naoms	1		1			1			
John Windefort	1	1	2	1					
Bernard Bush	1	1	1	2					
Jocum Robeson	1	1	2						
John Vanderbeck	1	1	1	1					
Conradus Do:	1	1	1	1					
William Pearce	1	3	2	3					
Robt Crannell	1	1	2	2					
Anne Marie		1		1					
John Thorn	1	1							
Richard Fleming	1	1		1					
Margt: ffordiz		2							
John Williams Romiere	1	1	1	1					
ies Dolse	1	1	1						
Jacob Hases	1	1	1						
John Peake	1	2	4	3					
John Leathing	1	1	1						
Edwd Anderson	1	1		1					
Peter Low	2					1			
Alida Wright		1		2					
Griffin Jones	1	1							
Powels Turke Junr	1	1		2					
Hendrick Johnson	1	1		3					1
Eliz: Wackham		4							
Thomas Coburn	1	1							
Richard Green	1	1		1					
John Lucas	1	1		1					
Sergeant Smith	1	1							
John Bowring	1	1		1					
Peter Fauconnier	1	3	2	2	1	1			

DOCK WARD.

MASTERS OF FAMILYS	Males from 16 to 60	females	Male Children	female Children	Male Negros	female Negros	Male Negro Children	female negro Children	all above 60
Phillip ffrench	1	1	1	2	3	2	1	1	
Mrs Mogon		1	2	2		1			
Zacharie Angeum	1	1		3					
Anthony Davis		1	1	1		1		1	
Elias Budinot	1	1		1		1		1	
Johan Hardenbrok	1	1	1	2				1	
John Parmiter	1	1	1	1					
Samuel Bayard	1	1	1	2	1	1			
Nicholas Jamin		1				5	1		1
Jno Casall	1	1				2			
Johannes Hoglandt	1	2	1		1	1			
Widow Alkfield		1	1	1					
Garret Dyking	1	1	2	2	1	1	1	1	
Catharin Potter		1		2		1			
David Jameson	1	1	1	2	1	2			
Moses Levey	3	2	1	1		1	1		
Robert Lurting	2	3	3	3		1	1		
Samuel Veach	1	2		1				2	
Widdow Taylor	0	1	2	1	1	1		2	
David Villat	1	1	1	1					

MASTER OF FAMILYS	Males from 16 to 60	Females	Male Children	female Children	Male Negros	female Negros	Male Negro Children	female Negro Children	all above 60
Mrs Allie	......	1	2	......	......	1	1	......	......
David Logall	1	1	1	2	......	1	......	......	......
Thos Burrough	1	1	1	2	1	1	......	......	......
Capt Simes	1	2	2	1	1	1	1	......	......
Robt Skelton	1	2	......	1	1	......	......	......	......
Charles Wooley	3	......	......	......	1	......	......	......	......
Garret Vanhorne	1	1	1	2	2	1	......	......	......
Paul Drulett	1	1	2	4	......	2	......	......	......
Lewis ffarree	1	3	2	2	......	1	1	......	......
Stephen D'lancey	1	1	2	......	3	2	1	1	......
Jno James Vanveale	1	1	......	......	......	1	......	1	......
Widdow ffaget	......	3	......	......	......	......	......	......	......
Hendrick Vand: Hull	1	1	1	1	......	......	......	......	......
John Shackmaple	1	2	......	......	......	......	......	......	......
Peter Hemoims	2	1	......	1	......	......	......	......	......
John Van horne	1	1	2	01	3	01	1	......	......
Jacobus vancourtlandt	1	1	1	2	2	2	1	......	......
Jacobus Decay	1	1	2	1	4	3	1	1	......
Mrs Cuylar	1	2	1	......	1	1	......	......	......
Jacob Ten Eyck	2	2	......	1	......	......	1	......	......
Abraham Governere	1	1	1	1	......	......	......	1	......
English Smith	......	2	1	......	......	......	......	......	1
Cornelius Jacobs	......	2	1	5	......	1	......	1	......
David Provost Junr	1	......	2	3	2	1	......	......	......
Widdow Sanders	......	3	......	......	......	1	3	......	......
Affey Tuder	......	1	1	......	......	1	......	......	......
Widdow D Roblus	......	4	3	1	......	1	......	......	......
Widdow Dillies & Nathaniei Masston in Ditto	3	4	1	5	......	1	......	......	1
Widdow Vanhorne	1	3	......	......	......	1	......	......	......
Abraham Sanford	1	1	3	2	......	......	......	......	......
William Walton	1	2	1	......	1	......	1	......	......
Christ pher Gillin	1	1	1	2	......	......	......	......	......
William Chambers	1	2	3	......	1	......	......	......	......
Johannes outman	1	2	1	......	1	......	......	......	......
Isaac D Markeys	1	2	1	1	1	2	......	1	......
Widdow Lawrence	......	1	3	2	......	......	......	......	......
Peter Lakerman	1	1	1	......	1	1	1	......	1
John Gurney	1	1	......	1	1	1	......	......	......
Widdow Sowalls	1	2	......	......	......	......	......	......	......
Coll. Nich: Bayard	......	1	1	......	2	......	......	1	......
ffrancis Garrabrant	1	2	......	2	2	......	......	......	......
William Barkely	1	3	1	1	......	1	......	......	......
Nicholas ffieldon	1	1	2	2	......	......	......	......	......
Bartholomew Hart	1	1	......	1	2	1	......	......	......
Overin	1	......	......	......	......	......	......	......	......
Thomas Wenham	1	1	1	1	2	3	......	......	......
Hibon	2	1	......	2	1	......	......	......	......
Vandemar	1	2	1	......	......	......	......	......	......
iv Cookers	......	2	......	1	......	......	......	......	......
John Scott	1	2	1	......	......	......	1	......	......
Widdow D. Pyster	......	1	......	2	1	1	......	......	......
John Lorring	1	1	1	1	......	2	......	......	......
Nicholas Garretts	......	3	2	2	1	0	......	1	......
Abraham V: D; waters	1	1	......	......	......	......	......	......	......
Harmanes Burger	1	1	1	1	......	......	......	......	......
Martines Criger	1	1	1	......	......	......	......	......	......
Andris Tenbrook	1	1	1	1	......	......	......	......	......
Rugert Waldron	3	1	1	1	......	......	......	......	......
John Davis	1	1	1	1	2	1	1	2	......
Widdow Buddinot	1	4	2	......	1	2	......	......	......
Richard Willit	2	1	......	......	......	1	1	......	......
• vis Gomas	2	2	3	1	1	1	......	......	......
John Harperding	......	1	......	1	......	......	......	1	1
Avert Elberseye	1	3	4	......	1	......	......	......	......
Roger Jones	2	......	......	......	......	......	......	......	......
Johannes Thiebout	1	1	1	......	......	......	......	......	......
Martin Coock	1	1	......	1	......	1	......	......	......
Albert Coock	2	1	3	2	1	1	......	......	......
Lawrence Vanhock	2	2	2	2	1	......	......	......	......
Cornelius Veilin	2	1	1	2	......	......	......	1	......
Abraham Mettelares	2	1	5	1	1	1	......	......	......
John Lansing	......	......	......	......	......	......	......	......	......
Evert Van D. watr	1	1	......	1	......	......	......	1	......
William Echeles	1	1	......	1	2	......	......	......	......
Edward Marshall	1	1	1	......	......	1	......	......	......
John Wanshares	1	1	......	1	......	......	......	......	......
John Vansent	2	1	......	......	2	1	......	......	......
William Bradford	2	1	3	2	......	2	......	......	......
Conrad Ten Eyke	4	3	1	......	1	......	......	......	......

MASTERS OF FAMILYS.	Males from 16 to 60	females	Male Children	female Children	Male Negroes	female Negroes	Male Negro Children	female Negro Children	all above 60
* rd Provost Sear	1	2		2		1			
John Everts	1	1		1	1				
Geesje ten Eges		1				1			
Hugh Crow	1	1	1					1	
Anthony Rutgers	1	1	2			1			
John Whitt	1	0	1	2					
Mr Legrand	1								
Nicholas Materbe	1	1							
Sa ull Leveridg	1	3	4		2	1			1
William White Junr	2	1							
Mary Wakham		4					1		
Henry Money	2	1							
John Stephens	2								
Richd Green	1	1							
* n Varickbookeouse	2	3	1	3					
* rence Vessells	1	1	2	2	3	1			
* aham Lawkerman	1	1	1		3	2	1	1	
Evardas Bogardus	1	2							
William Bickley	2					1	1	1	
Jannetie Van briekelen		3							
Abraham Splinter	2	1		2				1	
Gabrll Thiebod	1	1	2						
Widdow Colie	2								
Mrs Mashett		1	1						
Johannes Burger	1	2	4						
OUT WARD									
* Ritman	2	2	2	1	1		2		
* Kip	2	2		1	5	2	1		
* elus Bak	1	1	1	1					
* ids Widd		1	2	3					
Peter Bokho	1	1							
John Barr	2	1	1	3					
——— Solomon	1	2	2						1
* hn Peter	1	1	1	2					
* nl Carpenter	2	2	1						1
Abraham Brimer	1	1	4						
——— Gunoson	1	1		1					
John Dikman	1	1							
——— Tunsedes	2	4		2	1		3	2	1
John Devor	2		3	3					
Cornelius Drk	2	1	2	2					1
Cornelius Aker	1	1	4				1		
Tuns Cornelius	2	1	3	1	1		2		
Oranout Waber		1	1	1					1
Wolford Waber	1	1	1						
——— Solemon	1	1	2						
Will Da	1	1		1					
Hendrick Bordis	1	1	4	2	1				
* Moor	2	1	1	2	1				
* Griggs	1	1		2					
* Thomas	1	1		3	1			1	
* Gracklin									
Sam'l Mountaine	1	2	6	2	1				
Capt Sidmen	2	1	1	1	4	2	2	2	0
John Bronod	1	1	2	1	1		1	1	1
Rebeccah Van Scyock	1	1			2	1			
Wases Peterson	1	1	2	2	1				
Thoms Akerson	1	1	2	1					
Solomon Widdow	1	1	1	2					
Amanuel Franson	2	2		1					
Jacob Cornelius	2	1		2				0	1
Thomas Sekls	1	1							
John Clapp	1	1	2		2	1			
Abraham Bolt	1	1	3	6		1	1		
Capt Lock	1	1		1	1				
Hendrick Van Scyock		1	2						1
Philip Minthorne	1	1	3						
* ou	1	1	1	1	1	1	1		
* eabor		1				1		1	1
* way	1	1	1	1	5	1	1		
*		3	1	1	2		1		
* noute	1		1	2		1			
* Thomas	2	2	1	1					2
Walter Lamas				1					1
David Minvel	1	2	1		1	1			
* lin Pierson	2	1	2	4	1	1			
Agar Harman	2	2	1	4			2		
Jacob Conant	1	1		1			1		

* These names cannot be made out on account of the MS. being torn.

NAMES OF THE MINISTERS OF THE DUTCH REFORMED CHURCHES IN NEW-YORK AND NEW JERSEY.

[Naamregister der Predikanten; Te Leiden &c.]

1758.

Johannes Ritzema	*New York*	1744
Lambertus de Ronde	*New York*	1751
Reinhard Erichsohn	*Freehold*	1736
Fredericus Muzelius	*Tappan* Emeritus	1726
Gerard Haaghoort	*Second River*	1735
Georgius Wilhelmus Mancius,	*Kings Towne*	1732
Johannes Schuiler	*Hakkingsack &c*	1756
Johannes Casparus Fryenmoet,	*Menissink, Machakomich, Walpek and Smitsfield*	1744
Benjamin Meinema,	Pakeepsie & Fishkil	1745
Theodorus Frielinghausen, Thod. Jad. fil.,	*New Albany*	1746
Ulpianus Van Sinderin, Ulp. fil.	*Long Island*	1746
Johannes Henricus Goetschius,	*Hakkingsak end Schralenburg*	1748
Johannes Lyecht,	*Brunswick*	1748
Benjamin Van der Linden,	*Paremes*	1748
Samuel Verbryk,	*Tappan*	1748
David Marinus,	*Achuechnouck*	1752
Barent Vromans,	*Schonegtade*	1756
Thomas Romein,	*Queens County, Oyster bay*	1753
Johan. Caspar Rubel, Joh. Casp. fil.,	*Rhynbeck*	1755
Johannes Schenema,	*Kats-Kil & Cogsackie*	1753
William Jackson,	*Bergen & Staten Island*	1757

New Paltz, Schoggarie, Manor of Livingston } *Vacant* { Kinderhook, Klaverack, Kings County

1796.

Johannes Ritzema	*New York* Emeritus, 1784	1744
Ulpianus Van Sinderen, Ulp. fil.	*Kings Co Long Island*, Emer. 1784	1746
Johannes Lyecht,	*Brunswick*	1748
Benjamin Van der Linden,	*Paremes*	1748
Samuel Verbryck,	*Tappan*	1750
Lambertus de Ronde,	*New York* Emeritus 1784	1750
Barent Vrooman, 1722	*Sconectade*	1756
Thomas Romein, 1753	*Menissinck*	1761
Joh. Schenema,	*Cats-Kil & Cogsackie*	1753
William Jackson, A. L. M.	*Bergen & Staten Island*	1757
Jacob Rutsen Hardenberg	*Old Raritans*	1758
Eilardus Westerloo, Is. fil.	*New Albany*	1760
Johannes Martinus Van Harlingen,	*Millston & New Schonnick*	1761
Gerardus Daniel Cock,	*Camp & Rhinebeck*	1762

Hermanus Meyer, 1763 *Pomtan & Totoa* - - - - - - 1775
Isacus Rysdyk, *New Hackkingsack & Hopwel* - - - - - - 1765
Warmoldus Kuypers, 1769 *Hakkingsack & Schralenburg* - - - - 1771
Johannes Levingston, Th. Doct. *New York*, Eng Lang - - - - 1770
Johan Daniel Gross, *Kings-Town* - - - - - - - 1773
Christianus Fredericus Fuhring, 1770 *New York* German Lang - - - 1773
Joh. Gabriel Gebhard, 1772 *New York* German Lang.
Martinus Schoemaker, *New Haarlem & Gravesend*
[Dirck] Romein, Thom. fr. *Marbletown & Mombach*
[Wilm.] Linn, *New York*, Eng. Lang. - - - - - - 1784
Kuypers, Warm. fil. *New York* - - - - - 1784

Some Places, *Vacant*.

XXII.

PAPERS

RELATING TO

Long Island.

DIRECTOR KIEFTS PATENT TO THE TOWN OF GRAVESEND. ANNO 1645.

[Gravesend Records.]

Whereas it hath pleased the High & Mighty Lords the Estates Genl of the United Belgick Provces— His highness Fredrick Hendrick by ye grace of God Prince of Orange, &c. and the Rt Honourable ye Lords Bewint Heobers of the W. I. Company by theyr several Commissions under theyr hands and seales to give and grant unto me Wm Kieft sufficient power and authorities for the general rule & gouvernment of this Prouince called the New Netherlands, & likewise for ye settling of townes, collonies, plantations, disposing of ye land within this prouince, as by ye said Commissions more att large doth and maye appeare, Now Know yee whomsoever these Presents may any ways concerne that I, William Kieft, Gouvernor Generall of this Prouince by vertue of ye authoritie abovesaid & with ye aduice & consent of ye Councell of State heere established have given and graunted & by virtue of these presents doe give grant & confirme unto ye Honoured Lady Deborah Moody, Sr Hennry Moody Barronett, Ensign George Baxter & Sergeant James Hubbard theyr associates, heyres, executors, administrators, successours, assignes, or any they shall join in association with them, a certaine, quantitie or p'cel of Land, together with all ye hauens, harbours, rivers, creeks, woodland, marshes, and all other appurtenances thereunto belonging, lyeing & being uppon & about ye Westernmost parte of Longe Island & beginning at the mouth of a Creeke adjacent to Coneyne Island & being bounded one ye westwards parte thereof with ye land appertaining to Anthony Johnson & Robt Pennoyer & soe to run as farre as the westernmost part of a certain pond in an ould Indian field on the North side of ye plantation of ye said Robbert Pennoyer & from thence to runne direct East as farre as a valley begginning att ye head of a flye or Marshe sometimes belonging to ye land of Hughe Garrettson & being bounded one the said side with the Maine Ocean, for them the sd pattentees, theyr associates heyres, executors, adminisrs, successours, assigns, actuallie reallie & perpetuallie to injoye & pocesse as theyr owne free land of inheritance and it to improve & manure according to their owne discretions, with libertie likewise for them the sd pattentees, theyr associates, heyres, and successours and assignes to put what cattle they shall think fitting to feed or graze upon the aforesd Conyne Island, forther giving granting & by vertue of these presents Wee doe give & graunt unto the sd Patentees theeir associates heyrs & successours full power & authoritie uppon the said land to build a towne or townes with such necessarie fortifications as to them shall seem expedient & to haue and injoye the free libertie of conscience according to the costome and manner of Holland, without molestation or disturbance from any Madgistrate or Madgistrates or any other Ecclesiasticall Minister that may p'tend iurisdiction over them, with libertie likewise for them, the sd pattentees, theyr associates heyres &c to erect a bodye pollitique and ciuill combination amongst themselves, as free men of this Province & of the Towne of Grauesend & to make such civil ordinances as the Maior part of ye Inhabitants ffree of the Towne shall thinke fitting for theyr quiett and peaceable subsisting & to Nominate elect & choose three of ye Ablest approued honest men & them to present annuallie to ye Gouernor Generall of this Prouince for the tyme being, for him ye said Gouernr to establish and confirme to wch sd three men soe chosen & confirmed, wee doe hereby give & graunt full power & authoritie, absolutelie & definitiuely to determine (wthout appeal to any superior Court) for debt or trespasse not exceeding ffiftie Holland Guilders ffor all such actus as shall happen wthin ye iurisdictn of the above said limitt with power likewise for any one of the said three to examine uppon oath all witnesses in cases depending before them & in case any shall refuse to stand to the award of what the Maior part of the sd three shall agree unto, in such cases wee doe hereby give and graunt full power and authoritie to any two of ye sd three, to attache & ceise uppon ye lands goods, cattles & chattles of ye parties condemned by their said sentence & fourteen days after the sd ceizure (if ye partie soe condemned agree not in the interim & submitte himself unto ye sentence of the sd three men) the said three or three appointed men as affors d to take or ioyen to themselves two more of theyre neighbours discreete honest men, and wth the advice of them to apprise the lands, goods cattles & chattles wthin the above sd jurisdictn & belongs to the partie condemned as aforesd to ye full valleu & then to sell them to any that will paye, that sattisfaction & paiement may be made according to the sentence of ye appointed men; Likewise giuing & graunting & by virtue hereof wee doe give & graunt unto ye said Pattentees, theyre associates heyres, successours &c full power & authoritie to Elect & nominate a certaine officer amongst themselves to execute the place of a Scoute & him likewise to present annuallie to the Gouernor Generall of this Province to bee established and confirmed to wch sd officer soe chosene confirmed, Wee doe hereby give & graunt as large & ample power as is usuallie given to ye Scoutes of any Village in Holland for the suppression or prevention of any disorders that maye theyr arise, or to arrest and app'hend the body of any Criminall, Malefactouer or of any that shall by worde or act disturbe the publick tranquilletie of this Province or civill peace of the inhabitants wthin the above sd jurisdictn & him, them and her so arrested or apprehended to bring or case to be brought before the Gouernor Genll of this Province & theyre by way of Processe declare against the P'tie soe offending; farther Wee doe give & graunt unto the P'tentees theyr associates heyres &c free libertie of hawking, hunting, fishing, fowling within the above sd limitts; & to use or exercise all manner of trade & commerce according as the Inhabitants of this Province may or can by Virtue of any Priviledge or graunt made unto them, indueing all and singular ye sd patttees theyr associates, heyres &c with all & singular the immunities & priueledges allready graunted to ye Inhabitants of this Provce or hereafter to be graunted, as if they were natives of the United Belgick Provinces, allways prouided the sd patentes yr associates heyres &c shall faithfully acknowledge & reverently respect the above named High Mightie Lords &c. for theyr Superiour Lords & patrons & in all loialtie & fidellitie demeane themselves towards them & theyr successours accord'g as the Inhabitants of this prouince in dutye are bound, soe long as they shall [be] within this iurisdictn & att the experatn of ten yeares to beginne from the daye of the date hereof to paye or cause to bee paid to an officer thereunto deputed by the Gouernr Genl of this Provce for the time being, the tenth parte of the reueneew that shall arise by the ground manured by the plough or howe, in case it bee demanded to be paid to the sd officer in the ffield before it bee housed, gardens or orchards not exceeding one Hollands acre being excepted, and in case anye of the sd pattentees theyr associates heyres &c shall only improue theyr stocks in grasing or breeding of cattle, then the partie soe doing shall at the end of the ten yeares afforesaid paye or cause to be paid to an officer deputed as aforesd such reasonable sattisfactn in butter and cheese as other Inhabbats of other townes shall doe in the like cases: Likewise injoyning the said pattentees theyre associates heyres &c in the dating of all public instruments to use the New Style wth the wts & measure of this place. Given under my hand & Seale of this Prouince this 19th of December in the fort Amsterdam in New Netherland. 1645.

Signed WILHEM KIEFT.

Endorsed,—Ter ordonnantie van de Hr Directr Generael & Raden van Nieuw Nederlandt.

CORNELIS VAN TIENHOUEN, Secrety.

In the name of the LORD—Amen.

DESCRIPTION of the Founding or Beginning of New Utrecht, for the information of us and our successors. Together with their Grants and Privileges likewise the names of their officers and magistrates thereunto added and that from the year Sixteen hundred seven and fifty, also the names of the first Patentees and farmers, for the encouragement and information of their posterity.

A. D. 1657
1658
1659
1660

The beginning and progress of New Utrecht.

This land was originally granted to the Heer Cornelis Van Werckhoven, who was born in Utrecht in the Netherlands, and who here personally undertook to plant a colonie. After some years he returned to his Fatherland, where he died. On his return to the Netherlands he left in his place as his agent one Jacques Cortelliau. After the death of his late Lord, Cortilliau having no means in his hands to procure settlers to plant and found the colonie, was advised not to allow the beautiful land to lie unfruitful and without inhabitants, and as he was assured that such a course was in direct opposition to the orders and placards of the Noble and Right Honorable Lords Directors of the West India Company at Amsterdam, our Patrons, as also of the Noble Lord Director General Petrus Stuyvesant and the Counsellors Nicasius DeSille, and Johan Montagne Senor., he concluded to present to the Director General and Counsellors the following Petition:—

To the Noble and Right Honorable Lord Director General and Council of New Netherland:

Whereas no lands here can be laid out and settled except with your Honors' approbation and consent, therefore the petitioner addresses himself to your Honors for consent to found a Town on Long Island on the Bay of the North River.

was signed JA. CORTELLIAU.

Agent for the heirs of the deceased Cornelis Van Werckhoven.

In the margin stood " let the petition be granted, provided that they deliver by the first opportunity, a map thereof, to the Director General and Council. Dated fortress Amterdam in New Netherland, this 16th January A. D. 1657.

Underneath which was written, By Order of the Right Honorable Director General and Council of New Netherland. Subscribed by C. V. RUYVEN, Secretary.

Liberty being thus given to commence the settlement, Jacques Cortelliau laid out and surveyed the place, and divided it into 20 lots containing 25 morgen (50 acres) each, which lots were granted to the following patentees who were desirous of making a settlement;—

Jacques Cortelliau
The Lord Councillor & Fiscal Nicasius de Sille
Pieter Buys
Jacob Hellickers alias Swart
Joncker Jacobus Corlaer
Johan Tomasse
Rutgert Joosten
Pieter Roeloffse
Cornelis Beeckman
Johan Zeelen
Albert Albertsen
William Willemsen
Huybert Hoock
Pieter Jansen
Jan Jacobson
Jacobus Backer
Jacob Pietersen,
Claes Claessen,
Teunis Joosten.

The above named individuals having received their lots, came together so as speedily to advance the place by sowing, planting and building on their lots. Whereof the first was Jacob Hellekeers Swart, he having a small square house made of clapboards standing in Gravesend which he tore down and removed to the town. On this because they could not begin altogether and alike and for the purpose of setting a good example to the common people and for their encouragement, the Lord Councillor and fiscal (Attorney General) Nicasius De Sille, Peter Buys and Rutgert Joosten on the 8th of November 1657 sent for the above named Jacob Swart, who was a master builder, for the purpose of having each a house built, and warranted completed in May 1658. This could not be accomplished, because the house of the Heer de Sille was designed to be 36 feet in length, but afterwards on the 31st of May 1658, he directed 6 feet to be added, making it 42 feet, and this was the first house in the town which was covered with red tiles. It was, including the garden, enclosed with high palisades set close together. After the above 3 houses, Johnckeer Jacob Corlaer also erected a house, and then Cornelis Beeckman with his companion Willem Willemse erected one which shortly after was burnt.

Some of the above named 20 settlers abandoned their lots, and others came in their places by whom the cultivating and building were undertaken.

In 1659 it was evident that the village did not prosper in its buildings and agriculture; this induced the wellwishers of the same to employ Jacques Cortelliau, the surveyor, to carry to the Director General and his council, in the name of all of them, the following petition:

Petition.

To the Noble and Right Honorable Lord and Director General and Council of New-Netherland:

1. The town of New Utrecht, with your consent, at the great cost and expense of some, having been begun and founded, we therefore humbly desire that those who as yet have only gone to the expense of fencing their lots, may be warned also to build on the same, on pain of forfeiture of said lots.
2. That those who have sold their lots for considerable money, without having been subject to any cost except the simple fencing, may be ordered to restore the money received over and above the cost of same.
3. That every lot should be bound to have a man who shall keep the front of the lot in repair and remove whatever falls, so that men should not be bound to look after absentees, which cannot be done without incurring expense.
4. That Antony Jansen Van Sale may be warned to drive in the woods his horses, hogs, and cattle, the same as is practiced by others, so as to prevent their spoiling and eating the pasture from the meadows, by which the whole Town is injured, and we ask for power to place them in the pound when found in said meadows.
5. That Antony Jansen, maintaining the meadows to be his which he had bought of the Indians which could not be done without the approbation of you noble and right Honorable Lords, and he not having this, may be ordered to allow us the peaceable use of said meadows commenced by us with your consent, and peaceable possession of which was promised to the inhabitants of the town; the said Antony however, having dwelt many years in the place, to enjoy his lots and portion as well as others, but at the same time to be liable to bear his share of the costs and expenses.
6. That the meadow we have commenced using when divided in 23 or 24 lots, is not half enough to keep the cattle; we therefore petition you, noble and right Honorable Lords, for another place to be given us at Canarisy and immediately used.
7. That the inhabitants of the Town may have the benefit of the same exemptions and freedom that other new towns have.

Waiting hereupon for a favorable answer from you, noble and right Honorable Lords, I remain your humble servant Jacques Cortelliau; and this the community seek.

On this petition to the Noble and right Honorable Lord Director General Petrus Stuyvesant and Council, Nicasius de Sille first councillor, and Petrus Tonneman and Johan de Decker on the 12th of May 1659 gave the following answer:

On the above request being received and read, the following answer was returned:

The answer to the 1st point will be found published in the order of the 30th of January last, by which it is ordained that every one of what condition or quality soever he may be should cultivate, build, and live on the lot he had obtained, or cause the same to be cultivated and dwelt upon, within the period of six weeks, on penalty of forfeiture of his lot: and the Fiscal is authorized in the name of the Director General and Council, at the expiration of six days after proof of the delinquency of any person to assign his lands to such other individual as may be willing to comply with these regulations and to pay the first owner or occupant what his fencing and other improvements may appear to be worth.

The answer to the second is intermixed in the above; but further, no man may enjoy more than the true value of his fencing, and what he has expended in his cultivation of his lot including the value of his own labour: All received above the ascertained value shall be paid back to his successor. The Director General and Council are by no means however to be understood as authorizing the first occupants, who have neglected either personally or by others, to build, cultivate and labour on their lands, to seek for pay or profit in such manner as to retard cultivation.

On the 3d point it is ordered that every man, as well in the new begun Town of Utrecht as in other begun Towns consisting of one dwelling or a hamlet, who obtains a lot or building plot, also that all and every one from now forth who has sought or obtained lands, must seek and obtain therefor proper patents, and there obtained lands they must speedily undertake to plant and cultivate, and at the least from the proceedings of the patent have residing and kept thereon one able bodied man.

On the 4th and 5th points; the Fiscal was ordered to notify Anthony Van Zalee to keep his cattle and hogs out of the common meadows, and that if he claimed any more right to the meadows to make the same known to the Director General and Council: the Fiscal is directed to impound all cattle and hogs found on the meadows.

An answer to the 6th point will be taken into consideration.

On what is sought in the 7th point, consent is given, as in other towns, to an exemption from the payment of the tenth for the space of 10 years, with the exception of the plantation of the Heer Werckhoven.

Done in Fort Amsterdam in New-Netherland on the 12th of May 1659. Against the above stands, By order of the Noble and Right Honorable Lord and Director General and Council of the New-Netherland:

Witness, C. V Ruyven, Secretary.

The order of the 30th of January 1659 referred to in the answer to the 1st, is as follows:

Proclamation.

All persons are hereby notified and informed, that those who have obtained lots or plantations in the newly settled Town of Utrecht, are hereby directed within six weeks from the date hereof, to prepare to plant and fence the same, also to seek and obtain of the Secretary of the Director General and Council proper Deeds, on penalty of forfeiture of the lots, which will be given to others who may desire them. Of this all are hereby warned.

Done by order of the Right Honorable Director General and Council of New-Netherland, at Fort Amsterdam in New-Netherland this 30th January 1659.

Witness

C. V Ruyven, Secretary.

After the preceding there was another Proclamation applying to the town of Utrecht, first published by the Director General and Council on the 9th of October 1655, republished and renewed on the 30th December 1658 at Fort Amsterdam, and again on the 7th of January 1659 proclaimed from the Stadt-house at Fort Amsterdam for the benefit of the farmers.

Proclamation.

The Director General and Council of New Netherland daily hear great complaints that the posts, rails, clapboards, and other fencing, made with great cost and trouble of the inhabitants (for the preservation of the crops) around their sowed lands and gardens, are stolen during both night and day, the effect of which is that the cattle come in and destroy the crops, which discourages future planting and sowing, and we also fear that it will happen that in consequence of all the lands and gardens being bare of fencing during the coming winter, the sowed grain will not flourish, and that next season the crops will not be worth mowing: Therefore the Lord Director General and Council notify the Burgomasters and Schepens of their Towns not to allow and expressly to forbid injuries of this kind, and they also hereby notify all of what state or condition they may be, that they are hereby warned and expressly forbid from this time forth, not to make bare or strip any gardens, sowed, or planted places, of posts, rails, clapboards, or other fencing, on pain when found doing the same in part or in whole, for the first offence of being whipped and branded, and for the second offence of being hung with a cord till death follows, without favor to any person: and whoever after the date hereof shall give information of any person guilty of robbing the land of posts, rails, or clapboards, shall be rewarded therefor and his name concealed: every one is hereby warned.

All done in the Assembly at Fort Amsterdam in New Netherlands on the 9th of October 1655.

The inhabitants of the Town being diligent in the observance of the foregoing order or command, the Fiscal thereupon drew out of the Company's book the following copy concerning the meadow land, not knowing in whom it was lodged:

Petrus Stuyvesant Representative of the Noble High and Mighty the Lords States General of the United Netherlands, and the Lord Administrator of the Privileged West India Company, Director General of New Netherland, Curaçao, Bonayre Aruba, and the appendages thereunto belonging, hath with the consent of the Council, on the petition and supplication made to us on the date underneath written, showing the need of the inhabitants of the new begun Town of Utrecht and of those who might hereafter dwell there, allowed unto them as to others a parcel of meadow land lying on Long Island by the easterly Hook of the Bay of the North River, over against Conyen Island, including the kills, creeks, ponds, reeds, drowned and sand lands within its bounds, Containing 130 morgen (260 acres) Bounded on the westerly side by land of Antony Jansen Van Sale, north-easterly by the kill on which Gravesend mill is situated, East south-easterly by the same kill, and south-westerly by the Bay of the North River. Hereunto witness my hand and seal (in red wax) in Amsterdam in New Netherland this 27 August 1657.

Thereupon having assembled together in the Town of Utrecht in May A. D. 1659, for the purpose of drawing for the meadows, it being understood that the Director General and Council directed that the plantation of the Lord Werckhoven should draw two lots, and also Antony Jansen Van Sale two, and having divided the same into 24 lots, they were drawn as follows:

1. Jonker Jacob Curler,
2. Albert Albertse,
3. Jan Zėlen,
4. Jacob Backker,
5. Willem Willemse,
6. Hupbert Hook,

13. Nicasius De Sille, Fiscal,
14. Pieter Roeloffe,
15. Jaques Cortilliau,
16. Teunis Joosten,
17. Ruth Joosten,
18. Pieter Buys,

7. Peter Jansen,	19. Werckhoven,
8. Jacob Pieterse,	20. Ruth Joosten,
9. Jacob Swart,	21. Werckhoven,
10. Jan Tomasse,	22. Cornelius Beekman,
11. Klaes Blassen,	23. Antony Jansen Van Sale.
12. Jan Jacobse,	24.

In the meantime the inhabitants often disagreeing and disputing about their plantations, houses, and about the watch, the Director General, and Council ordained as follows:

The Director General and Council notify the inhabitants of the Town of New Utrecht to keep good watch, and for the purpose of keeping better order they have appointed and set, as in other cases, the person Jan Tomassen to the office of Serjeant: they therefore order the inhabitants of the Town to obey and acknowledge as Serjeant, the above named Jan Tomassen.

Done at Fort Amsterdam, the 2d of October A D. 1659.

Hereupon did the Fiscal N. DeSille send a Halberd.

Shortly thereafter the inhabitants of the Town complained, that they were badly provided with powder and lead, and also that some of them had no guns, they desired that the Fiscal would provide them at their own cost with the same, they having recourse to him inasmuch as they had heard the Director General and Council had appointed him Scout (Sheriff) over the Town of Utrecht.

The Lord General on the 6th cf October 1659, with many soldiers who were volunteers, a company of Citizens with the Orange banner, and a company of English wellwishers, went to Esopus to fight the Indians. Thereupon having charge of the Town on behalf of the company, I sent out of my own armoury as follows:

10 light muskets,	25 lb balls,
25 lb powder,	10 cartridge boxes,

2 bunches gun matches.

The Town therefore is charged at the following rate:—1 lb powder, one guilder in bevers, or 30 stuyvers in wampum, or 25 stuyvers in wheat; 1 lb lead, 6 stuyvers; 1 musket and cartridge box, 8 guilders in wampum and a match in proportion; also with one hour glass and a writing book.

Thereafter it happened that the inhabitants disputed, quarreled, and disagreed among one and another, in consequence of which Albert Albertse, Harmen Courten, Jan Sely, Jan Van Cleef, Teunis Ydessen, Cornelis Beeckman, Claes Claessen Smit, Jacob Hellekerse Swart, Huibert Jansen Hook, Willelm Willemse, Pieter Hesselse, and Jacob Van Curlaer, on the 11th of October 1659 united in a petition to the Director General and Counsel for relief, which they handed to the Fiscal for safe keeping, not being able to send it in consequence of the season and the Indians.

The Fiskal then gave orders to fortify and surround his house, which alone had a tile roof, with palisades for the safety of the inhabitants and as a place of refuge, which immediately was done and finished.

In consequence of many persons neglecting properly fencing their lots, keeping them in proper order, or keeping watch either personally or by deputy, dissatisfaction arose, so that Jan Tomasse, Huybert Janson Hoock, Cornelis Beeckman, Willem Williamse, and J. Van Curlaer, again on the 26th of January 1660, wrote to the Fiscal complaining of the damage daily done by the hogs, in consequence of the insufficiency of the fences, so that they had also had a mind to be neglectful if nothing was done to abate the evil.

The above and similar difficulties and disturbances caused the Fiscal much running about and made him weary, so that he did not know what immediately to do, and doubted whether or not to accept the office of Sheriff of the Town of Utrecht; he did as much as he could to make peace, so that the building and ploughing might go on, there being at that time but few houses; these were numbered on the 6th February 1660, as follows:

Nicasius De Sille,	Pieter Buyes,
Rutger Joosten,	Jacques Cortillau a barn
Jacob Swart,	Willem Willemse,
Jacob Van Curlaer,	Jan Sely
Jacob Pieterse,	Aelbert Albertse,
Teunis Ydesse,	Klaes Smit,

On the 21st of January 1660 the Fiscal demanded of the Surveyor Jacques Cortleyou his certificate of the survey of his house plot farm and meadows, which is as follows: A lot on the plain lying South East of the shore or strand way, and North-West of the land of Ruth Joosten, in width 12 rods, and in length 25 rods; the land known as lot No. 9 being in width 26 rods, and lying North-east against the land of Jacobus Backer, South-west by the village of New-Utrecht, stretching South-east and containing 25 Morgens (50 acres); also a piece in the meadows numbered 13, containing 3 morgens.

Now I shall insert in full the Fiscal's Patent, so that all persons may understand when they become liable to pay the tenth of the produce of their lands to the government, to which provision all are liable from the date of the first patent whether they take them up or not.

Patent.

Petrus Stuyvesant on the behalf of the Noble High and Mighty Lords the States General of the United Netherlands, and Noble Lord and Director of the Privileged West India Company of the Chamber at Amsterdam, Director General of New Netherland, Curacoa, Bonayre, Aruba, with their appendages, with the consent of the Noble Lords of the Council witness and declare, that We on the date hereunto underwritten, have given & granted to Nicasius de Sille, a parcel of land lying on Long Island in the Town of New Utrecht, known as number nine, in width 26 rods, bounded on the north-east by land of Jacob Backer, on the South-west by the village, and stretching South-east to the woods, containing 25 morgens (50 acres); also a piece of meadow land known as number 13 containing 3 morgens; also a building plot on the plain South-east of the shore or strand way, lying North-west of Ruth Joosten, in breadth 12 rods, and in length 25 rods; on the express condition and terms that the said Nicasius de Sille, or those who hereafter may obtain the same, acknowledge for his Lord and Patron, the Noble Lord Director above mentioned under the Sovereignty of the Noble, High and Mighty Lords of the States General, and in all things as a good inhabitant obey the Director General and Council, subject at the expiration of ten years after date, when required by the Lord Patrons, to the payment of the tenth, also to the other charges and services to which all the inhabitants of the land are liable when occasions arise to require the same; constituting over the same the beforenamed Nicasius De Sille in our place the actual possessor of the aforesaid parcel of land, giving him with the same, complete right, authority, and special charge of the aforesaid parcel of land for cultivation, dwelling, and use, the same as he might have with his other patrimonial lands and effects without our having any further claim thereon: But in behoof aforesaid desisting from all such from henceforth and forever, promising to keep firm, valid, and inviolable this conveyance, and to perform all its engagements justly, and to stand to the same without craft or subtlety, is this by Us subscribed, sealed in red wax, and confirmed; At Amsterdam in New Netherland this 22d day of January 1660.

Signed Petrus Stuyvesant.

(Here follows another Patent to De Sille for No. 8.)

On the 15th of February 1660, Jacob Van Curler, and Jan Tommassen who had the oversight and charge of the Town, sent to the Fiscal N. de Sille a letter of complaint and also one of enquiry, in the first of which they complained about the bad management in the Town of Utrecht to the injury of the well meaning; they also complained of certain ring leaders who they would not name, hoping they would repent and do better in future; they looked for and expected to have sent to them the promised Negroes of the Company to set palisades around the village as thought and spoken of by the Director General and Council: if they are not sent they desired to resign their situations and to have others appointed in their places.

Herewith they send to the Fiscal, draughts of rules which they desire to have put in operation in the Town and which in short are as follows:

1. An order relating to cattle and hogs jumping over and breaking the fences.
2. An order relating to the saving of powder and lead.
3. An order relating to the building plots of the inhabitants.
4. An order relating to those who own lands but neglect to cultivate and build on the same, and who remain outside the place.

When the Fiscal had read the above he drew the following Petition and joined to the same an Ordinance according to his own judgment, and on the 23 day of February 1660 delivered the same.

Copy.

To the Noble and Right honorable Lord and Director General and Council of New Netherland.

It is represented to your Honor by the orderly inhabitants of the Town of New Utrecht, that they have among them some absentees and evil doers, who refuse to listen to reason and act in an orderly manner, but always are contrary and troublesome, yea, will not obey the Serjeant Jan Tomasse, of which some time ago notice was given to you the Noble and Right Honorable Lord; several times the Fiscal has been written to in relation to the great trouble and injury caused by horses, cattle and hogs and consequent damages, also that they refuse to listen to and obey the orders of Jacob Curlear and Jan Tomasse in relation to cutting palisades; we therefore humbly seek in the first place that you Noble and Right Honorable Lord, will be pleased to send the promised Negroes for 8 days, and also to approve of the accompanying ordinances drawn for the Town, and to favour us with such others as you Noble and Right Honorable Lord, may think necessary:

This do, &c. Was subscribed,

To the Noble and Right Honorable Lord in the name of the orderly inhabitants of New Utrecht by your humble servant.

NICASIUS DE SILLE.

Amsterdam in N. Netherland this 23d Feb. 1660.

On the above written date the Fiscal personally delivered the following to the Council which was ordered to be enforced.

1. Those who have obtained lots and plantations in the Town of New Utrecht are notified properly to fence the same.
2. They shall acknowledge and obey as Serjeant the person Jan Tomasse.
3. Also to acknowledge the same Jan Tomasse and Jacob Van Curlaer as overseers over all, and to obey the orders they receive of the Noble and Right Honorable Lord Director General and Council, and to proceed in the first place with all hands with posts and rails properly to fence in the village, also the plantations.
4. Also that Village or Building lots be properly fenced, to prevent one and another receiving damage from horses, cattle or hogs.
5. So therefore to promote the prosperity of the Town and for the benefit of the in-dwellers and of those who may hereafter come, the Director General and Council directs, that they from now henceforth obey the person Nicasius de Sille as their officer and Jacob Corlaer and Jan Tomasse as his assistants for the purpose of allaying all differences that may happen.

6. Another, that all the inhabitants assist in inclosing the village (with palisades,) and that the work be divided among them, so that every one may know the portion he is to keep in order.
7. And, that every person who neglects to keep his part in order or tight, so that others in consequence receive damage, shall be liable not only to make good the damage, but also be fined 12 guilders for the first neglect and double that amount for the second.
8. Also, every person shall properly inclose his village plot, to prevent the neighbours receiving damage from cows, horses or hogs, on pain of the above mentioned penalty, but if the cattle break through, one or two of them may be caught and shut up in the public pound until the damage is made good and the penalty paid.
9. Also, the inhabitants shall build in the middle of the Village a good Blockhouse, in which they shall make provision for a grain mill for the convenience of the people, on the penalty of 12 guilders for every one that neglects to assist.
10. In like manner they shall build a public pound for the cattle which commit damage, on the penalty of 2 guilders for each person who refuses.
11. Also, they shall cut down all the trees standing within gun shot of the village, so that they may see afar off, on penalty of 6 guilders a-day.
12. Also those to whom powder and lead are given for the public are forbid to use it for shooting venison or game, nor shall they lavishly squander it, on penalty of restoring four times as much as given to them by the officer or his assistants.
13. And, for the purpose of purchasing and obtaining good ammunition, the Director General and Council order for the Town of New-Utrecht, that they who slaughter oxen, cows, calves, hogs or goats, for consumption in the town, shall be taxed for each guilder (40 cents) of their value, one stuyver (2 cents); and those who do not produce their animals for valuation previous to slaughtering shall forfeit the same for the benefit of the officer, the Town, and the informer.
14. And, those who absent themselves are notified to perform the part of the work which is allotted to them, for neglect of which their lots will be taken from them, and furthermore those who neglect to build around their village plots, will have the same given or allowed for building purposes to those who live outside the village.
15. And, that no man may pretend ignorance hereof, we direct that these our ordinances be immediately made public and that the Scout Fiscal and Assistants be notified to proceed to execute the same. And that without conniving, they proceed against those who transgress said ordinances, they being promulgated for the benefit of the Town of New Utrecht.

Thus done &c. 23d Feb. 1660.

On the 25th of February accompanied by my deputy Resolveertt Waldron, I came to the village of New Utrecht with the above ordinances, and made the same public, and also posted a copy of the same, signed with my hand and dated as above, on my house.

NICASIUS DE SILLE.

The original of the preceding is in the hand writing of the Secretary Jacob Curlaer and dated as above written.

N. B. This was forgotten to be entered in its proper place. The Director General and Council of New Netherland, hereby authorize and qualify the Noble Lord Nicasius de Sille, member of the Council and Fiscal to appoint a substitute to perform his duties as Scout (sheriff) in the Town of New Utrecht, until the Director General and Council see fit to commit the same to some other suitable person.

Done at Fort Amsterdam in New Netherlands this 23d February A° 1660 subscribed by me

PETRUS STUYVESANT &c

The Lord General P. Stuyvesant is pleased to learn that the new Village is pleasantly situated and he hopes it will prosper. He also on the 6th of February in the year 1660, in company with the Fiscal personally visited the place, and by word of mouth gave good directions and advice; he also called the people together and admonished every man in the first place to prepare, and make his own dwelling, and to keep a man or servant able to bear arms; also to enclose the village with a good heavy palisades, for which latter purpose the Director General and Council had promised several Negroes who should come on the 16th inst. following.

The inhabitants had the Prince's flag (given to the Town by the Fiscal) hoisted on a high pole in the centre of the village and unfurled to the breeze. Moreover Ruth Joosten prepared a dinner or public entertainment in as good a stile as the place could afford, in which he was assisted by the inhabitants. The Director General and his attendants remained but a short time at the banquet in consequence of the necessity of their departure to attend to other business.

On the 25th of said month of February I brought 7 Negroes, with Paulus Heymans as their overseer, who on the 26th inst. began with much strength to cut trees in the woods and split them for Palisades. There came however a soldier to fetch the Fiscal, who consequently could not remain longer. He was commissioned with the Burgomaster, Paulus Leenderse Van de Grist and Jacob Backer, Schepen, to proceed in the yacht Sea Bear to the South River (Delaware.) When he returned he found the Village inclosed with palisades to his contentment.

At this time Jacob Backer made known that he would not accept of his improved lot, its situation not pleasing him; the Scout and officer Nicasius de Sille therefore verbally warned him of the consequences, on which he answered that he would have nothing to do with the land; Will you have it? keep it. On this the Lord General gave it to the officer de Sille and on the 27th of May issued an order to the surveyor, to survey the same as follows: One lot known as No 8, in width 26 rods, lying on the Southwest side of the land of the said Fiscal and on the Northeast side of the land of Arien Willemse, stretching South East towards the woods containing 25 morgens (50 acres); and also a lot in the meadows known as No 4, containing 3 morgens. Besides the above, the Village plot attached to the aforesaid lands is also to be included in the patent.

At this time we discovered that we had an insufficient quantity of meadow to supply the wants of our increased quantity of cattle. We were advised to apply to the Lord General and Council for another piece of meadow for the use of the Town situated in the Canarse meadows. We therefore several times spoke to the Lord General in relation to said meadows.

On the 12th of June 1660, the General with the Fiscal and Van Ruyven came over and taking Curlaer and Jan Tomasse, went to the Canarse, where the meadows were shown to the Lords. Upon this the Lord General and Council made provision for the Town, and gave them a piece of meadow extending from Varckens (Hogs) hook to the Vischers (fisher's) hook, where the fisherman Hoorn had placed his house. The Secretary Cornelis Van Ruyven was notified of this and directed to deliver to the Town a writing securing to them the aforesaid meadows.

In February 1660, as well as previously, several proclamations and ordinances had been published, in which those who lived separately and outside the villages, were charged in the name of the Director General and Council of the New-Netherland, to abandon their separate dwellings and destroy them, or at least to unroof them, and to transport themselves and their goods into the adjoining villages, on the penalty, in the first place of the confiscation of all their goods upon all who from the aforesaid time are found residing in separate dwellings or farm houses. Those who do not remove by the 18 of May will also be liable to a penalty of 50 guilders, to be paid immediately and also to have their houses unroofed at their expense.

After this it happened that several persons who resided outside the village paid no attention to the above order, among whom was a Mr. Stilwel, who had purchased the land of Antony Jansen Van

Salee, Turck, but he made satisfaction to the Director General and Council for the same. Also another was Albert Albertse who hired a part of the plantation of C. Van Wreckhoven on the Na jack; he excused himself on the ground of being on hired land, and regarded not the Lords order, in consequence of which the fiscal ex officio brought him on the 19th of August 1660, before the high Council in Fort Amsterdam, and complained of his refusal to obey the ordinance He was condemned and sentenced as follows, after which he came and resided in the village of Utrecht, which lay near his lands:

By the Director General and Council of the New Netherland on a hearing of the parties; We condemn Albert Albertse alias Lintwever, to amends by paying the penalty of 50 guilders as per proclamation, and to stand imprisonment until the fine be paid.

On this sentence, after being imprisoned, he paid the fine and then removed within the village of New Utrecht.

In this year it happened that one Pieter Roeloffe sold his house and building lot in the village of Utrecht to one Jan Zeelen, and was about selling his farm and meadows, on which he had performed very little labour, to another man; on this Jan Zeelen applied to the Director General and council to have the said lands given to him, knowing that under the circumstances such lands fell to the Director General and Council. They granted his request and allowed and permitted to the said Jan Zeelen the lot in question known as No. 18, no man being allowed to sell lands for which he had no patent, without liberty first obtained from the public authorities, neither was it lawful to alienate the same. This took place on the 16th of Jan. 1660.

In the month of October of this year it came to the ears of the Fiscal, that an individual had done amiss in the village, from which evil consequences were likely to flow. To punish evil doers, frighten the vicious, and produce tranquility for the good, the Fiscal sent to the Village half a dozen shackels with an iron rod and a good lock.

Oderunt peccare Mali formidine pœnæ.
Oderunt peccare Boni Virtutis amore.

In this year 1660, the Fiscal, John Van Cleef and his friend, bought of Jacob Wolfertse Van Couwenhoven, for the use of the inhabitants of the town of Utrecht, a Horse Mill with the appurtenances which had been used for grinding in Amsterdam on the Manhattans. The mill stones and the mill work were brought and set up in the Village of Utrecht. The friend of Jan Van Cleef, without the knowledge of the Fiscal, sold out his third part to said Jan Van Cleef, the Fiscal being security for both of them, and having paid out already more than 400 guilders ($160) on account of the mill. The Fiscal seeing that Jan Van Cleef did not prosper, and that the last day of payment was near at hand, threatened to prosecute and compel him to act justly. On this Jan Van Cleef sought a buyer to sell the mill to, at the same time the people desired the Fiscal to buy the mill, but he refused, neither would he sell his third part, having in view the benefit of the Town and the convenience of the inhabitants. In consequence of this Jan Van Cleef was under the necessity of selling his two thirds to Albert Albertse, and the mill remained in the town of Utrecht, the Fiscal remaining unwilling to sell his third part.

Proclamation on Slaughtering.

The Director General and Council of New Netherland:

To all who see this Edict or hear the same read Health. Be it known that daily complaints are made to us, confirmed by proofs, of the taking from the plains, cows, hogs, and other cattle, belonging to the various nations of Indians, and slaughtering and selling of the same by Christians, or by men who go by the name of Christians; to prevent such acts this Edict is promulgated. The Director General and Council, to prevent the above mentioned evil practices, from this time forth hereby expressly interdict and forbid the slaughtering any cattle, calves, hogs, sheep, or goats, by any person or by the owners of the same, in the Towns, plains, villages, and Hamlets of this Province, unless the owner of such animals on the same day on which he intends to slaughter them informs either the magistrate of the town under whose jurisdiction he resides, or such person as may be authorized by the magistrate to act in his place, of his intention and obtains a permit for slaughtering said animal, on the penalty of the confiscation of the slaughtered animal, and also of paying double its value. For every permit the owner shall pay to the magistrate or to the receiver appointed for that purpose for the benefit of the community, one stuyver (2 cts.) on every guilder the slaughtered animal is justly valued at. In all places the money obtained for such permits shall be reserved for times of need or difficulty, and then be used to pay those who may be employed by the villages, to levy soldiers, and to purchase such ammunition as the occasion may require. The penalty for killing animals without a permit shall be divided as follows: one third to the informer, one third to the officer, and one third to the Town.

Done in Fort Amsterdam in New Netherlands, this 18th January 1660.

The above is the ordinance of the Noble Lord Director General of New Netherland.

Witness CORNELIUS VAN RVYVEN, Secretary.

On the 6th of Dec. 1660, I sent a petition to the Director General and Council, in which in consequence of my being confined to my house with a sore leg, I requested them to commit the supervision of the town of New Utrecht to the Heer Tonneman, Scout of New Amsterdam, and to authorize him, in my stead, to settle all controversies, misdeeds, and difficulties, also to stimulate the people to build dwelling houses, a block house and public pound, and to dig wells for the benefit of the community. My petition was sent to the General by my son Laurens de Sille, on which he sent me word that in 4 or 5 days he would personally go to New Utrecht for the purpose in the first place of putting every thing in good order. The Lord General in the mean time became sick and matters remained as they had been: I waited for his recovery and intend to wait and see what will follow.

I now close this Introduction or Commencement of the Records the Town, all the preceding have been written by myself and my son Laurens as gathered from various sources and memory. I now deliver this book over to Jacob Van Curiaer, Secretary of the town of Utrecht, and to his assistant Jan Tomasse, who I desire for our benefit and that of our successors to continue the same in the manner in which it begun.

Closed this 15th Decr A. D. 1660 in Amsterdam by me

NICASIUS DE SILLE.

(In the back part of the book from which the above was translated is the following:)

Short abstracts of proclamations or edicts relating to misdemeanors.

Sabbath days not to be broken.

1st. All persons are forbid selling Beer, Wine, or strong drink during divine service on the Sabbath, neither shall they allow it to be drank in their houses, as per edict of the last of May, 1647, the 26th Sept. 1656, and 12th July 1657.

Servants after 9 o'clock.

2d. All persons are forbid selling it to servants after 9 o'clock Ultimo May 1647.

To the Indians.

3d. All persons are forbid selling strong drink to the Indians according to the edict of the 26th Sept. 1656, and 12th July 1656.

Fences not to be injured.

4th. All persons are forbid entering into the gardens, farms, or orchards of others; they are forbid injuring the fruits growing in the same, also to break off the clapboards or other fencing with which the premises are enclosed. They are all directed to keep their fences in good order so that others receive no injury in consequence of their neglect, according to the Edict of July 1st 1647.

Fighting and striking.

5th. All fighting is forbid, drawing of knives, striking with the fist and wounding. Offenders to be punished as ordained in the edict of 15th Dec.

Inn keepers.

All tavern keepers to be held liable for willingly permitting fighting or wounding in their houses, and when such breaches of the peace take place, they shall inform the officer of the same, on penalty of having their trade stopped, and making the amends customary in Amsterdam, according to the edict of the 15th Decr. 1657.

Barbers.

The same law to operate in case fighting &c. should happen in the houses of Barbers according to the order of Amsterdam.

Servants.

Item. No person to create difficulties between Masters and Servants, nor induce Servants to come and live with him, neither shall he take in his service or harbour them in his house more than 24 honrs without acquainting the Officer or Fiscal of the same, for servants shall be obliged to fulfil their contracts and to follow the order of the 6th of Oct. 1648, and the custom of Holland.

Highways.

Item. No person may encumber or obstruct the highways by falling trees in them, or stones, but they shall be kept passable according to the edict of the 23d May 1650.

Waggon racing.

No person shall race with carts and wagons, in the streets within the villages, but the driver while passing through villages must walk by the side of his horses or vehicle, according to the edict of the 12th of July 1657.

Dead animals.

Item. No person shall have his dead beast on the highways or streets but must bury the same, on the penalty of 3 guilders for the first offence, 6 guilders for the second, and imprisonment for the 3d offence if he remains obstinate.

Privies

No person shall place privies on the highways or streets so as to allow the hogs to root up the filth in the same, on the penalty of 6 guilders for the first offence, 6 guilders for the second, and imprisonment for the third offence.

Weights and Measures.

Yard stick, measures and weights must be sealed and made alike, according to the custom of Amsterdam in Holland, on the penalty of 10 guilders for the first offence, 20 guilders for the second, and 40 guilders for the third offence, and also in addition to have their trade stopped.

Wages or hire of Indians.

Those who hire Indians for money, must pay them promptly and fulfil the engagement: for failure they shall be condemned to pay the hire and be punished according to the edict of the 28th of September 1648.

Concubinage.

All persons to be kept to the three publications of the bans before marriage and to wait one month thereafter so as to give opportunity for the making of legal objections if any exist; if after the expiration of that time either party refuse to marry without giving lawful reasons, they shall be liable to a penalty of 10 guilders for the first week and 20 guilders for every succeeding week until lawful reasons for refusal are given.

Further no man or woman may live together as husband and wife without being married, on the penalty of 100 guilders, or of as much more or less as the quality or ability of the offenders will warrant; if continuing to offend to be liable every month to pay the same penalty to the officer, according to the edict of the 15th of Jany 1658.

Conventicles.

No person may surreptitiously hold a meeting for public worship, or sing, read, or preach in the same, on the penalty of 100 pounds Flemish; and the hearers to be each liable to a penalty of 25 pounds Flemish, without regard to the religion or sect they may be of, as per the edict of the 1st of Feby. 1657.

Brewers not to be retailers of liquors.

These two occupations may not be followed by the same individual, neither shall they sell by the can, on the penalty of all the beer which may be found in their houses, and in addition of having their trade stopped for 6 months, according to the edict of the 12th of Jany 1648.

Goats.

The Goats which run at large without keepers, in consequence of their injuring fruit and other trees, may be seized by the officer and taken possession of according to the edict of the 16th of March, 1648.

Public instruments or papers.

No man may draft public documents or papers, unless authorized by the Director General and Council; offenders shall be brought to trial before the high court of judicature according to the edict of May 1649.

Receiving articles in pawn for liquor forbidden.

No man may take anything in pawn for liquors, on penalty of restoring the goods, and paying in addition 25 guilders for the first offence, 50 guilders for the second and double (100 guilders) for the third offence, and also to have his license taken away and trade stopped, according to the edict of the 3d of Dec. 1657.[1]

1 For the Translation of the above paper, the public is indebted to Teunis G. Bergen, Esq., of Kings Co.

GOV. COLVES CHARTER TO THE SEVERAL TOWNS ON LONG ISLAND. ANNO. 1673.

PROVISIONAL INSTRUCTION FOR THE SHERIFF AND MAGISTRATES OF THE VILLAGES OF MIDWOUT, (FLATBUSH) AMERSFOORT (FLATLANDS) BREUKELEN, NEW UTRECHT, GRAVESEND AND BOSWYCK SITUATE ON LONG ISLAND.

[Flatbush Rec.; also Alb. Rec.]

Art. 1. The Sheriff and Magistrates shall, each in his quality, take care that the Reformed Christian Religion be maintained in conformity to the Synod of Dordrecht without permitting any other sects attempting any thing contrary thereto.

2. The Sheriff shall be present, as often as possible, at all the meetings and preside over the same; but should he act for himself as party, or in behalf of the rights of the Lords Patroons or of Justice, he shall, in such case, rise from his seat and leave the Bench & in that event he shall not have any advisory much less a concluding vote, but the oldest Schepen shall, then, preside in his place.

3. All cases relating to the Police, Security and Peace of the Inhabitants; also to Justice between man and man, shall be finally determined by the magistrates of each of the aforesaid Villages, to the amount of sixty florins, Beaver, and thereunder without appeal: In case the sum be larger the aggrieved party may appeal to the meeting of the Sheriff and Councillors delegated from the Villages subject to his jurisdiction, for which purpose one person shall be annually appointed from each village who shall assemble in the most convenient place to be selected by them, and who shall have power to pronounce final judgment to the amount of fl. 240 Beavers and thereunder. But in all cases exceeding that sum each one shall be entitled to an appeal to the Governour General and Council here.

4. In cases of inequality of votes, the minority shall submit to the majority; but those who are of a contrary opinion may have it recorded in the minutes but not divulge it without the meeting on pain of arbitrary correction.

5. Whenever any cases occur in the meeting in which any of the Magistrates are interested such Magistrate shall, in that instance, rise and absent himself, as is hereinbefore stated, in the 2nd article; of the sheriff.

6. All Inhabitants of the abovenamed Villages shall be citable before said Sheriff and Schepens or their delegated Councillors who shall hold their meetings and courts as often as they shall consider requisite.

7. All criminal offences shall be referred to the Governour General and Council, on condition that the Sheriff be obliged to apprehend the offenders, to seize and detain them & to convey them as prisoners under proper safeguard to Chief Magistrate with good and correct informations for or against the offenders.

8. Smaller offences, such as quarrels, abusive words, threats, fisticuffs and such like, are left to the jurisdiction of the Magistrates of each particular Village.

9. The Sheriff and Schepens shall have power to conclude on some ordinances for the welfare and peace of the Inhabitants of their district such as laying highways, setting off lands and gardens and in like manner what appertains to agriculture, observance of the Sabbath, erecting churches, school houses or similar public works. *Item*, against fighting & wrestling and such petty offences provided such ordinances are not contrary but as far as is possible, conformable to the Laws of our Fatherland and the Statutes of this Province; and therefore, all orders of any importance shall, before publication, be presented to the Chief Magistrate and his approval thereof requested.

10. The said Sheriff and Schepens shall be bound strictly to observe and cause to be observed the Placards and Ordinances which shall be enacted and published by the supreme authority, and not suffer any thing to be done against them, but cause the Transgressors therein to be proceeded against according to the tenor thereof; and further, promptly execute such orders as the Governour General shall send them from time to time.

11. The Sheriff and Schepens shall be also obliged to acknowledge as their Sovereign Rulers their High Mightinesses the Lords States General of the United Netherlands and his Serene Highness the Lord Prince of Orange and to maintain their sovereign jurisdiction, right and domain over this country.

12. The selection of all inferior officers and servants in the employ of said Sheriff and Schepens, the Secretary alone excepted, shall be made and confirmed by themselves.

13. The Sheriff shall, by himself or deputies execute all the Magistrates' judgments nor discharge any one except by advice of the Court; he shall also take good care that the places under his charge shall be cleansed of all mobs, gamblers, whorehouses and such like impurities.

14. The Sheriff shall receive the half of all civil fines accruing during his term of office together with one third part of what belongs to the respective Villages from criminal cases; but he shall neither directly nor indirectly receive any presents forbidden by law.

15. Towards the time of election, the Sheriff and Schepens shall nominate as Schepens a double number of the best qualified, honest, intelligent and wealthiest inhabitants, exclusively of the Reformed Christian Religion or at least well affected thereunto, to be presented to the Governour, who shall then make his election therefrom with continuation of some of the old ones in case his honour may deem it necessary. Done in Fort Wilem Hendrick 1st October 1673.

NOTE. Similar instructions were sent to Flushing, Hemsted, Middleburgh, Jamaica, Oysterbay, Southampton, Southold, Seatalcot, Huntington and East Hampton, on L. I., to Swanenburgh, Hurley & Marbletown in the Esopus; to Elizabethtown, Woodbridge, Shrewsbury, Newarke, Bergen, Piscattaway and Middletown, behind Achter Cul; and to Staten Island & Westchester.

NAMES OF INHABITANTS OF THE TOWN OF HEMPSTEAD 1673.

[Vanderkemp's Transl. of Dutch Rec. XXII.]

John ———
John Smith Blew
Richard Geldersly, Sen
——— ———
Vrolphert Jacobs
Jan Carman
John Symons jun
Robert Jackson
Symon Tory
John Smith
Peter janse Schol
Richard Gildersly
Robbert Beedill
George Hallet
Samuel Allen
Richard Valentyn
Kaleb Carman
John Williams
Thomas Richmore
John Ellesson
Edward Spry
William Osborne
Edward Remsen
John Fossaker

John Sorram
James Payne
William Fixton
Samuel Denton
Robberd Hobbs
Thomas Sodderd
John Smith jun
Joseph Williams
Ralph Haal
Daniel Beedell
John Jackson
Johnathan Smith
John Champion
John Hobbs
John Langd
Jonhathan Semmes
John Bordes
Robbard Marisseu
Mos Hemmery
John Beets carpenter
Samuel Embry
Matthew Beedel
Comes
Thomas Ellison
Philip Davis
——— Hopkins
——— ———
Adam View
Edward Titus
Richard Eliison
John Seavin
Thomas Teasay
Thomas Ireland
Thomas Ellison
Joseph Gem
Thomas Champion
Joseph Pettet
Richard Fotter
John Beddell
Thomas Southward
John Beates
Calvet Goullet
Christoffel Yeomans

John Woully
Edward Banbury
Thomas Gowes
John Mavein
Wm Thorne
Joshua Watske
Benjamin Symenson
Jan Roelossen
Elbert Hubssen
Lewis Niot
John Ellison jun
Thomas Seabrook
Samuel Jackson
John Pine
Peter Jansen
William Waré
Solomon Semmar
Teunis Smith
Richard Valentin jun.
Joseph Wood
Herman Flouwer
William Dose
Symon Foster
Henry Mott
William Fourmer
Joseph Small
Walter pine
Josia Carman
John Peacock
John Quakerson
Thomas Daniels
John Napper
Richard Osborn
George Robbert
Charles Abram
Thomas Appelbe
Samuel Smith
——— Persell
Adam Mott Junr.
Samuel Jackson
Joseph Truax
Joseph Hoyt &
Nine others whose names are lost

THE ROLL

OFF THOSE WHO HAUE TAKEN THE OATH OFF ALLEGIANCE IN THE KINGS COUNTY IN THE PROVINCE OF NEW YORKE THE 26 : 27 : 28 : 29 AND 30th DAY OFF SEPTEMBER IN THE THIRD YEARE OF HIS MAYtsh RAIGNE ANNOQue DOMINE 1687.

[MSS. in Sec's Office.]

off fflackbush.

Willem Jacobs Van boerem was in this country 38 Jeare
Christoffel Probasco 33 Jeare
hendrick Rijcken 24 Jeare
Pieter Strycker native off this Province off N: York
Cornelis Pieterse native
Cornelis Peters Luijster native
Dirck Jansn Van Vliet 23 Jeare
gerrit Lubberse native
Ruth Albertse 25 Jeare
gerrardus beakman native
Jacob henk. hafften 23 Jeare
gerrit Dorlant native
Engelbert Lott native
Simon hanssen 48 Jeare
Jacob Willem Van bueren 38 Jeare
Reynier aertsen 34 Jeare
Pieter Lott 35 Jeare
Cornelis Barense Van Wyck 27 yeare
Jacob Remsen native
Jan harmenessen Van amesfoort 29 Jeares
Willem hendrickse native
Joseph hegeman 37 yeare
Claes Willkens 25 yeare
Willem guil Janse 47 yeare
Auke Reijnierse native
Jooris Remssen native
Jan Wourerse Van bosch 28 yeare
Lambert Jansen native
Jan Remsen native
Jan Dircks Van Vliet 23 yeare
hendrickus hegeman 36 yeare
Jan Spigelaer 25 yeare
adriaen hend aaten 36 yeare
Lefferd Pieterse 27 Jeare
Isaack hegeman native
Pieter guil Janse 45 Jeare
Pieter Willemsen native
Cornelis Jansse Seeu 27 Jeare
hendrick Lott native
Daniel Polhemius native
Jan Van Ditmaertz native
Denijs theunissen native
Jan Strycker 35 yeare
Isaac Van Cassant 35 Jeare
Jan barense blom native
Adriaen Reyerse 41 Jeare
Aris Vanderbilt native
Auke Janse Van Nuys 36 Jeare
Elbert adriaense native
Daniel Remsen native
Jacob Vandebilt native
Marten adriaense native
Christiaen Snediker native
Abram hegeman native
Jan Cornelissen Vander Veer native
Theodorus Van Wijck native
Thomas aaten native
gerrit Snediker native
hendrick Janse native
Roeloff Verkerck 24 Jeare
barent Janssen native
Jacobus hegeman 36 Jeare
hendrick Willemse 38 Jeare
Dirck Jan hooglant native
Jan Dircks hooglant native
Willem Dircks hooglant native
Jan oake 36 Jeare
gerrit Janse Strijker 35 Jeare
Rem Remssen native

off Breucklijn

Thomas Lamberse 36 Jeare
Jooris hanssen native
hendrick Vechten 27 Jeare
Claes arense Vechten 27 Jeare
Jan Aertsen 26 Jeare

hendrick Claaesen 33 Jeare
Jacob hanssen bergen native
Jooris Martens native
hendrick thyssen 21 Jeare
Mauritius Couverts native
Willem huijcken 21 Jeare
theunis gysbertse bogaert 35 Jeare
Willem bennitt native
hendrick Lamberse native
Jan ffredricks 35 Jeare
Jan Couverts native
Luijcas Couverts 24 Jeare
ffrans abramse native
gerrit aerts middag native
Simon Aertsen 23 Jeare
Matthys Cornelisen 24 yeare
Ephraim hendricks 33 jeare
Claes thomas Van dyck native
Jeronimus d'Rapale native
Jeronimus Remsen native
Casper Janssen native
Achias Janse Vandijck 36 yeare
Jacob Joorissen native
Jacobus d'beauvois 28 Jeare
harmen Joorissen native
Jacob Willemse bennit native
Jacob brouwer native
bourgon broulaet 12 Jeare
Jan Damen 37 Jeare
Cornelis Subrink native
hendrick Sleght 35 Jeare
Juriaen Vanderbreets native
Pieter Staats native
Abram Remsen native
Michiel hanssen native
theunis tobiassen native
Pieter Corsen native
theunis Janse Couverts 36 Jeare
Aert Simonssen native
Adam brouwer Junior native
Alexander Schaers native
Willem Pos native
Jan gerrise dorland 35 Jeare
Johannis Casperse 35 Jeare
Claes barentse blom native
Pieter brouwer native
Abram brouwer native
Jan bennit native
barent Sleght native
Jacobus Vande Water 29 Jeare
benjamin Vande Water native
Pieter Wiejnants native
joost ffranssen 33 Jeare
hendrick aaten native
Jan Janse Staats native
Claes Simons native
Anthonij Sauso 5 Jeare
Joost Casperse 35 Jeare
thijs Lubberse 50 Jeare
Paulus dirckse 36 Jeare
Adam brouwer 45 Jeare
Josias Dreths 26 Jeare
Pieter Van Nesten 40 Jeare
Jan theunisen native
Dirck Janse Woertman 40 Jeare
Daniel d'Rapale native
gijsbert boomgaert native
Volkert Vanderbrats native
Jan buijs 39 Jeare
gerrit Dorlant native
Abriaen bennit native
Tnomas Verdon native
Pieter janse Staats native

off New Uijtrceht

Tielman Vandermij 13 Jeare
karel Janse Vandijck 35 Jeare
Jan Janse Vandijck 35 Jeare
thomas tierckse 35 Jeare
Wouter Van Pelt 24 Jeare
Jacob Christiaense native
Lambert Janse 22 Jeare
Jan Van Deventer 25 Jeare
Cornelis Janse Vandeventer native
gijsbert thysen Laenen 24 Jeare
theunis Janse Van Pelt Laenan 24 Jeare
Anthony Van Pelt 24 Jeare
Jan Clement 22 Jeare
Cornelis wijnhart 30 Jeare
kreijn Janse Van Meteeren 24 Jeare
Joost Rutsen Van brent native
Aert theunissen Van Pelt native
Anthonij du Chaine 24 Jeare
Jan thijssen Laenen native
Jacob thijssen Laenen native

Laurens Jense native
Jan Van Cleeff 34 Jeare
Wellem klinckenberg native]
Nicolase Vandergrifft native
Jan Van kerck junior native
Jan Van kerck senior 24 Jeare
barent Joosten Ridder 35 Jeare
hendrick Matthysse Smack 33 Jeare
Cornelis Van kleeff native
Dirck Janse Van Sutphen 36 Jeare
Jan kierson 38 Jeare
Gerrit Courten Van Voorhuys native
Rooth Joosten Van brunt 31 Jeare
Pieter ffrancisco native
Jacques Cortejou 35 Jeare
Jacques Corteljou Junior native
Cornelis Corteljou native
Pieter Corteljou native
Willem Corteljouw native
gerrit Cornelis Van Duyn 38 Jeare
Cornelis gerris Vanduyn native
Denijs gerrisse Vanduyn native
Laurens Janse de Camp 23 Jaer
Pieter thyssen native
Swaen Janssen 33 Jeare
gerrit Stoffelse 36 Jeare
Jan hanssen bruynenburgh 48 Jeare
Stoffel gerritse native
Joost debaene 4 Jeare
hendrick Janse kamminga 9 Jaer
Cornelis Rutsen Van brunt native
barent Verkerck native

off Boswijck

Volkert Dirckse native
Pieter Janse de Witt 35 Jeare
Pieter Daniel 10 Jeare
Adriaen La fforge 15 jeare
Joost kockuyt 27 Jeare
Isaack La ffebre 4 Jeare
Pieter Schamp 15 Jeare
Wouter gysbert Verschier 38 Jaer
Pieter Loyse native
Jacqes ffontaine native
Pelegrom klock 31 Jeare
Volkert Witt native
Daniel Waldron 35 Jeare
Simon haecks 16 Jeare

Cornelis Loyse 36 Jeare
Jean Le quie 30 Jeare
Alezander Cockevaer 30 Jeare
Albert hendrickse 25 Jeare
Jean Miseroll junior 20 Jeare
Claes Cornelissen Kat 25 Jeare
Michiel Palmentier 23 Jeare
Vincent Bale 4 Jeare
Pieter Para 28 Jeare
Johannis ffontaine native
Jean de Consilie 25 Jeare
Josst durie 12 Jeare
Jan Janse 36 Jeare
Jacob Janse native
Peter Simonse native
Jacob dirckse Rosekrans native
Jochem VerSchuer native
hendrick Verschuer native
Laurens koeck 26 yeare

off fflackland

Elbert Elbertse 50 Jeare
Roeloff Martense Shenck 37 Jeare
Jan Roeloffs Schenck native
Jan Martense Schenck 37 Jeares
Jan theunis Van dyckhuys 34 Jeare
Court Stevense Van Voorhuys 27 Jeare
Pieter Nevius native
Abram Willemson 25 Jeare
Marten Roeloffe Shenck native
hans Janssen 47 Jeare
Albert Courten Van Voorhuijs native
Pieter Claasen wijckoff 51 Jaere
Simon Janse Van Aerts Daalen 34 Jeare
Cornelis Simonsen Van Aerts daalen native
gerrit Pieterse wijckoff native
Jan brower 30 Jeare
gerrit hanssen native
Evert Janssen Van Wickelen 23 Jaare
Claes Pieterse wijckoff native
Dirck brouwer native
gerrit hendrickse bresse native
Pieter brouwer native
Dirck Janssen Ammerman 37 Jeare
adriaen kume 27 Jeare
gerret Elberts Stoothoff native
Jacob Strijcker 36 Jeare
Dirck Stoffelse 30 Jeare

Stoffel Dirckse native
fferdinandus Van Sichghlen 35 Jeare
hendrick Pieterse wijckoff native
Willem gerritse Van Couwenhooven native
gerritt Willemsen Van Couwenhooven native
Jan Pieterse wijckoff native
Anthony Wanshaer native
Luycas Stevense 27 Jeare
Pieter Cornelis Luyster 31 Jeare
Jan Stevense 27 Jeare
Ruth bruynsen 34 Jeare
Willem Willemse borcklo native
Pieter Pieterse Tull 30 Jaer
hendrick brouwer native
Pieter Monffoort native
theunis Janse Van amach 14 Jeare
Thys Pieterse luyster 31 Jeare
Jan albertse terhuen native
Willem Davies 34 Jeare

Johannis Willemse 25 Jeare
off gravens End
Renier Van Siegelen native
Stoffel Janse Remeyn 34
Johannis Machielse native
John boisbilland 2 Jeare
had Letters off Denisatie
barent Jurianse 29 Jeare
Jan barense Van Zutphen 30 Jeare
Marten Pieterse native
Jochem gulick 34 Jeare
Cornelis buys native
Jan Willemsen Van borcklo native
Rem gerritse native
Adam Machielse Messecher 40 Jeare
Willem Willemse 30 Jeare
Jan Carstense native
Johannis brower native

AN EXACT LIST

OF ALL Y^e^ INHABITANTS NAMES W^th^IN Y^e^ TOWNE OF ffLUSHING AND P'CINCTS OF OLD AND YOUNG ffREEMEN AND SERUANTS WHITE AND BLACKE &c. 1698.

9 { Coll: Tho Willett and Mtrs
Alena his wife
Elbert, Cornelius, Abraham, John } Sones
Alena, Elizabeth } Daughters }
John Clement: Servt
Negros ffrancis
Jeffrey Hary Jack
and Dick Mary } 7
9 { Justice Tho: Hukes &
Mrs Mary his wife
Isaac: Benjamin—Charles
Wm Stephen Charley } Sones
Mary; daught }
Negros: Will Cuffee
Sherry ffreegeft & Jane } 6
Majr. Wm Lawrense
& Deborah his wife
William Richard
Obadiah Damell
11 Samuel John
Adam Debo: Sarah
Negros James Tom
Lew Bess 2 child } 6
Richard Cornell
& Sarah his wife
Sone Richard
6 { Sarah, Elizabeth, & Mary } Daugh
Negros Tom
Lewi Toby
Sarah & Dina } 6
5 { John Esmond &
Elizab: his wife
John & Mary
Wm Jewell serut }

Samll: Thorne &
Susanna his wife
Benjamin }
8 Samuell & } Sone
Nathan }
Jane Kesia }
& Deborah } Da:
Negros Coffe }
Dinah Kate } 5
Charles Tony }
James Clement
& Sarah his wife
Thomas }
Jacob }
Joseph & two } Sones
12 Samll & }
Nathan }
Mary }
Hannad }
Margarett } Daug
Bridgett }
Negros Toby

Dutch Inhabitants.

Cornelius Barnion
& Anna his wife
Johannis sone
Alke Anna }
7 Elizabeth & } Da:
Arante }
Negros Antony }
Jack Corose } 6
Mary Isabella }
Martin Wiltsee &
Maria his wife
6 Cornelius Hendrick
Johannis & Margrett.
Elbert Arinson &
Cataline his wife
5 Rem & Elbert sones
Anneke—negro Dick'r
Garratt Hanson &
Janneke his wife
10 Hance Rem Jan }
Peter Danll Jores } 6
Janake Cattaline Dau

Negro Jeffrey 1
Lorus Haff
Canuerte his wife
Jewrin Peter }
11 Johannis & Jacob } Sones
Stinchee Maria }
Tuntee Margaretta } Dau
Sauta }
Edec: Van Skyagg &
Ebell his wife
7 Cornelius ffrancis
& Arian
Elizabeth Rebecca
Poulus Amarman
3 and Abiena his wife
Abena: Daughter
Barn Bloome &
4 ffammily his wife
Garratt, Johannis.
Eliz Bloodgood
5 Wm & Elizabeth
one negro Will
Dirick Poules
& Sarah his wife
8 Peter Thynis
Rich'd: Wm Jon
Charles Sarah
one negro Tom
2 John Bloodgood
& Mary his wife
2 Powell Hoff
Rachell his wife
2 John Jores &
Maria his wife
Derick Brewer &
3 his wife Hannah
1 child

French Inhabits

John: Genung
3 & Margreta his wife:
John: sone
negros 2
ffrancis Burto &
Mary his wife
5 John ffrancis

Abigal: |Daug
Sarah Doughty
4 Benjamin } Sones
William
Sarah Seruant
Negros: Okee & Mary
2 Mary Perkins
Abigale Daug
Bess: Robin Maria } 3
Hanes
2 Ann Noble
Abigale serut.
Negros: Jack Jan 2
3 Mary Bowne
Annis Ruth; Daugh
Negros: James & } 2
Nell
Arther Powell &
4 Margrett his wife
Richard Arther sones
John Hinchman
& Sarah his wife
7 John James
Mercy Mary &
Sarah
Negroo Hetchtor 1
Richard Chew &
ffrances his wife
7 Rich'd Henry Tho
Hannah Charely
Mary Elizabeth
Thomas Runley &
4 Mary his wife
Thomas sone
Hannah
ffrancis Doughty
& Mary his wife
8 Elias Palmer
ffrancis Obadiah
Sarah Charely Mary
Negros Vester Rose 2
John Talman &
Mary his wife
7 John James peter
Mary Elizabeth
Charles Tom

Sarah 2 ch 5
John Thorne Senr &
5 Mary his wife
Hannah & Sarah Wm
Negros Alex wo: 3
William ffowler Carp
and Mary his wife
8 William John
Joseph Benj
Mary Rebecca
Negro Jack 1
John Thorne Jun'r
6 Katherin his wife
John Mary
Eliz: Deborah
Henry Taylor &
5 Mary Sarah his wife
Sarah phebe
Negro Tonny 1
Edward Greffin ju
4 Deborah his wife
Edward Mary
2 William Owen &
Mary his wife
2 Hugh Cowperthawt
Mary Southick
Negro Anthony—1
2 Henry ffranklin
& Sarah his wife
1 negro
3 Patience Cornelius
Elias: Mary—
Tho: ffarrington
& Abigale his wife
Thomas Robert
Benjamin—
8 Elizab: Bridget
Abigale
Negros—Mingo } 2
Winnee
Harman Kinge
6 & Mary his wife
John Joseph
Benj. ffrancis
Toby 1
William ffowler wea

3 & Judeth his wife
William sone
Thomas Willett
3 & Sarah his wife
Sarah—Daughter
Negro Lay—1
Thomas Hinchman
4 & Meriam his wife
Thomas & Sarah—
2 George Langley &
Rebeca his wife
Mary & Sampson 2
Matt ffarrington
5 & Hannah his wife
Matthew Sarah &
Edward
John Mariton
ffrancis John
5 Cornelius
Deborah Ebell—
Thomas Yeates
& Mary his wife
6 Mary ye mother
Wm Benj Jane.
Elias Doughty
Elizabeth his wife
5 Elias Eliz: Thomas
Negro: Jack—1
Charles Doughty
& Elizabeth his wife
6 John Charles—
Sarah Elizabeth
1 negro black boy 1
John Harrington
& Elzbth his wife
John Edward Matthew
13 Thomas Sam'll Robert
Mercy Margrett
Dorythy Anna—
Elizabeth
Sam'll Bowne
& Mary his wife
6 Sam'll Thomas
Ellmer Hannah
Negros Simon
Nany mingo 3
Joseph palmer

6 & Sarah his wife.
Dani'll Esther
Ric'h pricilla
Tho: Hedger &
Elizabeth his wife
Eliakim Thomas
11 Mary Hannah—
Jane Sarah Deborah
Elizabeth
Joseph Thorne &
Mary his wife—
Joseph William
11 Thomas John—
Benjamin Abraham
Hannah Mary Susan.
1 Negro Tom:—1
Sam'll Haight &
Sarah his wife—
10 Nicholas Jonathan
Dauid John Sarah Mary
Hannah phebe—
and 1 negro 1
Thomas fford and
3 Sarah his wife—
Thomas Child
2 Esther fford
William
Negro Anthony—1
John Embree and
6 Sarah his wife
Robert John Samll
Sarah
Hatham'll Roe and
3 Elizab'th his wife
Dauid
Charles Morgan
& Elizabeth his wife
7 Charles James Thomas
Sarah Ephraim Sophy
Negros: peter James
John Cornelius &
Mary his wife
10 John Dani'll Sam'll
Joseph Deborah
Mary phebe Sarah
Negro: Zambo: 1
Jona Wright Senr

and Sarah his wife
9 Sam'll Richard Charles
Job: Mary Hannah
John
Henry Wright and
4 Mary his wife
Hannah Sarah
Jona: Wright Ju
4 & Wine his wife
Jonathan Elizabeth
Dauid Wright and
4 Hannah his wife
Dauid phebe
Joseph Lawrense
4 & Mary his wife
Richard Thomas
1 negro Jack—1
2 John Hopper Peintr
& Christopher
2 John Hopper Jun
& Margarett his wife
John Harrison
& Elizabeth his wife
7 William Edward
Henry Eliz Ann
Negros Hechtor } 2
Kate }
Margery Smith
3 Judeth Hannah
Samuel Tatem &
Elizabeth his wife
6 Sam'll Eliza patience
Mary negro—1
Benj Hauileind &
5 Abigaile his wife
Adam Benj John
Abigale Bethia
William Benger &
5 his wife Elizabeth
John Jacob Eliz
John Heauiland &
3 Sarah his wife
John
Thomas Wildee
& Elizabeth his wife
8 Edward Rich'd
Tho Obadiah

Isaaih Eliz'bth
Edward Greffein Se
3 & Mary his wife
Deborah
Negro: Jack: 1
John Rodman
& Mary his wife
9 John Samuell—
Joseph William
Thomas An Eliz:
Negros—11
John Lawrence &
his wife Elizab'th
7 William Richard
Eliz: Mary Deborah
Negros James Rose
Bess Robin Moll—5
Benj ffeild and
Hannah his wife
6 Benj John Antho
Sam'll
Negros Jo: Betty—2
John Greffin &
Elizabeth his wife
5 John Benj Isaac
Joseph Elizab'th
Rich'd Greffin and
5 Susan his wife
Sam'll Sarah Rich'd
Dauid Roe Mary
3 his wife
Mary: Negro Sam 1
Rebeca Clery
4 Athelana Rebeca
phebe Negro: 1
Philip Odall &
his wife Mary
7 Philip Mary
John Elizab'th
Deborah
Joseph Hedger
& Hannah his
7 wife—Joseph
Margrett
Uriah Sarah
Hannah
Antnody Badgley

5 Elizabeth his wife
Anthony Georg—
phebe : 1 Negro 1
Dan'll Patrick &
4 Dinah his wife
Sarah James ffeke
One Negro 1
John Ryder & his
wife, John Robert
5 Hartie Wintie
one negro 1
2 Dennis Holdrone
Sarah his wife
Josiah Genning
3 & Martha his wife
one child
Edee Wilday
3 Rebecca & Mary
ffreemen-men
Tho: Lawrense
James Clement Ju'r
According to ye best of our Knowledges

John Clement
John Huker
Jacob Cornell
Thomas ffeild
Joseph ffeild
Derick Areson
Jon Areson
John Yeates
John Man
James ffeke
Robert Snelhen
Tho : Steuens
John Dewildoe
Abraham Rich
Robert Hinchmen

Inhabitants 530

Negros 113

JONATHAN WRIGHT
JAMES CLEMENT

[*Endorsed.*] a trew Lest as it is returned to us by the above constable and Clerk this Last of augost 1698

THO: HICKS
DAN'LL WHITE
JOHN SMITH
EDWARD WHITE
SAMUEL MOWETT
JOHN TREDWELL
WILLIAM HALLET

A LIST OF Y^E^ INHABITANTS

OF Y^e^ TOWNE OF SOUTHAMPTON OLD AND YONG CHRISTIANS AND HETHEN FFREEMEN AND SERVANTS WHITE AND BLACK A^nno^ 1698

William Jennings
Samuell Jennings
Benjn Haines
Benjn Haines Jur
John Haines
James Haines Jur
Thomas Shaw
David Frances
Frances Shaw
John Shaw
Samuell Clark
Samuell Clark Jur
Elish Clark
Eliphelett Clark

Clark
Clark
Jerhamiah Scott
John Scott
George Haris
George Haris Jur
Joseph Smith
Will Smith
Thomas Smith
Abiell Davis
Balhariah Davis
John Davis Jur
Eldad Davis
John Davis
Thomas Lupton
Joseph Lupton
Richard minthorn
Jeremiah Jager
Jeremiah Jager Jur
John Jager Jur
John Erle
David Erle
Samuell Cooper
James white
Ichabod Cooper
Peeter White
James Cooper
James Cooper Jur
John Cooper
Nathan Cooper
Abraham Cooper
John Reeves
John Reeves Jur
Thomas Reeves
Gershum Culver
Jerimiah Culver
David Culver
Jonathan Culver
Moses : Culver
Nahum Culver
John Bishope Jur
Joseph Poast
Will Mason
John Poastt
Richard Poast
Thomas Sayre
Will ffoster
Charles Topping
ffrancis Sayre
Iachabod Sayre
Caleb Sayre
Caleb Gilbord
Daniell Sayre
Ephraim Sayre
Nathan Sayre
John Bishop
Samuell Bishope
Josiah Bishope
John Bishope
Joshew Barns
Samuell Barns
Robert Wooly
John Wooly
Wooly Joseph
Isaac Bower
Jonah Bower
David Bower
Daniell Bower
John foster
John foster Jur
David ffoster
Jonathan foster
Jonathan ffoster Terts
Jermiah foster
Joseph Hildrith
Joseph Hildrith Jur
nathan Hildrith
Isaak Hildrith
Ephraim Hildrith
Daniell Hildrith
Jonathan Hildrith
John Woodrufe
Samll Woodrufe
Joseph woodrufe
Benjn Woodrufe
nathanl woodrufe
Jonathan woodrufe
Isaac woodrufe
John Burnat
Samuel Butler
Gidian Butler
nathaniell Butler
Obedia Roggers
obadiah Johnson

Ensn Joseph Peirson
Henry Peirson
Joseph Peirson
Ephraim Pierson
Small Peirson
Thomas Parvine
Thomas Pervine Jur
Lift Thomas Steephens
Isaack Willman
James Willman
Daniell Davis
and Will Hericke
Will Hericke Jur
John Herick
Herick
Thomas Hericke
Robert Patin
Ephraim Topping
Thomas Toping
Thomas Toping
Mr. William Barker Esq
Mr. John Wick
Job Wick
Arther Davis
John Carwith
Joseph Howell
Zebulon Howell
Joseph Howel Jur
James Howell
John ware
Jacob ware
John Ware Jur
John Jessup
Isaac Jessup
Jer: Jessup
Henry Jessup
Thomas Jessup
Mr. Edward Howell
Samuell Howell
Jonah Howell
Edward Howell Jur
Benjn Howell
Tho: Howell
Joseph foster
Christopher ffoster
Joseph foster
Daniell ffoster
nathan ffoster
John Howell
Manassa Kompton
Richard Howell
Richard Howell Jur
Hezeckia Howell
Edward Howell
obadia Howell
Chris: Howell
Joseph Goodale
Jonathan Goodale
Joseph Goodale
Will goodale
Benjn marshall
Jonathan Rayner
Jonathan Rayner Jur
Richard Wood
Isaac Halsey:
Ephraim Halsey
Nathaniell Howell
nehemiah Howell
Henry Howell
Ensn Joseph ffordham
Joseph ffordham Jur
ffellatia ffordham
John Willman
Mr Jonah fordham
Jonah fordham Jur
Mr Joseph Whitin
Samuell Whitin
Joseph Whitin Jur
Benjn whitin
Will Blyeth
Benjn Hildrith
Job Sayre
Benjn Sayre
John Maltby
Ephrm whit
Stephen white
Charles white
Isaac Halsey
Isaac Halsey Jur
Isaac Halsey Ters
Joshua Halsey
Thomas Halsey
Samuell Halsey
Samell Johnes

Samuell Johnes Jur
nathan Howell
Israell Howell
Ezekiel Howell
John Jager
John Jager Jur
Samuell Jager
Jonathan Jager
Benjn Jagger
Josiah Howell
Daniell Howell
Timoth : Hileyrd
Thomas Hongson
John Mowbry
Anning Mowbry
Samuell Clark
Jermiah Clark
Charles Clark
Will Clark
Richard Rounesfield
Richard Rounesfield
David Howell
John Rayne
Ephraim Howell
Ephraim Howell
Samuell Howell
Isaac Rayner
Daniell Halsey
Richard Halsey
Daniell Hallsey Jur
Lift abraham Howell
Abraham Howell
Charles Howell:
Philip Howell
Ebenezer Howell
John Sayre
John Sayre
Thomas Sayre
Lott Burnot
Joseph Burnott
David Burnott
nathan Burnott
Jonathan Burnott
Samiel Burnot
Isaac Burnott
Thomas ffoster
Benjn ffoster

David ffoster
Jonathan ffoster
Isaac ffoster
nathanel Hasey
Jonathan Howell
Jonathan Howell Jur
Isaa Howell
David Howell
Josiah Halsey
Josiah Halsey Jur
Jonathan Halsey
Benjn ffoster Jur
Henry Ludlom
Will Ludlom
Henry ludlom Jur
Jeremiah ludlom
Aibiell Cook
Abiell Cook Jur
Josiah Cook
Thomas Rose
Israell Rose
Humphrey Huse
John Parker
abner Huse
William Rose
uriah Huse
John masen
Jedadia Huse
James ffoster
John Huse
David Halsey
abraham Halsey
David Rose
James Rose
David Rose Jur
Anthony ludlom
James Herick
Aron Burnot
Aaron Burnot Jur
moses Burnat
Jonah Rogers
Jonah Rogers
Rogers
James Haines
Samuell Haines
Ellis Cook
Charles fordham

John Cook
John Cook Jur
Ellias Cook
obadia Cook
Ellijah Cook
Ensn John lupton
Christopher Lupton
Benj Lupton
Samuell Loome
mathew Loome
Samuell Loome
Isaac Mills
Isaac mills Jur
Thomas Cooper
Thomas Cooper Jur
Jonathan miles
Richard Cooper
Joseph more
Joseph more
Benjn more
Elisha Howell
Lemuell Howell
martine Rose
Jacob Wood
Lenard Hasy
William Tarbill
Will Tarbill Jur
John michill
John michill Jur
Jermiah Halsey
Jere : Halsey Jur
Benony nutton
Benjn nuton
Isaac nuton
Jonathan nuton
John nuton
James Hildrith
James Hildrith Jur
Joshua Hildrith
Ezekill Sanford
Ezekill Sanford Jur
Thomas Sanford
Samuell Barbur
Jonathan Strickling
nathaniell Resco Jur
Josiah hand
natha : Resco
Amij Resco
Peregrin Stanbrough
James Stanbrough
Doct nath. Wade
Simon wade
Alexander Wilmot
Joseph Wickham
Joseph wickham Jur
Thomas Diamond
Capt. Elnathan Topping
Stephen Tobping
Sillvanis Topping
Edward Petty
Ellnathan Petty
Edward Pety Jur
Josiah Topping
Josiah Topping Jur
Hezekia Topping
Robert Noris
Robert noris Jur
oliver noris
Mr. Ebenezer white
Elnath white
Lift Coll Henry Peirson
John Peirson
David Peirson
Theophilus Person
Abraham Peirson
Josiah Peirson
Bennony flint
John fflint
John morehouse
John morehouse Jur
Peter noris ———
Lift Thehopilus Howell
Theoph : Howell Jur
Cilley Howell
Theoder Peirson
Theoder Peirson
John Stanbrough
John Stanbrough Jur
Daniel Sayre Jur
Daniell Sayre terts
Dan Burnot
Ichabod Burnot
Dan Burnot Jur
The numbr of male Christians } 389

FFEAMALES

Ann Peirkins
Hannah Haines
Lidia Haines
mary Haines
mary Shaw
Susanah Shaw
Jeane Shaw
Sarah Clark
mary Clark
Ester Clark
Sarah Clark
mary Scott
Sarah Haris
Eunice Haris
mary Davis
mary Davis
Mary lupton
mary lupton
Hanah luptons
abigaill luptons
Abigaill Rose
Hanah Rose
Abigaile Rose Jur
Sarah Rose:
Hanah Rose
martha Rose
debro Rose
Hanah Jager
Sarah Jager
Hanah Jager.
Elizabeth Davis
mahitable davis
Jager
mary Erle
Mary Cooper
Sarah Cooper
mary Cooper Jur
Elisabeth Cooper
Elisabeth Cooper Jur
Jerash Cooper
Phebe Cooper
Elisabeth Cooper Jur
Johana Cooper
mahitable Cooper
mary Culver
mary Culver Jur

Rachell Reeves
Lidia Bishop
abigaile Bishop
marey Bishop
Eunis Bishop
Sarah Poast
mary Poast
mary Post Jur
Patience Sayere
mary Davis
Sarah Sayre
mary Sayre
mary Sayre
An Halsey
Abigaile Reeves
Elisabeth gilbord
Cethia Gilbord
mary gilbord
Hanah Sayre
mary Bishop
Susanah Bishope
Susanah Bishop Jur
Sarah Bishop
mary Bishop
Patience Barns
Sarah Barns
ann Woolly
Ann Woolly
Elisabeth woolly
Hanah woolly
Phebe woolly
mary woolly
Hanah Travely
Susanah Beswik
Ruth bower
mahitabell Bower
Sarah Erle
Sarah ffoster
Phebe foster
Hanah foster
Hanah foster
Hanah foster
Hana ffoster
Hanah Hildrith
Hanah woodrufe
Sarah woodrufe

Hanah Woodrufe
abigaile woodrufe
Elisabeth Woodrufe
Ellisabeth Butler
martha Buler
Sarah Butler
Amy butler
mary butler
mary Rogers
mary Roger Jur
mary Rogers ter
Sary Roegers
debro Rogers
Patience Rogers
mary Peirson
Rebeika Parvin
Elisabeth Steevens
Phebe Steephens
Susanah Stevens
Susana willman
hanah willmans
Elisbeth willmans
mahitable hericke
Ireniah Hericke
Phebe Hericke
mahitable Herick
Martha Herick
Debro Toping
Hanah Reeves
Temprance wick
Temprance Wick
Lidia Howell
Bothia Howell
ffreelove Howell
Elisabeth ware
Elisabeth Jesup
mary Jessup
Hanah Jessup
martha Davis
Sarah Jussup
mary Howell
mary Howell
Ireniah Roggers
mindwell Erle
Mrs. mary Howell
Sibell Howell
Elisabeth Simpkins

Johanah Howell
Abigaile ffoster
Sarah ffoster
mahitabell foster
Damary ffoster
Penellopie ffoster
Ellisabeth Howell
Dorkis Howell
Sary Howell
Sarah Howell
abigaile Howell
Elisabeth goodale
mary goodale
Hanah goodale
Sarah Rayner
debrah Rayner
Hanah Rayner
Sarah ffeild
mary Halsey
mahitable Halsey
mary Halsey
Sarah minthorn
Mrs. Susanah Howell
Prudence Howell
Hanah Howell
mahite Howell
martha Howell
mary fordham
mary fordham Jur
mary fordham 3d
Phebe fordham
Allath fordham
Deborah Whiting
Rebecca Whiting
Hanah whiting
Elisabeth whiting
Susannah Maltbey
Susanah Sayre
Ester fordham
Keziah fordham
Hanah fordham
Ruth White
Sarah white
mary Halsey
Elisabeth Halsey
Pheby Halsey
Hanah Erle

mary Poast
Sarah Poast
Dorithee Post
martha Poast
Debborah Poast
Ester Johnes
Phebe Johnes
Mrs. Mary Howell
Eunis Howell
Jerusha Howell
Hanah Jager
Lidia Jagger
Hanah Melvine
Margret Hilyard
Mary Howell
Mistris anning
Hanah Clark
Pheebe Clark
Hanah Rounsifield
Martha Rounsifield
Abigaill wilson
Hanah Howell
Sarah Howell
Hanah Howell
Judith Howell
Ann Howell
Grisill Howell
Amy Halsey
Hulda Erle
Ellisabeth Halsey
Debro Halsey
mary Ranr
Phebe Raynr
Hanah Raynr
Sarah Sayre
Sarah Sayre
Damorus Sayre
Phebe Burnatt
Lidia foster
Elisabeth white
Debro foster
Zeruiah foster
Annah Halsey
Hanah Howell
Zerusah Howell
mary Howell
Temprance Halsey
Sarah Halsey
Temprance Halsey
abigaile Halsey
martha foster
Bothy foster
martha foster
Sarah foster
Rachell Ludlom
Jane Ludlom
Abigaile ludlom
Rachell Ludlom Jur
ffrances Cooke
ffrances Cooke Jur
Hanah Rose
Hanah Rose
Sarah Hericke
Elisabeth Burnot
Elisabeth Burnott
Hanah Burnot
Mary Parker
Ester Rose
Hanah Halsey
Hanah Halsey
Prudence Halsey
Patience Ludlom
Patience Ludlom
Phebe Rogers
Phebe Rogers
Sarah Haines
Sarah Haines
Sarah nichill
Elisabeth Cook
Susanah Cook
Hanah Shaw
Elisabeth Cook
martha Cook
Hanah Lupton
Hanah Lupton
Lidia Lupton
mary laughton
Hanah Lome
Abigaile Lome
Hanah Loome
Johanah nuton
Johanah nuton
Ester leeming
Hanah Cooper

Sarah taping
Sarah more
Elisabeth more
Sarah more Jun
mary more
Hanah Sayre
Damones Howell
Elliner Howell
Penellopie Howell
Abiecah Howell
mary tarbill
mary Tarbill
mary Haris
mary haris
Deborah Hildrith
Deborah Hildrith
Hanah Sanford
Hanah Sanford
Elisabeth nuton
Phebe nuton
annah Halsey
annah Halsey
Johanah Resco
mary barbur
deliverance priest
mary barbur
mary Strickland
Mary hand
Abigaile wade
Sarah Stanbrough
Ollive Stanbrough
Eunis Stanbrough
Elisabeth Stanbrough
mary Willmott
Sarah Wickham
mary Topping

mary Baylee
Hannah Topping
Hanah Toping
Temperance Toping
Toping
martha huse
Hanah noris
Hanah noris
mary noris
Sarah noris
hanah leeming
mrs mahitable white
Elisabeth langton
Mrs Susannah Pierson
Abigaile toping
Hanah Pierson
Sarah Peirson
mary flint
mary flint
Hanah flintt
Sarah noris
Hanah noris
Elisabeth noris

———

Debro Howell
Phebee Howell
hanah noris
ffrances Peirson
Ann Peirson
martha Stanbrough
martha Stanbrough
Sarah Sayre
Hanah Sayre
Sarah Sayre
Abigaile burnot
feamale Christians 349

NEGRO MALES.

Will	Ceaser	Tom	Sambo
John	Jethro	Will	ned
Peter	Jack	Jack	Tobee
Dick	Titus	ffranck	Peter
Tom	Jefery	Ceser	Cisto
Guie	Lewis	Samson	brigitt
Jack	mingo	Jehue	———
Jack	Dick	Nero	40
Dick	Tittus	George	[7 names destroyed.]

NEGRO FEMALES.

Ann	bety	Rueth	molly
bety	Joane	Dorekis	Dinah
Isabell	Hager	Smony	Bess
bety	bety	Pegee	mariah
Elisabeth	Hanah	Philis	Simony
Perle	Rachel	hitabell	———
Abee	Judith	Sarah	females negro
Sarah	Judith	Sarah	persons 43
Hanah	Jinny	Rose	[6 names destroyed.]
Joane	Simony	margery	
Sarah	Rueth	hanah	

The number of Christian Males is - - - - - - -	389	738	821
The number of Christian ffeemales is - - - - - -	349		
The number of negro Slaves men is - - - - - -	040	083	
The number of women negro slaves is - - - - - -	043		

Indian males that are upwards of fifteen years—The Squas and children few of whom have any nam

Chice	Indian	Dick	Indian
Johnson	Indian	Plato	Indian
———	———	Tom-hodge	Indian
Arther	Indian	Denitt	Indian
Anthony	Indian	obedia	Indian
Thamanty	Indian	Cuttwas	Indian
Johnaquan	Indian	Abraham	Indian
queegano	Indian	Isaac	Indian
Lenard	Indian	Sam	Indian
Pisacomary	Indian	Steephen	Indian
Jefery	Indian	nodian	Indian
Rhicoam	Indian	Judas	Indian
Redhedwill	Indian	Weegon	Indian
Pomquaneo	Indian	Cough	Indian
Simon	Indian	Sam	Indian
Canady	Iudian	William	Indian
Tohemon	Indian	na	Indian
Coyemow	Indian	Chitty	Indian
ffranck	Indian	Hary	Indian
Toby	Indian	Joseph	Indian
macrobow	Indian	Tom	Indian
nabamacow	Indian	waynantuck	Indian
Philip	Indian	waneno	Indian
Sam	Indian	Titus	Indian
Tom lenard	Indian		

The nuber of Indians upwards of 15 years - - - - - - - - - -	52
The Indians Informes there is about The same number of woomen and as many Children	100
	152

The hethen are So Scattered To and frow that they can neither be Summonsed in [Manuscript torn]

The above listt of the Inhabitants of ye Town of Southampton, taken p me this 15th day of September 1698.

MATHEW HOWELL.

A LIST OF THE NAMES

OF OLD AND YOUNG, CHRISTIANS AND HEATHENS, FFREMEN, AND SERVANTS; WHITE; AND BLACK; &c. INHABITTEINGE WITHIN THE TOWN-SHIPP OF SOUTHOLD VIZ—

Isaac Arnold
Sarah Arnold
Rachel Arnold
Sarah Arnold Junjr
Susannah Arnold
Susannah Washbourn
John Washbourn
Thomas Mapes
Mary Mapes
Abigall Mapes
Margarett Edwards
Joshua Hobart
Peter Hobart
John Hobart
Ebenezer Way
Irene Way
Eliezer Way
Jonathan Horton
Bathia Horton
Jonathan Horton Junjr
William Horton
James Horton
Mehitobel Horton
Mary Horton
Abigall Horton
Patience Horton
Stephen Bouyer
Jonas Holdsworth
Joshua Horton
Mary Horton
Ephraim Horton
Mary Horton Junjr
Bathia Horton
Elizabeth Horton
Zerviah Horton
Jasper Griffiing
Hannah Griffing
Robert Griffing
Susannah Griffing
Edward Griffing
Robert Grffing Junjr
Samuel Griffing
John Griffing
John Youngs
Wm Walter
Theodor Ballens
Mary Griffing
Prudence Smith
John Booth
Hannah Booth
Mehitophel Booth
John Booth Junjr
Obadiah Booth
Daniel Booth
Hannah Booth Junj
Patience Booth
Thomas Emmons
Mary Emmons
Obadiah Emmons
Elizth. Emmons
Thomas Paine
John Tutthill
Sarah Tutthill
Daniel Tutthill
Nathaniel Tutthill
Ephraim Young

Mary Youngs
Ruth Terry
Thomas Youngs
Mary Youngs
Christopher Bradly
John Edwards
William Barnes
Mary Mayhew
Benjamin Lhommedieu
Patience Lhommedieu
Benjamin Lhommedieu Junjr
Hosea Lhommedieu
Eliza Sylvester
William Booth
Hannah Booth
Wm Booth Junjr
Samuel Booth
George Booth
Hannah Booth Junjr
Thomas Terry
Eliza Terry
Thomas Terry Junjr
Daniel Terry
Joseph Terry
Abigall Terry
Hannah Martin
John Rogers
John Conckline
Sarah Concklin
Sarah Conckline Junr.
John Conckline Junjr
Henry Conckline
Rachel Conckline
Thomas Conckline
Mary Concklin
Joseph Concklin
Abigall Concklin
Joseph Concklin Junjr
John Concklin
Phillip Gooding
Sarah Gooding
Amos Gooding
Phillip Gooding Junjr
ffreeloue Gooding
Christopher Youngs
Mercy Youngs
Abraham Youngs
Nathaniel Youngs
John Youngs
Charity Nashbourne
Thomas Terrell
John Terrell
Richard Terrell
Abigall Terrell
Nicholas Terrell
Catharine Terrell
Peter Hallock
Eliza Hallock
Bathia Hallock
Abigall Hallock
Peter Hallock Junjr
William Hallock
Noah Hallock
Richard Benjamen
Eliza Benjamen
Anna Benjamen
John Benjamen
Richard Benjamen Junjr
Jonathan Benjamen
David Benjamen
Joshua Benjamen
Joseph Benjamen
Daniel Terry
Sarah Terry
Daniel Terry Junjr
Samuel Terry
Eliza Terry
James Terry
Isaac Ouenton
John Ouenton
Thomas Ouenton
Thomas Goldsmith
Bathia Goldsmith
Joshua Goldsmith
Richard Terry
Prudence Terry
Abigall Coleman
Caleb Horton
John Reeue
hannah Reeue
Walter Reeue
John Reeue Junjr
Elisha Reeue
Abigall Reeue

Bathia Reeue
Margarett Giles
Peter Dickerson
Naomy Dickerson
Philemon Dickerson
John Dickerson
Mary Dickerson Junjr
Naomy Dickerson
Thomas Dickerson
Mary Dickerson
Mary Monjoy
Jonathan Reeue
Martha Reeue
Margarett Reeue
Mary Reeue
Martha Reeue Junjr
Matthew Reeue
Jonathan Mapes
Hester Mapes
Benjamen Youngs
Mary Youngs
Grover Youngs
John Bailey
Lott Johnson
Gideon Youngs
Sarah Youngs
Joseph Youngs
Jonathan Youngs
David Youngs
Gidion Youngs
Sarah Youngs
Hannah Youngs
Margarett Youngs
Mary Youngs
Hannah Wiggin widow
James Wiggin
Annis Wiggin
Eliza Wiggin
Patience Ryder
Thomas Hallock
Hope Hallock
Thomas Hallock
Kingsland Hallock
Ichabod Hallock
Zerobabel Hallock
Anna Hallock
Patience Hallock
Richard Hallock
Richard Howell
David Howell
Jonathan Howell
Richard Howell Junjr
Isaac Howell
Jacob Howell
Eliza Howell
Dorathy Howell
Mary Youngs Junjr widdow
Christopher Youngs Junjr
Anna Youngs
Phebe Youngs
Eliza Youngs
John Gattin
Sarah Gattin
Anna Gattin
Jonathan Brown
Eliza Brown
Jonathan Brown Junjr
Eliza Brown Junjr
Hannah Brown
Rachel Brown
Mary Giles
Edward Gattin
Mary Youngs widow
Daniel Youngs
William Youngs
Joshua Youngs
Samuel Turner
Mary Wiggans
Nathan Langdon
Hannah Langdon
Eliza Langdon
Nathan Langdon Junjr
James Langdon
Samuel Youngs
Joseph Sweazy
Mary Sweazy
Johannah Sweazy
Joseph Sweazy Junjr
Mary Swazy
Sarah Swazy
Samuel Swazy
Richard Swazy
Stephen Swazy
Bathia Swazy

Thomas Moor junjr
Jean Moor
Mary Moor
Rachel Moor
Isaac Osmond
Chaterine Osmond
Martha Osmond
Prudence Osmond
Isaac Osmond
William Downs
Abigall Downs
Abijah Downs Junjr
Samuel King Junjr
Hannah King
Samuel King
Zacharias King
John Swazy
Mary Swazy
Jno. Swazy Junjr
Susana. Swazy
Mary Swazy Junjr
Joshua & Phebe Swazy
Jacob Conckline
Mary Conckline
Jacob Conckline Junjr
Samuel Conckline
John Conckline
Gideon Conckline
Mary Conckline Junjr
Joseph Conckline
Joseph Conckline Junjr.
Mary Baily
Theophilus Corwin
John Harwood
William Brown
Catharine Brown
Wm Brown junjr
John Brown
Walter Brown
Silvanus Brown
David Brown
Mary Brown
Sarah Martin
John Corwin
Matthias Corwin
Samuel Corwin
Anna Corwin
Abigall Corwin
John Corwin Junjr
Sarah Corwin
Sarah Corwin Junjr
Eliza Corwin
Hester Corwin
Jacob Ozmond
Sarah Ozmond
Mary Ozmond
Sarah Ozmond Junjr
Eliza Ozmond
Hester Ozmond
Pinnina Ozmond
Hannah Ozmond
Martha Ozmond widdw
Sarah Ozmond
Dinah Blyth
Jno. Howel
Thomas Clark
Mary Clark
Thomas Clark Junjr
Elizabeth Clark
Mary Ozmond widdow
Deborah Ozmond
Phebe Ozmond
Johannah Ozmond
Mercy Ozmond
Samuel Ozmond
William King
Abigall King
Wm King Junjr
Hannah King
David King
Sarah Youngs
Daniel King
Robert Labe
Caleb Curtjes
Eliza Curtjes
Joshua Curtjes
Mary Curtjes
Samuel Curtjes
Sarah Curtjes
Hannah Curtjes
Richard Curtjes
Stephen Baily
Mary Baily
Hannah Baily

Israel Baily
Temprance Baily.
Jonathan Baily
Christian Baily
David Gardiner
Martha Gardiner
Mary Gardiner
Mehitober Corwin
Samuell King
Abigall King
Theophilus Case
hannah Case
William Case
Icabod Case
John Case
Eliza Robertson
Jasper Griffing Junjr
Ruth Griffing
Jasper Griffing
Ruth Griffing
Abraham Corey
Margarett Corey
Mary Corey
Abraham Corey Junjr
Jno Corey
Dorathy Corey
Patience Mayhew
Isaac Corey
Sarah Corey
Isaac Corey Junjr
David Corey
Jonathan Corey
Sarah Corey Junjr
Phebe Corey
Deborah Corey
Peter Aldridge
Annis Reeue widdow
Walter Brown
Joseph Brown
Daniel Brown
Gersham Aldridge
James Pattay
Experience Pattay
James Pattay Junjr
Mary Pattay
nymon Pattay
Experience Pattay

Thomas Ryder
Joseph Ryder
Providence Ryder
Jeremiah Ryder
Hester Ryder
Mehitobel Ryder
John Budd
Hester Budd
John Budd Junjr
Joseph Budd
Susannah Budd
Mary Budd
Martha Moor widdow
John Trusteen
Jonathan Moor
William Moor
Mary Trusteen
John Pain Junjr
Sarah Pain
Nathaniel Pain
John Pain
Samuel Crook
Joseph Crook
Sussannah Crook
John ffrancklin
Philla: ffrancklin
Jno ffrancklin Junjr
Mary ffrancklin
Samuel ffrancklin
Martha ffrancklin
ffrancis Noise
Perrsha Noice
Catharine Noise
Eliza Lewis
Mary Reeue widdow
Wm Reeue
Abigall Reeue
Margarett Reeue
Sarah Reeue
Thomas Reeue
Henry Tuthill
Batthia Tuthill
Henry Tuthill Junjr
Jonathan Tuthill
Nathaniel Tuthill
Barnabas Tuthill
Abigall Martin

Hester Hoaman widdow
Hester Hoaman Junjr
John Joanes
Thomas Hunter
Eliza Hunter
Eliza hunter Junjr
Zervia Hunter
Hannah Hunter
Sarah Horton Widdw
Peanellope Horton
John Pattay
Mary Pattay
Edward Pattay
David Pattay
Mary Pattay
Joshua Wells
Hannah Wells
William Wells
Jno. Wells
Joshua Wells
Deliurance Wells
Abigall Wells
Ann Wells
Mary Martin
John Owen
Thomas Booth
Mary Booth
John Booth
Thomas Booth Junjr
James Booth
Giles Booth
Mary Booth Junjr
Abraham Ozmond
Rebecca Ozmond
Joseph Ozmond
John Ozmond
Damarass Terrell
John Allowbin
hannah Allowbin Junjr
Mary Allowbin
Tabitha Allowbin
John Goldsmith
Eliza Goldsmith
John Goldsmith Junjr
Thomas Goldsmith
Richard Goldsmith
Nathaniel Goldsmith
Mary Goldsmith
Henry Wells
Mary Wells
Martha Carr
Samuel Glouer
Sarah Glouer
Samuel Glouer junjr
Martha Glouer
hanna. Glouer
Hester Glouer
William Glouer
Charles Glouer
Martha Glouer
Euan Davis
Mary Davis
Mordecai hoaman
William Coleman
Mary Coleman
Sarah Coleman
William Coleman Junjr
Mary Coleman Junjr
Sarah Coleman Junjr
Charles Booth
Abigall Booth
Mary Horton widdow
Jean Mappon
Charles Booth Junjr
Abigall Booth Junjr
David Booth
Jacob Aldridge
Caleb Horton
Jonathan Horton
David Horton
Barnabas Horton
Phebe Horton
Samuel Windes
Mary Windes
Wm Coe
Charley Edwards
Lott Johnson
Joseph Pattay
Mary Pattay
Daniel Pattay
James Reeue
Deborah Reeue
Mary Reeue
Isaac Reeue

Thomas Reeue
Mary Reeue
Richard Brown
Dorithy Brown
Richard Brown Junjr
Samuel Brown
Dorathy Brown
Abigall Brown
Mehitobel Brown
Henry Brown
Samuel Hutcheson
Elizabeth Hutcheson
Samuel Hutcheson Junjr
Gersham Terry
Deborah Terry
Gersham Terry Junjr
Deborah Terry Junjr
Abigall Terry
Richard Terry
Barsheba Terry
Mehitobel Terry
Eliza Cleaues
Jerediah Cleaues
John Cleaues
Eliza Cleaues Junjr
Mary Cleaues
Hannah Cleaues
John Cleaues Junjr
Abigall Cleues
Thomas Tusten
Priscilla Tusten, widdow
Eliza Tusten
Meriem Tusten
Grace Tusten
Carterett Gillam
Mary Gillam
Anna Gilliam
Arnold Gillam
James Gillam
John Wiggam
James Pershall
Margaret Pershall
Mary Pershall
Israel Pershall
David Pershall
Benjamen Pershall
Margarett Pershall Junjr

Thomas Terrell Junjr
Sarah Terrell
Thomas Terrell
Sarah Terrell Junjr
Joshua Horton Junjr
Eliza Horton
Eliza Horton Junjr
Patience Horton
Deborah Horton
Martha Horton
Henry Case
Tabitha Case
Henry Case Junjr
Samuel Case
Benjamin Case
Tabitha Case Junjr
Mary Case
John Bond
Sarah Rodman
John Barnes
Joseph Reeue
Abigal Reeue
Joseph Reeue Junjr
Benjamen Reeue
David Reeue
Ezikias Reeue
Solomon Reeue
Abigall Reeue
Mary Reeue
Margarett Hallock widdow
Dorathy Ozmon
Barnabas Windes
Mary Windes
Barnabas Windes Junjr
Samuel Windes
Bathia Windes
Peanellope Windes
Sussanna Willman
Bathia Horton
Susanna Windes
Martha Hutcheson widdow
Thomas Hutcheson
Mathias Hutcheson
Martha Hutcheson Junjr
Hanna Case
John Terry
Hannah Terry

John Terry Junjr
Nathaniel Moor
Jacob Cory
Ann Cory
Jacob Corey Junjr
Ann Corey Junjr
Abigall Cory
Jehoada Corey
John Corey
Benjamn Corey
Christopher Merrick
Hannah Merrick
Jeremiah Veale
Anne Veale
Thomas Veale
Jeremiah Veale Junjr
Mary Veale
Mary Moor
Joshua Sylvester
Joseph Moor
Martha Moor
Joseph Moor Junjr
Sarah Solmon widdow
William Solmon
Sarah Solmon Junjr
Mary Solmon
Amy Solmon
Elizabeth Youngs widdow
John Youngs
Benjamen Youngs Junr
Eliza Youngs Junjr
Christian Youngs
Jno. Coleman
Mary Harwood
William Allobon
Andrew Miller
Margarett Miller
David Miller
Eliza Miller
Margarett Miller Junjr
Hannah Miller
Gersham Tincker
Samuel Youngs
Mary Youngs
Margarett Youngs
Nathan Youngs
Zerobabel Youngs
Bathia Corwin
Joseph Youngs
Eliza Youngs
Mary Youngs
Thomas Youngs
Abigall Pain widdow
Abigall Pain Junjr
Mary Pain
Sarah Pain
John Daines
Sarah Moor, widdow
Abigall Moor
Patience Moor
Deborah Moor
Thomas Moor
John Moor
Nathaniel Moor
Martha Moor
Eliza Moor
Symon Grouer
Eliza Grouer
Martha Veale
Bedjamin Barns
Barnabas Horton
Samuel Bodman
Benjamen Moor
Abigall Moor
John Hutson
Mary Hutson
John Pain
Jemima Pain
Mary Pain
Martha Pain
Jemima Pain
Eliza Pain
John Pain Junjr
John Corwin
Benjamen Bedwell
Thomas Longworth
Deborah Longworth
Joshiah Youngs
Mary Youngs
Mary Youngs Junjr
Daniel Corwin
William Hallocke
Mary Hallock
William Hallock Junjr

Ruth Howell	Grace Veale
Prudence Hallock	John Veale Junjr
Zebulon Hallock	Daniel Veale
Mary Hallock Junjr	Samuel Veale
Mary Corwin	Obadiah Veale
Jabez Mapes	Mary Veale
Eliza Mapes	Abigall Veale
Sarah Mapes	Irene Veale
Eliza Mapes Junjr	Tabitha Veale
Hannah Mapes	Joyce Veale
Ealse Mapes	Mercey Pattay widdow
John Carter	Ralph Pattay
Ann Carter	Lucas Pattay
Gesia Carter	Moses Pattay
Hester Carter	Margaray Pattay
Eliza Rackett	Ann Pattay
John Rackett	Symon Rumsey
Ann Carter Junjr	Mary Rumsey
Mary Carter	Mary Rumsey Junjr
Joseph Mapes	Peter Symons
Ruth Mapes	Symons
Joseph Mapes Junjr	Symons
William Mapes	Symons
Hannah Mapes	John Tutthill Junjr
David Youngs	Mehitobell Tutthill
Mary Youngs	Waite Benjamen widdow
John Loring	William Benjamen
Richard Loring	Waite Benjamen Junjr
Samuel Loring	Anna Benjamen
John Loring Junjr	hanna Benjamen
Wm Loring	John Benjamen
Thomas Loring	William Rosebash
John Veale	Ann Rosebash

The Names of the Slaves, Men Weomen and Children.

Tony	Liddy	Grace	Cate
Maria	Jack	Cato	James
Semony	Betty	Semony	Jack
Mobsey	Peter	Rose	Betty
Titus	Nager	Tomm	Rose
Sombo	John	Robbin	huson
Tom	Santo	Dorrad	Titus
Prissilla	hope	Sarah	Sambo
Adrea	Pegge	Jenny a Girl	
Abigall	Jack	Jenny	
Grace	Bristol	Judah	In all 41

Indians ffreeman, Servants, men wemen and Children in number - - - 40
Whose Names Cannot be known because not Contant To any Name &c

One hundred thirty and two ffamelyes; Consisting of Christians, old and young;	- 800
Indians old & young - - - - - - - - - - - -	- 040
Slaves, old and young,— - - - - - - - - - - - -	- 41
In all - - - - - - -	- 881

Pr. ISA. ARNOTS
THOMAS MAPES

NOTES AND OBSERVATIONS ON THE TOWN OF EAST HAMPTON, L. I.

BY JOHN LYON GARDINER, OF THE ISLE OF WIGHT; APRIL, 1798.

The Town of East Hampton is bounded South-Easterly by the Atlantic Ocean, on which side the shore is a sand beach free from rocks. The sea gains on the shore, and it has been said by aged people that, in some places, the sea now washes the shore where Indian Corn has been planted by their Fathers. The sand near the shore is blown into hills on which nothing grows but a grass called "Beach Grass," and a shrub bearing the Beach plum. By this grass & the Bushes, the sand is, in some measure, prevented being blown over the adjacent pasture and mowing fields.

Easterly, the town terminates at Montauk's Point around which the tide runs very rapidly. Gardiners Island, or the Isle of Wight, lies on the North East side of Gardiner's Bay, and contains about 3,000 acres of good land. Its greatest length is from N. W to S. E. and is about 7½ miles. There is, besides, an Island called Rom (or Rum) Island, which belongs to it, and lies on the South part. The Shape of the Island is irregular. From its first settlement in 1639, it was a plantation by itself. As the Legislature in 1788 thought proper to annex it to the town of East Hampton, it will, in these Notes, be considered as a part of that Township. This Island is distant from the town 10 miles: and from Long Island shore about 3. It is assessed for about one sixth of the value of the Township. The shore on the North side of East Hampton is rocky and indented with bays, coves, and creeks, which lead into Ponds abounding with shell and scale fish, and are harbours for small vessels.

Westerly, the town is bounded by South Hampton.

The line between these two towns was in contention from the first settlement till 1695, when it was, finally, fixed where it now is, by persons mutually chosen by the two Towns. It begins at the sea shore on the south side, and crosses the eastern branch of the Island, to the North side & leaves but a small part of the houses, at Sag Harbor on the East Hampton side. This line is about miles in length, and was fenced about the year 1664 in order to keep the Southampton horses &c. from crossing over the bounds. This line is now much farther to the Eastward than where it was fixed by the General Assembly of Connecticut about 1660 to whose decision it was then referred.

The settlement of Sag Harbor is mostly in Southampton Township, and is a thriving place. It is exceedingly well calculated for the Whale and Cod Fishery.

By the Records, it appears that East Hampton was at first called *Maidstone*. This name does not appear after the year 1664, when they came under the Duke of York, and soon after received a Patent from Col. Richard Nicolls. By this Patent the Town is called East Hampton, though the records of the Town prior to the year 1664, mention that as the name of the place. It was probably called East, on account of its situation to the East of Southampton.

Some of the Free Settlers appear, by the Records, to have come from Stansted in the county of Kent in England. Probably some of them might have come from Maidstone in the same County. It is very evident from the Records, that some of the original 35 settlers and purchasers of the Town removed from Lynn in Massachusetts; and tradition informs us that they came from several of the towns on the Sea coast to the Eastward of Boston. These were, probably, natives of England, as New England had not been settled so long as to produce Native Immigrants when E. Hampton was first settled. Those who were received by the Original Settlers as "accepted Inhabitants," might have been born in America. None were received into the Town as Inhabitants but by a vote, and some were forbid settling on account of their principles and laziness.

There were, at first 35 purchasers. The names of 13 of these are now entirely extinct in the Town. The Christian & Surnames of many of the original settlers are now found to the 4th 5th & 6th degree, counting the first as one. Lands that were at first allotted, have descended in the family, and are, after a space of 150 years, occupied by one of the same family and name.

When the town was first settled only a home-lot at the South end of the Town, containing from 11 to 13 acres was laid out. This was done on both sides of the Pond, called the "Town Pond." This was probably on account of the convenience of getting water for themselves and cattle before they dug wells. It is probable a brook might have discharged itself into the Pond, which, since the land is cleared, has disappeared.

The next lands that was laid out to the Owners, were the Salt Marshes in various parts of the Town. The last of the Woodland was allotted to the owners about 60 years ago.

Excepting the Indian Deed for the Township, there is nothing of an earlier date on Record than the following:

"At a General Court holden at East Hampton, March 7th 1650 [o. s.] It is ordered that Ralph Dayton is to go to Keneticut for to procure the Evidence of our Lands, and for an acquittance for the payment of our lands, and for a boddie of laws.

"It was alsoe ordered that any man have libertie to sett gunns for to kill wolves, but not within half a mile of the town" &c &c. "No man shall sett any gun, but he shall look to it while the stars appear, and take the gunn up by the sunrising, and no man shall sell any dog or bitch, young or ould to any Indian upon the penaltie of paying of 30s."

Various town laws, similar to the above are on Record. They are styled "Orders." Many of them are relative to laying out vacant lands, making roads, destroying noxious animals &c. in short, laws that were necessary in a new settlement.

The Indian Deed for the land is on Record. It is from the four Indian Sachems, *Paggatacut*, of Manhansett: *Wayandanch* of Miantacutt: *Momoweta* of Corchaki: *Newodonah* of Shinacock.

It is dated April 29th 1648, and conveys the land, to the "Eastward of Southampton bounds, to the Worshipful Theophilus Eaton Esquire, Governour of the Colony of New Haven and the Worshipful Edward Hopkins Governour of the Colony of Conecticut and their assocyates . . . for and in consideration of 20 coats, 24 Looking Glasses, 24 hose, 24 Hatchets, 24 Knives, and one hundred Mucxs, already received by US, and reserve unto ourselves free Liberty to fish in all the cricks & ponds, and hunt up and down in the Woods without molestation, giving the English Inhabitants noe just cause of offence: likewise are to have the fynns & tails of all Whales cast up, and desire they may be friendly dealt with in the other part alsoe to fish for shells to make Wampum of, and if the Indyans, in hunting deer shall chase them into the water and the English shall kill them, the English shall have the bodie and the Sachem the skin." The witnesses were, Richard Woodhull, Thomas Stanton, Robert Bond, Job Sayre and Chectanoo (by his mark) the Interpreter.

There is recorded a receipt from Edward Hopkins to "Robert Bond—inhabitant of East Hampton for £34. 4. 8. being the amount of monies paid for the purchase of the Lands," and the certificate of the delivering to said Bond the writings of the said purchase and all the Interest that was thereby purchased dated 16th April 1651. On a blank leaf of one of the old Books of Records are seen these words "Robert Bond delivered unto the Govr for the purchase of our Lands, for the towns use the sum of £1. 3. 10. Robert Bond for his expenses, going to the Mayne land in the Town's service the sum is £1. 3s. 6d." It appears that the purchase was made by these two Governors in trust & in behalf of the Original Settlers of the Town.

The English & Natives appear to have lived on good terms. The lands on the East end of Long Island as well as the neighbouring Islands—Shelter Island, Gardiners Island, Plum Island & Fishers Island—were purchased of the Natives. Some French writers, I think Raynal, speaks in praise of the Great William Penn for having sett an uncommon Example in purchasing the Soil of Pennsylvania of the Native Indians, and which if it had been followed by the Settlers of New England and Virginia would have prevented some wars that took place. This Frenchman, like many European writers who have never been in the country, did not understand himself sufficiently on this subject The fact was that the Settlers of Virginia & New England purchased their lands of the Natives before Geo: Fox the Founder of the Quaker's Sect published their principles in England in Oliver Cromwell's time, and a long time before the celebrated William Penn settled in Pennsylvania. There is no doubt but the regular purchase & the warrantie deed from the four abovementioned Sachems, in 1648, prevented difficulties between the Natives & English. Some Indian writings on record in East Hampton speak of the friendship & amity of their neighbours the English about 1660.

Gov Winthrop in his Journal, page and Gov. Hutchinson in his History of Massachusetts, p. 88, mentions that in 1640, a number of families removed from Lynn to the West end of Long Island, and bought land there of James Farrett Agent to the Earl of Sterling: but getting into some quarrel with the Dutch, they removed to the East end, and settled at Southampton & chose one Peirson for their Minister. Probably Southampton was settled before East Hampton. Tradition informs us that, before East Hampton people built their first grist mill (which went with cattle), they went to Southampton to mill, and carried their grain on the back of a Bull that belonged to the Town for the use of their cows. If this is true, no doubt Southampton was settled first.

Govr Hutchinson says that in 1644 Southampton by an act of the Commissioners of the United Colonies was annext to the Jurisdiction of Connecticut. One might suppose that E. Hampton was settled from Southampton, but the method of pronunciation is quite different, although the Towns join. An East Hampton man may be known from a Southampton man as well as a native of Kent in England may be distinguished from a Yorkshire man. The original settlers of these Towns probably came from different parts of England. Besides the names that prevail in one town are not to be met with in the other. The names of Pierson, Halsey, Howell, Toppin, Sanford, Cooper White, Post &c are common in Southampton & confined there, as are the names of Mulford, Osborn, Conkling, Baker, Parsons, Miller, Gardiner, Dayton, &c. to East Hampton, The names of Hedges & Hand, are met in the Eastern part of Southampton but originally [they were] from E. Hampton. Very little intercourse took place between the two towns before the Revolutionary war. Since that, visits and intermarriages are more frequent.

What time East Hampton was first settled is not certainly known. Probably soon after Southampton. Neither of the Towns was settled as early as Gardiners Island which was settled by Lion Gardiner in March 1639. David, son of Lion Gardiner, in a petition presented to Gov. Dongan about 1683, mentions his father as the first Englishman that had settled in the Colony of New York. Southampton put itself under the Jurisdiction of Connecticut in 1644, as Southold did under New Haven in 1648. According to President Stiles History of the three Judges of Charles I., East Hampton was a plantation or Commonwealth as it is styled, in the Record—that was, Independent of any other Government from the first settlement till about 1657. The magistrates frequently asked advice in difficult cases "of the neighbour Towns of Southampton & Southold" and sometimes of "the Gentlemen at Hartford."

The three Towns on the East are styled the "Three Plantations." The government of the town of E. Hampton was purely republican. Their laws were enacted by all the citizens assembled in town meeting; this was stiled "the General Court" and a fine inflicted on such as did not attend.

In Decr 1653 by a vote of the General Court, "the Capital laws and the laws and Orders that are notic'd in the bodie of laws that came from Connecticut shall stand in force among us,"

Their public officers were few; three magistrates who were called Townsmen; were chosen annually. Their oath of office points out their duty; it was as follows:—

"You being chosen by the Court for the careful and comfortable carrying on of the affairs of this Town, do here swear by the name of the Great & Everliving God, that you will faithfully, and without respect of persons, execute all such laws and orders as are or shall be made & established by this Court, according to God, according to the trust committed to you during this year for which you are chosen & until new ones be chosen, if you remain among us, so help you God."

A Recorder & Constable were the only other public officers chosen; their oath points out their duty, and is *mutatis mutandis*, similar to the above. The Constable was always a reputable citizen and of great authority. He, by law, moderated the General Court. The Recorder, or Secretary not only recorded all orders of the General Court, but the decisions of the Magistrates, and by a vote passed in 1656, the depositions of witnesses, in trials at Law, for which he was allowed a stated price, as were also the magistrates and constable. Their trials were sometimes, with a Jury, but mostly without. From 1650 to 1664, about the time they came under Gov. Nicoll, there are about 50 or 60 cases at law on record. They were mostly for small debts & for defamation. By law, no one could recover more than £5 for defamation. In 165— Geo: Lee attorney to—— prosecuted "Lieut Lion Gardiner of the Isle of Wight in behalf of himself and the States of England for five hundred pounds Stg" before the magistrates in E. Hampton. It appears from the very lengthy depositions "that a Southampton man had hired a Dutchman to bring a freight (cargo) to that place from Manhadoes, & that the vessel was taken from the Dutchman & brought to the Isle of Wight to the Lieftenant who retook her for the Dutch owner" and was prosecuted by the original captors.

This affair was referred to the General Court at Hartford by the East Hampton Magistrates & both parties were bound to appear there. Lee obliged himself, if he did not prosecute the case there, it should be dropped. This was likely the result. This is the most important case on record where property was concerned.

"The three men were to meet the first second day of every month for the tryall of any cause according to an Order and to consider of those things that may concern the publick good of the place & whosoever of those Three men do not attend the day at 8 o'clock in the morning shall be liable to pay 5s."

"John Mulford, Robert Bone & Thos Baker chosen by this Court for the execution of those Orders, complied with their trust for this year. Ralph Dayton, Constable and Benjn Price, Recorder." Done at a General Court holden October 7, 1651.

The first General Court was in March 1650.

It was decreed October 1652 that "if any man be aggrieved with any thing that is done by the men that are in authoritie, that he shall have liberty to make his appeal to the next General Court, or when the freemen are assembled together for their publique occasions."

Their town Meetings were frequent and became burdensome on the people, but being their own law makers they made a multiplicity of laws for regulating the fences to fields pastured in common; for division of lands; making highways; building a mill or meeting house & this took up much of their time. The business of killing whales was regulated by law, and every one [was] obliged to take his turn to look out for them on the shore." Their houses were thatched and liable to take fire. Every man was obliged by law to provide himself with a ladder that should reach to the top of his house, and a man was appointed to see that the chimneys were well plaistered and swept. Severe laws were made against selling any Indians, guns, swords, powder, lead, flints, or any more than two drams of strong water at one time." Many of the laws appear curious, but in general they are mild, and the penalties not very severe. There are only three or four cases of corporal punishment and none of capital.

In the year 1653 the Indians were somewhat troublesome. Powder & shot were sent for to the mouth of the Connecticut River, and a watch by night of two, and a ward by day of one man was ordered to be kept by the Inhabitants in town. "April 26, 1653, It is ordered that no Indians shall come to the town unless it be upon special occasion, & none come armed, because that the Dutch hath hired Indians against the English, & we not knowing Indians by face cannot distinguish friends from enemies: &, because the Indians hath cast off their Sachem &c orders were given to shoot any Indian on third call or if they ran away." "Every man was obliged to go armed to the meeting house every Lords day, under penaltie of 12 pence," and four assistants were added to the three Townsmen. It does not appear by the Records that any battle was fought. Probably the Indians who were then numerous had not learned the use of Fire Arms. This was at the time Oliver Cromwell was at war with the Dutch Nation and an opinion prevailed through this country that the Dutch at Manhadoes supplied the Indians with arms, and urged them to destroy the English settlements. From the histories of those times, it is evident something was designed against the English by the Dutch & Indians. Oliver Cromwell about this time called on all the Colonies to assist in an expedition against the Dutch at Manhadoes, particularly New Haven and Connecticut who were nighest the Dutch. Major Sedgewick of Massachusetts was to have the command of the men that were to be sent from each Colony in a certain proportion. The following extract from the E. Hampton records probably refers to this:—

"June 29 1654. Having considered the letters that come from Connecticut wherein men are required to assist the power of England against the Dutch, we do think ourselves called to assist the said power."

The expedition did not take place, probably on account of Peace having been made soon after between the two Nations. Very little more is said about the Indians till the great Indian war which threatened all this country in 1675, when the people were again on their guard. But it does not appear that any lives were lost.

This was the most formidable combination of Indians that ever happened. Gov: Andross sent an armed Sloop to Gardiner's Island to protect it against the Indians. The English and the Indians were probably both on their guard against a surprise, but by 1675 the East end of Long Island had so many English settled that there was no great danger. The Five Nations joined this confederacy.

"Oct. 3. 1654. It is ordered that there shall be a copie of the Connecticut combination drawn forth as [soon as] is convenient for us and all men shall sett to their hands."

This combination was signed Oct 24, 1654, by about 40 and is now on Record by each on the Book. All excepting 3 or 4 write a plain legible hand for those days. These sign by making their mark.

This combination is to maintain and preserve the libertie and puritie of the Gospell of our Lord Jesus which we now profess as alsoe the Discipline of the Church which according to the said Gospell is now practiced among US. As alsoe in our civil affaires to be guided & governed according to such laws and orders as shall be made according to God and which by vote of the Major Part shall be of force among Us &c &c."

This Combination is similar to the one entered into in 163– by the 3 Towns of Hartford, Windsor & Weathersfield, and is a copy preamble of that as recorded in Hazards Coll: of State papers p—"

"March 19. 1657. It is ordered and by a Major vote of the Inhabitants of this Towne agreed upon, that Thomas Baker & John Hand is to go into Keneticut for to bring us under their government according to the terms as Southampton is, and alsoe to carry Goodwife Garlick that she may be delivered up unto the authorities there for the triall of the cause of Witchcraft which she is suspected for." It was afterwards agreed upon by the town "that Mr Gardiner shall be intrusted with the same power with Th^s Baker and John Hand for coming under Government.

In the Record the word is "interested." It doubtless should be intrusted.

It is evident from the Record that soon after this they were under the jurisdiction of that Colony, or rather composed a part of it, altho' nothing is said of their men's returning. Probably the General

Court at Hartford did not pay any attention to the latter part of the business on which Baker & Hand were sent. This poor woman had a trial in E. Hampton for Witchcraft, but nothing was done. It was referred to the Genl Court at Hartford.

At this day it appears surprising that not only those who settled in the American Wilderness should be so infatuated about Witches and Witchcraft but that King James I., Lord Justice Holt and some of the first characters in the English Nation should be so carried away with notions of this kind. If the affair of witches has made more noise in this country than it has in some Countries of Europe, it is not owing to their having been more executed for that supposed crime here: for I have no doubt there has been, during the same time, as many executed in England only, as there have been in all New England & Virginia, for it was not confined to New England but prevailed also in other parts. In Europe, the execution of a few individuals would be effaced from the page of History by more important events that were continually taking place during the last century. But in this country it was a singular affair, & has been handed down by our own writers, and dwelt upon, with wonder, by European writers who have endeavored to account for it from the enthusiastic ideas of the Inhabitants here, not considering that they acquired these ideas in Europe from books published by men of character & information. It is to be hoped this infatuation is done away among the Citizens of both sides of the Atlantic but it is not justice for one side to suppose that this infatuation prevailed only on the other. If King James, Lord Holt and others of information, who believed in witchcraft, are excusable, certainly those persecuted exiles who fled to a savage wilderness are equally clear of blame. Perhaps the law of Moses by which in many cases the first settlers were governed, was a Mean of urging them on in the belief of Witchcraft and its evils.

"November 29. 1662. It is jointly & fully agreed that Mr. T. Baker, Mr Thoss James, and Mr Lion Gardiner, Mr Robert Bond, Mr John Mulford, Thos Tomson and Thos Chatfield shall go to Southampton the next second day to compound a difference between Us & Capt. John Scott Esqr and Mr John Ogden about Meantaquit, and do hereby engage to ratifie and confirm what our committee shall conclude upon: & also we do empower this our Committee to joyne with Southampton and Southold about a Patten grant."

To whom they proposed to apply for a Patent I dont know. New York was then in the hands of the Dutch. It was either to King Charles 2nd or to the Government of Connecticut.

"Novemb: 23 1663. A committee was appointed to Join Southampton & Southold Committees and if they see cause, to establish laws for settling government amongst us, And what our Committee or a Major part of them shall doe herein we engage ourselves to stand unto."

It was, doubtless in contemplation to have the three towns join in one government as other towns on this continent have done.

"February 23. 1663. [o. s.] It was agreed that Muntauk shall pay fifty pounds of the 150 that is to purchase the pattent right."

March 25 At a Town Meeting, after long debate, it was agreed to that the Purchase of Pattent right should be borne by all the Inhabitants according to the land every Man Possesses.

"April 26. 1664. At a Town Meeting the Town doth desire those men, that doe goe to Hartford, to debate together with the Neighboring Plantations for the things of Mutual Government between Hartford & Us for our future Settlement, but to conclude of nothing, as understanding that the Governour will come over, or a Committee from the General Court."

Dec 21, 1664. The inhabitants of this Town—understanding that we are off from Connecticut, and the magistrates not willing to act further on that account, that we may not be without laws & Government, it is agreed the former laws shall stand in force till we have further order from York. It is agreed that the Constable of the Town shall be secured by the Town for not gathering the Rates."

The "rates" referred to in this Resolve probably refers to the adjudication that was made at New

York Dec. 1, 1664 by Gov. Nicoll & others on one part, and Gov. Winthrop and others, on the other, that Long Island should not be under the Government of Connecticut, but under His Highness the Duke of York &c. There appears from this time to have been some alteration in their Government. In April 1664 the Constable & Town Overseers were chosen; no mention is made of Townsmen.

Copy of James Farrett's Grant to Lion Gardiner.

Know all whom this present Writing may concern, that I, James Farrett of Long Island, Gent. Deputy to the Right Hon'ble the Earll of Starling Secretary for the Kingdom of Scotland, doe by these presents, in the name and behalf of the said Earll of Starling and in my own name also, as his Deputy, as it doth or may concern myself, Give & Grant free leave and liberty to Lion Gardiner his heirs, executors and assigns to enjoy that Island which he hath now in possession called by the Indians Manchonack, by the English the Isle of Wight; I say to enjoy both now & for ever, which Island hath been purchased, before my coming, from the ancient Inhabitants, the Indians; Nevertheless though the said Lion Gardiner had his possession first from the Indians before my coming, yet is he now contented to hold the tenor & title of the possession of the aforesaid Island from the Earll of Starling or his successors whomsoever, who hath a Grant from the King of England, under the Great Seal of the aforesaid Kingdom. Bee it known, therefore, that I, the said James Farrett doe give & hath given free liberty & power to the said Lion Gardiner, his Heirs, Exe'rs and Assigns and their Successors for ever to enjoy the possession of the aforesaid Island, to build & plant thereon as best liketh them, and to dispose thereof as they think fitt, and also to make, execute and put in practice such laws for Church and Civil Government as are according to God, the Kings and the practise of the Country, without giving any account thereof to any whomsoever and the aforesaid Right & title, both of land and Government to remayne with, and to them and their successors for ever, without any trouble or molestation from the said Earll or any of his successors, for now & forever. And as much as it hath pleased Our Royal King to give the Patten of Long Island to the aforesaid Earle of Starling in consideration whereof it is agreed upon that the trade with the Indians shall remayne with the said Earle and his successors, to dispose upon from time to time and at all times as best liketh him. Notwithstanding [allowing] the said Lion Gardiner to trade with the Indyans for Corne or any Kinde of victuals for the use of the Plantation and no farther: and if the said Lion Gardiner shall trade in Wampum from the Indyans hee shall pay for every fadome twenty shillings and also the said Lion Gardiner and his successors shall pay to the said Earle or his deputyes a yearly acknowledgment being the sum of Five Pounds, (being lawfully demanded) of lawfull money of England, or such commoditys as at that time shall pass for money in the country; and the first payment to begin on the last of Oct. 1643, the three former yeares being advanced for the use of the said James Farrett. In witness whereof the party has put his hands and seal the tenth day of March 1639. [o. s.]

(Signed) James Farrett (seal.)

Sealed and delivered in the presence of
ffulk Davis
Benj[n] Price.

XXIII.

STATISTICS

OF THE

Population of the Province of New-York.

1647—1774.

POPULATION—1647.

GOV. STUYVESANT TO THE STATES GENERAL.

[Hol. Doc. XI.]

I need not intrude on your Illustrious High Mightinesses with a long narrative as to the low condition in which I found New Netherland on my arrival—the Flattland so stripped of inhabitants that with the exception of the three English Villages of Hemstede, New Flushing & Gravesend, 50 Bouweries and Plantations could not be enumerated; and there could not be made out in the whole Province, 250, or at farthest 300 men capable of bearing arms.

1673.

[Vanderkemp Transl. of Dutch Rec. Vol. XXII.]

"They and as many of the Dutch nation as are yet residing under this Government is calculated to amount, Women and children included, to about Six thousand." (6.000). *Address of the Burgomasters &c to Bencks and Evertsen.*

AN ACCOUNT of the Number of Inhabitants in ye Severall Counties of ye Province of New Yorke taken by the High Sheriffs and Justices of the Peace in each respective County; as p order of His Excell. the Earl of Bellomont Governr &c. anno 1698

[Lond. Doc. XI.]

	Men.	Women.	Children.	Negros.
In ye County & Citty of Albany	380	270	803	23
In ye County of Ulster & Dutchesse County	248	111	869	156
In the County of Orange	29	31	140	19
In the City & County of New York	1019	1057	2161	700
In Richmond County als Staten Island	328	208	118	73
In ye County of West Chester	316	294	307	146
In Suffolk County within Nassau Island	973	1024	124	558
In Kings County within Nassau Island	308	332	1081	296
In Queens County within Nassau Island	1465	1350	551	199
	5066	4677	6154	2170

A true Copy	4667
(signed) BELLOMONT	6154
	2170
Total	18067 Population

POPULATION OF ALBANY COUNTY & INDIANS 1689—1698.

[Lond. Doc. XI.]

In pursuance of the Order from his Excell. Col. Benj Fletcher, Capt. Gen^ll^ & Govern^r^ in Chief dated the 3rd day of May 1697, to make a perfect reckoning of the Inhabitants of the City & County of Albany and how many families and particular persons in the said Citty and County are departed from the beginning of ye Warr, how many persons killed & carried away, & of what number ye Five Nations and River Indians there were, & how much they since are lessened, so that wee find that the Inhabitants of the Citty & County of Albany did consist:

in the year 1689			*and now*		
men	weomen	children	men	weomen	children
662	340	1014	382	272	805

*The Five Nations and River Indians vizt*

The Mohoggs	270	& now	110
The Onneydes	180	& now	70
The Onnondages	500	& now	250
The Cajouges	320	& now	200
The Sinnekes	1300	& now	600
The River Indians	250	& now	90
In the beginning of ye War	2800 Indians	& now	1320

The Christians departed from the Citty & County of Albany since the beginning of ye Warr

	Men.	Women.	Children.
Departed	142	68	209
Taken prisoners	16	”	”
Killed by ye enemy . . .	84	”	”
Dyed	38	”	”
	280	68	209

A true Copy

(signed) BELLOMONT.

COMPARATIVE TABLE OF POPULATION IN THE PROVINCE OF NEW YORK. 1703—1712.

[Lond. Doc. XIX.]

	1703	1712	*Increased.*
New York	4436	5840	1404
Kings County	1915	1925	10
Richd County	504	1279	775
Orange County	268	439	171
West Chester	1946	2803	857
	9069	12286	3217
Queens County	4392		
Suffolk	3346		
Albany City & County	2273		
Ulster & Dutches	1669		
	11680		

Of these Countys I have as yet no lists, nor from the Jerseys but hope to be able to send it to your Lordps by the next from Connecticut. I have so imperfect an account, that I am ashamed to send it but will endeavor to get a more perfect one.

In the five Countys whereof I have procured lists, the numbers were composed as followeth,

In the Year.	1703	1712	*Increased.*
Christians . .	7767	10511	2744
Slaves . . .	1301	1775	474
			3218

[NOTE.—In 1700 Population of Ulster Co. was 2005 of which 324 were Slaves.
In 1714 " " 2120 of which 433 were Slaves.
The Population of Dutchess Co. in 1714, was 445 Souls of whom 29 were Slaves.]

GOV. HUNTER TO THE BOARD OF TRADE, APRIL, 1716.

[Lond. Doc. XX.]

The number of the Militia of this Province by my last account is 5060. I cannot say that the inhabitants increase in that proportion (at least) as they do in the neighbouring provinces where the purchases of land are easier had, than with us, great numbers of the younger sort leave Long Island yearly to plant in the Jerseys & Pensylvania.

SAME TO THE SAME. AUGUST, 1720.

[Lond. Doc. XXI.]

Query, what is the number of the Militia?

Answer, About Six thousand.

AN ACCOUNT

OF THE FAMILIES OF GERMANS SETLLED ON HUDSON'S RIVER IN THE PROVINCE OF NEW YORK. 1718.

[Lond. Doc. XXI.]

On the East side of Hudson's River.

	families	Persons.
In Hunterstown	25	109
Kingsbury	33	104
Annberry	17	71
Haysberry	16	75
Rheinbeck	35	140
In Schoharie		
In Seven Townships	170	680
On the West Side		
New Town	14	56
George Town	13	52
Elizb : Town	9	36
Kingstown	15	60
Wessels pretended land	7	28
Kingstown Sopes	10	40
At New York and places adjacent	30	150
	394	1601

The widows & orphans are not included in this list.

This to the best of our knowledge is the Acc^{ot} of those people settled, amounting to 394 families, containing about 1601 persons.

JOSHUA KOCHERTHAL
JOHN FRED. HAGER.

[*Endorsed.*]

" New York, List of the Palatines settled in
New York Province Rec^{d} wth Brig. Hunters L^{r}
of 7 Aug 1718"

AN ACCOUNT OF THE NUMBER OF PEOPLE IN THE PROVINCE OF NEW YORK A. D. 1723.

[Lond. Doc. XXII.]

NAME OF THE COUNTY.	White					Negroes and other Slaves					
	Men	Women	Male Children	Female Children	Totall of White Persons	Men	Women	Male Children	Female Children	Totall of Negroes & other Slaves	Totall of Persons
New York	1460	1726	1352	1348	5886	408	476	220	258	1362	7248
Richmond	335	320	305	291	1251	101	63	49	42	255	1506
Kings	490	476	414	394	1774	171	123	83	67	444	2218
Queens	1568	1599	1530	1371	6068	393	294	228	208	1123	7191
Suffolk	1441	1348	1321	1156	5266	357	367	197	54	975	6241
West Chester	1050	951	1048	912	3961	155	118	92	83	448	4409
Orange	309	245	304	239	1097	45	29	42	31	147	1244
Dutchess	276	237	259	268	1040	22	14	2	5	43	1083
Ulster	642	453	563	699	2557	227	126	119	94	556	2923
Albany	1512	1408	1404	1369	5693	307	200	146	155	808	6501
Totall	9083	8763	8500	8047	34393	2186	1810	1178	997	6171	40564

ABSTRACT OF THE ACCOUNTS

OF THE NUMBER OF INHABITANTS OF THE SEVERAL CITIES AND COUNTIES IN THE PROVINCE OF NEW YORK, 2 NOV. 1731.

[MS in Sec's off.]

Citys and Counties	Sheriffs	Whites males above 10 years old	Whites females above 10	Whites males under 10	Whites females under 10	blacks males above ten	blacks females above ten	Blacks males under 10	Blacks females under 10	the amount in each county
City and County of New York	Henry Beekman	2628	2250	1143	1024	599	607	186	185	8622
City & County of Albany	Gosen Van Schick	2481	1155	2352	1212	568	185	346	174	8573
Queens County	Thos Hicks	2239	2175	1178	1139	476	363	226	199	7995
Suffolk County	David Corey 715 Indians	2144	1130	2845	955	239	83	196	83	7675
West Chester County	Gilbert Willet	1879	1701	1054	707	269	96	176	151	6033
Ulster County	John Wyncoop	990	914	577	515	321	196	124	91	3728
Kings County	Domini Van Der Veer	629	518	243	268	205	146	65	76	2150
Orange County	William Pullen	627	534	325	299	85	47	19	33	1969
Richmond County	Charles Garretson	423	471	263	256	111	98	51	44	1817
Dutchess County	William Squire	570	481	263	298	59	32	13	8	1727
		14613	11529	10243	6673	2932	1853	1402	1044	50289
		11529							1402	
		10243							1853	
		6673							2932	
		43508 Whites							7231	blacks

It is Remarkable that in New York there are above ten years 147 males & 995 females more than in Albany [and in Albany] 1029 males & 188 females [under ten] more than in New York Which is Accounted for by this parts being a trading place & many of the males go abroad of course many females Lye fallor & perhaps in the County they are better breeders & I believe many younger.

A LIST OF THE NUMBER OF INHABITANTS

BOTH WHITES AND BLACKS OF EACH SPECIES WITHIN THE PROVINCE OF NEW YORK ABOVE AND UNDER THE AGE OF TEN YEARS TAKEN IN THE YEAR 1737.

[Lond. Doc. XXVI.]

Cities and Countys	White males above 10 years	White Females above 10 years	White Males under 10 years	White Females under 10 years	Black Males above 10 years	Black females above 10 years	Black Males under 10 years	Black Females under 10 years	Total of each county	Total in 1731	Since increased
New York	3253	3568	1088	1036	674	609	229	207	10664	8622	2042
Albany	3209	2995	1463	1384	714	496	223	197	10681	8573	2108
West Chester	2110	1890	950	944	304	254	153	140	6745	6633	712
Orange	860	753	501	433	125	95	38	35	2840	1969	871
Ulster	1175	1681	541	601	378	260	124	110	4870	3728	1142
Dutchess	940	860	710	646	161	42	37	22	3418	1727	1691
Richmond	488	497	289	266	132	112	52	53	1889	1817	72
Kings	654	631	235	264	210	169	84	101	2348	2150	198
Queens	2407	2290	1395	1656	460	370	254	227	9059	7995	1064
Suffolk	2297	2353	1175	1008	393	307	203	187	7923	7675	248
	17393	17518	8347	8238	3551	2714	1397	1279	60437	50289	10148

AN ACCOUNT OF THE NUMBER OF INHABITANTS

OF THE PROVINCE OF NEW YORK TAKEN 4 JUNE 1746, BY ORDER OF HIS EXCELLENCY GOVERNOUR CLINTON.

[Lond. Doc. XXVIII.]

	Males white under 16	Males white 16 & under 60	Males white above 60	Females white under 16	Females white 16 and upwards.	Males black under 60.	Males black 16 & under 60	Males black above 60.	Females bl'ck under 16	Females bl'ck 16 & upwards	Total number
City & Co of N. Y.	2117	2097	149	2013	2897	419	645	76	735	569	11718
Kingston county	350	435	71	366	464	140	167	32	154	152	2331
* Albany county	......	......	......	......	......	......	......	......	......	......	......
Queens county	1946	1826	233	2077	1914	365	466	61	391	361	9640
Dutchess county	2200	2056	200	2100	1750	106	160	26	108	100	8806
Suffolk county	1887	1835	226	1891	2016	329	393	52	315	310	9254
Richmond county	445	376	35	421	414	92	88	13	95	94	2073
Orange county	536	763	67	871	721	82	99	34	51	44	3268
Westchester county	2435	2090	303	2095	1640	187	180	27	138	140	9235
Ulster county	1022	1044	116	972	1000	244	331	43	229	264	5265
	12938	12522	1400	12196	12816	1964	2529	364	2216	2034	61589

Total white 51,872.

* Not possible to be numbered on account of the enemy.

AN ACCOUNT OF THE NUMBER OF INHABITANTS

IN THE PROVINCE OF NEW YORK, TAKEN 10th MAY 1749, BY ORDER OF HIS EXCELLENCY THE HONOURABLE GOVERNOUR CLINTON.

[Lond. Doc. XXIX.]

	Males white under 16 y rs.	Males white 16 & under 60	Males white above 60	Fem'ls white under 16	Fem'ls white 16 & upwards	Total white.	Males black under 16	Males black 16 & under 60	Males black 60 & upwards	Fem'ls black under 16	Fem'ls black 16 & upwards	Total black.
City & Co. of N. Y.	2346	2765	183	2364	3268	10926	460	610	41	556	701	2368
King's county	288	437	62	322	391	1500	232	244	21	137	149	783
Albany county	2249	2359	322	2137	2087	9154	309	424	48	334	365	1480
Queens county	1630	1508	151	1550	1778	6617	300	386	43	245	349	1423
Dutchess county	1970	1820	160	1790	1751	7491	103	155	21	63	79	421
Suffolk county	2058	1863	248	1960	1969	8098	305	355	41	292	293	1286
Richmond county	431	420	36	424	434	1745	88	110	20	93	98	409
Orange county	1061	856	66	992	899	3874	62	95	16	84	103	360
Westchester county	2511	2312	228	2263	2233	9547	303	270	66	238	279	1156
Ulster county	913	992	110	810	979	3894	217	301	50	198	240	1006
	Total number of whites					62756	Total number of blacks					10692

Total number of Inhabitants, white and black, 73,448.

G. CLINTON.

GENERAL LIST OF INHABITANTS IN THE PROVINCE OF NEW YORK,

EXTRACTED FROM THE RETURNS OF THE SHERIFFS OF THE SEVERAL COUNTIES, IN PURSUANCE OF WARRANTS TO THEM, DATED 16TH FEBRUARY, 1756.

	WHITES.						BLACKS.					
Cities and Counties.	Males under 16	Males above 16 & under 60	Males 60 and upwards.	Females under 16	Females above 16	Total.	Males under 16	Males above 16 & under 60	Males 60 and upwards	Females under 16	Females above 16	Total.
City and County of New York,	2260	2308	174	2359	3667	10768	468	604	68	443	695	2272
City and County of Albany,	3474	3795	456	3234	3846	14805	658	786	76	496	403	2619
Ulster County,	1655	1687	156	1489	1618	6605	328	437	49	326	360	1500
Dutchess County,	3910	2873	203	3530	2782	13289	211	270	53	163	162	859
Orange County,	1213	1088	74	1083	998	4446	103	116	24	93	94	430
Westchester County	3153	2908	1039	2440	2379	11919	296	418	77	267	280	1338
Kings County,	417	467	84	358	536	1862	212	214	21	201	197	845
Queens County,	1960	2147	253	1892	2365	8617	581	563	55	500	470	2169
Suffolk County,	2283	2141	221	2265	2335	9245	278	297	40	194	236	1045
Richmond County,	344	411	107	334	471	1667	145	92	30	97	101	465

Whites 83,223 Blacks 13,542

Total 96,765.

LIST OF INHABITANTS

IN THE SEVERAL COUNTIES IN THE PROVINCE OF NEW YORK, TAKEN IN THE YEAR 1771.

Names of the several Counties.	WHITES.						BLACKS.						
	Males under 16.	Males above 16 & under 60.	Males 60 and upwards.	Females under 16.	Females above 16.	Total of whites in each county.	Males under 16.	Males above 16, and under 60.	Males 60 and upwards.	Females under 16.	Females above 16.	Total of blacks in each county.	Total of whites and blacks.
City & Co. of New York	3,720	5,083	280	3,779	5,864	18,726	568	890	42	552	1,085	3,137	21,863
Albany	9,740	9,822	1,136	9,086	9,045	38,829	876	1,100	250	671	980	3,877	42,706
Ulster	2,835	3,023	262	2,601	3,275	11,996	518	516	57	422	441	1,954	13,950
Dutchess	5,721	4,687	384	5,413	4,839	21,044	299	417	34	282	328	1,360	22,404
Orange	2,651	2,297	167	2,191	2,124	9,430	162	184	22	120	174	662	10,092
Westchester	3,813	5,204	549	3,483	5,266	18,315	793	916	68	776	887	3,430	21,745
Kings	548	644	76	513	680	2,461	297	287	22	261	295	1,162	3,623
Queens	1,253	2,083	950	2,126	2,332	8,744	374	511	271	546	534	2,236	10,980
Suffolk	2,731	2,834	347	2,658	3,106	11,676	350	389	59	320	334	1,452	13,128
Richmond	616	438	96	508	595	2,253	177	152	22	106	137	594	2,847
Cumberland	1,071	1,002	59	941	862	3,935	......	6	1	1	2	12	3,947
Gloucester	178	185	8	193	151	715	2	4	......	3	......	7	722
Totals	34,887	37,302	4,314	33,492	38,139	148,124	4,416	5,372	848	4,050	5,197	19,833	168,007

WM TRYON.

Estimated amount of Population in 1774.

[Lond. Doc. XLIV.]

Whites	161,098
Blacks,	21,149
Total estimated Population in 1774,	182,247

XXIV.

STATISTICS

OF

Revenue, Imports, Exports, &c.

1691—1768.

THE PRODUCE OF THE REVENUE

FROM THE 30th OF JANUARY 1690 TO THE 25th OF DECMBR. 1691.

[Lond. Doc. X.]

		£ s. d.
To customs, in, out, & up Hudsons River	£2521. 2.11¾	
To Inland Excise on retailed Liquors	203.12	
To the produce of the Weigh house	150	
To fines and forfeitures	306.10	
To Quit-rents received	21.12. 6	
		3202.17. 5¾
The produce of one year ended the 25th of Decr. 1692		
The Customes, as above	£2463. 3.11½	
To Excise of Liquors	834.15. 8	
To produce of the Weigh house		
To Fines and forfeitures	60. 8.	
		3358. 7. 7½
The year ended 25th Decr '93		
To Customs	£1916. 8. ¼	
To Excise	665.16. 6	
To Quit-rents	38.11.	
To Weigh house	90.	
To fines and seizures	229.17. 5¾	
		2940.13.
The year ended 25th Decr. '94.		
To customes	£3055.11. 3	
To excise	862. 4.10	
To Quit-rents	149. ½	
To Weigh house	218. 3. 2	
To fines and forfeitures	15. 7	
		4299.19.11
The year ended 25th Decr '95		
To Customes	£2313.17.10¼	
To Excise	919.18. 2½	
To Quit-rents	36.17. 6	
To produce of the Weigh-house	66.00.11¾	
To fynes and forfeitures	264.17. 4½	
		3601.11.11
Totall of receipts		£17403. 9.11¼

AN ACCOUNT OF HIS MAT'YS REVENUE IN THE PROVINCE OF NEW-YORK,

FROM Y^e 8th DAY OF JUNE 1698 TO Y^e 24th OF JUNE 1700.

[London Doc. XIII.]

1698	Arrears in ye time of ye late Collector	The Duty on Dry Goods	Duty on Wine imported.	Duty on Rumm imported.	Duty on Beavors exported	Duty on Goods carried up Hudsons River	Seizures	Excise	The Weigh House	Quit Rents.	Addiconal Duty.
From ye 8th day of June to ye 29th day of September	226.17.8½	393. 2. 8½	361.	401. .8	379. 8. 6¾	32. 4. 8	240. 8.5¾	181.15.	45.17.2½	8. 2. 3	....
From ye 29th day of September to ye 25th day of December	119.12.	208.13. 6½	158.	116.15.	103.13. 6	34.13. 8	43.11.8	181.15.	27.12. ½	3.15.	....
From the 25th day of Xber to ye 25th day of March 1699	....	36.19. 2¾	....	49. 7.4	12. 2¼	3.11. 4	....	181.15.	75.19.11	153. 7. 6	....
From ye 25th day of March to the 24th of June	....	511. 1. 5¼	6.10	268.10.	38. 7. ½	31.17.	....	534. . 6	46.	....	41.14.1
1699	346. 9.8½	1149.16.11	525.10	835.13.	542. 1. 3½	102. 6. 8	284. 1¾	1079. 5. 6	195. 9. 2	165. 4. 9	41.14.1
From ye 24th day of June to ye 29th day of September	....	648. 2. 5¼	204.10	284.12.4	310. 4½	43.11. 2¼	2. 5.4	119. 1.10½	27. 3	....	221.4.5¼
From ye 29th day of September to ye 25th day of December	....	178. 3. 5½	32.19	151.14.8	206. 6.11½	10.	....	134.11. 4	25.16.11½	3.16.	130.6.2¼
From the 25th day of Dec. to ye 25th day of March 1700	....	227. 1. 3	420. 5	20.12.4	5.	7.11.	....	142. 4.10	10.16. 5½	1.17.	114.4.4¼
From the 25th day of March to ye 24th of June	....	227. 1. 8	548.	355. 4.4	58 18. 7½	3. 6. 8	....	266.14. 6	23.18. 8	5. 6.	267.6.3¾
£	....	1280. 8. 9¾	1205.14	782. 3.8	571.10 11½	68. 8.10¼	2. 5.4	662.12. 6½	87.15. 1	10.19.	732.1.3¾

From the 8th day of June 1698 to the 24th day of June 1699, the totall sum rec'd is .... 5267.11.2¾ } £10668.10.9¼
From the 24th day of June 1699 to the 24th day of June 1700, the like rec'd is .... 5400.19.6½ }

A true copy
(signed) BELLOMONT.

Errors excepted
S. V. CORTLAND, Comr.

1721—1725.

AN ABSTRACT of the whole Amount of the Duties of the Several Commodities hereunder mentioned, from 5th of June 1721, until the 5th Day of June 1725 inclusive.

[From Journals of the General Assembly.]

Years.	*of Wine.*	*of Rum.*	*of Molasses.*	*of Salt.*	*of Cocoa.*	*of Dry Goods.*
1722	£496.10.6	£1165.14.9	£649.12. 4	£270.9.0	£192.19.6	£62. 2. 5
1723	1493. 2.0	1324. 1.9	711.18. 8	175.7.0	130.13.9	79.16. 4
1724	513. 0.0	1782.11.6	456.10.10	91.5.6	163. 3.3	115. 2.11
1725	961. 4.0	911. 8.9	728.15. 8	213.6.0	665.19.0	95.12. 9
	£3436.16.6	£5183.16.9	£2546.17. 6	£750.7.6	£1152.15.3	£352.14. 5

			1152.15. 3
1738	£2913. 6. 8		750. 7. 6
1740	2328. 4. 1		2546.17. 6
1742	2197. 7. 1¾		5183.16. 9
1743	2402. 8.10¼		3436.16. 6
1752	2704.15.11¾		
1753	1788. 8. 2½	Total	£13423. 7.11
1754	2566. 2. 0.		
1755	2447.19. 9¾	Average	£3355.16.11

1726.

AN ABSTRACT of the Several Branches of His Majesty's Revenue for support of Government in the Province of New York.

[From the same.]

From the 20th of April until the 1st October 1726 (5½ months) £3825.6.10½

GENERAL ACCOUNT of the Receipts of moneys, granted for the support of the Government of New York from 1st Sept. 1740, until 1st March 1741.

[From the same.]

Receipts, ... £5392.9.3¾

1st Sept. 1742 to 1 Sept. 1743 .... 6025.4.1¾

A GENERAL STATE OF THE PUBLIC FUNDS IN THE PROVINCE OF NEW YORK,

AND THE USES TO WHICH THEY ARE APPLIED. 1767.

[Lond. Doc. XL.]

Divers sums have been raised by different Acts of Assembly. We have an Act to lay a Duty of Tonnage on Ships, but the money is applied to sink certain Bills of Credit. Another for licencing Hawkers and Pedlers but it will expire soon and not be revived; and a third, commonly called the Duty Act. This last raises the money and for support of Government; it was passed the 12th Dec. 1753, and was limited to a year, but is annually continued. Tis entitled, "An Act for granting to

His Majesty the several Duties & impositions on Goods, wares and Merchandizes imported into this Colony, therein mentioned." The Dutiable Articles are Slaves, Wine, Cocoa, Rum, Brandy, Shrub, and other distilled Liquors, and European and East India dry goods, from the British Islands.

The annual produce of the Duty Act for ten years past stands, as digested from the Journals of the Assembly to whom the Province Treasury accounts yearly.

In the year 1755	£2447.19. 9¾	In the year 1761	£10318.16.11¾
1756	3171. 9. 2	1762	7108.12. 5¾
1757	3880.17.10¾	1763	8574. 0.10¾
1758	5207. 6. 2¾	1764	7596.12. 5¾
1759	8207. 2. 8¾	1765	4920. 5. 4
1760	10346. 9.11	1766	4811. 8.11¾
In value Sterling	£41180.12.9¾		74125. 3. 1

The last years amount being 4811.8.11¾ is in Sterling at the usual Exchange of £180 per cent £2673. 0. 6½

Out of this money we pay

To the Governor	2000
For Fuel and Candles for Fort George	400
To the Chief Justice of Salary & Riding the Circuit	300
To 3 puisne Judges each £200	600
To the Secretary for enrolling the Laws	30
To the Clerk of the Council	30
To the Doorkeeper of the Council	20
To the Public Printer	50
To the Guager of Dutiable Liquors	30
To the Land and Tide Waiters	50
To the Treasurers Standing Salary	200
To the same for Extraordinary Services	100
To the Agent in England	500
To the Attorney General	150
To the Clerk of the Assembly, each day of a session 20s suppose 50 days	50
To the Door Keeper of the Assembly each Day 6s suppose 50 days	15
To the Gunner & Store keeper of the Colony's Stores	20
Allowed for Contingents in the Service of the Colony	100
	4645 value Sterling £2580.11. 1¼
	£92. 9. 5¼

The Light house was erected in the year 1764. A Duty of 3d. *P.* Ton was laid on the Tonnage of Ships for maintaining it which produced the first year £487.6.9. & the expenses were £431.8.6.

The second year 415.16.1. D° 407.14.6.

From this State of the Civil List of the Province it appears that there is even this year a surplus beyond the whole Expence of supporting the Government, and it was heretofore very considerable. This Ballance has always been either borrowed in exigencies or applied by particular Laws to special uses.

The Annual account of Quit rents agreable to the list of Patents in the Receiver General's office is in Sterling - - - - - - - - - - - - - - - - £1806. 7. 9

The arrears of Quit rents agreable to the list in the said office amounts to - - 18,888.16.10

The above sums are as near as can be computed, the price of Wheat, Skins, Lambs, and Pease differing every year.

The following sums are paid out of the Quit Rents on the Kings warrants directed to the Receiver General.

To the Honourable Robert Cholmondely the auditor General of the Plantations	£100
To George Clarke Esp. Secretary of New York on two warrants for his salary and Incidents	60
To the Secretary for Indian Affairs	100
To the Receiver General's Salary	200
To the Honourable Robert Cholmondeley a Commission of £5 per cent of all monies received on auditing the accounts	
The Incidental charges of the Receiver Genls Office	

The owners of Lands in this Province have ever been so backward in the Payment of their Quit Rents that the sum collected annually has never been sufficient to pay off the above mentioned salaries, and some other orders which were formerly granted to different people by the Lords of the Treasury.

AMOUNT OF THE VALUE OF THE IMPORTS AND EXPORTS

FROM AND TO NEW YORK, FOR THREE YEARS FROM 1717, TO 1720.

[Lond. Doc. XXIII.]

IMPORTS.	£ s. d.	EXPORTS.	£ s. d.
From 1717 to 1718,	27.331.12.1	From 1717 to 1718,	62.966.16.3
From 1718 to 1719,	19.596. 6.5	From 1718 to 1719,	56.355. 3.9
From 1719 to 1720,	16.836.12.7	From 1719 to 1720,	37.397.19.5
Total Imports	63.764.11.1	Total exports	156.719.19.5
Medium	21.254.17.0¼	Medium	52.239.19.9½

The like account from 1720 *to* 1723.

	£ s. d.		£ s. d.
From 1720 to 1721.	15.681. 4.5	From 1720 to 1721,	50.788.10. 6
From 1721 to 1722,	19.564.15.4	From 1721 to 1722,	57.889.15.10
From 1722 to 1723,	28 518.12.6	From 1722 to 1723,	54.838. 9. 8
Total Imports,	63.764.12.3	Total Exports,	163.516.16. 0
Medium,	21.254.17.5	Medium,	54.505.12. 0

	£ s. d.
Total Export of the three last years,	163.516.16. 0
Total Export of the three preceding years,	156.719.19. 5
Exceeded in the Total Exports of the three last years,	6.796.16. 7
Which at a Medium has been an An'ual Increase in ye Exports	2.265,12. 2¼

An account of the Value of Furrs imported from New York for six years, from 1717 *to* 1723.

	£ s. d.		£ s. d.
From 1717 to 1718,	10.704. 3.11	From 1720 to 1721,	6.659. 4.11
From 1718 to 1719,	7.138. 2. 5	From 1721 to 1722,	7.045. 3.10
From 1719 to 1720,	7.487.16. 5	From 1722 to 1723,	8.833. 5. 4
	25.330. 2. 9		22.537.14. 1
Total of the three last years	22.537.14. 1		
Excess of the three first years	2.792. 8. 8	Medium,	930.16.2¼

AN ACCOUNT

OF THE ANNUAL AMOUNT OF THE IMPORTS AND EXPORTS FROM AND TO NEW YORK, FROM CHRISTMAS, 1723 TO CHRISTMAS 1728.

[Lond. Doc. XXIV.]

The several years.		Imports.	Exports.
		£ s. d.	£ s. d.
From Christmas 1723	To Christmas 1724	21191. 2. 3	63020. 0. 9
1724	1725	25316.18. 9	70650. 8. 0
1725	1726	38307.17.10	84850.18. 0
1726	1727	31617. 8. 1	67373. 6. 3
1727	1728	21005.12.11	78561. 6. 4

JOHN OXENFORDH A. I. Gen'l.

Custom House Inspect'r Gen'ls Office 17 Nov'r 1729.

NUMBER OF NEGROES IMPORTED FROM 1701—1726.

AN ACCO't of what Negro Slaves have been Imported into his Majesties Province of New York as taken from the Custom House Books between the year 1701 & this present year 1726.

[Lond. Doc. XXIII.]

YEAR.	From the West Indies.	From the coast of Africa.	YEARS.	From the West Indies.	From the coast of Africa.
1701	36	....	1717	68	266
1702	165	....	1718	447	70
1703	16	....	1719	104	....
1704	8	....	1720	81	....
1705	....	24	1721	76	*117
1710	....	53	1722	106	....
1711	....	55	1723	82	....
1712	....	77	1724	61	....
1714	53	....	1725	54	59
1715	17	38	1726	180	....
1716	19	43			
				1259	512
	314	290		314	290
				1573	8(2)8
		Totall 2395.		Should be	(0)

N. B. That all the Negroes in the foregoing account have been Imported by Private Traders and that none have been imported dureing that time by the African Company.

ARCH'D KENNEDY Coll'r.

New York 15 December 1726.

*Entered from the Coast of Africa but found afterwards to have been from Madagascar.

XXV.

PAPERS

RELATING TO THE

TRADE AND MANUFACTURES

OF THE

Province of New-York.

1705—1757.

Trade and Manufactures of the Province, 1705.

LORD CORNBURY TO SEC. HODGES.

[Lond. Doc. XVI.]

The Trade of this Province consists chiefly in flower and biskett which is sent to the Islands in the West Indians, in return they bring Rum, Sugar, Molasses, and some times pieces of Eight and Cocoa and Logwood; to Europe Our people send Skins of all sorts, Whale Oyle and Bone, which are the only Commodity this Country sends to Europe, of its own produce as yet, but if they were encouraged, the people of this Province would be able to supply England with all manner of Naval Stores, Pitch, Tarr, Rosine, Turpentine, Flax Hemp Masts and Timber of all Kinds and Sizes, and very good in their Kinds. . . . .

When I said on the other side that if the people were encouraged they would be able to supply England with all manner of Naval Stores, I mean (by encouraged) if they had a certain sure market for their produce; for as the Case now stands, they aply their land to Corn of all sorts, but chiefly Wheat, because they have a certain Market for that in the Islands, but if they had a sure market for Hemp and flax in England, they would greedily fall to the planting of hemp and flax, because they want Commoditys, to make returns to England for the goods they take from thence. Besides if part of their lands were employed to those uses, their Corn would fetch a better price; besides the want of wherewithall to make returns for England, sets mens wits at work, and that has put them upon a Trade which I am sure will hurt England in a little time; for I am well informed, that upon Long Island and Connecticut, they are setting up a Woollen Manufacture, and I myself have seen Serge made upon Long Island that any man may wear. Now if they begin to make Serge, they will in time make Course Cloth, and then fine; we have as good fullers earth and tobacco pipe clay in this Province, as any in the world; how farr this will be for the service of England I submit to better Judgments; but however I hope I may be pardoned, if I declare my opinion to be, that all these Colloneys, which are but twigs belonging to the Main Tree (England) ought to be Kept entirely dependent upon & subservient to England, and that can never be if they are suffered to go on in the notions they have, that as they are Englishmen, soe they may set up the same manufactures here as people may do in England; for the consequence will be that if once they can see they can cloath themselves, not only comfortably but handsomely too, without the help of England, they who are already not very fond of submitting to Government would soon think of putting in Execution designs they had long harbourd in their breasts This will not seem strange when you consider what sort of people this Country is inhabited by.

Mr CALEB HEATHCOTE TO THE BOARD OF TRADE, 3 AUG. 1708.

[Lond. Doc. XVII.]

My Lords—This comes chiefly to ask pardon for all the trouble I have given your Lordships in my severall letters relating to the Naval Stores. What I aimed at chiefly therein was the service of my Nation & I do assure yor Lordships (notwithstandg I may have been otherwise represented) is very dear to me. And what in the first place I aimed at by my proposals was, to have diverted the Americans from goeing on with their linen and Woollen Manufactorys & to have turn'd their thoughts on such things as might be usefull & beneficiall to Great Britain. They are already so far advanced in their Manufactoryes that 3|4 of ye linen and Woollen they use, is made amongst 'em ; especially the Courser sort, & if some speedy and effectual ways are not found to put a stop to it, they will carry it on a great deal further, & perhaps in time very much to the prejudice of our manufactorys at home. I have been discoursed with by some to assist them in setting up a manufactory of fine stuffs, but I have for the present putt it by, & will for my own part never be concerned in yt nor any thing of yt nature, but use all the little interest & skill I have to prevent it.[1]

GOV. HUNTER TO THE BOARD OF TRADE. 12 NOVR 1715

[Lond. Doc. XX.]

The Trade of this Province has consisted chiefly of provisions, We may reckon it considerably [decreased] since the late Peace, by reason that the Spaniards do not permit our Vessels to come on their coasts, as they did formerly, having lately, as I am well informed sent several ships, some of which are French with Spanish Commissns to Guard their Coasts from that Traffick, which formerly we had by private communications with them ; and these Provinces raising much more than serves for their own consumption and that of the West Indies, I can think of no solid way of preventg the total decay of Trade, and consequently the ruin of the Provinces but by setting on foot and carrying vigorously the production of Naval Stores, and if hemp were not so bulky a commodity, we know experimentally that our swamps and low land will produce as good of that kind as any in the world.

The People of this Town (N. York) and Albany, which make a great part of the Province wear no clothing of their own manufacture, but if the letters mentioned in your Lordships mean the Planters and poorer sort of Country people, the computatn is rather less than more, but the several sorts are coarser than what come from England ; I know no way to prevent it, than by encouraging them to go on some manufactures that may be useful to England & beneficial to themselves, for few that are able to go to the expense of English manufacture do wear home spun, and a law to oblige such as are not able to go to that expense to do it, under penalties, would be equivalent to a law to compel them to go naked, for your Lordships well know that Goods at 100 per cent advance are reckoned cheap here, nor does it consist with my knowledge that ever any home spun was sold in the shops.

1 Col. Heathcote the writer of the above, was Member of the Council, and an applicant for a contract to supply the Crown with Naval Stores & some small sloops of War for coasting purposes.

CADWALLADER COLDEN ON THE TRADE OF NEW YORK; 1723.

[Lond. Doc. XXII.]

The Trade of New York is chiefly to Britain & the British Plantations in the West Indies; besides which we have our wines from Madeira & a considerable Trade with Curacoa; some with Surinam & some little private Trade with the French Islands—The Trade to the West Indies is wholly to the advantage of this Province the balance being every where in our favor so that we have money remitted from every place we trade with, but chiefly from Curacoa and Jamaica, these places taking off great quantitys of Flower for the Spanish trade. The Trade to Barbadoes is more considerable than to any one of the rest Provisions being carried thither not only for the supply of that Island but likewise for Transportation to the Spanish coast while the Assiento Factors were settled there, & to the French Islands, so that tho' we consume more of the produce of that Island in Rum Sugar & Molasses than of all the others put together we have money frequently remitted from thence on Bills of Exchange for England. The Trade to Madeira is to our Loss this Province consuming more wine from thence, than can be purchased with our commodities which obliges the Merchant either to send money or to pay the Ballance of Bills of Exchange for London. But whatever advantages we have by the West India Trade we are so hard put to it to make even with England, that the money imported for the West Indies seldom continues six months in the Province, before it is remitted for England. The Current Cash being wholly in the Paper Bills of this Province and a few Lyon Dollars

In the time of the last war when the great scarcity of provisions happened in France, we had a very profitable Trade with Lisbon for wheat, by which several have made estates but that Trade was of no long duration, for the Distance made the carriage so chargeable being the Ships were obliged to return empty, that the Trade could not be carried on any Longer without Loss, after wheat fell to its usual price, tho the Wheat of America, be of greater value there than the European, & we cannot hope for a return of this Trade unless such a general scarcity of Provisions happens over Europe as did then

The Staple Commodity of the Province is Flower & Bread which is sent to all parts of the West Indies we are allowed to trade with, Besides Wheat, Pipe staves and a little Bees Wax to Madeira, We send likewise a considerable quantity of Pork, Bacon, Hogshead Staves, some Beef Butter & a few Candles to the West Indies. The great Bulk of our commoditys in proportion to their value, is the reason we cannot trade directly to the Spanish Coast as they do from the West Indies it being necessary to employ armed vessels to prevent Injuries from the Spaniards and Pirates, but we sometimes send vessels into the Bays of Campeachie & Honduras, to purchase Logwood & we have it imported from thence frequently by Strangers. This commodity is entirely exported again for England.

From Barbadoes we import Rum, Molasses & Sugar which are all consumed in the Province, from Antigua & the adjacent Islands, Molasses & some Rum for the country consumption, & sometimes sugar & Cotton for exportation to England, From Jamaica some Rum, Molasses & the best Muscovada Sugar for the consumption of the Country & sometimes Logwood, but the principal returns from thence are in Spanish money, From Curacoa the returns are in Spanish money & Cocoa which is exported again for England Surinam returns nothing besides Molasses and a little Rum which are consumed in the Province, in the time of War when the English could not trade with the French there was some considerable Trade to the Island of St. Thomas The Danes from thence supplying the French with our Provisions. We have Cotton from thence & now from the French Islands we sometimes have Cocoa Sugar & Indigo, the far greatest part of which are exported again from England.

Several of our Neighbours upon the Continent cannot well subsist without our assistance as to Provisions for we yearly send Wheat and Flower to Boston and Road Island as well as to South Carolina tho not in any great quantity Pennsylvania only rivals us in our Trade to the West Indies, but they have not that Credit in their Manufactures that this Province has

Besides our Trade by Sea this Province has a very considerable inland Trade with the Indians for Beaver other Furs & Peltry & with the French of Canada for Beaver, all which are purchased with English Commodity except a small quantity of Rum. As this trade is very profitable to England, so this province has a more considerable share in it than any other in His Matys Dominions & is the only Province that can Rival & I beleive out do the French, being the most advantageously situated for this Trade of any part of America

This Government (since the arrival of the present Governor) considering that the French of Canada buy yearly of the people of this Province great quantitys of English Goods in English Cloaths fit for the Indians use, & being convinced that the French cannot without great difficulty and expence import these goods directly from Europe & that without them they cannot carry out their trade with the Indians exclusive of the English: did by a severe Law prohibit the selling of any Indian Goods to the French. At the same time considerable encouragement was given to a number of young men to go into the Indian Country as far as the Pass between the great Lakes at the Falls of Iagara, to learn the language of these Indians, and to renew the Trade with the far Indians which our Traders have disused ever since the beginning of the Wars with France. This they could not be persuaded to undertake of themselves having of late fallen into the more safe and less toilsome Trade with the French tho less profitable

The Government has pursued this with a good deal of diligence notwithstanding many difficultys put in the way by the merchants who trade with the French & these measures are likely to have a very happy effect, to strengthen the British Interest on this continent. For if the Indians shall be once convinced that the French cannot supply them with the Goods they want or that they are furnished much cheaper by the English it will take off the dependance of the remote Indians on the French, which has been increasing of late to the Great Danger of this province, in case of a War, as well as to the loss of its trade in time of Peace, What is already done has had so good effect that but a few days ago 80 Indian Men, besides Women & Children arrived at Albany from the furthest nation who live about the place called by the French Missilimakenak 1200 miles distant from Albany, they could not be stopped in their design by all the art of the French who in several places endeavored to divert them. When they came to Albany they entered into a League of Friendship with this Government & desired to be added to the Six Nations under this Government, and that they may be esteemed the seventh Nation under the English Protection—The Language of these Indians is not understood by any Christian among us, & is the first time we have had any League with them—It is the opinion of many here that by the arts of Peace, with the assistance of a less sum than a tenth of what the expedition to Canada cost the Nation the settlement of Canada would be rendered useless to the French, and that they would be obliged to abandon it

It is evident that the whole Industry, Frugality & Trade of this Province is employed to ballance the Trade with England & to pay for the goods they yearly import from thence, & therefore it is undoubtedly y[e] Interest of Britain to encourage the trade of this Province as much as possible: For if the people here could remit by any method more money or Goods to England they would proportionably consume more of the English Manufactures. We have no reason to doubt that it is truly the desire of our mother country to make her colonys flourish—The only thing in question, is by what methods the produce and Trade of the Plantations can be best encouraged with the greatest advantage to England. It may be that many in England are not so well informed what their colonys are able to produce & by what means the people in the colonys will most effectually be put upon such Manufacture or Trade as shall be most beneficial to the Kingdom for the Colonys differ very much in the soil & inclination & humour of the Inhabitants.

It seems to be the desire of the Government of Great Britain that ye Kingdom be supplied with naval Stores from their Plantations, that they may not rely so much on the Pleasure of foreign Princes for what is so necessary to ye Strength & Wealth of ye Kingdom. Towards this end none of His Matys Provinces can be more useful than this & perhaps no country in the World is naturally better fitted for such produce or manufactures. There is not any where a richer Soil for producing Hemp than in many places in this Province—Such Land as has every year borne grain for above 50 years together without dunging in which I believe this excells all the other Provinces in North America. Our barren Sandy Lands bear great quantitys of Pitch pine for Tar, The Northern parts of the Province large white Pines* for Masts: & for iron we have great plenty of that Oar in many places close by the Bank of the River, where Ships of 3 or 400 Tuns may lay their sides the ground every where covered with wood for the Furnace and no want of Water Streams any where for the Forge

The reasons which have hindered the Inhabitants from going upon any of these manufactures are the difficulty with which people can be persuaded to leave the common means by which they have supported their familys to adventure upon any new methods which are always expensive in the beginning & uncertain in the profits they yield This reasoning has the more force because few of the Planters have any stock of money by them but depend yearly on the Produce of their Farms for the support of their Families. North America containing a vast Tract of Land every one is able to procure a piece of land at an inconsiderable rate and therefore is fond to set up for himself rather than work for hire. This makes labor continue very dear a common laborer usually earning 3 shillings by the day & consequently any undertaking which requires many hands must be undertaken at a far greater expense than in Europe & too often this charge only overballances all the advantages which the country naturally affords & is the hardest to overcome to make any commodity or Manufacture profitable which can be raised in Europe

The Merchant will not readily adventure his Stock in raising Hemp or making Tar being unacquainted with husbandry and will more difficulty be induced, because he knows the Farmer does not gain yearly half the common Interest of the value of his land & stock after he has deducted the charge of labor.

One of the methods already thought of for making this Province more useful as to Naval Stores, is a severe prohibition of cutting any white Pines fit for Masts, No doubt the destroying of so necessary a commodity ought to be prevented & it would be difficult to frame a Law for that end with many exceptions or Limitations which could be of much use on the other hand when the literal Breach of the Law becomes generally unavoidable it must loose its force, The Lands of this Province are granted upon condition that the Grantee within three years after the Grant effectually cultivate three acres for every fifty granted & it will not be supposed that it is the intent of the Law to put a stop to cultivating the Land which however cannot be done without destroying the Timber that grows upon it. One at first is ready to fear that the poor Planter is under a sad Dilemma. If he does not cultivate he cannot maintain his family & he must loose his Land; if he doos cultivate, he cuts down Trees, for which he is in danger of being undone by prosecution & fines—The Inhabitants cannot build Houses without pine for boards & covering, nor send Vessels to sea with-

* Neither the Pitch Pine nor White Pine are properly Pines according to the Botanists but are put by them under the class of ye Larix the White Pine being called by Tournefourt—*Larix orientalis fructu rotundiori obtuso* & by J Bonhim, Cedrus *magna, Sive Libani, Conifera.* I have not seen the true Pine to the Northward of Maryland.

out masts. It cannot surely be the intent of the Legislature to put the inhabitants under such extreem hardships by denying us necessary timber while we live in the midst of such Forests as cannot in many ages be destroyed—And the more that the King for whose use these Trees are reserved, does not or has not made use of one Tree for many years in this Province.

Nor need we mind the apprehensions of some who tell us of what ill consequences it may be if the People of the Plantations should apprehend that the people of England design to cut them off from the common body of English subjects by denying them the fundamental English Privilege of being tryed by their country. Our mother country the nursery of Liberty will never give up her children to the ravenous appetites of any one man nor will they loose the surest tye she has upon the affections of the people in the plantations especially in a Frontier Province in the neighbourhood of so potent & cunning a nation as the French are where the native English are less in number than Foreigners French & Dutch who at present think themselves happy under the English liberty, for the maxim that free subjects are more useful to their Prince than Slaves will be found as true in America as in Europe.

But suppose the People could be restrained from cutting any White Pines it will not answer the end for which it was designed, For if the King were to send People to cut down Masts in the place where they grow and to transport them to such places where they can be carried by water the charge will amount to treble the sum they might be bought for at New York, if the carrying of them were left to the Inhabitants themselves The King in this case must have a great many hands & overseers in constant pay He must buy horses, Oxen & Carriages & maintain them or hire them after the most chargeable manner—whereas the country people carry these Trees in the Winter upon the Snow & Ice when they cannot labor in the ground & are glad to make a little profit at any rate.

To balance any hard ship which the Colonys may apprehend themselves to be under The British Parliament has given such rewards & encouragements to their Plantations as no other nation has done the like for the manufacture of Hemp & Tar. The benefit of this however does not so immediately reach the Planters as the before mentioned penalties affect him, There is a considerable difference between encourageing the exportation & sale of a commodity which is already the manufacture of the country & engageing people to go upon a new commodity or manufacture in the first it is sufficient to give the merchant encouragement to buy & export in the other the encouragement would be more effectual if it were immediately applied to the persons who were to begin the Manufacture & run the whole risque of its turning to advantage or not.

Now I shall mention the means which I think most probable to make this Province useful in producing Naval Stores & which may with the least difficulty be put in practice—In the first place, to prevent the decay of Timber, fit for masts every one that improves Lands on which white Pines grow ought to be obliged to plant white Pines at proper distances all round his fields & enclosures when any of these shall dye or be cut down to put another in its place and some officer be obliged to see this punctually observed and for the encouragement of such as shall raise Hemp that the Receiver General be directed to receive Hemp when offered in lieu of money for the Kings Quit Rents at an encouraging price which Price the Receiver General ought to publish, pursuant to the directions he shall receive from England—The Commissioners of the Navy to appoint a Factor at New York whose credit must be punctually kept up to purchase Masts & Tar, made according to the direction of the Act of Parliament, who shall yearly publish the prices he will give for any of these commoditys & the Government to save themselves the Benefit of the Bounty. For some years the price to be allowed be above the intrinsic value of the commoditys, the loss of which to be defrayed by some publick fund, which I believe without great difficulty may be found & if these proposals be thought practicable & useful shall be the subject of another paper.

The Parliament appears desirous to encourage the importation of materials for dyeing which hitherto have been only brought from Foreign Parts I have seen fine Reds and Yellows & good black (the Country people say they have seen all colors) died by the Indians with some roots & weeds, which grow plentifully in the country. As the Indians know very little of the art of dying from what I have seen of their Reds I am apt to believe the root they dye that color with, may be very valuable & we may find some commoditys which at present are not in the Least thought of— When I go next to the Indians country I intend to procure some quantity of them sufficient to make a few experiments.

GOV[R] COSBY TO THE BOARD OF TRADE.

[Lond. Doc. XXIV.]

New York 18th Decr 1732.

My Lords—I acknowledge the receipt of your Lordpps to me of the 16th of June last, and in pursuance of His Matys directions to your Lordpps Board have made the strictest inquiry in respect to manufactures sett up, & Trade carryed on in this Province of New York & can discover none that may in any way affect or prejudice the Trade, Navigation & Manufactures of the Kingdom of Great Britain. As to the laws made here, I beg leave to refer your Lordpps to the acts which I shall transmit to your Lordpps so soon as they are engrossed which I fear I cannot have time to have done to send by this opportunity. The inhabitants here are more lazy & inactive than the world generally supposes, & their manufacture extends no farther than what is consumed in their own famillys, a few coarse Lindsey Woolseys for clothing, and linen for their own wear: the hatt makeing trade here seemed to promise to make the greatest advances to the prejudice of Great Britain, but that the Parliament having already taken into their consideration, needs no more mention, whatever new springs up that may in the least affect or prejudice the Trade or Navigation of Great Brittain, shall be narrowly inspected & annual returns of your Lordpps querries constantly sent In the meantime I have the honor to be with the greatest respect imaginable

My Lords
Your Lordpps most obedient
& most humble servant
(signed) W. Cosby.

SAME TO THE SAME 6 DEC. 1734.

[Lond. Doc XXV.]

Wheat is the staple of this Province, and tho' that comôdity seems literally to interfere with the product of Great Britain, it do's not so in fact, for it's generally manufactur'd into flower and bread, and sent to supply the sugar Collonys, and whenever a market in Spain Portugal or other parts of Europe has encouraged the sending it thither in Grain, the adventurers have often suffered by the undertaking, for at this remote distance, the intelligence of a demand reaches us so late, that the marketts are supplyed before our vessells come there, and even if it were otherwise our merchants lye under vast and certain disadvantages besides for freight of wheat from hence in time of warr was at least two shillings and six pence, and in time of peace is eighteen pence sterling per bushell, and by the length of the passage it often grows musty, at least cannot come so fresh to markett as from Great Britain; whence freights (as it's said) are not above one quarter part of what they are here.

The main bent of our farmers is to raise wheat, and they are like to remain in that way until the price of it becomes so low, that necessity puts upon some other way of Cultivation; which in process of time is like to happen, because the Sugar Islands cannot increase in the proportion which the Northern Collonys do, and whether some other encouragement may bring them over sooner I cannot affirm.

In this Collony are a great many lands extream fit for hemp, and there is not one farm in it but has land proper to raise flax; but little more of either is raised than w at is for private use, the former they apprehend to require more hands than they have to spare, and labour is still so dear that they cannot afford to hire people for that purpose. Nor do they (as I believe) well understand how to rost [rot?] and dress it.

Tarr Pitch and Turpentine may be got here, but more plentifully in some of the other Northern Collonys, in greater quantitys than can be made use of by the Navy or Nation of Great Britain, if the price at home will encourage it, which I am informed it has not done for several years past, notwithstanding the bounty allowed on the importation.

I am told your Lordships formerly sent hither the method used in Russia for making of Tar and that upon tryal thereof it was found not to answer here, which is attributed more to the difference of the nature of their pitch pine and that of this Country, than to the unskillfulness of our people.

In the Jerseys is an extraordinary rich mine and some others are discovered there which afford a good prospect but in this Province none have as yet been discovered, tho' a good deal of money has been expended in search of them.

Some lead mines have been found in several parts of this Collony but they hitherto not by farr quitted the cost expended on them, and if they happen to prove good, I believe the proprietor will rather send it home in Oar than be at the charge to erect smelt houses here

We have a great many Iron mines both of the bogg, and of the Mountain Oar but as yet no Iron Work is set up in this province if any encouragement was given upon the importing of it in Piggs and Bars, at least that it might be free of dutys, It is very probable that in a few years the Nation might be amply supplyed from her own Plantations and it is evident that the whole amount thereof wo'd be paid in the manufactures of Great Britain, who now pays ready money (as I am informed) for greatest part of the Iron It has from Sweden.

I am informed that when the Dutch were in possession of this Collony they sett up a Pottash work at vast expence but found it wo'd not answer, about twenty five years agoe it was attempted here again at the expense of a Gentleman in London but dropt for the same reason, and a like essay is lately set on foot in Jersey; which it is feared will be attended with the same fate.

ANSWER OF THE COLLECTOR OF NEW YORK TO QUERIES OF THE BOARD OF TRADE.—1747.

[Lond. Doc. XXVIII.]

The referred queries from the Lords of Trade and Plantations and the required Answer from the Collector of the Customs here as by direction of his Excellency the Governour of His Maj^tys Province, vizt

THE QUERIES.	THE ANSWER THEREUPON AS,					
	TRADING IN GENERAL.		Present No. of Vessels.	Their ton'ge pr Register.	and Number of Sea-men.	PRODUCTION & MANUFACTURE.
	INWARDS.	OUTWARDS.				
What is the trade of this Province, the number of Shipping, their tonnage and the Number of sea faring men with the respective increase or diminution within 10 years past ? What quantity and sorts of British Manufactures do the Inhabitants annually take from hence ? What trade has the Province under your Govermt with any Foreign Plantations or any part of Europe besides Great Britain ? how is that trade carried on ? what commodities do the people under your Govermt send or receive from Foreign Planta-t'ns ? What is the natural produce of the Country, staple commodities and Manufactures ? and what value thereof in sterling money may you annually export.	First: From Great Britain: European goods and those India with silk manufactures chiefly From Ireland: linnen and canvass as duly certifyed. From British Colonies: ennumerated commodities, Rum, Limejuice, snuff, piemento, sulphur, straw-plat, deer-skins, conch-shells, mahogany, ebony and Negroes. From Europe and both English and Foreign settlements in America together in Africa: Salt. From Africa, within the proper limits directed, Negroes now less than formerly bro't hither. From Madeira: Wines the growth thereof. From Northern &' Southern parts of this Continent: Cyder, Oil, Blubber, Whalefins, Flax-seed, hops, Flax, Bricks, Seal-skins & certain Wrought Iron, Brasury & Tin. Lastly from Plantations not under His Majties Dominions: small quantities of Molasses, Sugar & Rum, since the Act imposing new duties thereon, Snuff, Lign'-vitæ, Indico, Logwood & other dying woods, cotton wool, cocoa nuts, ettc.	First: To London & outports thereof, the latter seldom, the enumerated goods and other Merchandize legally imported. To Ireland: Flax-seed, Rum, Sugar, being prize effects & staves. To other parts of Europe: grain, hides, Elk-skins, Deer-skins, Ox-horns, logwood, Indico, cocoa-nutts, ettc., of foreign produce, lumber also, Sugar, Coffe, wines and other goods as prize effects be brought & in the Vice Admiralty Court adjudicated upon proper certifying. To Madeira & Azores: Grain and other provisions, Beewax and staves. To English districts North & South of this Continent & West Indies: provisions, chocolate, lumber, European & India goods with those species enumerated & such others as brought here for export regularly. Lastly: to the neutral Ports as St. Thomas, Curacoa & Surrenhaim: provisions, Lumber & Horses with provender.	99	4513	755	First: The Country people here have for many years, & yet their home spun (so termed) of wool & flax to supply themselves somewhat with the necessaries of clothing ettc. From the year 1715 or thereabouts, have been raised Linseed & milled into oil: hats made of Beaver-fur, the exporting whereof prevented by the Act, from Michelmas 1732, also Lamp-Black work'd up. From the year 1730 Sugar baking & its refining have been for home consumption, & transportation hence to other districts on the Continent & to the West Indies by regular certificates, & latterly the distilling of Rum & other Spirits, for there are three houses erected. In this Province are mines of Iron & Lead ores, the manufacturing of which have been of late proposed & the raising of Hemp likewise. Lastly: of these several besides, of grain of all sorts & other provisions, with Tobacco a diminutive quantity naturally produced out of this soil, yet being with such like brought hither from the Eastern & Western parts of this continent are saleable & indeed abroad cannot be distinguished as to ascertain the annual exporting of their value: neither practicable could it be from the imports thereof separated; because their prices according to the Markets currently vary in the respective species.
	There on each column are particularized as to the quantities as qualities in the quarterly lists of Trading Vessels: the transmitting whereof to their Lordshipps, is from the Naval Officer here, constituted by the Governour & also such Lists duly to their Honours the Commissioners of the Customs from their Officers, hence, thereby, may appear, that within the queries mentioned, time, how the increase or diminution differenceth respectively.					
What methods are there used to prevent illegal Trade, and are the same effectual ?	Such as are prescribed in the principal Laws of trade & aptly used hereat, whereby to effect the intended preventing any what contrary to those Laws; and that upon any breach thereof carefully inquired after by the deputed officers, process is issued against the same in the Vice Admiralty: or it happening sometimes in the Courts of records of this Province, for the Recovery of the subjected penalty on the fraud or abuse committed.					

Examined and compared at the Custom House of New York with the Books of Reports and entries therein by

ARCH'D KENNEDY Colletr.

5 January 1746-7.

NEW YORK IN AMERICA.

THE REFERRED QUERIES FROM THE LORDS OF TRADE AND PLANTATIONS; AND THE REQUIRED ANSWER FROM THE BOOKS OF REPORTS AND ENTRIES IN THE CUSTOM HOUSE AT ITS PORT BY DIRECTION OF THE GOV[r] OF THIS HIS MAJESTY'S PROVINCE. 1749.

[Lond. Doc. XXIX.]

Qre. What is the Trade of the Province, the Number of Shipping, their Tonage and the number of Seafaring Men with the respective Increase or Diminution within the years past? What Quantity and Sorts of British Manufactures do the Inhabitants Annually take from hence? What trade has the Province with any Foreign Plantations or any part of Europe besides Great Britain? How is that Trade caryed on? What Commodities do the People send to and receive from Foreign Plantations? What methods are there used to prevent Illegal Trade and are the same effectual?

Ansr. The Inward Trading in General is from Great Britain, European Goods, & those India with Silk Manufactures chiefly. From Ireland Linnen and Canvas Manufacturies certified duly. From British Colonies, enumerated Commodities, Piemento, sulphur, Strawplating, Lime juice, Coffee growth thereof, Hides, Deer Skins, Conch Shells, Mahogonie, Plank, Ebonie, & Negros. From Europe and Africa, besides from English Foreign Settlements in America, Salt. From the African Coast within the proper limits Directed, Negrôs: now less than formerly. From the Northern & Southern parts of this Continent; Fish, Oil, Bluber, Whale fins, Turpentine oil, Seal Skins, Hops, Cyder, Flax, Bricks, Cole, Lamp Black, certain wrought Iron, Tin & Braziery, Joinery, various Carriages and Chairs. From Plantations not under his May[s] Dominions, Molasses, Sugar, & Rum in no great Quantitys, since the Act imposing the new Dutys thereon, Lign. Vitæ, Drugs, Logwood and other Dying Wood, Indico, Cocoa Nutts, Cotton Wool, Snuff &c[a]. And the Outward is to London and its Outports, the latter more seldom, Naval Stores, Copper Ore, Furs and other the enumerated species, with the legal Import of divers Mercantile Wares, Plantation Iron, Oil, Spermaceti, Whale Fins, Lime Juice, Shruff, [snuff?] Myrtle Candles, Mahogany & Walnut planks, Reeds and Drugs. To Ireland Flax Seed, Rum, Sugar, being Prise effects, and Staves. To sev[l] Parts in Europe, Grain, Hides, Deer & Elk Skins, Ox Horns, Sarsaperila, Indico, Logwood, Cocoa Nutts &ca. And Foreign produce & Lumber, Moreover Argent Vivum, Coffee, Anatts, Elephant's Teeth, Beewax, Leather, Sarsafrax, Casiafistula, Wines & other goods as Prise effects hitherto brought and in the Vice admiralty Courts here and els where adjudicated upon proper certifying. To Madeira & the Azorts, Grain and other Provisions, BeeWax & Staves. To English Districts North & South of this Continent & West Indies, Provisions, Chocolate, Lumber European & India Goods with those enumerated in the Plantation Trade Acts, and such other Imported here for Conveyance home regularly. To neutral Ports as Curacoa, Suranhaim, and Saint Thomas; Provisions, Lumber, Horses, Sheep, and other live Stock with their Provender. All which are particularized as to the Quantitys and Qualitys in the Quarterly Lists of Vessells: the due transmitting whereof to their honours the Commissioners of the Customs from the offices hereat; thereby may appear within the Queries signifyed time what the Increase or Diminution respectively differenceth; Therefore upon comparing which it 'l be thus considerate, that the first is somewhat more than the other. As to the Shipping which at present belong here, the Number whereof is 157, the tons for registry 6406 & Navigated with 1228 men of Sea Employ, and for the preventive method of which happening illicite here, such prescribed in the principal Laws and aptly made use of, whereby to effect the same as contrary thereto; so that upon any Breach carefully inquired after by the Deputed Officers, process is issued against the like in the Vice Admiralty, or sometimes in the Courts of Record holden hereat, for recovery of the subjected Penalty on the Committed fraud & abuse.

Qre. What is the natural produce of the Country, Staple Commodities and Manufacture, and what Value thereof in Sterling Money may you actually export?

Ansr. The production and Manufacture is that the people in the Country here for many years & yet have their home spun, so termed, of Flax and Wool to supply themselves somewhat with necessaries of Clothing &c. That for thirty four years or thereabouts, have been raised Linseed & mil'd into Oil, Hats, made of beaver Furs, their Exportation prohibited by the act from Michaelmas 1730, also the working of Lampblack. That for nineteen years, Sugar baking and its refining in order to consumption here and transportation for other Districts on the Continent & the West Indies upon regular certificate; And Erecting Six houses latterly that rum and other Spirits may therein Distillable. That in the said Province are Mines of Lead & Iron ores; the Manufacturing of which hath been of late proposed; likewise Hemp raised; And that besides there are Grain of all kinds & other Provisions with Tobacco, a small quantity out of soil naturally productive: Yet such with the like hither brought from the Western & Eastern parts of this Continent being Vendible abroad cannot be distinguished as to ascertain the Prices of Annual Exports, neither could be practicable if from the seperated Exportness, because their current value according to the Markets in their respective Species vary.

G. Clinton.

New York 23[d] May, 1749.

GOVERNOR CLINTON'S CERTIFICATE ABOUT IRON ROLLING MILLS, &c., 1750.

[Lond. Doc. XXIX.]

By His Excellency Honble George Clinton Captain General, and Governor and Chief of the Province of New York and territories thereon depending in America, Vice Admiral of the same and Admiral of the White Squadron of His Majesty's Fleet.

In Obedience to an Act of Parliament, Entitled, "An Act to Encourage the Importation of Pig and Bar Iron from His Colonies in America; and to prevent the Erection of any Mill or other Engine for Slitting or Rolling of Iron; or any plating Forge to work with a Felt Hammer, or any Furnace for making Steel in any of the said Colonies" passed in the twenty third year of His Majesty's Reign His said Excellency doth hereby certify, that there is erected within the said Province, in the County of Orange, at a place called Wawaganda, about twenty six miles from Hudsons River, one plateing Forge to work with a Tilt Hammer, which belongs to Lawrance Scrauley of the said County a Blacksmith; has been built about four or five years, and is not at present made use. And further that there are not erected in his said Excellency's Government, any other or more plateing Forges, to work with a Tilt Hammer or any Mill or Mills, or other Engine for Slitting or Rolling of Iron, or any Furnace or Furnaces for making Steel. In Testimony, whereof his said Excellency hath subscribed these Presents, and caused the Great Seal of the Province of New York to be hereunto affixed. At Fort George in the city of New York the fourteenth day of December in the year of Our Lord one thousand seven Hundred and Fifty, and in the seventy fourth year of His Majestys Reign.

G. Clinton.

AN ACCOUNT OF IRON MADE AT ANCRAM,

IN THE MANOUR OF LIVINGSTON, BY ROB[t] LIVINGSTON JUN[r] ESQ[r].

[Lond. Doc. XXXIV.]

					MADE INTO BARS.					
Year.	T	C	qrs.	lbs.	T	C	Castings.			
1750	43	3	3	13	195	15	5	2	3	7
1751	606	6	3	17	164	12	6	1	2	..
1752	354	7	3	0	183	14	3	2	1	14
1753	22	9	2	0	215	6	2	3	0	21
1754	....	....	....	....	211	5	4	2	2	..
1755	722	2	3	0	149	16	36	2	3	7
1756	267	14	0	14	182	0	10	0	0	0
	2016	4	3	16	1302	8	66	15	0	21
	1302	8	0	0						
Total	3318	12	3	16						

Pr. DIRCK JANSEN,
Store keeper.

JAMES DE LANCEY TO BOARD OF TRADE.

New York 1st December 1757.

My Lords—I had the honour of your Lordships letter of the 9th of June directing me forthwith upon the receipt thereof to take the most effectual method for obtaining an account of the quantity of Iron made in this Province from the year 1749 to the 5th of January 1756. I accordingly wrote to Mr. Robert Livingstone who has the only Iron work in this Province which is carried on & I send your Lordships enclosed the account received from him as soon as it came to my hands. This Country abounds in Iron ore especially in the Highlands & several works have been begun but were dropt though the mismanagement or inability of the undertakers; of these there were two Furnaces in the Mannor of Cortland & several Bloomeries; but they have not been worked for several years past; it is probable after the war upon the Encouragement the Parliament of Great Britain are giving the Colonies in this Article these and several others will be carried on in this Province.

I have the honor to be Your Lordship's
most obed[t] & must humble servt
JAMES DE LANCY.

Right Honorable Lords Commissioners of Trade.

[Council Min. XXIII.]

At a Council held at Fort George in the city of New York,
Wednesday, 27th May 1761.

The Petition of William Hawkshurst praying a Grant for the sole making of Anchors and Anvills within this Province for the Term of Thirty years, or such other Term, and under such Regulations as shall be thought meet, was presented to the Board, and being read was rejected.

CIRCULAR.

THE BOARD OF TRADE TO ALL THE GOVERNORS ON THE CONTINENT OF AMERICA.

[Lond. Doc. XXXIX.]

WHITEHALL, August 1. 1766.

In pursuance of an Address of the House of Commons to His Majesty on the 27th March last, and of his Majesty's Commands thereupon, signified to us by his Grace the Duke of Richmond, in a letter to us dated the 11th ultimo, you are forthwith to prepare, and as soon as possible transmit to us, in order to be laid before the House of Commons in the next Session, a particular and exact Account of the several manufactures which have been set up and carried on within the Colony under your Government since the year 1734 and of the Public Encouragement which have been given thereto.

You are also from time to time Annually to transmit the like Account of any Manufactures which shall be hereafter set up, and of the Public Encouragement which have been given thereto.

We are &c.

DARTMOUTH.
ED. ELLIOT.
JOHN ROBERTS.
WM. FITZHERBERT.
PALMERSTON.

[Council Min. XXVI.]

At a Council held at Fort George in the City of New York on Friday the 7th day Novr 1766.

Present—His Excellency Sir Henry Moore Baronet, Capt. Genl &c

Mr Horsmanden | Mr Reed | Mr Apthorpe
Mr Smith | Mr Morris

His Excellency communicated to the Council a Letter to him of the 1st of August from the Right Honble the Lords Commissioners for Trade & Plantations requiring his Excellency, in pursuance of the Address of the House of Commons to his Majesty on the 27 March last, and of his Majesty's Commands thereupon, forthwith to prepare and transmit to their Lordships, in order to be laid before the House of Commons, at their next Sessions, a particular and exact Account of the Several Manufactures &c. [*As in the preceding Letter.*]

The Council declared, that no manufactures had been set up within this Colony since that Period, or received any public encouragement; nor did they know of any Manufacture of Wool or Woolen Cloth, but what was principally confined to private Families, for their own particular Consumption.

GOV. MOORE TO THE LORDS OF TRADE.

[Lond. Doc. XL.]

Fort George, New York, 12 Jany 1767.

My Lords—Having recd your Lordships' commands in a letter dated the first of August last, in which I was directed to prepare and transmit as soon as possible an account of the Several Manufactures set up and carried on within this Colony since the year 1734, I took the liberty of giving Mr Peter Hasenclaver a Letter of Introduction to your Lordships as he was then ready to sail for England, imagining that from his Character and Knowledge of the Country a more perfect Account might be obtained from him of what was required in the beforementioned Letter, than I could possibly give by that opportunity. I have since made all the Inquiries I could, and the whole of the Information given to me may be reduced to the following Heads.

There is a Small Manufactory of Linen in this City under the Conduct of one Wells, and supported chiefly by the Subscriptions of a set of men who call themselves the Society of Arts and Agriculture. No more than fourteen Looms are employed in it, and it was established in order to give Bread to several poor families which were a considerable charge to the city and are now comfortably supported by their own daily Labour in Spinning of Flax. It does not appear that there is any established Fabric of Broad Cloth here; and some poor Weavers from Yorkshire, who came over lately in expectation of being engaged to make Broad Cloths could find no Employment. But there is a general Manufactory of Woolen carried on here and consists of two sorts, the first a coarse cloth entirely woolen $\frac{3}{4}$ of a yard wide; and another a stuff which they call Linsey Woolsey. The Warp of this is Linen, and the Woof Woollen, and a very small quantity of it is ever sent to market. Last year when the Riots and Disorders here were at their height on the occasion of the Stamp Act, these manufactures were greatly boasted of, and the quantity then made greatly magnified by those who were desirous of distinguishing themselves as American Patriots, and would wear nothing else; They were sometimes sold for three times their value; but the manufacturers themselves shewed that they had more good sense than the persons who employed them; for they never cloathed themselves with the work of their own hands, but readily brought it to market, and selling it at an extravagant price there, bought English Cloths for themselves and their families. The Custom of making these Coarse Cloths in private families prevails throughout the whole province, and almost in every House a sufficient quantity is manufactured for the use of the Family, without the least design of sending any of it to market. This I had an opportunity of seeing in the late Tour I made, and had the same Accounts given me by all those persons of whom I made any inquiry, for every house swarms with children, who are set to work as soon as they are able to Spin and Card, and as every family is furnished with a Loom, the Itinerant Weavers who travel about the Country, put the finishing hand to the Work.

There is a Manufactory of Hats in this City, which is very considerable; for the Hats are not so good as those made in England, and are infinitely dearer. Under such disadvantages as these it is easy to imagine with what difficulty it is supported, & how short the duration of it is like to be; the Price of Labour is so great in this part of the World, that it will always prove the greatest obstacle to any Manufactures attempted to be set up here, and the genius of the People in a Country where every one can have land to work upon leads them so naturally into Agriculture that it prevails over every other occupation. There can be no stronger Instances of this, than in the Servants imported from Europe of different Trades; as soon as the time stipulated in their Indentures is expired they immediately quit their masters, and get a small tract of land, in settling which for the first three or four years they lead miserable lives, and in the most abject Poverty; but all this is patiently borne and submitted to with the greatest cheerfulness, the satisfaction of being Landholders smooths every difficulty, & makes them prefer this manner of living to that comfortable subsistence which they could procure for themselves and their familys by working at the Trades in which they were brought up.

The Master of a Glass-house; which was set up here a few years ago now a Bankrupt, assured me that his ruin was owing to no other cause than being deserted in this manner by the Servants, which he had Imported at a great expence; and that many others had suffered and been reduced as he was, by the same kind of misfortune.

The little Foundry lately set up near this Town for making Small Iron Potts is under the direction of a few private persons, and as yet very inconsiderable.

As to the Foundaries which Mr Hasenclaver has set up in the different parts of this Country, I do not mention them, as he will be able to give your Lordships a full account of them and of the progress he has already made; I can only say that I think this Province is under very great obligations to him for the large sums of money he has laid out here in promoting the Cultivation of Hemp, and introducing the valuable Manufacture of Iron and Pot Ash.

I have the honor to be &c.

H. Moore.

GOV. MOORE TO LORD HILLSBOROUGH.

[Lond. Doc. XLI.]

Fort George, New York, 7 May. 1768.

My Lord—I have the honor to transmit to your Lordship the copy of a letter I wrote in the beginning of the last year to the Lords Commissioners for Trade and Plantations, in answer to a letter I received from their Lordships in consequence of the Address of the House of Commons to His Majesty concerning the Manufactures of this Country, dated March 27th 1766. Another copy of this Address has been inclosed to me in your Lordships Letter marked No 3, to which I must make the same answer, as the Progress of Manufactures in this part of the world by no means corresponds with the pompous accounts given of them in the public papers. . . . . .

No mention is made in the former Letter of the great quantities of Leather being tanned in this Country, as this branch of business has been carried on for many years; the leather is greatly inferior in quality to that made in Europe; and they are not yet arrived to the perfection of making Soleleather. Your Lordship may be assured that I shall, from time to time, give every due information required in this address, and be particularly attentive to any new Establishment of which we have no instances since my last letter, except in the paper Mill begun to be erected within these few days, at a small distance from the Town.

I am &c. H. Moore.

XXVI.

REPORT

OF

GOVERNOR WILLIAM TRYON,

ON THE STATE OF THE

Province of New-York.

1774.

REPORT OF HIS EXCELLENCY WILLIAM TRYON, ESQUIRE,

CAPTAIN GENERAL AND GOVERNOR IN CHIEF IN AND OVER THE PROVINCE OF NEW YORK AND THE TERRITORIES DEPENDING THEREON IN AMERICA, CHANCELLOR AND VICE ADMIRAL OF THE SAME—ON CERTAIN HEADS OF ENQUIRY RELATIVE TO THE PRESENT STATE & CONDITION OF HIS MAJESTY'S SAID PROVINCE.

[Lond. Doc. XLIV.]

Question No. 1.

What is the situation of the Province under your Government, the nature of the Country soil and Climate: the Latitudes and Longitudes of the most considerable places in it: have those Latitudes and Longitudes been settled by good Observations, or only by common Computations, and from whence are the Longitudes computed?

Answer.

Situation of the province.

The Province of New York is situated on the Atlantic Ocean which washes its Southern shores: The Colonies of Connecticut, Massachusetts Bay and New Hampshire, lying to the East, Quebec to the North, and New Jersey, Pensylvania and the Indian Country to the West.

Nature of the Country and its soil.

The Face of the Country is everywhere uneven, with all the variety of Soil to be found any where. In the Northern Parts are lowlands enriched by the overflowing of Rivers, but little of this sort lies within seventy miles of the City of New York the Metropolis—the soil in general is much thinner and lighter in the Southern than in the Northern Parts and having been longer under Culture and subject to bad Husbandry, is much more exhausted.

Climate.

The Province extending nearly Four Degrees and a half of Latitude the difference of Climate between the Southern and Northern Parts is remarkable. In Summer the Heat is sometimes excessive, and in general much greater than in England—Melons and many other things are raised here by the natural warmth of the Climate which in England will require the aid of Hot Beds and Glasses—The Winter in all parts of the Province is more severe than in England, tho' the Latitude of London is about ten Degrees more North than the City of New York—Even in the Southern Part the Mercury in Farrenhight's Thermometer sinks some Degrees below 0 and rises to 90° but these extremes are always of short duration.—At Albany and to the Northward of that City the Harvest is about a Month later than at New York, and the Winter is much earlier. Hudson's River is generally frozen over many miles below Albany before the middle of December but no Quantity of Ice is found in the River within thirty miles of the City of New York, earlier than the Month of January—In March the Navigation is again open up to Albany; and it is observed the Seasons both as to heat and Cold grow more temperate.

Latitudes.

The Latitudes of the following places have been determined by good observations.

The Lignt house at Sandy Hook, - - - - - - - -	40°27' 40"
Fort George City of New York - - - - - - - -	40 41 50
Mouth of Mackhacamac Branch of Delaware, where the Line settled between New York & New Jersey terminates - - - - - - - -	41 21 37
City of Albany - - - - - - - - -	42 36 00
The South End of Lake George - - - - - - -	43 16 12
Crown Point - - - - - - - - -	43 50 07
Windmill Point - - - - - - - - -	44 57 18
Port au Pine - - - - - - - - -	44 58 48
Moores Point - - - - - - - - -	45 00 00

The Longitude of the City of New York has been found by good Observation of the Satellites of Jupiter to be 74° 38 West from London.

Longitude.

Question No. 2.

What are the reputed Boundaries, and are any parts disputed and by whom

Answer.

Boundaries of the Province.

The Boundaries of the Province of New York are derived from Two Sources.—First, the Grants from King Charles the Second to his Brother James Duke of York dated the 12th March 1663|4 and the 29 June 1674, which were intended to convey to the Duke all the Lands claimed by the Dutch, the first occupants of this Colony.—Secondly, from the Submission and Subjection of the Five Nations of Indians to the Crown of England.

As grounded on the Grants from Charles the 2d to James Duke of York.

The Descriptive part of both the Duke's Grants is in the same Words and exclusive of the Territory Eastward of Connecticut River, since granted to the Massachusetts Bay by their Charter of 1691, comprehends "All that Island or Islands commonly called Mattawacks or Long Island, together with Hudson's River, and all the land from the West side of Connecticut River to the East side of Delaware Bay." Connecticut River extends beyond, and Hudson's River takes its rise a little to the Southward of the Forty fifth Degree of Northern Latitude; And as a Line from the Head of the River Connecticut to Delaware Bay, would exclude the greatest part of Hudson's River, which is expressly granted to the Duke of York, the Boundary most consistent with the Grants to the Duke, and the claim of New York founded thereon, is a Line from the Head of the Connecticut River to the Source of Hudson's River, thence to the Head of the Mohawk Branch of the Hudsons River and thence to the East side of the Delaware Bay.

That this has been the reputed Boundary under the Duke's Title has been confirmed by the Grants of this Government extending Westward nearly to the Head of the Mohawk Branch of the Hudson's River, and Southward of that Branch to within a few miles of the North Boundary of Pensylvania.

No other Construction will justify the Terms of the Grants to the Duke, nor any Lines less comprehensive include the Lands patented by this Province or ceded to the Crown by the Indians, at the Treaty of Fort Stanwix in 1768.

And as grounded on the claim of the Five Nations of Indians.

The Second source of the Title of this Government is grounded on the Claim of the Five Nations who are in the Treaty of Utrecht acknowledged by France to be subject to Great Britain.

Soon after the English conquered this Country from the Dutch, pursuing their System of Policy, they entered into a strict Alliance with the Natives who by Treaties with this Colony, subjected themselves to the Crown of England, and their Lands to its protection, and from this Period were always treated as Subjects, and their Country considered by this Government as part of the Province of

New York, which probably gave rise to the extended Jurisdiction of the Colony beyond the Duke's Grants, signified by the Words "The Territories depending thereon" which are found in all the Commissions of the Crown to its Governors. Nor has the Crown except by the confirmation of the Agreement fixing the Boundary of Connecticut at about Twenty miles East of Hudson's River at any Time contracted the jurisdiction of the Colony Westward of Connecticut River & Southward of the Latitude 45 the Proclamation of His present Majesty of the 7th of October 1763, leaving the jurisdiction Southward of that Latitude as it stood before, tho' it prohibits for the present the further Extention of the Grants and Settlements into the Country thereby reserved to the Indians, to avoid giving Umbrage to that People who complained they were too much straitned in their hunting grounds. It is uncertain to this Day to what Extent the Five Nations carried their claim to the Westward & Northward but there is no doubt it went to the North beyond the 45 Degree of Latitude and Westward to Lake Huron, their Beaver Hunting Country being bounded to the West by that Lake, which Country the Five Nations by Treaty with the Governor of this Province at Albany in 1701, surrendered to the Crown to be protected and defended for them—Mitchell in his Map extends their claim much further Westwards and he is supported in this opinion by Maps and other anthorities very Ancient and Respectable.

The above Treaty of 1701 is to be found among the Records of Indian Transactions but it is recited and the Surrender made thereby confirmed in a Deed dated the 14th September 1726 by which the Seneca, Cayouga and Onondaga Nations also surrender'd their Habitations to King George the first, a Copy whereof is inserted in the article of the Appendix, Number 1.

Oswego on the South side of Lake Ontario was first established by this Colony about 1721, a Garrison of the King's Troops supported there at the Expense of this Government, and the Jurisdiction of New York actually exercised Westward to Oswego and its Vicinity until the Commencement of Hostilities in the late war.

His Majesty's Order of the 20 July 1764, confirming the Ancient Limits as granted the Duke declares "The Western Banks of the River Connecticut from where it enters the Province of the "Massachusetts Bay as far North as the Forty fifth Degree of Northern Latitude," to be the Boundary Line between the two Provinces of New Hampshire and New York: And if the Agreement lately concluded at Hartford should finally be ratified by the Crown, the Eastern Limits of this Colony where it borders on the Massachusetts Province, will extend about twenty miles only East from Hudson's River.

Description of Boundary supposing the Colony to include the Beaver hunting Country surrendered to the Crown by Treaty with this Province in 1701.

Without any view to the more Westerly claim of the Five Nations, supposing the Colony to comprize within its Limits or Jurisdiction the Country those Nations Surrendered to the Crown by the Description of the Beaver Hunting Country as before mentioned—The Boundaries of the Province of New York are as follows.

On the South.

The Atlantic Ocean, including Long Island, Staten Island and others of less note.

On the West.

The Banks of Hudson's River from Sandy Hook, on the Ocean, to the 41 Degree of Latitude, thence the Line established between New York and New Jersey to Delaware River—Thence the River Delaware to the North East Corner of Pensylvania or the Beginning of the Latitude 43, which in Mitchel's Map is by mistake carried thro' the whole of that degree—Thence the North Boundary Line of Pensylvania to the Northwest Corner of that Province, and continuing the same Line to a point in Lake Erie which bears due South from the East Bank of the Streights of D'Etroit and of Lake Huron to the Forty Fifth Degree of Northern Latitude.

On the North.

A Line from a point on the East Bank of Lake Huron in the Latitude of Forty Five East to the River St Lawrence, or the South Boundary Line of Quebec; Thence along the South Boundary Line of that Province across the River St Lawrence to the Monument on the East Bank of Lake Champlain fixed there in the 45 Degree of Northern Latitude; Thence East along the Line already run and marked to the Monument or Station fixed on the West Bank of the River Connecticut in the same Latitude.

On the East.

The Western Banks of the River Connecticut from the last mentioned Station to the South-west corner of the Province of New Hampshire, in the North boundary Line of the Massachusetts bay; and from thence along that Line, (if continued) and the Western limits of the Province of Massachusetts Bay, and the Colony of Connecticut.

In the Appendix N° 4, is a Map of the Province of New-York according to the preceding Description of its Boundaries.

Disputes that may still arise with Massachusetts Bay, in respect to the Limits of this province.

The Boundary of the Province of New York (in respect to the other Governments) being established in every part except where it borders to the East on the Massachusetts Bay, it was conceived the late agreement with that Province when ratified by the Crown, would extinguish every Controversy respecting the Limits of New York, the North Boundary Line of the Massachusetts having in the year 1740 been ascertained by a Royal Decree of the King in Privy Council in the Contest between that Province & New Hampshire. But the Massachusetts Commissaries at the late Meeting at Hartford in 1773 declared that they had no authority to settle their North Boundary which they considered as undetermined with respect to New York, and one of those Gentlemen intimated that they still left open their Western Claim to the South Sea.

Hence two very important Disputes may still arise of great Consequence to the Interests of the Crown, as well as the property of His Majesty's subjects of this Colony.

Observations on the Massachusetts Northern Claim.

The Massachusetts Northern Claim beyond the Line settled between that Province and New Hampshire, extends north from that Line about Fifty miles, and from thence Westward to within Twenty Miles East of Hudson's River, and after passing this Province, is commensurate with their Western Claim to the South Sea—The immediate object of their Northern Claim is a Country between Connecticut & Hudson's Rivers about Fifty Miles in length and about Forty in breadth and includes not only the greater part of the County of Cumberland, but a large District of the Counties of Albany and Charlotte.—The Lands there in question are wholly appropriated under Grants of this Province [and ?] of New Hampshire, and the Families settled thereon are not less than Two Thousand, tho' they probably exceed that number.

The Massachusetts Bay long acquiesced in the Royal Decree of 1740, the Line established by that Decision hath actually been run and marked from the south West Corner of New Hampshire Westward, to within about Twenty miles East of Hudson's River, and the Inhabitants of New York and the Massachusetts Bay have deemed that Line to be the utmost Extent of the Massachusetts North Boundary, whatever might have been determined as to their Western Limits And that this was the sense of the General Court of that Province soon after the Treaty of 1767, for settling the Boundary of the Two Provinces, appears clearly by their Resolution of the 23[d] January 1768 in these Words "Resolved that this Court will concede to and confirm the last proposal made by their Commissioners on the part of New York at their late Conference in the Words of the Report of the Lords of Trade and Plantations in May 1757, That a Streight Line be drawn Northerly from a point on the Southern Line of the Massachusetts Bay Twenty Miles due East from Hudson's River, to another point Twenty Miles due East from the said River, *on the Line which divides the Province of the Massachusetts Bay from New Hampshire*, be the Eastern Boundary of New York."

Nor can any Line more favorable to the Massachusetts Colony be hereafter established, without subverting the Principles, and calling in question the Justice of the Royal Decree pronounced in 1740 after full hearing of the merits of the Massachusetts claim on the appeal of both parties to the King in Privy Council; and which could it now be effected, must not only prove highly injurious to the Crown in respect to the right of Soil, its Quit Rents & Escheats, but be productive of the greatest disorder & confusion in that Country.

Remarks on the claim of Massachusetts Bay Westward to the South Sea, Showing a Defect in their Title as a Corporation and the propriety of raising this as an objection, should they prosecute their claim to a North Boundary beyond the present Line Established between that Province and New Hampshire, or their Western claim to the South Sea.

The Province of Massachusetts Bay ground their claim Westward to the South Sea on the Deed dated 19th March 1627|8 from the Council of Plimouth to Sir Henry Roswell &c. and their associates.—As also on the Charter or Letters Patent of Charles the First dated the 4 March 1628|9—The lands granted are the same in both, being in breadth about Sixty Miles, and extending as described in these Instruments "From the Atlantic and Western Sea and Ocean on the East part to the South Sea on the West part."

But the Crown being divested of these Lands by the Grant to the Council of Plimouth in 1620, could not pass them by its Charter of 1628|9, which had no other operation than to form the Massachusetts Bay into a Province, and to invest the same with Powers as a Body Corporate.

It became necessary therefore for the Massachusetts Bay after they were incorporated to obtain a Conveyance to the Corporation of the Lands granted to Roswell &c. and Associates —That they obtained such Conveyance has not been pretended —If they had, the Crown either became reseized of the Lands of the Corporation by the Judgment in 1681 which Vacated the Letters Patent of 1628|9 or the property reverted to the Grantees of the Council of Plymouth.

Had the Crown been reseized it might have passed the same Lands to the Massachusetts Province by the present Charter of 1691. But instead of so extensive and unreasonable a Grant of Three Thousand Miles in Length they obtained, it is true, by that Charter a great addition of Territory Eastward, but were confined in their Western limits which extend "towards the South Sea as far as the Colonies of Rhode Island, Connecticut and the Narragansett Country." This Description in strict Construction of Law will carry the Massachusetts Bay West no further than the Eastern Bounds of Connecticut, and by the most liberal interpretation do not extend their Boundary beyond the West Line of Connecticut, then and for some years before determined by Agreement between that Colony and New York to be upwards of Twenty Miles East of Hudson's River.

On the other hand admitting the Massachusetts Bay after their charter of 1628|9, and before it was vacated in 1684, did not obtain a Conveyance of the Lands granted to Roswell &c. and Associates, the Judgment which vacated that charter did not affect the Lands but left the Title in Roswell &c. and Associates, and the Crown could not by the Charter of 1691, grant them to the Massachusetts Colony; So that the Title, *if any exists,* must at this day be vested in the heirs or assigns of Roswell &c and Associates in their private right, and not in the Government of the Massachusetts Bay, unless transferred to or vested in the latter by some act of their Provincial Legislature, if such an Act could possibly have any Efficacy.

It is however presumed no Law of that Tendency has been passed, and if any should hereafter be presented for His Majesty's approbation, that it will be objected to (so far as it may countenance the extension of their Northern or Western claims beyond the Limits of their present Charter) as a measure calculated to divest the Crown of the right of Soil in that very large and extensive Territory, which lies Westward of the Colony of New York *to the South Sea.*

This claim had it been considered as well grounded wo ld long since have been prosecuted and brought to a decision.—The Massachusetts General Court or Assembly assert it in a Resolve they passed on the 23d of January 1768, but whether with an intention to maintain it, Time must discover.—A claim so long dormant, can hardly be expected under any circumstances to be now revived with a prospect of success, & whatever Judgment the Assembly of the Massachusetts Bay may have formed certainly their present Governor had no opinion of its solidity, when at a late Meeting of the Commissaries of both Provinces at Hartford in 1773 he declared "That it was a mere Ideal, Visionary project, in which he believed Nobody to be sincere," and discovered an anxiety least it should interrupt the progress of the Treaty.

Question No. 3.

What is the size and extent of the Province, the number of Acres supposed to be contained therein; What part thereof is cultivated and improved; and under what Title do the inhabitants hold their possessions?

Answer.

Size and extent of the Province.

The Extent of the Province from North to South is about 300 Statute miles. Nassau Island (commonly called Long Island) is situated to the South, its length from East to West, is about 150 miles, and its breadth on a medium fifteen miles; The breadth of the Province Northward of this Island is various. From the City of New York North about 20 miles up the Country, the breadth does not exceed 14 miles, and lies wholly on the East side of Hudson's River, New Jersey being bounded by the opposite shore—From the 41st Degree of Latitude the Province extends on both sides of that River; soon widens to about 60 miles; and increases in breadth up to the 42d Degree, where it is about 80 miles wide; supposing the Western Boundary to extend to the line mentioned in the Answer to the preceding Question No. 2, the extent from the 42d Degree to the North Line of Massachusetts Bay (a distance of 49 miles) is about 456 miles, and from thence to the 45th Degree, it extends East & West on a Medium about 500 miles, and on the like supposition the number of square miles contained within this Province exclusive of the Lakes is 82,112 or 52,551,680 acres, which is one fourth less than the number contained in the Province of Quebec.

Parts cultivated.

Nassau or Long Island which contains Kings, Queens and Suffolk Counties.—Staten Island which forms Richmond County and the Counties of New York, Westchester, Dutchess, Orange and Ulster, are all well inhabited, and not many large Tracts of improveable land are left uncultivated.—The County of Albany tho' the Inhabitants are numerous, and the Lands in general under Cultivation in the South, contains extensive and valuable Tracts unimproved in the North Part.[1] Tryon County tho' thinly settled, as its extent is great, has many Inhabitants.[2] The cultivated parts of Charlotte County are inconsiderable, compared with what remains to be settled and the same may be remarked with respect to the Counties of Cumberland and Gloucester.[3] In the Appendix is a list of the Inhabitants White and Black in the respective Counties, according to the returns of their numbers in 1771, since which they are greatly augmented, but it is to be observed that the new counties of Charlotte and Tryon were then part of Albany.[4]

1 Albany County at this date included the present Counties of Greene, Columbia, Albany, Rensselaer, Schenectady and Saratoga.

2 This County was taken from Albany County in 1772, and named in honour of Wm. Tryon then the Governor of the Province. In 1784 it was changed to that of Montgomery. When formed it embraced all that part of the State lying West of a line running North & South nearly through the centre of the present County of Schoharie.—*Campbell's Annals of Tryon County, New-York* 1831, *p.* 27.

3 Charlotte County embraced what now are Franklin, Clinton, Essex, Warren & Washington Countie in this State, and the West half of the State of Vermont; Cumberland & Gloucester lay on the West bank of the Connecticut river and extended from Canada to the Massachusetts boundary; the South line of the towns of Tunbridge, Strafford and Thetford being the division between the two. Westward they ran to the East bounds of Charlotte. Cumberland was erected in 1766; Gloucester in 1770, and Charlotte was taken from Albany in 1772, at the same time as Tryon.

4 For the Census table see ante p. 474.

The proportion of the cultivated to the uncultivated parts of the Province (the Limits as stated in No. 2) is as one to four; or one fifth only improved.

With respect to the Titles under which the Inhabitants hold their possessions; Before the Province was granted on 12 March 1663|4 by King Charles the Second to his brother James Duke of York, the Dutch West India Company had seized it, made setttlements and Issued many Grants of Land. In August 1664 the Country was surrendered by the Dutch to the English, and by the 3d article of the Terms of Capitulation it was stipulated "That all People shall continue free Denizens and shall enjoy their Lands, Houses, and goods, wheresoever they are within this Country and dispose of them as they please." Some lands of the Province are held under the old Dutch Grants without any confirmation of their Titles under the crown of England, but the ancient Records are replete with confirmatory Grants, which the Dutch Inhabitants were probably the more solicitous to obtain from an Apprehension that the Dutch conquest of the Province in 1673, might render their Titles under the former articles of Capitulation precarious; tho' the Country was finally restored to the English by the Treaty signed at Westminster the 9th Feby 1674.

Titles under which lands are held.

From that period it has remained in the possession of the English, and the Duke of York on the 29th of June 1674, obtained a new Grant from the King, of all the Territories included within the former Letters Patent in 1663|4.

During the life of King Charles the Second, the Duke of York as proprietor of the Soil, passed many Grants (by his Governor) in Fee, and since his accession to the Throne, Grants have continued to issue under the Great Seal of the Province, in consequence of the Powers given the several Governors by their Commissions and Instructions from the Crown—Two instances only occur of Grants or Letters Patent for Lands under the Great Seal of Great Britain.—One to Sir Joseph Eyles and others on the 15th May in the 4th year of His late Majesty King George the Second for a Tract of 62,000 acres, called the Equivalent Land from its having been ceded to New York by the Colony of Connecticut (on the settlement of the boundary between the two Provinces) in lieu of a like quantity yielded up to Connecticut by the Province of New York—The other lately, to Sir William Johnson Baronet—The Lands granted to Sir Joseph Eyles and his associates are not possessed by them or their assigns, Letters Patent under the Great Seal of the Province of New York having passed to others for the same Lands, before it was known here that the Royal Grant was obtained; and the Lands are now in possession of the New York Patentees or their assigns.[1]

These are all the different modes by which the Inhabitants have derived any legal Titles to their Lands within the Limits of this Province, whence it appears that all their lawful titles to Lands in Fee, except in cases of old Dutch Grants unconfirmed, originated from the Crown either *mediately* thro' the Duke of York before his Accession to the Throne, or *immediately* by Grants under the Great Seal of Great Britain or of this Province.

Purchases from the Indian Natives, as of their aboriginal right have never been held to be a legal Title in this Province, the Maxim obtaining here; as in England that the King is the Fountain of all real property, and that from this source all real Titles are to be derived.

Question No. 4

What Rivers are there and of what Extent & Convenience in point of Commerce?

1 This tract, otherwise called "The Oblong," lies along the eastern line of Putnam and Dutchess counties, extending from the north line of Cortland Manor to about the south bounds of Livingston Manor in Columbia co., as laid down in Le Rouge's Map of the Prov. of N. Y.; also in Sauthier's Map of New York, 1776, 1779. Further particulars regarding the controversy may be learned by reference to Book of Patents xi., 1.; Deed Books xiv. 133; xvii., 457, 471. (in Sec.'s Office.) Also Smith's History, ed. 1829-30, 1., 285-288; ii., 13, 29.

Answer.

Hudsons River is the only Navigable River in the Province, and affords a safe and easy Passage for Vessels of Eighty Tons Burthen to the city of Albany, which is about 180 miles from the sea—It has already been mentioned that it extends nearly to the Latitude of 45—but the Navigation, except for small Vessels terminates at or near that City.—To the Northward of Albany about Ten miles this River divides The Western Branch which (above the Great Cahoo Falls) is called the Mohawk River, or the Mohawk Branch of Hudson's River leads to Fort Stanwix, and a short cut across the carrying Place there might be made into Wood Creek which runs into the Oneida Lake, and thence thro' the Onondaga River into Lake Ontario

Rivers.

The other Branch being the continuation of the main River tends to Fort Edward, to the North of which it seems practicable to open a passage by Locks &c. to the Waters of Lake Champlain which communicate with the River St. Lawrence, passing over the Falls at St. Johns.

Both Branches are interrupted by Falls and Rifts, to surmount these obstructions an Expense would be required too heavy for the Province at present to support, but when effected would open a most effective inland navigation, equal perhaps to any as yet known.

Between Nassau or Long Island and the Continent the greatest Distance scarcely exceeds Twenty Miles. Near the City of New York it is less than one Mile, and is there called the East River, and from thence bears the appellation of the Sound. The River and Sound afford Navigation for Vessels of any Burthen towards the Collonies of Connecticut, Rhode Island and the Massachusetts Bay, in some degree hazardous however at the noted place distinguished by the name of Hell Gate about six Miles East of the City of New York.

Connecticut River where it divides this Province from New Hampshire is included within the Limits of the latter.

Question No. 5.

What are the Principal Harbours, how situated and of what extent; and what is the Depth of Water & nature of Anchorage in each?

Answer.

There is but one principal Harbour which is the Port of New York being that part of the East River fronting the City and lying between that and Long Island.—The harbour is in length from the North East to the Southwest about two miles, and its Breadth across to Long Island about one mile. The Depth of water from Four to Eight Fathom, tho' at some places no more at low Water than Ten Feet. In Nip Tides the Water rises about Four Feet and an half, at the Full and Change of the Moon, Six, and if at those Seasons a strong Easterly Wind prevails the rise of the Tides increase to Eight Feet. The Anchorage is good in a bottom of mud; there is only one remarkable Reef of Rocks about mid-channel, half a mile within the Entrance; And the Harbour being shelter'd in front by Long Island; to the East by a sudden bend in the River; and to the West by Nutten Island; Vessels during the hardest Gales ride in great safety, and are only incommoded a few days in the Winter by the floating Ice.

Harbours.

The Map in the Appendix marked N° 3, presents a full view of the Harbour, the situation of Sandy Hook, and shows the Depth of Water from thence up to the Port.[1]

Question No. 6.

What is the Constitution of the Government?

1 None of these Maps are in the London Documents. A copy of Sauthier's large Map, reduced one-half, engraved especially for this Vol. will be found at the end of this Report.

Answer.

Constitution of the Government.

By the Grants of this Province and other Territories to the Duke of York in 1663/4 and 1674, the powers of Government were vested in him, and were accordingly exercised by his Governors until he ascended the throne when his Rights as Proprietor merged in his Crown, and the Province ceased to be a charter Governm[t]

From that time it has been a Royal Government, and in its Constitution nearly resembles that of Great Britain and the other Royal Governments in America. The Governor is appointed by the King during his Royal Will and pleasure by Letters Pattent under the Great Seal of Great Britain with very ample Powers. He has a Council in Imitation of His Majesty's Privy Council —This Board when full consists of Twelve Members who are also appointed by the Crown during Will & Pleasure; any three of whom make a Quorum.—The Province enjoys a Legislative Body, which consists of the Governor as the King's Representative; the Council in the place of the House of Lords, and the Representatives of the People, who are chosen as in England: Of these the City of New York sends four.—All the other Counties (except the New Counties of Charlotte & Gloucester as yet not represented) send Two.—The Borough of Westchester, the Township of Schenectady and the three Manors of Rensselaerwyck, Livingston and Cortlandt each send one; in the whole forming a Body of Thirty one Representatives.

The Governor by his Commission is authorized to convene them with the advice of the Council, and adjourn, prorogue or dissolve the General Assembly as he shall judge necessary.

This Body has not power to make any Laws repugnant to the Laws and Statutes of Great Britain. All Laws proposed to be made by this Provincial Legislature, pass thro' each of the Houses of Council and Assembly, as Bills do thro' the House of Commons and House of Lords in England, and the Governor has a Negative voice in the making and passing of all such Laws. Every Law so passed is to be transmitted to His Majesty under the Great Seal of the Province, within three months, or sooner after the making thereof and a Duplicate by the next conveyance, in order to be approved or disallowed by his Majesty; And if His Majesty shall disallow any such Law and the same is signified to the Governor under the Royal Sign Manual or by Order of his Majesty's Privy Council, from thenceforth such law becomes utterly void.—A law of the Province has limited the duration of the Assembly to seven years.

The Common Law of England is considered as the Fundamental law of the Province and it is the received Doctrine that all the Statutes (not Local in their nature, and which can be fitly applied to the circumstances of the Colony) enacted before the Province had a Legislature, are binding upon the Colony, but that Statutes passed since do not affect the Colony, unless by being specially named, such appears to be the Intentions of the British Legislature.

The Province has a Court of Chancery in which the Governor or Commander in chief sits as Chancellor and the Practice of the Court of Chancery in England is pursued as closely as possible. The officers of this Court consist of a Master of the Rolls newly created—Two Masters.—Two Clerks in Court.—A Register.—An Examiner, and a Serjeant at Arms.

Of the Courts of Common Law the Chief is called the Supreme Court.—The Judges of which have all the powers of the King's Bench, Common Pleas and Exchequer in England. This Court sits once every three months at the City of New York, and the practice therein is modelled upon that of the King's Bench at Westminister.—Tho' the judges have the powers of the Court of Exchequer they never proceed upon the Equity side. The Court has no Officers but one Clerk, and is not organized nor supplied with any officers in that Department of the Exchequer, which in England has the care of the revenue. The judges of the Supreme Court hold their offices during the King's Will and Pleasure and are Judges of Nisi prius of Course by act of Assembly, & Annually perform a Circuit through the Counties.—The Decisions of this Court in General are final unless where the Value exceeds £300, Sterling, in which case the subject may be relieved from its errors *only* by an application to the Governor and Council, and where the Value exceeds £500 sterling an appeal lies from the Judgment of the latter to His Majesty in Privy Council.

By an Act of the Legislature of the Province suits are prohibited to be brought in the Supreme Court where the Value demanded does not exceed £20. Currency.

The Clerk's Office of the Supreme Court has always been held as an Appendage to that of the Secretary of the Province.

There is also in each County an Inferior Court of Common Pleas, which has the Cognizance of all actions real, personal & mixed, where the matter in demand is above £5 in value.—The practice of these Courts is a mixture between the King's Bench and Common Pleas at Westminister.—Their Errors are corrected in the first Instance by Writ of Error brought into the Supreme Court; and the Judges hold their offices during pleasure.—The Clerks of these Courts also hold their offices during pleasure and are appointed by the Governor, except the Clerk of Albany who is appointed under the King's Mandate.

Besides these Courts the Justices of peace are by Act of Assembly empowered to try all causes to the amount of £5. Currency, (except where the Crown is concerned or where the Title of Lands shall come into Question;—and Actions of Slander) but the parties may either of them demand a jury of Six Men.—If wrong is done to either party, the person injured may have a Certiorari from the Supreme Court, tho' the remedy is very inadequate.

The Courts of Criminal Jurisdiction are Correspondent to those in England.—The Supreme Court exercises it in the City of New York, as the King's Bench does at Westminister.—The Judges when they go the Circuit have a Commission of Oyer and Terminer and General Goal Delivery; and there are Courts of Sessions held by the Justices of the peace; the powers of which and their proceedings correspond with the like Courts in England.—The Office of the Clerk of the Sessions, is invariably connected with that of the Clerk of the Inferior Court of Common Pleas in the respective Counties.

By acts of the Provincial Legislature the Justices of the Peace have an extraordinary Jurisdiction with respect to some offences by which any three Justices, (one being of the Quorum) where the offender does not find Bail in 48 Hours after being in the Custody of the Constable, may try the party without any[1] or a jury, for any offence under the Degree of Grand Larceny; and inflict any punishment for these small offences at their Discretion, so that it exceeds [qy? extends] not to Life or Limb.—And any three Justices of the Peace (one being of the Quorum) and Five Freeholders have power without a Grand or Petty Jury to proceed against and try in a Summary Way, Slaves offending in certain cases, and punish them even with death.

The Duty of His Majesty's Attorney General of the Province is similar to the Duty of that officer in England, and the Master of the Crown Office: He is appointed by the Crown during Pleasure, and His Majesty has no Solicitor General nor Council in the Province, to assist the Attorney General upon any occasion.

There are two other Courts in the Province. The Court of Admiralty which proceeds after the Course of the Civil Law in matters within its Jurisdiction, which has been so enlarged by divers Statutes as to include almost every breach of the Acts of Trade.—From this Court an appeal lies to a Superior Court of Admiralty, lately established in North America by Statute; before this Establishment an appeal only lay to the High Court of Admiralty of England.

The Prerogative Court concerns itself only in the Probate of wills and in matters relating to the Administration of the Estates of Intestates and in granting Licenses of Marriage. The Governor is properly the Judge of this Court but it has been usual for him to act in general by a Delegate.

1 Blank in the orig.

The Province is at present divided into fourteen Counties, viz[t]—The City and County of New York—The County of Albany—Richmond (which comprehends the whole of Staten Island) Kings, Queens & Suffolk (which include the whole of Nassau or Long Island) Westchester, Dutchess, Ulster, Orange, Cumberland, Gloucester, Charlotte and Tryon.—For each of these Counties a Sheriff and one or more Coroners are appointed by the Governor who hold their offices during pleasure.

As to the Military power of the Province, the Governor for the time being is the Captain General and Commander in Chief and appoints all the Provincial Military officers during pleasure.

Question No. 7.

What is the Trade of the Province, the Number of shipping belonging thereto, their Tonnage, and the number of seafaring Men with respect to the Increase and Diminution within ten years past?

Answer.

Trade of the Province.

The Province carries on a considerable Trade with the British Settlements on the Continent of North America, supplying some of them with the produce of the Colony, others with British Manufactures and West India goods. The Trade to the British West Indies is extensive they having a constant demand for provisions and Lumber of all kinds, which articles are the natural produce of this Province.

The returns from the American Ports and West India Islands, are made in such produce and manufactures of the Provinces and Islands, as best suit the Trade and consumption of this Colony—There are also fitted out from the Port of New York several Whaling and Fishing Vessels.

Number of Vessels & Quantity of Tonnage & Number of Seafaring Men.

The above together with the Trade of Great Britain, Ireland, Africa and the foreign ports in Europe and the West Indias as stated in the Answers to Questions No. 8, and No. 9, include the whole Trade of the Province which employed

In the year	Vessels	Tons Burthen	Men
1762 - - -	477	19,514	3,552
In 1772 - -	709	29,132	3,374
	232	9,618	178

So that the increase of shipping in that period of Ten years is 232 Vessels and of the Tonnage or Burthen 9,618 Tons—And the Decrease of men 178. A less number of Hands being employed on board of Vessels in peace, than they sail with in time of War.

Question No. 8.

What Quantity or sorts of British Manufactures do the Inhabitants annually take from hence, What goods and Commodities are exported from thence to Great Britain, and what is the annual Amount at an average?

Answer.

Imports from Great Britain.

More than Eleven Twelfths of the Inhabitants of this Province both in the necessary and ornamental parts of their Dress are cloathed in British Manufactures, except Linen from Ireland and Hats and Shoes manufactured here. The same proportion of Houses are in like manner furnished with British Manufactures, except Cabinet & Joiner's Work, which is Generally made here.

When the number of Inhabitants are considered a better idea may be formed of the Quantity and variety of sorts of British Manufactures used in this Province, than can be done by enumerating the names under which they are imported.

Besides the Articles necessary for Cloathing and Furniture, there are imported from Great Britain, large Quantities of all kinds of East India Goods.—Grocery of all sorts (except Sugars, Coffee, and

Ginger) Ironmongery, Arms, Gunpowder, Lead, Tin, Sheet Copper, Drugs, Brimstone, Grindstones, Coals, Chalk, Sail Cloth, Cordage, Paints, Malt Liquors & Cheese.—There are indeed few articles the British Market affords, but what are in some proportion imported here, except such as are among our Staple Commodities, particularly mentioned in the Answer to No. 11.

If the Brokers in Great Britain employed as shippers of goods were for one year obliged to give in the value of the Goods when they apply for Cockets, the exact amount of what the inhabitants of each Province in America take from thence would be easily ascertained. In this Country it is not possible to make such a calculation with any Degree of Precision, for as the amount of Goods never appears in the Cockets, no Judgment can be formed of their Value from the Quantity or Number of pieces.—Silks for Instance come out from 25s to 2 shillings per yard, and in general the other Articles differ in the same proportion from the first cost of the highest to that of the loewst in quality.

Value of articles imported from Great Britain. When no particular stop is put upon trade with Great Britain, it is generally estimated here that the Annual Imports from thence into this Colony, amount on an average to Five Hundred Thousand Pounds Sterling.

Exports to Great Britain. The Goods exported from hence to Great Britain that are the produce of this Colony, are chiefly pot and pearl ashes, Pig and Bar Iron, Peltries, Beeswax, Masts and Spars, with Timber and Lumber of all kinds:—And of the produce of the West Indies and Honduras Bay, Log Wood and other Dye woods and Stuffs, Sarsaparilla, Mahogany, Cotton, Ginger & Pimento with some Raw Hides—And Tar, Pitch and Turpentine, the produce of North Carolina.

Value thereof. The Annual Amount of Exports to Great Britain on an Average, is One Hundred & Thirty Thousand pounds Sterling exclusive of the Cost of Ships built here for the Merchants in England to the Amount of Thirty Thousand pounds Sterling annually.

Question No. 9.

What trade has the Province under your Government with any Foreign Plantations, or any part of Europe besides Great Britain; how is that Trade carried on, what Commodities do the People under your Government send to or receive from Foreign Plantations, and what is the annual Amount thereof at an Average?

Answer

Trade with Foreign Plantations &ca. A considerable Trade is carried on from this to the Foreign West India Islands, Surrinam and Honduras Bay. Provisions and Lumber are the principal Articles with which they are supplied from hence.—The returns are generally in Sugar, Molasses, Dye Woods, Mahogany, Hides, Silver, and Bills of Exchange.

With Africa. There are a few vessels employed annually in the African Trade, their Outward Cargoes are chiefly Rum and some British Manufactures.—The high price and ready sale they meet with for their Slaves in the West Indies induce them always to dispose of their cargoes among the Islands.

Madeira & Teneriffe. To Madeira & Teneriffe the Trade from hence is considerable. The outward Cargoes are composed of Wheat, Indian Corn, Flour, Provisions in General, Lumber and Beeswax.—The returns are made in Wines, the greatest part of which are carried directly from Madeira to the British and foreign West India Islands, there sold and West India Cargoe purchased with which the Vessel returns.

Spanish & other Foreign Ports in Europe, Southward of Cape Finnistre. When Grain is Scarce in Europe there is also a very considerable Trade from hence to the Spanish ports in the Bay of Biscay and to other Foreign ports in Europe lying to the Southward of Cape Finnistre.—To these places are exported, Wheat, Rye, Flour, Indian Corn & Beeswax; and the returns are in Specie, Bills of Exchange and large Cargoes of Salt. Sometimes the

Vessels employed in this Trade take in a Load of Wines and Fruit, and call at some of the Outports in England for Clearances agreeable to Law.—The Trade is Carried on in Ships belonging to British Subjects and navigated conformable to the Acts of Trade.

The Annual amount of the Commodities exported from hence to Foreign Countries is on an aver-

Value of Foreign Exports. One Hundred and Fifty Thousand Pounds Sterling; and the Foreign Imports on an Average One Hundred Thousand Pounds Sterling.

Besides the Trade to the Foreign Ports in Europe, there is every year a great Quantity of Flax seed

Exports to Ireland. and Lumber and some Iron sent to Ireland, in ships generally belonging to that Kingdom, which come out annually with passengers and Servants, as also Linen, Beef and Butter.

The Province hath likewise some Trade with Gibralter and Minorca, the Cargoes out generally

To Gibralter and Minorca. consist of Grain, Flour, Provisions of other Kinds, Lumber, Naval Stores, and Rice.—As they are British Ports, it has ever been the practice here to allow enumerated Goods to be shipped to them, the Master of the vessel giving the enumerated Bond at the Naval Office. The Returns are Specie, Bills of Exchange and Salt.

Question No. 10.

What Methods are there used to prevent illegal Trade, and are the same effectual?

Answer

At this Port there is generally one of His Majesty's Ships of War, stationed near its principal

Means to prevent illegal Trade. entrance, except during the Four Winter Months, when she is obliged on account of the severe Weather and the Ice to come to the Wharf. The Custom House Officers are Eight in Number; viz. The Collector, Comptroller, Surveyor, and Searcher, Land Waiter, Tide Surveyor and Three Tide Waiters; There is also a Naval Officer. The Tide Waiters are mostly employed on Board of Vessels that arrive with dutiable goods, so that there are but three other out door officers to look after the business of a very extensive Harbour, lying on two sides of the town, which is situated on a point between two large Rivers.

As all Articles of Commerce, Provisions and Fuel are conveyed to Town by Water in a number of Small Boats, from Landings that lay on each side of both entrances to the Port, the strictest attention of the officers of His Majesty's ship, or the Vigilance of the Collector & Comptroller, (who speak favourably of their present Outdoor officers) cannot altogether prevent the illegal Trade in a port situated as this is; there can be no doubt therefore but that Assistance different from what the officers have at present, would be very necessary, and tend much to the increase of His Majesty's Revenues in this Province.

Question No. 11.

What is the Natural produce of the Country, staple Commodities and Manufactures, and what Value thereof in Sterling Money may you annually Export?

Answer.

The Natural produce & Staple Commodities of this Province are Wheat, Indian Corn, Oats, Rye,

Produce Staple Commodities and Manufactures. Pease, Barley and Buck Wheat, Live Stock, Masts & Spars, Timber & Lumber of all sorts, Furrs, Skins, Beeswax, Iron Ore, Pork, Beef, Flour, Pot & Pearl Ashes.—And its Manufactures are, the making of Pig and Bar Iron, Distilling of Rum and Spirits, Refining of Sugar, and making Chocolate; from Molasses, brown Sugar and Cocoa imported.—The Making of Soap and Candles, Hats, Shoes, Cordage and Cabinet Ware, Tanning, Malting, Brewing & Ship Building.

Value of those Articles Exported. The Annual Amount of the above mentioned Articles Exported (Hats excepted)[1] is on an average Four Hundred Thous[d] Pounds Sterling.

Question No. 12.

What Mines are there?

Answer.

There are few Mines yet discovered in the Province.—One of Iron Ore in the Manor of Livingston in the County of Albany belonging to Robert Livingston Esquire,—Another of Iron also in Orange County, the property of Vincent Matthews Esquire and one in the Manor of Philipsburgh in the County of Westchester lately leased for 99 years (pursuant to the Royal Order) to Frederick Philipse Esquire.—It is called a Silver Mine, but from the small Quantity of Silver the Ore has hitherto yielded, may perhaps more properly be classed among the Richer sort of lead Mines. The Works belonging to the First are carried on to great advantage.

Mines.

Question No. 13.

What is the Number of Inhabitants, Whites & Blacks?

Answer.

Number of Inhabitants. By the last account taken in 1771, the number of Inhabitants stood thus,

Whites		148,124
Blacks		19,883
Total number of Inhabitants in 1771		168,007

Supposing the Increase 1771 to 1774 to have been no more than the average Proportion of the Increase between 1756 and 1771, there must be added to compleat the Number of Inhabitants to the present time

Whites	12,974	
Blacks	1,266	
		14,244[2]
Total Number of Inhabitants in 1774		182,251[3]

Question No. 14.

Are the Inhabitants increased or decreased within the last Ten years; how much and for what Reasons?

1 In Feb. 1731 the Master Wardens and Assistants of the Company of Feltmakers of London petitioned Parliament to pass a law to prevent the Inhabitants of the American Colonies exporting Hats of American Manufacture to any place whatsoever, as the foreign Markets were then almost altogether supplied from the Plantations as well, also, as Great Britain to the great prejudice of the Trade.

This petition was referred to a Special Committee who reported the Evidence in which the number of Beaver Hats then Manufactured in New York & New England was estimated at 10,000 yearly; In Boston there were 16 Hatters one of whom was stated to have commonly finished 40 hats a week. The Exports were to the Southern Plantations, the West Indies and Ireland.

A law was accordingly passed the same Session (5. Geo. II. c. xxii.,) "to prevent the Exportation of Hats out of any of His Majesty's Colonies or Plantations in America and to restrain the number of Apprentices taken by the Hatmakers in said Colonies" &c. All such exported hats were declared forfeit; the exporter subjected to a fine of £500 and every Master, Mariner, Porter, Carter, Waggoner, Boatman &c aiding and assisting him became liable to a fine of Forty pounds; any officer of Customs passing an Entry for such Export was to be fined also £500. No person was to make Hats in the Colonies unless he served seven years to the Trade & no master could take more than two apprentices. This law continued in force in this country as long as it belonged to Great Britain and is still applicable to the existing Colonies. This explains the exception above made in Gov. Tryon's Report.

2 Incorrect: ought to be 14,240.

3 Ought to be 182,247.

Answer.

Increase of inhabitants. The number of Inhabitants in 1771 as appears in No. 13 was - - . 168,007

By the returns in 1756 from which year to 1771 no Census was taken, the numbers appear to have been

1756	Whites	83,233	
	Blacks	13,542	
			96,775

Which shews the Increase from 1756 to 1771 to be - - - - - - - - - 71,232

Admitting the Increase for the succeeding three years to be no more than the average proportion of this number which is much less than the Proportion at which it ought to be rated, there must be added for the Increase from 1771 to 1774 - - - - - 14,244

Increase of Inhabitants from 1756 to 1774 a period of 18 years - - - - - - 85,476

Hence by taking the proportion of the last mentioned number it is found that the Inhabitants of this Colony are increased during the last Ten years according to the lowest Calculation 47,480.

Causes of the Increase of Inhabitants. The reasons commonly assigned for the rapid population of the Colonies, are doubtless the principal causes of the Great increase in this Province.

The high price of Labour, and the plenty and cheapness of new land fit for Cultivation, as they increase the means of subsistence are strong additional Incitements to Marriage, and the people entering into that state more generally and at an earlier period of life than in Europe, the Proportion of Marriages and Births so far exceeds that of populous Countries, that it has been computed the Colonies double their Inhabitants by natural Increase only in Twenty Years.

The increase in this Colony has been nearly in same proportion, but it cannot be denied that the accession to our own numbers by Emigrants from the neighbouring Colonies and from Europe, has been considerable, tho' comparatively small to the number thus acquired by some of the Southern Colonies.

Question No. 15.

What is the Number of Militia and under what Regulations is it constituted?

Answer.

Number of the Militia. The White Inhabitants amounting to 161,102, the Militia may be supposed to consist of about Thirty two Thousand.

A law is passed annually or every two years for regulating the Militia; The act now in force directs

Regulation under which it is constituted. That every Man from Sixteen to Fifty years of age (a few excepted) shall inlist himself with the Commanding Officer of the Troop of Horse, or Company of Foot in the place where he resides.—That the Militia armed and equipped (as the Law prescribes) shall appear and be exercised twice a year.—And imposes fines on both Officers and Soldiers for every neglect of Duty, with other less material provisions relative to the service. The Officers are all appointed by the Governor, and the whole Militia is under his Command and subject to his Orders, agreeable to the power vested in him as Captain General of the Province by the Royal Letters Patent or Commission.

As no Act relative to the Militia was passed during the last Session of the General Assembly, the above regulations will cease on the first day of May 1774, when the present Militia Law expires by its own Limitation.

Question No. 16.

What Forts and places of Strength are there within your Government, and in what Condition?

Answer.

Forts and places of strength.

The City of New York the Metropolis, is protected by a Fort and a Range of Batteries at the Entrance of the East River or Harbour, in good order and capable of mounting about One Hundred pieces of Ordnance.—Albany and Schenectady are defended by Forts, and both places incircled by large Pickets or Stockades, with Blockhouses at proper Distances from each other, but which since the peace have been suffered to go to Decay and are now totally out of Repair.

The Western Posts are Fort Stanwix, and the Forts at Oswego and Niagara; the two former are Dismantled; a few men only are kept at Oswego.—Niagara is occupied by a Garrison of the King's Troops.

The Northern Posts are, Fort Edward which is abandoned.—A few men only are kept at the Works at the South End of Lake George to facilitate the Transportation to the next Posts, which are Ticonderoga and Crown Point; these are both Garrisoned by His Majesty's Troops, but since the fire which happened at Crown Point, only a small guard is kept there, the principal part of the Garrison being withdrawn and posted at Ticonderoga.

Question No. 17.

What number of Indians have you and how are they inclined?

Answer.

Number of Indians & how are they inclined.

The Indians who formerly possessed Nassau & Long Island, and that part of this Province which lies below Albany, are now reduced to a small number, and are in general so scattered and dispersed, and so addicted to wandering that no certain account can be obtained of them. They are remnants of the Tribes—Montocks and others of Long Island—Wappingers of Dutchess County—Esopus, Papagonck &c in Ulster County—and a few Skachticokes.

These Tribes have generally been denominated River Indians and consist of about Three hundred Fighting Men—They speak a language radically the same, and are understood by the Delawares being originally of the same Race. Most of these People at present profess Christianity, and as far as in their power adopt our Customs—The greater part of them attended the Army during the late War but not with the same reputation as those who are still deemed Hunters.

The Mohawks the first in Rank of the Six Nation Confederacy tho' now much reduced in Number, originally occupied the Country Westward from Albany to the German Flatts, a space of about 90 miles, and had many Towns; but having at different times been prevailed on to dispose of their Lands they have little property left, except to the Northward, and are reduced to Two Villages on the Mohawk River and a few Families at Schoharie. The lower Mohawks are in Number about One Hundred and Eighty Five, and the Upper or those of Canajoharie Two Hundred and Twenty one making together Four Hundred and Six; this nation hath always been Warm in their attachment to the English, and on this account suffered great loss during the late War.

The Nation beyond and to the Westward of the Mohawks is the Oneidas; the Villages where they reside including Onoaughquaga are just beyond the Indian Line or Boundary established at Fort Stanwix in 1768,[1] and their property within that Line except to the Northward bas been sold—This Nation consists of at least Fifteen Hundred and are firmly attached to the English.

The other Nations of that Confederacy and who live further beyond the Indian Line are the Onondagaes, Cayouges, Senecas and Tuscaroras and are Well inclined to the British Interest— he whole Six Nations consist of about Two Thousand Fighting Men, and their number of Souls according to their latest Returns are at least Ten Thousand; the Seneca Nation amounting alone to one half that number.

1 See Ante p. 379 for this Paper & Map.

Question No. 18.

What is the Strength of the Neighboring Indians?

Answer.

The Indians North of this Province near Montreal, with those living on the River St. Lawrence near the 45th Degree of Northern Latitude form a Body of about Three Thousand five Hundred. They are in Alliance with and held in great Esteem by the rest, are good warriors, and have behaved well since they became allies to the English previous to the Reduction of Canada.

Strength of the Neighbouring Indians.

The Tribes of Indians within the Province of Massachusetts Bay and the Colonies of Connecticut & Rhode Island &c. are under similar circumstances with those denominated River Indians and the Stockbridge Indians living on the Eastern Borders of New York may be considered as within it, as they formerly claimed the Lands near Albany, and still hold up some claim in that Vicinity. They served as a Corps during the late War and are in number about three Hundred.

Of the Susquehana Tribes many are retired further Westward, among which are some not well affected to the British Government—They are all dependants and allies of the Six Nations.

Within the Department of Sir William Johnson His Majesty's Superintendant of Indian Affairs there are Twenty Five Thousand Four Hundred and Twenty Fighting Men, and may be about One Hundred and Thirty Thousand Indians in the Whole, extending Westward to the Missisippa.

Total number within the Northern Department.

Question No. 19.

What is the Revenue arising within your Government, and how is it appropriated and applied?

Answer.

The Revenue of the Province arises as follows—First from the Duties on articles imported viz. Slaves—Wines, Distill'd Liquors, Cocoa, and all European and East India Goods from the British Islands in the West Indies—Also a Duty of Two per cent. on certain species of Goods sold at Public Auction or Outcry, and from Lycences granted to Hawkers and Pedlars.

Revenue.

The annual amount of the several Duties on an average of the last Five Years is £5000 Currency. Secondly from the Interest of £120,000 in Bills of Credit emitted by a Law of the Colony passed the 16th of February 1771 and put out on Loan at 5 per cent, by which a clear Revenue until 1776 is to be paid into the Treasury of - - - 5602

From the year 1776 One Tenth Part of the Principal Sum is to be paid yearly into the Treasury until the whole sum of £120,000 is paid, So that this Branch of Revenue decreasing annually in that proportion, will totally cease in 1785.

The Revenue arising from the Articles under the first Head as it is grounded on Laws annually passed, (except the Duty on Goods sold at Auction granted for three years) is appropriated by annual Laws towards payment of the salaries of the Officers of Government and other necessary Expenses for the Public Service enumerated in such Laws.

Application of the Revenue.

And the Interest Money arising from the Loan above mentioned, which is the Second Branch of Revenue, is annually applied in furnishing necessaries for His Majesty's Troops quartered in this Colony, for which there is usually granted £2000 Currency, and the Residue is occasionally applied to the payment of Debts contracted by the Province, such as repairs to the Fort & Batteries, the Governor's House, the making of gun carriages &c.

A Third Branch of the Revenue is the Excise on Spirituous Liquors.

By a Law passed the 8th of March 1773 This Fund is appropriated for Twenty Years as follows—

Particular Appropriation of the Excise on Strong Liquors

The sum of £800 (part of £1000 to be raised by the Excise in the City and County of New York) is to be paid Annually for Twenty years to the Governors of the Hospital now erecting in the city of New York for the support of that Institution, and the remaining sum of £200 is for the first five years to be paid to the Corporation of the Chamber of Commerce, for encouraging a Fishery on the Sea Coast for the better supplying the Public Markets of the City, and during the remaining Fifteen Years this sum is appropriated for repairing the Public Roads.

By the same Law the sums which shall be raised by the Excise in the other Counties subject to this Duty, are directed to be appropriated for the same period of Twenty years towards repairing the Highways and defraying the necessary charges of the respective Counties.

The whole produce of the Excise Fund before the passing of this Law usually amounted to about £1450 per annum.

Question No. 20.

What are the ordinary and extraordinary Expences of Government?

Answer.

The ordinary Expences are the Sallaries allowed by the Province to the Officers of Government,

Ordinary expense of Government.

which exclusive of the Salary of the Governor now paid by the Crown, amounted in 1773 to the sum of - - - - - - - - - - - - - £3120. 2.—

and will continue nearly the same while the salaries remain on the present footing.

The Extraordinary Expenses of Government are the allowance for the necessaries

Extraordinary Expenses.

with which the Troops quartered in the Colony are furnished usually amounting to - - - - - - - - - - - - - 2000.—.—

And the Expences arising from the settlement of the Boundary Lines of the Colony, Repairs to the Fortifications & the Governor's House,—Carriages and Utensils for Guns, Barracks &c. which in the year 1773 amounted to - - - 1807.11.4¾

For payment of Expresses and other small contingent articles of Expense there is annually allowed - - - - - - - - - - - 100.—.—

Question No. 21.

What are the Establishments Civil and Military within your Government and by what Authority do the Officers hold their Places, What is the annual value of each office Civil & Military, how are they respectively appointed, and who are the present possessors?

Answer.

The Civil Establishments in this Province consist either of the Officers whose salaries are paid by

Civil Establishments.

the Crown; or of such Officers as receive their Salaries by virtue of a law annually passed by the Provincial Legislature.

CIVIL ESTABLISHMENT PAID BY THE CROWN.

OFFICE.	PRESENT POSSESSOR.	BY WHAT AUTHORITY APPOINTED.	Salary or value of the Office. *Sterling Money.*
Governor	His Excy. William Tryon	By the Crown	£2,000 — —
Lieut. Governor	The Hon. Cadwallader Colden	Do	no salary
Chief Justice	Daniel Horsmanden	Do	500 — —
Auditor General	The Hon. Rob't. Cholmondely	Do	100 — —
Receiver General	Andrew Elliot	Do	200 — —
Attorney General	John Tabor Kempe	Do	350 — —
Secretary	George Clarke	Do	75 — —
Surveyor of the King's Woods	Adolphus Benzel	Do	300 — —
		OF HIS MAJESTY'S CUSTOMS.	
Collector	Andrew Elliot	By the Commissioners of the Customs in London by virtue of a Warrant of the Lords Commissioners of the Treasury	55 — —
Comptroller	Lambert Moore	By Do	55 — —
Surveyor & Searcher	Richard Nicholls Colden	By the Commissioners of the Customs at Boston by virtue of a Warrant from the Lords of the Treasury	60 — —
Land Waiter	John Coggeshal	By Warrant from the Commis'ners of the Customs at Boston	50 — —
Tide Surveyor	Anthony Kendall	By Do	60 — —
Tide Waiters	Thomas Bayeux	By Do	30 — —
	Henry Dufour	By Do	30 — —
	Thomas Kautzman	By Do	30 — —
Naval Officer	Samuel Kemble	By Mandate of the Crown	No Salary
		INDIAN DEPARTMENT.	
Superintendent & Sole Agent	Sir Wm. Johnson	By the Crown	1,000 — —
Deputies	Guy Johnson		200 — —
	Daniel Claus		200 — —
	George Croghan		200 — —
	Joseph Goreham		200 — —
Agent at Waubash	——— Maisonville		100 — —
Secretary	Vacant	By the Crown	100 — —
Two Smiths & Armourers with their Assistants	Names unknown		200 — —
Three Interpreters for the different Languages	Names unknown		162 10 —
Surgeon	Do		58 6 8
Storekeeper or Commissary of Provisions	Do		23 6 8
		COURT OF ADMIRALTY.	
Commissary or Judge	Richard Morris	By the Crown	No Sallary
Register	Richard Nicholls	Do	
Marshall	Thomas Ludlow	Do	

CIVIL ESTABLISHMENT PAID BY THE PROVINCE.

OFFICE.	PRESENT POSSESSOR.	BY WHAT AUTHORITY APPOINTED.	Salary or Value of the Office.
			New York Currency.
Governor	His Excy. William Tryon,	By the Crown—(No Sallary but allowed for fire wood & candles for Fort George)	£400 — —
Chief Justice	Daniel Horsmanden	By the Crown	300 — —
Puisne Judges of the Supreme Court	Robert H. Livingston	By the Governor	200 — —
	George Duncan Ludlow	Do	200 — —
	Thomas Jones	Do	200 — —
Attorney General	John Taber Kempe	By the Crown—Allowed by the Province of Extra Services	150 — —
Secretary	George Clarke	By the Crown	40 — —
Clerk of the Council	Do	Do	30 — —
Messenger of the Council	Christopher Bundel	By the Governor	30 — —
Guagers of Liquors subject to Provincial Duty	Thomas Moore	Do	30 — —
	John Griffith	Do	30 — —
Land & Tide Waiters for the like duty	Thomas Hill	Do	50 — —
	Josias Smith	Do	50 — —
Printer	Hugh Gaine	Do No sallary but the am't of his account annually paid	
Gunner and keeper of the Colony Stores	John Martin	By the Governor	20 — —
Treasurer	Abraham Lott	By the General Assem	300 — —
Agent	Edmund Burke	By Do	500 — —
Of the Gen. Assem ly. Clerk	Edmund Seaman	By Do	The four last mentioned officers are allowed no Salary, but are paid during their attendance on the General Assembly; The Clerk and his Assistant each 20*s* and the Sergeant at Arms and Door-keeper each 6*s* *p* diem.
Ass t Clerk	Gerard Bancker	By Do	
Doorkeeper	Alexander Lamb	By Do	
Sergeant at Arms,	John Scott	By Do	

There is no other Provincial Civil Establishment in the Colony. Most of the abovementioned Officers have Fees appertaining to their offices, the amount of which (if within the object of the present Enquiry) can only be ascertained by the Respective officers.

The Province has a Court of Chancery, the Governor is Chancellor, and the Officers of the Court are a Master of the Rolls newly created :—Two Masters :—Two Clerks :—a Register :—An Examiner, and a Serjeant at Arms.—There is also a Prerogative Court of which the Governor is Judge: Its officers are a Register and one or more Surrogates in every County.—In each of the Cities of New York and Albany there is a Mayor, Sheriff, Clerk and Corroner, and in each of the other Counties of the Province there are three or more Judges, and a number of Justices of the Peace; One Sheriff, one Clerk and one or more Coroners.—None of these Officers have any Salary, but have Fees annexed to their offices, and they are all appointed by the Governor.

Military Establishments. Military Establishments have only taken place in Time of War. The Province during the late War, raised, cloathed, and paid a large Body of Forces, which was disbanded at the Peace, and there is at present no Provincial Military Establishment unless the Militia may be regarded as such; The Officers of this Corps are as already observed appointed by the Governor, and having no pay their offices must be rather expensive than lucrative.

The Militia are not Subject to Garrison Duty, and all the posts where any Garrisons are Kept are occupied by the Kings Troops.

WM. TRYON.

LONDON 11th June 1774.

APPENDIX NO. 1.

DEED TO KING GEORGE THE FIRST RECITING THE SURRENDER BY THE FIVE NATIONS OF THEIR BEAVER HUNTING COUNTRY, AND CONTAINING AN ACTUAL SURRENDER OF THE CASTLES OR HABITATIONS OF THE SENNECAS, CAYOUGAS AND ONONDAGAS.

To all People to whom this present Instrument of Writing shall come.

WHEREAS the Sachems of the Five Nations did on the 19th day of July One Thousand Seven Hundred and One in a Conference held at Albany, Between John Nafan Esqr late Lieutenant Governor of the Province of New York give and render up All their Land where the Beaver Hunting is, which they won with the Sword then Eighty years ago to Coorachkoo Our Great King praying that he might be their Protector and Defender there for which they desired that their Secretary might then draw an instrument for them to sign and seal that it might be carried to the King as by the Minutes thereof now in the Custody of the Secretary for Indian Affairs at Albany may more fully and at large appear—WE Kanakazighton and Shanintzarouwee Sinneke Sachims, Ottsoghkoree, DeKanisoree and Aenjeweeratt Cayouge Sachims, Rachjakadorodon and Sadegeenaghtie, Confirm, Submit and Grant And by these presents do (for Ourselves, our Heirs and Successors and in behalf of the whole Nations of Sinnekes, Cayouges and Onnondages,) ratify, Confirm and Submit and Grant unto our most Sovereign Lord George by the Grace of God, King of Great Britain France & Ireland, Defender of the Faith &c. His Heirs and Successors for ever All the said Land & Beaver Hunting to be protected & Defended by his said Majesty, His Heirs and Successors to and for the Use of Us, our Heirs and Successors, And the said three Nations; And we do also of our own accord free & voluntary Will give, render, submit and grant, and by these presents do for Ourselves our Heirs and Successors give, render, submit and Grant unto our said Sovereign Lord King George, his Heirs & Successors for ever, All that Land lying & being sixty Miles Distance taken Directly from the Water into the Country, Beginning from a Creek called Canahogue on the Lake Oswego, all along the said Lake and all along the Narrow passage from the said Lake to the Falls of Oniagara called Canaguaraghe and all along the River of Oniagara and all along the Lake Cataracknui to the Creek called Sodoms belonging to the Senekes & from Sodoms to the Hill called Tegerhunkserode belonging to the Cayouges and from Tegerhunckserode to the reek called Caynunghage belonging to the Onnondages All the said Land being of the Breadth of sixty English miles as aforesaid. All the way from the aforesaid Lakes or Rivers directly into the Country and thereby including all the Castles of the aforesaid Three Nations with all the Rivers, Creeks & Lakes within the said Limits to be protected and defended by his said Majesty his Heirs and Successors for ever to and for Our Use our Heirs and Successors & the said Three Nations.

In Testimony Whereof We have hereunto set our Marks and affixed our Seals in the City of Albany this Fourteenth Day of September in the Thirteenth year of His Majesty's Reign Anno Domini 1726.

INDEX.

A.

B.

C.

D.

E.

F.

G.

H.

I.

J.

K.

L.

M.

N.

O.

P.

Q.

R.

S.

T.

U.

V.

W.

Y.

www.ingramcontent.com/pod-product-compliance
Lightning Source LLC
LaVergne TN
LVHW021259110826
845150LV00003B/429

* 9 7 8 1 4 2 5 5 6 0 6 9 0 *